Studies in Disorders of Communication

General Editors:

Professor David Crystal
Honorary Professor of Linguistics, University College of North Wales, Bangor

Professor Ruth Lesser
University of Newcastle upon Tyne

Professor Margaret Snowling
University of Newcastle upon Tyne

Dedication

To the memory of my father.

Communication Skills in Hearing-impaired Children

R. JOHN BENCH

Department of Communication Disorders
Lincoln School of Health Sciences
La Trobe University
Bundoora, Victoria, Australia

SINGULAR PUBLISHING GROUP INC.
SAN DIEGO, CALIFORNIA

Library of Congress Cataloging-in-Publication Data

A catalogue record for this book is available.
ISBN 1-56593-075-4

Photoset by Stephen Cary
Printed and bound in the UK by Athenaeum Press Ltd,
Newcastle upon Tyne

Preface

The topic of communication covers such a wide area that, even if limited to the hearing-impaired child, the potential coverage is very great. I am well aware that, using 'communication' in a general sense, one or more whole books could be written about the material summarised in each chapter of what follows. Thus, the present text can give the reader only a taste of, and hopefully for, the area. Nonetheless, it is surprising that in the narrower social sense of interpersonal communication the discussion of communication for hearing-impaired children is not well developed in the literature. The area of communication skills is even less well developed.

Two areas of endeavour which receive only passing attention in this book are the anatomical and linguistically oriented work of recent years. Although they are of abiding interest, I have not set apart a special section for them, as they have received extensive, expert and recent coverage elsewhere.

My brief was to write a book of around 125 000 words as an overview for the more senior undergraduate students in audiology, speech and language pathology, psychology, special education or related disciplines. The brief was also to update graduate students and practitioners. This book, then, assumes that the reader has a basic knowledge of psychology, acoustics and linguistics, and at least an elementary knowledge of work with hearing-impaired individuals. A glossary is included to help readers who may not be too familiar with the terminology, and where different terms are used in different countries. Mostly, I have chosen references which are accessible in the literature to make it easier for student readers to pursue points of interest, though this approach was not always possible.

The behaviour of hearing-impaired people, like that of human beings in general, presents as a seamless robe. Although it is possible to separate the facets of such behaviour conceptually, it is extremely difficult to design studies to isolate them at the empirical level, given the many practical constraints. The result is that salient variables are often confounded with one another, as the following pages clearly show. My approach has been generally to stick close to the published literature, giving enough detail for the reader to develop a feel for such difficulties, and limiting my own assessment and evaluation. In any case, the confounding of variables in investigative work, and the great diversity among hearing-impaired individuals, make it hard to be firmly prescriptive about methods of therapy or education. I myself make no such prescription, recalling Gallaudet's maxim of nearly 100 years ago: 'Nothing could be more unscientific, unprofessional, at variance with the testimony of experience, nor more cruel than to attempt to stretch all the deaf on the Procrustean bed of a single method' (British Deaf Mute, 1896, per National Union of the Deaf Steering Committee, 1982).

Not all authors have been specific about the hearing loss and other characteristics of their subjects. I have used the authors' terminology, however imprecise, in such cases. Elsewhere, I have avoided technical details in favour of commonly accepted terms whose meaning is clear and accurate enough. Thus I may refer to, say, 83 dB HTL in an original report as 'severely deaf'. Further, the term 'congenital' is used with two meanings in the literature. Some authors restrict the usage to issues occurring around birth, such as hypoxia, and exclude hereditary considerations. Others include both. I have generally followed the usage of the author. Also, I have tended to use the terms 'deaf' and 'hearing-impaired' as synonyms, thinking it a nonsense to restrict 'deaf' to those people, such as the 'stone deaf', whose numbers are vanishingly small, and declining to limit myself to the sometimes euphemistic 'hearing-impaired'. Where required, I have qualified either term with the relevant expression, such as 'moderately' or 'severely', to make the meaning clear.

Children whose hearing is within normal limits are referred to as 'hearing children' throughout. The terms 'preschool' and 'kindergarten' may have different meanings in different countries, or even in different states in the same country. Because it would have been tedious for the reader, I have not given the specific meaning for each instance.

This book played a part in a personal renaissance. Having spent most of the last 12 years or so in the gatekeeping role of an academic administrator, and having recently relinquished that role to return to teaching, clinical practice and research, I needed to bring myself up to date across the field. One thoroughgoing, if somewhat daunting, way of doing this was to write a book. The following pages are the result. I trust that, having perused the book, not too many readers will conclude that I should return to work in administration.

John Bench
Melbourne

General preface

This series focuses upon disorders of speech language and communication, bringing together the techniques of analysis, assessment and treatment which are pertinent to the area. It aims to cover cognitive, linguistic, social and education aspects of language disability, and therefore has relevance within a number of disciplines. These include speech therapy, the education of children and adults with special needs, teachers of the deaf, teachers of English as a second language and of foreign languages, and educational and clinical psychology. The research and clinical findings from these various areas can usefully inform one another and, therefore, we hope one of the main functions of this series will be to put people within one profession in touch with developments in another. Thus, it is our editorial policy to ask authors to consider the implications of their findings for professions outside their own and for fields with which they have not been primarily concerned. We hope to engender an integrated approach to theory and practice and to produce a much-needed emphasis on the description and analysis of language as such, as well as on the provision of specific techniques of therapy, remediation and rehabilitation

Whilst it has been our aim to restrict the series to the study of language disability, its scope goes considerably beyond this. Many previously neglected topics have been included where these seem to benefit from contemporary research in linguistics, psychology, medicine, sociology, education and English studies. Each volume puts its subject matter in perspective and provides an introductory slant to its presentation. In this way we hope to provide specialised studies which can be used as texts for components of teaching courses at undergraduate and postgraduate levels, as well as material directly applicable to the needs of professional workers.

David Crystal
Ruth Lesser
Margaret Snowling

Contents

Acknowledgements

My grateful thanks to Trish Collocott, Janet Doyle, Pierre Gorman, Jane Mulcahy, Elaine Saunders and Thein Tun for their advice on various sections of the text. Roslyn Doyle kindly allowed me to draw on some of her work in my discussion of pragmatics. Nicola Daly cheerfully helped with a multitude of details. The staff of the La Trobe University library, Carlton Campus, and Jane Mulcahy were invaluable in chasing up references. Heather Russell typed the draft manuscript with her customary zest. My deepest gratitude is due to my wife, Margaret, who had to put up with me as a semi-recluse during the preparation of the work. I owe her a great deal.

Chapter 1
The Nature of Human Communication

This introductory chapter considers the nature of human communication, its aims and goals, and communication as skilled behaviour. The discussion includes outlines of traditional approaches to communication from the referential and sociolinguistic viewpoints, the pragmatics of communication, and the biological and psychological features that affect the way in which communication is expressed. The chapter concludes with some remarks on the communication problems of hearing-impaired children, to set the context for the rest of the work.

Communication is about the transmission of information. Effective human communication relies heavily on language, a system of verbal and/or gestural symbols governed by rules in a sophisticated code, though some simple forms of communication, such as a handclap to attract attention, are non-linguistic. People communicate purposefully, but apparently without conscious effort. Yet the processes involved are among the most complex of human activities. As talkers, we choose from vocabularies of up to 50000 words (Newell and Simon, 1972) at a rate approaching five selections each second. At the same time we draw on a knowledge of syntax which sets rules for ordering these lexical choices; semantics which links words to accepted meanings; prosody which shapes the rhythms and stresses of speech; and pragmatics which relates to usage and users. In addition, we may have to switch frequently from language to metalanguage, as in using English to talk about English structure or meaning, when we want to illustrate, emphasise, or explain points of interest. We also use gestures and change our facial expressions while talking (Kendon, 1981a, b). So we make use of language, paralanguage, and kinesics, involving semantics and grammar, modulation of pitch and volume, and facial expressions in what Poyatos (1983) called the basic triple structure of human communication. There is probably no other human activity which requires such a high decision rate or involves interactions of such intricacy (Levelt, 1989; Pitt and Samuel, 1990), except perhaps that our complex behaviour as talkers is mirrored by matching activities as listeners.

The situation is further complicated by the need to perform roles as turn-takers, from talker to listener, and back again. Sometimes we deliberately break the usual conversational conventions, as with ironic or sarcastic statements, often cued by unusual emphasis or intonation. As well, the processes involved are subtly changed by the conversation itself when, as listeners, we come across new phraseology or meanings. Even as we converse, we are developing our conversational experience, which in turn shapes our ongoing discourse.

Communication by conversation, then, involves a high rate of word selection and recognition, while maintaining grammatical, semantic, rhythmic and pragmatic conventions and a readiness to slip into alternative or complementary forms. This high rate strongly suggests that, although the sounds of speech occur in an identifiable serial order, much of the processing of speech and language, in both production and perception, occurs simultaneously rather than in series. Whether we are speaking or listening, there simply is not time to process all the material item by item, though some serial processing may occur. Hence, simultaneous or parallel processing models have been introduced in the study of speech production and perception. The extent to which speech processing takes place serially or in parallel is a formidable task currently occupying the energies of speech scientists, linguists, cognitive psychologists and some philosophers, among others. The reader is referred to Garman (1990) and Levelt (1989) for comprehensive coverage of the area.

Human communication allows people to describe events, to teach and learn, and to share experiences and ideas. It is related to our ability to think in the abstract. It permits knowledge to be passed from one generation to another. Communication in some form is a feature of every known society, even the least well developed.

Forms of communication

Communication through speech, with its great flexibility, efficiency and variety, clearly excels where people need to relate closely and immediately to one another. There is no known society whose hearing members have to rely on gestures rather than words (Farb, 1973). Only a minority of members do not have speech as their main mode of communication. The fingerspelling and sign or gestural languages of some profoundly deaf and intellectually disabled groups offer two well-known examples. Although there is good reason for certain groups not to use speech as their main vehicle for communication, there is no doubt that failure to communicate in everyday activities by speech is socially isolating. Whilst blind people usually manage to communicate very well in speech with their sighted fellows, profoundly deaf signers have very considerable difficulty in communicating with most hearing people. They are detached from society at large. 'Many of us are shocked at the thought of deaf being able to communicate only with deaf' (Conrad, 1976).

People also need to communicate across distances, a need conveniently met by telecommunications devices. Distance communication now plays an important part in the everyday lives of most people in both work and recreation. It is particularly purposeful and goal directed. It takes extra effort to initiate and maintain, is more limiting than face-to-face communication, and has a financial cost. Distance communication is not initiated or maintained as casually as many face-to-face exchanges. Thus, although we tend to see human communication in real time as a face-to-face activity, we need increasingly to communicate at a distance via telephones, teletypes and computer terminals. Teletypes for the deaf, perhaps more correctly called telecommunications devices (Rittenhouse and Kenyon, 1987), are now commonly used by hearing-impaired people who would have difficulty in using the telephone (Erber, 1985). This use of teletypes has encouraged hearing-impaired people to improve their keyboard abilities for real-time communication.

Developed civilisations also make widespread use of written communication, so that writing is taken as one of the principal marks of a developed society. Some people spend more of their time in writing and reading books and articles than in other kinds of communication. Writing further offers a means not only to communicate in the present, but also to convey information to future generations. Despite recent developments in electrical data storage, the written word is still the most enduring general means of communication.

Interpersonal communication

Human communication is interpersonal. It involves the sharing of thoughts, meanings and ideas between people. Hearing-impaired children will develop their own manual communication system without instruction (Heider and Heider, 1941; Mohay, 1982), showing how pressing is the need to communicate with others. One act of communication usually requires a reciprocal act. Even without reciprocity, communication aims to affect the recipient, to add to or change the recipient's perceptions. It is thus remiss to describe communication in terms solely of methods and techniques, or of instruments and devices. A full understanding of human communication requires comprehension of the thoughts, motives and intentions of the communicator, the relationships between communicator and recipient, and the organisational setting in which communication occurs (Haney, 1973).

Communication skills are bound up with social skills, as shown by frequent use of the phrase 'interpersonal communication skills'. Argyle (1972), and Bellack and Hersen (1979) have developed theoretical reviews of interpersonal communication with an emphasis on social skills, whereas Ellis and Whittington (1981) have reviewed a number of attempts to train individuals in these skills. In an informative book, Hargie et al. (1981) identified and discussed the nature of social skills in interpersonal communication with the needs of 'interpersonal professionals', whose work involves communication with other people, in mind. They reviewed nine main skill areas in terms of social skills. However, it is clear that the social skills they considered are essentially interpersonal communication skills. Their review illustrated the extensive range of skills involved in interpersonal communication, showing that such skills are goal-directed, interrelated, defined in terms of identifiable behaviour, learned, and under the control of the individual.

Extensive research in this field is relatively recent, with most of the salient work emerging in the last 25 years or so. As yet, however, little similar work has been done with hearing-impaired people.

Goals of interpersonal communication

In communicating we adopt recognised roles and follow conventions or rules. Communication skills are directed skills, whether we are transmitter or receiver, which are applied to attain communication goals. These goals are interdependent for transmitter and receiver (Higgins et al., 1981) because each person influences, and is influenced by, the other.

In any interchange the transmitter and receiver not only play different roles, but also have different aims and goals. The transmitter's goal is to convey a message clearly to the receiver, and thus the transmitter needs relatively organised, unified and differentiated cognitive processes (Zajonc, 1960). The receiver, on the other hand, has to be ready to receive a broad range of possible messages, at least to start with, and hence needs cognitive processes that are not overly organised, unified and differentiated. In reviewing Zajonc's and similar studies, Higgins et al. (1981) concluded that, because transmitters need to convey clear and concise messages, they tend to polarise and can distort stimulus information more than receivers, who have to anticipate a wide range of messages. It is thus not unexpected that research in communication has sometimes found that the effectiveness of talkers and listeners is unrelated, or even negatively related. Talkers and listeners need and use different kinds of information processing in a communication 'game' (Rommetveit, 1974).

As well as the social goals of initiating personal contact and developing and maintaining personal relationships, communication may aim to develop a shared goal of social reality, particularly if that reality is ambiguous or difficult to establish (Stamm and Pearce, 1971). Shared goals of social reality develop from the exchange of beliefs and indications of personal awareness about issues, and expressions of self-worth. These goals can be tested by speculation and imagination, by recall of past circumstances, and by predictions of future events and outcomes. Elsewhere, Collins and Raven (1969) discussed communication goals where a group works together to solve problems. Such communication activities not only involve simple association with other people to solve the problem in hand, but they may also aim to influence the behaviour of others in the group to obtain control or power, and may benefit from coalitions among group members to attain objectives. Again, Goffman (1967) described face goals in the rituals of face-to-face behaviour, where the interchange aims at self-presentation and the maintenance of self-esteem. Other goals of interpersonal exchange include seeking reassurance, sympathy and the like through the expression of emotions and anxieties; obtaining relief from boredom and pursuing entertainment by the reading and writing of poetry, drama and song; the exchange of information by identifying an attribute, object, action or idea from a set of alternatives in referential communication; and the sharing of opinions and advice.

This short review of human communication has outlined its great richness and diversity. As we shall see later, only some of this variety has been studied systematically in work with hearing-impaired people.

Communication Skills as Skills

What constitutes communication skills? Is there a definable set of such skills? Are they acquired in the same way as other skills of the perceptual–motor kind? To answer these questions, we first consider the nature of skills and then proceed to discuss what skills may be involved in communication.

Because we are all versed in communication and see ourselves as expert in the use of communication skills, we may envisage that the answers will come easily. Nothing could be further from the truth. The reader is advised that the area is most complex and difficult, as the following pages will show.

Skills have a practical reference, with a strong element of training. Historically they have been considered in the context of motor behaviour, often in work situations such as typewriting, and of cognition, as in clinical decision-making (Harvey, 1991). Hence, besides motor or, more properly, perceptual–motor skills, we find skills across the whole spectrum of human behaviour. Early work showed that skills involve precision, speed, strength and rhythm (Seashore, 1951), and are characterised by low energy cost. Wolfle (1951), who investigated how skills are acquired, identified six principles which could be manipulated under practical training conditions: knowledge of results; avoidance of habit interference; variety of practice materials; methods used in training; knowledge of the procedures involved; and effectiveness of guidance. It is of interest to note in passing that Bode and Oyer (1970) used such principles in auditory training for speech discrimination in noise, for 32 adults with a mild inner-ear hearing loss, in one of the few published studies involving hearing-impaired subjects to do so.

Clarke (1958), working on the abilities and trainability of imbeciles in motor skills, referred to the importance of well-motivated subjects, achieved by setting realistic goals; task breakdown to basic constituents in a series of steps, to be mastered sequentially; spaced learning with overlearning; and verbal reinforcement.

The principles of Wolfle (1951) and Clarke (1958) translate almost exactly for normally developing children who are acquiring communication skills. The elementary skills are effected without awareness. Young children acquire their first skills in communication and language without deliberately setting out to learn them. To consider Wolfle's list first, the environment in which communication and language develop is one in which knowledge of results is usually immediate; inappropriate habits are discouraged by the caregiver; the caregiver naturally provides a variety of practice situations and materials; and several means are employed, from use of naturally occurring events to communication 'lessons'. Explicit, thoroughgoing knowledge of the principles involved is not found in the young child. A capacity for language and ongoing guidance by the caregiver ensure that the principles are internalised as they are introduced. Later, the child receives formal training at school from teachers, when most of the requisite principles are expressly learned.

In the case of Clarke's principles, young children are strongly motivated to communicate to attain other goals; the communication 'task' is broken down to basic constituents, or a series of steps in the right direction, by the capacities of the children themselves to which caregivers are sensitive; the acquisition of language and communication abilities is spread over months and years, with ample opportunity for overlearning; and verbal reinforcement is provided by the very nature of the situation.

We think of skills as relatively discrete attributes (Ammon, 1981): using the telephone; sharpening a pencil; reading some notes; or delivering a speech, for instance. However, skills can or may need to be combined (Wilson et al., 1989). For example, it helps to be highly practised in the skill of reading from notes in developing the complex skill of delivering a speech. A complex skill, as in speechmaking, hence relies on a number of subordinate skills, all or most of which are highly overlearned and are delivered smoothly and automatically. Some examples would be modulation of the voice, keeping an eye on the clock, and judging the reaction of the audience from time to time. Such subordinate skills may be relatively simple, or themselves quite complex, but all skills, even the most complex, can be reduced conceptually to a combination of individual skills. That such reduction is possible shows that all skills may be regarded as either unitary, or comprised of a number of unitary skills, even though it may be difficult to isolate individual skills in practice.

Work is now being done on general thinking skills and problem solving, particularly more complex problem solving (Chipman et al., 1985; Klahr and Kotovsky, 1989; Resnick, 1989). Sternberg (1983) outlined eight criteria for general intellectual skills training, which should: be based in the theory of information processing; be culturally relevant; offer direct instruction in the desired skills; consider the motivation of the subject and associated individual differences; relate to real-world behaviour; be effective through empirical test; be lasting over time; and transfer to related areas. Apart from the first criterion, the normal development of intellectual and communication skills progresses naturally from the young child's home and family environment according to these criteria, though this progression depends on the variety and sophistication of the experiences which that environment can offer. Several recent studies in the area of general intellectual and communication skills training have met many, if not all, of Sternberg's criteria (e.g. Larson et al. (1984) who studied transfer effects on verbal ability and cooperative learning, and Leinhardt and Greeno (1986) who explored the cognitive skills involved in teaching). Sternberg's list apparently omitted a feedback criterion. However, MacKay (1981, 1987) emphasised the need for external feedback, particularly during the early stages of skill acquisition, to ensure that an action has the desired effect. Without external feedback during the early stages, practice may strengthen the wrong associations. However, as the skill is developed, the strength of associations already formed can be further strengthened, without feedback, by mental practice.

There is recent and welcome emphasis on cognitive analyses of learning, performance and instruction, which has moved away from the study of training and learning processes themselves (Glaser and Bassok, 1989). Attention is now increasingly paid to the way in which knowledge is structured and to ecologically meaningful performance (Chi and Ceci, 1987; Greeno and Simon, 1988; Abkarian et al., 1990); the speed at which knowledge and skill are applied by experts and novices (Schneider, 1985); the translation of the content 'knowing what' into the procedural 'knowing how'; and ways in which knowledge is internalised through metacognitive processes (Bransford et al., 1986). So far, relatively little of this recent work has affected the management of hearing-impaired children, whether partially hearing or profoundly deaf. The view of the hearing-impaired child as a metasubject, for example, is rare in the literature.

Communication skills have frequently been considered in specific contexts, as in the work of King (1989) on Shulman's Test of Pragmatic Skills (Shulman, 1985), which covered ten conversational intentions in four scenarios for both listener and speaker roles. Nevertheless, the term 'communication skills' has often been used so generally and widely as to imply no more than communication behaviour. At times, it has been used to mean little more than 'social behaviour'. This global use of 'communication skills' confounds three important distinctions, conveniently separated by Ammon (1981): the distinction between skills and other forms of knowledge; the distinction between knowledge that is relevant only to communication and knowledge that is relevant to communication but not communication alone; and the distinction between knowledge and psychological factors other than knowledge that affect communicative performance.

Skills compared with other forms of knowledge

We have referred to 'knowing what' versus 'knowing how' – to content knowledge versus skill knowledge, respectively. Skill knowledge is practical, applied knowledge. When we use our skills we expect some result to follow. We employ our skills to achieve some desired end. As transmitters, we wish to influence the behaviour and/or the thinking of a receiver, and we shape our contribution to the communication to suit. As receivers, we may take notice of the communication or not. This situation does not hold in the same way for other kinds of knowledge. Content knowledge – knowing the names of the days of the week and the months of the year, for example – is not properly a skill in the practical sense. Such knowledge has practical consequences only when we employ it, as when, for example, we use the skills needed to set up the date of a meeting.

We may be able to recognise, and recognise the usefulness of, certain skills, but not be able to put them into practice. We may be able to state, from a study of the principles involved in communication, how a speaker should address a particular audience, but prove incompetent in the task ourselves. Thus factual knowledge about communication is not the same as possessing the practical skill.

Knowledge relevant to communication versus other knowledge

Communication skills could be defined as all those skills that are used from time to time in communication. Unfortunately, this definition includes a very large number of intellectual and social skills. As a result, it is of little practical use. Ammon (1981) pointed out that such a definition would be limited only by previous knowledge of the world. He argued that competence in communication should be restricted to those skills that arise only in communication tasks, thus forcing a focus on the competencies underlying communicative competence.

Knowledge compared with other psychological factors affecting communication

Skills that are used only in the observable aspects of communication are not enough to characterise communicative behaviour. Other skills, such as cognitive skills which are independent of communication, are clearly needed. This immediately raises problems for the analysis of any sample of communicative behaviour, since the social factors involved in communication will be tied up with other, psychological, factors. Further, although communication skills, narrowly defined, are needed for effective communication, they cannot account for individual variations in performance. Nor do they allow for the development of new communication skills in novel situations. This situation is so complex that few authors have attempted to grapple with it. Ammon (1981) is one of these few. He developed a rather complicated approach, which is not easy to follow, arguing for the analysis of communication skills into predicative and transformational schemas. His approach allows the educator to identify specific communication skills and to provide separate instruction for them, and for knowledge about communication.

Communication skills in hearing-impaired people

So far we have outlined some recent work on communication in hearing people. Only occasional reference has been made to findings related to hearing impairment. What, in more detail, have researchers into hearing impairment had to say about communication as a set of skills, and in the context of everyday communication?

Surprisingly little, for the most part. Although there are exceptions, most authors working with hearing-impaired people have not analysed in detail the communication skills of their patients or clients with an emphasis on skill as skill, despite the large literature with a pragmatic insistence on the abilities and attributes of hearing-impaired people (Prinz and Prinz, 1985). Reference to the contents list or subject index of books written about hearing-impaired people will rarely turn up the word 'skill(s)' or even the phrase 'communication skill(s)'. The approach to communication taken in such books may be full of analytical detail about hearing-impaired people, but not detail relating directly to the deployment, assessment and management of, or therapy for, skills as such.

On examining some well-known texts about hearing impairment and aural rehabilitation, we find, for example, that Clarke and Kendall (1976) referred to a number of areas (language, auditory training, speechreading and speech, fingerspelling and sign, and total communication) under the broad head of 'Language and communication skills', in training for methods of communication used in Canada. Schow and Nerbonne (1980a) discussed speechreading, auditory amplification procedures, aural rehabilitation, counselling, and psychosocial rehabilitation. They referred to the American Speech and Hearing Association description of the responsibilities of the audiologist (ASHA, 1974): '... evaluation of auditory disorders, development or remediation of communicative skills through training, use of devices to increase sensory input when indicated, guidance and counselling in terms of the auditory problem, re-evaluation of auditory function, and assessment of the effectiveness of the habilitative procedures.' Vernon and Ottinger (1980) remarked directly, if briefly, on communication skills in terms of assessment of both expressive and receptive skills, in addition to an audiological workup, as: ability with written language, evaluated through the use of school records, various educational and language tests, or sentence completion, with the verbal subtests of the Wechsler Intelligence Tests also yielding some information; speech and speechreading, which have relevance for the child at school and the adult at work; and evaluation of the clients' manual communication skills.

The justifiably well-regarded, but now somewhat dated, text *Deafness and Communication* (Sims et al., 1982) contains chapters more concerned with communication skills than most other such texts. Under the subhead 'Assessment of communication skills', the book describes hearing and speechreading assessment for the severely hearing-impaired child and for the deaf adult, speech assessment of the hearing-impaired adolescent, English skill assessment with the severely hearing-impaired, sign language assessment, and individual educational planning. Chapters on speech improvement by the deaf adult, the use of speech training aids, and functional speech therapy for the deaf child, follow under the subhead of 'Speech training'. In a section on receptive training, ensuing chapters deal with auditory training, speechreading, hearing-aid evaluation and cochlear implants. A subhead on English training covers English training for children of school age, and reading and writing instruction for young deaf adults. All these subheads are closely concerned with communication skills, as is much other material in the same text, but skills as skills were discussed relatively rarely.

Some of the chapters in Sims et al. (1982) emphasised the relevant skills, as skills, in those areas which may operate in roughly the same way in hearing and hearing-impaired people, such as interpreting. The use of skills was considered also where there is an extensive literature on the normal development or acquisition of the ability in question, such as acquisition of skills in English, and certain cognitive skills. On the other hand, skills in speech production and in hearing tended not to be considered specifically as issues of skill. The distinction perhaps occurred because authors working with the speech or voice production and hearing abilities of hearing-impaired people may be relatively less familiar with the literature on normal communication skills.

These conclusions are supported by contributions to Northcott's (1984) *Oral Interpreting*. In a discussion of speechreading in that book, Green and Green referred to vision and listening as skills. They also referred to the processes which underlie such skills, within a communication context which allows the receiver to 'size up' the communicative situation. They further remarked on inductive skills that affect a receiver's willingness to guess and/or form decisions on the basis of visual information. Siple, in the same text, mentioned the need to identify or analyse the precise skills needed to attain stated instructional goals, and the place of subordinate skills that can be shaped into a hierarchy of instructional events. Castle's chapter drew attention to the relationships between speechreading skills and education of the deaf, linguistics, phonetics, experimental psychology, audiology and speech and language pathology, as they bear on the role of the oral interpreter. She pointed to research (Berger, 1972) showing that speakers who are the easiest to speechread are also the most intelligible for a listener, concluding that precise articulation matters in understanding a message both through vision and listening. Careless, indistinct or exaggerated speech tends to interfere with speechreading. The relationship of these observations to communication skills is evident from work showing that better speech habits can be developed by training (Gonzalez, 1984).

In reviewing the relations between hearing impairment, auditory perception and language disability, Bamford and Saunders (1985) drew attention briefly to the dependence of linguistic abilities on cognitive skills in normal child development. Such skills allow the non-linguistic processing of experiences before language develops. Linguistic representations are thus 'mapped' onto meanings of events which have already been processed by non-linguistic cognitive skills, as a result of the desire to communicate (McAnnally et al., 1987). However, little is known about the extent to which these skills operate in hearing-impaired children.

Erber (1985, 1988) is one of the few workers in the field who has commented consistently on normal communication skills, and projected them to communication for hearing-impaired people. His views are well worth perusal. Erber (1985) summarised some of the work in children's referential communication skills. He showed that, in order to devise an adequately descriptive message and to succeed in communication, a child has to identify not only the critical attributes of the item concerned, but also the relevant characteristics of the receiver. Children come to realise that not everyone has the same knowledge or experience, and hence children need to learn the skills of shaping messages differently for different receivers. These skills form part of the talker's role. Alternatively, when children develop as listeners, they need to develop skills in the listener's role, which involves appreciation of the quality and completeness of the speaker's message. In time, children develop awareness that messages may often be fragmented, ambiguous or too complex for comprehension. Until such skills have developed, children are unaware of the limitations in their messages, and thus fail to give the required feedback to the talker. It seems, therefore, that hearing children need specific instruction or experience to develop good communication skills.

Since these skills are complex and hearing-impaired children have trouble in developing them, special techniques have been proposed to help their teachers and therapists (Brackett, 1983). The techniques that appear to be useful include role reversal, giving the child experience of both the talker's and the listener's viewpoints; confrontation training, which instructs the child directly about a spoken message and the listener's need; modelling relevant talker or listener behaviour; and active listening plans, to persuade and encourage the child to seek clarification when the message is unclear.

The 'talking heads' models of human communication, in which one hearing person converses with another, as when a teacher talks with a child, were seen by Erber (1988) as too restricted. He showed clearly and convincingly that conversations between two people can not only begin with either one of them, but that it can be difficult to identify the start of the conversation. Thus a teacher may appear to open a conversation, but in fact be responding to some non-verbal shift of a child's body position. Similarly, a mother may speak to her baby as a result of some bodily activity, other than vocalisation, on the baby's part. Erber saw verbal communication as a unitary skill with many components: a wish to communicate; recognition of the partner's interests; patterned communication activity, such as role-taking; non-verbal aspects, such as eye contact, posture, etc.; clear, intelligible speech; confirmation that the message has been received as intended; introduction of remedial strategies as needed, to keep the conversation going; judgement of success in attempts at clarification; and response to the partner's wish to change the topic of conversation. This list was developed especially with the needs of hearing-impaired partners in mind, but it is clear that the components are frequently found in conversations between hearing communicators.

A valuable account of developmental aspects in the assessment and enhancement of communication has been given by Moeller (1985). She commented on the difficulties of obtaining valid and reliable evaluations of communication skills in hearing-impaired children, especially when the children have additional handicapping conditions. Moeller argued that an adaptive approach is needed, in view of the marked individual differences shown by children with various kinds of disorder or disability. She also referred to a large number of formal tests covering social skills, communication strategies, and receptive and expressive language skills, many of which were developed on the basis of communication skills in hearing children. She remarked on the ways in which these may need to be adapted, especially when evaluating hearing-impaired developmentally disabled children.

Another valuable outline of the complex system that hearing children develop over their first few years of life, and which is important to communication and language development in deaf children, was provided by McAnnally et al. (1987). This outline included the need to communicate, which precedes the ability to communicate; the interaction which is essential to language development; the prosodic elements of language which can be more important initially than words; the form of adult input; feedback to children on how well they have represented their intended meanings; children's vocabularies, which grow rapidly and follow patterns; and children's syntax, which also grows rapidly and follows patterns.

McAnnally et al. were at pains to stress the very important point that language is learned through communication *for* communication. They were critical of the practice of teaching language through structured lessons, which stress patterning and imitation without reference to the underlying aim of communication. Language skills are to be learned or acquired as a subset of communication skills. Thus the teaching of language skills should make use of everyday experiences and events in the life of the child, about which the child is likely to want to communicate. McAnnally et al. would also stress that the teaching of language skills should follow the normal developmental sequence and structure of such skills. It should not, however, lose sight of the aim of promoting communicative competence, the ultimate goal of any language learning programme. McAnnally et al. further drew attention to inferencing skills, namely relationships between events that are not directly stated (Santrock, 1986), which play a significant part in human communication and which have attracted increasing interest (Wiig and Semel, 1984; Mason and Au, 1986).

Although this brief review of communication as a set of skills is incomplete, the various aspects are so many that to devise a catalogue of them all would be a very large and almost open-ended task. Whilst it is fair to say that most workers with hearing-impaired people have avoided detailed consideration of skills and skill hierarchies in communication, normal or otherwise, as a basis for their work, the magnitude of such a task, considered as a whole, is daunting. It seems only practical to consider those facets of communication skills which relate to particular communicative situations, to particular messages, and to particular communicative contexts (compare Hoemann, 1988). Henceforward, these aspects of communication are the ones we will consider.

Referential and Sociolinguistic Approaches to Communication

It has been traditional (Dickson, 1981) to consider research in the area under the two heads of referential communication and sociolinguistics. These two traditions have been highly influential in setting frameworks for the investigation of communication skills in hearing children, but they have not been nearly as influential in work with the hearing-impaired child.

The referential approach

The referential tradition, with its emphasis on the analysis of communication tasks involving the ability to give and understand specific information about objects or actions, stems from the work of Piaget (1926, 1929). Piaget believed that communication develops from the egocentricity of infants and young children to the socially orientated interchanges of adults. His studies were taken up by Flavell and colleagues (1968, 1977), who set out first to study the general skill area, especially its developmental aspects, seeking a general representation of what verbal communication skills and role-taking would imply. Secondly, they differentiated subskills in role-taking and verbal communication, proceeding from the general situation to specific role-taking or verbal communication activities. Thirdly, they sought tasks that measured the differentiated subskills. Data were then obtained from children of various ages who were attempting the tasks. Among his conclusions, Flavell (1968) specified five major attributes of communication for which a child has to develop knowledge or ability:

1. Existence – appreciating that different communication partners have different perspectives.
2. Need – realising that analysis of the partner's perspective in a given situation helps to obtain one's own goals.
3. Prediction – ability to undertake accurate analysis of the partner's perspective.
4. Maintenance – maintaining awareness of the predictions, namely, of the outcomes of the analysis of the partner's perspective.
5. Application – applying the awareness so developed and maintained to the communication in question.

These attributes have little to say about the causes of communication exchanges from which they are derived. They do not account for individual differences, nor do they explain the structure of role-taking, and so on. Nevertheless, they help to flesh-out Piaget's previous work. As children develop, they become increasingly aware of the needs of their communication partners. The egocentric speech of the young child, much of which occurs without reference to partners, gradually becomes attuned to partners' listening needs. Both Piaget and Flavell took the view that communication skills involve a developing ability to take communication partners' perspectives into consideration, with a gradual departure from the initial egocentrism.

More recent research, however, has shown that this view does not adequately explain the development of communication skills. For example, research now shows that very young children alter the nature of their communication behaviour, depending on the person to whom they are speaking. Children of preschool age address adults differently from young children (Shatz and Gelman, 1973; Sakata, 1989). Other research suggests that some of the egocentric speech of the young child is for the child's own passing use, perhaps as thinking aloud, since the speech may not only be largely meaningless to adults, but may not help the child to select referents (Asher and Oden, 1976).

Several reports have compared children's communication skills in role-taking with accuracy in communication. The general finding has been that correlations between abilities in these two areas are moderate or low, even though children improve in both areas as they grow older (Rubin, 1973; Johnson, 1977). The role-taking approach to the analysis of referential communication skills, then, does not explain the development of accuracy in communication. Asher and Wigfield (1981) observed that attempts to improve children's referential communication skills by training in role-taking had not been notably successful either. However, by observing a model verbalising the correct strategy, practising the strategy, and receiving feedback, communication accuracy in a verbal task was improved, with maintenance of the skills so trained, though there was no generalisation to other referential tasks.

Research in referential communication reviewed by Dickson and Mioskoff (1980), using meta-analysis techniques, showed that specific referential communication skills can be taught to children, as in the Asher and Wigfield study; children can be trained to realise that communication via referents is to appreciate and to describe differences; children can be trained to ask increasingly specific questions, yielding more accurate information exchange; and children can learn to understand that communication breakdown may be due to failure in the speaker's perspective, rather than in that of the listener. There was little evidence that referential communication performance is related to egocentrism or role-taking.

The area of referential communication skills was further reviewed by Bowman (1984), who considered listening plans, feedback and modelling. Referential tasks could be simple or complex, and should be relevant and stimulating. Bowman concluded that, although referential communication skills were seen to be important pragmatically between the ages of 2 and 9 years in normally developing children, little information was available on the referential skills of language-disordered populations, which would include hearing-impaired children, even though such children may have difficulty with this kind of communication.

Work on the normal development of referential communication has continued, notably in the researches of Sonnenschein and Whitehurst (1984) for skill hierarchies. The most recent review was published by Bunce (1991), who took up Bowman's call by offering some helpful guidelines for therapy.

The sociolinguistic approach

A tendency towards increasingly tightly controlled studies of hearing children's referential communication skills fell away somewhat in the 1970s, shifting towards more naturalistically oriented research with a sensible emphasis on the classroom and home environments. At the same time, there were developments in the complementary research tradition – the sociolinguistic approach. This tradition drew principally on the disciplines of linguistics, sociology and social psychology. The aim was to describe communication in a wide sense, in natural settings.

The sociolinguistic approach emphasises social and rhythmic rather than individual and cognitive aspects. Referential skills, it is argued, cannot be separated from social aspects of meaning (Erickson, 1981), though emphasis on the social aspects of communication may exclude referential exchange. The sociolinguistic stress is on ecological validity, on the grounds that communication exchanges are in part culturally determined. Communication exchanges have been analysed for interpretive cues, non-verbal communication and paralinguistic features – the 'how' of communicating as well as the referential content. The interpretation and misinterpretation of literal meaning has been a special area of study in the sociolinguistic tradition (Goody, 1978). The timing of aspects of communication can also be important, as role-taking alters at observable intervals in conversations (Erickson and Schultz, 1980), depending on the social relationship between conversational partners. Language can thus be used both to transmit information and to determine the social setting (Fasold, 1984). This dual function arises because a given message can be communicated linguistically in different ways. The form and the timing by which the information is transmitted are governed by the social situation.

Sociolinguistic analyses of the communication skills of hearing-impaired children have been few. Some interesting insights have been provided by Davis (1976), Montgomery (1976), Mitchell (1978), Scott (1978), and Hay (1978), but a thoroughgoing analysis of such skills in hearing-impaired people has yet to be done. However, an informative report on the sociolinguistic impact on its students of a residential school for the deaf has been provided by Evans and Falk (1986), and an instructive first book to define a range of sociolinguistic issues of concern to the deaf community has recently been published by Lucas (1989).

Contrasts between referential and sociolinguistic approaches

The contrast between the referential and the sociolinguistic traditions is highlighted in the sociolinguistic tradition by a more subjective, qualitative analysis, with emphasis on situational and social validity. Conversely, the research into referential skills emphasises quantitative and objective analysis, with the emphasis on reliability. Researchers adopting the sociolinguistic orientation have mostly used large numbers of observations, small numbers of subjects, realistic naturalistic tasks, broad competences in communication, social situations, and ecological contexts. A subjective approach has been accepted as unavoidable, and perhaps of special value. Research using the referential approach has made use of laboratory situations, specific and sometimes contrived tasks, small numbers of parameters or variables, large numbers of subjects, and cognitive explanations. Additionally, attempts to train subjects in communication skills have been made, often successfully, using the referential approach (Bunce, 1991). Training studies by researchers with a sociolinguistic orientation are relatively rare.

Despite the considerable influence of the referential and sociolinguistic traditions on the description and analysis of communication skills in hearing children, neither tradition has greatly affected the study of communication skills in the hearing-impaired child. Few texts in the field of hearing impairment even mention them. This is probably because the main problems in communication for hearing-impaired people have been seen as linguistic or cognitive. The focus for the education and rehabilitation of the hearing-impaired child has thus been on language, including sign language, and cognition. This focus is narrower than that on communication.

Notwithstanding these comments there is one area, associated with the sociolinguistic tradition and reflecting elements of the referential approach, which has made some impact on work with hearing-impaired people – the area of pragmatics.

Communication in Practical Contexts – Pragmatics

Pragmatics can be described (Moerk, 1977; Gallagher and Prutting, 1983; Prutting and Kirchner, 1983) as the use of syntax and semantics in the context of interactions between people. Recent research in pragmatics (Miller, 1981) has considered the unspoken rules people follow in conversing; the assumptions made by talkers about listeners in judging how to convey information, and how much to convey; and how the talker's intentions are expressed linguistically in different situations. Pragmatics therefore operates at a level above that of the words, phrases and clauses which form the immediate context of the message.

One of the more commonly cited definitions of pragmatics was stated by Morris (1946), who described its relationship to syntax and semantics as:

Syntactics – the relationships between signs.
Semantics – the relationships between signs and their referents.
Pragmatics – the relationships between signs and their users.

Bates (1976) criticised this definition, regarding it as too vague. It missed, she argued, an epistemological or recognisable difference between content and use, and a psychological distinction between objects and procedures. She related her preferred definition to the original work of Peirce (1932): pragmatics is the study

of linguistic indices – signs that relate to what they stand for because they participate in or are part of the event or object for which they stand. Hence a ringing
tone indexes a telephone, because both are part of the same phenomenon.
Further, it is not possible to describe the meanings of indices, but only the rules
for relating them to a context in which the meaning can be found. Nonetheless,
Morris's definition remains the one most generally accepted.

The emerging, but relatively sparse, literature on the pragmatics of communication in hearing-impaired people is considered in Chapter 8.

Pragmatics contrasted with metalinguistics

Before leaving this brief introduction to pragmatics, it may be well to distinguish
pragmatics as the skill of using language in a practical context, and metalinguistics
as awareness and self-regulation of language. Van Kleeck (1984) remarked that, in
conversing, neither talker nor listener particularly notices how the message is
being communicated until some unexpected, pragmatically deviant, conversational event occurs, as when a particular word is used incorrectly. Then the talker
and/or listener switch, if only momentarily, to a metalinguistic mode, shifting their
attention from the meaning of what is being said to the language being used to say
it. Thus a pragmatic slip in conversation produces a metalinguistic reaction in the
conversants.

While metalinguistics refers to thinking about language, metapragmatics refers
to bringing consciousness to bear on pragmatics, as when children make comments on the social use of language. Thus children may remark on what is being
discussed in a conversation; on turn-taking ('Let me finish talking!'); and on the
manner of the conversation ('Don't shout!'). Such remarks concern the social use
of language, namely pragmatics, as compared with metalinguistic remarks about
the grammar and meaning of the language itself.

Metaprocesses in connection with hearing-impaired children are discussed in
Chapter 7.

Biological Abilities and Learned Accomplishments

Like other issues in human behaviour, communication skills do not escape discussion of the relative importance of biologically or genetically based factors as compared with learned factors. Even with skills that are heavily influenced by learning
or other experiences, the so-called nature/nurture problem needs to be
addressed. Prelingually profoundly deaf people have great difficulty in acquiring
spoken language, and their cognition is usually very different from that of hearing
people and those who are profoundly deafened postlingually. This situation shows
that communication skills depend on systems or structures of the biological type.
The communication difficulties associated with prelingual profound deafness cannot be fully overcome by special training or learning of communication skills,
despite the remarkable achievements of some profoundly deaf individuals
(Epstein, 1980). Although we are unable to separate the variables necessary to
provide a definitive answer to the nature/nurture question by experiment, it

seems that the biological aspects relate to the learned aspects on a continuum. Research with congenitally profoundly deaf people shows that, even with the complete loss from birth of one of the senses primary for communication (the nature end of the continuum), it is possible for them to develop skills (the nurture end) to assist in interaction with their hearing fellows, though not completely so.

A most informative discussion of the area has been offered by Rieber and Voyat (1983) who reported the answers of Chomsky, Osgood, Piaget, Neisser and Kinsbourne to the nature/nurture question as regards language and thought. These answers are now described in turn.

Chomsky proposed that the language system is very complex, but is essentially the same over a range of individuals. The basis of language is thus determined genetically, despite its different manifestations in various cultures. There is an intrinsic, genetically determined factor in the growth of language, a 'universal grammar', which characterises the human genotype.

Chomsky's markedly nativist view of language on the one hand, and the behaviourists' extreme emphasis on learning at the other, were both opposed by Osgood. He stressed a role for prelinguistic cognitive activity, believing that both a child's innate cognitive capacities and learning through prelinguistic experiences are universal in human beings, so that children can acquire any language.

An important role for cognition was also accepted by Piaget, who believed that the development of cognitive structures proceeds by replacing exogenous knowledge, derived from experience, with endogenous or internal reconstructions which incorporate the experiences into existing systems. However, all exogenous knowledge presupposes an endogenous framework because knowledge is assimilated into endogenous forms.

Neisser's contribution turned the discussion back towards nativism. The influence of genetic factors in resolving the nature/nurture question turned out, according to Neisser, to be more important than originally expected, though he favoured an interaction between nature and nurture in explaining language development. He argued that research with deaf children born to hearing parents, who were advised not to teach sign language to their children, showed that, nevertheless, the children developed a rudimentary sign language by themselves. Neisser thought that this signing indicated innate pressures towards language development, although we might see the development of the rudimentary sign system as primarily reflecting a need to communicate with deaf others in the environment. Conversely, and indicative of a nurture effect, attempts to teach language to chimpanzees had turned out to be less successful than they originally appeared to be, when studies with chimpanzees reared in isolation were considered.

An interaction of genetic and environmental factors was also favoured by Kinsbourne, who believed that the child's brain is innately preprogrammed to provide a set of responses, the probabilities of which are biased to particular contingencies which will release them. Thus the environment imposes adaptive modifications on the initial predisposition, depending on the circumstances. The more instructive the environment, the easier it is for the child to modify response probabilities. Kinsbourne illustrated his view with reference to echolalia. Normal young children echo words in a holistic way to pick up phrases without a reference before they can analyse them into their components. The relatively high prevalence of echolalia among autistic children suggests that they cannot map their phonological system onto their cognitive system, as the lack of reference disconnects the children's verbal behaviour from their cognitive processes, giving a 'free-floating phonology'. Such instances show that the speech system and the cognitive system can develop independently (Bartak et al., 1975; Cantwell et al., 1978).

The debate on the nature/nurture question continues, and we will not be so rash as to attempt to resolve it here. We note, however, that the nature/nurture question is associated with the issues of cerebral hemispheric specialisation and neural plasticity. It is generally held that the hemispheres are relatively unspecialised and the neural circuitry is relatively plastic at birth, but become progressively less so as a child develops, though Efron (1990) has recently issued a forceful challenge to much of the rationale for hemispheric specialisation. Witelson (1982, 1985) argued that neural plasticity does not logically require hemispheric specialisation; in fact these two neural characteristics may be independent. Thus cerebral lateralisation may be fixed from birth, while neural plasticity is progressively reduced as the child develops, at least for some cognitive functions. Witelson (1987) further expressed a view that hemispheric specialisation exists from birth, and is not subsequently changed in nature or degree. She interpreted the apparent increase in hemispheric specialisation during childhood as an epiphenomenon of the child's increasing cognitive and behavioural repertoire. What does increase, she suggested, is the amount of cognition available for asymmetric mediation by the hemispheres. The implications of Witelson's position for the acquisition of language skills by prelingually hearing-impaired children may lie with the extent to which language, generally regarded as a left-hemisphere specialism, is mediated by the right cerebral hemisphere, or shared between the two hemispheres. The capacity of the right hemisphere to mediate language is not fully known. However, studies of children who have sustained left-hemisphere damage from birth show that many of these children perform roughly within normal limits on verbal intelligence tests (Woods and Carey, 1979). There is also increasing evidence to show that affective language is mediated in the right hemisphere, while propositional language is left-hemisphere mediated (Gorelick and Ross, 1987).

Age effects have been emphasised, particularly in work related to hearing-impaired children, through the concept of critical periods in language development, to be examined in Chapter 2. For the present we note that the concept has often been proposed to support the view that the experience of auditory and other stimuli during certain stages in child, and especially infant, development has profound and lasting effects on later behaviour, especially language behaviour. Should such experiences be denied, the child will experience long-lasting deleterious effects in the acquisition of hearing and listening skills and the development of speech and language.

There is a conceptual difficulty with the critical period hypothesis, because an argument based on critical periods insists on an irreversibility of the effects (Riesen, 1961). If some means can be found to change the effects back to normal, thus reversing the apparently irreversible, then the so-called critical period is not critical after all. Since it is not possible to be sure that the effects of some 'critical period' stimulation are irreversible, the usefulness of the critical period concept is frustrated by its own specificity. It may be more reasonable to forgo the concept of critical period, and replace it with 'sensitive period', or some such expression, allowing that certain periods in development may be very important for later behaviour, without forcing the notion of irreversibility (Bench, 1971). We may then allow that a child's brain is programmed to provide the child with a set of responses to certain stimuli for which, following Kinsbourne (see above) the probabilities are biased, even strongly biased, to particular releasing contingencies. For example, the infant's exposure to speech sounds shapes for the child a modification of the predisposition to develop language. Further, the richer the exposure to speech over time, the easier it should be for the child to release the potential for verbal language development.

The Interplay of Perceptual Cognitive and Linguistic Processes

Perceptions of simple, common events, such as the wind whistling through the telephone wires, will normally not attract our interest. This type of perception is not far removed from simple sensation. At most we register the percept, and then go back to what we were doing. But where the event forms part of a pattern which has significance for our activities, our perceptions are different. We bring our attention to bear on the relationship between the event and its context, as when we hear an ambulance siren while we are driving a car, and process the combination through pattern perception.

The perception of complex patterns allows us to recognise the relationships between external events and then to arrive at some hypothesis as to what is likely to happen next. To perceive complex patterns is to form conjectures (Gregory, 1974), in which we develop an internal running commentary about the status of the outside world, and our place in it. Perception, especially pattern perception, is thus central to cognition, to knowing and thinking about our circumstances. How we perceive complex patterns and associations and how, in response, we develop patterns of behaviour are thus at the core of the processes of cognition (Holland et al., 1986; Lakoff, 1987). Since we have language, we can mull over the complex pattern we have perceived and make judgements or calculations about it through a reasoning process. If we rehearse the situation to ourselves, we can also commit the complex percept and our cognitive response to our long-term memory.

To take an example from the hearing of speech, we know that the speech we perceive is a pattern of interrelated speech sounds or phonemes, which produces a pattern of sensations depending on differences of timing, frequency and intensity (Margolis, 1986). The meaning of a word, however, depends on the larger pattern the words in which it is embedded. The cognitive and linguistic processes of the listener then play an integral role in defining the semantic context of the word, as when the listener makes inferences about a talker's intentions, expectations and beliefs (Verbrugge, 1977). Thus, in using hearing to perceive speech, we bring our cognitive and linguistic processes to interpret the complex pattern percepts which are generated by the speech stimuli.

Oracy and Literacy

Human communication can be conveniently separated into oracy and literacy. Oracy involves the skills of speaking and listening. Literacy refers to reading and writing. There is a mutual relationship between each pair. To speak is to imply that somebody will listen to what is spoken, while listening in the context of human communication involves attending to speech. To write is to assume that somebody, if only the writer – as in the preparation of shopping lists, for example – will read what has been written, whereas reading requires that the substrate is written material. Whether the concern is for oracy or literacy, for speaking and listening, or for reading and writing, language is the foundation. Aspects of language, both expressive and receptive, are common to each pair. Skilled communicators, then, are skilled in language as a result of skills in at least one of these pairs, and usually in both. Whether we choose to speak, listen, write or read will differ with the need and context, but all deliver communication through language. Although the differences between good and bad readers, for example, can be due to differences in abilities in visual perception or visual memory, research has shown that the differences are related more to variation in the ability to process the material as linguistic material (Liberman et al., 1982; Vellutino, 1983).

Because of the common link through language, it helps to view oracy and literacy on a continuum rather than as opposites (Tannen, 1980; Westby, 1984). At one end of this continuum are found the pragmatic, participant (oracy) aspects of communication; at the other end are the deliberative, meditative (literacy) features. In reflecting these differences of function, oracy and literacy have rather different subject matter. Oracy aids direct understanding of immediate material affairs and the sharing of opinions. Oracy is particularly effective in communicating prosodic information and emotion (Olson, 1977) when the communication partners are together in space and time. Literacy lacks this aspect of mutuality. In order to avoid misunderstandings which cannot be put right at once, as with oracy, literacy relies on a more specific, formal and exact style of communication. Literacy excels in producing formal definitions and in making assumptions explicit, and therefore aids theorising of the more abstract kind. However, some oral styles, as in giving and listening to a lecture, seem analogous to literacy, and some written communications, like diary entries, are akin to oracy. Such instances fall towards the centre of the oracy–literacy continuum.

For most children, the main symbolic system is that of oracy. Children acquire their abilities in language by speaking and listening. Beginning with clause structures of the 'single word sentence' type where 'mama', for example, may mean 'I see mama', 'I want mama to pick me up', and so on, children elaborate their knowledge and use of language from the clause, phrase and word level up to clause coordination and subordination and the passive voice by about 4;6 years of age (Crystal et al., 1976), well before they begin to read and write. Hence hearing children base their literacy on their oracy. They draw on their abilities in speaking and listening to develop skills in reading and writing. Children who have poor oracy skills are likely to have problems with literacy, whatever the underlying disability. Since literacy, especially reading, helps children to develop their knowledge of the world, and to think about issues and events apart from context, children who are weak in oracy are doubly disadvantaged. First, their communication is impoverished by poor speaking and/or listening skills. Secondly their reading and/or writing abilities are impoverished because their language base, developed through oracy, is impaired. Such children need to develop special strategies to overcome their linguistic handicap in order to make sense of their environment.

Both oracy and literacy are facilitated if children develop that awareness of language known as metalinguistic awareness. Some metalinguistic skill is needed before children can manipulate their language to complement their perception of its immediate meaning (Liles et al., 1977; Donaldson, 1978; Robinson and Robinson, 1983). To be able to do things with words and phrases, to separate and integrate the individual sounds of a word or phrase beyond their actual meaning, seems to be possible only after extensive familiarity with the literal meaning. Thus this level of linguistic operation, too, is reduced for children whose oracy and literacy skills are poor.

Communication Problems of Hearing-impaired Children

At first thought hearing-impaired children seem to experience problems in communication simply because their hearing loss either prevents them from hearing speech at all, or enables them only to hear speech which is attenuated and/or distorted. Thus hearing-impaired children have difficulties in acquiring communication skills because they cannot hear, or find it difficult to hear, the sounds of speech. The relationship of speech sounds to hearing level is shown in Figure 1.1 (after Ballantyne, 1977), from which it is clear that children with mild to moderate hearing losses will experience some difficulty in hearing speech, while children with severe or greater deafness cannot perceive speech without amplification. However, this is only part of the problem.

Hearing children use their hearing for speech to acquire language. They subsequently employ their developing language base not only to elaborate the forms of their own talking and listening skills, but also to develop skills in reading and writing. There is also interplay between perception, language and cognition, which is important for the appreciation of the meanings of words and phrases and for thinking about language (metalinguistics). Hearing children learn to fit their communicative style to the context (pragmatics) and to deliberate about the appropriateness of such style (metapragmatics), as well as learn about other communication skills which suit interactions between people.

Depending on the degree and type of hearing loss, hearing-impaired children clearly have impaired speech perception. However, the problem does not stop here. Impaired speech perception leads to problems with language acquisition and cognition, which become evident in their communication. Then they

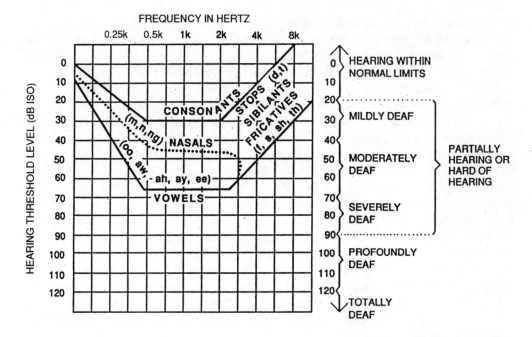

Figure 1.1 Pure-tone audiogram. (Source: Boole (1974), copyright *Perceptual and Motor Skills*, 1974.)

encounter difficulties in learning to read and write, since literacy skills depend on language and cognition. Their knowledge of affairs is reduced, also because of linguistic and cognitive factors. Such factors further deny them the normal range of the relevant metaskills. Again, hearing-impaired children come up against difficulties of a sociolinguistic kind. They have a lessened appreciation of the multifaceted nature of communication in a variety of social settings. They also have difficulties in acquiring the usual pragmatic skills.

It would be wrong, however, to imply that there is a simple additive relationship between hearing loss and/or these other features. For instance, some children with a given hearing loss perform linguistically and cognitively very much better than others with the same loss, because of their experiences, or because they can compensate with their intelligence or other forms of communication (Liben, 1978). Hence, characterisation by hearing loss alone can be very misleading.

Subsequent chapters explore the diversity in accomplishments of hearing-impaired children, the extent to which they experience communication problems, and to what extent they make use of compensating forms of communication.

Chapter 2
Early Assessment and Intervention

It is generally believed that for verbal language to develop adequately, children must be exposed to speech in their first 2 years or so of life. Congenitally deaf children will lack this exposure unless their hearing impairment is identified early and suitable treatment and therapy are begun without delay. This chapter presents the background to this view and considers the evidence for the effects of early auditory and linguistic deprivation on later communication ability. It also considers the effectiveness of early auditory remediation programmes for hearing-impaired children.

Children need to develop a language and cognitive base if they are to progress with communication, and such developments begin from an early age in hearing children. Babies are responsive to sounds from birth, and even earlier (Bench and Mentz, 1975; Kisilevsky and Muir, 1991). They can discriminate between phonemes at 3 months of age (Eimas et al., 1971), though their frequency discrimination as shown by psychophysical tuning curves is not then fully mature for the higher audiofrequencies (Spetner and Olsho, 1990). They produce their first words from 9 to 12 months. Babies also interact with their mothers at a very early age in games of the 'peek-a-boo' kind (Schaffer, 1977), their first experiences of communication involving turn-taking. By 3;6 years of age children have acquired the essentials of grammar, with virtually all grammatical skills achieved by 4;6 years (Crystal et al., 1976).

Sensitive Periods

Early experiences of communication, especially via speech, are important for the development of language. They may even be crucial. The latter view stems from the critical-period hypothesis, developed from the animal work of ethologists by Lenneberg (1967) and others, and influenced by the psychoanalytical school (Freud, 1915). Lenneberg argued for a critical period for human language development, seeing language development as associated with the maturation of the brain. The development would occur from exposure to a language environment from the age of about 2 years up to puberty.

Lenneberg thought that, below 2 years of age, the brain is not sufficiently mature for a critical period to start. In early life, the brain is characterised by a 'plasticity' which allows it to receive a variety of language inputs. The brain is then undifferentiated for the locus and degree of specialisation of function. Thus, the argument goes, the plasticity of neuronal function is greatest at birth, and in the months immediately following. Thereafter the plasticity gradually decreases and ends at puberty. As the plasticity declines, there is increasing specialisation of brain function and increasing localisation within the central nervous system for processing environmental stimulation. Beyond puberty, the brain loses the plasticity which previously allowed a dynamic interaction between children and their verbal environments.

Children who are prelingually profoundly deaf, that is, deaf at birth or soon after, will not experience verbal environments over the language-critical years unless their hearing loss is improved by amplification or otherwise. Hence they will be linguistically impoverished for life, because to miss out on the relevant experiences during a critical period causes irreversible damage. That all children born profoundly or severely deaf do have major problems with verbal language acquisition is frequently cited as evidence for the critical-period hypothesis (Tervoort, 1965; Downs, 1976; Bochner, 1982; Fisch, 1983; Anastasiow, 1990). Similar arguments have been advanced about second language learning (Davies, 1991; Scovel, 1981) and the use of pidgin (Anderson, 1983a).

As noted, Lenneberg (1967) postulated critical years from the age of about 2 years up to puberty for language acquisition. However, we know that the inner-ear structures are well developed before birth and that the human fetus in the last trimester of gestation is exposed to relatively intense low-frequency sounds from the maternal vascular system and borborygmi (Bench, 1968; Walker et al., 1971; Henshall, 1972). The fetus is responsive to audiofrequency stimulation (Johansson et al., 1964; Grimwade et al., 1971; Bench and Mentz, 1975; Kisilevsky and Muir, 1991), and many studies attest to the responsivity of the neonate and older babies to sound stimuli (Kagan and Lewis, 1965; Downs, 1967; Eimas et al., 1971; Bench et al., 1976a, b, c). We may therefore ask if early auditory, if not language, input is needed if children are to avoid retardation in language.

A firm answer to this question is virtually impossible to achieve for human beings. A definitive study would require well-controlled auditory deprivation experiments, which are not possible, for obvious ethical and social reasons. Hence recourse has been made to work with animals and to careful observations, in a few cases, of 'natural experiments' in which children have been raised in severe social isolation, though these instances provide evidence for deprivation which is linguistic rather than auditory.

Deprivation in animals

The clearest evidence on the effects of auditory or other sensory deprivation comes from work with animals. There is not only definite evidence (Kyle, 1978,

1980a; Webster and Webster, 1979; Fisch, 1990) that sensory deprivation from birth over several stimulus modalities has significant effects on cortical and behavioural development, but animal studies of auditory deprivation have shown damage to cortical structures associated with later auditory behaviour. It is difficult, even with animals, to show the effects of complete auditory deprivation, because it is virtually impossible to reduce ambient noise below threshold. However, work by Batkin et al. (1970), in which rats were raised in a sound-reduced environment, showed that they experienced later behavioural problems when auditory stimulation was reinstated. Evidence is also available at the molecular level. Aoki and Siekevits (1985) studied the effects in the cat of cyclic adenosine monophosphate, which transmits signals received at the nerve-cell boundary to specific sites within the cell. They found that phosphorylation was different before and after early periods in brain development, related to the presence or absence of sensory stimuli, both visual and auditory. However, whether the central auditory connections are complete in animals at an early age is not known.

Although there is thus clear evidence that auditory deprivation affects neural structures and behaviour in animals, we have reservations about the immediate relevance of findings from creatures who do not have speech. Animal work may lead us to presume that auditory deprivation will have similar effects on people, but does not prove it.

Auditory deprivation in children

The effects of either complete auditory deprivation or reduced auditory stimulation on human infants are less certain than for infant animals. In any case it has been argued (Bench, 1979) that for human infants the issue is more one of linguistic than of auditory deprivation, and that this issue has been confused by ascribing to sensory deprivation what should more importantly be attributed to linguistic deprivation (compare Conrad, 1980). This view was indirectly supported by Mayberry and Eichen (1991) who found that the age at acquisition of sign language was significant for all levels of linguistic structure in 49 prelingually deaf signers who acquired sign at ages from birth to 13 years. Hence we should not be so much concerned with the intrinsic problem of reduced auditory experience for the hearing-impaired child, apart from those born without any usable hearing. We should rather concentrate on the extrinsic aspect of developing more adequate aural rehabilitation programmes in the preschool years for infants with residual hearing. However, the results of such programmes at present are not generally grounds for great optimism (Conrad, 1979; Northern and Downs, 1984; Bamford and Saunders, 1985), perhaps because of insufficient emphasis on the use of residual hearing in natural social interaction, namely, in everyday communication (Wells, 1981). While hearing children acquire language and communication by natural interactive dialogue, deaf children have to be taught (Gregory and Mogford, 1981).

Hearing infants produce babble, which begins to assume the inflections of the spoken language of the culture into which the child has been born from about 5–6 months of age (Tervoort, 1965; Weir, 1966). Infants aged 6 months can identify phonemes which are not found in their native language, but seem to lose this ability by 1 year of age (Werker and Tees, 1984). Thus we might suppose that a 'critical period' for some aspects of language development begins by at least 6 months of age, and that the experience of spoken language becomes increasingly important over the next few months. If so, this argument is at variance with Lenneberg's (1967) position that the language-critical period begins around 2 years of age. Nevertheless, it could help us to understand the achievements of Helen Keller, who became deaf and blind at the age of 2 years following an attack of meningitis, since she would have had considerable, though not full, experience of aspects of spoken language before becoming deaf.

There is no firm agreement as to which months or years constitute the critical period as far as hearing in children is concerned. Such lack of agreement is illustrated by comparing a 'crucial' period posited by Pollack (1967) over the first year of life, and a critical period over the first 2 years by Northern and Downs (1984) and Welsh et al. (1983). Griffiths (1988) argued for a critical age of hearing from birth to 8 months, during which hearing-impaired infants are presumed to be responsive to auditory therapy. Griffiths (1967) further specified a maturation period for learning to listen and talk over the first 3 years, without specifying crucial or critical periods, though she assumed that the relevant maturation was complete by 3 years. Mischook and Cole (1986) also argued for the importance of the first 3 years of life. Kyle (1980a) accepted that the critical period is not easy to define in terms of time intervals, and cited evidence from Witelson and Paillie (1973) and Krashen (1973) that lateralisation of language function may not be complete until 5 years of age. Bench (1970) preferred a hierarchy or system of periods which may overlap in time (compare Ruben, 1986; Wood et al., 1986; Hoemann, 1988), thinking that a singular critical period is not a very sophisticated idea. Such a hierarchy or system is in keeping with knowledge that the auditory pathways are functional before birth and their myelinisation takes place between about 7 months and 4 years of age (Lecours, 1975). The pathways thus mature slowly (Aslin, 1981), extending the critical period over several years, during which children normally acquire most of their phonology and grammar (Anastasiow, 1986) though some aspects of language, such as vocabulary, continue to grow well into the adult years.

Instances of Extreme Deprivation

The undoubted problems of prelingually deaf children in acquiring verbal language give face validity to some kind of critical period hypothesis. What, then, of the findings of the few available 'natural experiments', in which children have been raised in gross social and/or linguistic deprivation which has denied them exposure to verbal language in their early years? Does such denial impose a handicap which stops them catching up on language once they have been discovered and treatment begun?

The results are not clear-cut. Some well-documented cases which yield somewhat conflicting findings are outlined below. Fromkin et al. (1974) and Skuse

(1984a, b) have cited other instances of sensory or social isolation which are not considered here because they are less relevant or less well documented.

Isabelle

Mason (1942) and Davis (1947) studied the same case of a 6-year-old girl, 'Isabelle'. They reported independently on Isabelle, and their accounts were not discrepant. At discovery, aged 6;6 years, Isabelle had no speech as a result of extreme isolation. Many of her actions resembled those of deaf children. However, following intensive therapy, she rapidly progressed through all the usual stages to full development of speech and language. Isabelle had spent most of her time with her mother in a dark room shut off from the rest of the mother's family. The mother was a deaf-mute, could not talk, read or write, was blind in one eye from the age of 2 years, and communicated with her family and Isabelle by crude gestures. Hence Isabelle had no opportunity to develop speech. Isabelle's remedial programme seemed hopeless at first. It took one week of intensive effort before she made her first attempt to vocalise. However, once she had begun to respond, she passed through the usual stages of learning typical of the years from 1 to 6, in the proper order, and remarkably quickly. Just after 2 months from her first vocalisation, Isabelle could produce simple sentences. After a further 9 months she could identify words and sentences in print, could write well, and could count to ten. She could also retell a story after hearing it. She attained a normal educational level by 8;6 years of age. Thus in 2 years she achieved the educational development which usually took about 6, and appeared to have been unaffected by any critical period over her first 6 years as far as language and educational development were concerned.

Koluchova's twins study

Koluchova (1972, 1976) reported on twin boys raised from the age of 1.5 to 7 years in severe social isolation by a psychopathic stepmother and an inadequate father. The twins were kept in a closet and a cellar. They grew up in almost total isolation. They were subjected to physical abuse and extreme neglect. Following discovery at age 7 years, the twins could barely walk, reacted with surprise and horror to everyday events and objects, and were very shy with people. Their spontaneous speech was very poor and they communicated with each other by gestures characteristic of younger children. They tried to repeat the speech of adults, but could manage only two or three words at a time with poor articulation, and could not answer questions. Further, they could not understand the meaning or function of pictures.

With care first in a children's home and then placement with an accepting family, and with education in a preschool, their intellectual and speech abilities increased markedly. At 8;4 years their full scale WISC scores were 80 and 72, with verbal IQs slightly lower than performance IQs. By 11 years of age, the full scale scores were 95 and 93, with verbal IQs slightly higher than performance IQs. Thus the twins made very rapid progress over a period of almost 4 years, towards normal WISC scores. Koluchova also remarked on the twins' remarkable improvement in writing, drawing and ability to concentrate, but could not predict how their intelligence might develop or what the course of their further development might be.

Commenting on Koluchova's (1972) paper and reports by others, Clarke (1972) remarked on the inadequacy of theories which stressed the overriding importance of early experience in forming later characteristics. Although Koluchova's case of the twins showed that, for their first 18 months, they would probably have developed the bases for later perceptual and linguistic development, following discovery they showed a responsiveness to remediation which underscored a natural resilience, with an obvious bearing on hypotheses concerning critical periods in development. Clarke further remarked that the pessimism surrounding the area may itself have contributed to passive approaches to the treatment of deprived children.

Genie

Fromkin et al. (1974) reported the case of Genie, a girl who had been isolated from the age of about 1;8 to 13;9 years. She was confined in a small room, with the door kept closed and the window covered. Genie was hurriedly fed and minimally cared for by her mother, who was almost blind. There was no radio or television in the house, and any sound stimulation which she could have received behind the closed door was minimal, as her father was intolerant of noise of any kind. She was punished physically if she made any sounds. Apparently her father and older brother never spoke to her although they barked at her like dogs.

On discovery, Genie was mute and socially unresponsive. Four weeks later she showed adequate hearing, visual and emotional responses, and good eye–hand coordination. She also showed much stimulus hunger. She did not appear to be mentally retarded or autistic. Within a few days Genie began to respond to speech and to imitate single words. Eleven months after her emergence, when she was able to cooperate in comprehension testing, Genie could understand individual words which she could not speak herself, but otherwise had little, if any, understanding of grammatical structures. She had physical difficulties in speaking, ascribed to her earlier repression of all vocalisations. Over time, her linguistic development became in many ways parallel to that observed in normal children, but with some differences. For example, her vocabulary was large in relation to her level of syntactic development. Her cognitive growth rate exceeded that of her linguistic growth. Fromkin et al. considered that, while Genie's language acquisition at age 16 years differed from that of normal children, she was continuing to learn language, and therefore at least some degree of language acquisition appeared possible past the critical period.

Alice and Beth

Douglas and Sutton (1978) described the case of twin girls, Alice and Beth, who were cared for by a variety of people during their first year of life. Then their mother, who was separated from their father, took the twins back and lived with them in a house due for demolition. She suffered from social isolation and depression requiring medical help. The twins received very little stimulation. They walked at the usual time but at discovery, when nearly 5 years old and about to attend school, they could not talk intelligibly except in a limited private language to each other. They thus had very limited language, although they had a friendly outlook towards others. Following discovery, the twins attended an infants' school. At the age of 6;4 years their language comprehension was between 5;1 and 6;0 years, with language expression between 5;3 and 6;0 years. They also scored 108 and 92 points (performance) and 102 and 85 points (verbal) in IQ. Thus their language and intellectual performance was at, or not far below, normally expected levels only 17 months after discovery.

Louise and Mary

The final cases considered here are those of Louise and Mary (Skuse, 1984a,b). These sisters, whose father could not be traced, spent their early years in the UK. They lived in a very deprived environment as their mother was intellectually retarded (IQ 55), microcephalic, and possibly psychiatrically disturbed. Louise and Mary were discovered at ages 3;6 and 2;4 years respectively. They took no notice of anybody, except to scamper up to and sniff strangers, while making animal-like noises. Louise had normal very early experiences, but Mary was deprived from birth, as her mother became very withdrawn after Mary was born. Mary had no speech and no hearing reactions at discovery, but made a few high-pitched sounds. Louise had the language abilities of an infant aged about 1 year. At the age of 13 years, Mary had a language comprehension score of 4 years, and a language expression score of 3;5 years. Her performance IQ was 94 at age 8;11 years. Louise, at 10;1 years, had a performance IQ of 80 and a verbal IQ of 77. At 14;5 years, she had appropriate language for her age. Thus, Louise had attained relatively normal ability, but Mary was linguistically very retarded.

Interim summary of outcomes

All the children described above had very limited verbal language abilities at discovery, having received much reduced or no exposure to language, although, apart possibly from Mary, they would have received some auditory stimulation. Subsequently, and with treatment, their language and cognitive abilities improved remarkably. Only Genie and Mary remained retarded in speech at the time of the latest reports, but Genie was not discovered till around the age of puberty, and there was known severe intellectual retardation in Mary's family history. Clarke and Clarke (1976) commented that the evidence was clear that in an improved environment, from the middle to the late childhood years, the speech of severely deprived children showed major gains.

Of the cases described, apparently only Isabelle and Mary were deprived of language from birth. Mary remained severely linguistically retarded, which may have been associated with her family history of severe intellectual retardation, but

Isabelle acquired language very quickly. It is possible that Isabelle's limited gestural communication with her mother may have been of some help here. However, Isabelle's case shows that deprivation of spoken language from birth to 6;6 years did not prevent her from making remarkable gains in spoken language by the age of 8;6 years.

Further observations of Genie

Curtiss (1977) reported extensively on continued work with Genie, making Genie's case very well known. Sometimes, Genie's case has been the only case of its kind to be cited in reference to critical periods, with potentially misleading conclusions (see below). Curtiss showed that Genie's language development continued to improve, but was by no means fully developed. Her language production and comprehension continued to be abnormally disparate. She showed unpredictable variability in the use of grammar, stereotypic speech, gaps in acquisition of syntax, and a generally retarded rate of linguistic development. However, Curtiss expressed the hope that Genie might develop far beyond what was described in the 1977 report.

Curtiss observed that Genie's language performance was in some ways similar to that of righthemisphere language learners. For example, Genie showed word-order discrimination problems similar to those found in child left hemispherectomies. Dichotic listening and other tests also suggested that her language was right-hemisphere based. These results may indicate that, after a 'critical period' for language acquisition, the left hemisphere cannot further control language acquisition. The right hemisphere then assumes this function, for which it is less appropriately 'wired', although Curtiss did not present evidence confirming normal left hemisphere functioning in Genie (Skuse, 1984b). However, the extent to which the right-hemisphere can mediate language is controversial. Work suggesting that language cannot develop as well in the right as in the left hemisphere is suspect (Bishop, 1988), as is the view that the special function of the left hemisphere is uniquely associated with language (Kimura, 1990). While Genie's case disproves the critical period hypothesis in a 'strong' form, namely, that children cannot acquire verbal language after puberty, it may support a weaker version of the hypothesis, that verbal language acquisition cannot occur fully beyond puberty.

In comparing the above cases it is, however, clear that Genie's case is unlike those of the others. First, Genie's language acquisition occurred around the menarche and subsequent years, namely around and post puberty. There was only limited exposure to language in the first, more 'plastic', years which are of interest for the early detection and remediation of hearing loss. Secondly, Genie was physically and emotionally punished in attempts at communication, whereas for the other cases, attempts at communication were not so treated, or at least to nothing like the same extent. The effects of this treatment were observed by Curtiss to have retarded at least Genie's speech development. The family environment accompanying her early attempts at communication were the very opposite of the encouragement which is given to hearing-impaired children. Thirdly, Genie was malnourished, which may have affected her neurophysiological development. Although we have no hesitation in agreeing with Kyle (1980a) that Genie's case is the most comprehensively documented, we cannot also agree that it is the one which allows meaningful evaluation in the context of congenital, or early-acquired hearing impairment (compare Mayberry and Eichen, 1991). More relevant cases are those outlined above, other than Genie, where the children were less harshly treated and were discovered at a younger age. Skuse (1984b) concluded that, in the absence of genetic or congenital anomalies and gross malnourishment, children experiencing severe environmental deprivation have an excellent prognosis. Although aspects of language may be more at risk than other factors as a result of some critical period effect, these cases suggest rather convincingly that all is not lost for young deaf children, even if they do not receive speech until school age, provided that they obtain suitable remediation.

We conclude that early linguistic deprivation may, but will not always, have lasting deleterious effects on the development of communication in some situations (compare Rutter, 1981). The dimensions of any critical period are not sufficiently well known for us to be more definite (Ruben, 1986).

Sam – a deprived deaf child treated in early middle age

Wolff (1973) described the case of 'Sam', a deaf–mute aged 43 years, and therefore well past puberty. Sam was born with a severe to profound hearing loss. He spent a short period in a school for the deaf and resided in a hospital for the mentally subnormal from the age of 12. Non-verbal intelligence tests showed Sam to be of about normal intelligence. At the start of treatment, Sam could say his own name indistinctly and 'shut the door' very indistinctly. He had no other speech and no comprehension of speech through hearing or speechreading. He knew the written alphabet almost completely in capital letters. He could write lower case letters, presumably learned in the school for the deaf, but was less happy with these, because of poor eyesight. He knew about three-quarters of the Standard Manual Alphabet used in the UK. His sister had taught him to write a few simple words, but his vocabulary was minimal. He had no knowledge of sentence structure.

With gestural communication, Sam would seek the words for pictures of objects of his own accord. His concepts and conceptual groupings of common objects, in object matching tests, were similar to those of normal people, although he had no spoken or written language. After a few months' teaching, Sam rapidly learned new names of objects, reflecting the 'naming explosion' of normal children. He was also taught syntax and semantics. Although at the time of Wolff's report Sam's language ability was limited and not fully productive in the linguistic sense (Chomsky, 1971), it seemed possible that he would make further progress. Wolff concluded that if Sam's efforts were accepted as rudimentary language, then that part of the language critical period which postulates that language learning is not possible after childhood, was disproved. The universality of the critical period concept was likewise disproved.

Congenitally profoundly deaf children

Recent studies show that verbal language can be acquired by at least a minority of congenitally profoundly deaf children, possibly through lipreading and/or the tactile sense. For example, Conrad (1979) found that five children in a group of 218 school leavers with severe to profound hearing losses had normal reading ability for their age, and possessed inner speech. Wood et al. (1986) showed that competence in reading and writing is associated with abilities in receptive and expressive speech in profoundly deaf primary school children. Thus work at literacy facilitates the development of listening to and expressing speech. Geers and Moog (1987, 1989) have shown that more than a small proportion of congenitally profoundly deaf children can learn verbal language. Hence some profoundly deaf children escape many of the effects ascribed to missing out on the 'critical period', and others can improve their verbal communication skills when they have missed out. We will return to these studies later. Meanwhile we observe that the issues, of course, are whether the improvement is adequate to some criterion, and how, and how far, it can be developed.

Early and Late Assessment of Hearing Impairment

A focus on the sequelae of auditory deprivation takes emphasis away from the development of improved approaches to aural rehabilitation, especially for language learning (Bench, 1978, 1979). Such a position is supported by the work of Williams (1970) who observed, in a study of maladjusted deaf children which is a lesson to us all, that early assessment of hearing loss had harmful effects on the later acquisition of speech. Williams found that early assessment of deafness was associated with a lower incidence of speech than when the assessment was not made till age 2 years. He studied 51 children aged 5–14 (mean 10) years, with severe to profound mainly prelingual losses, and neurotic, developmental and kinetic problems. Williams set aside five children with late-acquired deafness, expecting to find for the remainder that the earlier the assessment, the higher would be the incidence of children with speech. But the opposite was found. This result seemed so improbable that the data were reviewed. Cases showing educational subnormality and psychosis were discounted, whereupon the failure of early assessment of deafness to increase the incidence of children with speech became even higher. Those children assessed as deaf before their second birthday achieved speech in 27% of cases. Those assessed after their second birthday achieved speech in 80% of cases. There was no evidence to indicate that early assessment of deafness was associated with the severity of hearing loss, psychiatric disorder or social class.

Williams offered three reasons for these results. First, his early-assessed group could have contained a high proportion of children with central speech and language disorders. However, there was no evidence to support this argument. Secondly, some of the early-assessed children may have been fitted with unsuitable hearing aids, but this seemed unlikely as most of the aids would have had similar gain and frequency responses. Thirdly, early assessment which was not followed by appropriate rehabilitation and counselling may have led to parental indecision, depriving the child of affection unfettered by anxiety. The figures suggested, stated Williams, that to rely on early assessment and the fitting of a hearing aid is not enough. Intensive counselling and guidance are needed for all hearing-impaired children and their families. Although not directly considered by Williams, other factors may be at work. Children's linguistic competence reflects the language communicated to them by more experienced language users (Bruner, 1983; Wells, 1984). If parents are informed early that their infant has a hearing problem, they may modify their speech and other forms of communication, making it more difficult for the infant to experience natural language.

Features of parent–infant interaction

Generally, adult speech addressed to young children is characterised by simplicity, consistency, redundancy and exaggerated prosody (Snow, 1972; Gleason, 1975; Nienhuys and Tikotin, 1985), a 'motherese' which facilitates the child's acquisition of language. There are similarities between the speech of mothers and fathers to infants in mean length of utterance (MLU), though mothers use a simpler vocabulary and speak more than do fathers (Golinkoff and Ames, 1979), and mothers interrupt conversations more than children (Bedrosian et al., 1988). The child's abilities also influence adults' speech (Cross, 1977; Cross and Morris, 1980).

Similar findings have been found for hearing-impaired infants and their hearing parents, even though the poor intelligibility of the infants' speech and their reliance on idiosyncratic non-verbal cues makes parent–infant communication difficult (Kenworthy, 1986). Thus Tucker et al. (1983) reported similarities between mothers' and fathers' speech with 10 preschool children aged 1–4 years, who had severe or greater hearing losses, with fathers talking less, and using shorter and more variable MLUs, often employing single words to gain the children's attention. Blennerhassett (1984) described the communicative styles of a 13-month-old hearing-impaired infant, with a sloping mild to profound hearing loss, finding that both parents approached their child as a conversational partner and engaged in turn-taking exchanges. Both parents were seen as sensitive to feedback from the infant. Both adjusted their MLUs. The mother was more sensitive than the father in responding to the infant's topic shifts. Differences between the infant's style with her father and mother suggested that, even at 13 months of age, she adjusted to different communication situations, such as the more challenging demands of her father. Matey and Kretschmer (1985) compared mothers' speech to Down's syndrome, hearing-impaired and hearing children. In each of these three groups, children were studied at ages 18 months and 3 years. Mothers modified their speech to both Down's syndrome and hearing-impaired children, based on the perceived language level of the child. The 18-month-old Down's syndrome and hearing-impaired children received more direct imperatives than the hearing age-matched children. The 18-month and three-year-old hearing-impaired children were offered shorter MLUs, and the 3-year-old hearing-impaired children also received fewer questions. Similar results were reported for communication addressed to a hearing and a hearing-impaired child by Seewald and Brackett (1984). Likewise, Lartz and McCollum (1990) reported that a mother of 3-year-old twins addressed twice as many questions to the hearing as to the deaf twin.

Nevertheless, parental adaptations to interactions with their hearing-impaired infants may not necessarily be appropriate. Reduced syntactic and cognitive complexity of utterances, reduced use of expansions, more imperatives and different turn-taking aspects have been found in mothers' speech to hearing-impaired infants (Nienhuys et al., 1984, 1985). A pattern of reduced complexity and reduced variability in mothers' speech indicates that this speech may not be properly adaptive and could impede the infants' development of communication skills (Pratt, 1988; Power et al., 1990). Interestingly, women without experience of deaf people also tend to take a leading role in initiating interactions with unfamiliar deaf children (Lederberg, 1984).

Nienhuys and Tikotin (1985) further investigated the relative roles of vocalisation, hearing and gaze in maintaining mother–baby communication and the effects of babies' deafness on mother–infant interaction with infants aged 39–44 weeks. They concluded that hearing-impaired babies were less likely to be active in meaningful social and play interactions with their mothers than hearing babies. The hearing-impaired babies attended to their mothers or to objects, rather than playing with them. They did not engage in rhythmic periods of social involvement and play with their mothers, even though the mothers provided the opportunities. In similar vein, Spencer and Gutfreund (1990) suggested that mothers of hearing-impaired infants are as responsive in 'dialogues' with their infants as mothers of hearing infants, but since hearing-impaired infants produce less topic-initiating behaviour, their mothers come to dominate the interactions. We should, however, note that although hearing impairment will affect the nature of communication between infant and parents, it need not affect the quality of social attachment (Lederberg and Mobley, 1990).

In conclusion, we have seen that parents adjust their communicative style towards the linguistic and intellectual development of their hearing-impaired and hearing children. There is a nice, but important, distinction to be drawn between adjusting parental speech appropriately to suit the abilities of the child and reduction of speech because of pessimism or otherwise ('Why should I talk so much to my child if he can't hear properly?'). Unfortunately, published reports seldom allow the reader to appreciate this distinction. Although parents may be sensitive to the linguistic levels of their hearing-impaired child, only careful monitoring will show whether this sensitivity is appropriate, or results in non-optimal opportunities for the child to develop linguistically and cognitively. The astute therapist will monitor the mother–infant dyad carefully, and check that the parent is providing appropriate opportunities for the child.

Given these caveats, it is generally agreed that the earlier hearing loss is identified and therapy begun, the better for the development of communication. The effects of early intervention programmes on communication by hearing-impaired children are thus of particular interest (see below).

Some further technical considerations

It is increasingly possible to identify a large proportion of hearing-impaired babies within their first weeks or up to 1 year of age, and to fit them with hearing aids.

The introduction of behavioural hearing screening tests, as conducted by health visitors in the UK, maternal and child nurses in Australia, and public health nurses in Malaysia, for example, has led to the identification of many, though not all, instances of hearing impairment around 8 months of age. Recent technical developments, such as evoked auditory brain-stem responses (Stockard and Curran, 1990; Gorga and Thornton, 1990) and oto-acoustic emissions (Kemp et al., 1986) are used most cost-effectively in neonatal intensive care units in paediatric hospitals, where the numbers of babies with hearing impairment may be up to ten times the figure in the general population (McCormick et al., 1984).

Where a hearing-impaired baby is identified early and fitted with a hearing aid there are a number of practical problems to be overcome in following a successful communication programme. Parents are usually eager to learn how hearing aids will help their infant (Rushmer and Schuyler, 1984), but should be advised that the infant will probably not behave like a hearing child when the aids are first fitted. Parents also need advice and practice in the operation and maintenance of the aids and earmoulds. Where an infant spends much time lying down, it is often difficult to keep a behind-the-ear aid in place. A body-worn aid in a harness may be more suitable, though this can cause problems of noise from clothes-rub. Earmoulds can drop out of the ears of small children, in which case the mould and aid may be taped to the pinna or mastoid process. Some infants may pull on or pick at the aid or cord. Downs (1966) has outlined a familiarisation programme for such cases, which gradually increases the time in which the aid is in situ. Otherwise (Ross, 1975) it is probably best to fit the aid and mould, and leave them on.

Other technical issues complicate this situation further. Although parents may try to communicate normally with an infant assessed early as hearing-impaired and fitted with hearing aids, there will still be difficulties with speech and language acquisition. Speech perception via hearing aids may not reach the loudness which hearing children experience. Hearing aids introduce distortion to the speech signal, and amplify the background noise as much as the speech. Also, sensorineural hearing loss often involves poor frequency resolution (Wightman, 1981; Turner and Nelson, 1982). Thus the impaired ear causes distorted as well as attenuated hearing. Hearing aids and speechreading do not sufficiently redress the most severe and profound hearing losses (Erber, 1983).

Early intervention for the development of communication

Early intervention concerns the management of a hearing-handicapped child before the primary school years, and especially before 2 years of age. Late intervention generally refers to intervention after spoken language is normally acquired – say, after 3–4 years of age.

Although it is generally thought that early intervention programmes for the development of communication in hearing-impaired children are well-nigh essential (Northern and Downs, 1984; Riko et al., 1985), and although the advent of cochlear implants for young children has increased interest in early intervention, well-designed studies in the area are the exception. There are many descriptive comments and papers from teachers and therapists, but most papers have been concerned with an empirical rather than experimental approach to intervention, from which it is difficult to identify cause and effect. There is a dearth of quantitative studies, of specific hypotheses and of identifiable criteria by which to select children for, and to estimate the effects of, the intervention. Controls are often lacking, even same-subject controls. However, it would be hasty to discount this material. Although most of the evidence for early intervention is weak, this does not necessarily mean that early intervention does not work (see below).

As a result of such design flaws, the methods of therapy adopted in early intervention programmes are the subject of continuing debate. Liden and Kankkunen (1973) suggested that the decision as to what kind of educational or therapeutic method should be used in intervention would be helped by considering the difference between aided and unaided pure-tone thresholds. A large difference between these thresholds across the frequencies used in speech-hearing implies good candidacy for an aural–oral approach, namely the use of hearing and speechreading. Most children with moderate to severe hearing losses would be so suited. A large difference between aided and unaided thresholds at frequencies up to 1 kHz, and little or no difference thereafter, also implies candidacy for an aural–oral approach, as there is usable residual hearing. However, language development is likely to be slower and the eventual outcome questionable. Little or no difference between aided and unaided thresholds, with apparent hearing for low-frequency sounds ascribed to responses to vibrotactile sensation, implies candidacy for a manual approach from the beginning. Although Liden and Kankunnen's approach is relatively objective, it assumes a strong correlation between aidable, usable residual hearing, hearing for speech, and language development. However, the correspondence may not be very strong (Erber, 1974; Bamford et al., 1981). Further, Liden and Kankunnen's approach does not take into account motivational, cognitive and parental support variables. It emphasises the audiological status, rather than the 'educability' of the child.

Downs (1974) included both audiological and non-audiological factors in the Deafness Management Quotient (DMQ). This is a 100-point scale based on five items:

1. residual hearing (30 points);
2. central intactness – brain damage, perceptual dysfunction, intact central processing, etc. (30 points);
3. intellectual factors (20 points);
4. family constellation – support/no support (10 points);
5. socioeconomic status (10 points).

This scale was validated by post hoc data on young adults, showing that a DMQ of 81 or more was needed for success in aural–oral education.

The DMQ goes a long way towards meeting the criticisms of Liden and Kankunnen (1973) outlined above. Whereas Liden and Kankunnen weighted audiological factors at 100%, Downs weighted them only up to 30%. However, the DMQ is more difficult to apply to infants and young children than Liden and

Kankunnen's approach, because some factors such as intellectual level are hard to assess in infancy, and because the family constellation may change over time. Further, some DMQ factors need subjective judgement, which may be difficult to make. For example, estimates of family constellation would require considerable experience with the family to gauge familial support.

In a similar approach to that of Downs, Geers and Moog (1987) restated the need for objective data on which to base recommendations for oral communication, manual communication, or some combination of these two. They sought objectivity both at the initial placement stage and after the child had been enrolled in an educational programme. Geers and Moog developed the Spoken Language Predictor (SLP) Index in an attempt to overcome the perceived problems of the DMQ by: choosing factors which better predicted a hearing-impaired child's potential for spoken language acquisition; specifying more precisely the methods for assigning weights to the factors; and providing a category for those children for whom intensive instruction and periodic re-evaluations were needed. Five factors were chosen as affecting a child's success with oral teaching, and which could be estimated reliably in clinical evaluations from 3 years of age. Points were allotted to each factor by clinical judgement and a trial application to actual cases:

1. hearing capacity, 30 points;
2. language competence, 25 points;
3. non-verbal intelligence, 20 points;
4. family support, 15 points;
5. speech communication attitude, 10 points.

Total scores of 80–100 suggested a speech emphasis; 60–75 a provisional speech emphasis; and 0–55, a manual emphasis. The SLP procedures were validated concurrently against three teachers' estimates of oral language skills on a three-point (poor/fair/good) spoken language ability rating scale. All children ($n = 66$) aged 11–15 years enrolled in the Central Institute for the Deaf (CID) were assigned points from data and descriptive comments in the children's files, yielding a contingency coefficient of 0.71, and suggesting good validity. The SLP procedure was also validated retrospectively on 51 CID children aged 11–16 years, with complete information in their files before 6 years of age, again with a contingency coefficient of 0.71. A third study compared the reliabilities of the SLP over time on 51 children for preschool data and information obtained from 11 years of age, yielding a contingency coefficient of 0.74. Given that language competence may vary with different kinds of educational intervention, and that the estimate of family support seems rather subjective, as does that for speech communication attitude, the results are fairly impressive. However, even given the respectable contingency coefficients, a large amount of variation in spoken language was not 'explained' by the selected variables. As Geers and Moog accepted, more research is needed. Further, since it was designed for use with children aged 3 years or more, the SLP is of value only for children who will already have progressed some way in their cognitive and linguistic development.

As we have seen, there are moderate correlations between pure-tone thresholds and hearing for speech (Erber, 1974; Bamford et al., 1981), and it is possible to estimate pure-tone thresholds with fair to good accuracy in young children and infants with modern electro-acoustic methods. Therefore infants and young children with average pure-tone thresholds lower than, say, 85 dB HTL (hearing threshold level) may be fitted with hearing aids and instructed with aural–oral methods to begin with, and until other, non-audiological information becomes available to complement the measures of their hearing. The acoustic information in speech signals should be useful to most such children, and they should, for example, be able to use manner, nasal and place information from perceived speech (Davis and Hardick, 1981). If they can discriminate phonemes successfully, they may not require later manual supplements. Infants and young children with hearing losses of greater than about 85 dB, who will have difficulty in perceiving manner and place information, should probably be treated to both speech and sign simultaneously (Wolff, 1973; Conrad, 1980; Davis and Hardick, 1981) until it is clear if they will continue to require a combined method of communication, or if they will develop communication best with either speech or sign alone (see Chapter 9).

Early versus Late Intervention

Increasingly, early intervention programmes have emphasised a role for home-based treatment, and the involvement of parents (Schaefer, 1976; Meisels and Shonkoff, 1990). Training centres may model themselves on a home environment and encourage the involvement of parents in the child's training, not only as primary care-givers, but also as those with a primary responsibility for training, with the centre offering advice.

Design problems

Notwithstanding such precepts, it is difficult to establish unambiguous and easily defensible prescriptions for early intervention to develop communication skills for hearing-impaired children (Kretschmer and Kretschmer, 1978; Simeonsson et al., 1982; Greenberg and Calderon, 1984; Greenberg et al., 1984). On examining published work, the type of hearing loss has often been ambiguous. Although the severity of the hearing impairment and ensuing difficulties with spoken language and cognitive development are likely to have major influences on the effectiveness of early intervention, they have seldom been well described. Some important areas, such as cognition, may not have been considered at all. Most hearing-impaired children enrolled in early intervention programmes will be fitted with a hearing aid, but different aids are fitted to different children. Even if they were all fitted with similar aids, the child–aid interactions would be different. Therapist–child or teacher–child interactions are equally problematical. Ethical issues complicate the situation, because each child needs to receive treatment and such considerations make it difficult to design thoroughgoing research studies which withhold treatment from a control group. Prospective designs are difficult to implement as 'blind' studies. As Guralnick and Bennett (1987a) remarked, it is easy to reject much of the existing early intervention research outright and select data to fit one's own biases, or make unreliable generalisations through an uncritical acceptance of findings.

Although design problems bedevil research in early intervention, the area is too important to be ignored. Therefore, while maintaining a critical attitude, we now consider the effectiveness of early intervention with hearing-impaired children. Such intervention can only involve oral, aural or gestural aspects, or combinations thereof. The children are too young to read or write.

Selected studies

Meadow-Orlans (1987) did a major service in presenting a review of eight reports which compared early with late intervention – all that could be located at the time. These reports on early versus late intervention are now considered, with some additional data.

Craig (1964) described a programme in which 151 residential and day-school hearing-impaired children, with hearing losses of 60 dB or more, the experimental group, received oral preschool training between 2;10 and 4;6 years of age. The programme consisted of individual tutorials and group activities in two residential schools for the deaf. The parental role was not reported, but appears to have been minimal or nil. The experimental group was compared with a control group, which had no preschool training, of 92 hearing-impaired children who enrolled in the two schools between 5 and 7 years of age. Testing was completed between the ages of 6;8 and 16;6 years via speechreading and reading tests. Retrospective data analysis found no significant differences between the scores of the children with and without preschool training.

Early amplification and intensive treatment were emphasised by Horton and others (Horton, 1975, 1976). They compared the performance of an early intervention group of six children assessed as hearing-impaired (median loss 87 dB) and fitted with a hearing aid before 3 years of age (median age 2;3 years) with a late intervention group of five hearing-impaired children (median loss 84 dB) assessed and fitted after 3 years (median age 4;0 years). The parents of the early, but not the late, intervention group were involved in the treatment. A third group consisted of six hearing children, judged by teachers to be average achievers in the same second-grade classes as those of the early intervention group. The intervention consisted of visits to a demonstration home, working with the teacher, and weekly checks of hearing aids. Practice at home with parents was encouraged to develop the use of language in familiar, everyday situations. Children in all three groups were assessed in the second grade with Lee's (1966) Developmental Sentence Types, when the linguistic competence of the early intervention group was found to be similar to that of the hearing group. Statistically significant differences arose only in comparisons of the late intervention group with either the hearing or early intervention groups. The results thus suggested that early intervention with parental involvement allowed the early intervention group to express themselves in spoken language at a level comparable to that of the hearing children. The same suggestion would not apply for the late intervention group. However, the late intervention children were enrolled in a class for hearing-impaired children, rather than in regular classes, because their language was inadequate. This difference in class of enrolment was a confounding factor, leaving the interpretation of the results open to question. The testing was post-intervention only, with no allowance for uneven abilities of the children allocated to the two hearing-impaired groups.

An evaluation of early and late intervention with hearing-impaired infants in a strongly oral programme with an emphasis on parental support was reported by Greenstein et al. (1975). The mean ages at first enrolment for two groups of children who had hearing parents was 13 months ($n = 9$) and 21 months ($n = 10$). The mean enrolment age for another group with deaf parents ($n = 11$) was 7 months. The mean hearing losses for all groups were comparable (96–105 dB unaided; 42–54 dB aided). The intervention consisted of 90-minute weekly sessions with a teacher in an auditory training programme, plus weekly workshops for parent groups in which parents were instructed in the cognitive, linguistic and affective development of infants and young children, until the infants were aged 40 months. Assessments were made of language performance, mother–child interactions via videotape, and teacher ratings of communication skills by repeated comparisons of performance. The early-admitted children, whether of hearing or deaf parents, scored significantly higher on language performance at 24, 36 and 40 months of age, than the late-admitted group. In the early-admitted group the infants looked at, vocalised to, and moved to the mother more than the late-admitted infants. Also, teachers gave the mothers of early-admitted infants significantly higher communication ratings than the mothers of late-admitted infants. There were no significant differences between infants with hearing and deaf parents in the early-admitted groups. These results seem rather impressive. However, the infants were not randomly assigned to different groups and the hearing/deaf parents variable for the early-admission groups was confounded with admission age.

A retrospective analysis of reading and other academic achievements, from data in school files over 16 years from 1956 to 1971, was described by Balow and Brill (1975) for graduates of a residential school for the deaf. The intervention was oral-only preschool treatment with parental involvement. The children were considered in four groups: Group 1 ($n = 36$) attended a 6 week summer preschool with their parents at the John Tracy Clinic; Group 2 ($n = 15$) had attended preschool programmes at the clinic for 1 or 2 years; Group 3 ($n = 21$) had attended such programmes for 3 or 4 years; and Group 4 ($n = 240$) had access to the clinic programme via a parental correspondence course. With controls for IQ, Group 3 (3–4 years of clinic preschool programme) achieved the highest Stanford Achievement Test (SAT) battery scores (Gentile and Di Francesca, 1969) at high-school graduation. All groups achieved higher scores than students who had no contact with the clinic preschool programme. This study is of interest, but there were problems with the allocation of children to groups, which was non-random. Further, the extent of contact with the clinic preschool programme may have been affected by unknown but relevant variables.

In a comparison of North American programmes, Brasel and Quigley (1977) retrospectively reviewed several oral-only preschool interventions for children with hearing parents and manual interventions for children with deaf parents. The children with hearing parents were split into two groups: those who had experienced intensive oral training begun before 2 years of age; and those who experienced less intensive oral training begun between 2 and 4 years. The children with hearing-impaired parents were separated into those whose parents routinely used American Sign Language and those who used Manual English. Each group contained 18 children with a mean age of 14;8 years, mean performance IQ ≥ 90, and mean hearing loss > 90 dB. Deafness was confirmed before 1;3 years. The socioeconomic status was higher for the intensive early oral intervention than for the other groups. Parents were involved with the intensive early oral intervention group, and minimally involved for the less intensive oral intervention group. The involvement of the parents who were deaf was not stated. All children were tested with the SAT battery and the Test of Syntactic Ability (Quigley and Power, 1971). Those children who began intensive training before the age of 2 years attained higher levels of achievement than the children who partook of less intensive training begun between 2 and 4 years of age, with the latter scoring lowest of all four groups. The children whose parents used Manual English obtained the highest score of all groups, significantly so for the four language subtests of the SAT, with the children whose parents used American Sign Language scoring higher than the early intensive oral group. However, for the orally trained groups, although the group which began training before 2 years obtained higher scores than the group which began training between 2 and 4 years of age, the results were confounded by intensity of training, differences in parental involvement, and differences in parental socioeconomic status, besides the non-random allocation of children to groups because of the retrospectivity of the design.

Berg (1975, 1976a) and Watkins (1984) described the early intervention Ski-Hi programme developed between 1972 and 1975. The main features of this programme included baseline and periodic measures of hearing obtained until thresholds were established; two hearing aids often fitted soon after an estimate of the hearing loss was made; parents oriented to and provided with group counselling and instruction in adjustment to hearing loss in their child, and aspects of parent–home intervention; preparation of parents by home managers who were specialists in communication disorders and listening and language programming; and individual evaluation for each child regarding demographic information, significant dates, audiometric data, speech input, hearing aid data, and longitudinal data on measures of child and parental progress. Parents were given the options of oral-only or total communication training. Watkins compared four groups of children (each of $n = 23$) with comparable severe to profound hearing losses: a group experiencing home-based intervention before age 2;6 years; a group experiencing the same intervention after age 2;6 years; a group receiving centre-based (not Ski-Hi) rather than home-based training after 2;6 years of age; and a group with no training before enrolling in kindergarten at 5 years of age. The socioeconomic status of parents in the last group was lower than that of the parents for the other three groups. At testing, in the age range of 105–133 months, with Carrow's (1974) Elicited Language Inventory, the Peabody Picture Vocabulary Test

(Dunn, 1965), Lee's (1966) Developmental Sentence Types, and other tests, there were few differences between the early and late home intervention groups, or between the group with centre-based training and the group with no intervention before 5 years of age. However, the home intervention groups combined obtained a higher level of proficiency in 22 of the 24 test comparisons than the other two groups combined. The design weaknesses of this study were that the testing was post-testing only, and the children were not allocated to groups at random.

An oral-only intervention programme was reported by White and White (1987), which provided for strong parental involvement with spoken language training as the main emphasis. Teachers gave weekly 90-minute sessions of auditory training, and parent workshops were provided. Forty-six infants, with severe to profound hearing losses, were studied in four groups: group 1 ($n = 5$) had deaf parents and began the programme before 18 months of age; group 2 ($n = 4$) also had deaf parents and entered the programme after age 18 months; group 3 ($n = 9$) with hearing parents enrolled before age 18 months; and group 4 with hearing parents enrolled after 18 months of age. On testing by post-test, the hearing-impaired infants of deaf parents attained faster language development, on parts of speech and combinations of words and sounds, than the hearing-impaired infants of hearing parents, but not on all measures of a Revised Receptive and Expressive Emergent Language Test (Bzoch and League, 1971). However, infants with hearing parents scored higher than those with deaf parents for babble and jargon. Infants of hearing parents who enrolled before age 18 months scored higher than infants of hearing parents who enrolled after 18 months on 9 out of 10 comparisons, with no difference for one comparison. This finding was reversed for the infants of deaf parents. Here the early-enrolling group performed less well than the group which entered later. The design of this study, like some others above, allocated the infants to groups non-randomly, and the evaluation was done by post-testing. Also, the numbers of infants in the groups were small, especially for infants of deaf parents. It is therefore difficult to explain the differences between the groups.

In a comprehensive and well-conducted study of its kind, Levitt et al. (1987) identified all hearing-impaired children who were enrolled in US state special education schools or programmes, probably oral-only, in 1972, and who had been born in 1962. These children were tested in four successive years when the children were 10–14 years of age. Besides hearing impairment, data were collected on other variables, including hearing-aid use, IQ and socioeconomic status. The children were assessed with the Test of Syntactic Abilities (Quigley et al., 1978) and otherwise to obtain data for spoken and written expression, reading, speech perception, and speech intelligibility. Levitt et al. found that the age at which hearing aids were fitted was correlated with the age at which special education began. In turn, this age was correlated with high reading scores and high speech and language skills, when early intervention was begun at 3 years or younger. The correlation between early intervention and later speech and language development was particularly high in the oldest group of children, suggesting that early gains were maintained throughout the child's life. This investigation involved the use of sophisticated statistical techniques to unravel some important factors. It benefited, too, from repeated longitudinal testing, which was, however, post-test.

Conclusion

We are happy to conclude with Meadow-Orlans (1987) that, despite the problems of design and sometimes conflicting results, the balance of the evidence from these studies supported the case that early intervention increased the later achievements of hearing-impaired children, especially those achievements concerned with speech and language development. However, given some contradictory results, the situation was not clear, which could argue that any critical period effects were weak. In considering the above studies, and five others in which methods of early intervention were compared, Meadow-Orlans also concluded that early intervention programmes were likely to be successful if they had a strong emphasis on parent counselling, and access to experienced staff including audiologists to check and maintain hearing-aid performance. Although the evidence to support the distinction could be stronger, our own impression is that parental attitudes, and parental support and counselling, are probably more important for the success of early intervention than other differences in approach (compare Moores, 1989).

Our most important general conclusion concerns the plethora of poorly designed empirical work, not reviewed here, as compared with the scarcity of better designed studies which we have considered. Despite the practical and ethical difficulties, it is truly surprising that more of the better work has not been done in view of the great interest in, and the undoubted significance of, the area.

A further note

Very recently, Rittenhouse et al. (1990) presented the framework of an ongoing longitudinal study enquiring into the costs and benefits of early intervention for severely hearing-impaired infants. The programme includes a comparison of age at start of intervention, with one group of infants started before age 9 months and a second group started at age 18 months. Other important aspects are comparisons of different amounts of intervention, and a comparison of signed communication and oral approaches. Preliminary findings are available for the latter comparison only, for which no statistically significant differences were obtained across the several psychological domains assessed. The full results of this study, and especially for the effects of age at start of intervention, are awaited with interest. Meantime, and despite the authors' concern for reliable and valid work, we note that in starting the 18-month-old intervention group before the children were 3 years old (apparently because of a legal requirement) this study partly begs the question of early versus late intervention.

Chapter 3
The Speech Reception of Hearing-impaired Children

Speech reception involves both hearing and vision, requiring a discussion of both auditory speech reception and speechreading (lipreading). This chapter introduces the aural/oral area and discusses some important features of work with hearing aids, cochlear implants, and vibrotactile and electrotactile aids. There follows an account of speech perception by hearing-impaired children, with remarks on clinical applications. Finally, an outline is given of the processes involved in speechreading, and the extent to which it may be trained.

Although they use mainly their hearing to receive speech, communication by hearing children usually involves speech reception both by hearing and by vision – by hearing the talker's voice, and seeing the talker's lip movements, facial expressions and gestures. Speech reception is thus aural and oral. The oral features of speech are particularly helpful when listening to speech in a noisy background (Miller, 1947; Hawkins and Stevens, 1950; Festen and Plomp, 1990). For hearing-impaired children who communicate via residual hearing and speechreading (lipreading), the oral features are increasingly helpful as severity of hearing loss increases. For the greater hearing losses, the communication method is known simply as oral communication, or oralism, since stress is laid on the speechreading component. Reliance on speechreading alone is known as pure oralism. Thus oralism has no concern with manual communication. It disregards gesture, sign language and the like.

The hearing-impaired children who are expected to succeed best with the oral approach are those who have a significant degree of residual hearing, are fitted early with hearing aids, and are given early and ongoing training in speechreading and aural rehabilitation (Paterson, 1986; ASHA, 1990; Osberger, 1990; Smith and Richards, 1990).

Children with profound to total hearing loss who do not so succeed are sometimes referred to as 'oral failures'. Recent developments in cochlear implants and tactile devices offer to make speech perception more accessible to such children, and present a new impetus for the oral approach. We begin our review of speech reception in hearing-impaired children by briefly describing the use of hearing aids, cochlear implants and tactile instruments.

Hearing Aids, Cochlear Implants and Tactile Aids

There are few hearing-impaired children who are so deaf that they cannot receive some help from conventional hearing aids. However, they need training if they are to use the hearing aids to best effect. Even with training the benefit may amount to little more than perception of the suprasegmental stresses and rhythms of speech for children with profound losses. Further, there is a small proportion of profoundly to totally deaf children, whose deafness is such that they achieve little or no help from a hearing aid. Until recently these children would have relied on speechreading alone, or on manual communication, or on a combination of the two.

Conventional hearing aids

Electric amplifying hearing aids became available in the early 1900s. They soon stimulated work in aural/oral communication for children with usable residual hearing (Lou, 1988). The rationale is that, as soon as a significant hearing loss is determined, a child should have speech made accessible by a suitable hearing aid, with encouragement to use speechreading, thus increasing exposure to verbal language.

Technical progress with hearing aids progressed steadily. Electronic hearing aids were developed in the 1930s and 1940s, which saw the introduction of the first wearable hearing aids. Transistors permitted the miniaturisation of aids and the reduction of battery size in the 1950s. There followed further developments in solid-state electronics and the introduction of the microprocessor to develop signal processing aids, which shape the incoming signal to facilitate perception of speech. Microphones have been miniaturised and made directional. Amplification (gain) is now available up to 60–80 dB. Hearing aids have also developed cosmetically. Miniature hearing aids are now commonly fitted behind the ear or in the ear itself, and are made of inconspicuous flesh-tinted plastics. Yet the most sophisticated modern hearing aids, even those containing peak clipping, automatic gain control and/or noise-suppression circuits are only moderately successful in restoring hearing to normal, except for uncomplicated cases of conductive hearing loss. Hearing aids do not restore normal hearing as spectacles restore impaired vision to normal, not even the latest FM radio, speech coding, or digital noise suppressing hearing aids (Byrne and Walker, 1982; Flexer and Wood, 1984; Harris et al., 1988; Montgomery and Edge, 1988; McAlister, 1990; Thibodeau, 1990). The reasons are several. First, competing background noise intrudes on the speech signal (Chazan et al., 1987; McAlister, 1990). Secondly, the speech source will alter from one instant to another in distance or orientation from the hearing-aid wearer and hence is variously affected by background noise. Thirdly, most hearing aids are basically amplifying devices that weakly address the poor frequency resolution often found in inner-ear hearing loss (Turner et al., 1987). The best way to deal with background noise is to remove it at source. Unfortunately, however, in schools and other places where learning occurs few steps are taken to reduce background noise. As regards the third point, probably the most promising approach will be to undertake more detailed research into the characteristics of impaired hearing rather than to continue with the present technology-driven thrust in the design of hearing aids.

Selection of a hearing aid is a relatively complex procedure nowadays, but it was not always so. Just after World World II, prescriptive approaches were recommended by Davis et al. (1947) in the USA and the Committee on Electroacoustics, Medical Research Council (1947) in the UK. These approaches, developed independently in each country, recommended that the frequency response of hearing aids should be flat or increasing with audiofrequency, and that one frequency response would suit most hearing-impaired people. This resulted in a limited range of off-the-shelf hearing aids. It was criticised by Robbins and Gauger (1982) because many subjects in both studies had flat conductive losses. This criticism is fair, but hearing aids with frequency responses increasing with frequency, as most do, emphasise the middle to higher frequencies, notwithstanding that the earmould reduces the 2–4 kHz gain from the resonance of the open ear canal (Guelke, 1985). Such middle to high frequencies are important for understanding speech because salient speech information is carried by those same frequencies.

More recently, hearing aids have been selected to suit the individual's communication needs, as determined by psychoacoustic measurements. One commonly used method for sensorineurally impaired listeners (Byrne and Tonisson, 1976; Byrne and Cotton, 1988) involves selection of the in-the-ear frequency response of an aid such that the patient will hear all speech frequencies equally loudly, and with control of maximum power output. Preferred listening levels for aided speech occur typically between 1/3 and 2/3 of the interval between the hearing threshold and the level at which the speech is uncomfortably loud (Byrne and Cotton, 1987). This finding shows that it is better to amplify speech to comfortable listening levels, rather than seeking to restore hearing thresholds to normal. Ross (1975) has described a similar approach for preverbal children.

A child with measurable auditory responses up to about 500 Hz may be aided to perceive the first formant frequencies of most vowels, voicing and nasality cues, and the transitions of front plosive consonants, besides suprasegmental features. Auditory responses up to 1 kHz further allow access to the first formant frequencies of mid-vowels, the second formants of back and mid-vowels and the second formants of several voiced consonants (Stone and Adam, 1986). Hence, provided that they also get suitable guidance and instruction, even children with 'corner' or 'ski-slope' audiograms can use hearing aids to assist speech perception.

Despite such developments, there are often doubts that children are appropriately fitted with hearing aids (Matkin, 1981; Flexer and Wood, 1984; Diefendorf and Arthur, 1987), especially when the child has little or no speech with which to test the fitting. The emphasis has been on the electroacoustic functions of hearing aids, on technical aspects of selection and fitting, and on design features. It is disappointing that recent studies concerned especially with training in the everyday skills of using and maintaining hearing aids are few (Flexer and Wood, 1984; Stone and Adam, 1986), apart from instruction in simple maintenance (Diefendorf and Arthur, 1987). It is also of concern that little work has been published on the cosmetic or other psychological reasons why a child or parents may reject a hearing aid, even when properly fitted.

A small proportion of hearing-impaired children obtain no useful hearing for speech, even when fitted with the most powerful hearing aids. They perceive only grossly distorted speech or uncomfortable vibration. For these children the alternatives for speech perception, apart from speechreading, are cochlear implants or tactile devices.

Cochlear implants

Following earlier reports (Djourno and Eyries, 1957; Simmons, 1966; Michelson, 1971), but mainly since House (1976), those patients with an inner-ear hearing loss too great for them to be helped by conventional hearing aids have increasingly had the option of the cochlear implant prosthesis. The rationale is to bypass damaged hair cells in the cochlea and to stimulate the auditory nerve neurons (Parkins and Houde, 1982). Thus cochlear implants are designed to convert sounds into electrical energy to stimulate the auditory nerve fibres directly. The reader is referred to Northern (1984) for excellent descriptions of the relevant anatomy of the ear.

Work on cochlear implants developed fast. The ASHA Ad Hoc Committee on Cochlear Implants reported in 1986 that there were then more than 1000 cochlear implantees throughout the world (Ad Hoc Committee on Cochlear Implants, 1986). In the same year, House and Berliner (1986) considered that the House/37 cochlear implant system was no longer investigational and had become clinically feasible. Since then many more implants have been fitted, as teams of surgeons, engineers, speech and language scientists, audiologists and therapists have followed up the original advances. A small proportion of implantees can conduct a normal conversation without speechreading and some now use the telephone (Cohen et al., 1989). Reports on the management of communication for cochlear implantees are now appearing in quantity.

Cochlear implants can be grouped according to whether they are single-channel, with one active and one indifferent electrode, or multichannel devices, with up to 24 electrodes. House (1976) developed a single-channel device employing a carrier signal modulated by an analogue of the sound stimulus. Sounds relayed by this device appeared more natural than when the acoustic analogue was directly applied to the electrode placed in the scala tympani, but the device did not produce good speech perception without visual cues. Bilger et al. (1977) evaluated a number of single-channel implantees in the USA. These patients could identify some environmental sounds such as door-knocks, were assisted in speechreading because of intensity and timing information, improved their voice quality, and obtained some psychological benefits. All had good frequency discrimination up to 200 Hz, and a few up to 1 kHz. However, none had speech discrimination above chance level without visual cues. It is noteworthy that comparable results were obtained in the UK by Fourcin et al. (1979), using the much less invasive technique of an electrode on the promontory, within the middle ear.

Single-channel implants have been criticised for not operating according to the tonotopic structure of the organ of Corti, which functions as a series of bandpass filters, with low frequencies at the apex, towards the helicotrema, and high frequencies at the base, towards the oval and round windows. Thus, while single-channel work continued, other groups pursued multichannel devices, in which the active electrodes were distributed along the scala tympani, and hence along the organ of Corti. By the early to mid-1980s, patients fitted with multichannel devices were scoring above chance level on open-set word and sentence lists without visual information (Tyler et al., 1984; Dowell et al., 1985a). Subsequently, it has become accepted that multichannel implants offer more advantages for speech discrimination than single-channel types (Gantz et al., 1988; Spillman and Dillier, 1989).

Besides the number of channels and electrodes to be used, other important factors involve the design of the speech processor. This receives the sound signal, converts it to electrical form and then analyses and shapes it according to bandwidth, formant identification and selection output limitation, noise suppression, etc., before relaying it to the electrodes. This is a complex topic, beyond our present scope, but here, too, rapid advances are being made (Dowell et al., 1987; Wilson et al., 1988; Dorman et al., 1989; Skinner et al., 1991).

The performance of cochlear implantees was reviewed by Tyler et al. (1989) across five types of prostheses, with different numbers of channels and different processors, in France, Germany and the USA. Tyler et al. observed that all but one of the implant groups contained some patients who scored better than 10% on open-set words. They also remarked that the patients were selected as the better implantees in each clinic, so their results should not be seen as typical or average. Overall, performance on speech perception tests was modest, given that it was obtained from the better patients. Greater improvements can be attained with the addition of speechreading, though speechreading can be much improved with simple information such as speech envelope signals (Dorman et al., 1991).

Selection of patients for cochlear implantation

The earlier cochlear implant work was done with adults, especially bilaterally postlingually profoundly deaf adults, but some work was soon done with prelingually profoundly deaf adults (Eisenberg, 1982; Fugain et al., 1985). Eisenberg reported responses to gross sounds and music, with changes in voice quality, but not speech perception. Fugain et al. found similar results with postlingually and prelingually profoundly deaf adults. Generally, the amount of benefit that prelingually deaf adults can acquire from cochlear implantation is not certain. Ling and Nienhuys (1983) thought that at least three kinds of profoundly deaf patients were eligible for cochlear implantation: infants who were congenitally or prelingually deaf; adolescent or adult prelingually deaf people; and adults deafened postlingually through disease or injury. Each kind of patient would need a different kind of rehabilitation programme after implantation.

Experiments on the effects of cochlear damage in young animals (Trune, 1982; Chouard et al.,1983) led to suggestions for cochlear implantation at the earliest possible age. At present, the children most suited to cochlear implantation are those known to be bilaterally totally deaf. Even children born profoundly but not totally deaf may be more suited to conventional hearing aids. To assess definite bilateral total deafness before the age of 2 years is at present somewhat optimistic. Few children are considered for implanattion at so young an age. However, the number of reports showing improvements in life style, speech perception and speech production with cochlear implantation is increasing for children implanted at age 2 years and upwards (Bouse, 1987; Cunningham, 1990; Waltzman et al., 1990). Dawson et al. (1990) reported that of 21 implantees aged 3–20 years, five achieved significant scores on open-set speech perception tests using hearing without speechreading. Phoneme scores for monosyllabic words ranged from 30% to 72% correct. Word scores for sentences ranged from 26% to 74%. Four of these five patients were implanted before, and the fifth during, adolescence. Eight children, aged 3–11 years, could use auditory inputs in closed-set speech perception or vowel imitation tasks. The remaining implantees, aged 13–20 years, did not achieve open-set recognition but were all full-time implant users. It is likely that very young children will be candidates for implantation in the near future. The interest in early intervention for communication in hearing-impaired children suggests that this development will be a priority.

The remarkable feature of the advent of clinically viable and routinely available, if costly, cochlear implant programmes is that a prospect is in view in which most cases of total deafness may be eliminated. Many cases of profound deafness may be assisted to a handicap no greater than that sustained in severe hearing impairment. Even though there continue to be reports of patients who received minimal or limited benefit from the prosthesis (Abel and Tse, 1987) and the outcomes can be very variable (National Institutes of Health, 1988), such instances will decrease over time as surgical techniques become more apposite, the prostheses become more effective in converting speech sounds into appropriate electrical stimuli, and rehabilitation techniques become more sophisticated. In turn, this implies that over the coming years it will be increasingly possible for the profoundly to totally deaf to communicate via the auditory modality and, perhaps more significantly, for the prelingually hearing-impaired infant to receive therapy and education more effectively through aural methods.

So rapid have been developments in cochlear implantation that deaf people who communicate manually have seen cochlear implants as a threat to their existence as a separate culture within society. In some instances they have reacted negatively (Chapter 9). There is little doubt that this debate will become more acute in the next few years.

Vibrotactile and electrotactile aids

The use of vibrotactile stimulation was investigated long ago by Gault (1924) and Knudsen (1928). More recently, Oller et al. (1986) remarked that hearing individuals, with their hearing masked by noise, can learn to recognise a vocabulary of up to 150 words following 40–80 hours of practice on multichannel vibrotactile devices.

Such stimulation was not widely pursued as an aid to communication for hearing-impaired people until the advent of cochlear implants. Tactile stimulation now enjoys a new lease of life, especially as a supplement to speechreading (Oller et al., 1986; Terrio and Haas, 1986; Boothroyd and Hnath-Chisholm, 1988; Eilers et al., 1988a,b; Boothroyd, 1989). It offers both an alternative to implantation and a more exacting comparison or control for implant-assisted speech perception than conventional hearing aids, when patients are so deaf that they cannot perceive conventionally aided speech. Vibrotactile devices, using the sense of touch or vibration, can compete with cochlear implants if they are developed as wearable communication aids (Ling and Nienhuys, 1983; Blamey et al., 1988; Cowan et al., 1989).

The sense of touch has long been used with deaf–blind people, as the Tadoma method, to allow them to perceive aspects of speech and to develop some facility in language (Alcorn, 1932). In this method the subject places a hand on the talker's face to register mouth, lip and jaw movements, flow of air from the mouth and nostrils, and vibrations of the larynx (Reed et al., 1985; Chomsky, 1986; Leotta et al., 1988). The ASHA Ad Hoc Committee on Cochlear Implants (1986) observed that speech perception using the Tadoma method is similar to that of normal listeners for speech in noise, at signal-to-noise ratios of −6dB, and offers a standard for the comparison of tactile instruments. Proficiency in the method requires lengthy training and physical contact between talker and listener.

Plant et al. (1984a) reported on a single-channel vibrotactile aid, which provided additional information on duration of voicing and intensity in speechreading for an experienced subject. They found significant improvements at the phonemic, word and sentence levels when using the aid to supplement the visual signals, and in aided tracking of discourse. Other tests showed that the aid helped in perceiving word syllable numbers and types, stress and syllabic structure of sentences, and final consonant contrasts. In addition, the aid facilitated the identification of several environmental sounds.

Some people use a 'tactual phonology' to identify words by analogy with familiar ones (Frost and Brooks, 1983). Eilers et al. (1988a) have argued further that the close correspondence between tactile and auditory discrimination and identification of some vowels and consonants is evidence that aspects of speech are amodal.

Collins and Hurtig (1985) suggested that the maximum usefulness of tactile instruments in reducing ambiguities in speechreading cues could depend on phonemic recognition by tactile signals alone. They observed that the boundary for the voiced–voiceless distinction in hearing subjects occurred at longer voice-onset times (VOTs) for tactile than for auditory perception. Their results could explain the findings of Johnson et al. (1984) who explored the categorical perception of hearing-impaired children on a VOT continuum. Johnson et al. found normal VOT boundaries in some children. Other children, however, with longer than normal VOTs and who tended to be profoundly deaf, showed results similar to those for tactile stimulation in the Collins and Hurtig work. The similarity between their categorisations of speech sounds, and the categorisations of speech sounds presented to the finger tip in the Collins and Hurtig study, suggests that their responses were to tactile stimulation, as Collins and Hurtig pointed out. This conclusion is consistent with clinical suspicions that the audiometric responses of profoundly deaf children may be to tactile rather than hearing sensations for lower to middle audiofrequency stimuli.

Training in tactile representation of speech was illustrated well by Brooks et al. (1987) with an 18-channel tactile vocoder which presented stimuli via solenoids on the arm. Two prelingually profoundly deaf teenagers, with some skills in sign language and speechreading, attained 80% correct identifications for a 50-word vocabulary in 24 and 28.5 hours of training. Notably, the faster learning rate was achieved by the teenager with the better language skills. Next they were asked to place 400 random presentations of 16 CVs into five phonemic categories (voiced and unvoiced stops, voiced and unvoiced fricatives, and approximants), for which their mean accuracy was 84.5%. Then they were asked to place 400 random presentations of 12 VCs into four phonemic categories (unvoiced stops, nasals, unvoiced fricatives, and voiced stops), for which their mean accuracy was 89.6%. The mostly successful placing of the CVs and VCs into phonemic categories, shown on a stimulus list, indicated that the teenagers had acquired general rules about speech features with this multichannel device.

It is to be expected that results with different tactile devices will vary for different applications. Plant (1988) compared the performance of five commercially available tactile aids using a closed-set test of speech contrasts with five profoundly deaf subjects. Four of the devices were single-channel and the fifth was multichannel. Plant found marked task-to-task variation in the use of individual aids for speech contrasts. For example, one of the single-channel devices was best for suprasegmental contrasts, while the multichannel instrument performed best for segmental contrasts. The implication is that single-channel devices suit perception of the more unitary features whereas multichannel devices are needed to discriminate features which vary multidimensionally.

The sensation of vibration can also be elicited by electrocutaneous stimulation, where the signal stimulates the skin electrically (Blamey et al., 1988; Cowan et al., 1989; Blamey, 1990). Oller et al. (1986) described an elementary and preschool programme using vibrotactile and electrocutaneous vocoders in speech reception and production training with 13 profoundly deaf children aged 3–6 years. These children used an auditory training device at the same time. Their training included presentation of speech through touch (vocoders), vision (speechreading), and hearing (FM auditory trainer), in combination and isolation. Phonetic training was based on normal phonological development patterns, speech error patterns of the hearing-impaired, and the relative salience of the tactual speech features of the two vocoders. Further training was given with syllables, words and simple sentences. After training over an academic year, there were gains in speech production and reception, with rapid progress by most children, and generalisation of speech learning to situations that did not involve tactual aids. Those children who progressed the least were multiply handicapped, but even they showed measurable gains. Overall, the children progressed in speech learning in ways not found prior to training with tactual vocoders, and their results look impressive. However, adequate controls were not included for progress which might have been attained by conventional methods alone, or for 'halo' effects from the wearing of the vocoder devices. No differences were reported for comparisons of vibrotactile and electrocutaneous stimulation. Alcantara et al. (1990), however, found that the electrical stimulation of nerves under the skin was more reliable and comfortable than stimulation of tactile receptors and nerve endings in the skin itself, suggesting that subcutaneous electrotactile stimulation is a technique well worth pursuing.

To conclude, this brief review of work with tactile aids shows they can be used to distinguish speech feature contrasts, especially at the segmental level, by both hearing and hearing-impaired adults and children. Some speech features can be distinguished categorically with tactile stimulation, as with hearing, and some people can use a 'tactual phonology' in processing new words. It also seems that single-channel devices may be better for suprasegmental recognition, whereas multichannel instruments are better at the segmental level, but more work is needed before firmer conclusions can be reached.

Tactile devices versus cochlear implants

We suggested earlier that tactile devices could be an alternative to cochlear implantation for hearing-impaired individuals who obtain no usable benefit from conventional hearing aids. We also suggested that tactile devices offer a comparison or control when considering cochlear implantation. Further, tactile devices might be considered for very young children, until their hearing levels and other characteristics can be assessed sufficiently accurately for cochlear implantation to be contemplated. So, how does the use of tactile aids compare with the results of cochlear implantation?

This question was considered by Pickett and McFarland (1985) in a review of data on speech perception with implanted electrodes and with tactile aids. Pickett and McFarland compared speech reception data with a multichannel electrotactile aid (Sparks et al., 1979) with data from a Melbourne multichannel speech processor implant (Clark and Tong, 1982; Dowell et al., 1985a, b). They concluded that, despite difficulties in data comparison, speech reception via implants, even with a processor specially designed to transmit speech information, was not much better than tactile reception of speech. The main reason was probably that both devices conveyed the spectral information of speech very grossly. There was spread of electrical stimulation by the implant and poor spatial (frequency) resolution on the skin by the tactile device. In comparing other sets of multichannel implants and tactile instruments, their general conclusion was that the speech perception of implantees was not substantially better than that of subjects well-practised with tactile-devices. Perhaps their most significant conclusion was that neither implants nor tactile devices, either then or in the near future, could provide more than a modest aid to speechreading.

More recently, Skinner et al. (1988) reported different conclusions. They presented a comparison of the results from three different vibrotactile aids and cochlear implants (Nucleus 22 Electrode) for postlingually deaf adults. Four such adults were assessed with a 1- or 2-channel vibrotactile aid and, following surgery, with the multichannel cochlear implant. Skinner et al. concluded that the speech perception using the multichannel cochlear implant, a later model than that used in the review by Pickett and McFarland (1985), far surpassed that of the vibrotactile aids. A similar conclusion was drawn by Staller et al. (1991), who observed a clear trend towards continued improvements with longer-term use of multi-channel implants. More studies of this kind, with multichannel devices of both types and with controls for practice, are needed before the findings can be generally accepted as conclusive.

There is a theoretical consideration suggesting that cochlear implants may be preferred to tactile devices. Hearing people process speech through a phonological code. Cochlear implantation, designed to stimulate the hearing structures, is likely to bring these phonological coding mechanisms into play in processing spoken material. Although (Frost and Brooks, 1983; Eilers et al., 1988a) some people can use a 'tactual phonology' to process new words, and although Collins and Hurtig (1985) found a close correspondence between tactile and auditory perception of several speech features, there is some doubt as to whether tactile devices can take full advantage of such coding. There is much work to be done before this issue can be resolved.

Training in the use of cochlear implants and tactile devices

Since our interest is in communication skills, we should ask for more information on how users of cochlear implants and tactile devices have been trained in their use. The literature suggests that most studies have relied on a kind of guided practice. According to the ASHA Ad Hoc Committee on Cochlear Implants (1986), most centres involved with implants use a mix of analytic and synthetic approaches, with auditory-alone and auditory–visual practice to assist in the understanding of speech through the implant.

Speech perception via cochlear implants is believed to be only approximately speech-like. The advice is therefore to expose the implantee to a variety of speech and non-speech sounds, so that key features of both can be recognised. Even so, improved performance takes a long time for many implantees, suggesting that much practice is needed. The speech tracking procedure of DeFilippo and Scott (1978) is used for training and assessment in many implant programmes. In this procedure, a talker reads text phrase by phrase while the listener repeats each word. If the listener's response is incorrect, the talker repeats the phrase, or parts of it, until it is perceived correctly. Robbins et al. (1985) have described the use of this technique, finding that implantees who were previous hearing-aid users achieved a higher tracking rate than implantees with no previous experience of amplification. The technique can be quantified by measuring a 'communication rate', where the number of words in the text is divided by the amount of time needed to convey it. The procedure enables therapist and implantee to monitor progress, with instant knowledge of the results, but is more like guided practice than a training programme with predetermined goals.

Eisenberg (1985) is one of the few to have published specifically on training methods for implantees. Eisenberg recommended the use of tape recordings of both open- and closed-set stimuli, with the therapist directing the implantee's attention to time and intensity cues, together with cues from context. A set of responses ('yes-yes','no', 'please repeat') was offered by Castle (1984) to help an implantee in the use of the telephone, but only simple telephone communication is possible in this way, and only a few implantees appear to achieve success with it.

Tyler et al. (1986) found that previous experience with one type of implant could have a confounding effect on performance with another type later on. This study also provided evidence for generalisation of training, or experience, for the implantee investigated, though Tyler et al. saw it as a source of confounding.

Similar comments can be made about communication with tactile devices. Much of the training seems to have been based on guided practice. The work by Oller et al. (1986), outlined above, is an exception. In this study, which used tactile devices in a multisensory programme, training both speech production and reception, profoundly deaf children focused on tactile, auditory or visual speech features for syllables in articulation training, followed by a greater emphasis on word perception as phonological skills developed. They also focused initially on speech sounds as maximally contrasting pairs, progressing to word recognition in open sets in speech reception training. The training was hence based on normal phonological developmental sequences. Proctor (1990) followed the same kind of approach to tactile training with three hearing-aided profoundly deaf children who received multimodality experience in listening to and feeling sound while looking at the speaker. She found that the rate of progress in understanding oral language exceeded that expected of hearing children, though her small-scale study clearly needs replication with suitable controls and more subjects.

Auditory Perception of Speech by Hearing-impaired Children

Description of the communication skills of hearing-impaired children requires consideration of their speech perception at the level of the phoneme, word, phrase and clause. It also needs discussion in terms of the stress and intonation patterns of speech, which can vary within a single word or syllable ('Oh!' versus 'Oh?'), or across a sequence of connected speech, as when a sentence is changed from a statement to a question ('You caught the bus.' versus 'You caught the bus?').

Phonemic (segmental) aspects

The range of audio frequencies available to a hearing child is 20 Hz–20 kHz, but only the range from about 100 Hz–8 kHz is used in communication by speech. The first (F_1) and second (F_2) formants, the frequency bands of high energy associated with resonances of the vocal tract, which are needed for the recognition of vowels and voiced consonants, and the spectral energy of the voiceless consonants, fall in this range. However, the latter tend to have most of their energy distributed at higher frequencies than the vowel sounds. Hence children with high-frequency hearing losses have problems in perceiving the voiceless consonants characterised by place of articulation.

The consonants have less acoustic energy than the vowels as well as having their spectral energy concentrated at the higher end of the frequency range for speech-hearing. They are therefore more readily affected than vowels by a decrease in signal intensity or an increase in environmental noise.

Fortunately, neither vowels nor consonants usually have to be recognised alone. They are embedded in a context of syllables, words and sentences, which offer additional cues to their recognition. For the more easily lost or masked consonants it is often the transition component of the respective syllable, rather than the accompanying vowel in coarticulation, that aids consonant recognition. Transitions, like vowels, contain greater energy than consonants, and so the consonants can be recognised not only by the vowel but by the transition (Fletcher, 1953; Ladefoged, 1962).

Speech perception ability at the phonemic level is conveniently evaluated by lists of words spoken under controlled listening conditions. Error scores on such lists provide useful information as to where the child experiences phonemic confusions, and hence give pointers for training or therapy. A large variety of such word lists is available (Lyregaard et al., 1976; Keith, 1984; Martin, 1987). Some lists have been designed to meet special needs or purposes, but among those most commonly used are the open-response-set phonemically balanced word lists, designed to represent the phoneme balance used in the community. Examples are the isophonemic word lists of Boothroyd (1968) used in the UK and Australia, and the CID-W22 monosyllable word lists used in the USA (Hirsh, 1952; Hirsh et al., 1952; Studebaker and Sherbecoe, 1991). For young children the Wepman Test (1958) is used commonly in many English-speaking countries, though the Word Intelligibility by Picture Identification Test (Ross and Lerman, 1970) has many adherents.

The Boothroyd and CID-W22 word lists serve as 'general purpose' lists (Martin and Forbis, 1978; Evans, 1987). They are quick and convenient to administer, and have face validity as more 'natural' than nonsense syllables or synthetic word lists. However, they have been criticised when used in diagnostic audiometry to discriminate among individuals with differing degrees of sensorineural hearing loss, or as site-of-lesion tests (Geffner and Donovan, 1974; Lyregaard et al., 1976). Moreover, they are not particularly suited to testing for phoneme confusions, for which other tests are more informative. We shall return to this matter after considering impaired phoneme perception in more detail.

In a classic study, Miller and Nicely (1955) showed that hearing listeners used the articulatory and acoustical features of place of articulation, voicing and manner of articulation to identify phonemes. This work was later developed for both hearing and hearing-impaired listeners (Walden and Montgomery, 1975). For low-pass speech material, with middle and high frequencies missing, for example, hearing listeners confused place of articulation, whereas they perceived voicing and nasal manner correctly. As we have seen, hearing-impaired listeners who suffer from high-frequency hearing loss tend to present with the same confusions. Thus information is obtained on how the problem may be alleviated – by fitting a hearing aid with a high frequency emphasis, for example.

As stated, hearing-impaired listeners generally recognise vowels more satisfactorily than consonants. We now describe selected studies to give the reader some idea of the type of work involved.

Perception of vowels

A study of the vowels /i, u, ɪ, ɑ, ʌ, ɔ, æ / as recognised by 99 hard-of-hearing Gallaudet College students, was reported by Pickett et al. (1972). The students were in four groups with mean hearing losses of 67, 73, 82 and 88 dB HL. Allocation to these groups was made not by hearing loss but by scores on a version of the Modified Rhyme Test (MRT) (Fairbanks, 1958), with 50 monosyllabic words in a closed-set format presented to the better ear at 6 dB above each listener's most comfortable listening level.

Results were obtained for 20 initial and 20 final consonants, and 10 vowels. The respective vowel recognition for these groups was 91%, 76%, 62% and 48% correct. The group with the least severe mean hearing loss (67 dB), with 91% of vowels recognised correctly, produced minimal vowel confusions. For the 73 and 82 dB mean hearing loss groups the vowel confusions occurred mainly between vowels of similar F_1. Vowels with low frequency F_1 values were more readily confused than vowels which had F_1 values at the higher frequencies. For the 88 dB mean hearing loss group, vowels tended to be confused where their F_1 values were in the same frequency area, though vowels with low frequency F_1 values were the most confusable.

Vowel formant transitions, arising from the coarticulation of consonants and vowels, were investigated with a vowel synthesiser in three listeners with moderately severe, flat, sensorineural hearing losses by Martin et al. (1972). They found that, whilst this kind of hearing loss did not seem to impede the listener's abilities to use brief, small transitions in formant frequency as discrimination cues, it appeared to impede the ability to find such cues in listening to speech-like material, where the low-frequency formants masked the discrimination of transition cues in formants with higher frequencies. The effects were reduced by auditory training for some subjects.

The more severely hearing-impaired people can confuse vowels even when their formant frequencies differ considerably, as shown by Risberg (1976). He used a rhyme test with moderately to profoundly deaf Swedish children and young adults, aged 10–21 years, required to identify vowels in monosyllabic Swedish words. The vowels /u/, /o/ and /a/, which had frequency differences for F_1 and F_2 but had similar frequencies for F_3 and F_4, were used to determine hearing for formant frequencies below 1500 Hz. Hearing for frequencies above 1500 Hz was assessed by comparing /u/ and /i/, and /a/ and /æ/, for both of which pairs F_1 was similar but F_2 was different. Listeners with hearing losses between 60 dB and 69 dB showed the best recognition of vowels, though above 1500 Hz they partly confused vowels with different formants. Listeners with losses between 70 dB and 79 dB obtained recognition scores around 90% correct for vowels with different formants below 1500 Hz, and around 70% for vowels with different formants above 1500 Hz. A third group of listeners with losses of 80–89 dB obtained recognition scores of about 70% for vowels with different formants below 1500 Hz, and scores of only 40% for vowels with different formants above 1500 Hz. Risberg thus showed that listeners with the more severe to profound hearing losses tended to confuse vowels even when the vowels differed in formant frequencies. Listeners with moderate to severe losses, however, made confusions for mainly those vowels which were distinguishable by formants above 1500 Hz.

In similar work, Fourcin (1976) investigated vowel perception in hearing-impaired children with two-formant synthesised vowels /i/, /a/ and /u/, of which /i/ and /u/ had the same F_1 values but were distinguishable by the amplitude of F_2. The more severely hearing-impaired children were confused in recognising /i/ and /u/, but were able to recognise /a/ correctly. As with Risberg (1976), the children with the least severe hearing losses were able to recognise the vowels without great difficulty. More recent work (Pickett et al., 1983) has continued to show that, as hearing loss increases, it is more difficult to discriminate between vowels where the distinguishing acoustic features are of higher audiofrequency.

A different approach to vowel perception was taken by Bochner et al. (1988), who compared the perception of hearing and hearing-impaired listeners for changes in length of vowels and tonal complexes (filled intervals). Both hearing and hearing-impaired subjects showed greater acuity for the duration of filled as compared with unfilled intervals. The mean thresholds for filled, but not unfilled, intervals from the hearing listeners were significantly smaller than those from the hearing-impaired subjects, though a few of the latter showed acuity comparable to that of the hearing listeners under several listening conditions.

In an interesting twist, the usual experimental arrangement, in which perception of a given set of vowels is compared across various groups of subjects, was changed by Turner and Henn (1989) to allow for individual differences. They obtained measures of frequency resolution from individual hearing-impaired subjects to predict each subject's vowel recognition ability. Input filter patterns were obtained at six test frequencies from hearing and hearing-impaired listeners. These patterns were then used to compare frequency resolution with vowel recognition in the same listeners, to find the relationship between impaired frequency resolution and vowel recognition. This study therefore provided a link between individual differences in vowel perception by hearing-impaired subjects and the underlying problems of hearing loss and impaired frequency resolution. Taken with Bochner et al. (1988), it provides an increasingly complex, but increasingly complete, picture of the dimensions in which the vowel recognition of hearing-impaired listeners differs from that of hearing people.

Perception of consonants

There has been considerable research into consonant perception by hearing listeners (Pickett, 1980). However, research into consonant perception by hearing-impaired listeners is comparatively recent. It is generally agreed that moderately to profoundly deaf listeners have reduced access to speech contrasts and spectral cues, for example, in consonant distinctions (Boothroyd, 1984; Revoile et al., 1991a, b), and where frequency selectivity is impaired (Preminger and Wiley, 1985) or otherwise.

We now consider consonant perception by selecting from work on voiced and unvoiced consonants, and on the perception of consonants characterised by place of articulation. Space does not allow us to give more attention to this important area, but the outline which follows should give the reader an overview of salient aspects.

Voiced consonants

Perception of initial stop consonants was studied by Bennett and Ling (1973) for CV monosyllables by hearing and severely hearing-impaired children. The stimuli, with six stops, were prepared for systematic variations in voice onset time (VOT), the period after the initial stop before the onset of the following vowel. The CV stimuli, with varying VOTs, which are relatively short for voiced stops and longer for unvoiced stops, were presented binaurally at comfortable listening levels to ten children with severe or greater hearing losses. Whereas hearing children make the distinction between voiced and unvoiced stops at VOTs of between 20 and 40 ms, similar to hearing adults, the hearing-impaired children showed inconsistent performance. They tended to identify more unvoiced than voiced stops at VOTs of 60 ms or more.

An additional cue was introduced by Fourcin (1976) in a second test as part of the synthetic vowel perception study described earlier. He varied the cut-back of F_1, so that for some trials the F_1 cue did not coincide with the initial VOT cue as it would in natural speech. He concluded that hearing-impaired children needed both cues for correct phoneme identification. The children with the more severe hearing losses could not perceive the VOT contrast at all. This finding is generally consistent with that of Bennett and Ling (1973) – see above – and a study by Parady et al. (1981), which used synthetic /da/–/ta/ stimuli generated along the VOT continuum.

The upward spread of masking, in which the lower speech frequencies mask the higher ones, has long been suspected of causing, at least in part, the poor speech perception of the more severely hearing-impaired listeners (Martin et al., 1972; Pickett and Danaher, 1975; Wightman et al., 1977). To test this hypothesis, Dorman et al. (1985) eliminated F_1 entirely from the speech stimulus. They found, nevertheless, that removing the first formant did not improve the stimulus intelligibility for listeners with sloping mild to moderate hearing losses for levels above, at, or below the level of maximum intelligibility. In particular, they concluded that this and similar results (Trinder et al., 1980; Kaplan and Pickett, 1982) showed that spread of masking from the first formant was not a significant factor in the identification of voiced stop consonants.

The use of cues by moderately to severely hearing-impaired and hearing listeners in voicing perception of initial stop consonants was explored by Revoile et al. (1987). They prepared tests in which different parts of syllable onsets were either deleted or changed for syllables of cognate voicing, and they flattened the F_0 contour for syllable pairs. Twenty hearing-impaired subjects with mild to severe hearing losses, and six hearing Gallaudet College students were the listeners. The results confirmed that VOT was a strong voicing cue for both hearing and hearing-impaired listeners, supporting the findings of Parady et al. (1981) in that the moderately, and some severely, hearing-impaired students showed relatively normal use of the VOT cue. The results did not, however, support Bennett and Ling (1973), where VOT cues were not perceived by the children tested, though these latter children generally had greater hearing losses than the Gallaudet students (compare Fourcin, 1976).

Perception of place

Some consonants characterised by place of articulation can be distinguished by means of the rate of change in transition frequency in the formants of the preceding and/or the following vowels ('by' versus 'die'). In these instances the consonants are both voiced and articulated in a plosive manner, but differ in place (bilabial and alveolar respectively). The acoustic cue is a fast change in the higher part of the acoustic spectrum, which causes problems for many hearing-impaired people (Sher and Owens, 1974; Reed, 1975), unless they supplement perception of the acoustic feature distinction by speechreading.

For instance, Godfrey and Millay (1978) asked listeners with mild and moderate sensorineural hearing impairment to report on synthetically produced /bɛ/ and /wɛ/ sounds across a range of frequency transition durations from 10 to 120 ms, in 10 ms stages. Nine listeners identified /bɛ/ and /wɛ/ normally, by ascribing /bɛ/ to transitions of 40 ms or less and /wɛ/ to transitions of 80 ms or more. The remaining six listeners showed a variable response, both among listeners and within individual listeners, depending on the stimulus presentation level. Some of the listeners identified all transition durations as /bɛ/ or as /wɛ/, while some produced nearly random identifications of /bɛ/ and /wɛ/ across the range.

Ochs et al. (1989) examined place of articulation in the synthesised syllables /bi/, /di/ and /gi/ in a group of subjects with a high-frequency hearing loss and two groups of hearing subjects, one listening with, and one without, masking noise. Stimuli with a moving F_2 formant transition ('moving F_2 stimuli') were compared with stimuli in which F_2 was constant ('straight F_2 stimuli') to assess the F_2 transition in perceiving stop consonants. For both moving and straight F_2 stimuli, the performance of the three groups was similar in identifying /di/ and /gi/. However, performance of the hearing-impaired and noise-masked hearing listeners was below that of the unmasked hearing group for /bi/ for moving F_2 and especially for straight F_2. Errors with /bi/ most commonly involved confusions with /di/. Among possible explanations, Ochs et al. noted that Dubno et al. (1987) had observed that both /b/ and /d/ were harder to perceive than /g/ for listeners with a sloping high-frequency hearing loss. Such a loss may distort the onset of /b/ and /d/ more than the more compact onset of /g/.

The general conclusion from this selection of reports is that the vowel and consonant perception of hearing-impaired listeners is far from a simple attenuation or other modification of speech as perceived by hearing listeners, and controlled stimuli are needed to explore it. The reports also show that hearing-impaired listeners differ from each other in phoneme perception, depending on the type and degree of hearing loss. Hence it is important to have information about phoneme perception by hearing-impaired individuals in devising aural rehabilitation programmes to improve communication skills. Although, as expected, misperceptions of speech commonly occur in noisy situations, a hearing-impaired child can fail to understand speech because of inability to discriminate phonemes in the quiet. Fortunately the facility to synthesise speech sounds has considerably sharpened our ability to test the phonemic features which cause difficulty for a given hearing-impaired child (Damper, 1982; Kangas and Allen, 1990). We will consider the place of such tests shortly, but first some mention must be made of perception of the suprasegmental phonemes.

Perception of suprasegmentals

Little work has been done on the perception of prosody by hearing-impaired children, apart perhaps from the use of prosody as a supplement to speechreading (Grant, 1987a, b). Erber and Alencewicz (1976) have, however, developed the CID-CAT test, available in expanded form as the CID-MONSTER, which consists of four words to be presented in three different prosodic forms, as in monosyllables, trochees and spondees. The test is then scored in two ways, first by the percentage of words identified correctly and secondly by the percentage of correct stress patterns correctly identified. So, when a monosyllable is presented and the child responds with a monosyllable the response is scored once for reporting its phonetic form and also once for its prosodic feature. This test recognises that a child with a profound hearing loss, say, may be able to perceive the prosodic information in the word although the phonetic feature is elusive. Merklein (1981) also prepared a test related to perception of prosody in his short speech perception test for severely and profoundly deaf children. His time pattern item, involving the ability to perceive and count syllable pulses, as monosyllabic versus multisyllabic utterances, underscores the perception of rhythm and disjuncture.

A further test, designed to assess prosodic information in connected speech, is the Stress Pattern Recognition in Sentence (SPRIS) test of Jackson and Kerry-Ballweber (1979). This test contains four repetitions of 12 simple sentences, each of which consists of four monosyllabic words. A different word is stressed on each presentation of each sentence. The test is scored in the same way as that of Erber and Alencewicz (1976), with scoring both for identification of the sentence and for identification of the stress pattern of the sentence. Interestingly, the authors found that young adults with severe to profound hearing losses showed a wide range of performances on the SPRIS test which could not be predicted from audiograms. They suggested that individuals with relatively good auditory skills who relied on spectral cues could be given training based on word recognition, whereas individuals with poor auditory skills who relied on prosodic information should receive training in word pattern recognition.

Clinical and Practical Applications

The recent work in perception of acoustic features, or speech patterns, by hearing-impaired listeners presents a challenge to conventional speech audiometric assessment with phonemically balanced word lists of the type mentioned earlier. So far, however, this challenge has not been particularly well recognised in the clinic.

Phonemically balanced word lists versus 'speech pattern' tests

Merklein (1981) thought it puzzling that phonemically balanced word list testing persisted in the light of work on speech pattern tests. He criticised phonemically balanced word lists for their large, inappropriate vocabularies, open-response format and learning effects (see Byrne (1983) and Walker et al. (1982) for some examples and further comment). Merklein sought tests of speech-hearing which would produce more precise and valuable information for selecting hearing aids, assisting in educational placement, and for auditory training and speech therapy. He pointed to tests and observations such as those of Boothroyd (1972a), Erber (1974, 1978) and Erber and Alencewicz (1976), which considered spectral or speech envelope information for testing speech-hearing, as a way forward. He himself presented a short test for severely and profoundly deaf children, which assessed perception of speech-envelope versus spectral patterns, together with suprasegmental (prosodic) versus segmental (phonemic) aspects.

The routine clinical use of conventional phonemically balanced word lists probably endures because clinical audiologists, pressed for time, choose a procedure that will quickly give them an overview of their patient's phoneme perception via tests that are well known and widely used, facilitating communication of patient data. It may also be due to concern to identify peripheral neural lesions, which result in disproportionately poor speech recognition (Evans, 1987), particularly for vowels (Hannley and Jerger, 1985).

The research on acoustic features has generally shown that the greater the hearing loss, the greater is the difficulty in discriminating differences in vowel formants, especially in the higher audio frequencies. Children with severe to profound sensorineural losses have poor discrimination of F_2 transitions, perhaps more so in the presence of F_1, as occurs in natural speech. They also show poor discrimination of the rate of frequency transitions. As regards final consonants, some hearing-impaired subjects show poor perception when the preceding vowel-duration cue is removed, while others can use the remaining spectral cues (King, 1987). Perception of differences associated with VOT is difficult for severely to profound deaf children, as we saw.

King (1987) proposed sound pattern tests based on differences in acoustic features and reflecting also the sound patterns related to the prosodic aspects of speech. Other recent approaches which make use of spectral and similar pattern information have been suggested by Fourcin (1976), Erber (1980), Plant (1984), Hutchinson (1990), Hazan et al. (1991). The FAAF test (Foster and Haggard, 1979, 1984) further aimed to assess word identification scores rather precisely in the region of the maximum score as a function of spectral parameters. The PLOTT test (Plant, 1984) was also developed to assess the ability of hearing-impaired children to use spectral or time–intensity cues. It consists of nine subtests: Subtest 1 measures the ability to detect vowels and consonants; Subtests 2 and 3 measure the ability to use spectral versus time–intensity cues; Subtest 4 is a test of discrimination for very familiar non-confusable words; and Subtests 5–9 assess perception of vowel length, vowel discrimination, consonant voicing, consonant manner and consonant place, using a picture-pointing response. The results from the PLOTT test provide very useful data about a child's speech perception in hearing-aid use, but the test takes a long time to administer.

It may have occurred to the reader that techniques now available for the computer manipulation of speech features could provide selective enhancement of aspects of speech, making the speech more intelligible to hearing-impaired listeners. For example, it might be advantageous to increase the silent intervals in speech to reduce the possibility of forward masking (Cazals and Palis, 1991). It could also be helpful to amplify consonants, whose acoustic energy is usually below that of vowels, so that the energy of the consonants approximates that of the vowels. Montgomery and Edge (1988) have done this kind of study with adults. They amplified the consonants by computer enhancement to produce near-zero consonant/vowel intensity ratios. The duration of consonants was also increased to provide an additional 30ms of sound, with compensatory vowel shortening to maintain the original overall duration. A word stimulus set so manipulated was presented at 65dB SPL(sound pressure level) to one group of 20 adult listeners with a moderate sensorineural loss, and at 95 dB SPL to a second, similar group of 10 listeners. The amplitude processing gave an increase of 10–12% in intelligibility for the 65dB SPL stimuli, but there was no significant effect for the 95 dB SPL stimuli. Increase of consonant duration gave no benefit at 65dB SPL, but resulted in a 5% improvement at 95dB SPL. The effects of speech stimulus enhancement therefore appear to be relatively small and differ for different stimulus presentation levels. More research is needed in this area, especially with subjects who have different types and degrees of hearing loss.

Perception of Connected Speech

Children appear to perceive speech on the basis of sentences, not words alone (Houston, 1972). They learn about the functions of morphemes, syntax and vocabulary in the context of sentence perception (Streng et al., 1978). Further, the suprasegmental characteristics of connected speech, in the forms of stress, intonation, rhythm and phrasing directly affect the meaning of the speech, and thus inform the child further about the functions of the segmental aspects.

We saw that practitioners prefer phonemically balanced lists of words to other types of speech material for assessing the speech-hearing of hearing-impaired children. Such word lists are commonly used in routine clinical practice when connected speech material might be used to advantage. One of the main reasons is undoubtedly the extra time taken for sentence test administration unless a reduced number of test items (sentences) per list is provided but, for statistical reasons, reduction in the number of items leads to lower reliability in response measures.

Sentence tests estimate speech perception in daily communication with a much higher naturally appearing face validity than word tests. The case for the use of connected speech material for clinical testing and rehabilitation is persuasive when, for example, natural sentences – namely sentences with commonly occurring vocabulary, familiar syntax and semantics – are considered as an alternative to phonemic balancing in word lists. The main case for using sentences is that perception of words alone does not necessarily predict the perception of sentences, because it cannot estimate the grammar and semantics in sentences. Such aspects constrain words in sentences, but not isolated words. Sentences also permit systematic studies of the time domain, since they are usually sufficiently long to allow variations in the temporal properties of speech (Speaks and Jerger, 1965). It is likely that most of the time we operate on the basis of the largest speech or language units, and only use smaller units to resolve ambiguities or to accommodate the unexpected. It is also likely that we ignore a large part of the more detailed acoustic and linguistic information in speech in order to achieve high speed and accuracy in processing it (Boothroyd, 1978).

In what follows, we consider connected speech mainly in the form of sentences. Of course, not all connected speech consists of sentences, particularly single sentences. There is a role for continuous discourse, as in discourse tracking, currently popular in assessing the use of cochlear implants (see above), though discourse tracking is broken up into phrases because of the memory load. It may also be objected that, in conversations between people who know one another fairly well, natural speech is markedly context-bound, seems rather unconnected, is heavily pragmatic, and is more like a set of loosely connected phrases than sentences. This kind of conversation is characterised as much by short, phrase-like interruptions, interjections or questions ('So what?', 'Ridiculous!', 'Can't follow') as by sentences. These objections are recognised, but in the following material we choose to concentrate on the perception of sentences as the standard form of connected speech.

Hearing for speech in sentences by hearing-impaired people differs from their hearing for words. Niemeyer (1972) presented a study of dissociated hearing loss in which a zone of normal hearing, or mild hearing impairment, is juxtaposed with a zone of severe or profound hearing loss (the ski-slope audiogram). He argued that what is redundant in sentence material for hearing people is essential for communication in the hearing-impaired, allowing them to close the gaps in speech perception. Thus the contextual association between words in a sentence makes it easier to perceive words in sentences than the same words presented in isolation. This difference can be measured as an 'informational reserve'. Niemeyer proposed a sentence-specific informational reserve as: $X = (SD - WD)/SD \times 100\%$, where SD is the discrimination score of words in sentences and WD is the discrimination score of the words presented in isolation. For German speech material, the informational reserve was about 54% for hearing people. Hence, about half of the information in the sentences was due to context.

Being dissatisfied with sentence list tests then available for child speech audiometry in the UK and the USA (see below), which were lengthy and contained unfamiliar vocabulary, Bench and Bamford (1979) devised new sentence lists from a detailed linguistic analysis of spoken language samples of 208 hearing-impaired children. The resulting BKB Sentence Lists were deemed suitable for testing the speech-hearing of hearing-impaired children aged 8 years or more. These lists were available in picture-related and standard non-picture-related forms. Only the latter is considered here.

Bench et al. (1979) compared the speech-hearing abilities on these BKB sentence lists with other sentence list tests (Fry, 1961; Watson, 1967) and word list tests (Boothroyd, 1968; BKB word lists) on 129 partially hearing children, with losses mainly of prelingual sensorineural origin. They found that the BKB standard sentence lists gave steeper slopes for performance-intensity functions, lower speech reception thresholds and higher discrimination scores than the other sentence lists and, relevant to the present discussion, the Boothroyd Word Lists and the BKB words. A similar study, with similar outcomes, was reported by Bench et al. (1987), on the BKB sentence lists adapted for use in Australia (BKB/A lists). Consistently better speech-hearing was shown in tests with the BKB/A sentences than for other sentence lists and, importantly, than for word lists. It follows that to assess a hearing-impaired child's ability for speech-hearing in an everyday communication context with word lists will generally underestimate such ability, and sometimes markedly so.

The implications for aural rehabilitation are clear, though individual examples vary depending on linguistic competence, as further work showed. Thus Bench et al. (1987) also presented data from three individual children, all of whom had similar pure-tone hearing losses (62–69 dB three-frequency averages) and similarly shaped audiograms. Near-perfect scores were obtained for one child at 90 dB relative speech level for sentences, whereas the child obtained only about 63% for word lists at the same level. The second child obtained a score of 86% for sentences, but only about 18% for word lists, showing a large effect associated with the contextual aspect of the sentences. The third child obtained about 40% with the sentences and about 26% with the word lists in the range of 70–80 dB relative speech level, thus obtaining relatively little information from the contextual information in the sentences and suggesting poor linguistic competence, with the words in sentences perceived perhaps as strings of unconnected or loosely connected words.

The CID or CHABA sentences (Silverman and Hirsch, 1955) have been the sentence list material most widely used in the USA, particularly with adults. They are especially helpful in assessing postlingually hearing-impaired patients of more mature years, especially geriatric patients, who are unable to communicate adequately. However, they are too difficult for most children, and even for some young adults with severe to profound hearing losses (Webster, 1984), as the vocabulary is suited to adults and the sentences are rather long.

Speaks and Jerger (1965) developed the Synthetic Sentence Identification Test, in which the test materials do not form natural-seeming sentences. They are statistical approximations to English connected speech, and have found acceptance in aural rehabilitation, in the assessment of central auditory dysfunction, and may be used in assessing the use of hearing aids. Dubno and Dirks (1983) suggested ways in which their reliability may be optimised. They are not generally suitable for work with hearing-impaired children, especially young children, but rather with the postlingually deafened adult.

The North American Speech Perception In Noise (SPIN) test (Kalikow et al., 1977), adapted for use in Australia by Upfold and Smither (1981), has taken the use of context further. Half of the sentences, presented in speech babble, contain high-predictability, and half contain low-predictability, test items. The subject is asked to identify the final word in each sentence. The score is obtained from differences between the tallies on high- and low-predictability items. The SPIN test finds its main applications in aural rehabilitation, hearing-aid fitting, and assessing central auditory dysfunction, since the speech information is degraded by the babble, with a decrease in redundancy and consequently increased perceptual difficulty for the central auditory system.

Children do not discriminate speech in noise as well as adults (Mills, 1975), and the use of a signal-to-noise ratio of +9 dB was suggested by Keith (1981b) for standardised speech material, such as the WIPI or other word list tests, with children. Somewhat surprisingly at first thought, performance-intensity functions can be obtained for words and short sentences from children as young as 2 years of age. The Pediatric Speech Intelligibility Test (PSI – Jerger et al., 1981; Jerger et al., 1983; Jerger and Jerger, 1984) was developed with a restricted message set and concrete target words, allowing performance-intensity functions to be assessed for the perception of sentences and words in the quiet and at varying message-to-competition ratios.

Conclusion: Need for Clarification of Objectives

From overviews of recent work on the perception of speech by hearing-impaired children, such as those by Dermody and Mackie (1987) and Markides (1987), it is clear that speech perception tests are recognised as an essential part of the assessment of the child's hearing abilities. However, the plethora of available tests shows a lack of clarity about the use and purpose of techniques for measuring speech perception. A clarification of objectives is needed to put speech perception tests on a sound basis for regular clinical and educational use. To give one example of what might be done, research with hearing children (Bever, 1970; Strohner and Nelson, 1974) has indicated that in developing sentence comprehension strategies in English, young children tend to rely on pragmatic and semantic strategies, whereas older children rely mainly on word order to decide on the basic grammatical relations. However, following a cross-linguistic study, Bates et al. (1984) expressed caution about the existence of universal hypotheses of language structure. They felt that young children aged 2–5 years may not be able to make full use of some interpretative cues for sentence comprehension because they cannot appreciate the discourse functions of the cues.

Generally, the writer believes that for routine clinical work the most promising information about a child's hearing for speech will be obtained from speech pattern tests for phoneme perception and from sentence materials for perception of connected speech. As with Merklein (1981), it is difficult to see a continuing role for word lists.

Enhancement of the Intelligibility of Perceived Speech

On a different but related topic, work on speech perception in hearing-impaired children can suggest to teachers and therapists ways of enhancing their own speech to make it more intelligible to the children. There are many publications on the linguistic styles used by teachers and others to classes and groups of hearing-impaired children (Craig and Collins, 1970; Hutton and Whatton, 1981; Kyle and Allsop, 1982; Wood et al., 1986; Wood, 1991). There is also a long history of research on the characteristics of clear speech (Snidecor et al., 1944; Tolhurst, 1957; Nooteboom, 1973; Gay, 1978). However, studies of speech characteristics that affect the intelligibility of speech to hearing-impaired listeners are relatively recent.

Picheny et al. (1985) presented a set of nonsense sentences ('Their pail bails my tone') spoken by three male talkers to five adult listeners who had moderate to severe inner-ear hearing losses, increasing with frequency. The talkers recorded 40 'conversational sentences' alternating with 40 'clear sentences'. For conversational sentences, the talker was asked to recite the sentences in the way he spoke in ordinary conversation. For clear sentences he was asked to speak as clearly as possible, as if trying to communicate in a noisy environment or with a hearing-impaired listener. He had also to enunciate consonants more carefully and with greater vocal effort than in conversational speech, and to avoid slurring words together. Talkers were asked to stress nouns, adjectives and verbs in both types of sentence.

The results gave a 17% advantage overall in perception of clear versus conversational speech. The difference depended on the listener and talker to only a small extent, and was independent of presentation level and frequency-gain characteristics. Analysis of segmental-level errors showed that the increase in intelligibility with clear sentences occurred across all phoneme classes.

In a second study, Picheny et al. (1986) reported acoustic analyses of conversational and clear speech. They found that speaking rate decreased substantially for clear speech, and was achieved by inserting pauses between words and lengthening the durations of individual speech sounds. Also, while the vowels were modified or reduced and word-final stop bursts were often not released in conversational speech, the vowels were modified to a lesser extent and the stop bursts, as well as almost all word-final consonants, were released in clear speech. Further, the intensities for plosives, especially stop consonants, were greater in clear than in conversational speech. Interestingly, since the listeners were hearing-impaired with poorer hearing at the higher frequencies, the changes in the long-term spectrum were small, so that speaking clearly was not equivalent to giving the speech a high-frequency emphasis, though it would be of practical interest to try such an experiment.

Speechreading

Watching a talker's lips is like hearing speech by eye instead of by ear. Hearing speech by eye in speechreading shares the attributes of hearing written words by eye in reading (Williams, 1982), where inner speech serves a mediating role for most hearing people (Conrad, 1972a, b, 1979; Moores, 1970).

Speechreading assists hearing individuals in speech perception but, for most of the time, speech can be understood perfectly well without speechreading. The situation is quite different for profoundly and the more severely deaf individuals. If they wish to understand speech, if only imperfectly, they need to speechread. The use of residual hearing by itself seldom offers a full alternative.

Speechreading and hearing

A very useful test of primary modality for speech perception in hearing and hearing-impaired children was described by Seewald et al. (1985). The test material consisted of the four 25-item lists of the Word Intelligibility by Picture Identification (WIPI) test, which were video-recorded. Lists 1 and 2 were prepared for an auditory/visual conflict condition by pairing, for example, the visual production of the word 'school' from list 1 with the acoustic production of 'broom' from list 2, and so on, with the vowels matched but not the consonants. List 3 was used for auditory-alone, and list 4 for vision-alone testing. Responses from conflict lists were scored twice, once for accuracy for video-presented, and once for audio-presented, stimuli. Subtracting the visual from the auditory performance score gave the primary modality for speech perception (PMSP).

Results from 15 hearing and 69 mildly to profoundly deaf children aged 7;5 to 14;8 years, with known or suspected congenital hearing impairment, showed the PMSP score decreasing through the auditory portion of the PMSP continuum into the visual part, as hearing loss increased ($r^2 = 0.84$). All hearing children had PMSP scores which were strongly auditory, and all children with hearing losses greater than 90 dB HL were strongly visual. All children with losses of more than 95 dB HL had scores within the visual part, even with their auditory amplification functioning properly. The shift from auditory to visual speech perception as the primary modality occurred between 80 and 90 dB HL. Hearing loss and auditory word identification performance accounted for about 90% of the PMSP variance. The authors thus concluded that the relative use of hearing or vision in speechreading of words was almost entirely related to the children's hearing level and aided speech reception. Such clear-cut results are not often found for congenitally hearing-impaired children. It would therefore be of interest to replicate this study.

Although speechreading is like hearing by eye, speechreading is not as effective as hearing by ear in perceiving speech. Even highly skilled speechreaders have difficulty in perceiving some parts of speech. Many phonemes and words, such as the homophenous words 'man' and 'ban', look very similar on the lips. A large proportion of speech sounds cannot be seen on the lips, as they are produced in the rear of the mouth. Thus some of the vowels can be distinguished only with difficulty in speechreading, as their articulation is barely reflected in lip position contrasts. Also, vowel intelligibility may be poorer for CVCs with highly visible consonants, especially fricatives and labiodentals (Montgomery et al., 1987). Only about 40% of speech sounds in English are visible on the lips (Bode et al., 1982).

Hence speechreading skills depend heavily on filling the gaps between the visually apparent phonemes, or visemes, by drawing on linguistic and other contextual information. Skilled speechreaders are linguistically highly able. They are also practised 'gamblers' – or perhaps 'informed guessers' would be a better way to describe them (Lyxell and Ronnberg, 1987). For the profoundly deaf speechreader the knowledge of vocabulary and syntax, which informs the guessing of phonemes which do not have visemic counterparts, has to be learned via residual hearing and poor visual information to begin with. Such an impoverished cycle implies a difficult and protracted learning process for obtaining skills in speechreading, even though normal human vision, like hearing, has a wide dynamic range and can resolve fine time differences down to 20 ms (Geldard, 1972).

Hearing people can increase their speech perception in noisy situations considerably if they can see the talker's face. The advantage is equivalent to increasing the signal-to-noise ratio by about 15 dB (Sumby and Pollack, 1954). Seeing the talker's face increases speech perception from minimal to 80% correct or more for sentences presented at about 10 dB below the noise level, for noise of uniform spectrum from 100 to 7000 Hz (Miller et al., 1951). The reasons seem to be fourfold. First, acoustic cues for place of articulation, unlike the cues for voicing and nasality, are of low amplitude, are mainly above 1 kHz, and are defined by narrow, often transient, spectral features (Kryter, 1970). Conversely, speechreading is particularly effective for the visual perception of place (Binnie et al., 1976; Boothroyd, 1978). Secondly, seeing the lips of the talker provides additional reinforcing information to hearing speech at the segmental level. This redundancy of speechreading on hearing helps to reinforce perception of consonants, particularly the voiced consonants. It also aids perception of some vowels. Hence, when the auditory segmental information is masked by noise, it can be seen visually on the lips of the talker (MacLeod and Summerfield, 1987, 1990). Thirdly, speechreading allows the hearer to concentrate on the talker rather than the noise, by providing visual cues on the timing of the speech signal, and fourthly it provides paralinguistic information about the broader context, such as the communication environment and characteristics of the talker.

While the use of vision in speechreading assists the perception of speech in noise by hearing people, the use of hearing can help the speechreader. A number of studies (Utley, 1946; O'Neill, 1954; Brannon, 1961; Hull and Alpiner, 1976; Erber, 1979) found that vision alone permits the attainment of about 50% of speech intelligibility, which would be 100% in the auditory modality. Hearing, even at minimal levels, adds considerably to the comprehension of visible speech (Hull and Alpiner, 1976). Even auditory information limited to voice intensity cues, F_o or to low-pass (200 Hz) speech can lead to significant improvements in speech perception (Plant et al., 1984b; Grant, 1987b; Rosen et al., 1987), especially for listeners with no auditory frequency selectivity or who have narrow dynamic ranges above 500 Hz. Other work (Faulkner et al., 1990) suggests that profoundly deaf listeners who can use information from the manner of articulation are aided more in speechreading by selected speech pattern combinations than by exposure to whole speech.

Processing of speechread information

In a famous study, McGurk and MacDonald (1976) reported that hearing 'ba' while watching a video-recorded 'ga' on the talker's lips gave rise to the illusion of perceiving 'da'. This finding has been confirmed and extended by others, producing fusions, as in the above 'ba' + 'ga' = 'da', where the percept shares phonological features of the phoneme and viseme but results in the perception of a new consonant, and blends where both consonants are perceived, as in 'ba' (seen) + 'ga' (heard) = 'bda' or 'bga' (MacDonald and McGurk, 1978; Summerfield, 1979). Audiovisual fusions have also been reported for vowels (Summerfield and McGrath, 1984). Subjectively, the subject has the experience of hearing the illusory syllable. Even when told to report only the acoustic component, the subject reports the illusory compromise (Summerfield and McGrath, 1984).

This finding suggests strongly that both the heard and the seen syllables are processed at some stage by the same perceptual mechanism. What sort of process might this be? Both share a common source in articulation. It might therefore be that the speechreader refers both visual and auditory speech inputs to an articulatory processor. The modification of the auditory input by incompatible visual input in the audiovisual fusions supports such a view. However, such fusions are heard and not seen, and not some heard and some seen, which may raise problems for an explanation based only on an articulatory processor.

Audiovisual fusions have forced researchers in speech perception to take account of visual information besides the auditory input. That fusions or blends are obtained, rather than that either the visual or the auditory input is dominant, suggests that speech perception is to some degree amodal, and not as acoustically special as some would have it (Diehl et al., 1991; Fowler, 1991). Further, it raises the question of whether speechreading plays only a gap-filling function when speech is difficult to hear, or whether vision is of use in speech perception even when the speech sounds are heard clearly.

We know from our earlier discussion that speechreading serves to fill at least some of the gaps when speech is imperfectly heard. Further Reisberg (1978) reported that, when the speech is clearly heard, hearing subjects' performance in shadowing speech improved with vision, even when the visual information was only a loudspeaker grille. Thus, one function of vision while perceiving speech is to keep attention on the speech source. Reisberg et al. (1981) also showed that their subjects' auditory attention was associated with where they were looking. If they looked at a loudspeaker presenting the speech, their recall of the speech material was better than if they looked at a loudspeaker which produced irrelevant material. The conclusion is that we can better attend auditorily to speech while we are looking at the source than if we look at the source of alternative material. This conclusion confirms our everyday experience. It is of practical relevance for speechreading the teacher in noisy classrooms, where there are many possible competing speech sources from chattering children (compare Markides, 1989a).

In subsequent experiments Reisberg et al. (1987) showed that speechreading improved speech perception by 15% when shadowing a foreign language, when the speech material was hard to understand rather than hard to hear. Similar findings were obtained when shadowing complex speech material in English, the subject's native language. Thus speechreading added to the understanding of the speech, even when the acoustic signal was heard clearly. Together, these findings suggest that speechreading and hearing share the same perceptual processing system at some level. Tactile representations of speech can be perceived phonologically, as we have seen. There is thus a sense in which speech perception is amodal.

Costello (1957), Myklebust (1964) and Fry (1966) were among the first to develop the insight that speechreading, which monitors speech articulation, could be processed by a phonological code, based on hearing, which allows thinking to be done in words as inner speech. This view gathered adherents in subsequent years, covering reading and writing also (Morton, 1970; Locke, 1978). It is of interest to review the literature on speechreading and auditory speech perception from infancy, to assess to what extent speech perception develops synchronously in the two modalities.

We noted that the fetus is responsive to audiofrequency stimuli, that newborn babies are responsive to sounds, particularly complex sounds rather than tones, and that young infants of a few months old can make phonemic distinctions. Newborn babies and young infants show a preference for looking at human faces in a variety of test situations (e.g. Wilcox, 1969). According to Kuhl (1980), 4-month-old infants can distinguish all, or almost all, the acoustic cues at the segmental level of speech, while Spelke (1976) found that infants of the same age could associate sight with sound. With these findings in place, suggesting the potential in young infants for associating lip movements with speech, Dodd (1979) studied attention to speech by 12 hearing infants aged 10–16 weeks, when the speech and lip movements were in and out of synchrony. She found that the infants attended significantly more to the in-synchrony presentations, a result congruent with the view that the visual and auditory inputs are mediated by a single code, which is not specific to either modality. A similar conclusion can be drawn from Dodd (1972), who reported that the babbling patterns of 9- to 12-month-old infants were affected by auditory/visual stimulation, in the form of 'babbling' by the experimenter, and eye contact, probably including watching of lip movements, with the experimenter, but not by auditory or social (play) stimulation alone.

Although these studies suggested that infants can associate lip movements with hearing for speech in their first year of life, they did not show that the infants were speechreading. Therefore Dodd (1987) further studied a group of 18–36-month-old infants to test their ability to speechread known words presented in a carrier sentence ('Show me the _____') in a picture identification task. The target word was spoken by the experimenter in a pre-test and silently mouthed in the test condition. Although performance was poorer in the test (speechreading) condition than in the pre-test (heard) condition, the speechread task was completed significantly above chance level, showing that the infants could speechread familiar words. Interestingly, the infants understood easily that a speechread stimulus corresponded to a word.

These results indicate that speechreading and hearing for speech develop synchronously in infancy, and that speech stimuli in the auditory and visual modalities are processed together, suggesting that the processing is amodal. Infants combine the two speech-information inputs, rather than treating them separately.

Nevertheless, the correlation between scores on auditory-only and speechreading-only performance for the same test material may be low, or statistically non-significant. For instance, Raney et al. (1984) found no significant correlation between auditory and visual performances on CID Everyday Sentences for 30 normally hearing and sighted, or vision-corrected, young adults, implying that the ability to perceive speech in one modality provided little information about speech perception in the other. However, only one speaker was used, as was the case with most of the studies described above. The perception of speech can differ markedly between auditory and visual perception of different speakers (Lesner, 1988).

Speechreading and hearing impairment

Vision can play an important part in the perception of those consonants, vowels and diphthongs which are articulated on the lips and from the middle to the front of the mouth. The articulation of these speech sounds gives the hearing-impaired child the most help in speechreading. The lips, tongue and mouth opening provide the most useful information. Some visual cues are not easy to perceive, however, especially for cognate consonantal groupings, such as /f/ versus /v/, where the distinction is conveyed by slightly different positioning of the upper teeth on the lower lip, and /p/ versus /b/, where the lips are first shut and then separated. The reader is referred to Jeffers and Barley (1971) and Berg (1976b) for a description of the speechreading cues for English phonemes. There is a large literature devoted to the performance of hearing-impaired people on speechreading tests, and on test development, materials, talker characteristics, environmental conditions and non-verbal cues (O'Neill and Oyer, 1961; Berger, 1972; Berg, 1976b; Farwell, 1976; Davis and Hardick, 1981; Sims, 1982; De Filippo and Sims, 1988).

Although we know a great deal about the performance of hearing-impaired people on speechreading tests, and about many factors which affect their speechreading, we are not so well informed about how their linguistic ability affects their ability to speechread, despite the well-established connection between linguistic ability and hearing loss (Berger, 1972; Bench and Bamford, 1979; Conrad, 1979; Quigley and Kretschmer, 1982). It is difficult to know whether the performance of children in tests of speechreading is due to perception of information from the talker's lips and face, or whether it is the child's knowledge of language which is being assessed. Conrad (1979), for example, argued that there were two parts to the question of the proficiency of hearing-impaired children in speechreading. The first was how well the children use speechreading as a perceptual skill involving both vision and residual hearing; the second was how to devise the language material to be speechread.

A recent study by Fletcher (1986) has provided evidence that hearing-impaired children may have a special skill in processing visual information analogous to the lip openings characteristic of English vowels. He set up target dots on a video screen which could be moved vertically through intervals representing the range of lip openings found in the production of vowels. The children's task was to align a feedback dot with the target dot via small light-emitting diodes attached to their lips. Fletcher used children aged 5;7 to 14;1 years for this task. His group of 10 severely to profoundly deaf children showed higher velocities of lip movement, and shorter latencies in reaching goal positions, than a group of 10 hearing children, though both groups were equally accurate. Since the hearing-impaired children performed the task more quickly than the hearing children, it followed that they were more skilled. It was not clear, however, whether the higher skill lay in more rapid perception of the target shift, or in exercising the lips to align the feedback dot with the target, namely whether the skill was enhanced in the perceptual or motor aspects.

Coding for speechreading

Oral education of profoundly deaf children can also affect their speechreading ability, which raises the question of how the speechread information is coded in perception. Dodd (1976) showed that a group of prelingually profoundly deaf children aged 9–12 years consistently employed phonological rules in the use of consonants to name pictures. Their phonological processes were very similar to those of younger hearing children but, although it appeared normal, the phonological development of these profoundly deaf children was delayed. This finding raised the question of whether the phonology was acquired through an acoustic trace reinforced by speech teaching, or through internalising a speechread trace. In a second experiment with 12- to 16-year-old children, Dodd used nonsense words, which the children could not have been taught to speak, and which they could not hear in the experiment. In one condition the children had to speechread the nonsense words and, in a second condition, to read them. The results showed that the phonological rules had in the first, real word-naming experiment predicted the pronunciation of the nonsense words in the second. Further, the children speechreading the nonsense words performed more like the children in the first experiment, than when reading. These results implied that speechreading was the source for the development of the phonology. This outcome was supported by a further study (Dodd and Hermelin, 1977), in which profoundly congenitally deaf children made significantly fewer speechreading errors for homophone pairs predicted as easy to speechread than pairs predicted as hard to speechread.

The overall conclusion to be drawn from Dodd's work is that prelingually profoundly deaf children can acquire a spoken phonology derived from speechreading, similar to that of hearing children, but at a slower rate, possibly because of more slowly developing language ability. Those errors which do not follow the same pattern of errors found in hearing children can be explained on the basis of speech segments which are hard to speechread.

This explanation was supported by Campbell and Wright (1989), who assessed immediate recall for written CV lists in orally educated congenitally deaf teenagers and hearing controls. The deaf teenagers showed a significant consonant 'lipreadability' effect. Thus, the written syllables were harder for them to recall if those syllables contained consonants such as /D, SH and Z/, whose place of articulation is not visually distinctive. By contrast, syllables were easier to recall if they contained visually distinctive consonants, such as /F, TH and B/. Campbell and Wright concluded that phonological representation was poor for written consonants which are hard to speechread. No such effect was found for the hearing controls. Therefore, while the deaf teenagers were using a phonological code, that code produced a different performance in the immediate recall of written CV lists from that of the hearing children.

Conrad (1979) argued that we did not know, in an absolute sense, how well hearing-impaired children could speechread in everyday communication if we did not know about their language ability. In this sense the validity of results obtained on many tests of speechreading is open to question, with the exception of a few studies which have assessed both speechreading and language ability, usually finding a positive correlation (De Filippo, 1982; Meadow, 1968). Conrad's conclusion from his own work was that not only did children show a decline in speech comprehension with hearing loss because they knew less language, but they also speechread less of what they knew. Even when language ability was considered, the hearing-impaired children continued to have greater difficulty in speechreading with increasing hearing loss. A possible explanation is that hearing-impaired children are weak in the information-processing skills associated with speechreading (see below).

The large range of individual differences in the speechreading ability of hearing-impaired individuals has led to investigations of possible covariates, besides linguistic ability. Several reports have presented results for the effects of intelligence on speechreading. The results are generally very variable (Farwell, 1976; Conrad, 1979), with an overall picture of low to moderate positive correlations. Possibly the more intelligent hearing-impaired individuals are better able to use their language ability as a key to the sequencing and meaning of visemes in speechreading. However, the low values of the reported correlation coefficients suggest that speechreading is difficult to learn. Thus the view of speechreading as a learned communication skill is somewhat questionable. Speechreading appears to improve with age (Farwell, 1976) but whether this improvement is due to an increase in visual perception skills or in language ability (De Filippo, 1982) is unclear.

In conclusion, more research is needed on the development of speechreading skills and their coding, with suitable controls for language ability and intelligence.

Neurophysiology and speechreading

To date, neurophysiological covariates have not proved to be particularly illuminating in speechreading, though significant advances have been made in study of the hemispheric lateralisation of differences in visual information processing (Keenan et al., 1989). Earlier suggestions of a link between visual–neural speed and aspects of speechreading skill (Shepherd et al., 1977; Samar and Sims, 1983) were not supported in a more recent study by Ronnberg et al. (1989). The picture is complex, as Ronnberg et al. did find significant correlations for some context–free word discrimination and sign-alphabet conditions for visual–neural peak-to-peak amplitudes.

Further, the neurophysiology involved may be at a lower level of brain organisation. Mead and Lapidus (1989) reported that for 62 hearing and mild to moderately hearing-impaired children, of mean age 10;4 years, the ability to speechread sentences from a silent film was significantly related to psychological differentiation, as expressed in cognitive style, and pre-task skin conductance level, but not to hearing capacity or skin conductance level during the task. Speechreading ability was predicted best by performance on a Rod and Frame test and large increases in skin conductance from pre-task to task, implying that speechreading performance improves with a marked increase in level of arousal. This outcome is congruent with the research of Samar and Sims (1984), who suggested that sensitivity to the timing of a light flash was related to their subjects' expectations in speechreading.

Use of cues in speechreading by hearing-impaired individuals

We saw that only some 40% of phonemes are visible on the lips, and that speechreading is slow to be learned. Also, a relatively high proportion of hearing-impaired individuals have visual defects (Johnson et al., 1981; Gottlieb and Allen, 1985), a large proportion of the profoundly deaf population has poor acoustic short-term memory and coding skills for speech, and profoundly deaf people can have difficulties in dealing with information that is ordered sequentially (Hermelin and O'Connor, 1975; Grove et al., 1979; Grove and Rodda, 1984). We may therefore wonder if speechreading is a realistic option for many prelingually profoundly deaf children, despite some undoubted successes. Speechreading ability, even with the help of residual hearing, develops too slowly for many children to attain sufficient language ability in their early years, creating a linguistic lag which is difficult to overcome (Brasel and Quigley, 1977) and which, in turn, reduces the efficiency of speechreading.

Little is known about how profoundly deaf people who are good speechreaders go about perceiving speech compared with poor speechreaders, although the issue is not new (Kitson, 1915; Markides, 1989b). This means that the processes underlying speechreading are uncertain, although there are many clues – several of which have been described earlier – to go on. Although there is information about the background to speechreading, such as the articulation of the mouth and lips, the visibility of speech segments, styles of speech, types of speech material, lighting effects, paralinguistic cues, etc. (Lott and Levy, 1960; Erber, 1972; Franks, 1979; De Filippo and Sims, 1988; Markides, 1989b; Silverman and Kricos, 1990), little is known of how the expert speechreader uses them, or even if some of them are used to any great extent in any given condition. Research into the skills used by expert as compared with inexpert speechreaders is therefore a matter of pressing need.

A method of investigating some of the processes involved was suggested by the work of Busby et al. (1984), who investigated vowel perception in four profoundly deaf children aged 13–14 years in auditory-alone, vision-alone and audiovisual conditions. They used multidimensional scaling analysis of the confusion matrices to assess the underlying dimensions, and the individual differences found on the dimensions (compare Erber, 1972). Significant individual differences were found in parameter emphases in the auditory and audiovisual conditions. In a further paper, Busby et al. (1988) assessed the identification of consonants in /a/ – C – /a/ nonsense syllables by four profoundly deaf children aged 13–14 years. Performance was better with vision alone than with aided hearing alone. In an audiovisual condition the children predominantly combined the acoustic parameter of voicing with the visual signal. There was considerable consistency for the visual perception of vowels by lip opening, and consonants by place of articulation. These two studies suggest, in the context of identifying what makes expert readers, a method for assessing how vowels and consonants are perceived, which may be used with speechreaders of varying speechreading expertise.

Speechreading of connected speech in some hearing-impaired individuals seems to be influenced by their skills in information processing rather than their hearing loss. Lyxell and Ronnberg (1989), for example, explored verbal inference-making ability by sentence- and word-completion tests in hearing and in mildly to moderately deaf adults, finding that only sentence-completion was correlated with speechreading performance. The contribution from working memory and word-completion was mainly through their contribution to sentence-completion, for both hearing and hearing-impaired speechreaders, whose performances were similar.

Given evidence that hearing-impaired individuals are generally less able or no more skilled at speechreading than hearing people (Conrad, 1977b; De Filippo, 1984), do they use the same psychological processes in speechreading as hearing subjects? According to Dodd et al. (1983), orally educated prelingually profoundly deaf children could not be distinguished from hearing children in serial recall behaviour, including the recency effect, for speechread lists. They also reported that both hearing and profoundly deaf children did not demonstrate the recency advantage when the speechread lists are followed by a speechread suffix. Since it is likely that phonological processing is required for these effects to occur, it appears that both the hearing and hearing-impaired children used a phonological code. This is not so surprising since even congenitally profoundly deaf users of sign language show some evidence of phonemic confusions in recalling words (Hanson, 1982).

At the present state of knowledge, differences between speechreading in hearing and hearing-impaired people seem to be due principally to differences in information processing skills and language ability including inner speech, provided that allowance is made for possible visual defects.

Training in speechreading

We have referred to the study by Raney et al. (1984), who found that, for young hearing adults, the ability to understand CID Everyday Sentences presented in the audio-only mode did not correlate well with the ability to understand these sentences when presented by video-channel. This result suggested that auditory and visual skills can operate separately, as well as in conjunction. High-level visual skills do not necessarily imply high-level auditory skills, and generalisation of skills from one modality to the other need not occur. Although separate training for consonant perception of the visual and auditory systems will improve combined visual and auditory sentence recognition (Walden et al., 1981), unimodal training may be limited to the system used and not generalise well to other systems. However, Crawford et al. (1986) have argued that improvements in speechreading are likely to be affected by methodological and subject differences. It may be, for example, that subjects with low pretraining scores on speechreading tests will improve significantly with extended training, but show little or no change with short-term training.

Generally, it is hard to find evidence for successful training in the visual modality (De Filippo, 1990), which is a worry if we wish to regard speechreading as a skill which can be learned. However, Dodd et al. (1989) have recently described a study in which hearing-impaired students used a 3-hour videocassette containing nine lessons over a period of 5 weeks. The students showed a significant increase in speechreading performance in comparison with a control group which did not study the lessons. This report provided more convincing evidence than some of the earlier work on speechreading training, especially since speechreading generalised to unfamiliar speakers and materials.

Practice alone, rather than specific training, improves speechreading performance in both hearing and hearing-impaired subjects (Bannister and Britten, 1982; Squires and Dancer, 1986; Lesner et al., 1987; Warren et al., 1989). The improvement in performance typically ranges from about 3% to 10%. This percentage is of the same order as effects often ascribed to training, and occurs with both massed and distributed practice. Most subjects tend to show an increase in performance in the early trials, soon reaching a performance plateau, which continues for an extended period of time. Hence controls for practice effects are needed before claims for the efficacy of training in speechreading can be accepted as valid (Warren et al., 1989), particularly in the early phases of training. Few studies have included such controls up to the present time.

Given also that until quite recently there has been surprisingly little research on talker effects, which are known to be significant (Kricos and Lesner, 1985; Lesner, 1988), and that extended training may be confounded with improvements in language ability (Conrad, 1979), much of the research which argues for improvements in speechreading ability with training has to be regarded as suspect. The situation is yet further confounded with performance measures, type of material and task, type and amount of feedback, etc. (Fenn and Smith, 1987; Lesner et al., 1987; Small and Infante, 1988; Markides, 1989a).

In concluding, we note that the area is now the subject of extensive research, and hence useful findings can be confidently expected in the near future. Nevertheless, definitive work on training in speechreading will need to control for practice and language learning effects, which now bedevil the interpretation of most published research.

Chapter 4
The Produced Speech of Hearing-impaired Children

Deaf speech is characterised by features that give it distinctive properties, as described in this chapter. Also outlined are some approaches to speech training and work with speech-training aids. Deaf speech is generally difficult to understand. An account is given of studies that have attempted to explore some of the reasons for the poor intelligibility of deaf speech, with suggestions for further work.

Children who are born severely or profoundly hearing impaired or become deafened soon after birth have great difficulties in acquiring speech. Such children not only hear the speech of others very imperfectly, even if aided, they also have problems in monitoring the sounds of their own voices through auditory feedback. Thus differences in babbling have been found between hearing and hearing-impaired infants as early as the second 6 months of life (Oller et al., 1985). The greater the degree of hearing loss, the more difficult it is to learn speech, whether monitoring and controlling the loudness and the rhythms of the speech, in articulating speech sounds, or in co-articulating combinations of speech sounds (Smith, 1975a; Geffner and Freeman, 1980).

However, this is only part of the problem. Having learned some speech, hearing-impaired children need to maintain it. To do so involves monitoring their speech by hearing, touch and kinaesthesis, but this monitoring is impaired because of the impaired hearing, and so the speech tends to deteriorate. It is therefore not surprising that deaf children differ from hearing children in cerebral control of their speech production. Hearing children's cerebral control for produced speech appears to be left-lateralised, whereas deaf children show more symmetrical patterns of cerebral control (Marcotte and La Barba, 1985).

Older children and adults who become deafened after speech acquisition also experience deterioration in their speech, because they can no longer adequately hear what they are saying, but the order in which aspects of their speech deteriorate with time is controversial. It has been thought, following short-duration auditory feedback studies with hearing people, that the suprasegmental features deteriorate rather than features at the segmental level (Ladefoged, 1967; Ternstrom et al., 1988; Ball, 1991). Investigation of seven long-term postlingually totally deaf subjects by Waldstein (1990), however, indicated that all classes of speech sounds were affected. There is also evidence that the speech of people who become postlingually deaf in their earlier years deteriorates in both segmental and suprasegmental aspects more than for those who become deafened later (Plant and Hammarberg, 1983; Waldstein, 1990).

Since produced speech in hearing children is accompanied by monitoring the voice, speech is not so much a complex motor skill as a complex perceptual–motor skill. In developing speech, hearing children shape their speech sounds to match the phonology of their language by selecting those sounds which reflect the syntax and semantics of the language. For hearing children, learning to speak is a natural part of development. Hearing-impaired children on the other hand have to be taught their speech. Because they cannot, or can only partly, rely on auditory feedback in monitoring their speech, they have to use their visual, tactile or kinaesthetic senses to a greater degree than hearing children, depending on their degree of hearing loss. It proves very difficult to learn fluent speech through these senses, because the feedback they provide is less precise than feedback through hearing. As a result the speech of hearing-impaired children contains interjections (Smith, 1975b), is rarely as intelligible to the listener as that of hearing children (Bernstein et al., 1988) and the central phonetic processing as well as the speech may suffer (Fletcher et al., 1985).

Selected characteristics of the speech of hearing-impaired individuals will now be reviewed. We will also investigate how their speech may be trained. A substantial portion of the chapter will be spent on the intelligibility of deaf speech, as the understanding of speech is of major importance to communication.

Deaf Speech

The speech of hearing-impaired individuals tends to be characterised by features which set it apart from the speech of others, though the speech of a given deaf person does not necessarily show all of them.

Articulation

The classic study in the area of articulation is that of Hudgins and Numbers (1942), who found five types of vowel error and seven types of consonant error in the speech of 192 mildly to profoundly deaf children aged between 8 and 20 years. The vowel errors, in order of preponderance, consisted of substitutions, vowel neutralisations, creation of two syllables from one vowel, simplification of diphthongs by splitting them into two separate vowels or omitting one component, and vowel nasalisations. The consonant errors, also in order of preponderance, consisted of initial consonant deletions, devoicing of stops, insertions and deletions, final consonant deletions, denasalisations, substitutions, and vowel insertions.

✕   Deaf people learning to speak can develop a different kind of articulatory coordination from that of hearing speakers. For example, their jaw and tongue positions in vowel production following consonants may not vary consistently (Tye-Murray, 1987), although deaf speakers tend to move the body of their tongue in a similar way for all vowels (Tye-Murray, 1991). Further, the speech of deaf individuals is characterised by prolongations of vowels, even in multisyllabic words (Tye-Murray and Woodworth, 1989), associated with vowel neutralisation which involves overlapping of F_1 and F_2 formants (Angelocci et al., 1964; Monsen, 1976; Osberger, 1987).

Vowels are particularly difficult for prelingually profoundly deaf children to learn, probably because the articulators rarely come into contact in vowel production, preventing tactile feedback (Povel and Wansink, 1986). Monsen (1976) showed for hearing-impaired adolescents that F_2 remained stable around 800 Hz, irrespective of the vowel the speaker was attempting to produce. The result was reduced phonological space when accompanied by a restricted range for F_1. Similar findings have been reported for languages other than English (Shukla, 1989).

Vowel production is important in most spoken languages, including English, because vowels form the nuclei of words (Osberger, 1987). They often signal the adjacent consonant by formant transitions, so that a poorly produced vowel may result in misperception of not only the intended vowel but the adjacent consonant as well. Accuracy of vowel production is highly correlated with the speech intelligibility of profoundly deaf speakers (Monsen, 1976). Although F_1 is associated with changes in lower jaw movement and thus with vertical tongue movement, F_2 is associated with forward and backward movements of the tongue (Fant, 1962), which are difficult for hearing-impaired speakers to perceive. Monsen ascribed the difficulties in articulation of F_2 by his hearing-impaired adolescents to this reduced perception. Distorted articulation in the speech of hearing-impaired children is also defined by prolonged articulatory contacts (Angelocci, 1962), slow articulatory movements (Monsen, 1978), and slow articulation of syllables (Stevens et al., 1978; Osberger and McGarr, 1982).

Besides distortion, the speech of hearing-impaired children is remarkable for a high incidence of articulatory errors in the form of consonant omissions at the ends of words, phrases and sentences, which are the result of misplacing the tongue and of poor control of the aerodynamic flow (Markides, 1970; Smith, 1975a; Mencke et al., 1985). The reader will recall, however, that Hudgins and Numbers found consonants were omitted more commonly in the initial than the final position. The apparent discrepancy may be due to sampling differences and/or the type of test material (compare Geffner and Freeman, 1980). Markides (1983) reported for profoundly deaf and partially hearing children of primary and secondary school age that omissions were more common for final consonants, and substitutions were more common for initial consonants.

Smith (1975b) additionally noted interposed sounds in the speech of deaf children. She observed recurring patterns of excrescent or interjected sounds associated with movements of the articulators, and attributed them to slowness of movement, overshoot resulting in a greater than normal degree of constriction to yield affricate-like substitutions or glides, mistimed laryngeal action, and mistimed velar action. Tongue action was involved in 43% and lip action in 29% of the occurrences.

The speech of hearing-impaired people is also notable for the insertion of frequent and lengthy inter- and intra-word pauses (Osberger and McGarr, 1982; Stathopoulos et al., 1986). Their speech contains unusual segmentation, reducing its intelligibility, though Abdelhamied et al. (1990) were able to achieve automatic recognition of deaf speech by using these inter- and intra-word pauses to attain recognition rates as high as 93% and 82% for isolated words and connected speech respectively, only about 5% less than for the speech of hearing people. They argued that deaf speech has its own norm, showing typical and systematic patterns.

Suprasegmentals

Many profoundly deaf children produce suprasegmental features which are traditionally associated with 'deaf speech' (Angelocci et al., 1964; Martony, 1968; McGarr and Harris, 1983). Partially hearing children may show difficulties also, but not always if their language development level is considered (Weiss et al., 1985). Such errors or difficulties are described variously as problems with prosody, intonation, nasality, pitch, breath control and voice quality. Also, timing errors, involving prolonged stop closure duration where the time interval between starting the sound and releasing it with a burst of air is prolonged, have been described in semi-intelligible young hearing-impaired adults (Whitehead, 1991).

Typically deaf children speak stressed and unstressed syllables with the same duration or with less of a difference in duration than hearing children. Tye-Murray et al. (1987) suggested that it may be more problematical for deaf speakers to produce long stress patterns than short ones. Thus not only do hearing-impaired children need to be taught correct articulation at the phonetic level, where the sounds have relatively little individual meaning, but they must also be taught to combine these sounds into connected speech, and to appreciate the contribution of the suprasegmental aspects.

It is of interest to consider whether deaf speakers' problems in producing stress patterns are due to impaired motor control of speech or to linguistic factors. To answer this question, Tye-Murray and Folkins (1990) asked deaf and hearing subjects to speak sets of homogeneous syllable strings which they could tap out with a finger, and hence could understand. Strain gauges monitoring lower lip and jaw movements revealed that deaf and hearing subjects produced different durations and displacements for stressed and unstressed syllables. There was no evidence that motor abilities affected the production of stress patterns in the deaf speakers. Thus when the deaf subjects understood a given stress pattern they could speak it, even when they did not articulate the segments correctly. This outcome showed that the deaf subjects were not aware of phonemic distinctiveness via stress.

Voice pitch and quality

Voice pitch, which can be a suprasegmental feature as well as part of voice quality, is directly related to the function of the vocal folds. It is controlled during voicing by the tension of the vocal folds and the subglottal air pressure. In hearing children voice pitch tends to decrease and show lessening variability with age from early infancy (Robb and Saxman, 1985). Measurements of speech fundamental frequency (F_0) in hearing-impaired people, however, have presented mixed and conflicting results. Horii (1982) reported higher than normal F_0 values for 12 hearing-impaired girls aged 16–19 years. Leder et al. (1987) found more recently that F_0 was significantly higher in profoundly postlingually deaf than in hearing men, but not all studies have found voice pitch to be higher in hearing-impaired people. Whitehead (1987), using the pitch rating procedure of Subtelny et al. (1980), compared experts' perceptual judgements of pitch level with F_0 values for 156 young males of mean age 19;6 years and 104 young females of mean age 19;2 years with severe to profound hearing losses, on an oral reading task. The judgements of pitch level and mean F_0 values were significantly related for both male and female subjects. The mean F_0 values showed a range of vocal frequencies from below to substantially above normal. The results thus showed that most of the young adults had F_0 values not greatly different from those of young hearing adults, and they were judged to have a spoken pitch level at, or not too far removed from, the optimal level. Only a minority, of both males and females, produced spoken pitch judged much above optimal, with associated high F_0 values.

Hearing-impaired people may also have unusual voice quality, characterised by over-aspiration, spectral noise and so on. A frequent problem in deaf speakers is over-aspiration of initial voiceless stop and fricative consonants (Hutchinson and Smith, 1976; Whitehead and Barefoot, 1980). The over-aspiration, which may increase the tactile feedback for the speaker, gives a breathy quality to the speech and changes the temporal pattern. It is related to misarticulation rather than faulty laryngeal function.

Harshness of voice, related to spectral noise, in hearing-impaired children has been investigated by Thomas-Kersting and Casteel (1989). They compared spectral noise levels and ratings of perceived vocal effort in the voices of severely to profoundly deaf children in relation to hearing children in the age range of 6–11 years. The spectral noise levels were used as an index of the noise components from 100 to 2500 Hz for sustained vowel production. The results showed that the hearing-impaired children attained significantly higher spectral noise levels and were accorded significantly higher estimates of vocal effort. Thus, this group of hearing-impaired children appeared to expend more effort than the hearing children, which generated 'noisy' speech.

Children with severe to profound prelingual hearing loss have a particular problem in learning to coordinate control of their breathing in producing speech. Without experience to guide them they may attempt to speak on inspiration as well as expiration, using ingressive as well as egressive airstreams. They tend to produce short bursts of speech and then run out of breath, because they do not take sufficient breath before beginning to speak. Their spoken sentences are thus broken up by pauses, which interfere with the speech flow. The pauses make their speech stressful to listen to, and understanding of their message difficult (Hudgins and Numbers, 1942; Calvert and Silverman, 1975; Forner and Hixon, 1977; Monsen, 1979). These problems of coordinating breathing and phonation compound their errors in the articulation of vowels and consonants, and difficulties with suprasegmental features.

Speech Training

To learn speech, congenitally profoundly deaf children must expend very considerable effort and concentration on detail. It is therefore to be expected that so many of them produce speech which is difficult for people with good hearing to comprehend. Deaf children need to control breathing, laryngeal functions and movement of the articulators simultaneously to produce speech. They must do so by controlling these aspects within fine tolerances within accepted time intervals if their speech is to be intelligible.

Thus in training hearing-impaired children in the use of speech, the aims include: producing vocalisations, or phonations, as changes in modes of vibration of the vocal folds; control of voice quality; control of pitch, intensity and deviation; developing and practising imitations; developing, controlling and coordinating respiration, phonation and shape of the supraglottal vocal tract; using residual hearing; acquiring a multisensory feedback system by residual hearing, vision, tactile and kinaesthetic senses; articulating phonemes in meaningful contexts; progressing from phonetic skills to connected speech; and developing a recognition that speech is a means to manipulating and controlling the social environment (Siebert, 1980).

The training of hearing-impaired children to express themselves in speech is a complex, time-consuming and demanding procedure. It requires informed, systematic and sustained effort (Ling, 1976). None the less, even given prolonged training of intelligent, motivated hearing-impaired children by conscientious and competent teachers, it is very rare to find a prelingually profoundly deaf child whose speech is not characterised by some of the properties of deaf speech. Partly as a result of this, formal speech-training drills are losing popularity. The more recent emphasis is on integrating the various stages, especially in integrating phonetic level with phonological level skills (Ling, 1991) and in integrating the teaching of speech with the teaching of language (Ling, 1976, 1979, 1989; Subtelny, 1983; Perigoe and Ling, 1986). There is also emphasis on considering the child's environment, particularly the role of parents and family (Lieberth, 1982).

Besides recommending that speech production be taught with the teaching of language, many writers recommend teaching of speech production alongside training in speech perception (Berg, 1976b; Van Riper, 1978; McDonald, 1980; Novelli-Olmstead and Ling, 1984), because a child attempts to speak by using what has been heard or otherwise recognised. Also, hearing or residual hearing is used to monitor and control speech through auditory feedback and through reference to articulation, the so-called motor theory of speech perception (Liberman et al., 1967). Others have recommended the use of music and singing to facilitate speech and language development (Bang, 1980; Tait, 1986; Dawson, 1990; Heffernan, 1990). Moog and Geers (1985) have reported that intensive instruction with increased teaching effort can improve the academic development and speech production of profoundly deaf children.

A programme for speech training which has significantly influenced the approach of others (Martello, 1981), is that of Ling (Ling and Ling, 1978). Before training, the child's produced speech is assessed. Then the child receives speech therapy, ideally on a daily basis, to attain phonetic and phonological targets in a systematic fashion. This approach establishes stages of speech development, and thus provides targets and goals to be achieved for each stage, following the child from preschool to primary school.

Much of the earlier work had an intuitive–empirical base which has only recently become more experimentally based (Silverman, 1983). Most of the earlier reports were descriptive or anecdotal, without enough rationale, subjects or data, or with insufficient attention paid to experimental design, to permit estimation of their reliability and validity, and potential for generalisation to other cases. Nevertheless, some of the earlier texts remain in current use, because they contain a rich fund of insights, illustrations, tips and techniques on which the speech and language teacher can draw. A distinguished example of such writing is the book by Haycock (1933). The many reprintings of this book provide ample testimony to its usefulness over the years. Haycock (1933) is particularly recommended to the reader who wishes to gain an appreciation of the intricacies involved in the teaching of speech, and who may not have a grasp of the phonetic terminology required by the more modern texts. However, it is not concerned with the use of residual hearing in training speech production, having been written before the widespread use of hearing aids.

There is not space here to review the many recent accounts of speech training programmes, but one informative description is that of Osberger (1983), who considered the role of several important variables in training speech, although no controls were used. She employed an adaptation of Ling's system to conduct and evaluate a speech training programme in both segmental and suprasegmental speech for 21 severely to profoundly deaf preschool children. It appeared from her work that the rate of progress in speech production was very variable, requiring individual instruction. Many children could learn speech patterns through hearing alone, though others needed a very systematic and structured programme to develop their auditory–kinaesthetic or tactile–kinaesthetic feedback loops. The ability to produce a given speech pattern preceded and facilitated its perception. Hence training in the production of a particular speech pattern need not wait until there is evidence that it can be discriminated by hearing from other speech sounds – often a difficult task for young children.

Osberger (1987) has also described in some detail the improvement in vowel production by two profoundly deaf adolescents, one boy and one girl, in training again based on Ling's work. This study included controls for test learning effects, and for training, although the controls for training were hearing individuals. There may be some question about how far the findings can be generalised given the small scale of this study, and about the appropriateness of the controls given the highly individualised nature of the vowel changes observed during treatment. On the other hand, these queries illustrate how very difficult it is to design appropriate studies in this field.

Another noteworthy investigation is that of Abraham and Weiner (1985), who compared the use of meaningful and non-meaningful words with ten severely to profoundly deaf children of mean age 9 years. One group of five children was trained in eight daily sessions by direct imitation of words which could be illustrated by pictures. The words were spoken by the experimenter, with oral and aural cues. The other group of five children received nonsense syllables presented in the same way. Two phonemes were selected for each child from those which the child misarticulated with one phoneme, chosen randomly, as a training phoneme and the other as a control phoneme. Training was conducted with the training phoneme in the initial position for both words and syllables, while the control phoneme was not trained. Abraham and Weiner found that both word and syllable training improved the imitation of target phonemes. Word training was more effective than syllable training for improving correct spontaneous production of trained target phonemes in untrained generalisation words. They rightly pointed out that the efficacy of speech training is directly associated with how well it facilitates generalisation, a characteristic of a skill (Bennett, 1978).

A further well-designed study was that of Perigoe and Ling (1986), in which 12 profoundly deaf children aged from 5 to 8 years were arranged in two groups of six, matched as closely as possible for gender, age, hearing loss, phonetic and phonological speech ability and non-verbal intelligence, and who had similar language abilities. The 'context group' was taught speech by focusing on transferring old and new phonetic level skills to nouns and verbs. The 'function group' was taught by concentrating on transferring phonetic level patterns into the structural elements of language. The children's classroom teachers did not know to which group the children were assigned, though they had children from both groups in their classes. All children received phonetic and phonological training for 15 minutes daily for 40 sessions, and were tested over a year at 3-monthly intervals. Regular classroom speech training was given for the first 3 months, followed by 3 months of no intervention and a final 3 months of intensive speech training. The subjects in both groups improved significantly in both measures of speech after intensive training. The function group also improved significantly in language ability as shown by mean length of utterance scores, and scores on a word-morpheme index. Thus phonological training which emphasised the use of function words also enhanced selected language skills.

Descriptions and reviews of other interesting speech training programmes are conveniently offered by Ling (1976), Subtelny (1980), Lieberth (1982) and Blackwell (1983).

To summarise, we can see that there is increasingly good experimental, as opposed to empirical and descriptive, evidence showing that deaf children can be trained to improve their speech, though success is still limited. The evidence accrues from some well-designed and conducted studies which demonstrate significant gains in speech production for selected variables. It is less clear, however, that the gains persist over time or can be generalised to cognate speech skills. There is obviously a need for well-designed, multivariable speech training studies to resolve such issues.

Speech Training Aids

Boothroyd (1972b) identified many of the requirements for valid work in speech training. Until the early 1970s speech training aids mostly offered somewhat unsophisticated visual or tactile analogues of speech sounds. Most of the early devices were not fully evaluated as aids to speech therapy and, individually, they had relatively little impact on speech training (Prinz, 1985). Some of the devices presented oscilloscope traces of visual likenesses of rather gross aspects of speech sounds, such as the overall speech intensity envelope versus time. They were also physically cumbersome, and frequently fell into disuse after a short initial burst of enthusiastic work.

Some modern speech training aids

Recently speech training aids have become more sophisticated, with the possibilities of selection and identification of salient features of speech. They have also become better engineered to meet the needs of the user. Maki (1983) has reported on applications of the speech spectrograph display as an aid to the development of articulatory skills in adults, enabling identification by the user of significant spectral differences. Visual feedback is useful as an aid to speech therapy, since the visual information may be received confidently as a more objective and immediate source of feedback than the advice of a teacher or therapist (Risberg and Spens, 1967; Maki, 1980) and the user can practise alone once the visual display parameters have been set or modelled by the teacher.

In the 1970s work on the development of tactile vocoders accelerated (Oller et al., 1986). At about the same time the advent of the microprocessor offered increasingly sophisticated options at reasonable cost for speech training aids. A number of computer applications became available, with oscilloscope displays of intensity, frequency, voicing, aspiration, tongue position, etc., sometimes with a cartoon face that could be modified to display selected features. Although such instruments may provide the opportunity to work on a number of speech features, it is usual to concentrate on a few at any one time to avoid confusing the child (Martony, 1972). Boothroyd et al. (1975) used this kind of instrumentation on 42 hearing-impaired, mostly profoundly deaf, children, with both meaningful and non-meaningful speech material. The children were able to reduce speech errors in rehearsed, and to a lesser extent in unrehearsed, speech. However, their overall speech intelligibility did not improve, except in a few cases.

Because the use of most speech training aids requires considerable effort and concentration, they are not suitable for hearing-impaired infants and very young children. Hence, by the time they come to be considered for training with speech aids, these children will already have some speech, acquired from non-instrumental approaches. Invariably, this speech will contain errors. So a common way of beginning the use of speech training aids is in speech error analysis. For example, profoundly deaf children often produce stop consonants which are not clearly identifiable. They may, for example, produce a sound which is not clearly either /p/ or /b/, as a result of a voice-onset time (VOT) which is too short to be clearly /p/ but too long to be readily perceived as /b/. A speech spectrograph display can assist the child to produce /p/ or /b/ with less ambiguity by displaying the differences in VOT. Thus the error is first identified for the child, the correct production of the speech sound is illustrated, and the child is then given repeated practice, commonly as a set of drills (Houde, 1980).

Correct vowel production is difficult for hearing-impaired children, as already noted. The production of vowels may be aided by devices such as the laryngograph (Fourcin and Abberton, 1975; Ball et al., 1990; Ball, 1991), which measures the frequency of vocal fold vibrations via electrodes attached to the throat on either side of the larynx, and pitch extraction devices, such as the Visipitch (Key Elemetrics Corporation), which display voice pitch contours against time, with storage to allow for measurement and analysis of vowel formant frequencies. Povel and Wansink (1986) have described a computer-controlled vowel corrector, which provides information about the identity of vowels spoken in isolation or in monosyllables. The vowels appear on a screen in different locations, the coordinates of which are derived from the vowel spectra. Preliminary results showed that the device was useful for exploring vowel space as well as for learning global differentiation for the vowels. However, the discrimination of spectrally similar vowels was limited, as might be expected. Gulian et al. (1986) have also described a computer-based approach to vowel training with profoundly deaf children. Using the Computer Vowel Trainer to provide visual feedback, they found that changes in perception were feedback- and age-dependent. Younger children taught with the trainer showed more mobility in articulation, and they approximated target vowels more closely than control counterparts taught by conventional methods, with evident progress for back and central vowels particularly. There was also a marked reduction in substitutions with central vowels – a characteristic of deaf speech.

New speech training computer-based aids suitable for use with children have been described by Bernstein et al. (1988), Ferguson et al. (1988), and Mashie et al. (1988). They reviewed the characteristics of deaf speech, and proceeded to devise several computer-based aids. Included were two personal computer-based aids, one for use in the clinic, and the other for use in the child's home. The first assessed speech production by microphone, electro-glottograph, and pneumotachograph and was used for diagnosis, speech training and specification of speech exercises. The second assessed speech by microphone alone, and was used for practice at home between therapy sessions. This combination of personal computers was evaluated with five profoundly deaf children over a 1–2-week period, using an activity log and questionnaire completed by the children's parents. The first system, using both acoustic and physiological measures, was evaluated over 15 months with 15 children, when it was easily incorporated into the clinic and found useful for diagnosis and therapy. These preliminary findings appear encouraging, but further reports of more extensive use on larger numbers of hearing-impaired children are awaited.

Rosen et al. (1987) developed a body-worn microprocessor-based aid which presented only the larynx-frequency pattern of speech, as a sinusoid, because they believed it to be of greater value to profoundly deaf people than the complete acoustic signal. Seemingly, the presence of higher harmonics can give poorer labelling of isolated intonation contrasts, and often minimal gain in spectrally based segmental distinctions. Hence simplification of speech can lead to enhanced speech reception in the auditory modality. We might expect similar simplification of speech to be of advantage in speech training aids, because with some apparatus the complexity of the information provided can reduce the motivation of the hearing-impaired child to improve speech because of perceptual overload. This complexity may even embarrass the therapist with the number of available options.

We conclude on the basis of these comments that the human end-user of speech training aids needs to be considered carefully in the engineering of the device. We also conclude that the initial stages of speech training need to be completed thoroughly and to be well internalised before progressing to subsequent stages.

Cochlear implants as speech training aids

Conventional hearing aids and cochlear implants can be considered as speech training aids, because of the role played by the auditory feedback of speech in speech production. We do not discuss here the use of hearing aids as speech training aids, as this topic has been treated comprehensively elsewhere (e.g. Berg, 1976b; Northern and Downs, 1984), but a few words on the use of cochlear implants are in order.

We would expect cochlear implantees to show improved speech production, and this seems to be the case. Svirsky and Tobey (1991) concluded from a small-scale study that cochlear implantation helped in the production of some vowels. Tobey and Hasenstab (1991) found a significant increase in imitation of the non-segmental aspects of speech (loudness, pitch and duration) after the use of implants in a group of 78 profoundly, and mostly prelingually, deaf children. This increase occurred in only the first year after implantation, whereas imitation of segmental aspects, as in syllables, continued to improve with experience over 2 years. The children's speech intelligibility was significantly higher after implantation than before, though their mean length of utterance remained relatively low. Overall, the improvement in speech production was modest, as found also by Busby et al. (1991), who observed some improvements for consonant, but not vowel, production with training following the cochlear implantation of three prelingually profoundly to totally deaf patients with a multi-electrode device. However, the improvement for consonants rather than for vowels, and the lack of a general corresponding improvement in speech perception, suggested that the improvements were due to tactile–kinaesthetic rather than auditory feedback.

Despite the improved design and engineering of cochlear implants and other speech aids, which makes them increasingly more successful and easier to use, and despite some resulting improvements in speech characteristics and intelligibility, the speech of prelingually profoundly deaf children remains problematical. Apparently, to date, the developments in the engineering only partly help to address the formidable demands on the learning abilities of the deaf child.

Intelligibility of the Produced Speech of Hearing-impaired Children

The perceived intelligibility of speech depends on both its suprasegmental and its segmental features. Speech intelligibility is influenced by stress as the loudness/duration aspect which characterises the relative emphasis given to syllables, words and phrases (Levitt, 1971); intonation, or pitch variations across syllables; voicing, with the production of vowels, voiced consonants and diphthongs; the oral/nasal distinction, which governs the distinction between /m/ and /b/, /n/ and /d/, etc. ('met' versus 'bet', or 'not' versus 'dot'); the limitation of airflow through the oral cavity, which may be closed briefly for the stop/plosives (/b/ and /p/), relatively restricted for voiced consonants (/d/), and relatively open for the vowels; and the position taken by the tongue, lips and so on.

Children with mild to moderate prelingual loss of hearing develop normal articulation of vowels and normal or near-normal voice quality. Such children, however, will often have articulation problems with the liquid /r/ in the initial position, fricative consonants (/s/, /sh/, /th/) and the affricates (/dʒ/ and /tʃ/). They will often omit final consonants and voiced fricative consonants, and seldom produce voiced consonants with a back, lingual placement (/g/, /ŋ/, /ʒ/ and /dʒ/), as shown in a study of a 4-year-old hearing-impaired child by West and Weber (1973). Nevertheless, their speech is usually quite intelligible.

The situation is quite different for children with greater hearing losses. Because of problems in producing and harmonising the several facets of speech, their speech is generally hard to understand. Although the speech intelligibility of children with severe to profound losses varies considerably from child to child, the mean intelligibility figure is relatively constant for listeners not used to the speech of hearing-impaired children, at between 18 and 25%. The evidence on this point is very weighty. We now outline several studies to show just how strong this evidence is, though Monsen (1981) has indicated that clinically the speech intelligibility of hearing-impaired children is seldom measured.

A report of the Department of Education and Science in England and Wales (1964) on conversations by a medical practitioner with 359 children revealed that about one-third of the children with hearing losses in excess of 80 dB HL had unintelligible speech. This one-third may have been an optimistic estimate (see below). Brannon (1964) found that the mean intelligibility of 20 day-school students aged 12–15 years, with severe or greater hearing-losses, was 20–25%. He found also that their speech was more intelligible during sentence production than during the utterance of single words. Markides (1967, 1970) studied 85 day and residential school-children in two groups, one of 7- and one of 9-year-olds. For 58 profoundly deaf children, with a mean hearing loss of 95 dB HL, the intelligibility of spoken words was 19% for 'naïve' listeners and 31% for teachers of the deaf. The speech intelligibility for the remaining 27 partially hearing children, with a mean hearing loss of 57 dB HL, was 76% for naïve listeners and 83% for the teachers of the deaf. The product–moment correlation coefficient between hearing loss and speech intelligibility was −0.75 for naïve listeners, and −0.71 for the teachers. Thus teachers tended to score the speech intelligibility of hearing-impaired children higher than listeners who were not used to deaf speech, though Smale (1988) argued that hearing people who are not used to deaf individuals can improve their understanding of the speech of prelingually profoundly deaf adolescents after a short period of familiarisation.

Conrad (1979) also found that teachers tended to uprate very deaf children, but they downrated the partially hearing, while Doyle (1987) reported that audiologists given bogus audiograms rated a given speech sample as of poorer intelligibility if the audiogram showed a high degree of hearing impairment, and gave a high rating if the audiogram showed a low degree of hearing impairment. Such issues of listener experience in evaluating speech are clearly problematical. They have been discussed by Boothroyd (1985), who argued for a forced-choice paradigm to minimise their effects.

Forty-six severely to profoundly hearing-impaired residential school-children aged 3–15 years with hearing losses of 60 dB or more were found by Nober (1967) to have speech articulation age norms of 4 years if their hearing loss was 60–80 dB, and 3 years for hearing losses of 80 dB or more. Heidinger (1972) asked three experienced teachers of the deaf to score the speech of 20 severely to profoundly deaf residential school-children aged 10–14 years. For words in short sentences, only 20% were scored as intelligible.

The Department of Education and Science (1972) issued a further report in which 23% of 167 children with hearing losses of more than 80 dB were assessed, in a similar way to the 1964 investigation, as having unintelligible speech. This result was an apparent improvement on the 1964 report, but could have been due to differences in assessment and/or sampling differences. Also, 54.7% of the children had 'partly intelligible' speech, but it was doubted if the speech of many children in this group could readily be understood by people who were not familiar with the speech of deaf children. Again, 40 residential school-children with hearing losses of 80 dB or greater at 1 kHz and aged 8–10, and 13–15 years, were found by Smith (1975a) to have a mean spoken word intelligibility of 18.7%, and Weiss et al. (1975) obtained a mean speech intelligibility of 37% – a somewhat better result – on 60 preschool children from a number of day and residential programmes. However, the hearing losses extended down to some 75 dB. Levitt et al. (1976) repeatedly assessed the speech intelligibility of more than 100 hearing-impaired children aged 10 years, for whom no hearing loss data were given, but who were probably severely to profoundly hearing-impaired, from 10 schools over 4 successive years, to age 14. Scores of speech intelligibility in tape-recorded picture description tasks made by three listeners, who were familiar with the speech of hearing-impaired children, yielded more than 70% of children rated as impossible or difficult to understand on all test occasions.

On the other hand, 67 severely to profoundly deaf students aged 11 years and older at the Central Institute for the Deaf were assessed as having a mean speech intelligibility of 76%, atypically high, by 50 hearing listeners (Monsen, 1978). This high level was attributed principally to the shortness of the sentences of 4.5 syllables spoken by his subjects. Monsen found that three out of nine measures of consonant production, vowel production and prosody gave a multiple correlation coefficient of 0.85 with intelligibility scores. The mean VOT between /t/ and /d/ and the mean second formant difference between /i/ and /ɔ/ accounted for about 70% of the variance in speech intelligibility. The correlation coefficient between speech intelligibility and hearing loss was −0.60.

A wide-reaching study of speech intelligibility was conducted on 978 hearing-impaired children receiving special education by Jensema, Karchmer, Trybus and colleagues (Jensema et al., 1978; Trybus, 1980). For children whose speech was intelligible, or very intelligible, the percentage of children with hearing losses above 90 dB amounted to 23%. For hearing losses of 71–90 dB, 55% of children had intelligible or very intelligible speech, and for hearing losses up to 70 dB, 86% of children were rated as having intelligible or very intelligible speech. The correlation coefficient between hearing loss and speech intelligibility ratings was −0.68, reasonably close to that of Markides (1967, 1970). Taken together, the work of Jensema and colleagues, and Markides, indicates that up to half the variance for speech intelligibility is associated with degree of hearing loss. The effect of hearing loss is relatively small up to 85 dB, following which there is a marked effect.

In his investigation of 468 prelingually deafened children aged 15–16 years in the UK, Conrad (1979) tape-recorded the speech of each child speaking a set of ten sentences, and had the tapes judged by a panel of 4–6 inexperienced assessors, mainly housewives. He found that the speech of only 26.5% of the children with hearing losses of more than 90 dB had speech which was better than barely intelligible. Similar findings were reported by Geffner and Freeman (1980) who found that the speech intelligibility of 67 children aged 6 years, with a mean hearing loss of 104 dB HL, was only 24%.

Although several of the above reports may be criticised on various grounds, the general outcome shows very clearly indeed that only a minority of profoundly deaf children have reasonably intelligible speech. This depressing finding is universal, and is only moderately offset by differences in approach from one training centre to another. Markides (1983) felt that the only conclusion was that the speech of the large majority of these children was unintelligible to the layman.

Causes of poor speech intelligibility

The next steps in examining the speech intelligibility of hearing-impaired children are to consider, first, what factors are associated with it and, second, what it is about the speech of prelingually profoundly hearing-impaired children that contributes most to its poor intelligibility. Answers to both questions will be of great practical interest to teachers and therapists.

Intelligence, age and orosensory perception

We have seen that the degree of hearing loss is negatively correlated with speech intelligibility, a relationship found consistently by many workers over many years (Hudgins and Numbers, 1942; Markides 1967, 1970; Kyle, 1977; Monsen, 1978; Conrad, 1979; Sims et al., 1980; Whitehead, 1991). As for other factors, intelligence appears to be only moderately highly correlated with speech intelligibility, if at all (Quigley, 1969; Markides, 1970; Ling, 1976; Conrad, 1979). The effectiveness of speech training procedures which seemed to have little more impact on bright than on dull children was therefore queried by Conrad (1979). He wondered, alternatively, whether speech could be taught to deaf children any more than it is 'taught' to hearing children, thus casting doubt on its status as a skill. Correlations between age, beyond the first few years, and speech intelligibility are around zero (Babbini and Quigley, 1970; Jensema et al., 1978). Nor is speech intelligibility correlated with reading ability (Conrad, 1979). It does, however, appear to be correlated significantly with linguistic ability (Markides, 1967; John et al., 1976) perhaps because deaf children will be able to speak more fluently if they appreciate the rules of syntax and have a fair knowledge of vocabulary and semantics (Markides, 1983).

Despite Conrad's pessimistic remarks, there is evidence that deaf children can improve their speech intelligibility, if only moderately, with speech training (Wedenberg, 1954; Markides, 1967; Calvert and Silverman, 1975; Ling, 1976; Siebert, 1980; Subtelny, 1980; Lieberth, 1982; Hochberg et al., 1983; Osberger, 1983, 1987; Abraham and Weiner, 1985; Perigoe and Ling, 1986; Moores, 1987), even though several of these studies have design problems. This evidence is associated with a trend for speech and language specialists to enter the field (Silverman, 1983). Also, Markides (1967) reported that children who were making good use of their hearing aids showed significantly superior speech intelligibility to children who were not using their aids to such advantage. The implication of these studies is that to concentrate on spoken language development, use of hearing aids and aspects of speech training can bring about some improvement in the speech intelligibility of prelingually deaf children.

Since muscle movements are involved in the production of speech, we may suppose that problems of deviant articulation which contribute to poor speech intelligibility are related to a deficit in orosensory (tactile and kinaesthetic) feedback (Ringel et al., 1968; Fucci and Robertson, 1971; Fucci, 1972). Orosensory feedback is important to speech production by hearing-impaired individuals who lack adequate auditory feedback in monitoring articulation (Bishop et al., 1973; Waldstein, 1990).

Lieberth and Whitehead (1987) investigated the use of orosensory perception in hearing-impaired individuals by comparing the articulation errors and speech intelligibility of 75 young adults with a mean hearing loss of 92 dB HL to their errors on an orosensory test, modified from Ringel et al. (1970). They used stem-mounted forms (shapes) from the USA National Institute for Dental Research. Lieberth and Whitehead found no significant correlations for total errors between articulation, speech intelligibility, and orosensory perception. Nor did they find significant relationships between total orosensory perception errors and degree of hearing loss or history of amplification usage. However, between-class orosensory errors, in which the subjects did not perceive the shape of the objects, were correlated with vowel errors, phoneme omissions, and errors where the produced phoneme came from the same place as the intended phoneme. Substitution errors were significantly related to those orosensory test errors in which differences in size were not perceived. The orosensory test errors in which the subjects perceived two identical items to be different were related significantly to total articulation errors, and consonant, vowel and substitution errors. Lieberth and Whitehead concluded that the relationships between the types of errors could be used to develop strategies to remediate articulation disorders through further research.

In summary, apart from hearing loss, factors such as intelligence, age, type of training and orosensory perception seem to be only weakly related to speech intelligibility.

The characteristics of deaf speech and its intelligibility

What are the characteristics of the speech of deaf children which tend to make it unintelligible? We touched on some of these characteristics earlier, and now try to answer this question by considering the segmental and suprasegmental features of deaf speech in a little more detail. However, since the speech of children with the same number of segmental errors can show large differences in intelligibility (Smith, 1975a), it is possible that suprasegmental problems account for the differences. In other words, suprasegmental difficulties may or may not contribute to poor speech intelligibility caused by segmental errors (Markides, 1983).

At the segmental level, negative correlations have been found between vowel and consonant errors and speech intelligibility for the speech of hearing-impaired children (Brannon, 1966; Markides, 1967; Smith, 1975a). Generally the totalled vowel, diphthong and consonant errors contributed most to the problem, namely, up to about 80% of the variance ascribed to speech intelligibility but, within these totalled articulatory errors, difficulties with consonants caused more intelligibility problems than difficulties with vowels. Brown and Goldberg (1990) thought that VOT was a primary factor among consonant features. Initial and final consonants were roughly equally problematical, but consonant omissions caused more difficulties than substitutions or distortions, the latter having only a small effect. This finding is in alignment with that of Warren (1970), whose hearing listeners 'heard' speech sounds that had been removed from recorded speech and replaced by coughs, breaths or other non-speech sounds.

On analysing speech samples from 22 deaf children with an acoustic and a physiological distinctive feature system, Mencke et al. (1984) obtained moderate to high correlations with both systems for speech intelligibility scores. Higher correlations were found for final than for initial position-in-word phonemes, regardless of listener experience or feature system. More recently Porter and Dickerson (1986) investigated the relationship of syllabic complexity to speech intelligibility in 11 students who possessed some intelligible speech. These students were aged 12–18 years old, with hearing losses from 75–103dB. The results showed that their errors had a marked tendency to reduce syllable complexity, that is, to reduce the number of consonants preceding and following vowels. Also, hearing-impaired speakers with high speech intelligibility tended to make errors on the more complex syllables, thus reducing syllabic difficulty. The results implied that an appropriate approach to therapy for the speech production of hearing-impaired people should introduce phonemes systematically in increasingly complex syllabic structures.

Suprasegmental features were thought to play an important role in speech intelligibility by Hudgins and Numbers (1942), John and Howarth (1965) and Levitt et al. (1974). Hudgins and Numbers (1942) suggested that prosody had as much to contribute to speech intelligibility as articulation of consonants, and more than the articulation of vowels. Such observations led to a study of the importance of syllabic structure in explaining the phenomena associated with deaf speech (John and Howarth, 1965; Calvert and Silverman, 1975). However, correlations between prosody and speech intelligibility have proved to be rather small, perhaps not very surprising in view of the large proportion of variance taken up by articulatory features. Further, if deaf children can appropriately combine syllables into words and manage their phonation, the control of rhythm and intonation does not contribute very much to the intelligibility of their speech (Bernstein, 1977; Osberger and Levitt, 1979; Maassen and Povel, 1984; Maassen, 1986).

Suprasegmental deviations have led to the characterisation of deaf speech as 'staccato', with abnormal grouping of syllables (Gold, 1980), perhaps associated with control of breathing. There is also a relationship between the intelligibility of deaf speech and the number of pauses it contains (Parkhurst and Levitt, 1978). Removing the pauses decreases the intelligibility. Maassen (1986) attempted to compensate for the staccato nature of deaf speech by artificially inserting silent pauses between words, so that the word boundaries were acoustically marked. He therefore marked the word boundaries of 30 sentences spoken by ten prelingually profoundly deaf children aged 12–14 years with 160-ms pauses inserted between words. The insertions significantly increased the speech intelligibility, from 27% to 31%. Lengthening of phonemes to obtain the same sentence duration, as a control measure, showed that this effect was not due to the slowing of the speech. Thus Maassen obtained a small but useful improvement in speech intelligibility at the suprasegmental level.

In a particularly valuable study which produced information about the effects on intelligibility of both segmental and suprasegmental features, Metz et al. (1985) investigated three measures of speech intelligibility: single word identification using isolated words; contextual word identification using key words embedded in sentences; and scaled intelligibility of a paragraph of connected speech using direct magnitude estimation, for 12 segmental, prosodic and hearing parameters in 20 young adult speakers with a mean hearing loss of 91.5 dB. A regression analysis showed that speech intelligibility on isolated and contextual words was strongly associated with differences in VOT for cognate pairs, such as /p/ and /b/, and mean sentence duration.

A principal components analysis produced four factors, of which the first primarily reflected segmental production processes related to the temporal and spatial differentiation of phonemes, whilst the second reflected prosodic features and stability of production. Thus speech intelligibility had high positive loadings on both factor 1, showing differentiation of temporal and spatial events underlying the production of distinct phonemes, and on factor 2 which appeared to be due to prolonged sentence duration, instability in control of sentence duration, and instability in the production of cognate phoneme pairs. Factor 1 was positively, and factor 2 was negatively, correlated with estimates of speech intelligibility. Factor 1 accounted for twice the variance of factor 2 on isolated word intelligibility, for about four times the variance on contextual word intelligibility, and for slightly less of the variance for scaled intelligibility than for isolated words or contextual words.

This work confirmed the indications of previous studies by Monsen (1978) and others that speech intelligibility in severely to profoundly hearing-impaired speakers is determined independently by segmental features and by prosodic characteristics. Segmental features tend to be the more influential, though Metz et al. (1990a) found that the predictive capacity of the factor structure was somewhat reduced. The Metz et al. (1985) study revealed also that subjects with low speech intelligibility showed high variability in some aspects of speech production. This outcome was confirmed and extended by Metz et al. (1990b), who found that hearing-impaired speakers with poor speech intelligibility may fall into two groups: those who consistently produce aberrant speech, and those who have an inconsistent error pattern. Highly intelligible speakers were consistent in their speech patterns.

Given that there is available a corpus of knowledge showing that speech intelligibility in prelingually severely to profoundly hearing-impaired children can be impoverished primarily by segmental, but also by suprasegmental aspects, why do the problems of poor speech intelligibility persist? Ling (1976) suggested forthrightly that teachers did not have, or were not using, approaches which integrated current knowledge with compatible traditional strategies. Subtelny (1982), writing of adolescents, thought that, for segmental aspects, the errors were due to faults in hearing, faults in learning the morphological features of English, or to faults in control of breathing and articulation, especially for word, phrase and sentence endings. It was probable, she also thought, that poor speech intelligibility due to articulation errors was associated with poor linguistic ability (compare Abraham and Weiner, 1987). Thus a child who does not understand the significances of plural -s endings at the linguistic level may not produce them in spontaneous speech production (compare Markides, 1967; John et al., 1976). A similar explanation may account for problems in speech intelligibility at the suprasegmental level, where failure to appreciate the contribution of pausing, stress and intonation to the linguistic domain may go hand in hand with failure at the level of speech production.

Such arguments clearly suggest that training in language could be explored further as one key to improving speech intelligibility. Carney (1986) has recommended that clinical work to assess speech intelligibility should proceed on a basis of maximising contextual and experiential effects, as well as on a basis which minimises them. Meantime, we conclude that for most prelingually profoundly deaf children, and for many children who are prelingually severely deaf, the intelligibility of their speech is so poor as to cause the most serious problems for their communication. Speechreading of the deaf child by hearing listeners (Subtelny et al., 1980) may sometimes assist such communication. However, the situation is not clear, since Kricos et al. (1990) noted that visual information produces considerable variability in judgements of the speech-accuracy of hearing-impaired children.

Conclusion

Calvert (1986) wrote that, over 400 years, there was no clear record of steady improvement in teaching speech production to deaf children, nor had there been significant breakthroughs to reduce the effort required of the deaf child in learning speech. The speech intelligibility of deaf children has not been shown to have improved over the centuries either.

It appears from review of the area that much detail is now known about the characteristics of deaf speech, but less is known about why deaf speech gets to be the way it is and, in general, training for acceptable speech production and intelligibility is not successful. Notably absent in the literature are well-designed studies which compare different speech training procedures with different teaching styles and teacher–child interactions. Although the practical difficulties of conducting such work are very considerable, they are not insuperable. Without the information from such investigations, the present generally unsatisfactory situation seems bound to continue.

Chapter 5
Hearing Impairment and
Manual Communication

Most profoundly deaf individuals prefer to communicate with their deaf peers in sign, though they need to communicate verbally with hearing people. There has been fierce debate about whether deaf sign language is properly a language, rather than a communication system which is less than a full language. Following an account of manual systems other than sign language, this chapter considers the characteristics of sign language as language. It comments also on the neuropsychology of sign and the ways in which sign language is learned or acquired. The chapter concludes with a review of total communication, which is included here as its dominant mode is usually manual.

For mildly to moderately prelingually hearing-impaired children communication is oral and aural. Although such children may show delayed communication skills, and need special help in their linguistic and educational development, they should succeed with oral means of communication. The situation is less certain for the child with a prelingual severe hearing loss, and much less certain for the child with prelingual profound deafness.

Manual Communication

In 1880 an important International Congress on Education of the Deaf was held in Milan. This Congress was driven by a mood of change in European schools in the 1870s, resulting in a strong emphasis on oral communication. Despite this thrust by educators of the deaf, the dominant form of communication in the social inter-actions of one profoundly deaf person with another, especially if prelingually deaf, has been manual communication. We consider later the issue of which mode of communication may be used in the education and rehabilitation of the deaf. For the present we note that, despite the stress laid on oralism, the preferred com-munication mode of most profoundly deaf people amongst themselves is the man-ual mode. Manual communication is preferred, despite the availability of hearing aids and experience of aural rehabilitation.

The salient feature is the mode of communication which deaf people use among themselves. Clearly, only oracy will be effective in communicating with hearing people unless they have learned manual communication. Thus most orally educated deaf people communicate orally with hearing individuals and manually with their deaf peers. Profoundly deaf people who have not been educated orally, but by manual or by some mixed form of communication will, of course, have greater problems in communicating with the hearing world, and will be all the more predisposed to manual communication with deaf associates.

The Natural Language of the Deaf

When young profoundly deaf children are left to communicate among themselves, they develop a gestural system of communication. For example, Heider and Heider (1941) studied 14 profoundly deaf children at the Clarke School for the Deaf in the USA, who were observed in communication with other deaf children and with hearing adults. These children communicated by spontaneously acquired signs or symbolic gestures, different from conventional signs, whose meaning was inferred from the social context. The Heiders found that, while several gestures served genuine symbolic functions, considerable use was made of pointing and expressive movement. The communication was bound to the context, especially the social context. Some gestures were global, in that they could not be analysed into single word equivalents. Other gestures were combined in a kind of syntax to provide a 'phrase' or 'sentence', equivalent to the syntax of hearing children up to about 2;6 years of age. Thus gestural communication emerges naturally in groups of young deaf children, together with elementary syntax, without being taught. Such gestural communication is not a developed gestural language, but it shows that every deaf child has some means of communication, and the motivation to develop this means of communication is very strong.

Since most profoundly deaf people universally communicate with one another by some manual form, the suggestion has been made that manual communication is the natural language of the deaf (Charrow, 1975). Standard English is not the native language of deaf people who acquire a manual form of communication. Further spoken language is not perceived and acquired naturally by prelingually profoundly deaf children. If they are to learn it they have to learn it over a long period of instruction. Further, also their learning of standard English is imperfect. They make syntactic errors not made by hearing children; they are generally poorly skilled in reading and in writing; and they produce the unusual expressions commonly referred to as 'deafisms'. The outcome, according to Charrow, is 'Deaf English', a form of English equivalent to pidgin, which serves to cover the gap between manual and oral education for social interaction, and which crystallises in the teen years.

Most profoundly deaf children are born to hearing parents, and their first experience of language will be through oracy. However, it is likely that from an early age they will be brought into contact with other young deaf children, when some gestural communication will ensue. For these children, their first language is thus unlikely to be 'pure'. It will involve at least some gestural forms (Tervoort, 1979), and hence will involve aspects of bilingualism. On the other hand, the minority of profoundly deaf children who are born to profoundly deaf parents will have a monolingual manual form as their first language. Whereas profoundly deaf children born to profoundly deaf parents will have a unitary, gestural native language, the native communication system of profoundly deaf children born to hearing parents is likely to be some unsatisfactory mixture of attenuated standard English and gesture (Mohay, 1982).

The manual form of communication used by profoundly deaf people amongst themselves is deaf sign language. Until quite recently, this gestural form of communication was not seen as a language in its own right. Thus Furth (1966a) tended to argue that prelingually profoundly deaf children functioned as a group without language. He thought that since these children had no language, their performance would be weak in cognitive tasks, such as thinking and problem-solving. However, it became clear that, provided the tasks are not verbal, profoundly deaf children perform at about the same level as hearing children (Furth, 1971; Furth and Youniss, 1975). It also came to be recognised that verbal language is not essential for the performance of non-verbal cognitive tasks. This realisation left the way open for the exploration of deaf sign language as a language in its own right, as a code through which ideas could be communicated, with a vocabulary and semantics of its own, and with a generative capacity in the sense developed by Chomsky (1971).

Manual Systems Other than Sign Language

Before we consider deaf sign language further, it will be informative to cover briefly other forms of gestural communication used by profoundly deaf people.

Fingerspelling

Communication by fingerspelling for hearing-impaired people is one of the oldest known forms, though it has not received much research (Akamatsu and Stewart, 1989). It is sometimes used to connect signs into sentences, or to add stress in sign languages. Fingerspelling is particularly useful for introducing names, neologisms and technical terms, such as 'cruise missile' or 'virtual reality'. The manual alphabet is a one-to-one cipher for the letters of an alphabet on the fingers of the hand. In the UK the manual alphabet is two-handed, but elsewhere it is usually displayed on one hand. For English, there are 26 positions, or combinations of finger placements and handshapes, corresponding to the 26 letters of the English alphabet, which hence are shown without ambiguity and can be used to spell out a word with the fingers, as with conventional spelling of English letters. Clearly, fingerspelling is a slow form of communication. Bornstein (1979) has reported a maximum transmission rate of about 60 words per minute – roughly three times slower than rather fast speech or signed communication.

Fingerspelling is rarely used alone, but its frequent use in combination with signed communication has led to its partial integration into sign languages. American Sign Language (ASL) contains items borrowed from fingerspelling, and hence from standard English (Battison, 1978). Changes in handshape can show the first letter of the corresponding English word, a tactic known as initialisation (Evans, 1981). Thus although fingerspelt material is different from signs it may be 'borrowed' for use in sign language. Thereupon it becomes more sign-like and subject to the constraints of the sign language, such as not more than two parts in each sign. It takes considerable time to learn the rules for fingerspelling and its relationship to signs and to printed and spoken words (Maxwell, 1988).

Fingerspelling can be used in other ways. Evans (1981) suggested that, besides its direct use for names and technical terms, fingerspelling has a role as a lexical tool for the learning of such items, and can reinforce the written form of new words. He also observed that signs tend to communicate content words, whereas fingerspelling is useful for function words, such as articles, prepositions, etc. Thus fingerspelling plays a complementary role to signs, when it may significantly increase understanding of the signed message (Savage et al., 1981). Fingerspelling can be internalised in profoundly deaf subjects with poor speech (Locke and Locke, 1971). Their deaf subjects showed visual and dactylic confusions in their error patterns in recalling lists of consonants.

The Makaton Vocabulary

The Makaton Vocabulary was developed in the UK (Walker, 1976; Walker and Armfield, 1982; Walker and Buckfield, 1983). It was based on basic signs from British Sign Language (BSL) to produce a simple vocabulary of approximately 350 signs, graded to reflect difficulty in acquisition. The Makaton Vocabulary has been widely used in the UK, mainly with intellectually disabled people, for whom it appears to meet a keenly felt need (Kiernan et al., 1979). However, it is not generally suitable for the prelingually profoundly deaf population, as its vocabulary is limited to the 350 signs. Further, because it is essentially a lexicon of signs, its function is that of an elementary system of communication. It is not a language.

Linguistics of Visual English

Linguistics of Visual English (LOVE) was devised by Wampler (1971) for profoundly deaf children attending preschool and kindergarten. The LOVE signs were thought to correspond to the rhythms of speech. They consisted of hand positions as symbols for morphemes, designated in terms of meaning, speech sound similarity or spelling. The syllables of standard English could thus be represented by hand positions, one for each syllable. The LOVE system is of interest in that it represented an attempt to develop a manual system which in several respects was isomorphic with standard English. It is now little used, in part because it represents no natural system.

Mouth–hand systems

Mouth–hand systems use hand signals presented near the lips to supplement speechreading. In particular, they provide information about those speech sounds which are not readily seen on the lips. Hence mouth–hand systems may be described as oral communication with a manual supplement.

Mouth–hand communication systems have a long history. They were used in France in the mid-nineteenth century (Børrild, 1972). Early in the present century, the mouth–hand system was explored by Forchhammer (1903) in Denmark. Forchhammer recognised that speechreading was difficult because the speechreader could not see the position of the invisible speech organs. He set himself to illustrate these positions with one hand. Hand and finger positions were developed to illustrate the movements of the vocal folds, the palate, and the positions of the tongue. It was possible to illustrate all the vowels and consonants in this way. The system could be learned in 15–20 lessons, and could be used without slowing the speech rate. For well-trained users it gave a marked increase in the effectiveness of speechreading (Børrild, 1972). However, subsequent work showed that the users depended more on the hand than on the lip movements for speech perception, and even then only a small minority of users obtained mastery. Forchhammer's system thus proved in practice to be more like manual than oral communication, and for manual communication there were more natural alternatives.

The Rochester Method

The use of fingerspelling with speechreading, which came to be known as the Rochester Method, was developed in the USA in the latter half of the nineteenth century (Scouten, 1964). This method allowed the talker to write in the air, as it were, while speaking. Because fingerspelling is slower than speech, the use of simultaneous fingerspelling can only be used to indicate salient words or emphases, unless the speech is unnaturally slowed. A study of the Rochester Method was described by Moores (1987), who considered a number of programmes to find the preferred educational approach for a given child at a given developmental stage. The programmes investigated were auditory, oral/aural, Rochester Method and total communication (TC), in different settings (day or residential school), orientations (traditional nursery, academic, or cognitive), emphases (parent- or child-centred), and placements (integrated or self-contained). Moores found marked differences amongst the programmes, particularly for receptive communication. The programmes using the Rochester Method, as a combination of sounds, speechreading and fingerspelling obtained results superior to those using printed words, sounds alone, and sounds and speechreading, but not sounds, speechreading and signs.

Cued Speech

Despite some advantages, the Rochester Method is cumbersome. Although fingerspelling is still used to supplement speech (Savage et al., 1981), it is so employed rather informally and, as the Rochester Method, is no longer widely used. To some degree, the Rochester Method was superseded by Cued Speech (Cornett, 1967), which also uses manual gestures to supplement speechreading. Like Wampler

(1971), Cornett recognised that the rhythm, intonation and inflection of speech are intimately associated with the syllable, and hence designed Cued Speech to follow the spoken syllables precisely. Cued Speech allows for complete dependence on the lips for that part of speech information which they can supply, thus differing from Forchhammer's (1903) and the Rochester Method. The hands are used only for speech information which cannot be seen on the lips. The cues of Cued Speech cannot be read alone, which forces the hearing-impaired child to monitor the lips of the talker and to take only supplementary information from the hand. Also, the hearing-impaired child who is the talker must move his or her lips fairly normally to be understood, and cannot rely only on producing the hand cues. Thus (Cornett, 1972, 1985) Cued Speech requires complete use of and dependence on information from the lips. Any information besides that from the lips must be compatible in meaning and rhythm with the spoken form. All the essential detail of speech must be made evident and the method must be suitable for learning by the child in the home, namely, without formal teaching. Hence the method must be suitable for average parents to learn.

There is much to be said for Cued Speech. It does not disrupt the simultaneous talking, as occurs with fingerspelling. Cued Speech can keep up with speech (Nicholls and Ling, 1982) as it emphasises the syllables rather than individual phonemes. Since it signifies the syllables it is also in accord with the rhythms of the speech. It is therefore not necessary when using Cued Speech to single out hearing-impaired students in classes of mainly hearing students (Beaupre, 1985).

Cued Speech was heavily promoted, but there was little systematic study of its effectiveness in the years following its introduction (Quigley and Kretschmer, 1982), despite continuing favourable reports from many countries (e.g. Gregory, 1987). Clarke and Ling (1976) reported on a group of eight profoundly deaf children aged 8–12 years as receivers of 2 years of Cued Speech training. These children showed significantly improved reception of Cued Speech over this training period in their written responses to material presented via Cued Speech. They apparently performed at a level superior to that when using residual hearing and speechreading.

Three children, one severely and two profoundly deaf, aged between 1 and 3 years, were studied in a Cued Speech programme by Mohay (1983), with evaluation of their linguistic abilities before and after training in programmes of between 6 months and 2 years duration. She found a number of problems arising with Cued Speech. For example, the frequency of communicative gestures fell off with the introduction of the programme, but without a corresponding increase in the amount or the diversity of spoken language. As a result, there was an overall reduction in the frequency of communication. There was, however, a change towards the production of longer spoken utterances.

Although its use has been fairly widespread and it is employed in special applications, including the teaching of speech (Quenin and Blood, 1989), Cued Speech has not become highly popular in the USA (Calvert, 1986) or elsewhere. Only a proportion of deaf children manage to acquire full competence in perceiving and producing the cues, since they will have had no experience of the underlying speech sounds, and since they experience difficulties in responding to the complex combined visual inputs of lip and hand movements (compare Jensema and Trybus, 1978).

Seeing Essential English

Seeing Essential English (SEE$_1$) uses ASL signs together with introduced signs to cover the roots of words, and verbal inflections, namely prefixes and suffixes. This system, developed by Anthony (1971) closely followed standard English, with English words translated into the equivalent ASL sign plus a signed affix. The order of English syntax was maintained. Since ASL signs do not correspond exactly to English words the three criteria of meaning, spelling and sound were used to direct the choice of a sign. Compound English words often have a single sign as their ASL equivalent. In such cases, the sign for each component was used, unless the result appeared to be incongruent, when a new sign was introduced. SEE$_1$ has tended to be superseded by Signing Exact English (SEE$_2$), as shown below.

Signing Exact English

Signing Exact English (SEE$_2$) was produced by Gustason et al. (1972, 1983), because SEE$_1$ contained too many signs distanced from ASL (Bornstein, 1973). A distinction, then, between SEE$_1$ and SEE$_2$ is that generally SEE$_2$ uses signs to represent whole words rather than the roots of words. In SEE$_1$ these words would also need an affix if they were complex. SEE$_2$ requires only some 70 affixes, as opposed to the 118 affixes of SEE$_1$, 18% of modified ASL signs and 21% of introduced signs. Gustason (1983) claimed that in five SEE$_2$ school programmes across the USA children younger than 10 years performed better than their age norms on the Test of Syntactic Ability (Quigley, 1978). Writing samples from some of the children also proved to be superior. However, these results were indicative only, as this study was not designed as a controlled experiment (compare Gustason, 1981). SEE$_2$ can be used with young deaf children and has enjoyed widespread use. A difficulty for both SEE$_1$ and SEE$_2$ is that both are compromise systems, because words cannot be converted from the one language to the other with the same form and meaning. Further, the use of inflectional markers in the signed versions is inadequate for transmitting complex English, and they are onerous to learn (Bornstein, 1979). This results in constraints on learning by parents for use in the home, with consequent mismatches between the performance of child and parents (Moeller and Luetke-Stahlman, 1990), though Luetke-Stahlman and Moeller (1990) found that parents can be trained to improve their SEE$_2$ performance.

Pidgin Sign

Pidgin Sign, a variant of which is Siglish (Signed English, or Ameslish in the USA), may be used by deaf signers when they wish to use a manual form which approximates to standard English, rather than their native sign language. Pidgins arise when users of two separate languages meet, usually on a short-term basis, for social exchange. In such situations deaf signers may use signs or fingerspelling in the word order found with standard English, and without the use of English inflections. Such Pidgin Sign English (Bragg, 1973) is not a language, but an elementary communication system. It is far removed from the fluency and generative nature of a recognised language. Despite its limitations, however, Pidgin Sign proves to be remarkably persistent. It is found universally, because it meets a need keenly felt from time to time by deaf signers. Brasel and Quigley (1977) found that Pidgin Sign produced better linguistic and educational progress in early childhood than ASL or oral methods. It should however be noted that what is referred to as Pidgin Sign English, as used in the classroom between deaf children and hearing teachers, is a more developed form than a basic contact pidgin (Lucas and Valli, 1989).

The Paget–Gorman Sign System

The signs of the Paget–Gorman Sign System (PGSS) were developed in the UK (Paget and Gorman, 1968). They provide for a basic idea or concept together with a qualifier to convey specific meaning. Although originally designed for deaf people, the PGSS has more commonly been used for children with severe speech problems, and learning and intellectual disabilities (Fenn and Rowe, 1975; Kiernan et al., 1982; Rowe, 1982). The PGSS is a contrived system of signs devised quite separately from BSL, to which it bears little resemblance, apart from occasional correspondence of icons. Crystal and Craig (1978) thought that PGSS, with its 21 hand positions and 37 basic signs, could well represent standard English, with its logical progression of signs from the general to the particular ('cats' = animal + whiskers + plural marker). The PGSS has gone out of favour for use with deaf individuals probably because it is artificial when compared to deaf sign language, but it enjoys popularity in work with intellectually impaired children because it offers an alternative to standard English for children who have no natural and consistent sign system of their own.

Interim conclusion

Of the forms of manual communication for hearing-impaired people mentioned so far, we can say with some confidence that apart from TC, which is discussed later, and SEE 2 which in some ways resembles TC, only some form of Pidgin Sign is likely to endure in the future as a principal means of communication. Pidgin Sign is a special case. It meets a continuing need for communication when the users of two dominant but different languages, such as standard English and a sign language (see below), meet from time to time and share a need to communicate.

There is serious doubt about the lasting nature of any system which requires great learning effort by hearing parents for use in the home, which will not necessarily be used by the deaf child later in life, and which makes heavy perceptual or cognitive demands on hearing and deaf individuals alike. It is interesting that there are few indications that the systems so far considered have been put to anything like a thoroughgoing test in experimental studies, despite the clear desire of the authors for the utility of their systems to be well researched (e.g. Cornett, 1972). The efforts made to bring sign to conform to standard English, the use of manual supplements to standard English, and the development of contrived sign systems over the past 20 years or so, have generated much empirical work, strong statements of opinion, and a plethora of ideas and hypotheses. There is little consensus about their relative efficacy with deaf children, because the necessary research has yet to be done. For the reasons given, and the increasing recognition given to sign language (see below), we suspect that it may never be done, though others may be more optimistic.

Sign Language

A language is a complex code for conveying information to communicate meaning, and is governed by rules which are accepted by convention among users. These rules set the manner in which the meaning is to be conveyed. The simple sum of the rules does not make the language because, by themselves, the rules only partly direct the meaning. The message to be conveyed also depends on the selection of the words used. In standard English, however, the rules of syntax, governing word order, profoundly affect the meaning. The importance of syntactic rules in English is shown by the newsworthy sentence: 'The man bit the dog', where the rule that the subject normally precedes verbs of active voice makes it clear that the man did the biting, and not the dog. Not all languages ascribe such importance to word order. Some languages use verbal inflections to show subject, verb, object, etc. However, the language provides the meaning or message, not just the rule system. So a consideration of how a language functions must include an explanation not only of the arrangement of the words, but which words may be used, and the role of the words and word groupings in communicating ideas (Kretschmer and Kretschmer, 1990). The explanation must also allow for the generative capacity of languages to permit novel expressions.

The study of signed communication over the last 20 or so years, as used by hearing-impaired people, has shown that it is a complex and sophisticated means of communication. There is a sense in which sign is similar to spoken language if sign is considered as 'articulatory gesture' (Neisser, 1976), or if communication is seen as an articulatory as much as an acoustic phenomenon, where gestures take the place of speech, with their own rhythmic structure (Allen et al., 1991). Communication by signs is thus commonly referred to as communication by sign language (Bellugi, 1980; Bonvillian et al., 1980; Wilcox, 1990). However, not all workers in the field agree that sign language is indeed language. Some argue that sign has no grammar, cultural content or literary tradition, though these arguments have been challenged (Frishberg, 1988; Fromkin, 1988) and sign is gaining academic respectability as language (Wilcox, 1988). Notable amongst the critics of sign language as language is Van Uden (1986). His criticisms will now be considered, as they prove helpful in understanding the nature of sign language.

Van Uden wished to know whether sign language was comparable to pidgin, to a creole, namely, a 'language' developed from pidgin to form an elementary language with some syntax, noun declension and verb conjugation, or to a fully elaborated spoken language. He also wanted to know if sign language was none of these, but was unique. Although this is an argument about sign language as language, it is important to our interests. If sign language is not language, then signed communication is impoverished communication. Its users will not be able to exchange sophisticated messages as do users of verbal language.

Iconic and arbitrary signs

Van Uden began his analysis of sign language at the word level, asking to what extent signs were iconic (resembling reality, especially visual reality), esoteric (known only within a restricted circle of users), or arbitrary (arising adventitiously). For example, iconicity may be shown in sign by indicating whiskers, for a cat. In standard English, analogous instances would come from onomatopoeia such as the 'popping' of a cork. Esoteric signs are those whose meaning is not clear, or not immediately clear, except to a relatively small closed group of habitual users as, for instance, the terminology used in cricket. Many esoteric signs may be indirectly iconic, in that their iconicity becomes apparent when the meaning is explained. Some signs are arbitrary, where there appears to be no observable relationship between the sign and its meaning. However, most standard English words seem arbitrary if we do not delve into their etymology. Even then their origin may be arbitrary.

Sign languages are remarkable for their use of icons. The major proportion of signs is directly or indirectly iconic (esoteric). Only the minor proportion is arbitrary. Thus most signs are relatively transparent as to their meaning and only a minority are semantically opaque, though Miller (1987) found that even transparent signs were opaque to 3-year-old hearing non-signing preschool children. Van Uden argued that the dominance of iconicity in sign language sets it apart from spoken language. Such argument is accepted (Hoemann, 1975; Schlesinger, 1977b; Newport and Supalla, 1980; Sternberg, 1981; Luftig et al., 1983), but it is a relative argument, for both sign and spoken languages contain iconic forms, and esoteric and arbitrary items. It is the proportion that is different. Frishberg (1975) suggested that over the years there has been a trend towards more abstraction and less iconicity in ASL. To what extent this trend will progress, and the precise reasons for it, are difficult to estimate at present.

There is evidence that thinking via icons can retard thinking in the abstract (Furth, 1973; Paivio and Begg, 1981), but sign language does contain signs for abstract ideas (Bellugi and Klima, 1978; Klima and Bellugi, 1979). There seems to be no a priori reason to stop the development of more arbitrary signs to represent abstractions. A further consideration is that the opportunity for iconic, or indirectly iconic, representation is greater for a vocabulary expressed in sign rather than through oracy, which may aid memory in the learning of sign (Beykirch et al., 1990; Lieberth and Gamble, 1991). Intuitively it seems that most spoken vocabulary is simply not suited to iconic representation. Although sign language differs from natural spoken language in the ratio of iconic to arbitrary signs, this difference scarcely prevents sign language from consideration as a language.

Before leaving this aspect, we note that esoteric signs are esoteric only by the definition of the closed circle of users in relation to the culture. If we take the non-signing main culture as the reference, then signs used by deaf people, when the meaning is not apparent, are esoteric. However, if the population of deaf people is taken as the culture the signs clearly are not esoteric. It all depends on where we start from.

Phonology and cherology

We saw in Chapter 2 that a spoken language can be regarded, at one level, as comprising a number of phonemes. Although the acoustic nature of a phoneme may vary depending on the phonemes spoken before and after it, and with voice parameters, such as differences between male and female voices, its function for the listener remains constant.

In a classic paper, Stokoe (1960) proposed an analogous function in ASL. He argued that signs were comprised of a number of essentially meaningless individual features which could be combined in different ways to produce a vocabulary of signs. He named these features cheremes, or manual phonemes. Each sign could be considered as having three simultaneous features, a tabula (TAB) corresponding to the location, a designator (DEZ) corresponding to hand configuration, and a signation (SIG) corresponding to the hand movement. Some signs would need more than a single TAB or DEZ. For a sign to be recognised as a part of ASL, it would have to conform as to TABs, DEZs and SIGs to a set of rules. Stokoe identified 12 TABs, 19 DEZs and 24 SIGs, and gave each one a special symbol. He was thus able to produce a sign language dictionary (Stokoe et al., 1965) which was a marked departure from the 'pictogram' dictionaries in use up to that time. Sign language dictionaries, representing cheremes, have now been prepared for many countries (e.g. Johnston 1987 a, b, for Auslan). Lane et al. (1976) pointed to distinctive features in the geometry of the hand when used to indicate signs, analogous to the distinctive features of spoken language. Cognitive studies with deaf signers have shown that signs serve as perceptual units (Hass and Sams, 1987) and are coded in memory by Stokoe's features (Bellugi and Klima, 1975; Siple et al., 1977; Hanson, 1982; Shand, 1982).

Van Uden (1986) took issue with cherology for signs as analogous to the phonology of natural spoken language. He argued that the features of signs are determined by content, and are essentially iconic. Hence Stokoe's cheremes were integral parts of the icon of the sign, rather than arbitrary functional features, as with the phonemes of spoken language. It has to be admitted that the idea of cheremes seems to fit oddly with iconicity. However that may be, whether arbitrary features are present or absent does not tell us much about whether the system of which they are part is, or is not, a language, as Van Uden himself recognised. What is important is that the phonological, or cherological, rules of a language are the accepted convention, and that problems arise when they are broken.

Inflections

In discussing the morphology of sign language, especially ASL, Van Uden concluded that the morphology was extremely poor, particularly for expressing relationships. The morphological inflections of standard English to signify plural forms, comparatives and superlatives were largely absent in sign. However, as with iconicity, this is a relative argument. In standard English some nouns, for instance, are not inflected to show case. Van Uden quoted Stokoe (1978) to the effect that sign languages do not have the inflectional systems of Indo-European and related languages. However, this quotation missed the point. Sign language can be highly inflected, but it uses inflections in a different way to their use in standard English (Hanson and Feldman, 1989).

Singularity and plurality in English are commonly marked by the absence or presence of the suffix -s for nouns and for third person verbs. Instead of inflecting the sign, sign language uses repetition, or reduplication, of the sign, or precedes the sign by a number, to convey the plural marking. However, signs can be inflected to show classifiers. For example, Kyle and Woll (1985) described the BSL verb stem which means 'to go under a bridge', shown by moving the right hand under the left hand, where the shape (inflection) of the right hand conveys what is going under the bridge.

In an English sentence, such as 'The man bit the dog' the syntax shows that the man did the biting. In BSL (Kyle and Woll, 1985), the role, or who did what, is conveyed by inflecting the verb with conventionalised manual locations. Alternatively, each hand may be used in simultaneous articulation, not possible in a spoken language, by coding separate roles, one on each hand, following which the hands act on each other. Kyle and Woll (1985) illustrated other uses of manual morphology to represent time, aspect and quality, namely, manner or degree. Van Uden argued that purely functional inflexions, rather than the 'semantic' inflections of the type outlined, do not exist in sign language. Whether or not this is the case does not determine whether sign language can be regarded as a true language, however, if the meaning is conveyed in other ways.

Structure

In addition to his arguments that sign language has no 'phonology' and no functional morphology, Van Uden also argued that it has no linguistic syntax. In both ASL and BSL, for example, it is difficult to find a basic order of signs. However, it is arguable that a language must have a basic syntax, like the subject–verb–object (SVO) syntax of English. Rather, ASL and BSL may be topic-comment languages (Friedman, 1976; Deuchar, 1983), where the topic is first introduced and then elaborated. The characteristic structure thus shows semantic or pragmatic linkages rather than syntactic relationships (compare Fontana, 1990). Deuchar gave the example of 'TEN P PUT-IN' = 'I put in ten p', where ten p (pence) was the topic and was made first with the dominant right hand, then the right hand remained in the fingerspelling position for 'p' while PUT-IN was signed with the non-dominant left hand. Deuchar observed that studies of spontaneous signing (Hansen, 1975) accepted topic-comment as the base for signed sentences, whereas formal research using elicited sentences tended to find an SVO structure (Liddell, 1978b). She regarded the situation in which the sign was produced, or the influence of the dominant spoken language, as affecting the data. Hence both Deuchar and Friedman felt that indications of SVO structure in sign were caused by exposure to English, and were not basic characteristics of sign language. We conclude that Van Uden may not have been too far from the truth in stating that sign language does not possess a linguistic syntax, at least in the sense that sign language is not as dominated by word grouping or word order as English, though it does contain its own syntax-like arrangements (Wilbur, 1987; Lillo-Martin, 1990) for wh- questions, for instance. Natural, spontaneous sign language looks to be largely a topic-comment language. As such, there will be some sentence constructions in English which are difficult to convey directly via sign. Crystal and Craig (1978) have given some instances.

In response to Van Uden (1986), Stokoe (1987) observed that opposition to sign as language came from using the wrong kind of linguistics, originating from a particular social orientation. As we ourselves have argued, it depends where we start from. Although there is much to be learned about sign before it can be characterised fully and with confidence, the work reviewed fails to convince that sign language is definitely not language. It does show, however, that sign language has a very different structure from standard English. The real test of whether sign language is truly language depends, nevertheless, not so much on its structure, but on its success in carrying out its function. We need to ask, then, if sign language is as effective as English in coding meaning and information, in getting messages across, in generative capacity, and in facilitating the flow of discourse.

Communication by sign

How effective is sign language as a means of communication? For profoundly deaf individuals with no other form of communication it is 100% effective. Deaf children born to signing deaf parents know no other way of communicating. But we can look at this question in another way, asking how effectively is information transmitted by sign between deaf people in contrast to the transmission of the same information by speech between hearing people?

In one of the earlier referential communication studies, and in one of a number of experiments, Schlesinger (1971) found that deaf subjects had problems in conveying which one out of several pictures had been selected for communication. Each picture contained three characters in three roles – the agent, the object, and the indirect object ('A bear hands over a man to a monkey'). Six pictures, covering all possible permutations, made up a set, with each character appearing once in each role. The sender was required to describe one of the pictures, in Israeli sign language, following which the receiver had to select the correct picture from the set of six. The deaf subjects performed poorly. Schlesinger thought that the reason was because there was seemingly no rule in Israeli sign language which could be used consistently to distinguish between the subject, direct object and indirect object.

Schlesinger's work was criticised by Bode (1974), who thought it unreasonable to conclude that the main form of communication of any group lacked the means of conveying these relationships. Everyday communication required the frequent use of all three roles. Bode's well-founded criticisms included the absence of hearing controls using spoken language, who may also have found the task difficult. Bode also remarked on the lack of testing for competence in Israeli sign language, since some subjects may have been immigrants without developed skills in Israeli sign language. Bode's criticisms seem very pertinent. Schlesinger's (1971) study helps little to answer our question about the effectiveness of sign language in communicating meaning.

In an often-cited report, Hoemann (1972) compared information exchange by 40 mainly profoundly deaf and 40 hearing children in referential communication. The deaf group was acquiring ASL in a school where manual communication was allowed outside the classroom. The age of onset of hearing impairment, where known, was before 3 years of age. Half the hearing-impaired children had a mean age of 8;4 years and half of 11;4 years, while half of the 40 hearing children were of mean age 8;0 years and half 11;5 years. The genders were approximately equally distributed among all four groups. The two groups of hearing children had overall a higher performance IQ than the hearing-impaired groups. The children were studied in pairs of the same age grouping, as 8-year-olds with 8-year-olds, for example, and hearing status, as hearing with hearing and deaf with deaf. The pairs of children took part in three tasks: a description task, involving the description of various picture referents; a perspective task, requiring the construction of referent descriptions from the receiver's perspective; and a game-rules task, explaining the rules of a game.

Results for the description task showed significant differences for age and for hearing status, with no interaction, on sending scores. Older children obtained a higher communication accuracy than the younger children. Higher communication accuracy was also attained by hearing as compared with deaf children. Receiving scores were significantly higher than sending scores. Generally, the deaf children showed a 3-year lag in performance, as the scores of the 11-year-old deaf children were roughly the same as those of the 8-year-old hearing children, on all three measures assessed, namely sending, receiving and communication accuracy.

For the perspective task the hearing did better than the deaf children at both ages, and benefited more from a demonstration of perspective and from a prior experience as receivers. The older children, irrespective of hearing status, did better than the younger subjects, but the older hearing children only were able to establish whose perspective – sender's or receiver's – was to be taken. The younger deaf children produced more ambiguous or egocentric messages both before and after the demonstration, whereas the other groups changed their approach after the demonstration, but not always appropriately in all cases. The performance of the 11-year-old deaf children was again similar to that of the 8-year-old hearing children.

In the game-rules task, few deaf children explained the rules adequately. Both young and older deaf children behaved inappropriately, signing that they could not proceed, simply labelled the materials, or fixated on a single aspect of the game. However, all 40 deaf children were able to teach the game successfully when allowed to show the rules in action. Therefore, they knew the rules, but could not explain them manually. The 11 older deaf children, rated as explaining the rules adequately, used several manual modes of communicating, such as conventional ASL signs, fingerspelling and improvised iconic signs.

Hoemann concluded that peer-to-peer communication by deaf children was handicapped even for manual methods. The only tasks in which all his children succeeded were the descriptions of simple pictures. The 11-year-old deaf children were generally at the same performance level as the hearing 8-year-olds. Even when the hearing and deaf children were equated for IQ, the hearing children still showed significantly better performance on all three tasks. However, it is by no means clear that the differences between the deaf and the hearing children were due to differences in communication channel. As Hoemann himself pointed out, the relatively poor performance of his deaf children may have been due to a general experiential deficit affecting the acquisition of both linguistic skill and the development of formal communication skills. Hoemann's tasks were relatively formal. It is thus interesting to note that, in the game-rules task, the deaf children could convey the rules well by signing when allowed to demonstrate them in action, when they were able to draw on informal ways of communicating. Further, the deaf children would have begun school at 5–6 years of age with a poor knowledge of English, and with limited manual communication skills.

It would be instructive to repeat this study with deaf children of deaf signing parents as the group to be compared with hearing children. Such a comparison would allow a more balanced assessment of the effectiveness of conveying information by manual communication in referential communication tasks. That the performance level of Hoemann's deaf 11-year-olds was better than the deaf 8-year-olds suggested strongly that experience significantly increased formal communication skill, the learning of communication skill, and the learning of communication roles (compare Flavell, 1968). However, this study, though well designed in many aspects, does not allow us to decide whether sign language is sufficiently language-like in conveying meaning, as the deaf children were not necessarily competent users of sign language for their age.

Bode (1974) attempted to improve on the design used by Schlesinger (1971), described above, by trying to obtain comparable linguistic backgrounds for her hearing and deaf subjects. Her 16 English-speaking subjects were all native speakers of English. Her 16 deaf (probably profoundly deaf) subjects were ASL users. All but three had begun to learn ASL by 6 years of age. Those three acquired ASL at approximately 10, 14 and 17 years. All subjects were university undergraduates. All the deaf subjects were judged proficient in ASL by a mature deaf ASL user, who had acquired ASL from his deaf parents and siblings. Bode used one set of black and white picture referents illustrating three characters in which a first character handed a second character to a third, corresponding closely to the descriptions given in Schlesinger (1971). Another set of animals was prepared in which each character was of a different colour and shape and in which the depiction of time sequence was less ambiguous than in the first set ('a throws b overhand to c who stands with arms out' as in: 'The fish throws the cat to the pig'). Eight pairs of subjects were used for the spoken English part, and eight for the ASL part. For pairs of subjects, the two kinds of pictures and two kinds of instructions, brief and detailed, were balanced in two sequences. After a sender had described a picture indicated by the experimenter, and which the receiver could not see, the receiver tried to identify it from the complete set of six pictures.

For hearing pairs of subjects, 95% of the referent pictures were identified correctly. For the deaf subject pairs the proportion was 86%. Correct selection by chance would have been 17%. A comparison of the frequency of errors showed no significant difference between hearing and deaf groups. Nor were there other significant differences in scores. Bode concluded that ASL could communicate information about agent/object/indirect object which was comparable to that in spoken English. Her subjects performed uniformly well with both sets of pictures, when the linguistic abilities of deaf and hearing subjects were relatively comparable. Even so, and although they were judged to be proficient users of ASL, the deaf subjects had begun life with a marked communication disadvantage, as they had not begun to learn ASL till 6 years old. This delay, and the fact that they had not learned ASL naturally from deaf signing parents, may explain why their performance on the referential tasks was a little poorer than that of the hearing subjects, though not significantly so.

Before leaving this account of Bode's study, we comment on the nature of the referential communication task, which, as with Schlesinger (1971), was naturalistically very obscure. After all, man-handling bears and cat-throwing fish are not part of everyday experience. This obscurity was shown by some descriptions quoted by Bode, such as 'Fish hold cat/pig laugh' – a signed description – and 'On the bottom left there's a pink pig holding a yellow cat. On the right bottom there's a green glob' – a spoken description. These examples* show that some of both the deaf and the hearing children did not understand the action the pictures were meant to convey. Similar comments can be offered about the pictures used in other picture-description referential communication tasks. In a study by Oléron (1978), for example, sketches were intended to depict a man showing a boy to a woman, a woman showing a man to a boy, etc. It is not clear from the pictures what the action, namely 'showing', was meant to be. Hence the material was ambiguous. Such ambiguity adds 'noise' to the experimental design.

For all three studies reviewed, we have argued that a fair test of whether or not sign language can be used as effectively to transmit meaning as natural spoken language requires subjects who have been able to use sign as their natural means of communication from very early in life. Hence these subjects can communicate in a way that is comfortable and natural for them, and which they can fully understand (Erting, 1980). The use of signs by deaf children born to deaf parents begins before, or at least as soon as, the use of words by hearing children born to hearing parents, and the acquisition of a vocabulary of signs develops rapidly (Bonvillian et al., 1983). Hence it is particularly important to base studies of the effectiveness of sign by deaf users on those whose signed fluency approaches that of their parents. This emphasis on the use of deaf signers born of deaf signing parents is not trivial. Marmor and Petitto (1979) and Strong and Charlson (1987) have observed

---

* © *Perceptual and Motor Skills*, 1974; reprinted with permission.

that hearing teachers of the deaf may delete important signed information when speaking and signing to deaf children of school age. This observation clearly indicates that deaf children who learn to sign at school in TC may not experience full sign language instruction.

Use of parts of the body other than the hands

Important facets of sign language are produced with parts of the body other than the hands, though it is conventional to refer to sign language as a manual language. Parts of the body to which reference has been made include the face, eyes, head, upper limbs and trunk (Dittman, 1972; Baker and Padden, 1978; Baker 1980; Liddell, 1980; Ruggieri et al., 1982; Kluwin, 1983; Stokoe, 1991), for both hearing and hearing-impaired people. Generally, native speakers of standard English make relatively little use of kinesic communication (Harris, 1989), and as a result there has been a rather late realisation of the potential importance, in the sign language of deaf people, of signs other than the obvious manual gestures.

The signer's eye, face and head movements may help to form signs, serve a function as adverbs and adjectives, and indicate aspects of grammar (Baker-Shenk, 1985). Some signed communication may be conveyed with the face alone. Reduplicated verbs in Swedish Sign Language may be accompanied by different mouth positions. Such verbal modification is adverbial in nature. Another form, referred to as 'initial hold', is a modulation of degree meaning 'very'. Here, the movement begins with a short hold and is then completed quickly while the head is turned away to the side, giving a visual impression of an enlarged sign, since the distance between the hand and head is increased (Bergman, 1983).

Similar combinations, of which at least 20 are known, can occur in ASL (Baker-Schenk, 1985) when movements of the eyes, face and head serve as adjectives and adverbs to modulate the accompanying manual signs. Thus, to make the sign meaning 'write' whilst producing the facial adverb which means 'carelessly' produces the meaning of 'write carelessly'. Grammatical forms showing whether a message is a question, assertion, command, is conditional or negated, or includes a special topic or a relative clause, can also be indicated by movements of the eyes, face, head and trunk. In such instances, the grammatical signals are presented immediately before the relevant part of the message starts, and usually continue until it ends. The signal for the conditional part of a contingent message, for example, consists of raising the eyebrows and leaning the head and/or body to the side, and is offered throughout the presentation of the conditional segment. When this conditional segment has been completed another grammatical signal may be used to signify an ensuing 'main clause' statement, question, etc. Although 'if' may be signed manually in a conditional message, it need not be so signed when the non-manual conditional form is used. Even when it is signed manually, the signer still generally uses the non-manual signal throughout the presentation of the relevant segment. Similarly, a message which offers a negative statement can be presented with a manual sign for 'not' or with a non-manual negation signal which includes shaking of the head and a negative expression on the face with the corners of the mouth turned down. Baker-Schenk (1985) has presented pictorial representations of the above.

A combination of facial expression and head position marks topics in ASL where the eyebrows are raised with the head tilted slightly backwards (Bellugi and Fischer, 1972; Liddell, 1980). This combination is presented at the same time as the topic sign and then ceases. Liddell also described other non-manual signals giving grammatical information. Thus, head tilt is used to indicate relative clauses (Liddell, 1978a). Yes–no questions may be cued by raising the eyebrows, and leaning the head and body forward.

Research in facial expressions has developed to the degree to which a coding system is needed to record and analyse signed discourse, especially when overlaid with facial expressions of emotion. Baker-Shenk (1985) described a coding system based on the Facial Action Coding System of Ekman and Friesen (1978). This system uses 44 Action Units to describe the range of possible movements of the face which are closely related to movement of the facial musculature. It allows for separate coding of all positions and movements of gaze, face, head and trunk. Together with coding of manual signs, including onset and offset, via their English counterparts or glosses, the whole communication signal can be recorded against a timeline, giving a record of what was produced and when.

Baker-Shenk found that the affect of the signer could change the nature of the grammatical signal, so that it continued to be recognizable but changed its characteristics. Thus, the raised eyebrows in yes–no questions are usually at a mid-intensity level, with the upper eyelids slightly raised. But when the signer asks a question in surprise, the raising of eyebrows and eyelids increases in intensity and the jaw drops to leave the mouth open. Changes of facial expression in sign language are thus analogous to the role played by intonation in spoken English. Baker-Shenk remarked that facial movements could function as signs, components of signs, modifiers (adverbs), and as grammatical signals. Further, the movements and positions of the head of the signer had a function in the syntax of sign language. She felt that, as a result, sign languages should be referred to as visual–gestural, rather than manual, languages.

Mimicry and role-taking

Users of sign language may take the role of a person or animal to which allusion is being made, when the signer represents the person or animal with his or her own body, to show what that person or animal is doing. Such role-taking, mime, mimicry, or even dramatisation is very useful for representing indirect discourse (Hoemann, 1976, 1978a; Suty, 1986; Mindess, 1990). Hoemann (1976) reported the cumbersome indirect message: 'The doctor said that I should stay home. She said I could come to her office, but she told me not to go out for any other reason' as the signed 'STAY HOME. COME SEE ME, OK. OTHER OUT NO', with the signer acting in the role of the doctor. Signals that the signer has changed roles are given by facial expression, body posture and position, and manner of expression, in this case to simulate the authority figure of the doctor. Role-taking results in a considerable saving of effort. It may also produce a gain in clarity of who is saying what to whom, especially when the message involves a number of agents interacting with one another, when the role of each agent may be taken in turn.

Neuropsychology of communication by sign

To understand communication by sign, we need to appreciate the ways in which sign and other gestural forms, are organised in the brain. It is generally accepted that the left cerebral hemisphere plays the major part in monitoring and controlling speech functions in hearing people (but see Efron, 1990). It is also generally accepted that, for almost all right-handed people, speech functions are left-lateralised. The situation is less clear for left-handers. Their speech functions may be left-lateralised in about two-thirds or more of cases (Kimura, 1983). It is further well accepted that right-handed hearing people predominantly make right-handed gestures while talking. This effect is less marked for left-handers. Left-handers do not make left-handed gestures to the same extent as right-handers make right-handed gestures (Kimura, 1973a, b; Dalby et al., 1980; Kimura and Humphrys, 1981). The left cerebral hemisphere controls both the speech functions and the predominantly right-handed gestures which accompany speech in right-handed talkers (Kimura, 1973a).

Feyereisen (1983) concluded from work on non-fluent speech that gestures were related to speech function. Feyereisen reviewed evidence showing that, when hearing talkers are stuck for the correct words to communicate what they want to say, they may shift to use of gesture; gestures are more often used by bilingual people when using the less familiar of their two languages; and people with impaired speech, or expressive aphasia, use gestures more frequently than non-impaired people when communicating, but not in other activities. Were such gestures to occur more frequently on the right than the left side, when assessed against the proportions of right- versus left-hand gestures which occur during normal fluent speech, this finding would strongly support left cerebral lateralisation as mediating both speech functions and gestures in hearing people.

In his review of the rather slim evidence available, Harris (1989) observed that the increase in gesture was disproportionately greater on the right-hand side. He also took Kimura's (1973a) argument a stage further in concluding that the right hand is generally more expressive in serving communication among hearing people. In considering handedness and use of gestures by deaf people, the evidence suggests that right-handed deaf signers make gestures more with the right than the left hand (Harris, 1989). The inference is that signing is left-lateralised for right-handed deaf signers, but more work is needed before firm conclusions can be drawn. There is some suggestion that use of the dominant hand is less marked in deaf signers than is the use of the dominant hand for gestures during speech by hearing people, indicating that sign may not be as strongly lateralised as speech functions.

Further evidence of cerebral lateralisation in sign language comes from the area of the neuropsychology of visual perception – the so-called visual hemifield studies. Such studies are of practical interest because deaf children can identify signs presented well into their visual periphery (Swisher et al., 1989; Swisher, 1990), although studies investigating peripheral vision for signs and cerebral lateralisation have yet to be done.

Visual stimuli which impinge on one side of the retina are transmitted directly to one of the two cerebral hemispheres. Thus visual stimuli presented from the right side, that is, from the right visual field, go directly to the left cerebral hemisphere. If the stimuli move across the visual field from right to left, they will first directly stimulate the left side of the retinae and the resulting nerve impulses will travel from both eyes to the left hemisphere. They will then stimulate the right side of the retinae, with resulting nerve impulses travelling to the right hemisphere. Studies which demonstrate this effect require fixation on a central point, while stimulus material is introduced into the visual periphery. There is a right visual field (left hemisphere) advantage for verbal stimuli and a left visual field (right hemisphere) advantage for visual spatial stimuli (Mishkin and Forgays, 1952; Cohen, 1977; Hellige, 1980), though Moscovitch (1979) has argued that this kind of laterality effect occurs in relatively late stages of processing, and that analyses of the physical features of stimuli occur in both cerebral hemispheres. The right visual field advantage for verbal material seems to occur because the left cerebral hemisphere has an advantage in processing serial information, whereas visuospatial information is processed favourably by the right hemisphere (Cohen, 1977). Alternatively, the left hemisphere may be specialised for processing codes, while the right hemisphere may be superior in processing novel stimuli.

Neuropsychological processing has been studied in both deaf and hearing people. Phippard (1977), Ross et al. (1979) and Scholes and Fischler (1979) among others found that deaf signers showed a small left visual field (right hemisphere) advantage for words as compared with hearing individuals. Other workers (Poizner et al., 1979) have found a right visual field advantage in deaf subjects for English words, which was, however, less marked than the right visual field advantage for hearing subjects. Manning et al. (1977) observed that hearing subjects, as expected, showed a significant left hemisphere advantage for English words while deaf subjects showed only a tendency in the same direction. The results for the deaf subjects may have been due to variable familiarity of this group with ASL (Wilbur, 1979). Phippard (1977) studied a group of orally educated deaf and another group educated orally and manually, together with hearing subjects. The latter showed left hemisphere advantage for English letters and right hemisphere advantage for lines and faces. The orally educated deaf group showed right hemisphere advantage for English letters and lines (they were not presented with faces). The group educated both orally and manually showed no marked hemispheric advantage for different types of stimuli. Again, the extent of familiarity with the stimulus modality for the last group was not recorded, and may have been a confounding factor. The visual field effects found in these studies of verbal stimuli with deaf subjects were small and conflicting. This conflict may have been due to differences in method between the studies, or because of a lesser experience with written English amongst the deaf subjects (Zaidel, 1980).

For signs, both hearing and deaf people show a left visual field (right hemisphere) advantage when the signs are stationary (Manning et al., 1977; Poizner et al., 1979). Moving signs may show a small left visual field (right hemisphere) advantage (Poizner et al., 1979), but not when they are temporally redundant, such that parts of the signs are similar at the beginning and the end (Kyle and Woll, 1985).

These studies taken together do not present a convincing case that signs are processed in a neuropsychologically different way to standard English. More recent investigations tend to confirm that sign language, like English, is processed in the left cerebral hemisphere. Thus, while Boshoven et al. (1982) observed a left visual field advantage in deaf subjects for drawings, they did not find an advantage for words, dots or ASL, in comparisons with hearing subjects and interpreters for the deaf. Panou and Sewell (1984) also obtained a right visual field advantage in deaf subjects for English words and BSL signs. Poizner et al. (1984) found that four unilaterally brain-damaged deaf signers, fluent in ASL, processed linguistic and non-linguistic visual stimuli in essentially the same way as would have brain-damaged hearing people. Their three patients with left hemisphere damage were poor at processing linguistic signs, but processed non-linguistic visuospatial stimuli appropriately. The single patient with right hemisphere damage performed poorly with the non-linguistic visuospatial stimuli, but performance for the linguistic stimuli was adequate.

In a later significant review of neuropsychological work with deaf signers, Bellugi et al. (1988) concluded that hearing and speech were not necessary for hemispheric specialisation to develop. Hence hearing for speech was not crucial for hemispheric specialisation. This conclusion casts further doubt on aspects of the critical period hypothesis of the importance of early hearing ability for language development (Chapter 2), although auditory and sign languages may differ in other neuropsychological aspects. Bellugi et al. further concluded that patients with left hemisphere damage show marked deficits in the syntax of sign language, for example, but adequate facility for non-language visuospatial material such as spatial relations. Patients with right hemisphere damage showed the reverse. In sign language, although grammatical information is conveyed by the visuospatial modality, this did not appear to affect complementary hemispheric specialisation, which was similar to that by which hearing people process standard English and non-linguistic material. Bellugi et al. also found that aspects of sign language, such as lexicon and grammar, could be impaired selectively, suggesting that the brain's functional organisation for sign language may be modular. They concluded that the left cerebral hemisphere had an innate predisposition for language irrespective of language modality, and that views of hemispheric specialisation which based a distinction of function on a difference between language and visuospatial function were oversimple (compare Kimura, 1990). Sign language, in the visual modality and involving an interplay between visuospatial and linguistic relations, was processed neuropsychologically in the same way as standard English.

Similar conclusions were drawn by Bellugi et al. (1989) and Sanders et al. (1989). However, the situation is less clear for facial expressions. Corina (1989) found that deaf signers' visual field asymmetries for affective and linguistic expressions were affected by the order of presentation, whereas hearing subjects showed left visual field advantages for both kinds of signals. Thus for deaf signers, hemispheric specialisation for processing facial signals, which are of particular salience to them, may be affected by the differences which those signals serve. Sanders et al. (1989) have also presented results suggesting a left visual field advantage for semantic categorisation of words and static BSL signs, but their adolescent subjects were not all profoundly deaf and all had been instructed in sign-supported speech. The issue of lateralisation was therefore confounded with subject and experiential variables.

Although it may be relatively difficult to find them, work in this area will continue to be hard to interpret unless the deaf signers employed are congenitally profoundly deaf signers born to deaf signing parents, with no use of speechreading or residual hearing, and with no other interfering handicaps.

Acquisition and learning of sign language

Sign language is far from an elementary system of communication requiring only basic skills for its acquisition. It appears as a language in its own right, containing complex structures and its own intonation, semantics and pragmatics. Although its lexicon and sublexical material is relatively iconic, there is often an iconic correspondence between form and meaning in syntax and morphology (Fischer, 1978; Klima and Bellugi, 1979). Sign languages convey the meaning in communication pervasively by transparency and translucency of form.

Profoundly deaf children come from varying social and economic backgrounds. Their backgrounds also differ in whether their parents and siblings are hearing, or prelingually or postlingually deaf. Further, different members of their family may be deaf or hearing. What profoundly deaf children do have in common is a reliance on vision as their main means of acquiring language and communication skills (Russell et al., 1976). Where neither parents nor siblings are deaf, the deaf child will use speechreading supplemented by residual hearing and improvised gestures, or perhaps by manual communication if the parents have learned manual skills. On the other hand, deaf children will communicate most readily with deaf relatives by manual communication. There are thus different familial situations which direct a young hearing-impaired child's modality of communication. That modality seems likely to be purely manual only when both parents and any siblings are themselves deaf, and habitually use sign language in their everyday communication, including communication with visitors (Siple, 1978a). On attaining school age, deaf children born to hearing parents may communicate with each other in several ways, both in and out of the classroom. Much or all of this communication will be non-linguistic, a poor relation of sign language, especially if it is 'prohibited' by teachers (Lewis, 1968). It is likely to be an imperfect kind of communication (Tervoort, 1961). The reader is referred to Quigley and Kretschmer (1982) and Volterra and Erting (1990) for reviews of this area.

We now consider what is known of the early acquisition of sign language by deaf children born to deaf signing parents, where such children are congenitally deaf, or deafened before the acquisition of spoken language.

Schlesinger and Meadow (1972) reported a small study of two hearing children and one deaf child born to deaf parents. All three children learned to sign before they learned to speak, with the first sign for the deaf child produced at 10 months of age. Williams (1976) found that the first sign of a deaf child born to deaf parents was produced at 9 months. McIntire (1977), in a study of an infant with a borderline hearing loss, born to hearing-impaired parents, found 85 signs at 13 months of age and more than 200 signs at 21 months, with 2-sign productions at 10 months. Bonvillian et al. (1983) investigated 11 children from nine families with deaf parents. Both father and mother were deaf in seven families, one family was a single-parent family and one family had a deaf mother and a hearing father. Nine of the children were firstborn, with the remaining two second-born. Ten children were normally hearing, while the remaining one had a severe bilateral hearing loss. The children and parents were visited once every 5–6 weeks over a 16-month period. Seven children were studied from before their first birthday, from 4–10 months, together with a 12-month-old and an 18-month-old. Two older children, aged 2 and 3 years, for whom their parents had kept detailed developmental diaries, were also included. The infants' acquisition of the various motor milestones was in accord with accepted norms. While infants produce their first words between 11 and 14 months of age, the first sign was produced at an average age of 8.5 months. Ten signs were produced by 13.2 months as compared with norms of 10 words at 15.1 months, and the first combination of signs appeared on the average at 17 months as compared with norms for first word combinations at 18 to 21 months. Of the first ten signs produced, 30% were considered to be iconic, 37% were metonymic, being based on a relatively small or unimportant feature, and 33% were arbitrary. This distribution differs considerably from that discussed by Van Uden (1986), who reported relatively few arbitrary signs. The use of signs, then, was in advance of the norms for the use of words for these infants, who were all but one hearing, but all of whom had deaf parents who habitually used ASL in the home. Caselli (1983) reported on four deaf children without recording details of hearing loss or the hearing status of the parents. She concluded that the first gestures of both deaf and hearing children were deictic, such as pointing, and that these deictic gestures were then followed by signs, or words.

The parallel between the early acquisition of sign by deaf children of deaf parents and the acquisition of verbal language by hearing children of hearing parents continues into the later years. Thus Prinz and Prinz (1985) observed that 24 profoundly deaf children, mostly born to deaf parents and aged from 3 to 11 years, showed signed discourse strategies in peer interactions comparable to those used by hearing children in spoken conversations. They adhered to discourse rules, including soliciting attention, obtaining and holding eye contact, handling conversational topics, turn-taking, and remedial interruptions.

Deaf infants, then, acquire sign language at the same age as hearing infants acquire verbal language, or earlier, perhaps because the body-motor system develops earlier than the control of speech musculature (Sperling, 1978). The rate of increase in mean length of utterance with age, for example, is strikingly similar for deaf manually communicating and hearing verbally communicating infants around the age of 30–36 months. There are similarities, too, in infantile expressions or 'baby talk' (Siple, 1978a), and overgeneralisation of rules, similar to 'camed' and 'wented' in young hearing children acquiring standard English (Wilbur, 1979). It may therefore be argued that language acquisition develops in stages (Brown, 1973), which are not modality-specific (Schlesinger and Meadow, 1972; Collins-Ahlgren, 1975; McIntire, 1977). However, specific language structures, such as syntax, depend on particular mechanisms which may be modality-specific (Klima and Bellugi, 1979).

Although published research relates to studies of only small groups of children, it seems likely that deaf children acquire sign language structures developmentally in a similar way to that in which young hearing children acquire verbal language. Further, since languages need to be learned or acquired, this fact sets constraints on their structures (see below). Sign languages have the same type of analytic structure as spoken languages, in so far as both have a limited number of variables, each of which may contain a limited number of discrete values which shape language acquisition, together with a set of rules which control the ways in which the discrete values may be used. Further, the process of language acquisition sets limits on the structures languages may adopt, because languages are constrained by the processes of language acquisition (Newport and Supalla, 1980).

In learning any language, people like to establish one-to-one relationships between its basic semantic aspects and its surface forms. They also like to see clear relationships between meaning and form (Slobin, 1980). In the jargon used by linguists, people like the semantic aspects of a language to be transparent. Slobin argued that, in acquiring their first language, children strive for transparency and regularity, even beyond the natural regularity of the language, and only gradually adjust to the more opaque aspects of the language. He also argued that when the opacity is too great there is a shift to new and more transparent forms. These arguments suggest that the transparency of sign languages, and their noted iconicity, confers on sign a learnability beyond a characterisation of mere modality difference from spoken languages, and beyond the possible benefits of a clearly perceived association between signs and their referents. Under some circumstances, there is a tendency to regress towards transparency which seems to put sign languages at an advantage in their learning. It would also help to explain why the iconicity of sign is so pervasive and persistent.

Hearing children develop their expertise in spoken language subconsciously, without apparent effort. The same might be said of deaf children born to deaf signing parents and who have deaf signing siblings, in their progress with sign language. Older hearing children and adults are able both to acquire by unconscious assimilation and to learn by conscious effort in expanding their first language. They become aware, through learning, of its rule structure and lexicon, while retaining some continuing facility for acquiring it. The use of both acquisition and learning holds true for second-language learning by hearing older children and adults (Krashen, 1982), and for verbal language development by native deaf signers, for whom verbal language is a second language. For the orally communicating young congenitally deaf child, born to hearing parents and with hearing siblings, spoken language is the first language. But the difficulties imposed by poor auditory inputs are so great that a first spoken language for deaf children develops more like a second than a first language. The learning effort required is very considerable, and the part played by acquisition is small.

For most young deaf children who are born to hearing parents, sign language is a kind of second, second language, because the first oral language, with which they communicate with their parents, is nearly always imperfectly developed for their age. Thus most deaf children, who are those born to hearing parents, have to learn sign language. However, their motivation to communicate with other deaf individuals is likely to be so strong, especially if their oral communication is limited, that they usually become far more fluent in sign language, if permitted to do so, than hearing people who set out to learn it.

It is generally reported that deaf children born to deaf parents, or who otherwise begin their experiences with manual communication early in life, learn sign language more effectively and attain other advantages in cognitive skills and academic attainments. Nevertheless, there may be exceptions. Parasnis (1983) compared congenitally deaf college students, with deaf parents and who were native ASL users, with congenitally deaf college students who had hearing parents and learned ASL between 6 and 12 years of age. Comparisons were made of cognitive ability, the cognitive style of field dependence/independence and English language presented and produced in the spoken, written and signed modes. As expected, the subjects who had learned sign language performed significantly better than the native ASL group in speech perception and production. However, the latter group did not show differential effects which might be ascribed to early signed communication with their deaf parents. The lack of difference between the native ASL users and the group who learned to sign between 6 and 12 years may have occurred, however, because the relevant test involved English language presented via sign. Such a test would probably have been in a manual form more familiar to those who learned ASL rather than those who acquired it as their native language. Thus there was possible confounding with the type of test used, so Parasnis' work cannot be seen as clearly negating the general reports.

We saw earlier that young deaf children will develop a gestural form of communication for interaction with deaf peers, in the absence of any specific direction or modelling. Goldin-Meadow and Mylander (1984) have reported analogous findings for young deaf children of hearing parents, who developed a system of gestures for communicating with hearing individuals. Such gesture creation was observed in four deaf children aged 1;4 to 3;1 years, when each child, without usable conventional linguistic inputs, either oral or manual, developed a system of gestures comparable in semantic content and structure to the early spoken and signed systems of children acquiring conventional languages. As with Heider and Heider (1940) and Mohay (1982) the results suggested that signed communication can develop in markedly atypical language-learning environments, without a tutor's modelling or otherwise shaping the structure of the communication. It is not clear whether the development of such kinds of communication is acquired or learned. Certainly it will be far from the apparently effortless acquisition of the usual first steps in normal language development. Nevertheless, it is clear that the children themselves played the major role in developing these communication systems, as with the private verbal languages developed between hearing twins, implying that the gestural systems were not learned in the sense that they were not explicitly taught.

Research in volume into sign language learning has appeared only in recent years, and probably as much or more with hearing people and the intellectually disabled or communication-disordered as with the deaf child. This research followed earlier investigations of the nature of sign language, which emphasised the linguistic and psychological factors involved (Hoemann, 1975; Bellugi and Klima,

1976; Klima and Bellugi, 1979). The translucency of the sign and the correctness of its gloss were seen as important in sign language learning by Luftig and Lloyd (1981). Lloyd and Doherty (1983) considered production strategies that may be helpful for the learner of signing. Recent developments have been reviewed by Volterra and Erting (1990).

Much of this work has been conducted with the learning of sign language semantics and vocabulary – the relationship between the referent and its symbolic, manual representation (Robinson and Griffith, 1979; Orlansky and Bonvillian, 1984) in terms of iconicity, transparency and translucency. Page (1985a) also studied the perceived translucency between ASL signs and their glosses in hearing preschool and school-age children and adults. She found that her 4- and 7-year-old children and adults perceived signs that convey action, excluding stative verbs like 'feel' and 'is', to be more translucent or more iconic than signs representing nomination, which in turn were more translucent than signs conveying attribution. Page ascribed these results to Newport and Bellugi's (1979) categorisation of objects into the three levels of basic, superordinate and subordinate, as *chair* is basic to the superordinate *furniture* and the subordinate *recliner*, for which ASL has rather different forms in sign. Thus signs for basic terms are usually of single-unit form, signs for superordinates are compounds of basic level signs, and signs for subordinates consist of basic elements together with visual descriptive gestures. Page argued that translucency is that aspect of iconicity which is closest to usual sign learning, and that translucent signs are to be preferred to non-translucent signs in preparing materials for instruction in sign language.

Exploration of the relationship between signs and their verbal glosses should be a powerful tool for developing academic achievement. For example, Akamatsu and Armour (1987) drew the attention of six severely to profoundly prelingually deaf residential high-school students to signing, making explicit some of the ways in which signing differs from writing. Their results indicated that translating between sign and writing made the students more aware of the rule differences between sign and written English. In analysing the construction of ASL and Pidgin Sign English, the students began to perceive a common base to signed and written English modes of communication, signing in English and signing in ASL. A further useful outcome was that the students improved in the grammar of their written English more than a matched control group of deaf students who did not receive the analytical instruction.

This report by Akamatsu and Armour, showing a positive attitude to the use of sign in formal training of deaf children, also draws attention to the large proportion of teachers who now agree that sign input is very important to the development of communication skills in the profoundly deaf child, and to the level of skills needed for general conversation. This attitude now is regularly found in Australia (Ballge-Kimber and Giorcelli, 1989) though the development is recent (Treloar, 1985), Canada (Wickham and Kyle, 1987), the UK (Child, 1991) and the USA (Crittenden, 1986; Stewart, 1983). However, it is the majority view that signed English should be used in the classroom rather than sign language.

As regards the use of technology in the learning of sign language, Seal (1987) has discussed the preparation of instructional videotapes for signing deaf preschoolers. Slike et al. (1989) used an interactive video system to teach an introductory course of sign language vocabulary to 20 hearing students, while a control group, also of 20 students, learned the same signs by a traditional classroom method. Comparison of the groups after training showed no difference in the ability to recognise signs. However, the group that learned signed vocabulary via the interactive video system took only two-thirds of the time taken by the group learning the signs by the conventional approach. If these findings can be generalised to deaf students, then such students may be able to learn signed vocabulary more efficiently if use is made of interactive video technology.

Sign language learning clearly involves motor learning. It strikes the observer as involving perceptual motor skills rather more obviously than spoken language. There have been several studies concerned particularly with the motor aspects of sign learning to a greater or lesser degree. Dennis et al. (1982) proposed that motor factors played a part in facilitating the learning of sign vocabulary, since signs with high motor complexity will tend to dissuade the child from using them frequently. Hanson and Feldman (1989) devised a sign decision task in which deaf signers made a decision about the number of hands needed to produce particular ASL signs. They found significant facilitation of such decision-making by repetition among signs that shared a base morpheme, thus illustrating a practice effect in a motor aspect of sign learning. Also, a lexical decision task with English words showed facilitation by repetition of words that shared a base morpheme in both English and ASL, but not among words that shared a base morpheme in ASL alone.

Polar coordinates were used by Montgomery et al. (1983) to demonstrate patterns in signing, but the way in which students learn to express sign language movement patterns has only very recently been investigated by spatial analysis of motion. Thus Lupton and Zelaznick (1990) examined the changes in movement trajectories of two right-handed young female adult hearing students, from shortly after the beginning until the end of an introductory ASL course. These students had no knowledge of sign language to begin with. Lupton and Zelaznik, using infrared apparatus, found that the movement patterns increased in speed, symmetry and replicability, and became more limited in amplitude of movement as instruction progressed over a semester's course. Although users may show some preference for one-handed signs, interlimb coordination is important for many recognisable ASL signs. Thus (Battison, 1978; Hamilton and Lillo-Martin, 1986) there are constraints of symmetry in ASL such that when both hands are moving they display the same movement and shape, whether moving in- or out-of-phase. Because Lupton and Zelaznick's subjects developed such skill easily, their ease of learning supported the notion of such symmetry constraints.

From observations of an infant over age 13–21 months acquiring ASL in a family of deaf signers, McIntire (1977) suggested four stages, concerned with positions of fingers and thumb, in acquiring ASL handshapes, which are based on a child's developing cognitive and physical control of the weaker fingers. Thus the child became increasingly able to produce the more difficult features. McIntire's findings were similar to those observed in infants acquiring phonemic competence in spoken languages, where there are different stages for the acquisition of segments of speech sounds (Schick, 1990). In a study of the acquisition of classifiers, Schick explored whether handshapes were accurately produced in both structurally simple and complex predicates, and whether errors in production of handshapes occurred only because of anatomical factors. She found, in severely to profoundly deaf children aged between 4;5 and 9 years, that morphological complexity affected the accuracy of handshapes. But whereas earlier studies (Kantor, 1980) had suggested that the earliest handshapes used by children to form classifiers depended on both anatomical and cognitive complexity, Schick found that the children's production of handshapes was affected by complexity of morphology and by morphosyntactic aspects. There was no evidence, from analysis of hand-shape errors, to suggest that stages in the acquisition of handshapes depended only on anatomical complexity. Hence, in developing ability in ASL, the deaf child's performance depends on linguistic organisation rather than on motor learning or acquisition.

To summarise this section on the acquisition and learning of sign language, there is good evidence to show that deaf children born to deaf signing parents acquire sign readily, at a rate comparable to or faster than the acquisition of spoken language by hearing children. Deaf children born to hearing parents, however, have a harder time of it in learning sign, if such is available to them. A very recent area of research is the use of sophisticated techniques to investigate the geometry of sign, including the ways in which sign develops spatially. These techniques have revealed that sign develops as a coordination of speed and symmetry, with increasing replicability, in adult learners, and as a staged process increasing in complexity in infancy.

Total Communication

Despite the emphasis on oralism following the Milan Congress in 1880, a proportion of hearing-impaired children, especially those born to deaf parents, continued to acquire sign language as their first language, and used sign in communicating with other deaf individuals. To this day, both deaf children and adults who are competent in sign tend to seek out the deaf individuals in mixed groups of hearing and deaf people, and carry on communication in sign.

Sign language began to aquire official and linguistic respectability in the 1960s, notably boosted by the work of Stokoe (Stokoe et al., 1965), which initiated a status for sign as a language in its own right. This seminal work was followed by a burst of research into sign language, still continuing, from which it seems that the more that is known of sign language, the more accepted is its status as language. Further recognition of the potential of sign language came from the 'oral failures', an unfortunately large proportion of deaf children who had been educated orally but who did not perform well in academic achievement tests and whose speech was unintelligible. Those mentors who based educational attainment on the development of good communication skills argued that deaf child signers, who were expert in their native sign language, could benefit educationally from good signed communication with their teachers (Schlesinger, 1986). However, this attitude quickly ran into problems, because few of the teachers, who were mainly hearing, were fluent in sign language. Rather they used some form of signed English. The educational attainments of deaf children as a whole continued to be unacceptably low (see Chapter 6), whether the children were educated orally or manually.

The advent of TC

In the mid to late 1960s in the USA, soon followed in the UK (Montgomery, 1966), and Australia (Burch and Hyde, 1984) proposals were made to combine oral and signing approaches (Schlesinger, 1986) in what became known as Total Communication (TC), very similar to what is known as simultaneous communication (Newell et al., 1990). In theory, TC goes beyond oral plus manual approaches to permit other forms of communication. TC thus allows aural, manual and oral modes of communication (Gannon, 1981; Ling, 1984a; Johnson, 1988). In practice it may amount to not much more than a manual approach, occasionally augmented by other methods, such is the attraction of manual communication to the profoundly deaf. Hence TC is included in this chapter.

In retrospect, it is odd that it took so long to consider what seems to be an obvious alternative to oral-only or manual-only forms of communication. One reason was a fear that successful use of one alternative could be hindered by introduction of the other. The main reason, however, was probably that the positions of the oralists on the one hand, and the manualists on the other, were so entrenched, and defended with so much vigour and emotion, that for a long time consideration of a compromise was out of the question. However, in fairness, it should be pointed out that when a parent, therapist or teacher has expended great effort in learning an approach, the chosen approach will be defended stoutly and is unlikely to be altered except on the basis of very clear and overwhelming contraindications.

It was recognised at an early stage that TC should help to reduce the dominant position taken in class by teachers of the deaf, because TC would help to induce rapport between teacher and child, besides assisting a deaf child to communicate with hearing children and adults. TC also offered a prospect of the deaf child participating in an educational curriculum more like that of hearing children, and promised insights into spoken language learning by providing continuing opportunities for the deaf child to analyse and compare spoken and manual languages (compare Akamatsu and Armour, 1987). By 1975, White and Stevenson could report that in the USA the current trend was towards classroom use of TC.

TC and other communication methods

Since TC was introduced when oral and manual communication both had a long history, it is understandable that adherents of TC wished to 'prove' its usefulness against the established methods. White and Stevenson (1975) conducted an interesting study of the effects of learning-equated factual information by TC, manual communication, oral communication and reading by children in residential schools for the deaf. They were at pains to point out that most of the TC research conducted previous to their work was *ex-post-facto*, with recognised difficulties of interpretation, rather than experimentally based. Their subjects were all, or almost all, prelingually deaf with hearing losses of more than 65 dB, IQs in the range 60–140, and aged between 11 and 18 years, selected as a stratified random sample into nine subgroups, each of five children. An interpreter presented factual information from books at second- to fourth-grade level, following which the subjects were asked a standard set of questions about the information. All subgroups were found to have assimilated more information through reading, and more through total and through manual communication than through oral communication. No significant difference was found between total and manual communication, nor were there significant differences between high-, middle- and low-IQ children in assimilating information presented orally. However, the middle- and high-IQ children learned significantly more information than the children of low IQ when the information was presented by TC, manual communication or reading. There was thus an interaction between method of instruction and IQ, implying that conveying information orally to the brighter of these children resulted in them learning below their ability level. The addition of speech to manual communication (TC) did not increase these students' ability to learn the information but depressed it slightly, perhaps because the children lost information in shifting attention between speech and the manual signals, or because they experienced perceptual overload. This possibility is a continuing worry for adherents of TC (Nix, 1983). Further research is needed to establish to what extent it is a major issue.

The use of TC and oral communication in the UK were compared by Grove et al. (1979) with 26 adolescents, aged 16–21 years, all or most of whom were prelingually severely deaf. In this study each subject was presented with messages in their chosen mode of communication and instructed to tick a picture which meant the same as the message. Ten subjects relied on oral communication, and 16 on TC. The TC system was found to be the more effective method of communication for a number of different message structures. Grove et al. concluded that their results, and also the results of Montgomery (1968), and of White and Stevenson (1975), showed that TC and manual methods were no less effective in representing conventional language structures than oral communication, and were superior when used by those for whom they were the natural mode.

Grove and Rodda (1984) continued to obtain similar findings and to draw similar conclusions in a study of reading, TC, manual communication and oral communication with 118 severely and profoundly prelingually deaf subjects aged 9–20 years in Canada and New York. In checking pictures against a message, reading was the most effective method of communication, followed by TC and then manual communication. Oral methods were the least effective. From analyses of communication time, Grove and Rodda suggested that the relative weakness of the oral method was due to its low signal-to-noise ratio, and to short-term memory overload from ambiguous information caused by the hearing loss. Combining the oral and manual approaches, however, seemed to produce a stronger trace in short-term memory.

Using a video-taped test, five different communication modes – TC with audio, TC without audio, manual communication with no mouth movement, oral communication with audio, and oral communication without audio – were compared by Crittenden et al. (1986). The comparisons were made with 52 profoundly deaf children aged 6–12 years, all of whom used TC for their instruction over at least the previous 2 years and communicated outside the classroom in sign. The children were assessed on vocabulary, with a test standardised for deaf and hearing-impaired populations. The results showed that modes involving manual communication gave significantly better scores than all other modes. Oral communication added little to the manual mode for these children, confirming a view that deaf children communicating by TC communicate predominantly in manual language.

Despite such promising findings, TC has not been without its critics. Champie (1984) was concerned that although signs were used, preferably in combination with speech for TC, sign language was not being studied linguistically by deaf children. Their educational curriculum, she felt, should include the study of ASL as a language and as the communication system of deaf people. ASL was important for its effects on students' self-concepts, and because comparisons of ASL and English could improve their understanding of the rules of English, and hence their academic success. Nix (1983), mentioned earlier, took a more directly critical approach. He pointed out that the manual component of TC was typically either Manually Coded English (MCE), which required every word and morpheme present in the spoken version to be presented manually, or Pidgin Sign English (PSE), which was a conceptual approach that did not require a one-to-one relationship between the spoken and signed modes. On the one hand, the use of MCE cannot keep up in time with fluent speech, so that its users omitted up to 80% of it; on the other hand, users of PSE tended to decrease their speaking rate, but still spoke faster than they signed. They also omitted some of the signed material (compare; Marmor and Petitto, 1979; Strong and Charlson, 1987; Cokely, 1990). Nix's principal criticisms were that the overall transmission rate was decreased, the normal rate and rhythm of speech were changed, and the omission of MCE and parts of the spoken message produced ungrammatical and inconsistent models of English. Further, children using TC tended to show poor performance in specific areas related to spoken English, such as vocabulary and reading comprehension. However, Kluwin (1981) noted that more experienced teachers used more sign language, and less MCE, suggesting that as they became experienced they became more concerned with the function than the form of communication. It is hence interesting to note that Maxwell and Bernstein (1985) found MCE/sign mismatches in morphemes to be structural rather than semantic, and that the great majority of expressions conveyed the information appropriately, despite morphological differences. Certainly, the reader should not think that the problem is caused by the use of signs per se, as Emmorey and Corina (1990) have shown that fluent users of ASL can identify signs faster than has been found for spoken language. Much 'phonology' in sign is available simultaneously, in contrast to speech, resulting in faster lexical identification.

Knell and Klonoff (1983) obtained few differences between TC and orally educated severely to profoundly deaf children aged 7–11 years in verbal language output, but their orally educated children were significantly better in syntactic measures. Geers et al. (1984) also found that profoundly deaf children educated by TC experienced problems in the production of selected English language structures.

They assessed 327 children from oral/aural and TC programmes across the USA with the Grammatical Analysis of Elicited Language–Simple Sentence Level (GAEL-S) test, analysing the results separately for the oral productions of oral/aural children; the oral productions of TC children; the manual productions of TC children; and the combined productions of TC children. They found that the TC children gave oral productions substantially below the same children's manual scores, and below the scores of the oral/aural children for all sampled GAEL-S grammatical categories. The manual and combined scores of the TC children were significantly lower than those of the oral/aural children in over 50% of the grammatical categories, though the manual scores of the TC children significantly exceeded the oral/aural children's scores in up to 20% of these categories. This outcome suggested that spoken English did not develop along with MCE. Geers et al. also remarked that children in TC programmes, using MCE, did not show an advantage in the learning of English syntax over the orally/aurally educated children.

Much of the work described was conducted with single-item and/or short duration material, such as sentences. However, Gallagher and Meador (1989) found that in conversations between two adolescent hearing-impaired twin boys who had been TC-trained, there was use of an integrated bimodal form of English. Analysis of proportional frequencies of modes and the structural elements of spoken utterances showed that the bimodal English form used did not alter with the presence or absence of simultaneous signs in either the individual's or the partner's speech. Markides (1988) has found that in another specific area of spoken English, the speech intelligibility of a group of severely deaf children in a TC programme deteriorated over time. On the other hand, the intelligibility of the speech of a matched group in an aural/oral programme improved significantly over the same time interval.

A large number of studies which investigated the use of TC in educational programmes has been summarised by Schlesinger (1986), to which the reader's attention is drawn for a broader overview of the area. Her review concluded that, apart perhaps from deaf children whose background suggested that they would have success with oral methods and who could meet the demands a successful oral approach implied, such as well-educated and motivated parents of above average intelligence, TC could produce quite positive results. TC was valuable because it provided both a means of communicating and a way of assisting oral communication. TC could also help by stimulating the child's attention span, motivation, social interaction etc. As a recent report comparing oral, TC and cued speech approaches with hearing-impaired children in Hong Kong suggests (Lai and Lynas, 1990) TC could be also decrease behaviour problems. Schlesinger concluded her overview with a plea urging a truly bilingual approach, since for the great majority of deaf children, the situations with which they are faced require bilingual solutions involving both sign and speech.

In a considered and penetrating review, Maxwell (1990) has pointed out that TC or simultaneous communication mean different things to different people, and what is seen as a deficiency in a bimodal approach depends on the perceived purpose of the approach. Thus although a complete and exact translation of every spoken English morpheme into signed form is rarely achieved, except perhaps for the more simple or more easily translated constructions, such exactitude may not be the purpose of the teacher. It is therefore interesting to note (Mayer and Lowenbraun, 1990) that educators in kindergarten to fourth-grade educational programmes could produce a full manual representation (MCE) of their speech in TC. Proficiency in MCE may be affected by the teacher's attitude to the need to sign a complete message, the school's educational policy, and the degree to which teacher implementation of MCE policies is monitored. MCE was used in this study with a much higher accuracy rate (up to 90%) than that found by Marmor and Petitto (1979) at 10%.

Thompson and Swisher (1985) argued sensibly that TC was suitable for providing immediate and consistent language inputs for very young deaf children before eventual auditory perceptual skills could be determined. Such early inputs were important, they felt, because most hearing-impaired children have auditory discrimination or auditory perceptual problems which are difficult to assess thoroughly in early life. It also seems possible that TC is better suited to instruction for younger deaf children, who do not need such lengthy and complex linguistic inputs as the older deaf child. It may be particularly suited to deaf infants, who are too young for valid assessment of their hearing loss.

Conclusion

The adherents of TC argue that TC promotes communication, and a resulting increase in facility with language will assist academic learning and improve the production of speech. However, the academic abilities of hearing-impaired children who communicate in TC do not show conclusively that TC has major advantages over other methods. TC has not adequately met the high expectations of it (Eagney, 1987) for reasons such as those described above, although it is generally agreed to be valuable. The current trend is to proceed with TC, while contrary arguments continue.

Chapter 6
Hearing Impairment and Literacy Skills

There is an extensive literature on the reading achievement of hearing-impaired children, which shows a plateau in attainment at around 8–10 years of age beyond which it is difficult for the child to progress. This chapter outlines some of the studies documenting this effect. It then considers work which seeks to explain the processes underlying the reading performance of hearing-impaired children, and which promote intervention for the teaching of reading. An account is also given of the writing abilities of hearing-impaired children, and the reciprocal relationship between their reading and writing is discussed.

Besides the major handicaps imposed on oracy by severe and especially profound hearing loss, similar handicaps are encountered by the severely and profoundly hearing-impaired child in the skills involved in literacy. Such skills are learned by hearing children following the acquisition of oracy, most probably by building on inner speech. This inner speech mediates reading by the silent understanding and rehearsal of symbols or words, and recognition of sequential and contextual cues (Conrad, 1979; Wood, 1980; Nolen and Wilbur, 1984; Bamford and Saunders, 1985; Wood et al., 1986; Hanson et al., 1991). It also assists in the production of symbols or words in writing. Therefore, if children have problems with oracy they are also likely to experience problems with literacy (Vellum, 1979; Hanson, 1986), resulting in overall weak communicative fluency. This is generally also the case for deaf children.

Reading

We read to comprehend, and reading permits us to inform ourselves at our own rate of learning. Reading is particularly useful in allowing us to assimilate detail and considered ideas. Hence reading provides a deep basis of knowledge about events and concepts which add to the depth and flexibility of our communication. The increasing use of microcomputers, either as standalone devices, or more especially as aids to telecommunication, has produced a particular emphasis on skills in reading and writing (typing), not only for hearing people but also for the hearing-impaired, including deaf children.

Problems with reading can be experienced by hearing as well as by deaf children. Hearing children who are prone to hearing impairment as a result of chronic middle-ear infections may have difficulties in beginning reading (Webster et al., 1984; Webster et al., 1989). Also, young children with only a mild sensorineural hearing loss (20–45 dB) may show reduced performance in vocabulary acquisition and reading comprehension (Blair et al., 1985).

Hearing children of school age use complex grammatical structures and enjoy a large vocabulary. Their early reading primers, which contain grammatical constructs and vocabularies which are well within their grasp, are attuned to these linguistic skills. Hearing children can therefore concentrate on learning the skills involved in reading itself, on understanding printed material as a cipher that projects the linguistic code they already know (Smith, 1973).

The situation is quite different for the severely to profoundly deaf child who, in learning to read, is confronted with two main problems (Clarke et al., 1982). The first, and underlying, problem is that most such children are severely deficient in their knowledge of verbal language. The second problem lies in perceiving the written words as reflecting the language code. It is small wonder that, as a result, deaf children of school-leaving age commonly have a reading age of only about 9–10 years (Gentile and Di Francesca, 1969; Trybus and Karchmer, 1977; Conrad, 1979; King and Quigley, 1985). For most deaf children, learning to read means having to learn language as well (Webster and Ellwood, 1985). Of course, there are some deaf children, with well-developed linguistic attainments, whose reading ability is within normal limits, but unfortunately such children are in the minority. Even if a deaf child can recognise individual words, understanding of the written material will not happen without a sure base of language (Quigley and Kretschmer, 1982).

Reading achievement

Early work on reading achievement by deaf children has been reviewed by Quigley (1982), Quigley and Kretschmer (1982), Bamford and Saunders (1985), and King and Quigley (1985). Most of this work, in the USA, was based on tests of reading achievement standardised for hearing children, and was directed towards the demographic assessment of reading age or reading grade level (Pinter and Paterson, 1917; Pugh, 1946; Fusfeld, 1955; Wrightstone et al., 1963; Myklebust, 1964; Furth, 1966b; Balow et al., 1971; Hammermeister, 1971; Di Francesca, 1972; Trybus and Karchmer, 1977).

Quigley and Kretschmer (1982) pointed out that large-scale demographic studies may obscure the somewhat better results attained by some individual programmes, using the study of Lane and Baker (1974) to illustrate this point. Lane and Baker noted from Furth (1966b) and Wrightstone et al. (1963) that only 12% of more than 5000 hearing-impaired adolescents aged 10–16 years had a reading age of 11 years or more. On comparing the performance of this large group of adolescents with the scores of 132 hearing-impaired students of the Central

Institute of the Deaf aged between 10 and 16 years, Lane and Baker found that the CID group's grade level reading equivalent was much higher, though the reading attainment was still below that of hearing children. It was not clear, however, whether this difference was due to the educational approach, namely maximum use of residual hearing in continuous education at school and oral communication at home, as argued by Lane and Baker, or to the socioeconomic advantages of the CID group.

The depressing run of research which found low levels of reading achievement in the USA was supported by work in the UK. Hamp (1972) used a Picture Assisted Reading Test for words with children aged 9–15 years in eight schools for the deaf or partially hearing, to obtain a mean reading age of approximately 9 years for 15-year-old children. In associated assessments of reading comprehension, he found a mean reading age of around 8;10 years. Also in the UK, and using the Southgate Reading Test, Redgate (1972) measured the reading age of 698 hearing-impaired children aged 9–18 years attending 23 schools. At 15 years old the children had attained a reading age of 7;8 years. With the same test, Morris (1978) obtained a very similar reading age of 7;6 years for severely and profoundly deaf school leavers. Wood et al. (1981) found a mean reading age of 7;9 years for 60 children with a mean age of 11 years and a mean hearing loss of 87 dB, also with the Southgate Reading Test.

Conrad (1977a, 1979) used the Brimer Wide-Span Reading Test of sentence completion (Brimer, 1972) to measure the reading skills of 355 mostly orally educated deaf school leavers in England and Wales, all of whom were prelingually hearing-impaired, and aged 15–16 years. Conrad obtained a median reading age of 9 years for this group. He found no significant differences between groups of children with hearing losses in the ranges 86–95, 96–105, and above 105 dB HL. However, he did find that children with losses in the ranges of less than 66, and 66–85 dB HL attained higher reading ages than the children with severe and profound losses. Thus reading comprehension was greatly retarded with hearing impairment greater than 85 dB HL. Conrad also found a highly significant correlation between intelligence and reading age, with coefficients of between 0.30 and 0.53 for his five ranges of hearing loss, where the higher coefficients were associated with the lower levels of hearing loss. He concluded that there is a stage or plateau in the reading attainment of many deaf children which they cannot escape. Quigley and Kretschmer (1982) came to the same conclusion, finding that deaf children tended to progress to about the third- or fourth-grade level at 13–14 years of age, but progressed very little thereafter. This limiting stage or plateau may, however, be more apparent than real, because the reading achievements of hearing-impaired children tend to slow down as they reach the teen years. Also, the difference in reading attainment between hearing and hearing-impaired children increases with age, giving an impression of levelling-off of progress in reading by the hearing-impaired children (Myklebust, 1964; Serwatka et al., 1984).

Very different results, providing some grounds for optimism, were recently reported by Geers and Moog (1989) in a study of factors associated with literacy in profoundly deaf adolescents in the USA. Their aims were to record the literacy levels of a large sample of orally educated hearing-impaired school leavers, and to describe the factors which would predict competence in reading and writing. Their work is commended to the reader for its thoroughness of reportage, besides the significance of its outcome.

Geers and Moog's sample of 100 prelingually profoundly deaf adolescents, 49 boys and 51 girls, was aged from 15–18 years. Non-verbal IQ levels were not less than 85. All subjects had been enrolled in oral education programmes throughout preschool and elementary schooling. Their socioeconomic backgrounds were above average, being middle to upper middle class. Most families had at least one parent educated to tertiary level. Some 90% of parents reported that they had helped their children with speech production, language development and academic studies. Also, they had read to their children and had regularly discussed television programmes with them while they grew up. Only 15% of the subjects were enrolled in classes for the hearing impaired at the time of the research. The remainder were mainstreamed for all or most of the day, the average age at mainstreaming being 11;1 years (s.d. 4;6 years). Hearing aids had been fitted to 54% of the sample by 1 year of age, and to 90% by age 2 years. Seventy-five per cent of the subjects had enrolled in a parent–infant programme by 2 years of age, and 63% had attended a special education preschool by age 3 years. Forty-six per cent of subjects could identify some spoken words with their hearing aids; 36% could make speech pattern distinctions, such as one versus two syllable words, while only three subjects showed no speech perception skills. Fifteen per cent could correctly identify 90% of words in a closed-set word test. On the Minimal Auditory Capabilities visual enhancement subtest (Owens et al., 1985) the sample averaged 57% correct for lipreading alone, and 74% with lipreading and hearing. The mean performance IQ was 111, distinctly superior, probably partly a result of not including individuals with performance IQs of less than 85. The average verbal IQ score was 89, on the low side, as expected. On speech production tests (Monsen, 1981), 65% of the subjects obtained good to excellent results (above 80% intelligible). Sixty-two per cent of subjects knew no sign language, 9% could communicate in signed English, and 13% could converse in ASL. However, spoken English was the primary means of communicating for all.

The characteristics of this particularly well documented sample appears atypical of deaf adolescents. However, Geers and Moog estimated that it contained about 50% of the total American population of profoundly deaf 16 and 17 year olds who were educated orally. Although it comprised only about 5% of the population of all profoundly deaf children in this age range, the sample was thought to be representative of profoundly deaf children who continued in oral education.

In reading tests at the word level, the Woodcock Reading Mastery Test (Woodcock, 1973) was used to assess phonics skills independently of word knowledge, by using nonsense words. All subjects could perform this task. Half scored above, and half below the seventh-grade (13 year) level. Thirty-four per cent scored in the average range for hearing subjects of the same age. Word knowledge was measured with the vocabulary subtest of the California Achievement Test (1977), for knowledge of antonyms, synonyms and multiple definitions of words. Ninety per cent of subjects scored above the third-grade (9 year) level, and 54% above the seventh-grade level. Thirty per cent attained the levels for hearing children of equivalent age.

At the sentence level, recognition of syntactic structures was measured with the Test of Syntactic Abilities Screening Form (Quigley et al., 1978). Two-thirds of the subjects scored 90% or more. Ninety-two per cent scored above 75%, showing substantial mastery of the test's nine syntactic structures. Semantic skills at the sentence level were measured by the Peabody Individual Achievement Test – reading comprehension subtest (Dunn and Markwardt, 1970). Fifty-four per cent of the sample obtained scores below the seventh-grade level, but a quarter attained scores typical of hearing subjects.

At the text level, reading skills were assessed with the reading comprehension subtest of the Stanford Achievement Test (SAT: Gardner et al., 1982). Thirty per cent of the sample scored at their hearing grade-level equivalent, and 57% at the seventh-grade level. Special purpose tests were also devised to test top-down reading skills but as they were non-normed, these are not considered here. Skill at text-level reading was measured with the Gates McGinitie Reading Test (Gates and McGinitie, 1965). Sixty-three per cent of subjects scored at or above tenth-grade (16 year) level in reading speech, but only 44% scored at the same level for reading accuracy. Geers and Moog also included tests for writing and spoken language skills, and conducted a factor analysis for variables predictive of literacy, to be considered later.

For reading ability, it is apparent that Geers and Moog's sample had skills above the average for profoundly deaf adolescents, and above what may be expected on the basis of the studies reviewed earlier. For instance, their mean grade level on the SAT for reading comprehension was the eighth-grade level. Only 15% showed reading skills below the third-grade level, the mean level found for 16- and 17-year-old subjects by Schildroth and Karchmer (1986), while 30% performed at the same level as hearing subjects of the same age. Although this level of reading skill was encouraging, on the whole the sample did not attain the levels achieved by hearing 16- and 17-year-olds. Geers and Moog attributed this lower level of attainment to deficiency in vocabulary development, since the subjects' oral vocabulary was assessed at sixth-grade, and reading vocabulary at seventh-grade level.

Geers and Moog concluded, among other things, that by 16 years of age, profoundly deaf children could achieve, by reading, skills similar to those of hearing individuals, since between 24% and 34% of their subjects attained such skills. They also concluded that profoundly deaf children who had at least average non-verbal intelligence, early oral education, early auditory stimulation, and a middle-class family environment with strong family support, had the potential to attain much higher reading and other skills than generally reported for profoundly deaf people. They found the primary factors associated with the development of literacy in their orally educated sample were good use of residual hearing, early amplification, early educational management, and especially oral English language ability.

We have considered this work of Geers and Moog at length for good reasons. First, it is exemplary in its characterisation of the study sample. Few reports have taken the care to describe their subjects in such detail. Secondly, it is notable for reporting the good level of reading and other skills that can be attained by some profoundly deaf adolescents. The reported levels of reading suggest strongly that it is erroneous to generalise from the demographic studies of reading achievement to subgroups and individual cases. It is also notable that this study goes some way towards substantiating the claims for oral education put forward by its adherents.

However, although Geers and Moog may properly claim that a proportion of orally educated prelingually profoundly deaf children can achieve reading abilities approaching or equal to those of hearing children, the mean grade level, for reading comprehension on the SAT, was the eighth grade. Most members of their sample were retarded in reading ability with regard to norms for hearing children of the same age. Further, the sample was at a distinct advantage in terms of socioeconomic and environmental background. For this sample, the effects of oral education were confounded with environmental variables.

Two methodological aspects need special attention in interpreting the results of this study. The first is the high level of non-verbal intelligence (mean performance IQ of 111), which probably occurred in part because subjects whose IQ was less than 85 points were excluded. The findings were thus about *bright* orally educated prelingually profoundly deaf children. It is not clear how far the results were affected by such preselection. The second aspect concerns possible self-selection bias. The study was conducted at camps lasting 5 days. Although transport costs and other expenses were paid by the research grant, and not by the subjects, other self-selection criteria, such as willingness to leave home, could have played a significant part. Geers and Moog estimated their 100-subject sample as being about 50% of the prelingually profoundly deaf population aged 16–17 years, who had received an oral education. Thus there were approximately 100 other potential subjects, only a small proportion of whom would have included those subjects rejected because of IQ less than 85 points. In fairness, perhaps not all of these further 100 adolescents would have experienced an exclusively oral education throughout their preschool and elementary school years. But this still leaves us with a suspicion that self-selection may have biased the results. There is therefore scope for further investigation to discount these queries.

The results of Geers and Moog's USA study are at considerable variance with those given by Conrad (1979) in the UK (actually England and Wales). The reasons may include differences in national styles of provision for deaf education (USA versus UK), time of study (1974–1976 versus 1986), ages and age ranges of subjects (15–18 years versus 15–16 years), ranges of hearing loss (the UK study included subjects with moderate to profound losses), and possibly a less complete, less intensive or less demanding oral education in the UK. Also, the UK study reviewed the whole population of deaf school leavers and without selecting for intelligence. On the average the UK study subjects would have been less bright, and had no chance to self-select. There were thus considerable differences between the two studies in the characteristics of their subjects, which reflect a notable diversity among hearing-impaired individuals.

Processes associated with reading

Although recent studies of reading by deaf children have continued to confirm the thrust of earlier findings (Bennett et al., 1984; Allen, 1986), attention has turned from reading achievement to possible factors underlying the low levels of reading achievement generally observed.

Method of communication

It has been generally believed that prelingually deaf children of deaf signing parents are favoured in their cognitive and academic achievements. When the literature on the effects of parental method of communication on the reading attainments of prelingually deaf students was reviewed by Kampfe and Turecheck (1987), they confirmed this belief for reading. They concluded that deaf children of signing parents typically have more advanced reading skills than deaf children whose parents do not sign. This conclusion did not necessarily mean that there is a positive general relationship between the use of sign and reading ability. However, the evidence suggested some relationship between specific kinds of manual communication, level of parental skill in signing, and reading ability. Later, Kampfe (1989) reported results for the reading comprehension of 201 deaf adolescents, who used some manual form as their primary means of communication, in relation to the communication strategies and skills of their mothers. The method of communication used by the mothers, which included signing, speech and speechreading, gestures, made-up signs and pantomime, was not significantly related to their deaf children's reading comprehension scores on the SAT. For mothers who used manual communication, no significant relationship was found between reading comprehension and the age of the student when the mother began to sign. There was evidence that the students' reading comprehension was related to the level of skill used by mothers in signing. However, this relationship was not necessarily straightforward because mothers with higher manual communication abilities tend to have higher educational levels and children with higher IQs.

This interesting study thus had limitations. Kampfe also noted that the findings applied to students in residential schools, and the relation between mothers' signing skills and reading comprehension might have been greater had the children remained at home. Further, the measurements for mothers' skills and for students' reading comprehension, which were obtained by questionnaires, may have been applied differently in different schools.

A further complex mix of results was obtained by Moores and Sweet (1990), who assessed literacy skills in two groups of congenitally deaf children. One group had deaf, and the other hearing parents. The latter group was educated in TC from 4 years old. The data suggested similar factors associated with literacy for both groups. Measures of structure in English and vocabulary were important, whereas speech measures and hearing level were of less importance. Fluency in ASL was not correlated with reading or writing for either group.

To summarise, although there is evidence suggesting that native signing deaf children are better readers than deaf children who have learned to sign in later years, the situation is by no means completely clear. Reading competence may be more closely related to text-based competencies than to the type of face-to-face language which the reader brings to the reading task (Livingston, 1991).

Basic processes

Given that hearing-impaired children have problems in reading, we should ask in which aspects of reading are the problems found. In particular, do the problems occur at the more basic levels of letter and word recognition, or at higher levels, as with understanding meaning? Kyle (1980b) provided an answer to this question. He assessed the skills of profoundly deaf, partially to severely deaf, and hearing children of equivalent non-verbal IQ in discriminating letters, associating words with pictures, and reading comprehension. He found that the deaf children had similar vocabulary skills to the hearing children at 7 years of age. By age 9 years, their letter skills had caught up, although their vocabulary was then about 1 year behind. In contrast, at age 9 years, the deaf children had only just begun to read for meaning. The implication is that, since the hearing and deaf children performed at a roughly similar level in the basic skills of letter discrimination and vocabulary recognition, the difficulties experienced by deaf children in reading mostly occur at a higher level of processing, associated with reading for meaning.

The basic skills involved in letter and word matching and identification described by Kyle begin at the prereading level (Clay, 1979; Mason, 1980). Prereading skills need to be acquired or learned, as concepts about letters, words and stories, before children can learn to read successfully (Mason, 1980; Stanovich, 1980; Maxwell, 1986; Andrews, 1988). Normally, children acquire such concepts by identifying printed material in their everyday experiences, by printing letters and a few words, including their names, on their drawings and by listening to stories read from books by their parents. Andrews (1988) found for 23 prelingually deaf kindergarten and first-grade children with severe to profound hearing losses, who used speech, fingerspelling or signs, that all could identify a few written letters, while ten could read and understand simple sentences. The lesser-skilled children lacked practice in labelling pictures with signs, a variant of word recognition.

Tests of reading ability which estimate lower-level skills, up to the level of word recognition, tend to show relatively similar reading achievement in deaf and hearing children. According to Webster (1986), only with more demanding tests of reading ability, involving complex language skills and comprehension above a reading level of 8;6–9 years, will the performance of deaf children fall off sharply. He suggested that the plateau effect observed in tests of reading achievement with deaf children occurred at just this point, when the reading task passed from letters and words to a level of linguistic complexity beyond their abilities.

It seems necessary to qualify the implications of Kyle's (1980b) findings and Webster's (1986) arguments. Deaf children have more than their share of visual and visual perceptual deficits (Cooper and Arnold, 1981). Also, the eye movements of deaf children during reading may be different from those of hearing children of matched reading age and non-verbal IQ (Beggs et al., 1982). Thus deaf children, on average, are at a disadvantage in learning to read because of visual and visual perceptual impairment. However, the situation is not clear-cut. Spencer and Delk (1989) tested visual perceptual processing in 77 hearing-impaired children aged 7–8 years, finding that only those tests which had a memory component, or prevented an approach to a memory task through a non-sequential strategy, produced lower levels of performance than test norms for hearing children. Spencer and Delk's sample, however, contained a substantial proportion of children with moderate to severe hearing losses, who would have been less likely to experience visual perceptual processing problems than profoundly deaf children.

Reading tasks more complex than letter- and word-matching and discrimination are required in order to answer written questions about reading assignments. This point was illustrated by Scouten (1980), who observed that deaf students often tried to match specific words or phrases in a written question with the same word or phrase in the assigned text. This superficial visual matching resulted in the student's copying whole sentences, irrespective of the sense made in answering the question. Similar strategies have been observed by Webster et al. (1981), Wood et al. (1981), and Beggs and Breslaw (1983), where deaf children, unable to comprehend the text, based their responses to written questions on visual similarities of words and phrases, or picked the most interesting picture in a picture-assisted reading test.

This area was investigated further by LaSasso (1985), who compared the visual matching test-taking strategies of hearing and deaf student readers. She found extensive use of visual matching by deaf, but not hearing, students across several kinds of visual matching strategy. Her findings were supported by LaSasso (1986), in comparing the visual matching test-taking strategies on the SAT of 50 hearing children aged 14–17 years with those of a group of prelingually, profoundly deaf children of similar chronological and reading age. Although some visual matching was used by the hearing children, it was used far more by the deaf children. The implications are that care is needed in taking the results of some reading comprehension tests scores of deaf children at face value when the children have been able to look back at, or re-inspect, the text.

There are problems in assessing reading comprehension when the questions used to measure understanding of text are themselves liable to misinterpretation or confusion. Thus mistakes may be due to a failure to understand the question rather than the text. To overcome such problems, LaSasso (1980) and Reynolds (1986) used modified cloze procedures, where each reading passage might include a number of sentences with a single word omitted, with several alternative single word options provided for each omission. Cloze tests obviate errors attributable to the misunderstanding of questions in a comprehension test, and are more direct tests of reading comprehension. However, they have been criticised (Kretschmer and Kretschmer, 1986) because they stress syntactic knowledge in the sentence under consideration, and do not show a reader's competence in understanding the content of a passage of text, nor various literacy devices.

Cumulative cloze, a technique devised to overcome this problem, was proposed by Knight (1989). In cumulative cloze, the same noun, say, is deleted whenever it occurs in a paragraph of about 5 or 6 sentences. As the child reads the text, an increasing number of contextual cues to the missing noun is given by the text. If the missing noun is varied in its syntactic position, the effect of a given syntactic structure on solving for the missing noun is much reduced. Further, if readers are observed as they encounter each noun-gap, their predictions can be recorded. These predictions should be increasingly accurate as the readers receive an increasing number of contextual cues. Using cumulative cloze with ten prelingually deaf and ten hearing readers from each of the grades 4, 6, 8, 10 and 12, with six sentences in short paragraphs, Knight found significant differences between deaf and hearing children up to the sixth exposure point, that is up to the sixth sentence, for grades 4–6. However, there were no significant differences for grades 8–12. Both groups predicted meaning more accurately and their predictions were more semantically and grammatically acceptable as the contextual information increased. Hence, with a reduced load on their knowledge of syntax, the deaf children could improve their scores in reading for meaning. Knight also found that his deaf readers tended to abandon correct choices more often than his hearing readers, possibly because they focused more on the immediate context rather than on the progressive use of context.

Another extension of the cloze procedure was used by Andrews and Mason (1991) to explore decision making by prelingually profoundly deaf high-school youths, aged 17–20 years, in filling deleted words and phrases. Although born of hearing parents, these youths were all skilled signers in ASL. Besides predicting the missing word or phrase, the youths were asked to explain the reasons for their prediction. Andrews and Mason discovered that their deaf youths often relied on re-reading and background knowledge, whereas comparison groups of hearing readers relied more on cues from context. However, the use of re-reading and background knowledge were not as effective as were cues from context. The deaf readers' performance was poorer than that of the hearing readers because their background knowledge was poor in some instances, they experienced linguistic difficulties at the word, sentence and intra-sentence level, had problems with metaphor or recoding from print into sign or inner speech, or used inappropriate graphic similarities.

Cloze tests, free-response question tasks, and question tasks without permitting lookback were found by LaSasso and Davey (1987) to be very sensitive to vocabulary knowledge in 10–18-year-old prelingually profoundly deaf children, possibly because such tasks need more memory or more verbal ability than multiple-choice or lookback tasks. However, LaSasso and Davey observed that vocabulary knowledge, assessed by the Vocabulary Comprehension Subtest of the Gates–McGinitie Reading Tests, was a stronger predictor of reading comprehension, measured by the Reading Comprehension Subtest of the SAT, than cloze tasks, free-response questions, and no-lookback question tasks. Possibly, vocabulary knowledge was more strongly correlated with reading comprehension than the SAT.

Higher-level processes

Higher-level processes involved in reading include the understanding of ideas and meanings, which is associated with the structure of syntax. Here too, hearing-impaired children have difficulties. They develop linguistic skills later and in a different way from hearing individuals. A useful example of this situation was presented by Sarachan-Deily (1982), who examined both the syntactic and semantic relationships used by hearing-impaired readers. She asked 30 congenitally profoundly deaf and 30 hearing children aged 10–18 years to read a set of 12 sentences, one at a time. After reading a sentence once, the child was given a number-counting task for a period, to prevent rehearsal, and then had to recall the sentence in writing. The sentences varied in length from 5–9 words, and in syntax from active to passive. The deaf children, all orally educated, produced more syntactic errors in their recalled sentences than the hearing children, whose errors were relatively minor. Although nearly half their sentences contained syntactic errors, the deaf children produced sentences which preserved the meaning. Sarachan-Deily concluded that although their syntactic skills were frequently in error, the semantic patterns and processing abilities of the hearing-impaired children were similar to those of the hearing children. The syntactic errors, such as derivational or inflectional word endings, were not generally such as to destroy the semantic content.

However, things may not be so straightforward. Strassman et al. (1987) showed that profoundly prelingually deaf adolescents, aged 13–20 years and educated by TC, experienced problems with instantiation in a cued recall task, implying that they had some difficulties with semantics. In a typical instantiation task, the subject has to substitute a specific term, such as a specific noun, for a general term in a sentence to fit the meaning of the sentence ('The fruit was yellow' becomes 'The lemon was yellow'). The task thus requires familiarity with categorisation. Strassman et al. reported that their deaf subjects could instantiate when asked, but did not do so spontaneously. Their subjects' poor overall reading level possibly encouraged the use of verbatim, rather than inferential, recall. Alternatively, while their subjects may have been able to represent the semantics of individual words, the strength of the associations among and between the semantic representations could have been weak, limiting the use of context in comprehension. This study appeared to require a higher order of semantic representation than that of Sarachan-Deily (1982), which may account for the relatively greater difficulty in semantic processing observed in comprehending sentences. However, the studies used subjects of different ages and methods of communication. The large differences between the subjects make it impossible to compare the studies directly.

Conclusion

It appears that hearing-impaired children experience reading problems at both basic and higher levels of processing. The main reasons seem to be difficulties with syntax and the more complex aspects of semantics, and poor reading strategies. These problems become more obvious with age, as the differences between the reading performances of hearing and hearing-impaired children increase over time.

Neuropsychological aspects of reading

As noted earlier, neuropsychological studies of cerebral dominance have typically relied on the split-half visual field technique, in which the individual fixates on a central point while material is introduced into the left or right visual half-fields. Cerebral dominance is assessed by noting for which half-field the individual reports the greater amount of material correctly. This technique is useful in exploring the neuropsychology of reading.

In a test of 18 congenitally deaf undergraduate students, compared with 18 hearing control subjects, McKeever et al. (1976) found only minimal cerebral asymmetry for printed words among their deaf subjects, while their hearing subjects demonstrated left cerebral dominance, as anticipated. McKeever et al. concluded that deprivation of hearing resulted in very reduced asymmetry in cerebral processing. Similar results for word perception were obtained with congenitally deaf students by Manning et al. (1977). Letters were used by Phippard (1977) in work described earlier to compare visual hemifield perception in congenitally deaf students educated by TC or by oral methods, together with a group of hearing students. The hearing students showed dominance in the left cerebral hemisphere, as expected. The deaf students educated by TC showed no cerebral asymmetry, but those educated orally rather surprisingly showed a significant dominance of the right hemisphere. Phippard concluded that the orally educated group were coding the material visually rather than phonetically.

In reviewing these and related studies, Conrad (1979) commented that the differences between deaf and hearing subjects in tasks involving linguistic material was striking in all cases. He cautioned, however, that care should be taken, as the results were presented as group averages. Since a few profoundly deaf children had been shown to develop internal speech, it was not necessarily correct to assume that no deaf child would show left cerebral hemisphere dominance. Nevertheless, the clear implication was that most seriously hearing-impaired children have unusual neuropsychological function. Conrad also remarked that cases of left-hemisphere stroke in deaf patients resulted in disturbance to sign language performance, suggesting a common left cerebral hemisphere locus for all language processing (Chapter 5).

The work outlined above and a review and study with similar findings by Boshoven et al. (1982) were concerned with lower-level abilities associated with reading. As tests of reading ability, they were clearly incomplete. In other areas of reading in hearing children, and in hearing children with reading disabilities, the association of neuropsychological findings with reading is more comprehensive (Marcel et al., 1974; Kelly et al., 1989). In particular, processes associated with cortical function have been demonstrated for naming deficits (Vellutino, 1983), problems with serial order (Denckla et al., 1981), verbal dysfluency (Wolf, 1984), insensitivity to syntax (Rudel, 1985), selective attention (Rudel, 1985), and learning to read (Denckla, 1983). Investigation of neuropsychological processes associated with reading problems in deaf children in these latter areas remains to be carried out.

Bottom-up aspects of reading

Although tests of reading achievement are valuable in outlining the extent to which hearing-impaired children can read, they provide insufficient information about their reading skills. Similarly, the neuropsychological work related to reading suggests that reduced asymmetry in cerebral processing results in linguistic problems with reading, but does not show the nature of such linguistic skills that the hearing-impaired child may bring to reading. We now consider the cognitive processes involved in the bottom-up approaches to the study of reading, the approaches through which the reading difficulties experienced by deaf children were explored in detail by workers in the 1960s and 1970s.

Phonological coding

There is good evidence to show that poor readers do not make efficient use of phonemic information (Shankweiler and Liberman, 1976; Mann et al., 1980; Siegel and Linder, 1984; Hurford, 1988). Good readers bring to reading an ability to identify and discriminate among phonemes (Treiman and Barron, 1981) and hence can learn grapheme to phoneme correspondences (Gibson, 1972; Savin, 1972), where the written material is segmented and decoded into a phonological representation. This view is supported by electromyographic work showing that reading is accompanied by electrical impulses in the speech musculature, particularly when the reader is having difficulty with the material (McGuigan, 1970; Sokolov, 1972). Such phonological coding is thought to allow the reader to make use of inner speech, so that the reader covertly hears, as it were, the material which is being read. When phonemically confusible material, such as rhyming material which can interfere with phonemic coding, is included in sets of consonants (Conrad, 1970, 1972b, c; Liberman et al., 1977), words (Byrne and Shea, 1979; Conrad, 1979) or sentences (Mann et al., 1980), the recall of material is affected more for good than for poor readers. This outcome suggests strongly that poor readers do not rely, or rely less, on phonemic coding. Evidence for the use of weak phonemic coding in profoundly deaf children is found in work by Chen (1976) who reported that, when asked to put a stroke through all instances of the letter 'e' in a piece of prose, profoundly deaf students showed no difference in cancelling silent and pronounceable 'e's, as in 'name' vs 'net'. However, hearing students missed nearly twice as many silent 'e's as the deaf students. Locke (1978) obtained similar results. These studies suggest that hearing children decode written letters through a speech-like code, but that profoundly deaf children do not, or do not do so to the same extent.

Conrad (1979) found that hearing-impaired children who possessed inner speech were likely to be less severely hearing-impaired, better at reading, better at speechreading (compare Williams, 1982), more competent in language use, and to have more intelligible speech. He thus placed heavy emphasis on the possession of inner speech, particularly for phonology. His findings have since been supported by Quigley and Paul (1984) and Meadow (1980).

Visual coding

Conrad's emphasis on phonological coding may have been overdone. Bamford and Saunders (1985) pointed out that Conrad's conclusions were qualified by those of Hung et al. (1981), whose profoundly deaf 14–18-year-old students had to judge whether or not a pair of letters was identical. The deaf students' results were similar to those of hearing subjects in showing lower reaction times for name-identity conditions (*Aa*) as compared with physical-identity conditions (*AA*). However, the reaction times of the deaf students were considerably longer than those of the hearing subjects, showing that the processes associated with the coding of letters operated more slowly in deaf than hearing subjects. Slower encoding is to be expected because deaf children have less experience in reading letters but, as Hung et al. stated, slower decoding is also to be expected, for the same reason. Thus the reading deficiency of deaf subjects may be the result of a failure to develop fast automatic processing for low-level skills such as letter coding. If attention is then directed at letter coding, it is difficult to direct it to higher-level processing. Deaf child readers do limit their visual attention, at least to a word-by-word strategy, as shown in studies of reading and eye movements (Beggs et al., 1982).

Hung et al. also found that in a sentence/picture verification task, the deaf subjects seemed to use a visual imagery code rather than a linguistic code to verify printed sentences. However, this did not necessarily mean that the deaf students were unable to use a linguistic code. When they were given sentences with ASL signs in English frames, their verification reaction times showed a pattern consistent with a general linguistic model.

These observations provide an answer to the question of how those deaf children who do not possess inner speech, manage to code written material. If they do not use a phonological code, they may use a code based on visual imagery (Hirsh-Pasek and Treiman, 1982). Use of such a visual code can still result in reading problems as compared with readers who use inner speech, because if speech is 'special' (Chapter 1), then presumably inner speech is special too.

Use of a visual code is likely to persist into adulthood. Treiman and Hirsh-Pasek (1983) explored recoding strategies, as translation from printed text to some other form, in the silent reading of second-generation deaf readers, namely, congenitally deaf subjects born to deaf parents. Their 14 subjects, aged 28–63, all profoundly deaf and native ASL signers, who had never been fitted with hearing aids, took part in four experiments which recoded sentence material into articulation. The recoding involved phonological recoding, fingerspelling, ASL, or no recoding observed. Fourteen hearing young adult subjects, aged 18–25 years, none familiar with ASL, were used as controls. The deaf subjects did not appear to recode into articulation nor, as a group, did they recode into fingerspelling, even though most deaf individuals have a considerable fingerspelling vocabulary. However, they did recode into sign, as shown by the difficulty they experienced in reading and judging sentences whose sign versions contained similar signs. Thus these second-generation profoundly deaf subjects recoded written English into ASL, their native language, even though there are few direct spelling-to-sign correspondences. Treiman and Hirsh-Pasek concluded that the advantages to be obtained in memory and comprehension by using one's native language weigh heavily in choosing a system for recoding.

Studies of the type described by Hung et al. and Treiman and Hirsh-Pasek are not many, although few doubt that deaf children use some kind of visual code (Webster, 1986). Obviously, more work is required to identify how deaf individuals recode written material into sign and possibly fingerspelling, and the circumstances under which they do so.

Top-down aspects of reading

Conrad's (1979) approach to reading via phonological coding has been subject to a fair degree of criticism. To be fair to Conrad, his deaf poor readers almost all had problems with phonological coding and, besides, this criticism has been levelled at other proponents of bottom-up approaches (e.g. Locke, 1978; Hirsh-Pasek and Treiman, 1982). Bamford and Saunders (1985) remarked that arguments have been levied against non-lexical grapheme-to-phoneme conversion (GPC) processes from a psychological viewpoint (Henderson, 1982) in preference to explanations that unfamiliar words are spoken by analogy with familiar words. Also, fluent readers can use phonetic imagery to trace prosodic features from text. Such a suprasegmental level of operation argues for a higher arrangement of operation beyond GPC, and the emphasis on low-level phonological coding in GPC should be reduced in favour of higher-order factors This top-down thrust is reminiscent of the direction taken by such authors as Stanovich and West (1979), who argued that readers who otherwise performed poorly because of inadequate GPC rules could improve their performance by using top-down information to a greater extent than good readers.

Proponents of this top-down thrust would argue that use of a phonological code in short-term memory tasks does not necessarily imply the use of such a code in other tasks, including reading. Children can change tactics from one task to another, as shown by the different results obtained on reading tasks which force the adoption of different tactics. Since deaf individuals who use signing as their first language can be reasonably fluent readers, they probably use visual coding in reading, either alone or in combination with phonological coding. Further, reading involves more complex operations than phonemics alone. Higher-order linguistic processes have a most important part to play. Hence inner speech as speech may not always be involved in reading, and to rely principally on inner speech as phonological coding is too limiting (Webster, 1986, 1988).

Linguistic and cognitive considerations

Turning to linguistic considerations, Webster (1986) pointed out that deaf children can learn the simple declarative subject–verb–object (SVO) construction, although they have problems up to school-leaving age and beyond with more complex structures such as embedded clauses (Quigley et al., 1976b). Like younger hearing children, they may attempt to apply the SVO sequence not only to written SVO sentences, but to sentences which have other kinds of grammatical structure, using a simple tactic of visual order, in which the first occurring noun is taken to be the subject, followed by the verb, and then the object. Thus a sentence of the type 'The cat was bitten by the dog' may be reproduced as 'The cat bit the dog'. Another tactic that seems to be used frequently by deaf children is the 'Minimum Distance Principle' (MDP) of Chomsky (1965). This tactic makes use of visual contiguity in written text, so that a deleted subject is not inferred, but is taken to be the noun closest to the verb. Thus 'The dog bit the man and ran away' is interpreted as 'The man ran away'.

Both SVO and MDP tactics are used by young hearing children, though there is little agreement on how and why they are used (Romaine, 1984). The lack of agreement does not make it easy for us to explain their use by deaf children (Wood et al., 1986). However, we may explain why their use persists in older deaf children if we regard that persistence as a mismatch between the child's available grammatical skills and the more complex grammar of the printed text. In this case, the SVO and MDP tactics are simple devices to make sense of grammar beyond the childs' linguistic ability.

The issue of how deaf children read can be approached with tests of reading comprehension which permit study of the skills of deaf child readers at various levels. Webster (1986) presented a battery of graded reading material to 80 severely to profoundly deaf children aged 8–11 years. The test battery used familiar vocabulary in sentences with graded amounts of information and with increasingly complex grammar. The reading task was to look at a picture and to choose one sentence, out of 3 or 4, which matched the picture. Two scores were obtained for each child. The first approach scored the number of items passed when the child read sentences with complex grammar for meaning. The second approach scored the number of items where the child had to be shown the right vocabulary to pass the item. If a child failed on the first, but passed on the second, approach, it was assumed that the child was confused by the grammar.

Webster found that hearing loss was not of major importance in determining success in reading, but age was. The older the child, the better were the overall test scores, with little evidence of the plateau found in earlier studies of reading achievement. The plateau may thus be due to insensitive test instruments. The younger children were easily confused by the grammar, but usually succeeded when the vocabulary was highlighted (compare Sarachan-Deily, 1982). The older children made fewer overall errors, and approached 100% success. Many children found that the sentences with higher information (meaning) content were easier to get right, yet these sentences were more complex in their grammar. Webster suggested that deaf children can be helped if they are given more, rather than less, information in making selections from sentences. It is possible that Webster's results could be due in part to guessing. If the children were making guesses, then the greater the amount of information, the more directed would be the guesses. Hence the provision of more information with complex sentences would yield more accurate guessing.

We may envisage that the reading tactics of deaf children can easily be disrupted by imposing a load on their short-term memory. In an extension of his work, Webster (1986) made use of just this technique. For 20 severely to profoundly deaf children aged 11 years, 20 hearing children aged 8–9 years, and a group of 11-year-old hearing children, he set a further task of matching a picture with one of a set of sentences. First, both picture and sentences were presented. Then the sentences were offered without the picture, so that cross-referencing could not occur. After a 10-second delay, the picture was presented, but the sentences were removed. The children were asked to recall which of the sentences fitted the picture. Under the first condition, the deaf children scored beyond 90%, but under the memory test, scores dropped to around 45%. The younger hearing children attained 70% correct scores under the first condition, falling to 52% under the memory test. The older hearing children obtained scores of more than 90% and more than 80% in the first and memory tasks, respectively. Webster concluded that the top-down reading strategies of deaf children are easily disrupted. He explained this outcome by suggesting that deaf children lacked inner speech in which to conduct articulatory rehearsal in short-term memory. He therefore accepted the importance of inner speech in reading, but ascribed its importance not to phonological coding, but to a top-down use in memory rehearsal via an articulatory loop. Deaf children are limited in rehearsing verbal material via inner speech in short-term memory, which explains their problems in tasks related to verbal language.

Others have also been critical of Conrad's (1979) bottom-up approach to the study of reading ability in deaf children. Thus Wood et al. (1986) also argued for a top-down orientation, drawing on a model of poor reading skills developed by Stanovitch and West (1979). This model views poor readers as weak in using automated GPC rules. Poor readers try to make more use of top-down information than good readers by using their general world knowledge and language knowledge to cover the gaps in their poor reading. Such a reading strategy requires considerable conscious effort, is time-consuming, error-prone, and requires a copious store of valid general knowledge if it is to succeed (compare Stanovich, 1986; Andrews and Mason, 1991). Wood et al. believed that deaf children were in exactly this situation.

However, deaf children generally have poorer linguistic and general knowledge than poor hearing readers, giving them an additional handicap. They are likely to use various tactics, some of which may be non-linguistic. They will stretch their intelligence in using general knowledge, and such elementary devices as word associations, to make the most of cues from the reading task and its context to augment their limited linguistic ability. This error-prone approach results in frequent failures, which is hardly encouraging for the deaf child reader. Making a somewhat similar observation, Hanson (1986) suggested that deaf readers with poor speech, likely to be poorer readers, may compensate for their low level of ability in spelling to process nonsense words, consisting of legal consonant and vowel strings, by relying on the statistical redundancies of the orthography.

Storytelling

Several workers have begun to recommend that more attention be paid to conversation and storytelling as foundations for literacy in teaching reading to deaf children (e.g. Gaines et al., 1981; Wood et al., 1986). Their case is supported by the role found for linguistic prediction in reading for hearing individuals (Goodman and Burke, 1980). Studies of the cloze procedure with deaf children (Marshall,

1970; Odom et al., 1967; LaSasso, 1985, 1986) show that they have severe problems in using grammar or vocabulary to complement written material with missing words. The findings of these studies also relate to problems of linguistic prediction, supporting the view that failure to predict grammatical sequences markedly slows the attainment of literacy (Kretschmer and Kretschmer, 1986).

However, conversation and storytelling are more promising as foundations for the discourse and content levels of reading. There are two main types of discourse: narration and exposition (Hidi and Hildyard, 1983; Kretschmer and Kretschmer, 1986). Narration is relatively tightly organised, around a situation of conflict, for instance, and is more easily recalled, whereas exposition is less tightly organised and less easily recalled. Both types of stories have been used in relation to reading by hearing-impaired children.

Tales with a narrative structure can be employed to assess how well hearing-impaired children identify significant intelligence in the story. Thus stories with a narrative structure were presented together with scrambled stories to groups of hearing-impaired and hearing children by Gaines et al. (1981). For scrambled or distorted stories, the children had to rearrange the material to create the story. Both groups of children recalled significant information better than significant detail. The hearing-impaired children recalled more total information from the scrambled stories, but this information was not always about the more important parts of the story. Generally, the hearing children made better use of the narrative stories than the children with impaired hearing.

Expository stories have been used to explore the ways in which hearing-impaired children respond to organisational styles of text. Gormley (1981) found that familiarity with content facilitated the ability of third-grade hearing-impaired children in reading comprehension. Familiar paragraphs were better understood than unfamiliar paragraphs, even though they were structurally equivalent. Gormley (1982) extended this study by comparing the reading comprehension skills of hearing-impaired children at the ages of 8 and 15 years. Seven children formed the younger group, while eight children were the subjects in the older group. All children had hearing losses of 80 dB ISO, or more, and came from a TC day programme. The children read silently short (100-word) expository paragraphs about sports and insects. Two paragraphs were about familiar material (baseball and mosquitoes), and two were of unfamiliar content (curling and aphids). The paragraphs were equivalent in sentence structure, word frequency, readability level (third-grade), argument repetition and idea units. Apart from the reading of the text, communication between child and interpreter was by TC. Having been checked for prior knowledge, the child read the paragraph and then retold it. Additional information could be probed by text-based questions.

Gormley found that children from different age groups did not differ in prior knowledge or understanding of the text. However, familiarity with the material was a significantly differentiating factor for both age groups. Even though the third-grade level text was too difficult for the 8-year-old children at a technical level, they recalled paragraphs with familiar content better than those where the content was unfamiliar. This finding was important, because it showed that hearing-impaired children can obtain a fair reading comprehension of prose, which is too difficult for them at a technical level, if they are able to use their intelligence and general knowledge to assist their knowledge of grammar (compare Wood et al., 1986). Similar comments have been made by Banks et al. (1991a) and Gray et al. (1991) in discussing the use of story schemata in deaf children asked to reproduce a written story by arranging a set of pictures in sequence, a technique aimed to encourage the children to read for meaning and reducing the effect of syntax.

Figurative material

It has been generally thought that deaf children are not able to cope with figurative material in their reading or otherwise, and findings to this effect continue (Payne and Quigley, 1987). However, Fruchter et al. (1984) noted a surprisingly high level of non-literal understanding of idioms, where 13–15-year-old severely to profoundly deaf children read a sentence and then chose one of four pictures to explain the meaning.

In a later study of figurative language, Rittenhouse and Stearns (1990) also observed good figurative understanding in deaf children. Their moderately to profoundly congenitally deaf children aged 8–18 years were given a short original expository story to read. After reading the story, the children answered ten written yes/no questions, with lookback permitted. Vocabulary help was offered as needed. The 14 children were randomly assigned to two groups. One group read a literal version of the story; the other group read a figurative version, in which all textual answers to the questions were marked in figurative phrasing. Results showed that both groups answered the questions, which were all presented in literal form, above chance level. The figurative version of the story was no more difficult to comprehend than the literal version. Therefore figurative language need not always cause problems in reading comprehension for severely deaf children. Rittenhouse and Stearns observed that teachers were often reluctant to expose hearing-impaired children to figurative language, because the children did not use it spontaneously. However, hearing-impaired children can come to understand figurative language, even though they do not use it spontaneously, as also found (Iran-Nejad et al., 1981; Rittenhouse et al., 1981) in studies of hearing-impaired children's experiences with metaphor. It may be that failure to use higher-level skills, such as semantic representation, instantiation and metaphor, spontaneously is the result of over-exposure to low-level reading materials and markedly verbatim recall tasks (Davey and King, 1990).

Intervention in reading

There is a very large number of approaches to the teaching of reading. For example, reading in volume (Eller et al., 1988) and varied reading contexts (Nagy et al., 1987; Sternberg, 1987) have been promoted for vocabulary learning. Regression or lookback has been recommended as a reading strategy (Daneman, 1988; Davey and King, 1990). We cannot hope to conduct a detailed exploration of such methods here. Instead, we offer a few words about selected studies with hearing-impaired children.

Deaf children in UK classes have been been found to stop reading of their own accord more often than hearing children (Wood et al., 1986). They were also stopped in their reading more often than hearing children by their teachers, because they did not pronounce words correctly, and to teach the meanings of words. Generally teachers stopped deaf children in reading both more often, and for more varied reasons than they stopped hearing children. Teachers of the deaf thus viewed deaf children as having a wider range of reading difficulties than did teachers of hearing children. Teachers of hearing children viewed breaks in the reading of their hearing children as signalling breakdowns in grapheme/phoneme relationships, assuming that the children knew the vocabulary and syntax. Furthermore, hearing children tended to be praised more often in relation to the number of breaks than did deaf children.

A spoken reading rate of less than 40 words per minute suggests that the child does not comprehend what is being read, and many deaf children read below that rate (Wood et al., 1986). They thus have difficulty in understanding what they are reading. What is nominally a reading lesson becomes a lesson in the expression of speech and in language learning. Since they read slowly, deaf children have reduced opportunity to use intonation or stress patterns appropriately in their reading. Because of their reduced hearing, they have a more difficult task in dividing their attention between reading materials and the teacher. Together with a less than fully developed vocabulary for their age, and with problems in understanding syntax, it is not surprising that their reading achievements are weak. A possible solution would be to delay the teaching of reading until the child has acquired greater mastery over vocabulary, grammar and speech. Wood et al. also remarked that when the number of breaks for the teaching of language and speech expression are greater than those for teaching reading itself, then clearly the reading text is too difficult. More emphasis might be given to silent reading, as speech articulation is problematical for so many deaf children. Also, more attention could be given to story-telling and to conversations to provide a basis for the development of literacy.

A quite different approach was suggested by Serwatka et al. (1984). Instead of working directly on the children, they chose to promote the educational role of classroom teachers, dormitory teachers who were teachers acting as surrogate parents in after-school hours, and parents. Classroom teachers were treated to workshops by external consultants and project staff, instructional videotapes, and newsletters containing reviews of recent research in language and reading. The dormitory teachers, who had received little instruction as language and reading teachers, were also given workshops by external consultants and project staff, and newsletters on techniques for encouraging reading. The parents of the hearing-impaired children, too, were given workshops by project staff, and newsletters. The 43 students in this study were aged 11–16 years, and had taken the same level of the SAT over at least 2 years. They were thus in a group which appeared least likely to improve in reading without special intervention. Significant gains were found on the SAT for students who were in the project for at least 1 year, albeit less than those gains that would have been attained by hearing children. The results were not fully conclusive, however, as no controls were included. Also, it was not clear as to which of the classroom teachers, dormitory teachers or parents were most responsible for the improvements in reading skills, and/or whether the apparent improvements were due to improvements in language, or reading itself.

The reading material may be based on the ideas and experiences of hearing-impaired children themselves, to improve the meaningfulness or relevance of texts for reading purposes. This approach will help the children to learn that meaning is conveyed by print, as well as other forms of communication. This experiential method for language learning and reading is the Language-Experience Approach (LEA). The emphasis is on the use of whole language, as the text for subsequent reading is based on the child's use of lexicon, grammar and semantics in dictating the original material. LEA thus makes use of oracy and literacy in the preparation and reading of text, into which a child's drawings or pictures may be incorporated (Ewoldt and Hammermeister, 1986). LEA is derived from a sociolinguistic base, emphasising the interactive nature of language, and is aimed to promote the child's interest and motivation, so that success in language-related tasks is more assured. Further, since the original material is generated by the child in dictation to the teacher on an individual basis, there is no need for external controls for familiarity with vocabulary, grammar or semantics. The child's signed or spoken dictation offers its own constraints.

Other advantages for the LEA technique in reading are that a child who uses signs can see how the signed experience is translated into text. The translation does not require matching on a word-by-word basis, but does require the introduction of punctuation. Children who have individually dictated a common experience to the teacher will be keen to see how their peers have reported the same experience, and how it appears in the LEA texts of other children. This interest, so the argument goes, will help the child to learn that a given experience can be reported and written down in a variety of linguistic styles and conventions.

Despite these seeming advantages, LaSasso (1987) found in the USA that basal reader approaches, such as that devised for hearing-impaired children by Quigley and King (1984), were used more often than LEAs as the primary approach to instruction at all teaching levels. This finding was robust, as LaSasso surveyed 478 educational programmes for hearing-impaired children. The 'Reading Milestones' approach of Quigley and King was regarded favourably because it contained appropriate vocabulary, grammar, figurative expression and phonics emphasis.

LaSasso questioned the appropriateness of the continued use of basal readers. However, she remarked that although the LEA method was used quite extensively, it could lack uniform effectiveness, since comprehensiveness and continuity require careful coordination. More than two-thirds of programmes using LEA reported that teachers made independent decisions about which specific vocabulary and reading skills to introduce. This finding highlights criticisms of the LEA technique. First, in its purer form, where the teacher keeps closely to the dictated material of the child, the scope for introducing new vocabulary, grammar and semantics is reduced. However, if the teacher is too adventurous, familiarity with the reading material, one of the main advantages of LEA, is likely to be lost. Secondly, LEA does not prescribe how the teacher should go about the teaching of reading skills. It is only to be expected that teachers of hearing-impaired children more often preferred the basal reader approach. A further possible reason why the LEA method was not as favoured as it might have been, is that teachers of hearing-impaired students may be only moderately accurate in judging the reading interests of their students. When Stoefen-Fisher (1990) asked 20 teachers of the hearing-impaired to judge the top two areas of reading interest for each of 82 severely to profoundly deaf students in residential programmes, their judgements were only partly accurate.

Computer-assisted instruction in reading

Several authors have remarked on the advantages of using computer-assisted instruction with hearing-impaired students, the first really influential computer system for such purposes being Plato (Watson, 1979; Richardson, 1981). Most of the emphasis has been on the use of computer-aided instruction for language learning and problem solving, but some studies have also been concerned with reading (Geoffrion and Goldenberg, 1981; Richardson, 1981; Geoffrion and Geoffrion, 1983; Prinz et al., 1985). MacGregor and Thomas (1988) commented that much of the earlier instructional software for the deaf student required only a simple response to questions or statements. This was a serious disadvantage because it relied on drills and practice exercises. More recent developments include the introduction of computer-mediated text (CMT), in which the computer program changes the text to allow for interactions not possible on the printed page. CMT can also be used in conjunction with such tools as computer dictionaries, text paraphrasing and reciprocal questioning. Thus CMT reduces some of the student's processing load and encourages more interaction between the student and the program (Reinking and Schreiner, 1985). The following two examples show the type of use to which CMT is being put.

MacGregor and Thomas (1988) used five versions of a CMT system plus an electronic dictionary with 45 hearing-impaired children in grade levels 4–6, who had reading abilities between first- and third-grade levels. The children, aged between 7 and 13 years, were severely to profoundly deaf. The five CMT versions included activities with intrinsic motivation in a vocabulary game, extrinsic motivation in a post-reading passage test in the form of a vocabulary and comprehension check, or no given motivation. The information supplied by the electronic dictionary was also varied. Some versions showed a standalone definition, while others gave the definition together with a sentence showing the use of the word in context. The results indicated that the extrinsic motivation activity, assessed with a post-reading vocabulary and comprehension test, was the best motivating condition for developing vocabulary, comprehension and expository writing. The evaluation concentrated the children's attention on the need to know the meaning of words and to understand the text passages. Use of the expanded electronic dictionary, giving a definition of a word and an exemplar of the word in a sentence context, did not however result in improved reading or writing, for reasons which were not clear.

Braden et al. (1989) studied the effects of microcomputer-assisted telecommunication, analogous to reading and writing text, on the language and literacy of 48 hearing-impaired children between sixth- and eighth-grade levels, with a mean reading grade equivalent of 2.76 years. One group of children used microcomputers to telecommunicate with hearing children, another group telecommunicated with hearing-impaired peers, and a control group was given computer-aided instruction without telecommunication. Results showed that the two telecommunication groups improved their syntax skills in comparison to the control group, but not on other measures. However, there was a general tendency for the hearing-impaired to hearing-impaired telecommunication group to outperform the hearing-impaired to hearing group on all measures of improvement, namely in unstructured telecommunicated conversations, written language and scholastic achievement test scores, with both of these groups doing better than the control group. This finding is perhaps of greater importance than the microcomputer-assisted telecommunication. It suggests that it is not so much the language expertise or language model that promotes an increase in language and literacy skills as the need to match like with like, namely to present hearing-impaired children with text at a level familiar to them, though Braden et al. argued that it was the disequilibrium of experiencing conversations frustrated by other weak users of language which prompted the gains in language and literacy skills.

Much work remains to be done in this rapidly developing area, since computers are now favoured as a teaching tool in schools for the deaf. Although they are used commonly to present academic work, and to provide for practice in question-and-answer program, this is a traditional and rather limited expression of their potential. As computers become more sophisticated and user-friendly, we expect to see them being used in an increasing variety of educational applications, including CMT, for instruction in reading.

Writing

Since what is read has been written, and because both reading and writing skills depend on a common knowledge of vocabulary, syntax and semantics, it is to be expected that achievements in reading are related to achievements in writing (Graves, 1983; Walmsley, 1983). Further, most material is written in order to be read but, because reading is the skill learned first, writing is learned after the attainment of some skill in reading. Thereafter achievements in reading and writing tend to progress in tandem.

Useful discussions of the purposes of writing, and of the processes involved for hearing individuals are presented in several papers in volume 87 (1985) of the *Volta Review*. A recent summary of disorders of written expression is available in Gregg (1991). A full review of writing ability would involve consideration of spelling. However, spelling does not play as primary a role in written communication as other factors, and it is not considered here.

The principal purposes of writing for hearing individuals are to communicate information and ideas in a lasting form. Deaf people, however, also write to communicate everyday ideas to persons beyond their nuclear family and their circle of friends. If they do not receive sufficient help from amplification and/or speechreading, they need to rely heavily on written communication. They also need to rely on writing if they communicate manually or if they cannot articulate reasonably clear speech (White and Stevenson, 1975). Remarkably, there is very little published research in this important area. Most reports of writing by hearing-impaired individuals have been concerned with written exercises of hearing-impaired children at school, or similar activities. Necessarily, this is the material which we review.

Written grammar

Writing by hearing-impaired children has been the subject of considerable study and research, conveniently summarised by Quigley and Paul (1984) and Yoshinaga-Itano and Snyder (1985). Although there are large differences between good and poor deaf writers in both content and linguistic style (Gormley and Sarachan-Deily, 1987), the weight of research shows clearly that severely and profoundly deaf children produce grammatical errors in their writing. Even partially hearing children have problems in writing grammatically correct sentences which they can say (Arnold et al., 1982). Children with greater hearing losses tend to omit function words, such as articles, auxiliary verbs and prepositions – a characteristic which continues into post-secondary years (McAfee et al., 1990). In addition to these omissions, their sentences tend to be short, because of problems with some conjunctions, leading to 'jumps' from one sentence to another. Many of their sentences are of the SVO type. Some have no apparent grammar at all (Webster and Ellwood, 1985), or may be grammatically deviant. Overall, the impression for the reader is one of a rigid style of writing, with omissions, sequencing problems and occasional grammatical infelicities ('deafisms') which make it difficult to follow the train of thought (Ivimey, 1977c; Harrison et al., 1991). The semantics of the written message are hence thrown off track for the reader, who may have to study the writing with repeated regression and progression to understand the meaning of such instances as: 'The girl take pencil and drop. Pick-up. Drawing in book. Rub-out'. Inevitably problems of interpretation arise, which cast some question on the validity of syntactic and semantic analysis of the writing (Rodda and Grove, 1987).

Earlier studies approached the analysis of writing from the viewpoint of traditional grammar, with tallies of words, sometimes classified as traditional 'parts of speech' (nouns, verbs, adjectives, adverbs, etc.), and sentences. Studies of type–token ratios were popular, where types referred to the number of different words and tokens to the total number of words (Heider and Heider, 1940; Simmons, 1962; Myklebust, 1964; Schulze, 1965). Some of these earlier authors suggested that the writing of hearing-impaired children resembled that of normally developing children of a younger age. Others (Fusfeld, 1955) saw the writing as a tangled collation of words in a disorderly array, without sequencing or inflections reflecting accepted grammar.

Following Chomsky's (1957, 1965) transformational generative grammar, the analysis of writing by hearing-impaired children was approached in another way (Ivimey, 1976; Quigley et al., 1976a). Instead of traditional approaches, the writing was analysed for syntactic structures which, while not usual, none the less appeared consistently. Hearing-impaired children were seen to have problems with the inflection of nouns and verbs, and with articles and auxiliary verbs into the teen years, although they had mastered straightforward active declarative sentences, such as SVO forms.

Particular problems were experienced with the less concrete verbs, such as 'to be' and 'to have'. Control of verb tenses was weak, and in some cases non-existent (Ivimey, 1981), so that the one verb tense could be used to indicate past, present and future, but modified by an external marker ('He came now'). Similarly, noun modifiers were used to show plurality ('The two cup'). Articles were often appropriately used with the subject but were often omitted for the object ('The family go on picnic'), though the use of determiner and noun as subject was often over-used. Relative and other embedded clauses were used rarely. Indeed, Wilbur (1977) argued that hearing-impaired children tended to approach writing as a clause by clause, or sentence by sentence, task rather than as a task in whole composition. There were also difficulties in using the passive voice (Power and Quigley, 1973). However, because these results were found consistently between and within deaf children, it was argued that the writing was not lacking in grammatical rules but had a rule system of its own, or that hearing-impaired children used the standard English rules of grammar together with their own constructions (Quigley et al., 1976b).

It is now generally accepted that the writing of hearing-impaired children is both linguistically delayed and different, or deviant (Webster, 1986). The use of unusual or deviant written grammar is a real problem, because society cannot be expected to cope with idiosyncratic use of grammar. Even if there are consistent patterns of deviancies across groups of hearing-impaired children, there will still be a major problem for them in communicating their ideas to hearing individuals. Thus from the communication viewpoint, it is a pressing issue to discover the extent of the use of deviant grammar in the writing of hearing-impaired children. Papers by Bamford and Bench (1979), Williams and Dennis (1979) and Williams (1986) using the Language Assessment, Remediation and Screening Procedure of Crystal et al. (1976) illustrate methods of how this issue might be explored further.

To explain the findings, it has been suggested that function words are short in duration and often unstressed, so that they are difficult to hear or speechread and hence are poorly learned. The over-use of the definite article with subject nouns and other features has been ascribed to rigid teaching, though Bunch (1979) found no difference in the use of rules of grammar with natural versus formal methods of teaching for hearing-impaired children aged 9–16 years. Problems with writing standard English have also been ascribed to interfering effects from the learning of sign language (Dawson, 1981).

More recent work (Geers and Moog, 1989), discussed earlier in the section on reading skills, has shown that some orally educated profoundly deaf adolescents aged from 15 to 18 years can write at levels much better than the main thrust of the literature would indicate. Geers and Moog reported that the majority of their children could write acceptable essays and business letters, with only some mechanical and grammatical errors. Such reports show that caution is needed in generalising about the abilities of deaf individuals. However, Geers and Moog's subjects were atypical of deaf adolescents as a whole. McAfee et al. (1990), mentioned earlier, reported findings for severely deaf post-secondary students which showed that the written English skills of these students were consistent with the earlier reports, with a high occurrence of errors in function words. Klecan-Aker and Blondeau (1990) have also presented results which confirm the earlier work for use of clauses, and coordinating versus subordinating conjunctions.

Some of the unusual aspects of the writing of hearing-impaired children are similar to the early efforts at writing of young hearing children, an observation which lends weight to the idea that the writing skills of hearing-impaired children are delayed, at least in part. Although the writing of hearing-impaired children improves with age (Myklebust, 1964; Power and Wilgus, 1983), this improvement is relatively slow, as with improvement in their reading skills. It seems that the older children attempt to express more complex thoughts in writing as they develop, but their grammatical ability holds them back. One result is 'deafisms' or deviant grammar. Although the vocabulary may be adequate, the way in which words are put together reflects a less sophisticated style of writing because of imperfectly learned grammatical structures. It seems, then, that difficulties of a linguistic kind, and especially with grammar, retard the ability of hearing-impaired children in both reading and writing. Since reading is problematic for hearing-impaired children, it is scarcely surprising that they also have problems with writing. Difficulties in both reading and writing can be explained by failure to develop an internal language (Quigley and Kretschmer, 1982).

It will be recalled that manipulation of memory rehearsal can shed light on the reading strategies of hearing-impaired children (Webster, 1986). Given a reciprocal relationship between reading and writing, it would seem that manipulation of rehearsal could also be a useful tool in the investigation of writing. In a novel experiment, Webster (1986) has indeed studied the effects of rehearsal on the writing skills of hearing-impaired children, particularly for the writing of longer items. Such longer items need to be held in memory, and hence a child who has poor inner language will be unable to rehearse the material, just before it is written down, through 'articulatory feedback loops' or some similar strategem (Baddeley, 1979). The child will therefore have problems in the fluent writing of sequential connected prose. Webster studied 20 severely to profoundly deaf children aged 11–12 years, and 20 hearing children of the same age. The children wrote about a picture under two conditions. For the first condition, the children were given a sheet of paper and asked to write for 30 minutes about what they saw. In the second condition, the children performed the same task, but wrote with an expired pen on a sheet of paper, under which was a sheet of carbon paper overlaying a second sheet. Thus the children could see what they had written in the first condition, but not in the second.

Webster found, first, that hearing children used fewer sentences and made fewer grammatical errors than the hearing-impaired children. The latter used simple sentence structures, more content words such as nouns and verbs, fewer function words, and many non-standard grammatical forms, confirming earlier work. Secondly, in comparing the two conditions, he found that writing without visual feedback in the second condition did not affect the performance of the hearing-impaired children. The possibility, in normal circumstances, of looking back at what they had written did not affect their subsequent writing, because their use of feedback mechanisms was already disrupted or weak. The hearing children, however, performed badly in the second condition, increasing their errors and reducing their production of complex sentences. Some hearing children produced deviant structures similar to deafisms, such as omission of determiners and auxiliaries. They also used inappropriate word endings. Thus feedback from material already written and rehearsal of material play an important role in writing skills, especially for prose containing more complex structures.

The poor achievement of hearing-impaired child writers can be attributed, in part, to failure to rehearse the material because of difficulties with inner language which prevents rehearsal from taking place. This conclusion is supported by Wood et al. (1986) who found that hearing-impaired children who wrote relatively well also produced relatively accurate spoken messages, suggesting that inner language assisted both writing and speaking. Interestingly, Webster's study suggests that the primary failure, namely failure to rehearse the material, is a cognitive rather than a linguistic problem.

Learning to write

The literature is weak on how hearing-impaired children begin to learn writing skills. In a free-choice exercise, Conway (1985) found that hearing-impaired children of kindergarten age were interested to express meaning and content in their writing rather than form. He argued for an educational focus on the child's capacity to learn rather than on the writing deficits. Ewoldt (1985) used a natural composition approach to teach fluent writing over a period of 3 years to ten hearing-impaired children, born to hearing-impaired parents. The programme began with children at ages 4–5, concluding at ages 6–7 years. Her results, however, did not indicate clear advantages for a natural language approach to writing as a means of overcoming the rigid productions of hearing-impaired children. In any case, and as we saw above, Bunch (1979) found no difference between natural and formal approaches in teaching written grammar.

More informative results were obtained by Truax (1985), who described a 3-week programme of near-daily meetings for 6- and 7-year-old hearing-impaired children. The teacher modelled stories, after which each of six children told short stories, in turns, with the teacher asking questions for clarification. Then the children drew pictures to show the main characters, settings and events in their stories, and retold the stories, which were written up in front of the group. This programme continued, with the children writing words to add to the pictures and progressing to more sophisticated forms of writing. The interaction of the children in telling and writing stories was highly motivating. Presenting their ideas in writing to others, with verbal storytelling and group discussion, spurred them on. Truax's programme appears to be worth pursuing further, particularly as it attempted to integrate reading and writing with group communication. However, her work lacked controls, such as a matched group of children learning to write through traditional methods, which makes the significance of the report difficult to estimate.

The approaches of Conway (1985), Ewoldt (1985), and Truax (1985) look promising as teaching vehicles because they were motivating. The focus was on content, narrative or semantic aspects rather than grammar. Yoshinaga-Itano (1986) continued with this theme. She reported an attempt to expand the semantic properties of the written compositions of hearing-impaired children using a propositional analysis. She also studied the semantic–syntactic links between sentences (Yoshinaga-Itano and Snyder, 1985). She compared the writing of 49 prelingually deaf children aged 10–14 years, who had moderate or greater hearing losses, with the writing of 49 hearing children. A quadratic trend was found for semantic written language variables, peaking at age 12 years for hearing-impaired children and at age 13 years for hearing children. Both groups, however, showed a linear developmental trend for syntactic variables. This linear trend increased with age, with the hearing children outperforming the deaf group. Hence the difference between the two groups was greater in syntactic than semantic performance.

Increasing numbers of researchers have begun to study the written narratives of hearing-impaired children as narrative discourse in the last few years. We have already referred to work in this area by Webster (1986). Sarachan-Deily (1985) gave an account of the ability of hearing-impaired high-school students to recall explicit propositions and inferences, going beyond the literal meaning, by reading and then writing a given story. Although the hearing-impaired students recalled significantly fewer propositions than hearing subjects, they included a similar number of inferences in their written narratives. Further, the better readers among the hearing-impaired students recalled propositions more accurately, but did not differ in recalling implicit content.

Somewhat dissimilar findings were presented for stories written and signed for severely to profoundly deaf children, or written and told for hearing children, aged 8–15 years by Everhart and Marschark (1988). Their hearing children produced comparable numbers of non-literal constructions in spoken and written stories, whereas the deaf children produced significantly more non-literal constructions in sign than in writing, where the non-literal constructions were very few. The deaf children were linguistically much more creative in sign than in writing. However, the children studied by Sarachan-Deily on the one hand, and by Everhart and Marschark on the other, differed in age and otherwise. As Everhart and Marschark remarked, different children may have different preferred ways of creative expression. To separate the different effects and causes would require comparisons of individuals who are matched carefully for their abilities in sign, speech and other relevant variables.

Intervention programmes

Given the emphasis on writing in education, it is not surprising to find many reports of educational programmes to improve the written communication skills of hearing-impaired children. Besides the more conventional approaches, we note the advent of computer-assisted training using word-processing programs (Schilp,

1989), and the use of a journal or notebook to prompt interactive dialogue (Staton, 1985; Teller and Lindsey, 1987). Journal-writing is helpful since it is much more like face-to-face interaction than formal writing assignments, especially where dialogue journals are exchanged between deaf and hearing children (Kluwin and Kelly, 1991). Research on dialogue journal exchange approaches the need we mentioned at the start of this section for studies of the use of writing in everyday communication by hearing-impaired children. Unfortunately to date, reports of dialogue–journal exchange are as far as the literature goes.

We next consider the effects of combining communication modes on the development of writing skills. In one of the better designed studies, Akamatsu and Armour (1987) assessed the effects of complementary teaching in sign language, transliteration as writing in letters of another alphabet, and translation and editing skills on the writing skills of six severely to profoundly deaf students in a residential high school for the deaf. The students had auditory discrimination scores of less than or equal to 15%, and reading comprehension grades between 3.5 and 6.0 on the SAT (hearing-impaired version). Following a pre-test with a spontaneous writing sample and a receptive signing transfer test, the students were instructed twice a week for 45 minutes over a 10-week period. The instruction included information on communication, the way in which sign systems convey information, transliteration and translation skills, and editing/grammar skills for English, to make the students more aware of these features and their interrelationships. Both literal and figurative aspects were taught. In comparison with seven matched controls, no significant differences were found between the groups on pre-test measures, but the post-test scores for the experimental (instructed) group were significantly higher than those of the control (no instruction) group for spontaneous writing and sign-receptive transfer for grammar and accuracy of information. These results showed that drawing the experimental group's attention to signing, and ways in which signing differed from writing, improved aspects of their writing ability. Akamatsu and Armour went on to argue for an increased role for bilingual education in the classroom, with a broad range of teachers. Their results are stimulating. However, as they were aware, their design confounded instructor effects for the experimental group. Also the use of editing skills in writing was confounded with the instruction. Clearly, further clarificatory work needs to be done.

The work we have considered so far has been concerned with identifying the reasons for poor writing performance in hearing-impaired children, and remediating it. There has been little reference to writing as communication. There is, nevertheless, one approach which has taken written communication as its focus. In a particularly interesting paper, Harrison et al. (1991) reported a bold approach where there was no intervention to teach vocabulary or syntax for writing, and written syntax was never corrected. The aim was to allow the child's writing to be judged on its ability to communicate ideas. Samples of the writing, from usual school routines, of 86 moderately to profoundly deaf children aged 5–17 years, who were integrated in ordinary schools in Leicestershire, UK, were grouped into categories according to their syntactic maturity or completeness. Harrison et al. found that 85% of the writing contained fluent and expressive use of complex language allowing easy extraction of meaning, though with immature syntax, up to normal use of syntax. Seventy-seven per cent of the profoundly deaf children also produced writing in this range. The authors believed that the achievement of sentences with the completeness of adult usage was an inappropriate and unnecessary goal for many hearing-impaired children. They concluded that a non-corrective approach to writing enabled the children to develop a confidence and fluency of expression which allowed them to express their ideas using their available linguistic knowledge, and to use writing as a means of communication. This study offers much food for thought. Confirmatory reports of its findings and reports of the degree of community acceptance of its goals are keenly anticipated.

Concluding Remarks: Reading and Writing

This chapter concludes with some comments on the relation between reading and writing as it affects hearing-impaired children.

A first point to note is that although reading and writing depend on both syntax and semantics, the semantic aspects of writing are more closely related to reading comprehension than are the syntactic aspects (Yoshinaga-Itano and Snyder, 1985). The reason is that, within limits, syntax indicates how verbal material is to be processed rather than what it means. This point is particularly relevant to communication, because communication is concerned with the transfer of meaning. In everyday communication, errors of syntax can be accommodated, provided that they are not too glaring. Semantic errors are likely to be much more troublesome.

The relationship between reading comprehension and writing skills may be observed by asking children to read a passage of prose, and then to provide a written summary of it. One such study is that of Peterson and French (1988) with 30 hearing and 30 hearing-impaired college students. Each group read and summarised two expository scientific passages which were controlled for the number of topic or main idea sentences, and which had been judged earlier for the importance of the 'idea units' they contained. The two groups' performances were similar in their use of summarisation strategies, except for the inclusion of comments or opinions in the summaries. The hearing-impaired group was less sensitive to the importance of ideas. They made less frequent use of important ideas, choice of topic sentences, creation of topic statements, and integration of ideas within and among paragraphs. The hearing-impaired college students thus had basic skills in writing summaries, but used summarisation strategies less effectively than the hearing students. However, this study may have underestimated the abilities of the hearing-impaired group. Given a chance to read and revise their own narrative drafts, hearing-impaired high-school students can produce revised drafts which are better than the first (Livingston, 1989).

Arnold (1981) and Exley and Arnold (1987) drew attention to the propensity of deaf children to make fewer written spelling errors because of phonemic confusions than hearing children, since deaf individuals code and store words as visual sequences of letters. The analogy with processes involved in the reading abilities of deaf children, outlined above, is clear. Although deaf children may have this advantage in avoiding written errors caused by phonemic confusions, it is far out-weighed by their lack of inner speech, which causes major difficulties with both reading and writing.

We recall that assessments of deaf children's ability in reading were criticised when based on reading tests for hearing children. The criticism was that such tests are based on expressive language skills which deaf children may not have (Davey et al., 1983). It is tempting to promote a similar criticism of the assessment of deaf children's writing skills. The problem is, however, that there is no general alterna-tive mode such as sign in which to write, for written sign systems are little used. Although Quigley and Kretschmer (1982) suggested that video-recording of signed communication be used in lieu of writing, this novel suggestion is seldom pur-sued. It proves cumbersome in practice.

The reciprocal relationship between reading and writing is known to hearing-impaired children themselves (Hollingshead, 1982). Practice in the one should therefore promote attainment in the other. Both depend on well developed inter-nal language, which itself depends on a communication system which can convey a wide and complex range of meaningful experiences to the child (Quigley and Kretschmer, 1982). However that may be, it is unfortunately the case, as we have seen, that most severely to profoundly prelingually deaf children presently do not learn to read and write adequately. They are accordingly denied communication via literacy with wider society.

Chapter 7
Hearing Impairment and Cognition

This chapter is divided into three sections dealing with cognition, metaprocesses and central auditory dysfunction in communication. The first section considers cognitive skills in relation to the hearing-impaired child's understanding of speech. There follows a discussion of cognitive processes including memory, temporal processing, semantics and higher-level aspects, and then some comments on the cognitive processes of deaf signers. The section on metaprocesses, where the literature is very slim, reviews virtually all the published research on metaprocesses in hearing-impaired children. The final section on central auditory dysfunction outlines the nature of the phenomenon, making a distinction between central auditory disorders and language learning problems.

Because of the pervasive influence of language in everyday communication, language supports not only oracy and literacy, but thinking, understanding, memorising and so on (Hayes, 1990). The closeness of cognition and language can be seen in questions, for example, where deaf children may experience problems with both the linguistic form of a question and in comprehending its meaning (LaSasso, 1990). In earlier work, language was seen as primary to cognition (Sapir, 1949; Whorf, 1956). Although it was accepted that the very young infant develops some cognitive abilities before language begins to appear, as soon as language emerges it was thought to dominate cognitive development. The work of Chomsky (1957, 1968), which emphasised a unique role for language, added impetus to this direction.

With Piaget's influential work on concept development (Chapter 1), the so-called Whorfian view that language dominates cognition fell out of favour. In its place emerged the idea that language builds on pre-existing cognitive activity. According to this view, cognition is primary to language (Bever, 1970; Slobin, 1979). Language is built on concepts and ideas which have already developed without a linguistic basis. Apparent evidence to support this view comes from research into deafness (Furth, 1964a, 1970; Bond, 1987; Christensen, 1990), since cognitive activity in the signing deaf occurs in the absence of verbal language.

However, since we cannot be sure that such activity occurs without mediation by sign language, the evidence is questionable. More convincing are the studies of object permanence by Corrigan (1978), who found in hearing infants that the beginning of search for objects removed from view occurred at the same time as production of the first words. The early deprivation reports (Chapter 2) also offer support, since several of these reports showed that cognitive activity can develop with little language.

At present, the cognitive-dominant view is the accepted one (King and Quigley, 1985; Christensen, 1990), but the issue is by no means settled. It may be that phonology and syntax are acquired satisfactorily even with severe cognitive impairment, but that semantics and comprehension cannot be (Cossu and Marshall, 1990). Much remains to be discovered about the nature of cognitive and communicative development early in life, before the first words are spoken. We have already seen that active communication takes place between mother and infant in this period, setting the stage for further cognitive and linguistic development, when the need to communicate thoughts and intentions drives the development of language. For the time being, we will settle for a parallel interaction between cognition and language, after early infancy (Schlesinger, 1977a; Wells, 1979). According to this position, thinking, intention and meaning can be developed through experience of language, as much as language may be expanded through cognition. In taking this position we recognise, of course, a distinction between language associated with cognition, and language as a basis for communication (Wood, 1991).

Cognitive Skills

In discussing cognition, it is common to refer to studies by Piaget, reflecting his concern with cognitive development (Duckworth, 1979; Rittenhouse et al., 1981; Peterson and Peterson, 1989; Christensen, 1990). These references relate to Piaget's focus on developmental stages and the interaction of the child with the environment in acquiring knowledge, though Affolter (1985) has argued that developmental patterns follow a continuous developmental progression rather than stages.

It is also common to give an account of cognitive subskills, ranging from such 'lower-order' skills as attention, psychophysical discrimination, and short-term memory, through such 'middle-order' skills as temporal sequencing and rehearsal, to higher-order skills, such as thinking, concept formation, problem-solving and reasoning (Sloan, 1980; Davis and Rampp, 1983; Rodda and Grove, 1987; Gruneberg et al., 1988). There is a logical sense to this kind of treatment, following, as it does, the sequence from sensation and perception to the mental activity which ensues. Also, it allows us to think about cognitive ability in an orderly way. However, the lower-order skills tend to be directly involved in the acquisition of the higher-order skills. In hearing children, for example, an articulatory loop, the phonological memory component of working memory, is directly involved in language acquisition and development, and in the development of oral comprehension (Hulme, 1987; Gathercole, 1990). Further, although it is feasible to analyse cognitive activity into a range of subskills at a conceptual level, it is very doubtful if hearing individuals, in their ordinary conversations, process speech inputs by analysing the speech sounds in detail, and then bring some such sequence as that outlined above to bear on the interpretation of the results. The sheer rate of speech production in even a simple conversation can scarcely allow it (Chapter 1).

We will consider the way in which the information contained in speech becomes accessible to cognition by viewing the task as an exercise in information processing constrained by the phonetic and linguistic properties of running speech.

Information processing

A useful place from which to start is the situation as described by Ivimey (1977a, b, c). He pointed out that the acoustic properties of conversational speech are quite different from what might be supposed from analysis of the 40 or so phonemes identified by classical phonetics. It is false to view the phonemes as making a set of relatively free-standing sounds, some representing vowels and some representing consonants, with each taking between 10 and 100 ms to produce and which, in combination, produce the sounds of speech. The true situation is much more complex. Speech sounds occur concurrently as much as sequentially. There is a relatively slow sequence of vowels which are modified at their beginnings and endings by formant transitions in the production of adjacent consonants. The acoustic cues for consonants are usually different when the same consonant is paired with different vowels, when the consonants are in different positions (initial, medial or final) and for the kinds of cues (manner, place and voicing) that are used (Liberman et al., 1967).

Instead of discriminating among some 40 stable phonemes, the listener has to choose from about 300–400 possibilities. The complexity does not stop there, because different speakers produce distinctly different speech sounds. Male, female and child's speech sounds are quite different. Also, in running speech, the 'target' sounds that the speaker intends to produce are not fully realised because, as one sound is pronounced, the vocal organs are already being positioned to produce the next one. The anatomical speech structures do not have time to attain the ideal configuration for the production of a given speech sound before they start to alter to produce the next. Thus, instead of bringing perceptual and cognitive processes to bear on a relatively small range of speech sounds, presented in a clearly sequential fashion, the listener has to contend with up to perhaps 1000 possible different sounds, many of which are coarticulated, and many of which only approximate what the speaker intended to produce. The task for the listener primarily involves identifying the main bursts of energy, the vowels, which may not be on target, and the initial and final modifications to those bursts of vowel energy, representing the consonants. These identifications must be made so that relative differences between speakers do not disrupt the process. The listener does not so much analyse speech in minute acoustic detail, as analyse for the overall pattern of the speech. Clearly, much more is at issue than the acoustic properties of the speech signal. The listener has to decode an apparently confusing and rapidly changing complex of sounds.

Phonological, prosodic, grammatical and semantic constraints

The interpretation of speech sounds in conversations is greatly facilitated by the characteristics of the language in which the speech is produced and received, because languages are subject to phonological, syntactic and semantic constraints. Under these constraints, only a limited number of sequences is allowed. The result is a marked reduction in the cognitive load on the listener in understanding what is being said. For example, when listening and then repeating a new word, or when reading aloud a new word for the first time, people articulate the word on the basis of the accepted phonology. It is thus easy to articulate a nonsense word such as 'poad' to rhyme with 'road' or 'goad'.

Several authors have attempted to describe how segmental information is processed in spoken words. Salasoo and Pisoni (1985) examined the sources of knowledge from which spoken words can be identified; Grosjean and Gee (1987) reported on the effects of prosodic structure on the perception of spoken words; and Slowiaczek et al. (1987) explored the effects of phonological priming, a form of prompting to manipulate phonological salience, on word recognition. Slowiaczek (1990) manipulated lexical stress by varying the stressed syllable in sets of words. Some stresses were correct and some incorrect ('YELlow' versus 'yelLOW'). She reported that correctly stressed words were produced faster than incorrectly stressed words in shadowing experiments which involved speaking a word immediately following its presentation. Correctly stressed words were also classified faster than incorrectly stressed words in a lexical decision task between words and non-words ('YELlow' vs. 'GHELlow'). Her work further suggested that sequential information was relied on more heavily when the correct lexical stress was absent. Thus prosodic information, and in particular lexical stress, is subject to constraints which must be observed to make sense of a message.

Speech sounds are subject to grammatical constraints of syntax and morphology. For instance, besides using syntax to put words into permissible sequences, we use syntax to organise morphemes. The morphemes can exist alone as free morphemes ('boy', 'girl') or bound morphemes, which have meaning only when joined with other morphemes (-s in 'boys', or -ed in 'played'). Syntax organises morphemes as part of grammar. A sentence such as 'The boys shout and run away' is allowable, whereas 'The boy shout and run away' is beyond the rules.

At the semantic level, the overall context is of particular importance in understanding connected speech. Whereas semantic information is conveyed by the meaningfulness of the words in an isolated sentence, under natural conversational conditions the context of the conversation sets the scene for the whole utterance. In such conditions whole words may be replaced experimentally by noise bursts, analogous to the replacement of phonemes discussed above, and yet the listener may insist that the original word was present (Warren, 1970). At this level of semantic processing expert knowledge of language and everyday affairs is central to skill in communication.

Occasional problems with speech production or perception, such as occasional mispronunciations or mishearings, are no problem because the context and the speaker's and listener's knowledge of the world allows such lacunae to be bypassed. Hearing people who have well developed central cognitive processes and who are well versed in the world of affairs have considerable leeway in overcoming such errors, gaps and breaks. Even when words that make up a sequence of connected speech cannot be perceived, the listener may still be able to make sense of the message if isolated speech fragments can be fitted together in the listener's internal schema (Bever, 1970, 1973). What is said has to be heard as making sense. The constraint is derived from meaning.

The constraints on the semantics produced by the speaker are less particular than constraints at the phonological, morphological and syntactic levels (Garrett, 1980; Meyer, 1990). This relaxation of constraint at the semantic level for the speaker can be matched by the listener's concentration on the meaning of what is being said, as shown by supplying words or phrases for which the speaker is temporarily stymied, with the words or phrases on the tip of the tongue.

Cognition and Hearing Impairment

The outline just presented will have reminded the reader of the huge task that faces the would-be orally communicating prelingually severely or profoundly deaf child. We now consider first some aspects of cognition in deaf children concerned with speechreading, information processing, memory, time perception, semantics and higher-level processes. We consider secondly some cognitive features of sign.

The field is difficult to conceptualise clearly because of its pragmatic orientation and historical development. The methodologies are various and there are few clear theoretical directions. For instance, most of the earlier work was done with deaf children who were educated orally, especially in Europe, while later work has involved children who are more likely to use sign in some form as their main means of communication.

Cognitive delay or cognitive difference?

An interesting model has it that the major constraint on the perception of connected speech is not so much in the nature of the available sensory data as in the extent to which a listener is versed in the interacting sets of phonological, morphological, syntactic, prosodic and semantic rules of a language. This view of speech perception predicts that even profoundly deaf individuals whose cognitive and linguistic competence is high will be able to communicate well through such residual hearing as they may have, and through lipreading. That postlingually profoundly deaf individuals generally have good levels of communication, that communication skill is only partly explained by level of hearing loss, and that lipreading and use of residual hearing are correlated with linguistic competence and knowledge of the world in the prelingually profoundly deaf is good supportive evidence for this model. Recent studies have given further weight to the argument. Lyxell and Ronnberg (1989) found no differences in speechreading ability between postlingually mildly to moderately hearing-impaired adults and hearing adults in a sentence-completion test. Rather, the use of information-processing skills was the important factor, as shown by inference-making or guessing abilities

(Burke and Nerbonne, 1978; Paniagua, 1990; Lyxell and Ronnberg, 1991).

The particular issue, then, for the prelingually profoundly deaf child is to develop linguistic competence and a high degree of associated cognitive skill when hearing loss obstructs or diverts the development of such competence and skill. It is this and related problems that we now consider.

Some earlier workers saw the cognitive processes of hearing-impaired children as normal in type. However, language development would be affected by restricted interaction with the environment and a lack of sufficient chances for learning (Furth, 1966a, b), resulting in linguistic delay. The solution, according to this view, is to provide enriched opportunities for linguistic development.

An alternative view (Myklebust, 1964) is that the diminished auditory input results not only in language delay but in different cognitive processes from those of hearing children which, in turn, compound the linguistic problems. Different cognitive mechanisms result from reliance on other sensory modalities such as vision or touch, from which hearing-impaired children develop different cognitive and linguistic styles. Adherents of this view argue for alternative methods of communication for hearing-impaired children, such as communication by sign or, to a lesser extent, by tactile signals.

Since these two extremes were first expressed, more has become known about the cognitive and linguistic processes of hearing-impaired children. However, such evidence has not clarified the situation completely in the direction of one argument or the other. Hearing-impaired children have come to be seen as a very heterogeneous group (Bamford and Saunders, 1985), differing in degree of hearing loss, age at onset of loss, motivation, familial and social background, educational environment and so on.

Environmental factors, such as social and educational background, turn out to be at least as important, and possibly more important, than the hearing loss itself. Since the child's social and educational background is all but impossible to control, the debate is likely to remain confounded. What is clear is that most, but not all, prelingually severely and profoundly deaf children do have different cognitive styles in processing linguistic material. On the other hand, in demonstrating a near-normal level of linguistic and cognitive performance, a minority of such children function as though they had been deafened postlingually.

Working in the UK, and hence at the time with mainly orally-educated hearing-impaired children, Ivimey (1977c) argued that they perform like hearing children, but show marked performance delay. Such phenomena as 'deafisms' were due to a lack of exposure to English, not hearing loss per se. Considering the processes involved in the acquisition of grammar by deaf children, Ivimey thought that they acquire grammar in the normal way, but differ from hearing children in the age of acquisition. They use their experience to form tentative grammatical rules, and generalise these rules to other situations by analogy in a sequence of stages characterised by increasing linguistic and cognitive complexity. This sequence of stages and the association of linguistic and cognitive complexity is reminiscent of a classification of the language of teachers (Blank et al., 1978), where language is ordered according to its level of cognitive demand. Although concerned mainly with teachers' questions addressed to children, the classification allows language to be scaled from low-level cognitive demand items, such as names of objects and their attributes, to higher-level demand for the relationships between objects and events. The highest level of cognitive demand in this scheme is concerned with reasoning and planning. Hence the level of demand increases from the concrete towards inference and abstraction.

The explanation for Ivimey's stages was that deaf children first learn words as individual units and in meaningful sequences, as the simplest tasks, and then proceed to the more complex forms such as noun plurals, and the more concrete prepositions identifying location such as *to* and *in*. Later come the final *s* in verbs and the dative use of *to* which may be used inconsistently. The genitive use of *s*, and the use of prepositions in a correct but less than common way ('*on* the train' as opposed to '*on* the table') are used much later, if at all. The progression illustrates increasing complexity in the underlying concepts, and involves increasing demands on cognition.

Ivimey's argument has force. Prelingually hearing-impaired children experience many similar circumstances to hearing children in understanding their environments. In acquiring language, both groups are likely to make many similar linguistic 'mistakes' as their facility with language and their accompanying cognitive processes are developing. There is no doubt that hearing-impaired children have greater difficulty, at a given age, in coping linguistically and cognitively with their environment. There may, however, be a trade-off between IQ and hearing loss in that high IQ can offset the effects of hearing loss to some degree (Gallaway et al., 1990). Hence some prelingually deaf children do manage to develop a remarkable degree of sophistication in their linguistic and cognitive development, provided that they have a supportive and educationally sophisticated environment.

Nevertheless, as Conrad (1979) and Rodda and Grove (1987) have pointed out, although the tasks involved in the perception of speech have some similarities for hearing and hearing-impaired individuals, the cognitive processes involved are not comparable in most cases. Children with hearing within normal limits, or a mild to moderate hearing loss, learn to perceive speech mainly via the auditory channel, and develop a phonological or inner speech code in processing language. On the other hand, severely and especially profoundly deaf children have limited access to the auditory channel, which may additionally distort the auditory input. They are thus denied the opportunity to develop inner speech, except in a minority of cases where speechreading can be used successfully to supplement residual hearing (Myklebust, 1964). Prelingually deaf children in the main appear to process language through a visual code (see below).

We now examine such cognitive differences in greater detail, and begin by asking what sort of memory code is used by deaf children.

Hearing impairment and memory

Memory plays a significant role in communication. As short-term memory, it is important for hearing, speaking, speechreading, writing and reading, because it is difficult to continue with communication if we are unaware of what we have just been expressing, or what has just been expressed to us.

Memory codes

In an early study of short-term visual memory (Blair, 1957), severely and pro-foundly deaf children were assessed on the Memory for Designs Test and the Knox Cube Test, for which the order of stimuli has to be recalled. The deaf children per-formed at a significantly higher level on these tests than hearing children matched for age, gender and intelligence. They also performed better, but not significantly so, on a test of object location, where they had to remember the position of every-day objects on a card. However, when they were required to recall stimuli in sequence, the deaf children performed below the level of the hearing controls. Blair suggested that the reason was that the deaf children had a problem with auditory memory, associated with their low attainment in reading. Subsequent work, discussed at length in the well known and highly influential text by Conrad (1979), confirmed this view.

Conrad (1979) set out to investigate the operation of sequential memory, which is the order in which items are organised in memory, and the use of memo-ry codes, in a large group of deaf school leavers. The children were shown printed words, one at a time, and asked to write them down from memory in the right order. Stimulus trials used either homophone words, which sound the same as one another, or non-homophone words. The effect of hearing loss on recall errors, with scores adjusted for non-verbal intelligence, was statistically significant, but not great, when all words were scored across all trials. The effect of hearing loss was less than that of intelligence. By adjusting the scores for intelligence, and by classifying the children with a separate test for the ability to use internal speech, Conrad then showed that the hearing loss had a negligible effect on per-formance. More importantly, the availability of internal speech was the significant variable, and the availability of internal speech was associated with hearing loss. The original effect of hearing loss on the error scores in the memory tasks was indirect. The use of inner speech, then, was the important factor. Accordingly, the apparent relationship of error scores to hearing loss was due to the extent of use of inner speech, which was negatively correlated with hearing loss.

Conrad also showed that the children with internal speech made fewer errors in the serial recall of non-homophonous words than those without internal speech. This was to be expected. The children with internal speech, who used a phonemic code, would be less likely to confuse word items with words which would not sound the same if pronounced than those children using some other code, such as a visual one.

When errors were considered in the serial recall of the homophonous words, no difference was found for the availability or not of internal speech. The reason given was that children with internal speech produced a fairly high rate of errors as the words were phonemically confusible. For children who did not have inter-nal speech, but who presumably used a visual code in their memory, the error rate was also fairly high, because a visual code is not effective for serial-order tasks (Paivio, 1971; Hanson, 1982).

Conrad showed, then, that hearing loss by itself had little effect on serial mem-ory for words. He also showed that the use of a phonemic code was less likely with increasing hearing loss, even though a few profoundly deaf children appeared to use it, and that the effectiveness of the memory code interacted with the material to be memorised. A next step was to match hearing-impaired children with hearing children on the basis of internal speech, and hence use of a phonemic code. These two groups should then show the same performance in memory for words. This Conrad did, but he found a difference between the two groups of children which just attained statistical significance. On considering the possible effect of differences in intelligence between the two groups, however, he concluded that their performances were similar.

The importance of Conrad's work for communication in hearing-impaired children is that their verbal communication, whether expressed through oracy or literacy, is highly likely to be impaired when they have no internal speech, rather than because of hearing loss itself. Those hearing-impaired children who, though profoundly deaf, have access to inner speech will be good communicators in ordinary society. They are able to hold in short-term store the immediately preceding spoken or written words as an aid to understanding words that follow. Conrad also argued that the use of inner speech was of major importance not only for memory, but also for speechreading, speech intelligibility and reading.

Although several studies have shown that deaf children have particular problems with memory tasks in which verbal mediation is required, or confers an advantage (Locke and Locke, 1971; Conrad, 1972a, c, 1979; Wallace and Corballis, 1973), deaf children recall as well as or perhaps better than hearing children in tasks that involve motor or visual mediation (O'Connor and Hermelin, 1976; Siple et al., 1977). The likely explanation is that deaf and hearing children use different kinds of coding. Hearing children use a speech-like code, though young hearing children may use a visual rather than a phonemic code, as shown by their higher visual than phonemic confusions in recall tasks (Campbell and Wright; 1990). Deaf children generally seem to use a visual or spatial code. Nevertheless, some can use a speech code, and Campbell and Wright (1990) have argued that orally educated prelingually profoundly deaf children may use speech-based codes in specific situations, such as naming pictures in a serial-recall task, as well as using visual or meaning-based codes in other contexts. The next question is: how is the material to be memorised put into any given code?

Memory encoding

The usual encoding mechanism suggested is that of rehearsal, the recounting or repetition of the material as it is held in short-term memory, before it is transferred into longer-term mental storage. For hearing individuals, the memory span appears to be closely related to the internal speech rate (Standing and Curtis, 1989), implying that memory span is related to the maximum rate of rehearsal. When asked to recall items in serial order, the child aged 5–6 years typically recalls correctly fewer items than older children. Yet the younger child can improve recall performance if instructed in how to rehearse (Kingsley and Hagen, 1969; Bebko, 1979), showing that the child perceives the stimuli and can label them, but does not usually rehearse them.

Several reports have described the use of rehearsal in recall tasks by deaf children. The general finding has been that the type of rehearsal is related to the preferred method of communication. Orally well educated students tend to use verbal rehearsal, students used to the Rochester Method employ fingerspelling, and signed rehearsal is used by students in sign language and TC programmes (Beck et al., 1977; Shand, 1982; Bonvillian, 1983; Morariu and Bruning, 1984; Krakow and Hanson, 1985; Shimizu and Inoue, 1988). However, Krakow and Hanson (1985) observed that deaf signers who were college students, and deaf graduates, used a sign-based code to recall ASL signs, but not to recall English words. Hence well educated deaf signers may not translate into sign, their primary language, when the material to be recalled is in printed English.

Although deaf children encode in the mode of their familiar modality of communication, there is evidence of flexibility to use other modes, depending on experience. In a study of 58 subjects comprising six groups with different hearing levels and linguistic experience, Hamilton and Holzman (1989) showed that individuals can encode flexibly in short-term memory tasks, with the code selected being biased by the properties of the incoming stimulus: oral, manual or both modalities. Subjects with both speech and sign experience recalled simultaneous oral and manual expressions more readily than expressions presented manually or orally alone, suggesting enhanced encoding as a result of linguistic experience. The total linguistic experience affected recall accuracy rather than the selection of the code.

The problems of children with rehearsal are due to failure to make use of rehearsal, rather than in not having rehearsal available. Bebko (1984) reported findings which cast light on rehearsal strategies in severely to profoundly congenitally deaf children aged 5–15 years. Twenty-nine of these children were educated orally and 34 were educated by TC. Following the presentation of various colour stimuli there was a 15-second delay. This delay interval was either unfilled, allowing spontaneous rehearsal, or the children were induced to rehearse by demonstration, or were prevented from rehearsal by counting digits. As expected, the orally educated children tended to rehearse verbally, while those educated by TC rehearsed in sign. Both types of spontaneous rehearsal seemed to be equally effective. However, although the serial position patterns in spontaneous rehearsal (first/mid/last) were similar to those of hearing children, they were delayed in performance level by several years for both orally and TC-educated children, a delay attributed to impaired linguistic and educational experience (compare Ivimey, 1977b, c). When rehearsal was prevented or induced, the deaf recalled as well as, or better than, the hearing children. Thus the memory and rehearsal spans of the deaf children were at least as good as those of the hearing children. The difference was that the hearing children used spontaneous rehearsal effectively whereas the deaf children tended not to use the opportunity for spontaneous rehearsal to good effect. The deaf children did not have difficulty with the content, or differences in memory span per se, but their strategy for remembering was poor. This outcome is reminiscent of the writing study of Webster (1986, and Chapter 6), which indicated that the poor writing skills of hearing-impaired children were due to lack of regression, or looking back at what they had just written – another kind of strategy problem.

Bebko and McKinnon (1990) extended this work by investigating whether the language history of deaf children was related to age delay in the use of spontaneous rehearsal. Forty-one prelingually severely to profoundly deaf children aged 5–15 years and educated in a TC programme were compared with 45 hearing children aged 5–8 years in a memory-for-colours task requiring serial recall. Their language experience was defined as chronological age both for hearing children and for signing deaf children born to deaf signing parents, and as years of training in their dominant communication mode for the remaining deaf children. As with Bebko (1984), a lag of several years was found in the emergence of spontaneous rehearsal. Discriminant function analysis showed that language experience was a very good explanation of the relation between age and use of rehearsal. In other words, the use of rehearsal in serial-order recall was strongly associated with years of experience in the use of language, whether verbal, signed or mixed. Experience in the use of language provided both hearing and deaf children with an effective medium for rehearsal. The deaf children born to hearing parents took longer to make use of such a strategy because of their delayed language ability.

A similar explanation can be given for the results of earlier studies of recall in deaf subjects. For example, Koh et al. (1971) reported on the free recall of lists of words by prelingually deaf and hearing adolescents aged 13–14 years and young adults aged 18–20 years. Two types of word lists were used. The first type was mixed, for which the words were chosen at random. The second type was organised in semantic categories. Although the free recall of the hearing subjects was superior to that of the deaf, the older deaf subjects performed almost as well as the older hearing subjects, suggesting that, by 18–20 years, increased language experience permitted the use of more effective rehearsal strategies in memory. The implication is that the material to be memorised should be meaningful in terms of its potential for integration with the subjects' cognitive schemata, and should suit their long-term memory and linguistic rule-generating skills. This maxim finds support from observations (Mills and Weldon, 1983) that hearing adults who are learning sign as a second language, recall signs more readily if the signs are grouped by semantic category rather than by cheremic category. Such sign-naïve people possess a schema for semantic categorisation, but not for cheremically grouped signs (Fuller and Wilbur, 1987).

Temporal processing

Hearing has been described as the 'time sense' (Fraisse, 1964). Hearing people can detect up to 1000 interruptions per second in a white-noise signal, but only 60 flashes of bright light per second (Miller and Taylor, 1948). Beyond the sensory level, O'Connor and Hermelin (1986) have suggested that successive judgements of time depend mainly on hearing. When hearing individuals had to perform a task in which practice with auditory verbal stimuli preceded practice with a visual representation of the stimuli, they tended to repeat the auditory pattern subvocally, to improve their timing for the visual stimuli.

Earlier studies of temporal processing by prelingually deaf people suggest that they have problems with temporal order, although the findings are not very clear (Blair, 1957; Conrad, 1979; Bross and Sauerwein, 1980; Hanson, 1982). Whether or not hearing-impaired individuals have problems with temporal processing is important. In order to communicate in speech, for example, sensitivity to temporal aspects of the speech signal matters in perceiving speech sounds continuously or categorically (Liberman et al., 1967) as part of the speech code. Temporal differences are also related to cortical processing of ASL signs (Poizner et al., 1979), though temporal contrasts are more important to communication by speech than by sign (Poizner and Tallal, 1987). Indeed, the temporal order of signs is relatively less important than the order of words in verbal English, as is the case in all inflected languages.

Short-term auditory deprivation studies with hearing individuals have shown enhanced visual temporal resolution for rapidly flashing visual stimulus (critical flicker fusion frequency) thresholds (Bross et al., 1980). Hence we might suppose that longer-term auditory deprivation in the form of congenital severe to profound deafness would produce enhanced visual temporal abilities, provided that there were no visual or central visual problems. Poizner and Tallal (1987) investigated this possibility by comparing critical flicker frequency thresholds in congenitally deaf adult signers and hearing subjects. No significant differences were found, in this and related experiments. Deaf signers, then, appear to have the same sensitivity to rapid visual changes as hearing people. Further, long-term auditory deprivation, in the form of deafness since birth, does not seem to affect visual temporal processing. In other experiments on perception and memory for rapidly changing non-linguistic visual forms there was likewise no difference between deaf and hearing subjects. However, Ronnberg et al. (1989), working with mildly to moderately adult deaf subjects, found a relationship between the speed parameters of visual-evoked brain potentials and performance speed on a long-term memory non-semantic letter-matching task. They also found a correlation between performance in a complex short-term memory test and neural speed.

The results of both studies seem to be associated with visual processing speed, and suggest some relationship between hearing loss and temporal processing. It is difficult, nevertheless, to relate them. We have to conclude that this more recent work leaves the area little clearer than the outcomes of the earlier reports mentioned above.

Since hearing is the 'time sense', at another level we may expect hearing-impaired people to experience difficulties with rhythm, which depends on timing and intensity. Levine (1986), for example, suggested that congenitally hearing-impaired people will have problems in coordinating inputs from sensory pathways. Studies of rhythm production and perception in hearing-impaired children are not numerous and their implications are not very clear. One of the earlier papers was presented by Swaiko (1974) on the use of rhythm in deaf education. Asp (1984), Guberina and Asp (1981) and Rosen et al. (1981) reported on the use of methods that may aid the perception and production of the suprasegmental components of speech, which have important rhythmic properties (Darrow, 1984).

In one of the better controlled experiments, a rhythmicity-testing protocol was developed by Liemohn et al. (1990) to assess whether rhythmic performance in tapping could be improved with training and whether the stimulus modality, visual versus tactile, affected performance. The subjects, 46 children aged 11–14 years with moderate to profound hearing losses, were instructed to tap with their hands in time to various stimuli. In a pre-test an experimental group of 23 of the 46 children were trained in a variety of rhythmic activities, including locomotor tasks, manipulative tasks, dance, and hopping routines, with accompanying rhythmic stimuli such as drum beats, strobe lights, etc. A control group, consisting of the other 23 children, participated in usual physical education routines, without rhythmic stimuli. Post-test tapping in time with the original visual and tactile stimuli was undertaken after the training or control activities, when the quality of rhythmic tapping was found to be related to stimulus modality. The tactile stimulus was judged more accurately than the visual stimulus by both experimental and control groups, indicating that modality-specific encoding was in use. The effects of the training were less conclusive, though training appeared to suggest an improvement in rhythmic tapping.

To summarise, it is generally unclear whether deaf children use different temporal processing from hearing children. Given the importance of the area for the development of communication, there is obviously a need for more research.

Semantic factors and cognition

Long-term memory for the way in which the world is organised and operates has an important bearing on the considerations of semantics and is perceived as increasingly important for the development and use of communication skills (Rodda and Grove, 1987). We have seen that hearing-impaired children are more likely to take note of the spatial proximity and semantic associations of words in reading and writing tasks than hearing children, whose reading and writing take account more readily of syntax and conventional phonology and orthography (Hanson et al., 1983). It seems, then, that the knowledge of the world should help their literacy by developing and reinforcing their semantic associations.

Early studies of the development of semantics in hearing-impaired children often used the word-association approach, in which children are asked to produce words which they believe are associated in meaning with a given word. Such work showed that hearing-impaired children produced more associations of a visual kind, and produced a smaller number of associated words than hearing children (Bonvillian et al., 1973). Also hearing-impaired children were less able than hearing children to match the syntactical form of the stimulus word. This evidence confirms that hearing-impaired children have a relatively weak world knowledge, as shown by fewer word associations, and grammar as demonstrated in a lesser ability to match for syntax.

The semantic differential technique has also been used to assess semantic structures in hearing-impaired children and their knowledge of the world. Green (1974) and Green and Shepherd (1975) used the semantic differential to describe the semantic structure of 33 severely to profoundly deaf subjects aged 9–17 years.

They used a combination of scaling and association methods to present several pairs of antonymous adjectives like 'good–bad', separated on a 7-point scale. The children were given a concept, such as 'teacher', 'spider', etc., and asked to rate it on the 7-point scale. Factor analysis of the results showed the semantic system of the deaf children to contain the rather concrete Evaluation ('rich–poor') and Potency ('little–big') dimensions found with hearing children. A third dimension appeared to be related to vision and the sense of touch ('round–square'), unlike in hearing children, for whom the third dimension related to Activity ('slow–fast'). Further, the deaf children's Evaluation and Potency dimensions accounted for more of their semantic associations than found with hearing children, whose semantic structure was less restricted and contained the dimensions of Warmth ('cold–hot'), and Novelty–Reality ('new–old'), etc. Thus this study also suggested relatively limited world knowledge.

The semantic organisation of older deaf students was investigated by Tweney et al. (1975), who studied 63 deaf adolescents, aged 16–18 years, together with 63 hearing adolescents of the same age range. Subjects were presented with cards showing sound words, common nouns, and drawings corresponding to the list of noun words. They were asked to put items they did not know into a separate pile, and then to sort each of the three sets into categories of similar meaning, using as many or as few categories as they wished. Instructions were both spoken and signed. Hierarchical cluster analysis was then used to compare the semantic structures of hearing and deaf subjects. The two groups showed only minor differences for noun words and pictures. However, the deaf group did differ from the hearing subjects for sound words, for which they would have had little or no auditory experience. Even when the deaf subjects offered some category structure, it was not always semantically based. Although 'meow–bark' was clustered, so was 'whack–whine' which may have been based on similarity of lettering. The latter type of grouping was not found for noun words or pictures, suggesting that the deaf subjects used a rationale based on visual similarity when they lacked sufficient semantic reasons as a basis for categorisation.

In a second study, Tweney et al. (1975) presented stimulus words which differed in imagery but were of equal frequency of occurrence. Again, the differences between matched sets of high and low imagery words ('chair' versus 'cost') were comparable for 63 deaf and 63 hearing adolescents. The overall results of neither study supported an argument that deaf subjects are relatively more dependent on some visual mediating process than hearing subjects. The absence of an auditory mediating process such as phonological coding did not weaken the deaf subjects' performance. Tweney et al. thus argued that the subjective lexicon of deaf individuals is comparable to that of hearing people. Further, since linguistic material appeared to be organised in semantic dimensions which were independent of the receptive channel providing information to the lexicon, the central linguistic and symbolic processes of deaf individuals were seen as abstract, and not limited to concrete operations.

As indicated by Rodda and Grove (1987), this outcome contradicted the commonly held assumption that deaf individuals are relatively limited to concrete, high-imagery ways of thinking. Rodda and Grove argued that abstract verbal materials are treated in a similar way by deaf and hearing individuals when, as in the Tweney et al. study, there are no demands on syntactic skills. However, age may be an important confounding variable. There is evidence (Green and Shepherd, 1975) that younger deaf children operate semantically at a relatively concrete level, which may not persist into late adolescence. There is also evidence (Johnson et al., 1982; Liben, 1979) that, although hearing-impaired children develop networks of associations in their lexical systems, the networks are relatively weak in terms of relationships between word meanings. Further, Marschark et al. (1986) found decreasing use of lexical inventions with age.

Studies of semantics in hearing-impaired children which use such methods as closed response sets, forced choice, word associations, word sorts, picture identification and so on are open to criticism (Conway, 1990). Conway argued that these methods not only require minimal linguistic responses but preclude assessment of how the children construct word meanings and demonstrate their knowledge in definitions. He urged the use of non-restrictive methods such as open-ended questions, which would encourage the elicitation of linguistic responses to prompt search of the children's semantic systems ('Tell me about ...'; 'Tell me some more about ...'; 'What else do you know about ...?').

Conway examined the amount, type and complexity of the semantic relationships in the word meanings of two groups of prelingually profoundly deaf children differentiated by age, with a mean age of 7 years for the younger and 9 years for the older group. Employing Norlin's (1981) open-ended questions to prompt the expression of semantic relationships to ten common nouns, and using each child's preferred mode of communication, Conway found that the younger group produced significantly fewer semantic relationships than the older group. Otherwise, the performance of the two groups did not differ. However, for both groups the definitions produced were at an immature level, similar to that of younger hearing children. Studies of semantics that use non-restrictive methods can all too easily confound semantics with syntax, where the syntactic relationships provide clues to meaning (Rodda and Grove, 1987). Conway's analysis used semantic case relationships (subordinate, coordinate, purpose, attribute etc.) and does not seem to have confounded semantics with syntax in this way. Nonetheless, the situation is not clear because the more complex semantic associations may require some sophistication in syntax to express them (Watson, 1985). Clearly, more work needs to be done in this area.

Higher-level aspects

Taxonomies of levels of thinking have been devised to help analyse the processes involved in the formation and use of concepts and ideas (Bruner, 1973; Moore, 1983; Quinsland and Van Ginkel, 1990). Such taxonomies include the intellectual, knowledge, comprehension and evaluative levels among others, and may be investigated through tests of intelligence as well as purpose-designed tests.

Most earlier studies of the assessment of intelligence concluded that severely to profoundly deaf children were retarded by about 2 years or so (Pintner and Reamer, 1920). Realising the need to discount verbal reasoning abilities, Pintner and

Paterson (1923) in the USA developed a non-verbal performance scale, one of the first of its kind, involving digit/symbol substitution tests. However, here too they found a retardation in ability by some 2–3 years. A review of 22 reports by Lane (1948) narrowed the intelligence gap to less than 1 year, though a few years previously Drever and Collins (1944) using carefully devised performance tests found that the intellectual abilities of hearing-impaired children were on a par with those of hearing children. Confirmation of the latter findings was obtained by Murphy (1957) in the UK, who reported that scores for the Wechsler Performance Scales of hearing-impaired children fell within the normal range for hearing children.

Since Furth (1971), it has become generally accepted that the intellectual abilities of hearing-impaired children are of the same order as those for the hearing child, except where verbal factors have a part to play (e.g. Watson et al., 1986), though Savage et al. (1981) concluded that the data are still rather disorganised and somewhat conflicting. The reader is referred to Lewis (1968) and Quigley and Kretschmer (1982) for historical reviews.

The abilities of hearing-impaired children in the learning and use of various concepts were described by Furth (1961, 1963, 1964b). In a task for sameness, his subjects had to choose stimuli with defined properties; in a symmetry task they had to pick a stimulus showing symmetry; and in an opposition task subjects chose the opposite size stimulus to the one identified. The deaf subjects attained similar scores to hearing children on the sameness and symmetry tasks and did only slightly less well on the opposition task possibly because of weak verbal reasoning. In a pictorial choice task, deaf children were required to identify a 'part–whole' concept concealed in a confusing visual ground. Again, no differences were found between deaf and hearing children, but age and intelligence did have significant effects.

Since severe to profound hearing loss generally leads to altered cognitive function, and probably to altered perceptual function, it is likely to affect motor function in some way, especially in perceptual–motor tasks. Accordingly, it is of interest to remark that Wiegersma and Van der Velde (1983) observed lower performance in both general dynamic movement and visual–motor coordination in young deaf as compared with hearing children. Savage et al. (1981) specifically asked if deafness leads to altered perceptual organisation and hence influences aspects of motor function. They used the Minnesota Percepto-Diagnostic Test (MPDT), in which the child has to reproduce figures shown on stimulus cards, and the Digit/Symbol and Block Design Subtests from the Wechsler scales as tests of perceptual–motor function, with a sample of 55 deaf children aged 8–13 years. No significant difference was found for the MPDT between deaf and hearing children when the data were corrected for age and gender. On the Wechsler coding (digit/symbol) measure, however, deaf and hearing children differed significantly. Further, the poor and especially the very poor readers in the deaf group obtained significantly lower coding level scores than the better deaf readers. The deaf and hearing groups also differed significantly on the Block Design test. It appeared then that deafness can affect performance on perceptual–motor tasks, and that the relationship is connected with verbal ability. A similar conclusion was reached by Bolton (1971) in a factor analytic study of the communication skills and non-verbal abilities of deaf individuals. It seems likely that the use of inner speech is associated with verbal ability in some kinds of perceptual–motor tasks.

It is of interest to learn if there are differences between hearing and hearing-impaired children in higher-level cognitive processes which do not involve linguistic, and especially syntactic, mediation. Although reports in the area are few, they all point to the same conclusion. Thus, Rittenhouse et al. (1981) found that hearing loss and poor linguistic ability do not directly affect tasks involving the understanding of metaphor or tasks involving the principles of conservation. Such tasks can be undertaken using cognition alone, and in general deaf children perform them at the same level as hearing children of the same age. Any slight retardation of performance that has been noted can be ascribed to difficulties in understanding the instructions or to lesser experience of the world in general. Also, weak linguistic ability need not have much effect on the understanding of idiom, which is largely a cognitive activity. The comprehension of idioms seems to be based on memory for literal and figurative meanings in a way similar to memory for single words and single word meanings (Fruchter et al., 1984). Thus although hearing-impaired students may have difficulty in understanding idioms, they have the cognitive structures needed to understand them and can be trained to discriminate among them (Fruchter et al., 1984; Israelite et al., 1986).

The material reviewed above suggests that, provided care is taken in recognising the effects of any confounding linguistic variables, the higher-level cognitive skills of deaf children are roughly equal to those of hearing children. Although prelingually deaf children do not seem to use the same coding in their cognitive processing, such as inner speech, as do hearing children (Conrad and Rush, 1965; Conrad, 1979), this is not to say that their cognitive capacity is inferior to that of hearing children. When allowance is made for the difference in experience, especially linguistic experience, of deaf children, their cognitive performance is close to that of children who hear (Conrad, 1979). Accordingly, in a review of several papers on cognitive strategies and processes, Wolff (1985) remarked that apparent cognitive deficits in deaf subjects were generally attributable to linguistic competencies and to secondary handicaps. When such variables were taken into consideration the papers reviewed showed, on the whole, a resounding lack of difference between hearing and deaf individuals.

Such experiential differences may partly explain reports of stimulus over-selectivity in deaf children who have especially poor communicative competence, where they have not learned to focus on the relevant cues from a given complex stimulus and to ignore the irrelevant ones (Fairbank et al., 1986). Hence the specific cognitive problems experienced by some deaf children are a manifestation of a more general weakness in knowledge of the world.

Some Cognitive Aspects of Sign

Some authors (e.g. Morariu and Bruning, 1984) have commented that deaf individuals have a visual orientation, regardless of any training in sign, that leads them to develop a sign-based system of coding which predisposes them to react to sign as a familiar language. Such a position implies that deaf signers should develop a high competency in sign. Accordingly, it is to be expected that the communication ability of deaf signing children is similar to that of their hearing peers when signed performance is weighted equally with verbal performance (Arnold and Walter, 1979; Christensen, 1988).

Memory coding in deaf signers

Although the code used by many deaf children in short-term memory is spatial or visual (O'Connor and Hermelin, 1973), it may be based on fingerspelling (Hoemann, 1978a) or on signs (Bellugi et al., 1975; Shand, 1982; Bonvillian, 1983; Hamilton, 1985; Bonvillian et al., 1987). Coding by sign implies that concepts are represented by coding through the cheremes or the shape of the hand, hand position and movement, and so on. Thus, when items in a list of words have signed forms which are similar to one another we may expect them to be confused in a memory task (Poizner et al., 1981), because the coding process uses signed forms in a way analogous to the phonological coding used by hearing individuals.

We would expect to find a number of experiments that illustrate the use of a visual code in short-term memory for signs, analogous to the use of phonological coding for words, and such is the case. Bellugi et al. (1975), for instance, instructed their deaf subjects to write their responses in a serial-recall-for-signs task. Serial position effects, such as primacy and recency phenomena, were demonstrated in a similar form to those found in recall of lists of words by hearing subjects. Substitution errors occurred for items with confusable signs. The writing of English glosses for the signs may be thought to have put the deaf subjects at a disadvantage, although Klima and Bellugi (1979) argued convincingly that such was not the case.

Such issues were avoided by Kyle (1981), who both presented stimuli and permitted responses in sign or in words. Kyle described serial-recall tasks for deaf and hearing bilinguals, equally fluent in sign and spoken English. The bilingual subjects produced results similar to those obtained with English speakers, showing effects for phonological coding, such as homophone versus non-homophone differences, and verbal rehearsal superior to silent rehearsal. The deaf subjects, who preferred to recall in words, showed no overt rehearsal effect for words. Using silent serial recall of similar-sounding words, or signs with the same handshape, as a baseline for comparing the effects of overt rehearsal, Kyle found that both bilingual and deaf subjects showed similar recall effects when responding in sign, but when recalling in words, the bilingual group showed a marked advantage, due to facilitation by overt rehearsal of words. Hence effects due to 'signing aloud', the equivalent of verbal rehearsal by hearing people, seems relatively weak for deaf signers – at first thought a rather surprising result. However, this result is not so surprising when we remember that sign coding in serial recall is not found reliably in deaf people (Hanson, 1982), possibly because sign language is less order-bound than verbal language, and that hearing-impaired children can be averse to rehearsing in sign unless instructed to do so (Manion and Butcher, 1986).

If discrete coding in a given modality is employed in short-term memory, it should be possible to demonstrate it by switching the material within a memory task from one mode to another, and seeking a change in behaviour. Hoemann (1978b) used this technique in modality-switching studies with English and manual alphabets, or English words and ASL signs. Deaf students experienced in ASL and written English, and hearing adults with ASL experience, were presented with this material in short-term memory tasks. These tasks contained a number of stimulus trials, where proactive interference would build up quickly on repeated trials. On the last trial, the stimuli were switched from one modality to the other. If the modalities operated with different memory stores, then bilingual subjects who were switched to the second mode for the final trial should show increased recall scores because of release from proactive interference. Hoemann described three experiments showing just such an effect. A further study was reported by Hoemann and Koenig (1990) on hearing students beginning instruction in ASL, with 3–5 weeks' experience. The students were given a task in which proactive interference would increase rapidly with repeated trials. On their last trial, the stimuli were switched from manual alphabet to English alphabet, or vice versa. The students in the manual-to-English alphabet switch showed release from proactive interference, but those in the English-to-manual alphabet did not. Hoemann and Koenig were at a loss to explain this asymmetrical result. However, they concluded that the characters of the manual and English alphabets were coded separately in different memory stores, even with hearing people who were just beginning to learn ASL as a second language.

We saw that studies of visual short-term memory in deaf signers produced outcomes analogous to those of verbal short-term memory in hearing subjects. The results showed that the cognitive processes were similar when modality differences were taken into account. But the reader is cautioned that it is not easy to demonstrate this situation convincingly, as a study by Spencer et al. (1989) has shown.

Spencer et al. studied short-term memory in severely to profoundly prelingually deaf adolescents with lists of written words presented visually for 10 s. Their 17 deaf and 10 hearing students were asked to recall the words after a 10 s distraction task of adding pairs of digits. The different word lists were devised as signable with a single sign, with compound or a combination of signs, or with fingerspelling for unsignable words. Hearing students recalled significantly more words than the deaf in each of these categories. Both deaf and hearing students recalled significantly more single signable words than those in the compound/combination or unsignable (fingerspelling) categories. Differences between the latter two categories were not significant. The results showing that the hearing subjects recalled more written words than the deaf subjects were congruent with the results of previous studies, which showed that deaf individuals can recall words at the same performance level as hearing individuals when the words are signed for them rather than written (Poizner et al., 1981; Bonvillian, 1983).

Spencer et al. had hypothesised that the errors made by their hearing subjects would show use of a phonological code, and the errors of the deaf subjects would reflect a sign code, but such effects were not observed, perhaps because the error rates were low and the subjects were unwilling to guess when unsure of the correct item, though instructed to do so. This study is of particular interest in that the expected outcome was not attained, and for the methodological issues the authors raised. As they noted, many studies in this area have not used a hearing control group. Also, it is necessary to ensure that the subjects understand the task by writing, speaking or signing the instructions to them as needed, that the material is equally familiar to experimental and control groups, and that care is taken with imagery value and word-frequency effects, because the more frequently used words tend to have a single sign.

Thinking, reasoning and semantics in sign

Thinking and reasoning concern manipulations of the meanings of terms, and involve the area of semantics, where thinking, reasoning and language come together in a complex way. Furth (1966a) was one of the first to observe that the impoverished experience of deaf children was likely to show deficiencies in these areas. However, Green and Shepherd (1975, see above) found that deaf children had many similar semantic concepts to those found in hearing children, though they had an extra factor involving touch and vision, and appeared weak in structures for abstract meaning.

Developmental trends

Developmental trends in the use of sign to communicate reasoning and use of meaning in young hearing-impaired children are of special interest, since they are important for the child's education and achievement as well as everyday communication. The literature is slim in this area, but one useful report is that by Ellenberger and Steyaert (1978), who studied representation of action in a single deaf child between the ages of 3;7 and 5;11 years. In this child's learning of ASL as a first language, they found a developmental trend in the sequence: decrease in the use of gesture, pantomime or citation forms as action signs increased; gradual increase in using abstract signs while iconic re-enactments of events decreased; change from the function of actor to that of narrator in storytelling; developing ability to structure the space in which action signs moved; and increasing ability in using signs about agents in the activities described. Overall the child showed a developmental progression. Early on, the child used citation forms which were not usually modified spatially. Later, adult-like spatial structures of signs were used, illustrating a relatively advanced mastery of cognitive skills associated with semantic aspects of spatial relations.

Complex semantic representation

The notably iconic appearance of sign suggests to the unsophisticated observer that sign language has difficulty in conveying complex meanings. In fact, sign uses inflections and combinations of signs to do a remarkably good job. Bellugi (1980) explained how signs may be used to express complex semantic notions for various concepts. She also argued that there were mechanisms in ASL, used on a daily basis in conversation, which could expand the lexicon to allow for new concepts and ideas, including signed neologisms to depict advances in modern technology, such as 'genetic engineering' and 'microwave oven'. Thus the single sign glossed as LOOK could be varied to convey 'reminisce', 'sight-seeing', 'watch', 'look forward to', 'prophesy', 'look around aimlessly', 'stare', 'gaze at', and so on. The modifications or inflections to produce these various meanings involved spatiotemporal features overlaid on the basic sign. ASL processes of an inflexional kind included: Referential Indexing in the use of verbs to indicate the main actors in a sentence; Reciprocity shown by mutual action or mutual relation; Grammatical Number with verbal inflections for different plurals – dual, triple, or multiple; Distributional Aspect with verbal inflections signifying indivisible or separate action, actions occurring at certain points of time, order of occurrence of action, and relation of actions to the participants; Exhaustive Inflection shown by actions distributed to individuals in a group; Allocative Determinate Inflection in the actions distributed to individuals at specific points in time; and Allocative Indeterminate Inflection with actions distributed to unspecified individuals over time. ASL verb forms could also be inflected to convey Temporal Aspect or Temporal Focus, conveying a specific point in time or enduring activity, and Manner and Degree as in changing basic verbs to nouns or adjectives, or adjectives to nouns or verbs, etc. Further complex notions could be conveyed by the compounding of signs (GOOD + ENOUGH = JUST GOOD ENOUGH, with a different meaning from GOOD ENOUGH). Other inflections giving semantic differences have been illustrated by Klima and Bellugi (1979).

Factors associated with thinking and reasoning

Studies of thinking and reasoning among deaf users of sign language have not been numerous if we omit consideration of tests of intelligence used to determine IQ. Montgomery (1968) and Bolton (1971) used a range of tests to investigate the factors underlying communication and reasoning in deaf subjects as deaf schoolleavers and rehabilitation clients, respectively. Bolton showed that both studies identified four main factors: non-verbal reasoning, oral communication, manual communication, and psychomotor ability. Arnold and Walter (1979) conducted a similar investigation on 25 congenitally profoundly deaf students with a mean age of 19 years, but included hearing controls who could sign, hypothesising that verbal reasoning would distinguish deaf and hearing signers the most. They thought, secondly, that the performance of deaf adults on non-verbal reasoning and perceptual speed tests would be similar to that of hearing people. The first hypothesis was confirmed. The deaf group had the greatest difficulty on a test of verbal reasoning. No significant difference was found for performance on tests of oral reception and manual reception, which was consistent with the second hypothesis.

Storytelling

There has been a tendency to consider sign language from a 'bottom-up' viewpoint, involving the identification of sign units followed by a consideration of how they are used (Kyle, 1983a). On the other hand, and from the psychological viewpoint, grammar, for instance, is organised through higher control processes. Syntax and propositional structures are thus controlled by higher-level semantic processing. Some kind of centrally mediated linguistic plan decides how we express our thoughts and, indeed, how we understand the language we use. Typically, storytelling has been used to illustrate the processes involved. Using the storytelling technique, Kyle (1983a) concluded that deaf and hearing individuals show differences in their accounts of a story, with deaf storytellers signing a richness in their depiction of events in a way not found in English, and with deaf storytellers tending to recall events rather than to make inferences as English speakers tend to do. Such differences do not occur necessarily because of different perceptions of the world. English speakers tend to report the events of a story in relation to the overall schema in their mind's eye, whereas deaf signers produce a version which is more directly related to the events in the story. Sign language, and presumably the thinking associated with its use, tends to be more literal in its account of events, is more imaginal in its presentation, and deviates less from the sequence of events than standard English. Sign language consequently makes use of 'mime', in re-enacting events, rather than in making great use of referential communication. In Kyle's view, sign is imaginal and uses an event structure, whereas English speech is referential and tends to modify the propositional arrangements, namely, the small units that convey items of meaning. The tendency of deaf signers to use referential devices less often than hearing individuals to communicate their meaning may explain their lower performance level in referential communication tasks (Hoemann, 1972).

The extent of use of literal presentation in sign language, however, is not clear. Everhart and Marschark (1988) compared the linguistic flexibility of prelingually, mostly severely to profoundly, deaf and hearing children from 8 to 15 years of age, in stories written and signed by the deaf, and written and spoken by the hearing children. They found for the latter group, that both written and spoken stories contained similar numbers of non-literal constructions, including figurative language, gesture and pantomime, whereas the deaf children produced significantly more non-literal constructions in their signed than in their written stories. Further, the deaf children used more non-literal constructions in their signed stories than did the hearing children in their spoken stories. The confusion may have arisen because Everhart and Marschark did not distinguish between literal ways of signing events and imaginal sign styles, such as the use of mime, for such literal presentations.

As an example of what may be observed, recall of a short silent comedy film by deaf, hearing and bilingual subjects was investigated by Kyle (1983b). Having watched the film, subjects were asked to recall the story for a deaf or hearing person who had not seen the film. After a 1-hour interval, they were asked to retell the story again. The story contained 15 main visual events which were related in time and cause. Both the deaf and hearing subjects recalled the main events equally well, but the hearing subjects kept less to the temporal sequence of the events after the time interval than the deaf subjects. The bilingual viewers' performance was in between those of the deaf and hearing subjects. Kyle (1983b) argued that the system of tenses and conditional structures in English makes it easy to refer to events out of sequence. Perhaps it was easier to present the events out of sequence to simplify the story. If so, the deaf subjects used this device less often, even though BSL, as an inflected sign language, permits a flexible approach to the construction and use of propositions, which in English most commonly occur as clauses (Kyle and Woll, 1985).

Cognitive development and signing/non-signing parentage

Although it has turned out to be a controversial topic, it has often been supposed (Brasel and Quigley, 1977; Sisco and Anderson, 1980; Zwiebel, 1987) that deaf children of deaf parents attain higher levels of linguistic, academic, communication and cognitive development than deaf children of hearing parents, because of early and continuing exposure to language through manual communication. In particular, native deaf signers are thought to present English more effectively than deaf individuals born to hearing parents, and to be more adept at code switching (Hoffmeister and Moores, 1987). One reason for such beliefs is the greater acceptance of the child's deafness by deaf parents. Noting that deaf children of deaf parents scored higher on the WISC-R (adapted for deaf children) than deaf children of hearing parents, and higher than hearing children of deaf parents, Sisco and Anderson (1980) concluded that deaf parents may be particularly suited to provide the kind of care appropriate for intellectual growth in deaf children. However, Conrad and Weiskrantz (1981), who found no superiority in the cognitive performance of deaf children of deaf parents in a study carefully devised to allow for environmental differences between deaf and hearing children, concluded that earlier investigations were lacking in their methodology. This outcome led Kyle and Woll (1985) to regard as a myth the idea that deaf children who learn sign at an early age have a cognitive advantage, even over hearing children.

However, more recent work has re-opened the issue. Zwiebel (1987) tested the hypothesis of Kusche et al. (1983) that children who were deaf for genetic reasons would show superior performance on cognitive tests, irrespective of whether their parents were deaf or hearing. He investigated 122 deaf boys and 121 deaf girls aged 6–14 years, attending regular and special educational programmes in Israel. Most (80.5%) were deaf from birth and 94.6% were deaf by 2 years of age. The great majority (85%) had a hearing loss of 70 dB or more. The children were divided into three groups: a group with deaf parents and deaf siblings ($n = 23$); a group with hearing parents and deaf siblings ($n = 76$); and a group with hearing parents and hearing siblings ($n = 144$). The groups were similar on a range of demographic and hearing-loss variables, except that the children with hearing parents and deaf siblings contained more girls and had a lower mean socioeconomic status, more children of Asian and African background, more cases of acquired hearing loss, and a greater use of hearing aids. Zwiebel found a continuum in Israeli Sign Language, the manual communication system used at home, ranging from good with deaf parents and deaf siblings to partial with hearing parents and deaf siblings, to a lack of mastery with hearing parents and hearing siblings. Findings from tests of cognition showed that the children exposed to signing gained cognitively from the exposure. Children with deaf parents and deaf siblings achieved a higher cognitive performance level than the deaf children not exposed to signing, and indeed achieved a level equivalent to that of hearing children. Comparison of the other two groups suggested that even moderate exposure to sign was of benefit in building intellectual performance.

The children with deaf parents and deaf siblings were considered to have hearing losses due to genetic factors, and used sign language. The children with hearing parents and deaf siblings had hearing losses with a genetic component and a mixed communication environment, with an emphasis towards oral communication. The children with hearing parents and hearing siblings had no overt genetic element and an oral home environment. The results of tests showed that the children using sign language scored at a higher intellectual level than those children not using sign language, and that the genetic background made no difference. Hence the hypothesis of Kusche et al. (1983) was not supported. However, the conclusions are not completely convincing, as the necessary comparison group of deaf children who used sign language, but had no genetic basis for their hearing loss – that is, signing deaf children born to hearing parents – was not available. It may also be argued that the lower scores in tests of intellectual ability of the children with hearing parents and deaf siblings could have been due to their lower socioeconomic status, rather than the genetic component, as Zwiebel appreciated, although he thought that the pattern of test performance argued against this view.

This study shows that the intellectual development of deaf children with deaf parents and siblings, and consequently using sign language, is equal to that of hearing children under certain conditions, contrary to Conrad and Weiskrantz (1981). Zwiebel concluded that the effect of early exposure to sign language on the cognitive development of deaf children is a positive one. Weisel (1988) has also shown, in a well designed investigation, that deaf children of deaf parents attained a higher level of reading comprehension, emotional adjustment and motivation for communication than deaf children of hearing parents.

Age at exposure to sign

The age at which a deaf child is exposed to sign language affects subsequent semantic processing. Mayberry and Fischer (1989) found that native and non-native sign language acquisition showed different effects on sign language processing. Their subjects were all congenitally deaf and used sign language for communication, but acquired it at different ages ranging from birth to 18 years of age. In a first study, deaf signers simultaneously watched and reproduced sign language stories presented in ASL and Pidgin Sign English, in good and poor seeing conditions. In a second study, deaf signers recalled and shadowed grammatical and ungrammatical ASL sentences. The native signers were more accurate in their tasks, understood better, and when they made lexical changes, they changed signs related to sign meaning independent of the phonological aspects of the stimulus item. Conversely, the non-native signers tended to make changes of sign related to the phonological characteristics of the stimulus independent of the lexical and sentential meaning. Semantic lexical changes were positively correlated, and phonological lexical changes were negatively correlated, with processing accuracy and understanding. This result occurred across sign dialect, seeing conditions and processing tasks. Thus the native signers processed lexical material automatically, allowing them to attend to lexical meaning and sentential meaning. The non-native signers tended to pay more attention to the identification of phonological aspects, so that they were less well able to attend to lexical meaning.

Concluding comments

We indicated earlier that recent research into semantic processes and the thinking and reasoning of deaf signers has been relatively sparse. What has become clear, however, is that our knowledge and understanding of this area may be limited, unless we concede that sign language may be quite unlike standard English, as suggested from a 'top-down' rather than a 'bottom-up' approach. Also, as with study of any natural language, we need to seek an explanation of sign language processing which can take account of discourse and reasoning. Such an explanation will need to offer a description of the relations, within and between 'sentences', which are used by the signer, and the processes by which they are derived. So, research in this area needs to study the kinds of representation which are used for discourse and reasoning. Such work would involve a study of how assumptions relate to the network of propositions in reasoning, and how attention, interpretation and inferencing are brought to bear. This field is being actively researched in verbal language (Myers et al., 1986) and hence leads are available to guide similar work in sign.

General Conclusion on Hearing Impairment and Cognition

Research into cognition and hearing impairment is both challenging and exciting. At the same time it must be agreed that some of the findings are confusing. There is little by way of consistent theoretical direction, apart perhaps from elaborations on the work of Piaget. The research methodologies also are disparate, making it difficult to compare results. There is thus a compelling need to produce clear theoretical directions to explain the salient issues concerned with cognitive processes and strategies in deaf individuals (Wolk and Schildroth, 1984) and for clear and comprehensive descriptions of subjects and research methods, to allow for closer comparison of results.

Metaprocesses

We have chosen to consider metaprocesses in this chapter on cognition as they require the application of higher-level cognitive processes, such as thinking, reflection, comparison and comprehension.

The metaprocesses (metacognition, metalinguistics, etc.) derive from work in cognitive psychology in the 1970s (Cazden, 1976; Flavell and Wellman, 1977; Brown, 1978). The field now has the status of a recognised field of inquiry in its own right, although reference to metaprocesses, in other terms, can be found in the literature going way back into the past. 'Meta' is used in the general sense of 'beyond' or 'transcending'. Thus 'metalinguistics' implies the relation between linguistics and other features of behaviour. More specifically metaprocesses, reflecting their place in cognitive psychology, have come to be associated with awareness and control in the sense of self-regulation. In reading a text in order to learn from it, for example, the effective reader needs to be aware of the logical structure of the text (Brown and Smiley, 1978), and of such possible shortcomings as ambiguities and irregular use of grammar or semantics (Harris et al., 1981).

Tunmer and Bowey (1984) have described four stages of metalinguistic awareness, thought to be particularly important in learning to read: awareness of words, phonology, pragmatics, and form. Awareness at the word level associates the spoken with the written word. Phonological awareness not only involves knowledge of phonological elements, but the ability to segment a word into its phonological parts, and the synthesis of the parts into a word. Pragmatic awareness relates to knowledge of the relationships within linguistics, between linguistics and context, and attention to a listener's knowledge. Form awareness involves the ability to reflect on the internal grammar of sentences.

The development of metaprocesses is related to proficiency in learning (Armbruster et al., 1982). Generally, younger hearing children, with less developed psychological processes, are less able to understand how the several variables involved in learning affect learning outcomes, and are less able to monitor and regulate their own abilities. Younger and poorer-hearing readers, for instance, tend to lack the two important aspects of metacognition: knowledge and control. Metaprocess training can help to overcome such problems, by bringing the learning substrate, strategies for processing it, and a knowledge of themselves as learners, to children's awareness.

Hearing children aged 7–11 years show considerable understanding of listening, although age plays a part within this range (McDevitt et al., 1990). McDevitt found that older children depended less on behavioural factors and more on comprehension in their definitions of good listening. Children felt that appropriate listening tactics depended on the situation. When confused by mothers' speech they thought it best to seek clarification directly by asking questions, but when confused by teachers, they thought that they should listen more carefully. Young hearing children tended to blame the listener if that listener could not identify an object described by a speaker, even when the description was inadequate or ambiguous (Robinson, 1981). They only ascribed some responsibility to the speaker when the nature of the problem was made explicit.

Metaprocesses and the hearing-impaired child

Hearing-impaired children frequently have problems in suiting the style of their messages to the needs of the listener, even in adolescence, resulting in breakdown of communication (Maxwell, 1980; Murphy and Hill, 1989). Such problems of adapting their behaviour to the needs of other individuals suggest that they are egocentric and non-reflective, failing to think about the consequences of their behaviour on others (Howarth and Wood, 1977). Research is needed in the metaprocesses of hearing-impaired children, so that the knowledge so acquired can be used to train them to gain insights into how they relate to others and how they themselves can help to shape their communication. We remarked earlier that research in the pragmatics of communication by hearing-impaired children leaves much to be desired. We also saw that research in the deployment of social skills by hearing-impaired children is sparse. There is also little research on hearing-impaired children's metaprocesses.

Quigley et al. (1976b) were among the first to conduct research in the area for judgements of grammaticality. Kretschmer (1982) referred to a role for metaprocesses in a discussion of decoding in reading readiness by hearing-impaired children, commenting that many teachers find that such children have problems in mapping speech elements onto their orthography. Kretschmer saw a place for metaprocesses in reading by hearing-impaired children, ranging from what the children think reading is to the use of various study skills. He drew a parallel between developed metaprocesses and an internal locus of control, noting that hearing-impaired children, whose metaprocesses seem relatively undeveloped, show behaviour characteristic of an external locus of control, associated with a reduced self-image, lack of motivation, lack of confidence, and a feeling of being controlled by the environment.

An example of the use of a metalinguistic approach is to be found in Zorfass (1981), who studied the ability of 11 prelingually severely to profoundly deaf children, aged 4–7 years, who used Signed English, to segment Signed English sentences into words. Words which did not have signs were fingerspelt. Zorfass sought to assess the children's metalinguistic abilities in segmenting sentences into words. She grouped her subjects into four classes based on four factors: class 1, sentences or groups of words not segmented; class 2, major parts of sentences segmented; class 3, major parts of sentences and some function words segmented; and class 4, whole sentences segmented. The concept of segmentation was taught with the help of toys when, for example, the tester moved a toy along a roadway in short stages, with pauses in between, and speaking segments of a sentence while the toy was moved. This task focused the children's attention on the segmentation of the sentences. In the experimental part of the study, the children increasingly omitted words as sentence length increased from two to five words. Class 1 subjects omitted two to three words in five-word sentences, while class 4 subjects omitted either no words or one word. Subjects in classes 1, 2 and 3 omitted function words and forms of the verb 'to be', but preserved content words. Zorfass suggested that such performance was associated with telegraphic information given to them by hearing teachers, who tended to delete words other than content words when presenting the signed part of Signed English (compare Marmor and Petitto, 1979). Her hearing-impaired children also omitted inflectional morphemes (-ed, plural s, and -ing), with the proportion of omissions increasing from class 4 to class 1. Zorfass ascribed such omissions to the failure of the children to use inflectional morphemes in their speech.

This study by Zorfass was a preliminary one, and did not include controls for various factors. However, her subjects showed varying metalinguistic abilities which generally increased with age and a developmental pattern similar to that found with hearing children (Ehri, 1975).

The general literature on hearing-impaired children contains allusions to the young hearing-impaired child who can listen, but who cannot integrate that listening into everyday life. The problem seems to be that the child associates listening with listening time in class, and fails to generalise classroom listening skills to listening outside the classroom. Fisher and Schneider (1986) attributed this problem to the kind of instruction, especially segmented curricula, and argued for group teaching, to indicate to the child the place of listening in a range of social contexts. However, it is also possible that the problem is a problem of metacognition. In this case, listening is not just a process in cognition, but needs for its full use in communication an appreciation and control of its functions by the child. Fisher and Schneider's hearing-impaired children were preschoolers, too young for the full development of metaprocesses. Nevertheless, Fisher and Schneider's reference to communication clarification, formulating hypotheses, explaining cause and effect, attention and awareness, suggests strongly that weaknesses of metaprocesses are part of the explanation for the effect which they described.

Wood (1991) has taken this kind of argument much further to criticise the high control by adults of both deaf and hearing children. According to Wood, such control can result in low initiative, short utterances, and a lack of speculation, hypothesis formation and imagination, leading to a meagre linguistic diet and little space in which to develop flexibility, creativity and self-expression. He suggested that difficulties in communication were a cause of this high control, which has been observed in some teachers of deaf children. Although he did not specifically address metaprocesses, it seems clear that the effects of high control will be to reduce opportunities for reflection and speculation, and thus will retard the development of metaprocesses in deaf children.

The metalinguistics of fingerspelling was investigated by Hirsh-Pasek (1987) in a study of phonological awareness related to reading ability. Phonological awareness is prerequisite to reading because it facilitates the decoding and recoding of text, and assists the identification of words and storage in short-term memory. Hirsh-Pasek assessed the metalinguistic ability of 26 congenitally deaf children of elementary and secondary school age to segment and manipulate their fingerspelt lexica. She found that metalinguistic competence in fingerspelling, shown by the children's direction of their attention to fingerspelt words, was correlated with achievement in beginning reading, even for the children of elementary school age. Metalinguistic competence in fingerspelling was not correlated with indices of intelligence, such as skill at mathematics. Training in fingerspelling helped with word identification for the words in the children's fingerspelt lexica. Since word identification is a good predictor of reading ability, this result suggests that decoding text into fingerspelling may assist beginning readers to progress to more advanced reading comprehension. Hirsh-Pasek concluded that decoding by fingerspelling allowed children who have problems with speech analysis to develop a phonological system which maps language onto print. Grapheme-to-handshape correspondences could thus help beginning deaf readers who have problems in recognising phonemes.

The use of metalinguistics in three sign systems, Signed English, Pidgin Sign English and American Sign Language, as the primary form of communication in 20 severely to profoundly prelingually deaf children aged 5–8 years was studied by Borman et al. (1988). These children, who were educated by TC, were presented with a synonymy judgement task for which they saw pairs of videorecorded sentences. They were to decide if the sentences had the same or different meanings. This task was metalinguistic because the children had to compare two sentences and judge whether their meaning was the same, thus involving attention to content and evaluation of synonymy. No differences were found between sign systems, but overall the girls' results were better than those of the boys. The children performed only slightly above chance level on the judgement of synonymy task in all three sign systems, showing that they lacked the metalinguistic awareness for judging synonymy of pairs of sentences. However, more sentence pairs with different meanings were processed correctly than synonymous sentence pairs, suggesting that gross differences could be detected before similarities could be recognised, as found with hearing children (Hakes, 1980). As the authors recognised, this study requires replication with control or comparison groups, such as older hearing-impaired children. Hearing children as direct controls would be problematical because of the different systems of communication used.

Since not much is known about how deaf learners apply cognitive strategies, the area of metacognition in the deaf may repay investigation, especially with reference to instruction and remedial education. It is thus pleasing to note that Krinsky (1990) has described an investigation into the 'feeling of knowing', an aspect of metamemory, in 40, mainly residential, moderately to profoundly deaf adolescents, aged 14–20 years, who used American Sign Language as their preferred form of communication. These subjects were asked to define words from the Peabody Picture Vocabulary Test (PPVT – Dunn and Dunn, 1981), beginning at the place appropriate for their reading level. They were then asked to rank words which they had missed for the difficulty which they would expect to experience in choosing a picture of the missing word. Thus, they were asked to make judgements of their feeling of knowing for the words which they had missed. They were then assessed with the PPVT as a test of accuracy for their ranked judgements. The results showed that the deaf adolescents were not able to judge accurately their feeling of knowing for the words missed, but control groups of hearing adolescents of the same age, and hearing children of the same reading level were able to perform this task. Krinsky explained this outcome on the basis of unfamiliarity. Familiarity, or the degree of prior learning, had been shown to affect the feeling of knowing (Nelson et al., 1982). The normative difficulty of the PPVT vocabulary items was uncertain for the deaf adolescents, although it was known for the hearing controls. These hearing controls had most probably heard all the words at some time, and were in this sense more familiar with the words than the deaf adolescents. The deaf adolescents were also less likely to guess at a solution and, when they did guess, they based their guesses on the visual appearance of words. Krinsky's findings will be interesting to therapists and teachers, since the monitoring of memory is becoming of increasing importance in research on cognition (Armbruster et al., 1982; Flavell, 1985).

Andrews and Mason (1991), mentioned earlier, pointed out that metacognitive strategies are used in fluent reading. They compared the performance of prelingually profoundly deaf high-school boys, hearing reading-disabled high-school boys and hearing boys of elementary school age in filling deleted words and phrases in expository texts. After making replacements to fill the gaps, the boys explained their decisions in sign or verbally, as appropriate. The deaf boys relied on rereading and background knowledge, whereas the hearing readers relied more on context cues in the text. Andrews and Mason recommended the teaching of metacognitive comprehension strategies to deaf students as tools to comprehend English texts, but noted that such strategies would not by themselves guarantee successful reading comprehension. For example, metaprocesses cannot take the place of seriously deficient linguistic or general knowledge. The use of learner-generated semantic mapping, in which a spatial representation or diagram is constructed of the main ideas in the text, with emphasis on active processing, looks to be a fruitful approach in developing metaprocesses in reading by deaf children, as it makes the strategy explicit (Banks et al., 1991b).

Conclusion

We have referred to reports of metalinguistic and metacognitive studies with hearing-impaired children of various ages, which have explored awareness of syntax, phonology, synonymy and pragmatics, in reading and in signed communication, a facet of memory, and strategies in reading comprehension. In view of the considerable interest in metaprocesses in other applied fields, such as language delay and learning disorders, let alone the developments on metaprocesses in normally developing hearing children, it is surprising that so little work has been done on children with hearing impairment. As there is little doubt that children's awareness of and insights into their learning are part of that learning, there is clearly a deficiency here in research with hearing-impaired children which needs to be addressed.

Central Auditory Dysfunction

Central auditory dysfunction refers to difficulties in hearing associated with the retrocochlear neurological pathways and processes, which convey sounds up to, and include, the higher cortical areas of the brain. The terms 'psychogenic' or 'functional hearing loss' are used to describe the same condition, as is the quaint 'non-organic hearing loss' beloved of otologists (Dixon and Newby, 1959). Such usages do not usually impute definite absence of physical pathology, except in cases of malingering, which are rare in children (Dixon and Newby, 1959). Rather, they describe a dysfunction for which the neurology is currently unknown or obscure (Oberklaid et al., 1989). It is usual to refer to such conditions as problems, disorders or dysfunctions, since some people with the condition show no signs of hearing loss when tested by conventional audiometry in the quiet. The disorder commonly appears when stress is placed on the auditory system (Tallal, 1980). One common technique to produce such stress is to reduce the redundancy present in speech, using such techniques as filtering or presenting the speech or other stimuli under difficult listening conditions, as in rapid switching between the ears, or in noise. Individuals with disordered auditory processing skills then have problems in reproducing the speech. Other techniques involve special psychoacoustic tests (Pinheiro and Musiek, 1985a; Tobin, 1985).

Site of lesion

There has been a continuing industry to devise audiometric tests to identify the site of a neurological lesion from sites immediately posterior to the cochlear up to and including the auditory cortex. In view of the possibility of eighth nerve tumours and similar phenomena, the importance of such tests scarcely needs comment. Because, however, the emphasis of this book is on perceptual rather than physiological or anatomical features, we make only brief mention of site of lesion here. The reader is referred to the several comprehensive chapters in Katz (1985) and Pinheiro and Musiek (1985b) for a considered treatment.

Functional aspects

A convenient synopsis of factors reportedly associated with central auditory dysfunction, or disordered auditory processing skills, was outlined by Davis and Rampp (1983). These factors, which are interrelated, include attention, auditory discrimination, analysis and synthesis, and memory and sequencing. It is apparent that problems with any of these factors will interfere with normal communication.

As regards attention, children with problems of auditory processing typically find it hard to focus their attention selectively over time on a particular task. They find it difficult to direct their attention to the salient sounds in their environment, with the result that all the sounds in the environment are treated as 'foreground' sounds. Such children are able to understand speech, especially non-complex speech, when it is presented at comfortable listening levels in the quiet, but fail to understand speech in noise, especially in speech noise. This situation may be described as one in which the children hear, but do not listen.

Most children suspected of an auditory processing disorder also have problems with auditory discrimination, sometimes assessed with the Wepman Auditory Discrimination Test (Wepman, 1975) or the Goldman–Fristoe–Woodcock Test of Auditory Discrimination (Goldman et al., 1970). Auditory discrimination is the ability to distinguish between one sound and another ('goat' vs 'coat') and hence its assessment requires tests which use such phonemic contrasts. The phonemically balanced word lists presented in the quiet, commonly used by audiologists, and often referred to as speech discrimination tests, do not use such contrasts, and hence present no special difficulty to children with auditory processing problems. A test for auditory discrimination requires the discrimination of a test stimulus from another signal. Problems with auditory discrimination can present as 'auditory distractibility', as when a child has problems in following a teacher's speech in a noisy classroom. Wepman (1960) regarded poor auditory discrimination as correlated with problems of articulation and reading disabilities. It interferes with reading and language acquisition.

Auditory analysis and synthesis are the ability to separate wholes into parts, and combine parts into wholes, as in separating sentences into words and syllables, and combining syllables and words into sentences. Tests in this area are few, but Kirk et al. (1968) have offered a sound blending test which assesses the ability to combine phonemes into words, for which the phonemes must be held in serial order and then run together to produce a common word (d-o-g = dog).

Memory and sequencing are often involved in auditory discrimination, which enables us to distinguish between sounds following one another in time, as well as distinguishing a sound from a noise background when the two occur simultaneously. Davis and Rampp (1983) have drawn attention to auditory chunking, in which the sounds to be retained are processed as combinations of phonemes (syllables), combinations of syllables (words), and combinations of words (phrases). Auditory memory is conventionally tested as memory for digits or for words and syllables, including nonsense syllables (Kirk et al., 1968). Auditory memory is typically described in age level terms. Children with auditory processing disorders frequently present with auditory memory skills 1–2 years below their chronological age.

Auditory sequencing is the ability to process auditory stimuli in serial order, a skill of relevance to English language processing, where word order is crucial to meaning. An auditory–vocal sequencing test has been described by Kirk et al. (1968), which bears some relationship to reading difficulties.

Davis and Rampp (1983) described the status of tests for auditory processing disorders as woefully inadequate. The available tests were dated and in several cases were of doubtful validity and reliability. They were often gross measures, and confounded one specific disorder with another, because they tended to assess several factors at the same time. For example, because auditory stimuli are sequential in nature, all auditory tests which involve more than one component in time necessarily involve auditory memory.

A degree of structure which escapes confounding can be introduced by separating auditory processing disorders into two classes: those which are associated with language disorders, and those which are not. Some language disorders are caused by an auditory, rather than by a linguistic or higher-order cognitive problem. In such disorders, children typically have auditory problems in discriminating between consonants presented in minimally different word pairs ('goat' vs. 'coat' mentioned above) for reasons other than sensory end-organ disorder. Tallal (1976) described a test for rapid auditory processing in which items of auditory information are presented in quick succession, which may identify auditory processing problems of the above type and problems that appear independent of any language difficulty. In the latter type of auditory processing problem, language functions assessed by conventional tests may be within normal limits, but the child may have problems of attention, memory, etc., which retard the development of skills in reading and writing.

With young children, it may be difficult to measure central auditory processing problems because of the plasticity of the central nervous system, which was considered in Chapter 2. If the functions under investigation have not become set, because of immaturity in cortical specialisation, then they will be difficult to assess. Also, it is increasingly necessary to use linguistic, or language-like, stimuli when the nervous structures associated with the central auditory processing problems are located higher along the auditory pathway. However, because language contains considerable redundancy, language stimuli presented in the quiet tend to make auditory processing too easy for test purposes. Hence we frequently find the use of time-compressed speech, filtered speech, speech in noise, dichotic listening, in which different material is presented to each ear, etc., as test stimuli. The trick is to reduce the redundancy in speech to a minimum without reducing it so far as to prevent people with normal central auditory processing functions from perceiving the content clearly. There may be objections to the use of acoustic manipulations to speech on the grounds of naturalness. A partial way round this criticism is to use statistical approximations to English, in which the syntax and semantics are manipulated to produce material which looks like some kinds of poetry ('Battle cry and be better than ever', Jerger et al., 1968).

A typical case

Because of the possible immaturity of the central nervous system in young children, and because the test materials are relatively difficult to perceive, the child typically assessed for central auditory processing problems is about 6–8 years old. He is more often than not male, underachieves academically, and yet has normal to high intelligence. However, we should note that there is generally a positive correlation between intelligence and auditory discrimination ability (Watson, 1991). The child has little or no peripheral hearing problem. He is often left-handed, as may be one or more of his close relatives. His fine and gross motor skills are usually good, and he has no apparent neurological problems.

This outline of a typical case was presented by Page (1985b), who also commented on poorly developed auditory memory as a glaring characteristic. The child may perform well when simple, straightforward directions are presented to him in quiet conditions, but appears confused when given instructions, especially instructions which contain more than one direction, in a noisy environment such as a classroom. Further, he may have problems with reading and writing. His visuospatial skills are good, so that he can draw and paint adequately. His health is good, but there may be a history of chronic middle-ear infections (compare Greville et al., 1985; Aplin and Rowson, 1990).

As far as treatment is concerned, some tests may suggest a specific lesion in the auditory pathway, which should be drawn to the attention of the neurologist or neuro-otologist. Frequently, however, these tests do not suggest a specific lesion, nor do other, neurological tests. In such a situation, the findings can be drawn to the attention of therapists and teachers, who may be able to devise remedial programmes, using carefully structured lessons given on an individual basis in quiet surroundings, to develop the child's reading, writing and related skills (Butler, 1981; Katz and Harmon, 1981; Sloan, 1986). Its seems to the author that speechreading could be helpful in therapy for some central auditory disorders but, rather surprisingly, this approach is not evident in the literature.

Some criticisms

On occasion, it may be possible to associate the functional problem with a neurological lesion, but frequently this is not possible. There remains a clear functional problem, but it is often none too clear what lies behind the problem, nor how best to treat it. 'Central auditory processing disorders', 'central auditory dysfunction', and so on, are concepts which appear 'woolly', and can be used to cloak mixed and disorderly findings of obscure aetiology.

Several authors have commented on this aspect (Sanders, 1977; Lyon, 1977) and notably Rees (1973, 1981). The auditory processing explanations, remarked Rees, are used in two different ways. On the one hand, they are used by professionals remediating children with speech, language or learning problems. These professionals tend to assume that complex communication skills can be broken down into a set of less complex subskills for assessment and remediation, hence the identification of auditory discrimination, auditory memory and auditory sequencing. On the other hand, professionals more concerned with diagnosis use a 'site-of-lesion' approach, and have developed the central auditory processing disorders emphasis. The latter group of professionals tends to focus on test development rather than on remediation.

Rees commented on the wide variety of tasks used to establish auditory processing skills, which presented a plethora of empirical endeavours devoid of any coherent or unified theory. She proceeded (1981) with a critique of efforts to identify the units to be sequenced in tests of 'auditory sequencing', citing studies which showed that phonemes, syllables, words and clauses might at different times each be the units to be sequenced. No one of these units appeared to be more salient than the others for auditory sequencing, and there was no compelling evidence for a specific problem in auditory sequencing as an explanation for failure in language and in learning. The search for units reflected associationism, the approach which seeks to reduce complex behaviour to components in order to explain it, but left us wondering about the psychological reality of the units thus identified. Rees went on to criticise the use of 'auditory synthesis' and 'auditory closure' as auditory abilities, seeing them rather as metalinguistic skills which required the child consciously to perceive words as made up of phonemic units, rather than the usual unconscious linguistic processing of the sounds of connected speech. She further criticised the use of 'auditory discrimination' for speech sounds as an 'auditory' rather than a linguistic skill involving phonological, lexical, syntactic and semantic aspects, and she was severe with the approach which treated memory as a unitary phenomenon, since it consisted of sensory, short-term and long-term aspects.

Rees was kinder in her treatment of the various tests based on reducing the redundancy of natural speech, concluding that they may be assessing functions which were more auditory than linguistic, unlike the tests for auditory discrimination, memory and sequencing. However, the relevance of tests which reduced the redundancy of speech to language acquisition and learning was not clear. The field of central auditory processing skills was, she concluded, in an exploratory state.

Conclusion

Rees performed a valuable service in subjecting the area of central auditory processing disorders to rigorous criticism. There is, however, good evidence that some children who perform poorly in tests which reduce the redundancy in speech do have problems with language, learning and reading. Devens et al. (1978) found auditory localisation problems in learning-disabled children and McGroskey and Kidder (1980) found auditory fusion difficulties among similar children. Elliott and Hammer (1988) observed long-term (3-year duration), weak, fine-grained auditory discrimination results in children with language learning problems, though Tallal (1990) has claimed that fine-grained deficits in children with language learning problems are not specific to the auditory modality nor to speech perception. Tallal et al. (1985) observed that auditory perceptual variables requiring rapid temporal analysis were highly correlated with the extent of receptive language deficit in dysphasic children. Further, in a recent report, Hartvig Jensen et al. (1989) described the administration of a battery of psychological tests, both verbal and non-verbal, to right- and to left-ear hearing-impaired children aged 10–16 years. Children with a unilateral right-ear hearing loss performed significantly worse than the left-ear hearing-impaired children, particularly in verbal tests which were sensitive to minor input or processing damage. Results from WISC Digit-Span and WISC Similarities subtests suggested that the right-ear impaired children suffered from a subtle deficit at a high cerebral level. However, Rodriguez et al. (1990), working with normally hearing and cognitively intact elderly adults, have reported central auditory processing problems without a decline in linguistic competence.

From the communication viewpoint, children with auditory processing difficulties usually communicate well enough when involved in clear, individual to individual, conversations which have a straightforward grammatical and semantic structure. However, they commonly have problems in following conversations which include complex sequencing of syntax and semantics. They often experience problems in following conversations presented against a noisy background. They have problems also with reading comprehension, especially with irregular verbs and embedded clauses and phrases. They thus may have problems with verbal communication of the more complex kind, while simpler verbal communication poses few problems. Given a normal level of intelligence, this situation can give rise to frustration for the child and bewilderment for parents who suspect a problem but cannot define it.

At the time of writing, the field remains unclear. The site-of-lesion approach continues to attract the development of sophisticated auditory tests with some success (Musiek and Pinheiro, 1987; Musiek et al., 1990), central auditory problems occurring together with cochlear loss have been studied (Speaks et al., 1985), and specific auditory perceptual dysfunction in the form of an isolated auditory-phonological processing problem has been reported (Jerger et al., 1987). Keith (1981a) emphasised that work directed to the evaluation and remediation of central auditory dysfunction needs to proceed, while the debate continues on terminology and the relationships between auditory perceptual disorders and language learning problems. His advice still holds.

Chapter 8
Individual and Social Aspects

There has been debate over the years as to whether deaf people have more than their share of psychiatric or psychological problems, and whether there is a 'deaf personality'. This chapter reviews the area, and then proceeds to consider deaf children in social contexts. Finally, an overview is presented of the emerging interest in pragmatics, the use of communication in social interaction.

In one of the earlier reviews of psychological and sociological factors associated with hearing loss, Vernon (1969) observed that for deaf and hard of hearing individuals there was an essentially normal distribution of intellectual potential and cognitive capacity. However, the hearing-impaired population was grossly below national (US) averages in educational achievement and vocational attainment. Vernon presented data on marriage patterns, organisations, mental illness and communication among the hearing-impaired community, noting inter alia that 95% of deaf people married other deaf people, that deaf individuals formed their own strong social organisations, and that most deaf employees worked in manual labour requiring varying skill levels. They did not aspire to higher levels of employment. This situation has been slow to change. For example, Sharp (1984) reported that deaf adolescents had more stereotyped attitudes than their hearing peers to gender roles and 'appropriate' occupations. They aspired to the less prestigious occupations, having limited knowledge of the characteristics of the workforce. Cole and Edelmann (1991) have recorded worries about employment opportunities and capabilities for work in British deaf adolescents, because of perceived problems with communication and employer discrimination.

Psychopathology

The greater the hearing impairment, the greater is the degree of relative social isolation, even within the most caring and sympathetic environment. Such relative isolation affects the communication behaviour of the hearing-impaired child and, in turn, this behaviour affects education and remediation (Myklebust, 1960), and might be thought to predispose to psychopathology.

First, we consider the question of whether hearing impairment is associated with a frequency of psychiatric disturbance higher than that found in the hearing population. Some earlier studies suggested that the deaf community has a relatively high population of schizophrenics, in line with a suggestion (Editorial, *Lancet*, 1981) that perceptual disturbances can cause schizophrenia. Matzker (1960) reported that, in the then Federal Republic of Germany, the incidence of deafness among a large sample of schizophrenics was unusually high. Myklebust (1964) found a tendency towards schizophrenia in a group of profoundly deaf adults as indicated by the Minnesota Multiphasic Personality Inventory. He was, however, careful to point out that feelings of isolation and detachment could have been the cause, and that his findings did not necessarily imply that deaf people suffered from schizophrenia.

Other studies have not supported a link between deafness and schizophrenia. Altschuler and Sarlin (1963) concluded that schizophrenia was no more common in deaf than in hearing people, while Kallman (1963) and Rainer and Altschuler (1971) found that schizophrenia was a little less common in psychotic deaf individuals than in hearing psychotics. Interestingly, prelingually profoundly deaf schizophrenics may experience a kind of auditory hallucination, although it is not clear that their subjective experiences are actually auditory (Critchley et al., 1981). Although they may complain of voices inside their heads (Bowman and Coons, 1990) or getting at them (Kitson and Fry, 1990), they cannot state what the voices are saying, which suggests that the hallucination is not auditory as such, but reflects visual images of people talking. Kitson and Fry (1990) concluded that, although the reliability of the data is questionable, and although the area of psychiatry and prelingual deafness has been neglected, schizophrenic psychoses are not found more frequently in deaf than hearing individuals. However, they reported that deaf schizophrenics required high doses of antipsychotic drugs, often in combination with mood-stabilising medication, to remedy their condition.

There is no reliable evidence to indicate whether or not deaf people suffer more than hearing individuals from depression or obsessional states (Moore, 1981; Evans and Elliott, 1987), even though it is sometimes said that deaf people have somewhat rigid personalities, and this rigidity constrains their communication. The one psychiatric area where there may be an association between psychopathology and deafness is that of paranoia associated with late-acquired hearing loss (Cooper, 1976). It is scarcely surprising that losing a faculty which is so important to communication and everyday living should lead to an increased incidence of paranoia in people deafened adventitiously (compare Harvey, 1989).

Although the area of deafness and psychopathology is under-researched, especially in deaf children, it seems that such children, particularly those who are prelingually deaf, are no more likely to experience serious psychiatric problems than hearing children. There is even a suggestion (Moore, 1981; Kitson and Fry, 1990) that prelingual deafness protects a child against affective disorders. However, deaf children do appear to experience a relatively high occurrence of mild psychiatric or behaviour disorders (Meadow, 1981; Prior et al., 1988) and these aspects have interested the psychoanalyst. Mendelson et al. (1960) found that the characteristics of the dreams of severely to profoundly deaf young adults were reported as vivid, brilliantly coloured and frequent. Where affect was prominent in dreams, primitive signs were reported. These characteristics were most marked in the prelingually deaf, less marked in those subjects with deafness acquired before 5 years of age, and least prominent in subjects deafened after 5 years of age. More recently, Hurst (1988) argued that communication has a peculiar dynamic in deaf people's dreams, where it is symbolically significant if interaction in a dream is spoken, signed, or represents 'pure communication', in which neither speaking nor signing are used. Thus if a deaf, signing child dreams of signing to a non-signing parent, this can indicate a wish for increased conversational exchanges. On the other hand, if the dreamed conversation occurs in speech, a desire to conform to the expectations of the hearing world is suggested.

Some unusual dream characteristics of deaf adolescents and adults have been recorded by Rainer (1976), who posed questions about their relationship to ego development and object representation. His observations led him to conclude that profound hearing loss from birth or early childhood led to a greater or lesser immaturity, a lack of empathy and stereotyped social behaviour, together with relatively shallow, short-duration, labile and detached affective responses. Rainer referred to the work of Schlesinger (1972) on the battles in communication which develop between a mother and her deaf child aged from 18 months to 3 years, as in word training, fearfulness of adult disapproval, and the pursuit of adult caring. Schlesinger stressed that parents who are afraid of the autonomy of their deaf child impose stringent measures, resulting in the child's habitual loss of autonomy and interference in the child's development of inner controls and self-concepts, as can occur also with hearing children. However, Freedman (1981) argued that young deaf children can establish a well-differentiated sense of self, and can form relationships between external objects and internal object representations if able to communicate effectively.

These extracts from the writing of some psychoanalysts may give the impression that, although deafness may not lead to psychiatric problems, it may nonetheless exert a traumatising influence on the deaf child. There is no doubt that deafness produces considerable frustrations for children, and leads to great demands on them and their parents (Brinich, 1981). There is also little doubt that deaf children show a relatively high frequency of behaviour problems, arising from difficulties in communication, which hinder the rehabilitation of their deafness. It would however be premature to conclude that the psychoanalytic view of the deaf child is a settled one. Work in the area has been relatively slight and spasmodic. Psychoanalysts seem no less prone to disagree with one another than members of the other occupations concerned with deaf children. Further, the divergent style of communication used by severely and profoundly deaf signers may make them difficult subjects for psychotherapy (Hoyt et al., 1981; Stokoe and Battison, 1981). The findings we have considered are therefore suggestive rather than conclusive.

Psychological Aspects

Given that deaf individuals can show unusual personal characteristics in childhood and in adulthood (Myklebust, 1966; Knutson and Lansing, 1990), we may ask: 'Is there a deaf personality?' or 'Is there a psychology of deafness?' (Vernon and Andrews, 1990).

A deaf personality?

Some of the earlier work in the area (Pintner, 1941; Brereton, 1957; Levine, 1960; Lewis, 1968) referred to an immaturity in deaf children of hearing parents which may appear in differences of arousal and expression of feelings. In the face of frustration such children are prone to tantrums, which seldom persist beyond infancy in hearing children, suggesting unusual personality development. Basilier (1964) described a condition of 'surdophrenia', involving emotional immaturity associated with weak ego development. Pintner (1941) and Lewis (1968) suggested that deaf children may be retarded in the way they relate to the affective aspects of language, such as the word 'mother', which releases in us all a complex emotional reaction. However (Lewis, 1968), differences in linguistic measures were clearly correlated with differences in personal and ethical traits, rather than with differences in emotional and social traits. Lewis' results indicated that the children who were the most mature in their personal and ethical development showed the greatest sophistication in features of the semantics of their language. His data support the view that a deaf child's personal development, in terms of self-confidence, initiative, determination and self-reliance influences the development of (oral) language, and hence communication.

A review and a justifiably fierce criticism of previous psychological research studies of affect in deaf people was presented by Donoghue (1968). He found that three studies described the deaf as reality-orientated, four reported them as passive in attitude, and two reported them as having hostile feelings. Attributes of rigidity in thinking featured in seven studies, impulsiveness in three, and egocentricity and insensitivity in five. One study proposed deaf neurotic symptoms, while another indicated psychosis. Three studies viewed deaf individuals as confused, and several saw the deaf as restricted in their ability to form concepts.

Donoghue concluded that because of the heterogeneity of the samples and variations in research methodology, the only reliable finding was that, as a whole, deaf individuals showed excessive rigidity. He was puzzled by the divergent findings, which ranged from serious emotional maladjustment to relatively normal social adjustment. His solution to this puzzle was to castigate the researchers for their improper approach and methodology in psychodiagnostic evaluation. Their conclusions, he argued, were at best speculations based on the questionable use of subjective reasoning and an obviously inadequate reference matrix. Few of the studies reviewed had been able, or had even attempted, to communicate with their deaf subjects to ensure a valid interchange between tester and subject. There was excessive reliance on fingerspelling and speechreading, when in many cases the preferred mode of communication by the deaf subjects was sign. With such a restricted opportunity for communication, it was not surprising to find reports of weak thinking in the abstract, rigidity, and so on. The result was a bias towards describing deaf individuals as having a constricted personality.

Donoghue ended his indictment by observing that the thinking of deaf individuals was possibly similar to that of hearing people. However, the way in which this thinking was expressed would vary with the educational and social backgrounds of the subjects. Mere professional competency in test administration needed to be complemented by an appreciation of the communication and cultural patterns of the deaf (compare Freeman, 1989).

Fortunately, nowadays a gross stereotyped view of hearing-impaired people, of the type described by the publications reviewed by Donoghue, is no longer held by professionals. Nevertheless, there is evidence of subtle and complex labelling. For example, when hearing and hearing-impaired teachers were asked to assess the behaviour of 8-year-old hearing and profoundly deaf children, on the basis of written information only, the hearing teachers were more likely to lable hearing children as behaviourally impaired whilst hearing-impaired teachers were more likley to use this label with the deaf children (Murphy-Berman et al., 1987).

In view of Donoghue's conclusions, we may wonder whether other approaches can lead to more valid results. Communication in the subject's preferred communication mode looks to be the obvious way to go, but indirect, projective methods could also be of value. Being aware of the methodological problems, Hess (1969) used a projective technique combined with non-verbal methods in a version of the Make-a-Picture Story Test – MAPS (Schneidman, 1948). The MAPS test consists of 22 background scenes and 67 figures with which to populate them. Hess found that deaf boys and girls used more, and more varied, figures than hearing children, interpreted as a leaning towards release from restrictions in the interpersonal relationships of their daily lives. Once chosen, the figures were rarely changed by the deaf children, unlike their hearing peers, suggesting that the deaf children were less flexible and realistic in interpreting their surroundings. Evidence for emotional instability and confusion was deduced from the deaf children's sorting of figures into the categories of 'happy', 'sad', etc., when the deaf attributed multiple affect to the same figure, suggesting weak concepts of emotional states. The deaf children chose significantly fewer figures as likeable, and designated more as sad and fewer as happy, than hearing subjects. Hess argued that since other investigators had found an association between accepting oneself and a tendency to look favourably on others, the deaf children felt less satisfied with themselves as they did not see their environment as particularly accepting (compare Bachara et al., 1980).

Although Hess used a projective technique, with likely uncertainties as to validity and reliability, and although it is only too easy to read into the results the interpretation which is sought, Hess's study was relatively robust because it included a group of emotionally disturbed children among the hearing controls. In general, where their performance was dissimilar to that of normal hearing children, the deaf children performed similarly to the emotionally disturbed children. Also, Hess's findings confirmed the results of an earlier study of deaf and hearing children with MAPS by Bindon (1957), who also found that differences in MAPS responses between hearing and deaf adolescents were greatest when the interactions showed the most frequent and personal relationships of daily life.

There is evidence that deaf children with different communication backgrounds differ in their personal and emotional adjustment. Weisel (1988) found that congenitally profoundly deaf Israeli children of elementary school age, born to deaf parents, performed significantly better than similar children of hearing parents in emotional adjustment, self-image, motivation for communication and reading comprehension, but not in social adjustment. Since the deafness of all the children was of genetic origin, this outcome offered support for the influence of environmental factors, such as family circumstances, and early and continuous exposure to sign language, on personal and cognitive development. Weisel's study had relatively good control over the effects of heredity, gender, age distribution and hearing loss. Its findings supported the view that the reading achievement and, more important to the present discussion, the emotional development of deaf children born to deaf parents are superior to those of deaf children born to hearing parents, as proposed earlier (Quigley and Kretschmer, 1982; Moores, 1987).

Impulsivity

The literature contains scattered reports to the effect that deaf children are more impulsive in their behaviour than hearing children. Wishing to discover the influence of such cultural factors as paternalistic practices in education, which could lead to a dependent and egocentric orientation promoting impulsivity, Altschuler et al. (1976) undertook a large-scale psychological testing of deaf and hearing adolescents in American and Yugoslavian schools. Their subjects were aged 15–17 years with IQs between 85 and 115, and with prelingual profound hearing losses in the case of the deaf adolescents. Subjects with brain damage or severe personality disorder were excluded. Altschuler et al. studied 50 Yugoslavian deaf subjects and 50 hearing controls from several states and schools, and 50 American hearing subjects and 50 deaf subjects from schools in New York. With an eye to validity, objectivity and reliability, in which they were only partly successful, they used relatively non-verbal and culture-free measures, such as assessments of long-range planning ability, impulsivity, emotional stability and flexibility versus ego-rigidity. They used the Porteous Maze test, the Draw-A-Line (DAL) test, the Id–Ego–Superego (IES) test, and the Rorschach, all of which were to have been correlated with a criterion measure of impulsivity from the ratings of two teachers. Unfortunately, the variance between the teachers was so great that their ratings had to be discarded.

Both Yugoslav and American deaf subjects showed greater impulsivity than the hearing subjects in the respective countries on the Porteous test, and on the Ego scores of the Arrow–Dot, the Picture Story Completion subtests of the IES, and the DAL test. The results of the Rorschach test were only slightly less marked. The Yugoslav subjects, whether deaf or hearing, were in general more impulsive than the American subjects. Since most findings were obtained via objective and language-free tests, they may be regarded as escaping criticisms of the type put forward by Donoghue (1968) – see above. However, for all subjects, whether deaf or hearing, the correlations between scores on one measure and scores on any other measure were close to zero, though all were devised to measure impulsivity and several clearly separated the deaf from the hearing subjects. Altschuler et al.

concluded that what is regarded clinically as impulsivity may be a final compendium which reflects a number of different personality variables.

Commenting that impulsivity continued to be a significant psychosocial problem in deaf individuals according to educators and clinicians alike, O'Brien (1987) took the concept further to ask whether the impulsivity might not only be shown by deaf individuals in their overt behaviour, but also in their underlying style of thinking. She assessed the relationship of the cognitive dimension of reflection–impulsivity to communication mode (oral or TC) and age in 71 prelingually severely to profoundly deaf and hearing boys aged 6–15 years. The Porteous Maze test, and a Matching Familiar Figures picture-matching test (MFFT), were administered to all the boys in the classroom.

The results of MFFT errors showed that the deaf boys were more impulsive than the hearing boys. On the Porteous Q scores, which were a weighted sum of errors in execution and thus related to reflection–impulsivity, there was a significant difference between the hearing and deaf TC boys. There was also a significant difference between the hearing and the deaf oral boys on MFFT responses. There were no other significant differences between deaf and hearing groups. This is not too surprising. Not all tests for emotional or personality factors used with deaf children show the anticipated findings (compare Cates, 1991). No significant differences were found between the oral and TC groups, but the older deaf and hearing groups, aged 11–15 years showed less impulsivity than the younger deaf and hearing groups aged 6–10 years. O'Brien also found some suggestion of a difference between deaf children with deaf parents and deaf children with hearing parents reminiscent of Harris (1978), who reported that deaf children with deaf parents were less impulsive than deaf children of hearing parents.

The findings of Harris (1978) and O'Brien (1987) show that the different experiences of deaf children of deaf or hearing parents affect the children's impulsivity in different ways. Possibly a greater acceptance of the child's deafness by deaf parents reduces the child's impulsive behaviour. O'Brien noted that several intervention programmes were being used to reduce impulsive behaviour in hearing children, but that only one (Kusche et al., 1987) was in progress to reduce the impulsivity of deaf children through language mediation techniques, despite the perceived need for this type of intervention programme.

Self-concept

Self-concept involves an individual's view of personal attitudes, traits and social standing. It has been argued that hearing loss leads to problems of adjustment in children, because problems with communication produce barriers to social development which are difficult to overcome. In turn, these barriers cause problems in social adjustment (Freeman et al., 1981; Schlesinger, 1978; Kusche et al., 1987) and interfere with the development of a concept of self like that of the hearing child.

In an exploratory investigation, Warren and Hasenstab (1986) studied the combination of demographic and impairment-related variables, and parental attitudes in the prediction of self-concept in 58 severely to profoundly deaf children of 5–11 years of age. The causes of deafness were congenital, illness or unknown. Almost all the parents were hearing. The children were asked to decide whether pictures showing normal home, play or school situations were happy or sad by circling faces corresponding to the pictures (the Picture Game – Lambert and Bower, 1979), a task believed to provide an index of self-concept. Parental attitudes to child-rearing were assessed with the Maryland Parent Attitude Survey – MPAS (Pumroy, 1966), to distinguish between indulgent, protecting, rejecting and disciplinarian attitudes. The parents were asked to select the different parent types, balanced for social desirability, which most reflected their views.

The results showed a clear association between the child's self-concept and parental indulgence, protection, discipline, and the child's level of language and communication at the onset of hearing loss. Warren and Hasenstab saw the results as indicating that, although the hearing parents of deaf children wish to do their best by them, most parents have problems in coping with their hearing-impaired child, and may in fact contribute to maladjusted behaviour. They argued that there was a clear need for more support for the families of deaf children.

Similar results were obtained by Loeb and Sarigiani (1986), who, in an important large-scale project, asked if hearing impairment affected children's personalities in a clear and consistent way. They studied 250 children aged 8–15 years from 33 schools with mainstream special education programmes. There were 64 hearing-impaired children, 74 children with visual impairments and 112 children with no sensory or major emotional, mental or physical impairments. Sixty of the hearing-impaired children attended schools using oral methods. The remaining four hearing-impaired children came from TC programmes. The children were assessed with the Children's Locus of Control Scale (Nowicki and Strickland, 1973) in a form which was linguistically simplified for hearing-impaired children, and which measured the extent of children's perception of their control over their life space; a Q-sort technique (Schwartz et al., 1975) requiring the children to sort into five piles 15 cards containing descriptions of human characteristics, such as 'happy', and then requiring a repeated sorting into how the children perceived they would like to be; the Children's Self-Concept Scale of Piers and Harris (1964), which is easy to read and offers a measure of self-esteem together with such components as behaviour, intellect, physical wellbeing, anxiety, popularity and happiness; a tower-building task (Loeb et al., 1980) in which they were blindfolded and asked to build two towers from irregularly-shaped blocks in a set time period; and a sentence-stem completion task, used as a projective method to indicate the issues and concerns of the greatest importance to them. Checks were made that the children understood all the tasks.

The hearing-impaired children, whose hearing losses ranged from mild to profound but were mainly moderate to severe, were lower in self-esteem (Piers–Harris' test) than the other groups, but level of hearing-impairment did not interact with self-esteem. Significant effects were found also for behaviour and popularity, with higher popularity being significantly related to later onset of hearing impairment. Girls were more anxious than boys, and black children obtained lower scores than white children on the Appearance item. The locus of control test (Nowicki and Strickland, 1973) produced no main effects. However, there was a significant interaction between race and handicap. The hearing-impaired white children showed a more external locus of control than the hearing-impaired black children. From the Q-sorts, which compared the children's ranks for items as they saw themselves and how they would have wished to be, the hearing-impaired children reported that they would have liked to be less shy and more likeable than they were. The children with later onsets of hearing loss were less satisfied with themselves than the children with early onsets. From the tower-building data, the predictions of the group of hearing-impaired children for a further tower were lower than those of the two other groups, based realistically on the lower towers they had built earlier. The height of the towers built correlated negatively with the severity of the hearing loss. From the sentence-stem completion task the hearing-impaired children appeared more often sad because of name-calling, and tended to identify a special activity or playing as most liked instead of their family or friends, unlike the children from the other groups. They were also more likely to select some aspect of their environment, such as their room, home or school, as what they would most like to change, rather than some characteristic of themselves.

Their teachers saw the hearing-impaired children as having more problems with school work, shyness, getting on with other children and adults, and lacking in confidence more than the other children. The mothers thought that their hearing-impaired children had no greater problems than the visually impaired or non-sensorially handicapped children, apart from their education, where the mothers of both the hearing-handicapped and the visually handicapped children reported more problems than the parents of the children without sensory impairments.

We have considered this report by Loeb and Sarigiani at length because of its importance in assessing a variety of self-perceptions on a large sample over several schools, with comparison groups for type of impairment and absence of impairment. Its major limitation was its restriction mainly to hearing-impaired children who were educated orally. However, it is likely that hearing-impaired children who used other modes of communication would have a similar or more pessimistic outcome in the same environment.

The results showed that orally educated hearing-impaired children in mainstreamed programmes had self-assessed problems of several kinds. They were not popular with peers, found it hard to make friends and were not often chosen as playmates. They tended to be shy, an obvious impediment to the development of communication. Surprisingly, they saw their ideal selves as less likeable than they were, and they were more interested in changing their environment than themselves, suggesting that they accepted their communication problems as a major obstacle. It appears difficult to motivate such children to develop their social interaction and their communication. They would seem, rather, to prefer to stay within the limited environment they know. However, Loeb and Sarigiani thought it encouraging that the hearing-impaired group were not more external in locus of control than the other groups. Further, from the Q-sort measure of overall self-satisfaction, the hearing-impaired children saw themselves as having a normally positive outlook, as shown also by some of the responses to the sentence-stem completion test.

In summary, this research by Loeb and Sarigiani indicates not only that hearing impairment, gender, age and race affect children's self-perceptions, but that they do so in a complex way. The differences between the children reinforce the view that each child develops self-perceptions uniquely. It is misleading to emphasise any one variable to the exclusion of the others. Having stated that, the study shows that most hearing-impaired children need special assistance to develop several personality characteristics which most people would see as desirable and which would assist their communication. In this context, the current emphasis on mainstreaming in deaf education is a cause for concern if it is not adequately supported by services. With minimal support services, mainstreamed hearing-impaired children tend to have lower self concepts (Reich et al., 1977).

As an additional comment, it is rather disconcerting that research instruments purporting to assess self-concepts or self-perceptions tend to be indirect, such as tower-building, or to have uncertain validities, as in the use of certain projective tests. Little work has generally gone into the development of personality tests for hearing-impaired people (Freeman, 1989), although Oblitz et al. (1991) have recently described a self-concept scale for older hearing-impaired children which may help to overcome some of these concerns. It is also important to estimate whether the self-concepts themselves reflect a valid situation. This situation is of particular concern since deaf individuals may have quite false self-concepts. Thus Cole and Edelmann (1991) found that some profoundly deaf adolescents described themselves as 'a bit deaf' or believed that in time they might become hearing.

Some hearing-impaired individuals may encounter special circumstances in which their personal characteristics and needs are less than sufficiently recognised. For example, problems that are incipient in the early years of life and in elementary schooling, become more obvious in the more demanding and competitive environments of tertiary education settings (Flexer et al., 1986), requiring the services of a support group. There is some indication (Israelite, 1986) that the hearing adolescent siblings of hearing-impaired children define themselves not only as individuals in their own right, but also as the siblings of hearing-impaired children. The latter definition may add to siblings' feelings of inadequacy in social situations, since adolescents do not like to appear different or deviant (Sherif and Sherif, 1964). In turn, perception of feelings of inadequacy on the part of their siblings may affect the personalities of hearing-impaired children. This is a topic for further research.

Conclusion

As regards the question: 'Is there a deaf personality?' our stance is necessarily somewhat equivocal. The test instruments used and the studies published to date have not generally been as vaild, objective and reliable as desired (Freeman, 1989). Further, hearing-impairment itself does not create personality differences as much as do the ensuing problems of communication. Such communication problems may grow less over time, as methods of communication by and with hearing-impaired people are researched and extended. Nevertheless, and for the time being, hearing-impaired individuals do seem to differ in personality from hearing people. We are content to accept the suggestion of Rodda and Grove (1987) that the concept of a deaf personality or 'surdophrenia' has some uses, provided that it is not over-emphasised or misused.

Social Aspects

In this section we consider the social interaction of hearing-impaired children outside their family. Parent–infant interactions were described in Chapter 2.

In a conference discussion on social and vocational adjustment by deaf individuals more than 25 years ago (Stuckless, 1965), it was considered that the deaf community, school and family were so active in helping deaf individuals that there was no real need for assistance from social agencies. Since 1965, not only has our knowledge of such social needs expanded, but it is also clear that much work remains to be done, both in research in the area and in the provision of services. Further, the nature of social interaction between hearing and hearing-impaired children, and between one hearing-impaired child and another, proves to be far from simple.

Some 20 years after the above conference, Hummel and Schirmer (1984) reviewed the work of programmes concerned with the social development of hearing-impaired students. There had, they thought, been a tendency to focus too much on cognitive and linguistic factors, to the exclusion of affective factors. Increased attention needed to be paid to the social development and social interactions of both handicapped and non-handicapped children. Since communication skills are acquired or learned in a social context, and since such skills need to be maximised if the child is to learn effectively, the arrangements for the education of children – hearing as well as hearing impaired – need to involve consideration of the child's development of social skills. Hummel and Schirmer commented that the existing literature in the area was relatively scanty and methodologically and conceptually weak. We might add that some of it was overly descriptive or anecdotal (e.g. Altschuler, 1974; Feinstein, 1983). The yield of the existing research did not allow Hummel and Schirmer to form firm conclusions. However, the thrust towards the integration of hearing-impaired with hearing children in educational settings was forcing more attention to be paid to well-conducted research in the area, with some promising work emerging on useful intervention strategies.

The shift, in the 1980s, towards the study of the interplay of language, cognition and social interaction, as in research on the analysis of discourse in social situations (Seewald and Brackett, 1984) and on social cognition (Peterson and Peterson, 1989), is likely to prove illuminating about the communication skills of hearing-impaired children. As regards social development itself, we begin with the review of Hummel and Schirmer, taking note of their incisive criticisms, and commenting where other, or more recent, research suggests meaningful progress.

Hummel and Schirmer (1984) remarked that, at the time of their review, much of the published research in the social development and social interaction of hearing-impaired children had been concerned with whether they had deficits in social skills. Most of this research, they observed, had taken a traditional, normative approach, involving comparisons of the behaviour of hearing-impaired with that of hearing children. It entailed estimates of the frequency with which the hearing-impaired children showed non-normal, and thus often undesirable, social behaviour, and the extent to which such behaviour was beyond norms from hearing children. Such a normative approach was criticised, first, because of insufficient standardisation of the test instruments. It was an inadequate basis for intervention, because the knowledge base was not sufficiently robust to show clearly which apparently non-normal behaviour required intervention. There were no proper test norms for hearing-impaired children. Such norms as did exist were derived from tools for describing the behaviour of hearing children. Similar conclusions were drawn by Delgado (1982). It would be preferable to have norms for hearing-impaired children and norms for hearing children of the same ages, at least until more information was forthcoming about the relation between hearing impairment and specific behaviour problems.

The second basic difficulty with the normative approach was that of judging which behaviour patterns were desirable or undesirable. It is clear in a general sense what this criticism means, but it seems somewhat unfairly levied. The judgements are not necessarily normative themselves, but reflect child conduct departing from the behavioural norms, even though some people regard conforming, or alternatively, aberrant behaviour, differently from others (Togonu-Bickersteth, 1988). There is now, however, a developing literature on the attention paid by teachers, case managers and counsellors to the social and communication skills of hearing-impaired children (Beck, 1988; Murphy and Hill, 1989; Cates and Shontz, 1990; Maxon et al., 1991).

Hummel and Schirmer stated firmly that research which shows that the behaviour in question is linked to current and/or future adjustment greatly helps the making of decisions about intervention. They referred to evidence that decreases in aggression (Feshbach, 1970) and positive peer interaction (Hartup, 1976) are desirable goals in intervention for hearing students, since these are linked with emotional adjustment, academic achievement and ethical development. A similar association was imputed for hearing-impaired children.

Peer interaction

There have been a number of reports of the social interaction between hearing-impaired children with one another and between hearing-impaired children and their hearing peers. We now outline several of these reports, following which we offer general conclusions.

The use of sociometric ratings to explore the acceptance and rejection by one another of 200 severely to profoundly deaf students aged 7–17 years was discussed by Hagborg (1987). The lowest-scoring 29 and the highest-scoring 29 students were classed as rejected and accepted groups respectively. Members of the accepted group had been enrolled in the school for a longer time, were more likely to be female, and were rated by teachers as having a more favourable behaviour adjustment than the rejected group. Thus social acceptance by peers was partly related to behavioural adjustment.

Social interactions between preschool hearing and hearing-impaired children were described by Brackett and Henniges (1976), who found that the hearing-impaired children, with a wide range of mild to profound hearing losses, began more social interactions during free play than in structured language sessions. We would expect the more linguistically competent hearing-impaired children to interact more frequently than those with weaker language skills, and this was the case. Further, the latter interacted socially with other hearing-impaired, rather than hearing children. Arnold and Tremblay (1979) obtained similar results, but found in addition that hearing children preferred to interact with other hearing children, presumably mainly because of greater ease of communication. It seems then that, where hearing and hearing-impaired preschool children play together, children with strong language ability and good communication skills, whether hearing or hearing-impaired, use that ability to choose partners in play. Otherwise, age, gender and ethnicity are the important variables in the choice of preschool deaf children's play partners (Lederberg, 1991).

For school-age children, McCauley et al. (1976) and Antia (1982) concluded that hearing-impaired children with moderate to profound hearing losses looked to teachers for positive interactions. It is not therefore surprising that the hearing-impaired children interacted at a significantly lower rate with their peers than did the hearing children. Antia (1985) suggested that, since one of the goals of main-streaming is social integration, the teacher's role needs to be considered. If teachers decrease their social interactions with the school-aged hearing-impaired children, the latter may be prompted to participate more in the play of their peers.

Hearing-impaired children are not necessarily more disposed to social interaction with hearing-impaired peers than are hearing children, as shown by Vandell and George (1981). They matched preschool children aged 14–64 months for age and gender in dyads consisting of two hearing children, two hearing-impaired children, and one hearing and one hearing-impaired child. The hearing-impaired children, who had a wide range of hearing losses, used a combination of speech and Signed Essential English. The hearing-impaired dyads began more social interactions than the hearing dyads, but these interactions were more frequently rejected or ignored by partners. Such rejection was even more marked in the mixed dyads. Hence both hearing and hearing-impaired preschoolers tended to discount the communication initiatives of their hearing-impaired partners. Also, they often began interactions which could not be perceived by their hearing-impaired partner. Accordingly, the hearing-impaired children were less likely to respond to the approaches of the other children, whether hearing or hearing-impaired.

According to Antia (1985), this study showed that lack of understanding of the needs governing the communication of hearing-impaired children was as much a barrier to interaction with peers as linguistic competence, and that the results had implications for intervention programmes for hearing and hearing-impaired children alike. The social integration of hearing-impaired children could be helped by teaching the communication skills needed to begin and to maintain positive interactions. Structured situations for positive interactions with peers would therefore increase the social acceptance of hearing-impaired children, by promoting the appropriate use of communication skills such as greetings, invitations and acceptances, asking questions about the interests of others, and turn-taking (compare La Greca and Mesibov, 1979).

Physical distance in a school playground was identified by Jones (1985) as another factor in dyadic interactions. She measured the distances between 40 hearing and 40 hearing-impaired dyads whose members were aged 6–8 years, prior to mainstreaming, when the hearing-impaired dyads were separated by about 25% more space than occurred for the hearing dyads. The effect does not seem to have been due to space needed for signing, as the hearing-impaired children were educated orally. The reason for the effect is not clear, and it may not persist with increasing age (Holton, 1978), though physical propinquity is of obvious relevance to communication. Jones thought her results could have implications for positive interactions between hearing and hearing-impaired children, if distancing formed an important part of children's interpretation of communication interchange. However, such interchange was not part of this investigation.

There is, then, an emerging literature which shows that positive peer interactions are problematical and/or different for hearing-impaired children. Their attempts at social interaction are rejected relatively often by potential hearing and hearing-impaired partners alike. In particular, their interactions will be fewer if they show poor behaviour adjustment or low levels of linguistic ability. The teaching of communication skills to both hearing and hearing-impaired children, and the opportunity to practise them in free play with limited teacher presence, could improve this situation.

However, a cautionary comment has been injected by Magen (1990), suggesting that the situation may be age-dependent. Using a questionnaire, Magen found that the intensity and frequency of interpersonal experiences were higher for hearing-impaired than for hearing adolescents. Hearing-impaired adolescents, with severe or lesser hearing losses, reported positive interpersonal experiences equally distributed between experiences with hearing-impaired and hearing individuals. It appeared that positive interpersonal experiences may be the rule, rather than the exception among hearing-impaired adolescents, though they may have had to work especially hard at developing them. However, the adolescents concerned were less than profoundly deaf. Also, the use of the questionnaires is an indirect reporting instrument which does not necessarily yield the most valid findings.

Aggression

Aggression in the social interactions of hearing-impaired children is another area where the literature is slim. In one of the few studies that reported detailed findings on aggression Maxon et al. (1991), using a self-report social awareness test, found that severely to profoundly deaf children aged 7–19 years perceived themselves differently on items relating to the verbal expression of emotion, verbal aggression, physical aggression and social interaction, when compared with hearing children. Age and gender differences were also found. The deaf children reported themselves as less verbally aggressive than the hearing children, possibly because of reduced verbal emotional expression, but they saw themselves as more aggressive physically. Overall, they saw themselves not as necessarily less or more aggressive, but as releasing their aggression in different ways. If these perceptions were true reflections of the actual state of affairs, and there is supporting evidence for this (McCane, 1980; Meadow, 1980), there are important implications for the development of positive social interactions. Initiations of social interactions could be more successful for hearing-impaired children if they were a little more verbally aggressive, and less physically aggressive, than hearing children. As Maxon et al. indicated, the problem may be greater for hearing-impaired girls, as the hearing-impaired girl who is physically aggressive will appear more socially inept than the aggressive hearing-impaired boy.

Levels of aggression may differ with the extent to which hearing-impaired children cope with feelings of frustration or inadequacy in communicating through different modes. Aggressive acts were recorded by Cornelius and Hornett (1990) in two groups of mainly lingually hearing-impaired kindergarten children, aged 5–6 years. One group attended an oral programme which used no sign. The other group used TC. Play was observed as functional play, namely, simple and repetitive muscular activity with or without objects, constructive play in manipulating objects, dramatic play in assuming a role, and social play. The groups did not differ from each other in functional and constructive play, but they varied significantly in dramatic and social play. Children using TC showed higher levels of social play, and engaged in more frequent dramatic play than the children using the oral-only mode. They touched, gestured and vocalised almost twice as much as those using the oral-only mode. Further, 17 aggressive acts were noted for the oral-only class, whereas only two such instances were observed with the group using TC. The aggressive acts were forceful, including pushing, hitting and pinching other children. Cornelius and Hornett remarked that the child's communication mode should not only allow but encourage positive play and social interaction. The introduction of sign may promote such developments for orally educated children if the reason for their aggression is frustration because of poor ability to establish communication.

Social skills training

Although there have been many recommendations for developing the social skills of hearing-impaired children, Hummel and Schirmer (1984) remarked that, at the time, there had been few reports about the implementation of such recommendations. Becker (1978) described an oral training programme conducted with 14-year-old hearing-impaired children in Montreal, designed to develop personal and social maturity, with which the staff were very satisfied. A programme of skills in attending, spontaneous interaction, communication clarification and social fluency, which were taught directly and simultaneously, at levels suitable for the age of the child, was developed by McGinnis et al. (1980). Hummel (1982) reported success in developing social skills with a structured learning approach which involved modelling of target skills, role playing, performance feedback with various methods of reinforcing children's attempts to practise the skill in daily life, and transfer of training.

Training programmes in social skills have since developed, though several show serious design or reporting problems. There has been emphasis on appropriateness of communication, response latency, smiling, eye contact and gestures. Lemanek et al. (1986), for example, noted an increase in such skills following the use of a social skills training package with 11–18-year-old hearing-impaired adolescents. A procedure to increase toy sharing among five hearing-impaired children of kindergarten age was described by Barton and Osborne (1978). Kreimeyer and Antia (1988) drew on this work in devising a social interaction intervention programme for hearing-impaired preschool children with a wide range of hearing losses, to increase positive peer interaction. They also wished to know whether the taught interaction skills would generalise to free play. Positive peer interaction was found to increase with teaching, and the taught social interaction skills could be generalised to free play, but only when specific generalisation strategies were used. Generalisation for interaction with peers occurred only when toys used in the initiation of social interaction skills were offered during free play. Peer interaction did not generalise to free play on the introduction of toys which had not been used in instruction. This outcome is reminiscent of trained skills in other areas, which we have discussed in previous chapters. Hearing-impaired children clearly have problems in generalising trained skills of various kinds, an issue which begs for further research.

Situations devised by the children themselves should be particularly conducive to social skills training. Using this approach, six profoundly deaf children aged 12–13 years were trained in a programme designed by Murphy and Hill (1989) to improve their communication abilities. The children were trained in weekly 1.5 hour sessions over 8 weeks, using video-recorded enactments of situations by pairs of children thought up by the children themselves. Between-session analyses were reported to show marked improvements in communication between partners, which was generalised from one situation to another. However, no data were given. Further, Cates and Shontz (1990) have found that role-taking behaviour is not reliably related to some measures of social behaviour in moderately to profoundly deaf children. The results of Murphy and Hill are therefore open to question.

Conclusion

Despite later advances in research, including work in areas more peculiar to deaf individuals such as signed communication (Hall, 1989), there is still a dearth of well designed and executed studies on the development of social skills in hearing-impaired children. Even the work on pragmatics (see below) improves insufficiently on this situation. There is no doubt, however, of the need for further knowledge which may assist the integration of hearing-impaired children in mainstream education and elsewhere, especially given concerns that the grouping of hearing-impaired with hearing children does not necessarily produce social interaction or social acceptance (Antia, 1985). In view of advice on techniques and approaches, such as video-recording and analysis procedures (Johnson and Griffith, 1985), creative drama (Davies, 1984), and the application of the Vineland Adaptive Behavior Scale to the study of socialisation (Dunlap and Iceman Sands,

1990), we may expect to see more comprehensive and methodologically more robust future reports in this difficult and demanding area.

Pragmatics

Traditionally, analysis of the language of children with impaired hearing focused on deficits in lexical, syntactic and, to a lesser extent, phonological development. The perspective has now broadened to include the ways in which hearing-impaired children put language to use in pragmatics to attain specific goals, as in posing questions to obtain information, describing events, making promises and cracking jokes (Pien, 1985). Hence, the development of competence in communication requires mastery of stylistic variation in the use of language as well as mastery of language itself, whether in sign or verbal language (Lou et al., 1987; Mounty, 1989).

A focus on pragmatics leads to considerations of language use with fundamental implications for language assessment, intervention and teaching. A pragmatic orientation suggests change in language assessment towards evaluating various communicative functions that the child expresses. Also, the pragmatic focus suggests changes in intervention and teaching methods. The primary goal of intervention and teaching becomes the facilitation of general communicative functions, for which vocabulary, syntactic structures and phonology are tools used in context (Bates, 1976).

The relevance of pragmatics to communication is in the skills used in interpersonal communication. Conversations, for example, are conducted by means of rules which have to be learned, and the learning of the rules of pragmatics in conducting conversations is as important for communication as the learning of syntax and vocabulary. Hearing-impaired children may have difficulties in introducing a topic of conversation, or in shifting from one topic to another during conversation, because they do not sufficiently consider the needs of the listener (Moeller et al., 1983). Further, Geoffrion (1982) observed that hearing-impaired partners pass on the burden of keeping up a conversation, even in communication by teletype. Considerations of pragmatics and syntax show that relationships between the two pose special difficulties for hearing-impaired children, as when difficulty is experienced with conjunctions such as 'although' which signal a shift of topic. Also problematical for hearing-impaired children is the development of communication repair strategies (Kretschmer and Kretschmer, 1980), which require skills in pragmatics to restore a broken conversation by seeking clarification, or by repeating what is said for confirmation, or by offering additional information. Other desiderata in pragmatics for hearing-impaired children involve a readiness to seek information by repeated questioning, so that the child can continue as an effective communication partner by acquiring enough information to keep a conversation flowing, and offering prompts, as in paraphrasing, to elicit specific information.

The description of the field which follows has been divided into two main areas: Communicative Intentions and Conversation.

Communicative intentions

The study of communicative intentions, or the functions that utterances are intended to serve, are of special interest because of the relationship between intentions and linguistic forms of expression.

Skarakis and Prutting (1977) described the semantic and pragmatic components of language in the spontaneous communication of four hearing-impaired preschool children aged 2–4 years. The children had received oral language instruction, were functioning intellectually at or above their chronological age, and were severely to profoundly deaf. Data were collected by written transcript of the child's communicative acts in four different situations: free play, snacktime, and group and individual lessons, over a 4-week period. The data were analysed for semantic functions and communicative intentions. There are several advantages in using this twofold approach: first, pragmatics and semantics can be examined separately; secondly, communication skills can be studied independently of specific linguistic skills; thirdly, the children's knowledge of the world, and behaviour reflecting such knowledge, can be distinguished from their knowledge of language.

Analysis procedures were derived from Greenfield and Smith (1976) for semantic function, and from Dore (1974) and Bates (1976) for communicative intent. The communicative intent was covered by the categories Labelling, Response, Request/Demand, Greeting, Protesting, Repeating, Description and Attention. The procedures used the following evidence to determine the appropriate aspect: the relation between the child's utterance and the context; the child's utterance, gesture, facial expression, actions and body orientation; and the adult's or peer's response. In addition, physical context including the referent, events involving the child, and the prior linguistic experience of the child were considered.

Verbalisation and gesture were used by all subjects. Verbal behaviour was used predominantly by one subject, with the other three using gesture as their main means of communication. The results revealed positive implications for hearing-impaired children. First, subjects showed semantic functions and communicative intentions in spontaneous speech. Secondly, although direct comparisons were not cited, some of the communicative intentions and semantic functions were similar to those identified by Dore (1974) and Greenfield and Smith (1976) in younger hearing children. The results showed that the hearing-impaired children expressed similar semantic functions and communicative intentions to those of hearing children at the prelinguistic and one-word stage. Skarakis and Prutting thus suggested that hearing-impaired children progress through this early stage of language development in the same way as the hearing child.

A further study of the semantic and pragmatic development of young hearing-impaired children was conducted by Curtiss et al. (1979), as both an expansion and a refinement of Skarakis and Prutting (1977). A larger sample size of 12 preschool children constituted the study group, with a wider age range, from 22–60 months. Hearing impairment ranged from severe to profound deafness. Data were collected from four different environmental settings, and videotapes were used instead of written transcripts. Dore's (1974) categories were modified to facilitate the recording of behaviour of hearing-impaired subjects, resulting in 16 speech act categories. Greenfield and Smith's (1976) semantic function categories were also modified and expanded to include gestural communication. The pragmatic intention and semantic content, whether verbal or non-verbal, were recorded.

The results revealed that children of all ages used the full range of pragmatic intentions. Age was an important variable for semantic functions. Two year olds displayed limited semantic ability, but there was an increase in the expression of semantics with increasing age. Pragmatic and semantic functions expressed in combination revealed that as their semantic abilities expanded, the children were also learning pragmatics. Non-verbally, all children expressed the full range of pragmatic functions, but several categories were not expressed verbally. Individual data showed marked differences between children in the same age group. One of the most pertinent findings was that hearing loss played only a small role in non-verbal pragmatic and semantic ability. However, only individual scores were considered and statistical computations, such as correlation coefficients between different abilities, were not reported. Curtiss et al. also found that the number of combinations of pragmatic and semantic behaviours increased with age, seeing these interactions as illustrating the relational nature of communication.

A major finding of this study was that children with impaired hearing coded a variety of pragmatic intentions and semantic functions, using both verbal and non-verbal means. They showed considerable communicative ability, a finding in agreement with Skarakis and Prutting (1977). Semantic functions appeared to develop at a slower rate across all age groups than did pragmatic intention, a finding supported by a more recent report (Swanson, 1987) of the effects of self-instruction training for one profoundly deaf child, which showed that self-instruction was immediately effective on the child's signed pragmatic behaviour, with a slower effect on signed semantic behaviour. Curtiss et al. felt that the difference between the development of pragmatic and semantic functions may have been the result of difficulties, in some instances, of coding meaning through non-linguistic means. As for the effects of the hearing loss on communicative skill, Curtiss et al. pointed out that further research using aided rather than unaided loss may be a better predictor of communicative ability.

This pattern of results was continued by Day (1986) with five prelingually profoundly deaf children aged 35–42 months, who were learning Manually Coded English. Deafness did not limit the amount of communicative interaction between these children and their parents, as they communicated successfully and often with their signing hearing mothers, frequently using invented gestures beyond the sign system they were learning. The children produced highly differentiated sets of communicative intentions which were readily identified by the mothers, although the children's vocabulary and syntax were limited.

At a quite different level, in a study offering insights into communicative intentions in context for older subjects, Foster et al. (1989) investigated the meaning of communication for a group of 23 first-year hearing-impaired college students who had sustained moderate to profound hearing losses from an early age. These students, from 15 states in the USA, were interviewed in depth. They were encouraged to pursue their thoughts, though the interviews were constrained by a set of core topics about communication. The great majority of these students had some familiarity with both speechreading and manual communication. The interview transcripts were organised into categories of language-modality, affective, situational and sociopolitical. Of these, the third, situational category is relevant to the present discussion. It offers some useful insights, although because of the study design, these insights were given at a descriptive level only.

First, in the situational category, and not surprisingly, the students reported that ease of communication varied widely with the background of the communication partner. The distinction between friend and stranger was given most frequently. Friends were seen as more likely to understand the students' communication and to be more interested in keeping a conversation going. Awkward situations were seen as less likely to happen with friends and, when they did, could be handled with less difficulty.

Secondly, the purpose or topic of the conversation was seen to bear importantly on the success of the communication. Many students reported that communication was easier when the topic was of mutual interest, and that communication was more likely to fail in the absence of shared interests.

Thirdly, the environment or place in which the communication occurred was important, with environmental noise perceived as a significant impediment to successful conversation. Regional accents could also be a problem.

Fourthly, the modality of communication and situational styles were at issue. Communication was particularly difficult when the modality was unfamiliar to the students (e.g. signing versus talking), and the ability to switch between modalities was perceived as most important for handling complex communication. Support services and special equipment were seen as essential for good communication by some students. Problems could arise when equipment, such as hearing aids, could not be used, as when swimming.

Fifthly, time was mentioned as affecting all of the above, because the time expended in setting up the communication had a major influence on the quality of the subsequent relationship. Longer periods of time helped the development of communication skills and in accustoming hearing communication partners to acquire an understanding of the students' communication problems.

The purposes of communication showed a strongly social and pragmatic emphasis, as in getting a point across, sharing ideas, solving problems and so on. It was clear that the students had a very good perception of the importance of successful communication for understanding events and conditions, and for relating to other people. Their motivation and intention to succeed in so doing came through very strongly.

Conversation

A well-known and well-conducted study of language functioning in sustained communication, using video-recorded conversations between pairs of preschool hearing-impaired and hearing children engaged in play, was presented by McKirdy and Blank (1982). The hearing-impaired group, probably severely to profoundly deaf, comprised 24 children with congenital or prelingual hearing losses, whose ages ranged from 52 to 64 months. Twenty-two of the children were educated in TC programmes, with the remaining two educated orally. The hearing-impaired children were paired with hearing children of the same age, gender and non-verbal IQ. The children were arranged in same-gender dyads based on teacher's rank-order rating of preferred playmates, and placed in a room with a range of toys.

This study by McKirdy and Blank stands apart from most similar studies of its time in the use of a matched control group, and in employing statistical tests to evaluate the results. A coding system (Blank and Franklin, 1980) was used to score each participant in a dialogue, who was seen as assuming two separate roles, one of speaker-initiator; and the other as speaker-responder. As initiator, a speaker's signed and spoken utterances were judged for their level of cognitive complexity or their explicitness of demand for a response. As responder, a speaker's utterances and behaviours were judged for their appropriateness to the speaker-initiator's preceding utterance. The cognitive complexity for speaker-initiator allowed any utterance to be placed along a single continuum of complexity, divided into four levels: I Matching Experience, which involved words as symbols or labels for non-linguistic concepts already developed; II Selective Analysis of Experience, where the utterances were still tied to experience but represented a higher level of discrimination; III Re-ordering Experience, where language took on a directive function; and IV Reasoning about Experience, concerned with reasoning and problem-solving. The speaker-initiator scales also coded some pragmatic functions as to whether or not an utterance contained an explicit demand for a response. Explicit demands were termed 'Obliges' and their counterpart utterances which were not demands were 'Comments'. A scale for speaker-responder coded utterances for their appropriateness to the initiating speaker's remarks within the categories Adequate, Inadequate, No response and Ambiguous.

Communication between hearing and hearing-impaired children differed markedly. The hearing-impaired children initiated 27 conversational turns as against the hearing children's 57, reminiscent in part of Curtiss et al. (1979). Fifty-seven per cent of initiations of the hearing-impaired children's were Obliges, whereas the predominant form (57%) for the hearing children was the Comment. For both groups Obliges served to attract the partner's attention. The complexity of the interaction expressed in percentages revealed that the majority (92%) of the hearing-impaired children's initiations occurred at Level I (Matching Experience) with few occurrences at Levels II (Selective Analysis of Experience) and III (Re-ordering Experience), and none at Level IV (Reasoning about Experience). Level II accounted for 49% of the hearing children's initiations, with Levels I (29%) and III (21%) occurring in roughly equal percentages. Little use was made of Level IV (1%).

Although the percentage of responses to different levels of initiation at Levels I and II differed for hearing and hearing-impaired children, the patterns of response were similar. For both groups, Obliges were more effective than Comments in eliciting adequate responses. For example, the percentage of adequate responses to Obliges and Comments at Level I were 70% and 12% respectively for deaf children, and 65% and 34% for hearing children. The percentage of adequate responses for the deaf children decreased as the level of initiation increased from Level I to Level II, showing that the children were affected by the complexity of the formulations. Re-coded utterances, namely, utterances that were coded twice, first as responses to previous Comments, then secondly as initiations, were also examined to assess the extent to which there was a sustained exchange. Again, differences were observed. Re-coded data were obtained for all hearing children, but for only five out of the 24 hearing-impaired children, indicating the difficulty experienced by the deaf child in keeping dialogue going.

This work by McKirdy and Blank dealt with several interesting points. First, there was a difference in the rate of verbal productivity, with hearing-impaired children producing fewer messages at any one time than hearing subjects, as found by Curtiss et al. (1979). An explanation was offered that the deaf children's hands, needed for communication in sign, were occupied in playing with toys. Secondly, the range of levels in the deaf children's initiations was restricted in comparison to that of the hearing children, being limited to events and objects in the immediate present. Thirdly, the deaf children were learning their sign system, but had not proceeded very far. Instead, they relied on self-generated signs which, though adequate for signalling for attention, produced problems in coping with ideas beyond the immediate present. Fourthly, difficulties were more marked for the deaf children as speaker-responders than as speaker-initiators. They were less likely than the hearing children to respond to Comments, and offered fewer appropriate responses to Level II initiations, though the responses of deaf and hearing children to Level I initiations was similar.

As noted, a major difficulty in this study was the use of self-generated signs, which created restrictions, particularly in recording the symbolisation of ideas. The study might have achieved clearer results had children with a greater mastery of sign, such as signing deaf children born to signing deaf parents, been studied. McKirdy and Blank remarked that a pair of deaf children who were fluent in ASL had about the same initiation rate as the hearing children.

Examination of the breakdowns in conversations can provide a good indication of skills in pragmatics. Hughes and James (1985) found that TC-educated prelingually severely to profoundly deaf children aged 5–8 years were effective in dealing with communication breakdowns when the experimenter simultaneously spoke and signed: 'What?' in conversations, by revising or repeating their messages. The higher the children's grammatical skills, the more likely they were to revise their message. This use of pragmatics skills was similar to that found with the hearing child. It should, however, be appreciated that the 'What?' probe was a unitary and easily identified marker of communication breakdown. How deaf children cope with more complex breakdowns remains to be investigated.

Communication patterns in classrooms

A frequently cited study of communication patterns in classes for moderately to profoundly prelingually deaf children is that of Craig and Collins (1969, 1970). They used a modified Flanders Interactive Scale (Flanders, 1965), which contained several interactive categories, in direct observation of classroom communication.

Overall results for categories of interaction showed that in the structured areas of teaching, teachers markedly dominated classroom communication in all schools and for all ages of students. 'Questioning' and 'informing' were the categories used most frequently by teachers and students in language-dependent and specialised classes in initiating communication, though the teachers used them much more than the students. Assuming that the study was undertaken in the traditional setting where the teacher–pupil relationship is heavily structured and teacher-dominated, this finding is hardly surprising, though it is useful to have it put on record. The same comment can be made about the second overall finding, that a higher proportion of behaviour in the student 'response' category was observed when teacher 'questioning' comprised a high proportion of teacher-initiated behaviour. The very small 1% of 'confusions' showed the extent of teacher dominance. Thirdly, 'no communication' generally predominated when teacher-initiated interaction was relatively low.

Results for mode characteristics showed a predominance of the oral mode in structured situations at the primary and intermediate level classes. In language-dependent situations at the high-school level, the predominance of the oral mode continued in one school, while manual, written and combined modes were used roughly equally in another.

In the schools for the deaf investigated, limited emphasis was placed on the purpose of the students' communication, with the most obvious finding being the high level of teacher-initiated communication at all student ages. It is not clear to what extent this outcome occurred in schools for the deaf as compared with schools for the hearing, since none of the latter were included. The results of the work of McKirdy and Blank raised two main questions which their study, by design, was not able to resolve. Did the hearing-impaired students lack the ability to initiate communication? Or did they not get the chance to initiate it? Further research is required into learning under different conditions and in a variety of settings, to determine what changes in student communication would occur if differing proportions of interactions were controlled by teachers.

A subsequent investigation exploring classroom communication patterns and communication modes was conducted by Lawson (1978) to assess whether deaf students spend more classroom time on compliant, rather than self-directive, communication. Lawson adapted her method from Craig and Collins (1969), dividing it into the self-directive communications of the students and student-compliant communications. These two main categories were further subdivided to include self-directive behaviour addressed to the teacher or to another student. Lawson's study differed from that of Craig and Collins in recording exchanges not only between teachers and students but also between students themselves. However, no specific data were presented on teacher influence. Lawson gathered data from five intermediate level classrooms with student ages ranging from 10 to 13 years. One class was slow, three were average and one was advanced in achievement. Lawson offered no further information as to the degree of hearing loss of the subjects, how achievement levels were determined, or the reliability between the two observers who recorded the data. The results showed that both student-directive and student-compliant communicative behaviours occurred. The most frequent student-directive communication was 'informing', with 'following directions' being the most frequent student-compliant communication act. Students communicated during 64% of the observation period, with over half of this communication being student-compliant .

Lawson drew a number of parallels between her work and the earlier studies of Craig and Collins. First, the most frequently used category initiated by students in both studies was Informing, followed by Questioning. Secondly, there were few counts in the Development category. In order to find the extent of teacher-dominated communication, Lawson combined the categories of teacher communication with student-compliant communication for comparison with Craig and Collins' teacher-initiated communication. A large difference was found, with less teacher domination occurring in Lawson's study. Lawson suggested that this difference could be attributed to the didactic methods used with the lower grades investigated by Craig and Collins, and the possibility of changing communication involvement patterns in classrooms for the deaf, over time. However, the drawing of parallels between the two studies is questionable given the differing populations used. Further, Lawson's objective was not specifically to consider teacher dominance, since she used a category system where all teacher communications were grouped together. Combining teacher communication with student-compliant communication did not therefore necessarily facilitate a valid comparison with Craig and Collins' teacher-initiated communication category. Little information was given by Craig and Collins about the teaching methods used in their study, while Lawson provided no evidence in support of any change in communication involvement patterns in deaf classrooms. Lawson suggested that the lack of communication in the category of Development may show that hearing-impaired children do not actively integrate information into their own thinking. This view was shared by Craig and Collins (1969), but requires further investigation.

Craig and Collins' work also influenced Wolff (1977), who developed a Cognitive Verbal, Non-Verbal Observation Scale (CVNV) for in-service training of teachers in the area of cognition. This scale was used to investigate communication patterns in classes for deaf children employing different communication modes. It was based on an affective–cognitive system in which a category of communication intent, a level of cognitive implication of the communication, an indication of the mode, and a tally for the direction of communication were recorded. The CVNV schedule was based on a modified version of Craig and Collins' (1969) adaptation of the Flanders' Scale, with cognitive levels based on Piaget's levels of development. In contrast to Craig and Collins, but in line with Lawson (1978), the CVNV was able to assess student-to-student communication. However, Wolff's work differed from both in that data were provided on the cognitive levels at which the interaction generally occurred.

Limited data were provided about the population used in Wolff's study, which incorporated a wide age range of students from preschool to high-school level. No further information was given concerning the degree of hearing loss, mode of communication or classroom environment. Comparisons were drawn between traditional and cognitive classrooms, but definitions were not supplied. The lack of data and explanation in this study makes it difficult to ascertain exactly what the author was trying to achieve. The results, expressed as percentages, were compared with those obtained by Craig and Collins. Wolff, and Craig and Collins, found that 'teacher talk' comprised 47.3% and 48.5% respectively of the total talk in the primary school. At the intermediate and high-school levels, Wolff found teacher talk to be 43.4% of the total talk, while Craig and Collins found it to be 56.4% at the intermediate level, and 57% to 59% at the high-school level, depending on the subject matter. A comparison between the teachers in Wolff's study and those in Flanders (1965) and Craig and Collins (1969) at the primary level, showed that CVNV-trained teachers were 17% less immediately directive. Consequently, the students in Wolff's study showed 17% more student communication. Similar findings were reported at the intermediate level.

Taking into account the differences in the systems of analysis and the fact that teachers in Wolff's study had been trained to encourage non-directive language-supportive instruction, these results are to be expected. Wolff concluded that CVNV-trained teachers of the deaf are less immediately directive and that, as their skills improved with his training, their classes would communicate more. However, a comparison group was not used to compare direct and indirect communication, and comparisons with previous studies need to be interpreted with care. In considering the percentage of communication with cognitive intent, Wolff found that the content centred around activities involving memory and classification, with little attention paid to inference building. There was a tendency for TC classes to show more open communication than the oral classes, while those classes which employed only fingerspelling were the least open in communication. Wolff pointed out that there were differences in the three methods which could have influenced his findings about cognitive behaviour. However, whether these findings were a function of teacher style or the methodology used is unclear.

Interim summary

The studies reviewed so far showed that linguistic control of classrooms for the deaf has tended to be in the mouth and hands of the teacher, regardless of communication mode or ages of the children. However, there were indications that teachers needed to be more sensitive to the communication needs of deaf children. The studies attributed deficiencies in communication skills solely to deafness, though this conclusion cannot be fully accepted in the absence of data specifying the influence of age, IQ, hearing loss, family environment and so on. Also, several studies had design flaws, making their interpretation difficult.

Recent work with teachers

More recent work by Wood et al. (1982) examined the influence of classroom environment and the influence of the teacher in relation to deaf children's limited conversational abilities. The aim was to determine how far deaf children were capable of complying with conversational demands, and whether the ensuing conversations were governed by similar dynamic principles. Moderately to profoundly deaf children aged from 6 to 10 years from 16 different classrooms were involved.

Their non-verbal IQs ranged from 81 to 126. Data were collected in a 'news session' in which the children were asked to tell the teachers and the other children of their experiences outside school. The validity of such sessions is questionable when studying conversation, because it largely involves a monologue from the child who stands in front of the class, when a number of unconsidered child-related variables may be operating. However, an analysis of teacher talk and its relationship to averaged measures of child talk was presented. Transcripts were coded in two ways. First, the conversational moves of both teacher and child were classified into levels of control, and secondly, teacher speech was analysed in terms of the functions in each utterance. The authors were interested in the nature of the children's responses to different linguistic demands and the extent of their mean length of turn (MLT). The predictor variables were the various levels and functions of teacher moves in dialogue. A teacher power ratio was obtained from the percentage of questions and requested repetitions. Child-initiated measures were obtained from the percentage of questions, elaborations and contributions. The results were compared with an earlier study by the same authors of adult–child conversations involving young hearing children.

Initial analysis revealed that deaf children responded to the structure of teacher talk in a similar way to hearing children. Where teachers asked a high proportion of questions, children tended to display low initiative, indicating a strong effect of teacher style on the conversational capabilities displayed by children, whether hearing-impaired or hearing. In more detailed analysis, the deaf children were found to elaborate on their answers to questions only 14% of the time. They tended not to ask for repetitions or clarification, 'read' the basic force of teacher moves and seldom confused open and closed questions, and made their own contribution by developing a theme.

The relationship between moves and functions in teacher speech was also examined to reveal that some moves in teacher speech were associated with longer utterances from the children than others. This could have been a reflection of differences between the children and/or conversational style. A significant correlation was observed between MLT and hearing loss, with the least hearing-impaired children producing longer utterances. A significant correlation was also found between the frequency of move and hearing loss, where teachers tended to ask open questions of the least hearing-impaired children. It should be noted, however, that MLT does not necessarily enlighten us as to the child's conversational abilities. It could have been more informative to consider either syntactical complexity or conversational intent. Further, information about the mean number of utterances addressed to each child, the number of children in the group and perhaps even the topic of conversation is required before firm conclusions can be drawn on the correlation between teachers' conversations and hearing loss.

Continued investigations were reported by Wood et al. (1986) into why, after many years in school, most deaf children leave with low levels of linguistic and academic achievement. A summary of their conclusions, which relate mainly to orally educated children, is relevant to the consideration of pragmatics in communication. Wood et al. concluded that the disruptions, which occur for younger hearing-impaired children in mother–child and teacher–child interactions, are caused by specific difficulties in communication. An example would be the division of attention which occurs when the hearing-impaired child has to use vision to attend to both acts and objects of communication. However, adults, including teachers, may express unhelpful and even counterproductive behaviour which denies the child access to the naturally occurring non-verbal communication that helps hearing children to acquire an understanding of speech. Wood et al. concluded that the central role played by adults in guiding and promoting a child's progress through the stages involved in acquiring verbal communication is often not fulfilled for hearing-impaired children, especially where the child needs to learn how to distribute attention between communication partner and the object of the communication (compare Huntington and Whatton, 1981, 1984, 1986).

Despite the accumulating evidence of its occurrence, the didactic, overly-controlling, non-contingent ways of adult communication with hearing-impaired children continue (Lai and Lynas, 1990), though they occur more in the classroom than the home (Bodner-Johnson, 1991). Harrison et al. (1987) found, for example, that teachers interacting with four severely to profoundly deaf preschool children used labelling, modelling and correction techniques extensively. Little use was made of expansion or completion of a child's utterances, nor of reinforcement, repetition or amplification of utterances. Wood et al. (1986) were particularly critical of the question–answer exchange, which typifies many teacher–child interactions in school. This theme has been continued by Wood (1991). Wood et al. further saw teachers' language in the classroom as making no greater linguistic demands of older than of younger deaf children. The teacher's language was therefore probably not sufficiently challenging of the linguistic competence of the older children. It will be recalled that, in Chapter 2, we raised a similar query in asking whether parental language is properly 'tuned' to the linguistic abilities of hearing-impaired infants.

Nevertheless, it is unfair to single out teachers. Tests of reading designed for hearing children have also been criticised as insensitive to the linguistic abilities of hearing-impaired children, and hence poorly reflect their competencies and needs (Wood et al., 1986). Appropriate tests are important because oracy is closely involved with the development of literacy, and hence relevant tests are needed to assess both spoken and written language. The mismatch between the linguistic competence of hearing-impaired children and the demands of texts may lead to teaching strategies that teach special tactics for understanding reading material, rather than assisting the development of true literacy.

We have noted that it is sometimes said that teachers use relatively less figurative or idiomatic language with hearing-impaired children. In work by Newton (1985), communicative patterning in the classroom was investigated with a focus on the teachers' use of non-literal language as part of the linguistic environment. Newton remarked that whereas the poor English language abilities of hearing-impaired children had been attributed to impaired hearing or inadequate teaching, research was needed on the kind of language models used. He chose to study teachers' use of non-literal language because this aspect was commonly seen as deficient in hearing-impaired children. Newton compared the language spoken to hearing-impaired and hearing children to assess the influence of teachers' perceptions of the children's needs, and the influence of constraints in their children's linguistic ability on teachers' adaptations. For example, did teachers who used an oral-only approach with hearing-impaired children, use less non-literal language than teachers communicating with hearing children of comparable linguistic ability? Did teachers communicating by TC use less non-literal language than teachers using an oral-only approach when addressing hearing-impaired children?

Newton examined the use of two kinds of non-literal language: idiom ('That's kind of funny') and indirect requests ('Why don't you sit down?'), commonly used to communicate with hearing children. His subjects were 30 teacher–child dyads: 10 with hearing children; 10 with hearing-impaired children using aural/oral communication; and 10 with hearing-impaired children using TC. Each group consisted of dyads from two different programmes in two different cities. For hearing teacher–child dyads, the children were aged 2–3 years with a mean length of utterance (MLU) of at least 2.0. The teachers were those who normally worked with the child. For hearing-impaired teacher–child dyads, all children were prelingually profoundly deaf. Language matching was based on MLU data, though the hearing-impaired children had higher MLUs of at least 3.0. These children were also cognitively, physically and socially more mature, with ages ranging from 5 to 9 years. All their teachers were of normal hearing, had taught hearing-impaired children for at least 3 years, and were well-acquainted with the child in their dyad. Two tasks were assigned to each dyad – spontaneous communication and storytelling. Only the oral component of the TC teachers' language was assessed, as their greatest use of non-literal language always occurred in this oral component.

For idiomatic usage, no differences were found in the teachers' use of non-literal language between speech addressed to hearing and to oral hearing-impaired children on either task, although there was less use of idiomatic language, in both the oral and signed components, when TC was used, especially for the signed component. No significant differences were found in the oral component for indirect requests between the three groups, though few indirect requests were actually presented to the hearing children. However, only 55% of these requests were presented non-literally in the signed portion of TC.

Thus the results did not support a hypothesis of greater use of idioms by teachers with hearing than with oral hearing-impaired children, but the expected difference between oral- and TC-educated hearing-impaired children was found. For the hearing-impaired children educated via TC, their teachers seldom used idiomatic structures, and when they did, about two-thirds were not signed for the children to observe. Teachers used no more indirect requests with the older and cognitively and socially more mature hearing-impaired children. The explanation is unclear, as the maturity variables between hearing and hearing-impaired children were not adequately matched.

In conclusion, both the earlier studies (Craig and Collins, 1969, 1970; Wolff, 1977; Lawson, 1978) and the more recent reports (Wood et al., 1982; Newton, 1985; Wood et al., 1986; Wood, 1991) reveal an inappropriate, overly directing orientation in teachers of the deaf towards their students, which Wood (1991) has ascribed to the effort involved in coping with individuals who have weak communication skills. This style seems universal where there is a large mismatch in communication between hearing adult and deaf child. It may partly explain why similarities are found in the approaches to coping with classroom conversations in hearing-impaired and learning-disabled children (Weiss, 1986).

It would be informative to discover if overly directing approaches by native deaf signing teachers of the deaf do not occur towards native deaf signing students, who would communicate well in sign. There is some evidence that this is the case. Observations by Mather (1989) suggested that, of two teachers, one who was a native deaf signer encouraged wh- questions, risk-taking, role-playing, etc., in her deaf preschool students more than a hearing teacher using signed English. Also, Murphy and Hill (1989) and Musselman and Churchill (1991) have concluded that communication by TC, with its sign component which puts hearing teachers and deaf children on a more even communication footing, is effective in developing pragmatics skills in deaf children, allowing the children to obtain more conversational styles or more conversational control. However, the results of Newton (1985) are grounds for scepticism about such a conclusion. TC may have the potential to assist the development of skills in pragmatics, but this potential may not be realised.

Interactive communication patterns

The next group of studies to be reviewed consider the interactive communication patterns of hearing-impaired children, beginning with work on referential communication, which relates globally to pragmatics.

We start with the study by Hoemann (1972), in which the accuracy and quality of peer-to-peer referential communication in prelingually profoundly deaf children who used sign was compared with that of hearing children using spoken English. Half the subjects had a mean age of 8 years and half of 11 years. Half were hearing and half were deaf. The reader is referred to Chapter 5 (page 112) for other details of design and methodology.

Receiving scores were higher than sending scores for all four samples. As this finding was most marked in the 8-year-old deaf subjects, it suggested that their low communication accuracy score was due more to poor messages than to poor receiving skills. The hearing subjects manifested two achievements lacking in the deaf children, namely, establishment of a social contract over whose perspective to take, and description of pictures in left–right trials according to the receiver's right or left hand. In the task of explaining the rules of a game, results were recorded both before and after prompting, and classified as adequate, fair or deficient. Little difference in deaf subjects was noted before and after prompting, whereas the hearing children were able to add rules they had omitted. Younger and older deaf subjects with deficient explanations behaved inappropriately. However, all 40 deaf subjects were able to teach their peers how to play the game when permitted to demonstrate the rules in action, suggesting that although they knew the rules, they were unable to communicate them manually to their peers.

Whilst Hoemann's study indicates that deafness was a handicap in peer-to-peer communication, there are other aspects to be considered. Was the poor performance of the deaf children due to the channel properties of sign? Hoemann noted some instances where gestural communication presented special difficulties, but it is unclear whether they were sufficient to account for a generally deficient performance. He hypothesised that a general experiential deficit could account for the handicap, presenting evidence in the form of overlapping contributions of scores, in which some deaf subjects did as well as their hearing peers. Further, the role of experience in developing communication was indicated by the improvement with increasing age. There are several other factors which need to be investigated before accepting this explanation. Previous experience with similar tasks needs consideration, as does the developmental stage of an individual's manual communication skills. Also questionable is the extent to which formal referential tasks may have restricted the use of non-verbal modes of communication (Chapter 7). Hoemann's study provided an interesting basis for further work on interactive communication patterns of deaf children. However, it was limited in terms of furthering our knowledge of deaf children's communicative competence in social communication.

Similar remarks can be passed on the work of Jordan (1983), who studied pairs of hearing-impaired children ranging in age from 3 to 15 years, and a hearing group, pairing the children by age. They were asked to describe 25 pictures to an age-matched listener, so that the listener could identify the picture from a picture set. Differences were found with age in communicative accuracy across age groups of hearing-impaired subjects and between hearing-impaired and normally hearing children, but statistical evaluations were not reported.

Other workers, however, have not found differences between hearing and hearing-impaired children on referential communication tasks. Thus, Breslaw et al. (1981) compared groups of hearing-impaired children with a mean hearing loss of 88 dB and a mean age of 8 years, from different educational backgrounds, with groups of hearing children. Each child had to place coloured blocks on a board and tell a listener about it, so that the listener could perform the same task. The performances of the hearing-impaired and the hearing children were generally not significantly different.

It is of interest to enquire further into whether communication mode affects the conveying of information in referential communication. This question can be answered by comparing the performance in the same task of hearing-impaired children who communicate in different modes. For instance, message-formation skills involved in referential messages from differently communicating hearing-impaired children to their mothers were studied by MacKay-Sorota et al. (1987). The children were aged 6–10 years, and came from oral or bimodal, namely, oral plus manual programmes. They were tested in two tasks. In the first task, the children described a specified picture in a set of four, so that the mothers could identify the referent from the alternatives. In a second task, the children viewed a single picture, and subsequently had to identify it from a set of four related pictures. Nevertheless, although their hearing losses were greater, the bimodally educated children produced more differentiated messages than the orally educated children. They also gave better reformulations of messages that at first were inadequate. Although the mothers of the orally educated children received inferior messages, they were as successful as the mothers of the bimodally educated children in selecting the correct referent. This result is odd. It suggests that the picture-description task was too simple to be a good test of differences in modality in conveying the information as compared with forming it. Both groups of children were near-perfect on the picture recognition task, showing that the differences in the first task were due to differences in skill at message formation rather than differential visual perceptual processing of the task materials.

More detailed research is needed in the area of referential communication with hearing-impaired children to answer the several queries which we have raised. The results outlined are insufficiently clear, and conflicting.

We now consider a selection of other work on interactive communication, to illustrate further interactive communication patterns.

Interactive communication in group work has been described by Pendergrass and Hodges (1976), who observed children involved in group problem-solving. Six groups, comprising 4–6 severely to profoundly deaf children each, were brought together to solve a problem presented to them by the examiner. The Bates' (1950) Interactive Process Analysis (IPA) procedure was used to evaluate the quantity and quality of communicative interactions. The IPA has a standardised set of 12 categories, and interaction can be considered in a number of ways – in relation to the 12 categories, the four major areas into which the 12 categories can be grouped, and/or pairing specific categories with each pair representing a typical problem in group interaction.

The six groups were divided so that four contained younger, 6–9-year-old, children with limited formal communication skills. The other two contained older, 11–13-year-old, children with more refined skills. Two problems were presented. The first was a puzzle, and the second involved unscrambling letters to form words that matched pictures of animals. Pendergrass and Hodges stated that the problems could be solved for the most part with limited formal communication skills, but they encouraged maximum communication between students. Data were recorded in relation to the child initiating the interaction, the child being addressed, and the category of communication.

While the distribution of communication activities among the 12 categories revealed the use of all categories, few interactions were recorded in a 'questioning' category, implying that these deaf children lacked the general ability to ask for information, make suggestions, provide orientations, or seek clarification of the opinions of others. Interactions within the four major categories saw 'attempted answers' ranking the highest, followed by 'positive social–emotional areas'. 'Questions' ranked the lowest. A comparison of positive and negative social emotional areas for each group found little difference between them, in the groups of younger children. However, a higher percentage of interaction in the positive area was found in the groups of older children. This may indicate that, with maturity, the deaf child becomes more task-orientated.

Without a comparison group of hearing subjects, it is not clear whether the degree of interaction between the hearing-impaired subjects would differ significantly from that for hearing subjects. Whether the problems presented actually encouraged interaction is also questionable. Considered with the other studies reviewed above, problem-solving tasks by pairs or larger groups present some difficulties in their application to informal social communication. They do, however, permit not merely an estimate of how well a message was communicated or received, but also a systematic analysis of communicative intent and social interaction.

It is of special interest to study the pragmatics of communication in deaf infants in their first few months of life, before the emergence of recognisable language. We need to know, for instance, how early prelingual communication patterns develop so that we can interpret the mapping of communication through verbal or sign language on to prelinguistic forms. A longitudinal study which offered insights into this process was conducted by Scroggs (1983) on the communicative interactions between hearing-impaired infants and their parents. Four hearing-impaired infants identified in their first year were video-taped for half an hour once a month in play sessions with their parents. Observations concentrated on the communicative strategies used by the children and their parents. The preliminary observations involved the behaviour used by the parent or child to initiate 'conversations', the simultaneous and sequential turn-taking behaviour used to sustain conversation, and the procedures used to end them.

The first observation was that rhythmical behaviour occurred when the parent and infant were communicating. This behaviour played an important role in engaging the infant's attention, in cueing the infant into a familiar play sequence, in checking the infant's interest in a particular game, and in continuing the conversation through imitating the infant's behaviour. In addition, a coordinated rhythmic behaviour was observed, which served as a turn-taking strategy. The infant became familiar with a behaviour pattern and would wait until the mother had finished before taking his turn. This rhythmic behaviour was seen as playing a fundamental role as the basis for successful communication. The communicative strategies used by deaf infants and their parents differed little from those of hearing infants. Vocalisations were not the major factor in conversations, which may explain why the auditory component does not, at this stage of development, cause serious disruptions to communication, and also why deafness in infants is not easily suspected by parents at early developmental stages. Scroggs did not, however, point out that the parents' knowledge of their child's deafness may have influenced some or many of the interactions observed.

All too often the education of hearing-impaired children has emphasised the acquisition of vocabulary and syntax, without an equal and necessary emphasis on the use of language for interaction in communication (compare Duffy, 1984; Giorcelli, 1985). Facilitation of interactive communication patterns was investigated by Antia and Kreimeyer (1985), who introduced social interaction routines to assist peer interaction in preschool hearing-impaired children. They devised a programme consisting of a number of social skills and social interaction routines. The programme was administered to three groups of preschool children, with 3–5 children in each group. The children were aged 3–5 years, with normal IQs and mild to profound hearing losses. All wore hearing aids which were checked daily. Two groups used oral communication while the third used signed English. The programme was conducted for 20–30 minutes each day over 1 year.

Data were collected from observation of the frequency of peer interaction, and from a questionnaire for parents and teachers, on which they rated the children on changes in interaction skills at home and in class. The data showed that positive interactions increased from an average of 6% to 12% of recorded intervals before the programme to 30–38% during the programme. Questionnaire data indicated increases in Praising and Cooperating for some 80% of children and increases in Sharing and Assisting for 70%. Teachers reported no change in negative behaviour for 80% of the children, while parents reported a decrease for about 70%.

Like several others in the field, this study of Antia and Kreimeyer was not designed so that the effectiveness of the programme, which looks impressive, could be validly assessed. There was no matched control group which did not receive the programme, nor were data offered about the progress which might be expected over 1 year by hearing children of similar age. The results are therefore more indicative than compelling.

Summary and conclusions

Analysis of the communication of hearing-impaired children has, in the past, focused on the linguistic aspects of vocabulary, syntax and, to a lesser degree, phonological development. However, with a growing emphasis on pragmatics, in the fields of normal and specific language impairment, researchers have begun to broaden their perspective to include pragmatics in considering how hearing-impaired children put language to use. The available literature is small and has to date made little use of pragmatic theories and systems of analysis.

Our review has examined the research in two main areas – communicative intentions and conversation. There are few general conclusions that can be drawn from the research, for several reasons. First, research in this area is scanty (Foster et al., 1989). Secondly, the majority of studies used a research design which had lacunae in one or more of the following:

1. Did not draw on benchmark measures, which could have been obtained by incorporating control groups.
2. Did not assign children randomly to experimental and comparison (control) groups or, where matched groups were used, did not use appropriate matches.
3. Made limited use of statistical methods to test the reliability and significance of results.
4. Omitted to measure or record salient subject variables.

In fairness we should note that such design issues are not limited to work on the pragmatics skills of hearing-impaired children. They are to be found also in other areas (Beisler and Tsai, 1983; Prinz and Ferrier, 1983; Damico et al. 1984).

Investigations of the functions that utterances serve revealed that hearing-impaired children code a variety of communicative intentions. The work of Skarakis and Prutting (1977), Curtiss et al. (1979) and Scroggs (1983) showed that hearing-impaired infants and young children express similar semantic functions and communicative intentions to those of hearing children at the prelinguistic and one-word stage. For older individuals, the interviews conducted with college students by Foster et al. (1989) suggest practical contexts where future work may be undertaken to advantage. All these studies have implications for assessment and remediation. Analysis procedures could be used as assessment tools. Parallels drawn between hearing-impaired and hearing subjects can provide the language teacher with guidelines for the content and sequencing of language remediation programmes. Results illustrating the interdependence of semantics and pragmatics also hold implications for remediation. It may be worthwhile, for example, to teach the use of a particular semantic function with a number of different pragmatic intentions. In addition, it could be shown that one feature in pragmatics can be used to express a variety of semantic functions. The extent to which the hearing-impaired differ significantly from hearing individuals in this area is not clear and further research is needed for the planning of adequate remediation programmes.

McKirdy and Blank (1982), who evaluated language within a communication framework, pointed out that past discussions of language programmes have seldom concerned communication or the multiple roles that communication demands. The assumption had been that if a suitable linguistic system was available to the child, it would invariably be followed by the ability to communicate through that system. Their study showed that this is not necessarily so. In conversation, their hearing-impaired children functioned both as initiators and responders, but their pattern of performance differed in quantity of conversational turns, and the quality and complexity of the interaction. The data showed that communication ought not to be considered as inevitably following from given language abilities.

Work which considered communication patterns in the classroom indicated that the degree and type of communication used by the students was heavily dependent on the teacher. There were a number of limitations in each of these studies, and differences across groups and methods of analysis did not enable adequate comparisons to be drawn between the studies. However, the reports provided information on measuring instruments, such as the instrument devised by Craig and Collins (1969), modified by Lawson (1978), and by Wolff (1977). The reports also contained implications for investigating teaching methods. Some suggestions for further research have been indicated.

The rationale within our schools for the deaf is to provide not only academic training, but also language-supportive and language-stimulating instruction. Granted these goals, there are clear implications for reassessing teaching methods. The degree to which hearing-impaired children in the classroom have the opportunity to initiate and engage in interactive communication should be queried (Wood et al., 1982, 1986; Wood, 1991). Further research is thus required into learning in different communicative roles and in a variety of settings. This research would determine the degree of change in student communication when faced with varieties of teacher talk.

A weaker performance by hearing-impaired children, in comparison with hearing children, was found by Hoemann (1972) and Jordan (1983) in the accuracy and quality of peer-to-peer communication, though Breslaw et al. (1981) found otherwise. Whether it is hearing loss that causes this possible handicap, and/or the manual method of communication, and/or other factors, requires further investigation. One means would be to conduct studies with children who are proficient in manual communication, or those using an alternative means of communication. In this context, Newton's (1985) report suggests strongly that the use of idiom is restricted by normal forms of communication.

The study by Pendergrass and Hodges (1976), which considered interactive communication patterns through a group problem-solving task, showed that deaf children were limited in their ability to question and that, with increased maturity, the deaf child became more task-orientated. This study may help educators of the deaf with teaching group problem-solving tasks. It is implicit that small group analysis provides a structured tool for the identification of specific strengths and weaknesses of pragmatics skills in hearing-impaired children. The findings suggested that for educators to help hearing-impaired children in these skills they may need to devote more time to intensive training in questioning skills, in reinforcing social maturation by teaching positive social skills in group problem-solving situations, and in training the skills needed for attention to tasks. The findings of Antia and Kreimeyer (1985) pointed in the same general direction.

Some of the fundamental groundwork for the understanding of the pragmatics skills of hearing-impaired children has been laid. The continuation of research in this area is important not only for the understanding of communication in hearing-impaired children, but for the ongoing development of remedial programmes. The studies reviewed raise a number of issues to which more fundamental research can now be addressed.

By way of final comment, we note that no published studies have focused on the development of pragmatics skills in young cochlear implantees. Given that certain pragmatics skills in communication are known to precede the use of language in hearing infants, this is astonishing. Some of the procedures currently used in the rehabilitation of young implantees should benefit from increased attention to the pragmatics of communication, rather than concentrating quite so much on the use of hearing and aural rehabilitation in the narrow sense. Techniques of the type described by Tait and Wood (1987), covering the progression from non-verbal communication to language, and involving visual attention-sharing and turn-taking, suggest some paths to be explored.

Chapter 9
Management of the Hearing-impaired Child

This chapter outlines selected 'milestones' seen as historically important in approaches to the management of the deaf child. It then considers a number of issues of a practical nature which bear on education and therapy. The chapter concludes with a consideration of the options available to parents with young severely to profoundly deaf children, and remarks on several areas about which there is continuing debate.

Up to about the 1960s, the approach taken towards the rehabilitation of hearing-impaired individuals was based on the defectology model. Hearing-impaired people, especially those deafened before acquiring verbal language, were regarded by and large as 'defective' (Garrison and Tesch, 1978; Murphy-Berman et al., 1987). Although such individuals could gain from rehabilitation and education, it was generally believed that their communicative abilities remained problematical, and they could not attain the life styles of hearing individuals. Nor should they aspire to do so. A particularly moving account of the experiences of deaf individuals in such a climate is given by Petkovsek (1961), and a very readable collection of the varied experiences of deaf people can be found in Taylor and Bishop (1991).

Negative attitudes towards deaf individuals among professionals have changed, but they have far from changed elsewhere, in both children and adults (Dengerink and Porter, 1984; Sacks, 1989). Attempts to modify these negative attitudes meet with mixed success (Strong and Shaver, 1991).

Some Milestones

Professional attitudes towards hearing-impaired individuals and their rehabilitation have been subject to fashion and change no less than other topics in human affairs. As a result, certain areas in the treatment of deaf people have varied in prominence over the years. We comment now on several, not necessarily directly connected, topics which have affected the management of hearing-impaired children over the last few decades.

Linguistic deviancy

Some expressions produced by hearing-impaired children have been represented as 'deafisms', a kind of linguistic deviancy, most marked in commentaries about the attempts of deaf children who are trying to grasp verbal language. Such deafisms have been ascribed to children with the more severe hearing handicaps, especially the profoundly deaf. This topic is important. The implications are weighty if deafisms are so pervasive as to constitute a deaf communication system or language (deaf English), because it will be hard to develop communication skills if the linguistic base is obscure to others (see below).

Linguistic deviancy can be associated with various impairments besides deafness. Hence, if deafisms are unique, it must be shown that their linguistic divergence differs qualitatively, or shows marked quantitative differences, from other deviances. It is easy to confound linguistic deviancy with language delay, as when a certain expression appears to be deviant at first sight, given the age of the child, but on inspection is seen to be due to delayed rather than divergent language development. If deafisms are uniquely divergent, they should occur uniquely in the language of hearing-impaired children and not occur in the early development of hearing children or elsewhere.

Deviancy is, by definition, difficult or impossible to analyse with the conventional tools used in language analysis. Such a situation will at once alert us to a possible deviancy. However, we will need several instances of such deviancy if we are not to regard it as an idiosyncrasy or slip of the tongue, or as an unwitting error or lacuna in writing. We also need to be careful lest the apparent deviancy represents an accepted local form, for example: 'She's having a maggot' – a seeming semantic deviancy, used by a hearing-impaired child in Oxfordshire, UK, to describe to the writer's colleagues a picture containing an obviously annoyed woman.

Fusfeld (1955) saw the deviances of hearing-impaired individuals as a state of non-language, because the words were not aligned in an orderly way. Myklebust (1964) gave instances of linguistic deviancy, but did not seek any systematic characterisation among them. As he remarked, we need to know not only whether hearing-impaired children have reduced linguistic skills, but whether their errors show characteristic patterns. Brannon (1968) studied the picture-elicited spoken language of hearing, partially hearing and profoundly deaf children with a mean age of 12;6 years. He found a marked decrease in the number of words used as hearing loss increased. He also found that of 14 parts of speech analysed, the partially hearing differed notably from hearing children only in the use of adverbs, pronouns and auxiliaries, in which the deaf children were the most deficient. These deaf children used all classes of words, except conjunctions, less than the hearing children. Brannon confirmed Goda's (1964) previous finding that the speech of profoundly deaf children contained relatively fewer 'function words' (auxiliaries, prepositions, etc.) than the speech of hearing children. However, because of the method of analysis, the distinction was presented quantitatively, and hence the observed differences were of degree rather than kind, even though the speech of the deafer children seemed 'telegraphic' (Goda, 1964).

Similar findings were obtained by Pressnell (1973) for the comprehension and spoken syntax of 47 profoundly deaf and partially hearing children with an age range of 5–13;3 years, using the Northwestern Syntax Screening Test (Lee, 1969) with a set of pictures. While analysis showed that the performance of the older was superior to that of the younger hearing-impaired children, further analyses of spontaneous utterances, scored according to Lee and Canter (1971), showed that the children had the greatest difficulty with compound verbs. Relatively little difficulty was found with uninflected verbs and the copula. The results revealed particular difficulties with auxiliary verbs and morphology, but again the differences were in degree rather than in kind.

Wilcox and Tobin (1974) used a sentence-repetition task to assess the spoken language of hearing and hearing-impaired children. Special attention was paid to verb constructions. Results for their 11 congenitally mildly to severely deaf children, of mean age 10 years, and 11 hearing children of the same mean age, showed that verb constructions were significantly poorer for the hearing-impaired than for the hearing group. Wilcox and Tobin concluded that the performance differences across the verb forms were distinguished in quantity rather than in quality, since the patterns of scores were similar for both groups. However, they remarked that there was a marked divergence in performance for (have + en) and negative passive. Use of the negative passive in particular showed a considerable difference between the groups. These instances suggested a difference in kind, tantamount to a qualitative difference. Also, the relatively marked difficulty with (have + en) was similar to the findings of Pressnell (1973) – see above – indicating that hearing-impaired children have a characteristic difficulty with this verb form.

Ivimey (1976) commented that evidence of deviant skills abounded in the literature and, in reviewing studies such as those described above, asked if the many defects and deviances in the language of the deaf were sufficiently consistent and widespread to justify classing them as a system that is the only one of its kind, namely, a peculiar language that differs to a greater or lesser extent from normal English. This is an interesting question because, if the language of the deaf is different in kind from normal language, then deaf people will have qualitatively distinct communication skills. Ivimey thus asked whether the language of deaf children was systematic and, if so, whether it was congruent with the language of hearing children. If not, was it to be considered a deviant subsystem or as a language in its own right?

To answer such questions requires the analysis of a large corpus of material from a large representative sample of deaf children, because the need is to show whether the majority of deaf children exhibit the linguistic behaviour in question. The effort involved in such a task is so great that it has not been attempted on the scale desired. Rather there are a number of relatively small-scale or individual studies. One such study was that described by West and Weber (1974) for a partially hearing girl aged 4 years, who produced a number of non-standard English forms, such as bound morphemes like 'badboy', in addition to conventional English. Other interesting reports include that of Davis (1977), who found that one group of hearing-impaired children with moderate hearing loss, and another group with severe to profound hearing loss, had difficulty with linguistically advanced forms. Since the hearing-impaired children studied by Davis and the other workers cited above had problems with the more difficult linguistic constructions, it is not clear that their language was deviant. Rather, it could be argued that the language was retarded.

Most of the quoted examples of deviancy in the literature have been obtained from written rather than spoken examples. One of the few large-scale studies of spoken language from hearing-impaired children was reported by Bamford and Mentz (1979). They found no syntactic deviancy in a detailed grammatical analysis of picture-elicited speech in a sample of 263 children aged 8–15 years with mild to profound hearing losses. However, their sample overall comprised partially hearing rather than profoundly deaf children.

The studies outlined so far were mainly concerned with grammar. Studies of semantics in hearing-impaired children are relatively rare, although this area overlaps that of cognition, which has received considerable attention. Investigations that show semantic deviancy are even rarer. One such investigation, noted in Chapter 8, was recorded by Green and Shepherd (1975), who explored the adjectival semantic structure of the language of 33 severely to profoundly deaf children, aged 9–18 years with performance IQs of 80–125, with the semantic differential technique as adapted by Di Vesta (1966). The data from 28 scales were subjected to factor analysis, yielding six factors. The first two factors reflected the Evaluative ('good–bad') and Potency ('weak–strong') dimensions respectively, as seen also in the semantic systems of hearing children. However, the hearing children's Activity dimension ('slow–fast') was displaced by a dimension involving sensory judgements associated with visual and tactile modalities ('wet–dry', 'round–square'). Other factors found in the semantic systems of hearing children were missing. Hence Green and Shepherd found an unusual pattern of semantic factor structures with this group of deaf children.

More recently, Schaefer (1980), who was interested in the semantic relationships underlying the categories which capture verb meaning, prepared videotapes of situations encoded by the categories 'cut', 'break', and 'open', which were arranged as expected- and unexpected-choice pairs. Various groups, including deaf and hearing children, matched as the 'same' one choice from a pair to a video-taped sample of the expected category. The choices for the children, as compared with adults, showed that unexpected choices were preferred as a match, with the choices of younger and older hearing children following a developmental pattern. Although the basis for their choices was not clear, the deaf children did not fit this pattern. Their performance may have been associated with problems of developing meanings for words as independent entities (Lewis and Wilcox, 1978). More studies of this type, concerning boundary features of words, which minimally constrain judgements of 'sameness', would be of value.

Commentaries on linguistic deviancy in the spoken language of deaf children have fallen away in recent years, though Bamford and Saunders (1985) observed that even if 'deaf English' was denied as a system, deafisms were still commonly found. In part, the reduced emphasis on deafisms is due to an emerging realisation that hearing-impaired children do not form as homogeneous a group as originally thought. Hearing loss is only moderately positively correlated with linguistic development, and other factors such as age, intelligence and auditory perceptual and cognitive processes need to be considered. For the present, a convincing case, based on substantial data and thoroughgoing analysis, has yet to show that the language of deaf children, or of any well identified deaf subgroup, contains linguistic deviancy to such a degree as to confirm the existence of a deaf verbal language. The language of hearing-impaired children generally approximates to standard verbal language, though it is characterised by difficulties with linguistic forms more complex than simple SVO constructions (Leslie and Clarke, 1977; Tate, 1980).

For some hearing-impaired children these problems will be temporary. They will go on to master the more complex forms in due course. For others, there will be a level beyond which they will find it difficult to proceed (compare Charrow, 1975). We have considered some of the reasons for this situation in previous chapters. It is particularly disconcerting to have to remark that the cause of unusual language in deaf children is repeatedly ascribed not so much to deafness itself, but to the ways in which the deaf child's education has been managed (Arnold, 1978; Gormley and Franzen, 1978; Wood, 1991).

Advent of hearing aids

The development of the wearable hearing aid, in the years leading to and following the Second World War, did much to reveal to administrators, educators and therapists, and hearing-impaired people themselves, that hearing-impaired individuals could be divided broadly into two groups. The majority had usable residual hearing in the region of mild to severe hearing loss. For most of the individuals in this partially hearing group, the fitting of a hearing aid made the speech of others accessible. Even though distorted, as the hearing aids of the time were rather crude audio-amplifiers, and given also the distorting effects of inner-ear hearing loss, access to the speech of others allowed the child to communicate fairly well. Although partially hearing children with prelingual hearing loss experienced difficulties in language development, and even those children who became hearing-impaired postlingually had real problems, they were nonetheless generally able to acquire language and speech. They were hence able to communicate at levels not too different from those of their hearing peers, especially when given sufficient therapeutic and other support. One result was that a large proportion of hearing-impaired children formerly regarded as 'defective' could be seen as more like hearing children, though the obvious clumsily packaged body-worn aids of the time continued to mark them as different.

Conventional hearing aids were, and are, of much less help to the child with profound hearing loss. Although high-gain and other sophisticated aids give the child a perception of the rhythms of speech, and can assist with the discrimination of some speech sounds, it was and has remained generally the case that many, if not most, children with profound prelingual deafness do not acquire sufficient speech, let alone intelligible speech, despite the strenuous efforts of parents, teachers and therapists.

Part of the problem is that hearing-impaired children, particularly those who are born profoundly deaf, have problems in generalising from one stimulus situation to another. Although a given communication skill, such as distinguishing one phoneme from another, may be learned, it proves difficult for the child to translate the skill to other phonemic contexts. Also, while a particular approach to the perception of speech may be taught and learned sufficiently thoroughly for a given purpose, it is not transferred to other parts of the programme (Fisher and Schneider, 1986). We noted similar problems in our discussion of social skills in Chapter 8. It is as though the child comes to regard what is taught in a given situation as specific to that situation, and not to be used, or not of use, outside it. The problem may arise from the approach taken to the child's remediation or education, where segmented teaching produces segmented communication skills. Or perhaps it is a characteristic of deaf children, who have problems in understanding the value of listening (Smith and Richards, 1990).

Various authors have remarked on ways to overcome the difficulty (Ling, 1976; Fisher and Schneider, 1986), but further research is required. Increased use of group discussion in the classroom, which is designed to allow the practice of skills taught to children individually, and which forces the use of a variety of communication skills if the child is to contribute, may be one way forward. Even so, and although there were, and continue to be, remarkable exceptions (McCartney, 1986), generally the profoundly deafened ear yields aided hearing which is too limited or too distorted for the acquisition of speech and language, and hence severely reduces opportunities for everyday communication (Maxwell, 1989).

Aided hearing is improved only modestly by speechreading. As noted in Chapter 3, only about half of the phonemes can be perceived visually. Only about eight can be identified without ambiguity, and that under good seeing conditions such as short distance, good illumination and limited angle of regard (Erber, 1979). These conditions are not easy to meet in the classroom. Given that speechreading often has to take place in less than good seeing conditions, that only some phonemes can be perceived visually, that most prelingually profoundly deaf children do not have well developed skills for coding speech, and have a weak verbal language which makes it unproductive for them to guess, it is scarcely surprising that the use of speechreading and what little residual hearing they may have is often ineffective (Conrad, 1979).

Where the use of speechreading appears to be efficacious, the perception of the speech may be due more to a lack of control for gestures and to the level and use of residual hearing, which is such that the child is severely rather than profoundly deaf. Erber (1972, 1979) has shown that the contribution of speechreading to speech perception in hearing-impaired children is relatively small, and is about the same for profoundly and severely deaf children. Younger postlingually profoundly deaf children are in only a moderately more advantageous position as regards aided hearing, depending on the extent to which they could recognise speech sounds before the deafness occurred. Although then, the advent of wearable hearing aids may have helped to remove the stigma of defect from partially hearing children by improving their verbal communication, it did less to help children who were profoundly deaf.

Recognition of sign language

Profoundly deaf individuals who communicate by sign continue to be seen as in some way defective. The use of sign marks them as very different from hearing people. Historically, because hearing people have not understood sign, they have held it in contempt (De l'Epée, 1784). The recognition of sign as language was also held back because the field of linguistics was insufficiently advanced and because those who used it as their first language, namely deaf signers, did not have the academic background to research it. However, in the 1960s, the work of Stokoe and his colleagues (Stokoe, 1960; Stokoe et al., 1965) began to change the perceptions of professionals about sign and its users. The earlier perceptions that the gestural means of communication used by profoundly deaf people was less than an accepted language began to alter. Although there are dissenters (see Chapter 5), it is now generally accepted that deaf sign language is a language in its own right (Lane, 1988). Its native users are increasingly seen as different rather than deficient, which can only assist in the management of the deaf child.

Sign language is increasingly used in schools for the deaf, although it has yet to be used extensively in deaf education (Woodward and Allen, 1987). An impressive token of its acceptance in the community is that sign language is now offered to hearing students in schools and colleges as a second language (Chapin, 1988; Selover, 1988).

Diversity in communication ability

Research over the last 20 years or so has shown that, within limits, hearing loss or deafness is not the sole determinant of difference. Nor does it make sense any longer to lump together all individuals with a given degree of loss, such as severe or profound deafness. Research has shown that deafness leads to cognitive and linguistic differences which are the proximal causes of several communication problems, with hearing loss itself being the distal cause. There is, for example, particular diversity in communication ability in children who are severely deaf. Some severely deaf children behave like other children with lesser degrees of hearing loss, and communicate orally. Others operate more like the profoundly deaf child who prefers to sign. The difference is probably associated with the child's development of inner speech (Conrad, 1980). However, even profoundly deaf children seem to have at least some elements of coding for inner speech (Geers et al., 1984), perhaps developed through residual hearing, speechreading or kinaesthetic stimulation, while hearing individuals, who operate on the basis of inner speech can also acquire coding processes for signs (Crittenden, 1974). As we have seen, there is conflict in research findings on the oral and manual communicative abilities of severely and profoundly deaf children. This conflict is often a reflection of the considerable diversity in communicative abilities found among hearing-impaired individuals of all ages, even within narrow ranges of hearing loss.

Acknowledgement of diversity in communication, the increasing recognition of sign as a language, the development of combined communication methods such as TC and cued speech, the use of signed forms which approximate the syntax of spoken English, and research showing the limitations of the oral approach, have dealt severe blows to the former dominant position of oralism in deaf education and therapy. It is all the more surprising, in view of the displacement of oralism, that the movement towards integration or mainstreaming of hearing-impaired children into normal schools was prosecuted with such vigour and resolution in the 1970s and 1980s. It is, however, clear that the impetus to mainstreaming is here to stay, though not all would have it so (Branson and Miller, 1989). The advent of combined methods helped to promote such mainstreaming but, more importantly, the move to decentralise deaf education was the result of new thrusts in political philosophy (Trybus, 1987). Drives towards social equity and equal opportunity in access to society's resources have included hearing-impaired individuals in a trend which accepts difference and diversity, but not separatism. Whatever the merits or disadvantages of mainstreaming for education or remediation, one positive effect is that of providing for recognition of diversity and hence reducing the stigma of defect associated with separatism.

'Deaf power'

A further force to challenge oralism, with obvious implications for the management of communication for the deaf child, is the movement to promote deaf–mutism in the form of deaf culture – 'deaf power' (Nash and Nash, 1981; Sacks, 1986, 1989; Rutherford, 1988). This movement is characterised by its own institutions, attitudes and ways of socialisation, in addition to striving to raise the status of sign language (Humphries, 1991). The deaf culture movement has become very active in recent years, notably among and for the severely and profoundly deaf. The origins of this increased activity stem largely from the notions of equity discussed above, but also from a rejection by deaf pressure groups of the paternal orientations of institutions for the deaf. These institutions have usually been administered by hearing individuals, and many have tended to perpetuate, sometimes insensitively, their own practices and agendas rather than those of their clientele (Schowe, 1979; Lane, 1990). The deaf culture movement is notable for the emphasis it has given to the recognition of sign language which 'belongs' to the deaf community, and which the movement has promoted as a communication mode to be recognised as having a rightful place of its own.

In understandable zeal for its recognition as a linguistic minority using sign, the deaf culture movement has opposed the promotion of medical technology where the technology aims to assist the deaf to communicate by hearing, and especially against research in and application of cochlear prostheses. Such has been the vehemence of this clash that some members of the deaf culture movement see the advent of the cochlear implant prosthesis as threatening to eliminate deafness and hence the very existence of deaf culture, in a kind of genocide (National Union of the Deaf Steering Committee, 1982). It is presently too early to ascribe such a threat to cochlear implant programmes, for the reasons given in Chapter 3, though the situation could change quickly with developments in technology.

Lane (1990) was particularly critical of implant programmes. He argued that the increases in speech perception and production gained with a cochlear implant are modest; that about one in 30 implants develops surgical complications; that a partially successful implant may be worse than none at all as it may hinder or delay the acquisition of sign language on which the implantee will have to fall back; and that there were insufficiently considered ethical issues. Among these ethical issues was the likely rejection by signing deaf adults of an implant were they to be offered one (Evans, 1989), and hence a possible wish by implantees, later in life, that they had not been implanted as children. Wilbers (1988) mused that, if a cure could be found for all deafness, some hearing-impaired people would choose not to avail themselves of the remedy, while nearly all would lament the break-up of a close-knit community. The view here is that the deaf community is defined by a common language, a common means of communication in sign and a common culture, and not by a handicap. The difficulty is that there are no clear and unambiguous rules for deciding how to separate diversity from deviance (Lane, 1990).

Practical Issues Affecting Management

This section discusses some practical issues closely related to hearing for the child with mild to moderate, and severe to profound hearing loss. Next follows consideration of some social aspects of practical relevance, such as involvement of the family in assessment and remediation, the relationship of child and family with professionals, and the relationship of the hearing-impaired child alone with professionals. This then leads to an outline of mainstreaming (integration) activities.

Mild to moderate hearing impairment

The child with a mild to moderate hearing loss will communicate with parents and peers, and embark on programmes of instruction at school via hearing. Such children usually develop and progress in ordinary ways, although their language development and academic achievements may be retarded. The identification of these children is frequently made around the age of 1–5 years or so, when slowness in language development and other behavioural milestones leads to a check of their hearing status. Preschool and school-age hearing screening programmes also identify large numbers of children with mild to moderate hearing losses.

A few of these children will have inner-ear losses, but the greater number will have a middle-ear problem. A high proportion of these middle-ear problems, especially in the case of mild hearing losses, will resolve themselves as they are caused by a cold or other upper respiratory tract infection, which is of short duration and remits spontaneously. Mild losses due to transient infections are very common – so common, indeed, that it is preferable to check for their continued presence some 4–6 weeks after the first detection, rather than to make immediate referrals for medical treatment, unless there are clear signs of pathology such as suppuration or inflammation. Persistent mild to moderate hearing losses of middle-ear origin should, however, be referred for treatment without undue delay. There is evidence that a persistent, or fluctuating hearing loss delays the acquisition of language and academic progress (Bamford and Saunders, 1985). If untreated, the condition may develop into the more serious problem of secretory otitis media or other sequelae.

Where, following medical treatment, there continues to be a mild to moderate conductive or inner-ear hearing loss, and where there are no medical contraindications of serous otitis or otherwise, the fitting of a hearing aid may restore the hearing threshold to normal. However, the fitting of aids may not be very helpful with mild losses, if the child spends much time in noisy surroundings. In any case, the child will continue to acquire information orally, though parents and teachers should be advised on management techniques which will minimise the effects of the hearing impairment on communication and learning. Children with unilateral hearing losses, even if quite severe, will also learn to communicate orally, though they will experience communication problems, especially in noisy environments, which are likely to compromise their educational development (Bess and Tharpe, 1984).

Severe to profound hearing impairment

The situation is very different when we consider children with severe to profound hearing losses. Fortunately, the greater the hearing loss, the easier it is to detect (Upfold and Isepy, 1982). Thus children with marked hearing losses are usually identified fairly early. The proportion of such children in the general population has declined considerably since the late 1960s, due in large part to the success of rubella immunisation and other programmes (Upfold and Isepy, 1982). Yet although the incidence of congenital moderate to profound hearing impairment is reduced nowadays, children with such degrees of impaired hearing continue to be found. Services to assist in the development of their communication skills are constantly required.

For reasons considered earlier, there is a very considerable difference required in the management of the prelingually and postlingually hearing-impaired child. A postlingual hearing loss, occurring after the age of 2 years or so, and certainly by the age of 3–4 years, means that the child will usually have acquired sufficient language through hearing and sufficient inner speech to continue with oral education. There is no doubt that the education will at times be very difficult, but generally there will be a firm base in oral language and communication from which residual hearing and speechreading can be used to make significant progress. For the prelingually hearing-impaired child the situation is quite dissimilar, especially where the child is born to signing parents, as we have seen.

Granted the very considerable diversity across many variables among prelingually deafened children, which has been a recurring theme in this book, a child's inclinations towards oral, manual or combined communication can be reinforced from an early age, by taking a cue from the child's preferred means of communication (Conrad, 1980). A problem arises, however, when the approach is not limited to the supportive or remedial, but becomes what Lewis (1968) has called prophylactic – when we foster the child's tendencies in a direction which *we* prefer. Then there arises the question of which communication method to teach.

At this point, we need to review our previous consideration of early intervention and its effects (Chapter 2). We saw that all, or almost all, reported early intervention programmes included some aspect of oral training, even in programmes where manual communication was fostered, and all, or almost all, such programmes fitted hearing aids. Early intervention programmes which relied entirely on a manual means of communication were very rare or non-existent. This is to be expected in the case of deaf children born to deaf parents: manual communication is their natural communication mode. The children themselves are the experts, and early manual-only intervention would be a nonsense. There is, however, a case for the early teaching of a gestural form of communication to deaf children born to hearing parents, and to the parents themselves, whether to supplement the use of residual hearing, as with cued speech, or to enable such children to learn a sign system or language to communicate with deaf peers. Such signed intervention is worth considering because most deaf children born to hearing parents learn sign language from other deaf children, and hence their learning of sign is impoverished and parochial (Stokoe, 1983).

Irrespective of mode of communication, the great majority of prelingually severely to profoundly hearing-impaired children do not develop verbal language and academic skills appropriate for their age, as shown time and again in the literature (McConckey Robbins, 1986). Yet the studies of early intervention reviewed in Chapter 2 suggest that significant gains can be made in language development over various periods by the young hearing-impaired participants in these programmes. Thus, although early-intervention programmes may produce important gains, almost all the hearing-impaired children who participate in such programmes still show delays in verbal language and academic achievement throughout their development. Although they may follow the same path as hearing children, their progress is slower and there is some evidence of deviancy. As a result, continuing attention is being paid to the identification of the relevant factors and their manipulation in management strategies and educational curricula (Cole and Mischook, 1985; Mischook and Cole, 1986). Until such research provides more illuminating information than is currently available, it is premature to close off the options for communication mode, by arguing exclusively for one mode versus others.

As the field develops, new and sometimes disturbing findings emerge concerning some of the effects of early intervention. For example, we saw that listening skills, involving hearing, attention and understanding, may be learned in task-specific situations, but frequently fail to generalise to daily life. The problem could be due to a failure in management to teach listening skills in settings which promote communication as a social activity. We also saw that educational practice has been criticised for teaching language, especially syntax and vocabulary, by overly formal techniques. It now appears that similar criticisms can be levelled at some early intervention activities (Fisher and Schneider, 1986). Socialisation begins from birth, and accompanies the development of communication in hearing children until they are able, on entering school, to divorce the social aspects of communication from the academic ones. By school age, hearing children have a sure social, language and communication system which supports the more abstract levels of language learning offered in school. However, younger hearing children acquire their linguistic and communication skills in the strong social context of the family. It therefore seems clear that language and communication need to be taught in a socially relevant way in early intervention programmes, especially while the rudiments are being learned.

Family involvement

For the severely to profoundly deaf child born to deaf signing parents, the child's signing family environment is most probably the normal communication environment. This situation is implied by the almost complete silence on the topic in the literature, though that very silence makes us cautious about being too dogmatic on the subject.

For hearing parents, the discovery that their child is deaf or has a severe hearing loss often results in a period of extreme stress (Moores, 1987). Ogden (1984) and Ogden and Lipsett (1982) have described a sequence of reactions through which parents pass: shock; recognition; denial; acknowledgement; and constructive action. Some parents may stay indefinitely at one stage in this sequence, without proceeding through all the stages.

Parents' usual initial reaction is one of shock when told that their child has a serious hearing impairment. This reaction may extend over a few hours or a few days, and is characterised by a stunned withdrawal. After the initial shock there follows a period of recognition, in which the parents begin to explore the implications of their child's hearing impairment, and to learn about the medical, social, educational and communicative aspects. At this stage, the parents may experience feelings of anger, frustration, guilt, blame and grief. As they realise the demands which will be placed on them and their child in coping with the hearing impairment, they may attempt to deny the fact of the child's hearing loss. Nevertheless, they usually come to acknowledge the existence of the problem, and discuss it with their relatives and friends. Finally, they set themselves to learn more about the child's hearing impairment and participate in the child's rehabilitation and education. In such a sequence of stresses, parents need support and advice in the management of their child. Indeed Luterman (1979) has argued that, to begin with, the parents need more attention than the child. As Mischook and Cole (1986) have pointed out, the parents are not to be seen as intruding on the management and rehabilitation of the child. Although their initial reactions of shock, confusion and so on may not be in the best interests of the child, it is of great importance for therapists and teachers to resolve such emotional responses in order to recruit the parents to work for the child's remediation.

As they begin to overcome their emotional reactions, parents feel daunted by the task of assisting in the development of their child's communication, and especially by the effort involved in teaching language. They may feel inclined to back off, though achieving reciprocity in parent–child interaction is seen as highly important for the child's social progress and the development of communication skills (Hadadian and Rose, 1991). At this stage, professionals need to be competent to explain the nature of the task, to facilitate decisions about which communication mode to use, and to promote the child's development. Parents and other family members can be encouraged to start by observing and recording the child's efforts to communicate. Such observations and records will not only help the family to adjust to the problem, but will greatly assist the work of the professional. They will also help to orient the family, and especially the mother, who usually takes the lead in deciding on the communication method to be used (Kluwin and Gaustad, 1991), towards managing the child's communication, rather than relying too heavily on professional help. The professional then becomes the adviser to the family, rather than being the immediate agent for change.

Cole and St Clair-Stokes (1984) presented a procedure for video-recording and analysing those caregiver–child interactions which can facilitate or hinder the child's communication. Video-recording can be introduced from an early stage, as soon as the parents are ready to accept and use it. As a guide, the literature contains several papers (Bromwich, 1981; Blennerhassett, 1984; Matey and Kretschmer, 1985; Nienhuys and Tikotin, 1985; Connard and Kantor, 1988; Plapinger and Kretschmer, 1991; and others) describing communicative behaviour between caregiver and child for hearing, hearing-impaired and other children, from infancy to school age. Video-recording techniques can be used (Cole and St Clair-Stokes, 1984) to illustrate such desiderata as talking in a normal way within the range of the child's hearing ability; using normal gestures appropriate to the topic and the child's age; avoiding the use and elicitation of single words; using connected speech with the appropriate length and level of complexity, depending on the child's age and ability; allowing the child to take a turn; keeping up with the interests of the child for a significant part of the time; responding to all, or almost all, of the child's attempts to communicate; talking about people and objects in the immediate context; and using various strategies to maximise hearing. This list implies an oral approach. However, it may be adapted where the communication mode is manual, or where some auditory/manual combination is used.

The use of video-recordings helps to involve other members of the family in the rehabilitation of the child, gives them a feeling that they can make useful contributions, and guides them in matching their communication behaviour to levels and activities which suit the child. At the same time, those aspects of the communicative behaviour of members of the family which do not help the child can be identified, and discouraged in further interaction. The use of video-recording in this way is somewhat similar to that of keeping a diary of caregiver–child interactions (Pearson, 1984). However, video-recording provides for replays of detail in ways that a diary cannot.

The understanding of the child's message in response to parental communication requires concentration and guessing. Further, whereas the parents of hearing children can continue with other activities while talking to their child, these other activities have to stop when communicating with the hearing-impaired child. Parents cannot take it for granted that their messages will be received by their hearing-impaired child and need to check on message reception and understanding. The availability of radiofrequency hearing aids assists only a little in coping with this situation. Communication between parent and hearing-impaired child needs to be explicit. As the child develops, parents and other family members become concerned with issues other than communication, such as concepts in ethics and morality, for example. Getting across to the child such abstract concepts as moral behaviour involves a considerable effort (Ogden, 1984). Much research is needed in this area.

Although many publications suggest that the quality of interaction between hearing-impaired children and their families is of considerable importance, there have been few well designed empirical studies in the area. Bodner-Johnson (1985) described some activities and interactions between families and their pre-adolescent hearing-impaired children. In this study, the parents of 125 prelingually severely to profoundly deaf 10–12-year-old children were interviewed in their homes. Parents' responses were factor-analysed to produce representative dimensions, which were subsequently used in a discriminant analysis to investigate those dimensions in the family environment that distinguished the children's levels of achievement in reading comprehension and mathematics. Children with high levels of achievement in reading and mathematics had parents who were attuned to their child's hearing loss and pressed the child to achieve.

Interestingly, family involvement in the child's academic learning was less important in attaining levels of achievement than the parents' acceptance of the hearing impairment and their thrust for the child to achieve. These parents reported that they had accepted their child's hearing loss early on, and had integrated the childs' needs, including special communication needs, into the family routine. They tended to use methods of simultaneous communication and were permissive, rather than over-protective, in their child-rearing. They praised the child's school work, had made plans for the child's future education, and had relatively high expectations for the child's further education and occupation. The parents viewed their child's hearing loss as a personal characteristic of the child rather than as a handicap. They had also dealt with each crisis in a rational way, while recognising their own emotional responses. They saw their lives as a sequence of more or less difficult stages, and recognised the difference. In their treatment of the child, they gave similar supervision to that expected for a hearing child. They did not so much change their rules for their hearing-impaired child's behaviour, as modify their style to take account of the hearing loss.

In work on the parental experiences of mothers of severely to profoundly deaf adolescents aged 12–18 years, Morgan-Redshaw et al. (1990) interviewed five hearing mothers who were willing to share their experiences, from a pool of about 50. At a first interview, the mothers were allowed as much time as needed to relate their experiences as mothers of deaf children. There followed an interval of 2–3 weeks, during which the mothers kept a record of their further thoughts and feelings, and incidents during the interval which related to mothering. They were then interviewed again and, when offered additional information, they elaborated on responses to some points raised in the first interview, and discussed the themes in the first interview.

The main themes were several: the mothers' personal growth, which was extended by their experiences; the mother–child relationship, which showed more dependence of the child on the mother than occurs for hearing children;

parent–professional relationships, which included a mix of positive and negative aspects; school programmes, some of which were highly praised while others were described as unpleasant, non-challenging or non-facilitating; fluent communication, where fluency in communication was seen as more important than the method of communication; and sources of support. These sources were multi-faceted, with hearing siblings being generally supportive but not always so because, particularly in the earlier years, the hearing-impaired child needed much of the mother's time, and the siblings had to assume additional responsibilities because of the needs of the deaf child.

The five mothers participating in this study were a small group, but represented a range of parental experiences. A major methodological drawback was that the mothers were selected for their willingness and ability to share their experiences, and were possibly non-representative of mothers of hearing-impaired children as a whole. However, the study has value in showing that the mothers' varied experiences could be represented in six main themes, which were identified and discussed. It is reassuring to note that the mothers were fond of their hearing-impaired children, generally thought of them highly as individuals, and had managed to establish satisfactory communication. However, the mothers found the absence of a cure, and their inability to prepare the children for a full life painful and frustrating. Although as the child grew older these negative feelings grew less, they continued to surface occasionally.

Hearing-impaired children, families and professionals

A variety of recent research reports referred to the roles of various professionals (e.g. Harvey, 1989; Erlbaum, 1990): factors associated with the selection of modes of communication in various settings (Caccamise et al., 1983; Raimondo and Maxwell, 1987), the communication skills of professionals in sign language (Caccamise et al., 1990), the effects of different ethnic backgrounds (Cohen et al., 1990), competencies for teaching (Luckner, 1991a) and the attitudes of deaf adults to sign systems used in classrooms (Kautzky-Bowden and Gonzales, 1987). With the placement of hearing-impaired children in schools catering mainly for hearing children – the mainstream or integration approach, reviewed for its history by McCartney (1984) and more recent developments by Schildroth (1988) – many papers have dealt with factors guiding parents and others about placements (Jones, 1984; Bunch, 1987; Goldberg et al., 1989), the classroom participation of mainstreamed hearing-impaired students (Saur et al., 1986, 1987), and reverse mainstreaming, which involves bringing hearing children into classes for hearing-impaired students (Dean and Nettles, 1987). These papers raised a plethora of stimulating findings and equally stimulating questions, which we cannot cover here.

Of immediate interest, however, is the way in which hearing-impaired children, their families, and the therapists, teachers, and other professionals interact. Since the information that their child has a hearing impairment is so often stressful for parents, some earlier workers suggested that a professional discipline be formed for parent counselling (Whetnall and Fry, 1964; Northcott, 1975). Such calls have not been made in recent years. Most families seem to get over an initial crisis and, as with Ferguson and Watt (1980), who found no more anxiety in mothers of severely mentally handicapped children than in mothers of normally developing children, continuing maladjustment to the child's hearing handicap was probably never of frequent occurrence.

Nonetheless, parent counselling needs to be handled sensitively. The way in which parents of hearing-impaired children saw how they were informed of their child's hearing loss and how they were advised in coping with the situation was investigated by Williams and Darbyshire (1982). They interviewed 25 families with severely or profoundly deaf children under 11 years of age who were educated in a variety of placements. The parents, who covered a wide range of social backgrounds and came from predominantly rural and small town areas in Canada, had little or no contact with other parents of hearing-impaired children. Their experience is probably typical of parents in rural areas in other countries also.

The age at which parents first suspected a problem ranged from 4 months to 6 years, with a mean of 28 months, but the responses of family physicians led to the postponement of diagnosis of hearing impairment. Eighty per cent of the family physicians appeared to disagree with or dismissed the parents' suspicions. The mean age of the child at diagnosis was 48 months, following several steps of professional involvement (physician, otologist, audiologist etc.), but the diagnosis, rather than the delay, caused severe negative reactions in 80% of parents. Most (84%) were unable to understand all the information given at diagnosis.

Only a minority of the families received professional in-home training. Although parents accepted the value of home training, they themselves did little of it, except for the parents of deaf preschoolers who had experience of the government's peripatetic preschool teaching programme. The service offered by the preschool visiting teacher was praised consistently, though not more than one-third of the sample had experienced it. Parents commonly complained that they did not know of the services available. Also there was little follow-up by the professionals who had made the diagnosis. Eighty-eight per cent of the parents stated a need for more factual information about hearing impairment, what the hearing loss meant for their child, the future prospects for the child, child management problems, and correspondence courses. Few parents realised that they could be the main agents for change in managing their child. This situation seems unfortunately to have been all too common up to the 1970s and, in predominantly rural areas, up to the 1980s.

The provision of family therapy is worth considering for families in which there are hearing parents and at least one deaf child whose preferred mode of communication is manual. The provision of family therapy in such situations, together with the use of an interpreter for communicating in sign, was proposed by Harvey (1984a). The therapist was seen as knowledgeable about the psychosocial and cultural aspects of deafness, and should preferably be able to communicate in sign language and signed English, although it was not feasible for the therapist to interpret for all the family while providing treatment. Harvey thought that the use of an interpreter went beyond the facilitation of communication between family members who used spoken English and the deaf child who preferred manual communication. The interpreter could help the therapist to modify family rules that denied the implications of deafness and forbade the use of sign. The interpreter could also help to modify the balance of power in a family threatened by allowing the child to communicate, through the interpreter, in sign, and to encourage parents to bring to awareness their emotional responses by projecting, transferring or displacing to the interpreter their feelings about their deaf child.

Scott (1984) took issue with aspects of Harvey's approach. Scott viewed the approach as condescending towards the families, who were seen as incompetent without the therapist's intervention, blaming of the families for compounding the deaf child's problems, overly focusing therapy on the disability and on communication at the expense of other family problems, sidestepping the family's natural pace of transactions in order to communicate at the speed that the therapist thought was adequate, and antagonistic towards the family rather than encouraging it to develop its resources. In a spirited defence, Harvey (1984b) referred to the controversy pervading the provision of psychological services to deaf individuals. He saw the controversy as rooted in communication, namely, how and to what degree communication takes place between deaf and hearing people. His case for the use of interpreters was for families whose deaf child preferred manual communication when hearing members of the family communicated verbally. Such families commonly, though not always, prohibited the use of sign. Harvey listed specific points for family therapy: it was impossible to do therapy and be an accurate interpreter at the same time; the therapist must respect each individual's model of the world, and preferred mode of communication; and the therapist must be a competent family therapist and be knowledgeable about deafness. He saw no need for condescension or lack of respect.

Hearing-impaired individuals and professionals

A short review of communication between health care professionals and deaf individuals, primarily as hospital patients, was published by Ludders (1987). He saw most hospital staff as knowing little about deafness and how deaf people communicate. The first encounters with hospital staff caused deaf patients to experience a high degree of anxiety. The problems may have dated back to the deaf patient's early family experiences as a sick child, when all communication took place between the usually hearing parents and the physician. No one may have made the effort to explain the illness to the child (Di Pietro et al., 1981). Ludders suggested a role for social workers as advocates for deaf patients. Such social workers would not be expert about deafness, but should be trained to be sufficiently knowledgeable in identifying and resolving communication problems between deaf patients and health care professionals.

The counselling of families of hearing-impaired children by Australian and United States audiologists was investigated by Martin et al. (1989), using a questionnaire approach. Audiologists reported parental denial of hearing loss more frequently than the parents themselves. It is thus interesting to note that parents in both countries appreciated 'honesty' in the audiologist. For both countries also, many parents gave sorrow as a typical subsequent response. There was a suggestion that many audiologists did not realise how long a parent's sorrow about their child's hearing loss may persist. Most parents and audiologists in both countries found it helpful for parents to watch the assessment of the child's hearing ability. A similar proportion of parents in both countries stated that they had received the same kinds of information about the child's hearing impairment at diagnosis, with a high proportion of parents remarking that they wanted details of the hearing loss at diagnosis. However, several parents' wished to receive details later when they felt less emotional, or to receive written information for later perusal. Martin et al. recommended that, because parents' reactions were so varied, audiologists should follow parents' leads in presenting factual information. Referral to a parental support system was strongly recommended.

The importance of parental counselling, support and case management of the hearing-impaired child continues to be recognised by audiologists. However, audiologists are divided on the issue of how much responsibility they should assume for case management, with many realistically seeing this responsibility as shared with other professionals, such as the classroom teacher (English, 1991).

As hearing-impaired children attain school age, they could themselves be asked how they perceive the approach used by the professionals responsible for their development. It would be of particular interest to learn how hearing-impaired children feel about their experiences during the difficult time of transfer from home or preschool to primary school. There have been reports of this transition, and the transition from school to community, which refer to family issues, both for children with hearing-impairment only and for children with hearing-impairment and other disabilities (Elliott and Powers, 1988; Davis and Bullis, 1990). However, little is known specifically about the children's views.

There is a considerable literature on the attitudes of teachers to students and to their work with them, teachers' views of their own abilities, and to the views of older students of their teachers' and interpreters' instructional ability (e.g. McKee and Dowaliby, 1985; Murphy-Berman et al., 1987; Foster and Brown, 1989; Mertens, 1991). In one such study, differences were found by White (1990) in the way in which teachers of hearing-impaired children perceived their ability to teach speech, their own ability to understand deaf speech, and the ability of hearing-impaired children to use speech. Not surprisingly, teachers from schools which differed in the communication mode taught to hearing-impaired children differed in expectations for the children to attain speech. As also expected, teachers with greater oral experience held higher expectations for a child's speech than teachers with experience of TC. Teachers with oral experience also had the most confidence in their ability to teach speech, and placed the greatest importance on the use of speech. However, some teachers who used an oral approach in a residential school were less confident about the children's potential to achieve speech than teachers in oral day schools.

White argued that, although they may have held a good opinion of their abilities to teach speech, their work in a residential school gave them a different, and lesser, expectation of the children's speech potential. He also argued that variables associated with the attitudes of teachers to speech development were among the most important variables involved in speech instruction. He felt that significant gains might never be made in developing speech in hearing-impaired children until there was a fuller appreciation of the emotions underlying the teaching and learning of speech. In this sense, the social environment in which the child is managed may be as important for speech development as knowledge about speech, and the effort put into its teaching. There is evidence to support this view showing that the social environment created by teacher expectations has a significant effect on a child's performance (Martinek, 1980; Ryan and Levine, 1981).

Mainstreaming (integration)

In the 1980s, teachers in schools for hearing children became increasingly concerned with the education of a variety of handicapped children who had moved from special schools and institutions to normal schools. The mainstreaming, or integration, of these children greatly stretched and expanded the skills of teachers. Initially there was much comment from the teachers themselves and in the media about the strains that integration imposed on the teachers and on the handicapped children, despite some obvious benefits such as the decrease in stigma associated with handicap, as hearing individuals became more aware of handicapped children.

The management of the hearing-impaired child in the normal, or regular, classroom is difficult because the hearing child learns largely through speech, and spends about half of the time at school in listening (Berg, 1987). On the other hand, effective teaching of hearing-impaired children is generally best attained by the use of more visual, pictorial material supplemented with spoken information (Waldron et al., 1985). Even so, hearing-impaired children need to be able, in a mainstreamed setting, to operate their hearing aids, to change the batteries, and to use such messages as: 'I can't hear you'; 'I don't know'; 'Please say it again'. Deaf children often just shrug their shoulders when addressed, making it difficult for the teacher to follow what is meant (Cochrane, 1991).

We saw that the attitudes of teachers can have significant effects on the achievements of their charges, and Strong et al. (1987) have remarked that in some cases, the teacher's willingness to accept hearing-impaired children into classes hitherto designed for hearing children has been a factor in the children's placement (compare Salend and Johns, 1983).

Chorost (1988) asked: what were the attitudes of such teachers who were relatively or absolutely untrained for teaching hearing-impaired children; did their attitudes change when hearing-impaired children were placed in their classes; what support services did they think were helpful; and what could be achieved to make the placements a more positive experience? Chorost studied the integration into regular classroom settings of six children with congenital mild/moderate to profound hearing losses, ranging in age from 3 to 12 years. Support was provided by special materials and access to a teacher of hearing-impaired children. From a survey of teachers' initial feelings on learning that they would be teaching hearing-impaired children, five of 15 teachers surveyed were negative or very negative, and eight were positive or very positive about the forthcoming experience. Two were neutral. All teachers expressed initial anxieties. At the end of the school year, only one teacher rated her feelings as very negative as compared with three teachers who had given very negative initial ratings. Eight teachers rated their experience at the end of the year as very positive, whereas only two teachers had given initial ratings of very positive. Four teachers felt the same at the end as at the start of the year, but the remainder felt more positive. Thus there was an important overall shift towards positive feelings by the teachers between the start and end of the year, but not by all teachers. Importantly, no teacher felt more negative at the end than at the start of the year.

Sixty per cent of the teachers felt that the placement was appropriate for the children, especially given a support structure. However 40% thought the opposite, indicating that a given child was so far behind classmates that little mainstreamed academic learning took place, and that too much of the teacher's time was taken up by such a child, to the disadvantage of the hearing children. The teachers reported different experiences on the amount of extra time spent with the hearing-impaired children, ranging from an extra 5–15 minutes, up to an extra 1–2 hours per day. Eight of the 15 teachers became comfortable with the child in their class during the first month, while two more teachers took 1–3 months. One-third of the teachers never felt comfortable with the hearing-impaired child placed in their classes. The teachers used the support resources to different extents. On being asked what else could have helped, they cited observations of other classes with integration children, extended use of a class aide, more visual and manipulable teaching aids, and advance notice of the child's characteristics, including secondary handicaps.

Chorost concluded that, although much extra time and effort was generally demanded of the teachers, most thought that the time and effort was well spent and saw the experience as a positive one. The teachers of the younger children, from kindergarten age to grade 2, felt less positive than the teachers of the older children in grades 3–6, perhaps because the older children were able to work more independently. It is not clear whether the younger children were among the more severely hearing-impaired, which could also account for this result. However, Chorost did indicate that children with mild or moderate hearing losses could be viewed more positively by teachers than children with severe to profound losses. The lack of information and adequate preparation of teachers found by Chorost has been reported by others (Hull and Dilka, 1984; Martin et al., 1988). It is a severe criticism of the lack of planning by employing authorities.

The overall situation has been assessed very recently by Luckner (1991b). He sent a questionnaire to members of three organisations for teachers of the hearing-impaired, who were asked to pass it on to normal education teachers who had a hearing-impaired child in their classrooms. A 58% response rate ($n = 354$) was obtained from teachers working with hearing-impaired children aged 4–18 years. The 16 questions in this survey were adapted from Chorost (1988) and addressed teachers' attitudes to working with hearing-impaired children, the amount of extra time entailed, the type of administrative support received, the type of help given by teachers of the hearing-impaired, their perceptions of the functioning of the hearing-impaired student in the normal classroom, their perceptions of how they might be better prepared, and any suggestions they had for teachers of hearing children who had hearing-impaired children in their classes.

Most respondents stated that when mainstreaming began, they felt positive or very positive towards the forthcoming experience. Only 6% recalled negative feelings, while 31% were of neutral outlook. At the end of the year, 89% felt positive to very positive and wished to continue with another hearing-impaired child. They also replied (86%) that they felt comfortable with the hearing-impaired child in less than 1 month, and that the child needed only an extra 5–15 minutes attention each day. The teachers received only minimal administrative support, and consulted the teacher of the hearing-impaired less than six times per month. Almost all (95%) of the teachers regarded the placement of the hearing-impaired children in their classrooms as appropriate. The perceived socialisation of the hearing-impaired children was variable. About 12% did not socialise well or worse, some 26% had adequate socialisation skills, about 28% had good socialisation abilities, and about 34% showed high socialisation skills.

Generally, then, the teachers participating in this survey felt positive about working with integration hearing-impaired children, on whom they did not spend a great deal of extra time. They saw the children as appropriately placed in their classes and often socialising well, implying that the placements were suitable for the educational management of the children, and that the children were able to develop and use communication skills with their hearing classmates (Ross et al., 1982; Saur and Stinson, 1986). However, the teachers lacked appropriate preparation and assistance. Also, plans specifying objectives for placements, programmes and services were not sufficiently delineated, and systems for evaluating the progress of the hearing-impaired children were insufficient. Powers (1990) has expressed similar concerns. Further, the effects of the changes caused by integration programmes on teachers of the hearing-impaired, who often acted in a consulting role, had yet to be considered in detail. Luckner recommended that teachers of the hearing-impaired should be instructed, as trainees, in the role of collaborative consultants for teachers in integration classes.

Luckner's work is reassuring in many of its findings, apart from the weaknesses reported above by the respondents. However, it would have been informative if the paper had given some indication of the effects of age and hearing loss of the child on the teacher's perceptions. It is also rather worrying that the response rate was only 58%. The reader is left wondering whether a large proportion of the 42% of non-respondents did not reply because of mainly negative experiences of integration. Finally, as Luckner himself pointed out, positive perceptions by the teachers does not necessarily mean that the educational needs of the children were being met, or that they were making adequate educational progress. To address the latter issue requires a longitudinal study with controls, and hence a long-established programme. No such experiment is known, but one study without controls has been desribed by Saur et al. (1986), in which path analysis was used to investigate the contribution of academic performance, mainstream experience and employment concerns in a model of the relationships of mainstreaming and achievement. The level of mainstreamed experience was moderately positively correlated with measures of academic achievement, but around zero with job satisfaction. The most interesting outcome was that hearing loss was not significantly related to the other variables.

Without controlled longitudinal studies, the efficacy of mainstreaming for academic achievement and career prospects remains obscure. However, some investigators have shown that deaf students in secondary and tertiary education experience limited interaction with hearing peers, both in and out of school (Ladd et al., 1984; Brown and Foster, 1991), implying that mainstreaming amounts to physical placement rather than integration. Hearing-impaired mainstreamed college students may be lonely, though no difference in loneliness was found between hard of hearing and profoundly deaf students by Murphy and Newlon (1987).

Conclusion

The approach to the management of hearing-impaired children has changed considerably in recent years. Formerly, the child would be put into the charge of a teacher or therapist, with little parental involvement. From the 1970s, parents have been actively encouraged to participate in the management of their child in both educational and therapeutic settings. Increasingly, parents are accepted as members of a team which plans for the education of the child and devises programmes for therapy (Crickmore, 1988), though progress towards a team approach varies from one country to another. It is likely that parental involvement of this kind has been accelerated in those countries which have introduced integration programmes, since for most of these programmes the specialist professional functions more as a consultant and less as the main day-to-day agent for change. This distancing of the specialist professional forces increases reliance on everyday resources and thus promotes the involvement of the child's family. The involvement of parents and family may be all the more important since deaf children in mainstreamed programmes do not seem to socialise well with hearing students.

As hearing parents were becoming more involved in the management of their hearing-impaired child, and as hearing-impaired students were increasingly placed in mainstreamed environments, events elsewhere took another turn. Profoundly deaf adults concerned for the education of their young deaf children, and for the acceptance of the deaf signing culture by the hearing community, began to argue forcefully that their children should be taught sign language, and should otherwise be taught in sign by deaf adults who had sign as their first language. Prelingually profoundly deaf children born to deaf parents represent only 5–10% of the profoundly deaf population (Arnold, 1985), and therefore represent only a very small proportion of the overall population. However, the strength of the movement should not be underestimated.

Options for Parents with Deaf Children

This section considers possible approaches to the management of the deaf infant and child in the current climate where, as we have seen, the complex, diffuse and sometimes conflicting findings of recent research have made few management choices easier than hitherto. It is stressed that the material which follows attempts only to provide some thoughts for deliberation; it does not present firm prescriptions for management. We have repeatedly emphasised the diversity to be found among hearing-impaired children, even within narrow ranges of hearing loss. Such diversity, together with the complex and sometimes perplexing outcomes of research, make it foolhardy to be dogmatic over management. The emphasis is therefore on options and not on rules.

Deaf parents with a young profoundly deaf infant will usually choose for their child to use sign language as a means of communication. They seem very unlikely to opt for use of residual hearing and speechreading. To opt for sign by no means implies that the child's development will be impoverished. We have seen that deaf children of deaf parents can do better academically than deaf children born to hearing parents, who communicate orally, via a combined method, or signed English. There is also evidence that deaf children born to a fluent signing family develop higher intelligence than deaf children born to hearing parents, presumably because fluent communication aids cognitive development (Conrad, 1979: Zwiebel, 1987).

Unfortunately, the integration movement has complicated the issue of communication for deaf children born to deaf parents. Although communication by sign within the family and among the deaf community appears to be generally accepted as the way for them to go, problems arise when signing deaf children encounter mainstreaming on entering school. Present integration policies impose on the child some kind of bilingualism, such as the additional learning of signed English or a combined method, unless the parents can arrange for the education of their child at separate, signing classes for the deaf.

Despite such problems, the deaf child born to hearing parents presents more complex issues. So, what advice is to be given to the hearing parents of an infant who has been newly diagnosed in the first 2 years of life as profoundly deaf?

Auditory assistive devices

One option is to fit a hearing aid and to begin an aural rehabilitation programme, though the parents should appreciate that this approach requires much time, advice, effort and skill, and hence is likely to be directly or indirectly costly if it is to succeed. Having started, if the infant appears to make good use of the aid, then the use of the aid can be continued. Some infants seem to do well with this approach, especially if they have intensive rehabilitation from an early age, well motivated parents, and are of above average intelligence. Others, however, will perform poorly. Evidence suggests that the less bright child born into the lower socioeconomic groups may have problems. There is thus a wide range of individual differences (Brookhouser and Moeller, 1986), and unfortunately, the extent of progress in language and communication will not usually become clear until the infant is in the 3rd or 4th year.

If the infant does not appear to benefit from the aid, a further option is cochlear implantation, not necessarily right away, but after the parents have considered the issues, if the child is thought to be of suitable disposition, and when the child is considered ready to withstand the stress of hospitalisation. Some factors considered to be associated with successful implantation have been described by Hellman et al. (1991) and Beiter et al. (1991).

The best that can presently be achieved with cochlear implantation is the substitution of something like severe deafness in place of the profound deafness. Since what is achievable is most often something between the two, parents need to realise that implantation is not likely per se, to change the situation all that much for the child or for themselves, as compared, say, with the use of hearing aids, unless the child is profoundly to totally deaf. One advantage of implantation is that it holds the promise, but not the certainty, of indicating to the child what may be perceived with residual hearing, a perception which may be more difficult for the non-implanted child who is fitted with a conventional hearing aid. Another advantage is that implantation extends the promise, but not the certainty, of easier integration into mainstreamed schooling, by modestly improving residual hearing, though special training programmes will be needed both for the child and for teachers (Robbins, 1990; Moog and Geers, 1991). Some readers will see at once that cochlear implantation could result in a revival of oralism, since there is usually some improvement in residual hearing with implantation. However, the improvement at present ranges from none to modest, so that any fresh impetus to oralism will be rather weak.

Screening for oral skills

If not implanted, the child will continue to be profoundly deaf. Also, a minority of cochlear implantees seem to obtain little or no advantage from the implant. Where do we go from here? The USA Commission on Education of the Deaf (1988) has recommended, among other things, that the facilitation of vocal, visual and written English language is a paramount concern, and that positive action should be taken to enhance the quality of education for children with limited proficiency in English whose native language is American Sign Language. This suggests that deaf children should be screened for oral skills before their method of instruction is set. We saw that this topic has been addressed (Northern and Downs, 1984; Geers and Moog, 1987), but such evaluation cannot be done until the child has entered the postlingual years. It will not help the hearing parents of a newly diagnosed deaf infant. Although there is some prospect that ability for speechreading may be assessed by measuring averaged visual evoked responses (Samar and Sims, 1983), more work remains to be done in this area with young children. The technique may give parents a pointer towards their child's likely success with an oral approach, but it is not routinely available.

Bilingual approaches

Faced with this situation, how do we begin to advise hearing parents with a deaf infant? Conrad (1980), from his research with English deaf school-leavers, argued for a close association between the degree of hearing loss and speech intelligibility. In turn, speech intelligibility was associated with the likelihood of using internal speech, namely of thinking verbally or orally. The use of speechreading and residual hearing proved to have been a very poor way of learning language for Conrad's population of deaf school-leavers, and severe retardation in reading was a result. His findings held with but few exceptions for his prelingually profoundly deaf school-leavers, and for a substantial proportion of his partially hearing children, though these findings may have been somewhat pessimistic (Chapter 6). Conrad's solution was to leave the choice of communication method to the children, when they were old enough to make that choice, and not to wait until they had failed with the oral method they were currently using. He argued for an early bilingual approach, allowing the child to use speechreading and residual hearing for verbal English language, and sign for the other language, as suggested earlier by Wolff (1973). There are some problems with this approach (Maxwell, 1990). For example, one problem is that lip and facial movements may be used in sign as well as verbal English. It is also by no means clear which sign language or system should be taught. Fluent communication in sign language is very difficult for hearing parents or teachers to learn, which is why sign language alone is not generally recommended. It may also be queried when the child has sufficient maturity to make the choice (see below).

The family of sign systems known as signed English use the syntax of English, not that of native sign languages, although they are contrived systems which result in impoverished communication when compared with native sign languages. Conrad did not see this as a daunting problem. He thought that use of signed English would suit in the early stages, when only a relatively simple syntax and a small vocabulary would be needed, though deaf infants would need plenty of practice in it. Since parents already know the syntax, they would only have to learn a vocabulary of signs. These signs are for the most part the same in signed English and sign language, so that the child would not have to learn a new sign vocabulary if sign language was subsequently chosen as the preferred means of communication. Further, signed English, but not native sign, would facilitate simultaneous communication, as the spoken and signed versions would be largely isomorphic.

Any problems occurring with such an approach to the early development of communication would, Conrad implied, be greatly outweighed by the advantages. His approach has much to commend it, but considerable research remains to be done. Since this bilingual approach offers a relatively straightforward solution to a complex problem (Moores, 1991), it is surprising that it has only very recently received more serious consideration. A particular advantage is that, where there is uncertainty, a bilingual approach appears to keep the communication options open, and would seem to insure against failure with any one choice. The child will be too young to appreciate such an advantage, but it could be attractive to parents, especially if the child is likely to be enrolled eventually in a mainstreamed educational programme, and needs to communicate with deaf and hearing children.

What should be done for the deaf child in preschool or beginning primary school? Here, the question of which sign approach to use has generated yet more choice and controversy. Gustason (1981) among others concluded that young deaf children using Signing Exact English in TC attained improved English language, though such findings have not always been supported (Nix, 1983). Similar criticisms have been addressed by Rodda and Grove (1987), with the conclusion that the sign system to be chosen is the one which allows the greatest degree of isomorphism between signed English and sign language, which seems reasonable enough. Few other authors, however, have accepted Conrad's (1980) suggestion that signed English could be followed by a transition to sign language at the appropriate time, if the child so chooses. If such a choice were not made, bilingualism would continue to be a communication option. The child needs to become comfortable with the communication approach if it is to be used successfully (Palmer et al., 1990).

Debates continue

Given the diversity among deaf children and research findings, it is not surprising that debates about the preferred approach to communication continue, largely because of insufficient well designed studies in the area (Pudlas, 1987; Lou, 1988). The debates were given a further stimulus from proposals that American Sign Language should be the primary language for American deaf children in bilingual programmes. Lieberth (1990) presented a detailed and powerful criticism of this movement, arguing that the curriculum should be one which allows access for deaf children, and there is no one best way, at present, for deaf children to learn to communicate. In addition, she pointed out that considerably more research is needed on the appropriateness of applying the principles of bilingual education in the following topics: the effects of offering two languages in different modalities; the effects of changing from a visual–gestural to an auditory–verbal language; the development of competency in English through writing; the way in which ASL is learned or acquired; the degree of competency in sign required of parents; the relationship between child and parents; the heterogeneity of deaf children; and so on. Stuckless (1991) shared some of these concerns. Some of the necessary research is being put in hand, especially as regards the acquisition of grammar and the learning of writing (e.g. Jackson, 1989; Davies, 1991).

There are also findings of equipotentiality between gestural and vocal modalities in deaf and hearing infants around 1 year of age, with gestures and vocalisations both going through decontextualisation to become signs and words early in the first year. The choice between the two modalities eventually depends, if the child has a choice, on the efficacy of the linguistic input which the child receives (Volterra and Caselli, 1986). It would seem wise, however, not to allow the child to make such a choice until there is good evidence that the child has attended assiduously to both modalities and has the maturity to make a considered and reasonably informed decision. This area needs urgent research.

In view of our discussion of the diversity of deaf children, the definition of 'best' is at present as much a political and socioeconomic issue as an argument about the effectiveness of communication. The problem is, of course, that once professionals and deaf people themselves have invested considerable time and effort in a given approach to communication, they feel obliged to defend it. This seems especially true when a condition is made the subject of an infirmity model (Lane, 1990). In this context the education and training of the professionals should repay study.

Chapter 10
Concluding Comments

This short concluding chapter summarises several of the points made in the preceding pages and reinforces the emphasis on communication.

The material reviewed in the areas of oracy and literacy, the debate over the status of sign as language, the contentions about method or mode of management or instruction, the discussion of individual and social aspects, and the current concern for the rights of deaf people point to deafness not only as a problem of impaired hearing but also as an issue in communication (Schuchman, 1988). To be deaf is to communicate differently from hearing people. It is this situation, as much as lack of hearing, which affects the daily life of deaf individuals.

Until quite recently, 'ownership' of the concept of deafness was the preserve of hearing professionals, especially medical practitioners and other clinicians, educators and psychologists. These hearing professionals developed models of deafness which attempted to explain what was seen as inadequate, defective or deviant behaviour resulting from the pathology of sensory impairment (Gregory and Hartley, 1991). Deafness as an issue of communication was downplayed until the work on sign in the 1960s and the advent of more recent insights, such as the suggestion that speech may be amodal, forced the acceptance of a broader view. Somewhat more emphasis is now placed on communication as the paradigm to direct work in the field though, as we have seen, the study of communication in deaf individuals has a long way to go. It seems that although many professionals in the field would not be unhappy nowadays to be described as involved in the area of disordered communication, allegiances to individual professional disciplines can still obstruct the recognition of such a broader view.

With the discussions of multiculturalism in the wider community and the 'discovery' of the deaf community as a cultural minority, there has been some increase in recognition of a place for deaf culture in pluralist society. On the other hand, the alternative movement towards cultural assimilation, as seen in integration or mainstreaming programmes, has diminished the significance of deaf culture. Each of these two developments has increased the familiarity of hearing people with the characteristics of hearing impairment, as the adherents of each position have indulged in public discussion which has brought issues affecting deafness to popular attention. Unfortunately, however, such debates have at times been shrill.

One result has been to sharpen the awareness of many parents of deaf children to issues of management, without ameliorating management dilemmas. These dilemmas are of very real concern to hearing-impaired children and their parents, as shown in the preceding chapter.

Problems in this area are essentially to do with communication, because they are intimately bound up with the role of the deaf child as a communicating individual in the complex world of modern society. Presentation of the alternatives of speech, sign and the various combined methods, as *choices about communication*, and the skills needed to develop that communication, should help hearing-impaired children, their parents, and professionals to organise their thinking on how to conceptualise the numerous issues involved.

Using the concept of communication to provide the framework will offer a greater unity of approach and reduce apprehension about the fragmented and perplexing nature of the field. To start from a basis of communication should ensure consideration not only of face-to-face interaction, which tends to dominate initial concerns, but also the part to be played by literacy, by cognitive styles and by the various social and environmental factors. The concept of communication can also provide a useful framework for considering the often confusing outcomes of research studies, which amply illustrate the complexities of hearing impairment, but which at present cannot direct our approaches to education and therapy as well as could be desired.

By way of final comment, attention is again drawn to the diversity in abilities and performance found among hearing-impaired children, which has been one of the recurring themes in this book. Such diversity means that 'controlled group experiments' can only go so far in informing us about the complexities involved. A good argument can be made for more work on case studies, especially case studies of treatments (Leutke-Stahlman, 1984). This is not to say that the purely descriptive case study is necessarily the way to go. Properly conceived experiments of the single-case design type would seem to offer more exact intelligence.

Treatments in education and therapy for hearing-impaired individuals, and others, are concerned with serially correlated behaviour over time. It is therefore puzzling that so little use has been made of the techniques of time series analysis (Gottman, 1981; Kendall and Ord, 1990) in evaluating these treatments. Perhaps the mathematical complexities of time series analysis have proved off-putting, or the emphasis on controlled group experiments has crowded out such an approach. However, neither reason should obstruct the pursuit of well-designed single case studies of changes in behaviour with time, to complement the more traditional controlled group work. Such studies using time series analysis should be of particular value to the practising teacher or therapist.

Glossary

adventitious
accidental, acquired (as opposed to hereditary)

ambient
environmental, surrounding

American Sign Language (ASL)
native sign language in the USA

audiometry
measurement of hearing, normally with electro-acoustic apparatus

auditory training
instruction in the use of hearing, especially in listening, and the use
of hearing aids and similar devices

aural
related to hearing

aural rehabilitation
treatment or therapy in the use of hearing

Australian Sign Language (Auslan)
native sign language in Australia

binaural
involving hearing with both ears

brainstem evoked response audiometry (BSER)
assessment of sound-evoked computer-averaged electrical responses from the
brainstem, sometimes known as auditory brainstem response audiometry (ABR)

British Sign Language (BSL)
native sign language in the United Kingdom

central auditory dysfunction
malfunction of processing of sound stimuli in the higher centres of the brain

cerebral dominance
priority taken by one side of the brain over the other

chereme
manual analogue of phoneme

closure
making up the whole from the presentation of a part

cochlea
spiral organ of hearing in the inner ear

cochlear implant
surgically-implanted device which stimulates the cochlea directly and electrically with an external signal received at the ear, processed by a body-worn unit and transmitted to an induction coil inserted under the skin near the ear

cognition
thinking, knowing or apprehension, in contrast to emotion or impulse

combined method
use of speech, speechreading and fingerspelling (compare Rochester Method and Simultaneous Method)

conductive hearing loss
hearing loss associated with pathology of the outer and/or middle ear

confounding
forgoing information in failing to separate the effects of two or more variables

contralateral
on the opposite side of the body or head

cued speech
natural English speech accompanied by hand movements next to the lower part of the face, especially to indicate speech which cannot be seen on the lips

dactylic
related to the fingers, as in fingerspelling

decibel (dB)
a level of measurement on a ratio scale, for which the reference may be specified or implied

dichotic
relating to each ear separately

diotic
relating to each ear identically

discriminant analysis
statistical technique to maximise the difference between groups relative to the spread of scores within groups

distinctive feature
property which distinguishes a given phoneme from other phonemes

distortion
perversion of a sound or waveform resulting in false reproduction

dyad
pair functioning as a unit (e.g. mother–child)

dyslexia
disability in learning to read and spell

electroacoustic
interface involving electrical and acoustic properties

electrotactile
use of electrical signals to stimulate the sense of touch or vibration

factor analysis
statistical technique to determine how many distinct attributes can be ascribed to data, and to find the relationship between these attributes and the data

filter
device, usually electrical, which passes some frequencies and attenuates others

fingerspelling
manual communication where letters of the alphabet are shown by the position of the fingers

formant
energy peak in the spectrum of a phoneme

free field
area with acoustically unimportant or non-reflecting perimeters

frequency
number of times a signal repeats itself in a given time interval

frequency modulation (FM)
variation of frequency as used in varying a carrier wave to convey information

gain
amount of amplification

gloss
explanation or translation (of a sign)

grammar
syntax and morphology

handicap
disadvantage

hard of hearing
mildy to severely hearing-impaired (21–90 dB HL)

hearing level (HL)
level relative to the hearing threshold of young, normally hearing adults

hearing threshold level (HTL)
see hearing level

homograph
word which is written the same as another, but pronounced differently (e.g. present and past tenses of 'read')

homophene
word which appears the same on the lips as another word (e.g. 'fat', 'vat')

homophone
word which sounds the same as but is written differently from another (e.g. 'due', 'dew')

impairment
diminished function or structure

impedance
resistance to the flow of alternating electrical or acoustic energy

incidence
number or proportion of new cases of a condition over an interval of time in a given population

inner ear
cochlea and related structures

intelligibility
degree to which speech is understood

intensity
energy per unit area per unit time

interaural
between the ears

intonation
modulation of the pitch of the voice

ipsilateral
on the same side of the body or head

lacuna
gap or hiatus

language
complex generative code for conveying information

latency
period between stimulus and response

lateralisation
sensation or perception of a stimulus within one ear or within but to one side of the head

learning disability
want of ability in learning, not associated with sensory impairment

lesion
wound or injury

lexicon
all the words in a vocabulary or language

Linguistics of Visual English (LOVE)
sign system emphasising English morphemes and speech rhythms

localisation
perception of the locus of a stimulus in space

mainstreaming
placement or integration in a class in a normal school

Manually Coded English (MCE)
any one of several systems where signs represent the more important aspects of English (e.g. SEE_1, SEE_2)

masking
suppression of the perception of one sound by another

mental handicap/mental retardation
condition associated with low intelligence

middle ear
cavity containing ossicles which transmit sound from the eardrum to the oval window in the cochlea

mildly deaf
hearing loss of about 20–40 dB HL

modality
any primary method of sensation or communication

mode
see modality

moderately deaf
hearing loss of about 40–70 dB HL

monaural
involving hearing with one ear

monotic
relating to one ear only

morpheme
smallest meaningful linguistic unit

morphology
study of morphemes

noise
unwanted sound or signal

oralism
method of perceiving speech using residual hearing and speechreading

otitis media
inflammation of the middle ear

outer ear
pinna and ear canal, terminating at the eardrum

partially hearing
see hard of hearing

performance–intensity function
plot of speech correctly identified versus the relative intensity of the speech

phoneme
smallest unit of speech distinguishing one speech item from another

phonetic balance
pattern of phonemes which simulates the phonemic pattern of everyday speech

Pidgin sign English
attenuated communication system using signs or fingerspelling in the word order of English

postlingual
after the development of language (after 2–3 years of age)

prelingual
before the development of language (before 2–3 years of age)

prevalence
number or proportion of cases of a condition at a given time in a given population

profoundly deaf
hearing loss greater than about 90 dB HL

prosody
intonation, stress of speech

psycholinguistics
study of the interaction of linguistics and behaviour

psychometric
related to the measurement of intellectual abilities

pure oralism
method of speech perception using speechreading only

redundant
that which can be lost without decreasing the information

rehabilitation
therapy to improve impaired function

residual hearing
usable hearing of a hearing-impaired individual

retrocochlear
posterior to the cochlea, especially relating to the auditory nerve

Rochester Method
communication by speech and fingerspelling

Seeing Essential English (SEE$_1$)
modification of ASL to resemble English word roots and affixes

semantics
the field concerned with meaning

sensorineural hearing loss
hearing impairment associated with lesions in the inner ear

sequela
after-effect, consequence

severely deaf
hearing loss of about 70–90 dB HL

sign language
language conveyed by gesture and facial expressions

Signed English (Siglish)
sign system using ASL signs for English words

Signing Exact English (SEE$_2$)
modification of ASL to resemble English words, with sign markers to denote English grammar

Simultaneous Method
use of speech, speechreading and sign

sound pressure level (SPL)
level of sound relative to 20 mPa or 0.0002 dyn/cm^2

spectrum
range of frequencies

speechreading
lipreading plus monitoring of facial expression and gestures, often including use of hearing

suprasegmental
variation in voice pitch, intonation, stress etc. (see prosody)

syntax
relation of words to one another, especially in word order

total communication (TC)
rationale in which all means of communication are allowed

transducer
device which changes one form of energy into another form

verbotonal method
use of residual hearing, tactile sensation and body movements to perceive speech

vibrotactile
using touch to sense vibrations

viseme
smallest unit of speech which can be seen on the lips

vocoder
device which transposes the frequencies of speech into some equivalent signal, such as vibratory stimulation

References

ABDELHAMIED, K., WALDRON, M. and FOX, R.A. (1990). Automatic Recognition of deaf speech. *Volta Rev.* **92**, 121–130.

ABEL, S.M. and TSE, S.M. (1987). The Nucleus implant: rehabilitation and results. *J. Otolaryngol.* **16**, 295–299.

ABKARIAN, G.G., JONES, A. and WEST, G. (1990). Enhancing children's communication skills: idioms 'fit the bill'. *Child Lang. Teaching Ther.* **6**, 246–254.

ABRAHAM, S. and WEINER, F. (1985). Efficacy of word training vs. syllable training on articulatory generalization by severely hearing-impaired children. *Volta Rev.* **87**, 95–105.

ABRAHAM, S. and WEINER, F. (1987). The effects of grammatical category and syntactic complexity on articulation of severely and profoundly hearing-impaired children. *Volta Rev.* **89**, 197–210.

AD HOC COMMITTEE ON COCHLEAR IMPLANTS (1986). Report of the Ad Hoc Committee on Cochlear Implants. *ASHA* **28**, 29–52.

AFFOLTER, F. (1985). The development of perceptual processes and problem-solving activities in normal, hearing-impaired, and language-disturbed children. In: Martin (1985).

AKAMATSU, C.T. and ARMOUR, V.A. (1987). Developing written literacy in deaf children through analyzing sign language. *Am. Ann. Deaf* **132**, 46–51.

AKAMATSU, C.T. and STEWART, D.A. (1989). The role of fingerspelling in simultaneous communication. *Sign Lang. Stud.* **65**, 361–373.

ALATIS, J.E. (Ed.) (1980). *Current issues in bilingual education.* Washington, DC: Georgetown University Press.

ALCANTARA, J.I., WHITFORD, L.A., BLAMEY, P.J., COWAN, R.S.C. and CLARK, G.M. (1990). Speech feature recognition by profoundly hearing-impaired children using a multiple-channel electrotactile speech processor and aided residual hearing. *J. Acoust. Soc. Am.* **88**, 1260–1273.

ALCORN, S. (1932). The Tadoma Method. *Volta Rev.* **34**, 195–198.

ALLEN, G.D., WILBUR, R.B. and SCHICK, B.B. (1991). Aspects of rhythm in ASL. *Sign Lang. Stud.* **72**, 297–320.

ALLEN, T.E. (1986). Patterns of academic achievement among hearing impaired students: 1974 and 1983. In: Schildroth and Karchmer (1986).

ALTSCHULER, K. and SARLIN, M. (1963). Deafness and schizophrenia: a family study. In: Rainer et al. (1963).

ALTSCHULER, K.Z. (1974). The social and psychological development of the deaf child: problems, their treatment and prevention. *Am. Ann. Deaf* **119**, 365–376.

ALTSCHULER, K.Z., DEMING, W.E., VOLLENWEIDER, J., RAINER, J.D. and TENDLER, R. (1976). Impulsivity and profound early deafness: a cross cultural inquiry. *Am. Ann. Deaf* **121**, 331–345.

AMERICAN NATIONAL STANDARDS INSTITUTE (1969). *American National Standards Institute. Specification for Audiometers.* New York: ANSI s3.6.

AMERICAN SPEECH AND HEARING ASSOCIATION (1974). The audiologist: responsibilities in the habilitation of the auditorily handicapped. *ASHA* 16, 68–70.

AMERICAN SPEECH AND HEARING ASSOCIATION (1990). Aural rehabilitation: an annotated bibliography. *ASHA Suppl. No. 1*, 1–30.

AMMON, P. (1981). Communication skills and communicative competence: a neo-piagetian process-structural view. In: Dickson (1981).

ANASTASIOW, N.J. (1986). *Development and Disability: A Psychobiological Analysis for Special Educators.* Baltimore, MD: PH Brooker.

ANASTASIOW, N.J. (1990). Implications of the neurobiological model for early intervention. In: Meisels and Shonkoff (1990).

ANDERSON, G.B. and WATSON, D. (Eds) (1987). Innovations in the habilitation and rehabilitation of deaf adolescents, Proc. Second Nat. Conf. on the Habilitation and Rehabilitation of Deaf Adolescents, University of Arkansas.

ANDERSON, R.W. (Ed.) (1981). *New Dimensions in Second Language Acquisition Research.* Rowley, MA: Newbury House.

ANDERSON, R.W. (1983a). Introduction: a language acquisition interpretation of pidginization and Creolization. In: Anderson (1983b).

ANDERSON, R.W. (Ed.) (1983b). *Pidginization and Creolization as Language Acquisition.* Rowley, MA: Newbury House.

ANDREWS, J.F. (1988). Deaf children's acquisition of prereading skills using the reciprocal teaching procedure. *Except. Child.* 54, 349–355.

ANDREWS, J.F. and MASON, J.M. (1991). Strategy usage among deaf and hearing readers. *Except. Child.* 57, 536–545.

ANGELOCCI, A.A. (1962). Some observations on the speech of the deaf. *Volta Rev.* 64, 403–405.

ANGELOCCI, A.A., KOPP, G.A. and HOLBROOK, A. (1964). The vowel formants of deaf and normal hearing eleven to fourteen-year-old boys. *J. Speech Hear. Disord.* 29, 156–170.

ANTHONY, D.A. (1971) *Seeing Essential English.* Anaheim, CA: Anaheim Union High School District.

ANTIA, S. (1982). Social interaction of partially mainstreamed hearing impaired children. *Am. Ann. Deaf* 127, 18–25.

ANTIA, S. (1985). Social integration of hearing-impaired children: fact or fiction? *Volta Rev.* 87, 279–289.

ANTIA, S.D. and KREIMEYER, K.H. (1985). Social interaction routines to facilitate peer interaction in hearing-impaired children. *Aust. Teacher of the Deaf* 26, 13–20.

AOKI, C. and SIEKEVITS, P. (1985). Ontogenetic changes in C 3'-5' monophosphate stimulatable phosphorylation of the cat visual cortex proteins, particularly of microtubule-associated protein 2 (MAP 2): effects of normal and dark rearing and of the exposure to light. *J. Neurosci.* 5, 2465–2483.

APLIN, D.Y. and ROWSON, V.J. (1990). Psychological characteristics of children with functional hearing loss. *Br. J. Audiol.* 24, 77–87.

ARGYLE, M. (1972). *The Psychology of Interpersonal Behaviour,* 2nd edn. Harmondsworth: Penguin.

ARMBRUSTER, B.B., ECHOLS, C.H. and BROWN, A.L. (1982). The role of metacognition in reading to learn: a developmental perspective. *Volta Rev.* 84, 45–56.

ARNOLD, D. and TREMBLAY, A. (1979). Interaction of deaf and hearing preschool children. *J. Commun. Disord.* 12, 245–251.

ARNOLD, P. (1978). The deaf child's written English – can we measure its quality? *J. Br. Assn. Teachers of the Deaf* 2, 196–200.

ARNOLD, P. (1981). Recent research on the deaf child's written English. *J. Br. Assn. Teachers of the Deaf* 6, 174–177.

ARNOLD, P. (1985). Experimental psychology and the deaf child. *J. Rehab. Deaf.* 19, 4–8.

ARNOLD, P., CROSSLEY, E. and EXLEY, S. (1982). Deaf children's speaking, writing and comprehension of sentences. *J. Aud. Res.* **22**, 225–232.

ARNOLD, P. and WALTER, G. (1979). Communication and reasoning skills of deaf and hearing signers. *Percept. Mot. Skills* **49**, 192–194.

ASHER, S.R. and ODEN, S.L. (1976). Children's failure to communicate: an assessment of comparison and egocentrism explanations. *Devel. Psychol.* **12**, 132–140.

ASHER, S.R. and WIGFIELD, A. (1981). Training referential communication skills. In: Dickson (1981).

ASLIN, R.N. (1981). Experimental influence and sensitive period in perceptual development: a unified model. In: Aslin et al. (1981).

ASLIN, R.N., ALBERTS, J.R. and PETERSEN, M.R. (Eds) (1981). *The Development of Perception: Psychobiological Perspectives.* New York: Academic Press.

ASP, C.W. (1984). The verbo-tonal method for establishing spoken language and listening skills. In: Perkins (1984).

ATKINSON, R.C., HERRNSTEIN, R., LINDZEY, G. and LUCE, R.D. (Eds) (1988). *Stevens' Handbook of Experimental Psychology.* New York: Wiley.

BABBINI, B.E. and QUIGLEY, S.P. (1970). *A Study of the Growth Patterns in Language, Communication, and Educational Achievements in Six Residential Schools for Deaf Students.* Urbana, IL: Institute for Research on Exceptional Children.

BACHARA, G.H., RAPHAEL, J. and PHELAN, W.J. (1980). Empathy development in deaf preadolescents. *Am. Ann. Deaf* **125**, 38–41.

BADDELEY, A.D. (1979). Working memory and reading. In: Kolers et al. (1979).

BAIN, A.M., BAILET, L.L. and MOATS, L.C. (Eds) (1991). *Written Language Disorders: Theory into Practice.* Austin, TX: Pro-Ed.

BAKER, C. (1980). Sentences in American Sign Language. In: Baker and Battison (1980).

BAKER, C. and BATTISON R. (Eds) (1980). *Sign Language and the Deaf Community: Essays in Honor of William C. Stokoe.* Silver Spring, MD: National Association of the Deaf.

BAKER, C. and PADDEN, C. (1978). Focusing on the non-manual components of American Sign Language. In: Siple (1978b).

BAKER-SCHENK, C. (1985). The facial behavior of deaf signers: evidence of a complex language. *Am. Ann Deaf* **130**, 297–304.

BALL, V. (1991). Computer-based tools for assessment and remediation of speech. *Br. J. Disord. Commun.* **26**, 95–113.

BALL, V., FAULKNER, A. and FOURCIN, A. (1990). The effects of two different speech-coding strategies on voice fundamental frequency control in deafened adults. *Br. J. Audiol.* **24**, 393–409.

BALLANTYNE, J. (1977). *Deafness.* 3rd Edn, Edinburgh: Churchill Livingstone.

BALLGE-KIMBER, P.J. and GIORCELLI, L.R. (1989). The perceptions and attitudes of hearing teachers towards sign language: an Australian study. *Aust. Teacher of the Deaf* **30**, 54–73.

BALOW, F., FULTON, H. and PEPLOE, E. (1971). Reading comprehension skills among hearing-impaired adolescents. *Volta Rev.* **73**, 113–119.

BALOW, I.H. and BRILL, R.G. (1975). An evaluation of reading and academic achievement levels of 16 graduating classes of the California School for the Deaf, Riverside. *Volta Rev.* **77**, 266–276.

BAMFORD, J.M. and BENCH, J. (1979). A grammatical analysis of the speech of partially-hearing children. In: Crystal (1979).

BAMFORD, J. and SAUNDERS, E. (1985). *Hearing Impairment, Auditory Perception, and Language Disability.* London: Edward Arnold.

BAMFORD, J.M. and MENTZ, D.L. (1979). The spoken language of hearing impaired children: grammar. In: Bench and Bamford (1979).

BAMFORD, J.M., WILSON, I.M., ATKINSON, D. and BENCH, J. (1981). Pure tone audiograms from hearing-impaired children, II: predicting speech-hearing from the audiogram. *Br. J. Audiol.* **15**, 3–10.

BANG, C. (1980). A world of sound and music: auditory training of hearing-impaired pre-school children. *Scand. Audiol. Suppl.* 10.

BANKS, J., GRAY, C., FYFE, R. and MORRIS, A. (1991a). An investigation of story schemata in deaf children using a new picture arrangement test. *J. Br. Assn. Teachers of the Deaf* 15, 9–19.

BANKS, J., MACAULAY, M. and GRAY, C. (1991b). The use of semantic mapping and cloze inferencing in the reading instruction of deaf children: an exploratory study. *J. Br. Assn. Teachers of the Deaf* 15, 46–59.

BANNISTER, M. and BRITTEN, F. (1982). Linguistically based speechreading assessment. *J. Commun. Disord.* 15, 475–479.

BARTAK, L., RUTTER, M. and COX, A. (1975). A comparative study of infantile autism and specific developmental receptive language I: the children. *Br. J. Psychiat.* 126, 127–45.

BARTON, E.J. and OSBORNE, J.G. (1978). The development of classroom sharing by a teacher using positive practice. *Behav. Modif.* 2, 231–249.

BASILIER, T. (1964). Surdophrenia. *Acta Psychiat. Scand. Suppl.* 40, 362–374.

BATES, E. (1976). *Language and Context: The Acquisition of Pragmatics.* New York: Academic Press.

BATES, E., MacWHINNEY, B., CASELLI, C., DEVESCOVI, A., NATALE, F. and VENZA, V. (1984). A cross-linguistic study of the development of sentence interpretation strategies. *Child Devel.* 55, 341–354.

BATES, R. (1950). *Interaction Process Analysis: A Method for the Study of Small Groups.* Cambridge: Addison-Wesley.

BATKIN, S., GROTH, H., WATSON, J.R. and ANSBERRY, M. (1970). The effects of auditory deprivation in the development of auditory sensitivity in albino rats. *EEG Clin. Neurophysiol.* 28, 351–359.

BATTISON, R. (1978). *Lexical Borrowing in American Sign Language.* Silver Spring, MD: Linstock Press.

BEAUPRE, W. (1985). Phonetics for the hearing-impaired university student: an alternate strategy. *Volta Rev.* 87, 345–348.

BEBKO, J.M. (1979). Can recall differences among children be attributed to rehearsal effects? *J. Psychol.* 33, 96–105.

BEBKO, J.M. (1984). Memory and rehearsal characteristics of profoundly deaf children. *J. Exp. Child Psychol.* 38, 415–428.

BEBKO, J.M. and MCKINNON, E.E. (1990). The language experience of deaf children: its relation to spontaneous rehearsal in a memory task. *Child Devel.* 61, 1744–1752.

BECK, B. (1988). Self-assessment of selected interpersonal abilities in hard of hearing and deaf adolescents. *Internat. J. Rehab. Res.* 11, 343–349.

BECK, K., BECK, C. and GIRONELLA, O. (1977). Rehearsal and recall strategies of deaf and hearing individuals. *Am. Ann. Deaf* 122, 544–552.

BECKER, S. (1978). An approach to developing personal and social maturity. *Volta Rev.* 80, 105–108.

BEDROSIAN, J.L., WANSKA, S.K., SYKES, K.M., SMITH, A.J. and DALTON, B.M. (1988). Conversational turn-taking violations in mother–child interaction. *J. Speech Hear. Res.* 31, 81–88.

BEGGS, W.D.A. and BRESLAW, P.I. (1983). Reading retardation or linguistic deficit? (III): a further examination of response strategies in a reading test completed by hearing-impaired children. *J. Res. Read.* 6, 19–28.

BEGGS, W.D.A., BRESLAW, P.I. and WILKINSON, H.P. (1982). Eye movements and reading achievement in deaf children. In: Groner and Fraisse (1982).

BEISLER, J.M. and TSAI, L.Y. (1983). A pragmatic approach to increase expressive language in young autistic children. *J. Autism Devel. Disord.* 13, 287–303.

BEITER, A.L., STALLER, S.J. and DOWELL, R.C. (1991). Evaluation and device programming in children. *Ear Hear. Suppl.* 12, 25–33.

BELLACK, A.S. and HERSEN, M. (Eds) (1979). *Research and Practice in Social Skills Training.* New York: Plenum.

BELLUGI, U. (1980), How signs express complex meanings. In: Baker and Battison (1980).

BELLUGI, U. and FISCHER, S. (1972). A comparison of sign language and spoken language: rate and grammatical mechanisms. *Cognition* 1, 173–200.

BELLUGI, U. and KLIMA, E. (1976). Two faces of sign: iconic and abstract. In: Harnad (1976).

BELLUGI, U. and KLIMA, E.S. (1975). Aspects of sign language and its structure. In: Kavanagh and Cutting (1975).

BELLUGI, U. and KLIMA, E.S. (1978). Structural properties of American Sign Language. In: Liben (1978).

BELLUGI, U., KLIMA, E.S. and POIZNER, H. (1988). Sign language and the brain. *Res. Publ. Assoc. Res. Nerv. Ment. Dis.* **66**, 39–56.

BELLUGI, U., KLIMA, E.S. and SIPLE, P. (1975). Remembering in signs. *Cognition* **3**, 93–125.

BELLUGI, U., POIZNER, H. and KLIMA, E.S. (1989). Language, modality and the brain. *Trends Neurosci.* **12**, 380–388.

BELLUGI, U. and STUDDERT-KENNEDY, M. (Eds) (1980). *Signed and Spoken Language: Biological Constraints on Linguistic Form.* Weinheim: Verlag Chemie.

BENCH, J. (1970). On the implications of the critical period concept for early diagnosis. Proc. Internat. Congr. Educ. Deaf., Stockholm. 128.

BENCH, J. (1978). The basics of infant hearing screening: why early diagnosis? In: Gerber and Mencher (1978).

BENCH, J. (1979). Auditory deprivation – an intrinsic or extrinsic problem? Some comments on Kyle (1978). *Br. J. Audiol.* **13**, 51–52.

BENCH, J. and BAMFORD, J. (Eds) (1979). *Speech–Hearing Tests and the Spoken Language of Hearing-Impaired Children.* London: Academic Press.

BENCH, J., BAMFORD, J.M., WILSON, I.M. and CLIFFT, L. (1979). A comparison of the BKB Sentence Lists for children with other speech audiometry tests. *Aust. J. Audiol.* **1**, 61–66.

BENCH, J., COLLYER, Y., MENTZ, L. and WILSON, I. (1976a). Studies in infant behavioural audiometry, I: neonates. *Audiology* **15**, 85–105.

BENCH, J., COLLYER, Y., MENTZ, L. and WILSON, I. (1976b). Studies in infant behavioural audiometry, II: six-week-old infants. *Audiology* **15**, 302–314.

BENCH, J., COLLYER, Y., MENTZ, L. and WILSON, I. (1976c). Studies in infant behavioural audiometry, III: six-month-old infants. *Audiology* **15**, 384–394.

BENCH, J., DOYLE, J. and GREENWOOD, K.M. (1987). A standardisation of the BKB/A Sentence Test for children in comparison with the NAL-CID Sentence Test and the CAL-PBM Word Test. *Aust. J. Audiol.* **9**, 39–48.

BENCH, R.J. (1968). Sound transmission to the human foetus through the maternal abdominal wall. *J. Genet. Psychol.* **113**, 85–87.

BENCH, R.J. (1971). The rise and demise of the critical period concept. *Sound* **5**, 21–23.

BENCH, R.J. and MENTZ, D.L. (1975). On the measurement of human foetal auditory response. In: Bench et al. (1975).

BENCH, R.J., PYE, A. and PYE, D. (Eds) (1975). *Sound Reception in Mammals.* London: Academic Press.

BENNETT, C. (1978). Articulation training of profoundly hearing-impaired children: a distinctive feature approach. *J. Commun. Disord.* **11**, 433–442.

BENNETT, C. and LING, D. (1973). Discrimination of the voiced–voiceless distinction by severely hearing-impaired children. *J. Aud. Res.* **13**, 271–279.

BENNETT, R., RAGOSTA, M. and STRICKER, L. (1984). *The Test Performance of Handicapped People: Report No. 2: Studies of Admissions Testing and Handicapped People.* Princeton, NJ: Educational Testing Service.

BERG, F.S. (1975). Evaluation section. In: Clark (1975).

BERG, F.S. (1976a). Programming beginning during infancy. In: Berg (1976b).

BERG, F.S. (1976b). *Educational Audiology: Hearing and Speech Management.* New York: Grune and Stratton.

BERG, F.S. (1987). *Facilitating Classroom Listening: A Handbook for Teachers of Normal and Hard of Hearing Students.* Boston, MA: College Hill Press.

BERGER, K.W. (1972). *Speechreading Principles and Methods.* Baltimore, MD: National Educational Press.

BERGMAN, B. (1983). Verbs and adjectives: some morphological processes in Swedish language. In: Kyle and Woll (1983).

BERNSTEIN, J. (1977). Intelligibility and simulated deaf-like segmental and timing errors. *Proceedings of the IEEE International. Conference on Acoustics, Speech and Signal Processing* 25, 244–247.

BERNSTEIN, L.E., GOLDSTEIN, M.H. and MASHIE, J.J. (1988). Speech training aids for hearing-impaired individuals: I. overview and aims. *J. Rehab. Res. Devel.* 25, 53–62.

BESS, F., FREEMAN, B. and SINCLAIR, S.J. (Eds) (1981). *Amplification in Education.* Washington, DC: Alexander Graham Bell Association.

BESS, F.H. and THARPE, A.M. (1984). Unilateral hearing impairment in children. *Pediatrics* 74, 206–216.

BEST, C.T. (Ed.) (1985). *Hemispheric Function and Collaboration in the Child.* Orlando, FL: Academic Press.

BEVER, T.G. (1970). The cognitive basis for linguistic structures. In: Hayes (1970).

BEVER, T.G. (1973). The influence of speech performance on linguistic structure. In: Flores d' Arcais (1973).

BEYKIRCH, H.L., HOLCOMB, T.A. and HARRINGTON, J.F. (1990). Iconicity and sign vocabulary acquisition. *Am. Ann. Deaf* 135, 306–311.

BILGER, R.C., BLACK, F.O., HOPKINS, N.T., MYERS, E.N., PAYNE, J., STENSON, N., VEGA, A. and WOLF, R. (1977). Evaluations of subjects presently fitted with implanted auditory prostheses. *Ann. Otol. Rhinol. Laryngol. (Suppl. 38)* 86, 1–76.

BINDON, M.D. (1957). Make-A-Picture Story (MAPS) test findings for rubella-deaf children. *J. Abnorm. Soc. Psychol.* 55, 38–42.

BINNIE, C.A., JACKSON, A.P. and MONTGOMERY, A. (1976). Visual intelligibility of consonants: a lipreading screening test with implications for aural rehabilitation. *J. Speech Hear. Disord.* 41, 530–539.

BISHOP, D.V.M. (1988). Can the right hemisphere mediate language as well as the left? A critical review of recent research. *Cognit. Neuropsychol.* 5, 353–367.

BISHOP, M., RINGEL, R. and HOUSE, A. (1973). Orosensory perception, speech production and deafness. *J. Speech Hear. Res.* 16, 257–266.

BLACKWELL, P.M. (1983). Training strategies in functional speech routines. In: Hochberg et al. (1983).

BLAIR, F.X. (1957). A study of the visual memory of deaf and hearing children. *Am. Ann. Deaf* 102, 254–263.

BLAIR, J.C., PETERSON, M.E. and VIEHWEG, S.H. (1985). The effects of mild sensorineural hearing loss on academic performance of young school-age children. *Volta Rev.* 87, 87–93.

BLAMEY, P.J. (1990). Developments in tactile devices. Tutorial Day Notes, Proc. SST-90 Conf. Melbourne: Australian Speech Science and Technology Association.

BLAMEY, P.J., COWAN, R.S.C., ALCANTARA, J.I. and CLARK, G.M. (1988). Phonemic information transmitted by a multichannel electrotactile speech processor. *J. Speech Hear. Res.* 31, 620–629.

BLANK, M. and FRANKLIN, E. (1980). Dialogue with pre-schoolers: a cognitively-based system of assessment. *Appl. Psycholing.* 1, 127–150.

BLANK, M., ROSE, S.A. and BERLIN, L.J. (1978). *The Language of Learning: The Preschool Years.* New York: Grune and Stratton.

BLENNERHASSETT, L. (1984). Communicative styles of a 13 month old hearing-impaired child and her parents. *Volta Rev.* 86, 217–228.

BOCHNER, J.H. (1982). English in the deaf population. In: Sims et al. (1982).

BOCHNER, J.H., SNEIL, K.B. and MCKENZIE, D.J. (1988). Duration discrimination of speech and tonal complex stimuli by normally-hearing and hearing-impaired listeners. *J. Acoust. Soc. Am.* 84, 493–500.

BODE, D. and OYER, H. (1970). Auditory training and speech discrimination. *J. Speech Hear. Res.* 13, 839–855.

BODE, D.L., TWEEDIE, D. and HULL, R.H. (1982). Improving communication through aural rehabilitation. In: Hull (1982).

BODE, L. (1974). Communication of agent, object, and indirect object in signed and spoken languages. *Percept. Mot. Skills* **39**,1151–1158.

BODNER-JOHNSON, B. (1985). Families that work for the hearing-impaired child. *Volta Rev.* **87**, 131–137.

BODNER-JOHNSON, B. (1991). Family conversation style: its effect on the deaf child's participation. *Except. Child.* **57**, 502–509.

BOLTON, B. (1971). A factor analytic study of communication skills and non-verbal abilities of deaf rehabilitation clients. *Multivar. Behav. Res.* **6**, 485–501.

BOND, G.G. (1987). An assessment of cognitive abilities in hearing and hearing-impaired preschool children. *J. Speech Hear. Disord.* **52**, 319–323.

BONVILLIAN, J.D. (1983). Effects of signability and imagery on word recall of deaf and hearing students. *Percept. Mot. Skills* **56**, 775–791.

BONVILLIAN, J.D., CHARROW, V.R. and NELSON, K.E. (1973). Psycholinguistic and educational implications of deafness. *Hum. Devel.* **16**, 321–345.

BONVILLIAN, J.D., NELSON, K.E. and CHARROW, V.R. (1980). Languages and language-related skills in deaf and hearing children. In: Stokoe (1980).

BONVILLIAN J.D., ORLANSKY, M.D. and NOVAK, L.L. (1983). Developmental milestones: sign language acquisition and motor development. *Child Devel.* **54**, 1435–1445.

BONVILLIAN, J.D., REA, C.A., ORLANDSKY, M.D. and SLADE, L.A. (1987). The effect of sign language rehearsal on subjects' immediate and delayed recall of English word lists. *Appl. Psycholing.* **8**, 33–55.

BOOTHROYD, A. (1968). Developments in speech audiometry. *Sound* **2**, 3–11.

BOOTHROYD, A. (1972a). Audiological evaluation of severely and profoundly deaf children. In: Fant (1972).

BOOTHROYD, A. (1972b). Sensory aids research project – Clarke School for the Deaf. In: Fant (1972).

BOOTHROYD, A. (1978). Speech perception and sensorineural hearing loss. In: Ross and Giolas (1978).

BOOTHROYD, A. (1984). Auditory perception of speech contrasts by subjects with sensorineural hearing loss. *J. Speech Hear. Res.* **27**, 134–144.

BOOTHROYD, A. (1985). Evaluation of speech production of the hearing-impaired: some benefits of forced-choice testing. *J. Speech Hear. Res.* **28**, 185–196.

BOOTHROYD, A. (1989). Developing and evaluating a tactile speechreading aid. *Volta Rev.* **91**, 101–112.

BOOTHROYD, A., ARCHAMBAULT, P., ADAMS, R.E. and STORM, R.D. (1975). Use of a computer-based system of speech training aids for deaf persons. *Volta Rev.* **77**, 178–193.

BOOTHROYD, A. and HNATH-CHISHOLM, T. (1988). Spatial, tactile presentation of voice fundamental frequency as a supplement to lipreading: results of extended training with a single subject. *J. Rehab. Res. Devel.* **25**, 51–56.

BORMAN, D.L., STOEFEN-FISHER, J.M., TAYLOR, N., DRAPER, L.M. and SCHMIDT-NEIDERKLEIN, L. (1988). Metalinguistic abilities of young hearing-impaired children: performance on a judgment of synonymy task. *Am. Ann. Deaf* **133**, 325–329.

BORNSTEIN, H. (1973). A description of some current sign systems designed to represent English. *Am. Ann. Deaf* **118**, 454–463.

BORNSTEIN, H. (1979). Systems of sign. In: Bradford and Hardy (1979).

BRRILD, K. (1972). Cued speech and the mouth–hand system. A contribution to the discussion. In: Fant (1972).

BOSHOVEN, M.M., MCNEIL, M.R. and HARVEY, L.O. (1982). Hemispheric specialization for the processing of linguistic and non-linguistic stimuli in congenitally deaf and hearing adults: a review and contribution. *Audiology* **21**, 509–530.

BOUSE, C. (1987). Impact of a cochlear implant on a teenager's quality of life: a parent's perspective. *Hear. J.* Sept. 24–29.

BOWMAN, E.S. and COONS, P.M. (1990). The use of hypnosis in a deaf patient with multiple personality disorder: a case report. *Am. J. Clin. Hypnosis* **33**, 99–104.

BOWMAN, S.N. (1984). A review of referential communication skills. *Aust. J. Hum. Commun. Disord.* **12**, 93–112.

BRACKETT, D. (1983). Group communication strategies for the hearing impaired. *Volta Rev.* **85**, 116–128.

BRACKETT, D. and HENNIGES, M. (1976). Communicative interaction of preschool hearing impaired children in an integrated setting. *Volta Rev.* **78**, 276–285.

BRADEN, J., BOOTH, K., SHAW, S., LEACH, J.M. and MACDONALD, B. (1989). The effects of microcomputer telecommunication on hearing-impaired children's literacy and language. *Volta Rev.* **91**, 143–150.

BRADFORD, L.J. and HARDY, W.G. (Eds) (1979). *Hearing and Hearing Impairment*. New York: Grune and Stratton.

BRAGG, B. (1973). Ameslish – Our American heritage: a testimony. *Am. Ann. Deaf* **118**, 672–674.

BRANNON, C. (1961). Speechreading of various materials. *J. Speech Hear. Disord.* **26**, 348–354.

BRANNON, J.B. (1964). *Visual Feedback of Glossal Motions and Its Influence on the Speech of Deaf Children*. Evanston, IL: Northwestern University: unpublished Doctoral Thesis.

BRANNON, J.B. (1966). The speech production and spoken language of the deaf. *Lang. Speech* **9**, 127–136.

BRANNON, J.B. (1968). Linguistic word classes in the spoken language of normal, hard-of-hearing and deaf children. *J. Speech Hear. Res.* **11**, 279–287.

BRANSFORD, J., SHERWOOD, R., VYE, N. and RIESER, J. (1986). Teaching thinking and problem solving: research foundations. *Am. Psychol.* **41**, 1078–1089.

BRANSON, J. and MILLER, D. (1989). Sign language, oralism and the control of deaf children. *Aust. Hear. Deaf Rev.* **6**, 19–23.

BRASEL, K.E. and QUIGLEY, S.P. (1977). The influence of certain language and communication environments in early childhood on the development of language in deaf individuals. *J. Speech Hear. Res.* **20**, 95–107.

BRERETON, B. le G. (1957). *The Schooling of Children with Impaired Hearing*. Sydney: Commonwealth Office of Information.

BRESLAW, P.I., GRIFFITHS, A.J., WOOD, D.J. and HOWARTH, C.I. (1981). The referential communication skills of deaf children from different educational environments. *J. Child Psychol.* **22**, 269–282.

BRIMER, A. (1972). *Wide-Span Reading Test*. London: Nelson.

BRINICH, P.M. (1981). Application of the metapsychological profile to the assessment of deaf children. *Psychoanalyt. Study of the Child* **36**, 3–32.

BROMWICH, R. (1981). *Working with Parents and Infants: An Interactional Approach*. Baltimore, MD: University Park Press.

BROOKHOUSER, P.E. and MOELLER, M.P. (1986). Choosing the appropriate habilitative track for the newly identified hearing-impaired child. *Ann. Otol. Rhinol. Laryngol.* **95**, 51–59.

BROOKS, P.L., FROST, B.J., MASON, J.L. and GIBSON, D.M. (1987). Word and feature identification by profoundly deaf teenagers using the Queen's University tactile vocoder. *J. Speech Hear. Res.* **30**, 137–141.

BROSS, M., HARPER, D. and SICZ, G. (1980). Visual effects of auditory deprivation: common intermodal and intramodal factors. *Science* **207**, 667–668.

BROSS, M. and SAUERWEIN, H. (1980). Signal detection analysis of visual flicker in deaf and hearing individuals. *Percept. Mot. Skills* **51**, 839–843.

BROWN, A.L. (1978). Knowing when, where and how to remember: a problem of metacognition. In: Glaser (1978).

BROWN, A.L. and SMILEY, S.S. (1978). The development of strategies for studying texts. *Child Devel.* **49**, 1076–1088.

BROWN, P.M. and FOSTER, S.B. (1991). Integrating hearing and deaf students on a college campus: successes and barriers as perceived by hearing students. *Am. Ann. Deaf* **136**, 21–27.

BROWN, R. (1973). *A First Language: The Early Stages*. Cambridge, MA: Harvard University Press.

BROWN, S.C. (Ed.) (1974). *Philosophy of Psychology*. London: Macmillan.

BROWN, W.S. and GOLDBERG, D.M. (1990). An acoustic study of the intelligible utterances of hearing-impaired speakers. *Folia Phoniat.* **42**, 230–238.

BRUNER, J. (1983). *Child's Talk: Learning to Use Language*. Oxford: Oxford University Press.

BRUNER, J.S. (1973). *Beyond the Information Given*. New York: WW Norton.

BRUNER, J.S., JOLLY, A. and SYLVA, K. (Eds) (1976). *Play – Its Role in Development and Evolution*. Harmondsworth: Penguin.

BUNCE, B.H. (1991). Referential communication skills: guidelines for therapy. *Lang. Speech Hear. in Schools* **22**, 296–301.

BUNCH, G. (1987). Designing an integration rating guide. *Volta Rev.* **89**, 35–47.

BUNCH, G.O. (1979). Degree and manner of acquisition of written English language rules by the deaf. *Am. Ann. Deaf* **124**, 10–15.

BURCH, E. and HYDE, M. (1984). Deaf adults and total communication: a questionnaire survey of knowledge, attitudes and use. *Aust. Teacher of the Deaf* **25**, 34–38.

BURKE, L.E. and NERBONNE, M.A. (1978). The influence of the guess factor on the speech reception threshold. *J. Am. Audit. Soc.* **4**, 87–90.

BUSBY, P.A., TONG, Y.C. and CLARK, G.M. (1984). Underlying dimensions and individual differences in auditory, visual and auditory–visual vowel perception by hearing-impaired children. *J. Acoust. Soc. Am.* **75**, 1858–1865.

BUSBY, P.A., TONG, Y.C. and CLARK, G.M. (1988). Underlying structure of auditory–visual consonant perception by hearing-impaired children and the influences of syllabic compression. *J. Speech Hear. Res.* **31**, 156–165.

BUSBY, P.A., ROBERTS, S.A., TONG, Y.C. and CLARK, G.M. (1991). Results of speech perception and speech production training for three prelingually deaf patients using a multiple-electrode cochlear implant. *Br. J. Audiol.* **25**, 291–302.

BUTLER, K.G. (1981). Language processing disorders: factors in diagnosis and remediation. In: Keith (1981b).

BUTTERWORTH, B. (Ed.) (1980). *Language Production, Vol. I, Speech and Talk*. New York: Academic Press.

BYRNE, B. and SHEA, P. (1979). Semantic and phonetic memory codes in beginning readers. *Mem. Cognit.* **7**, 333–338.

BYRNE, D. (1983). Word familiarity in speech perception testing of children. *Aust. J. Audiol.* **5**, 77–80.

BYRNE, D. and COTTON, S. (1987). Preferred listening levels of sensorineural hearing-impaired listeners. *Aust. J. Audiol.* **9**, 7–14.

BYRNE, D. and COTTON, S. (1988). Evaluation of the national acoustic laboratories' new hearing aid selection procedure. *J. Speech Hear. Res.* **31**, 178–186.

BYRNE, D.J. and TONISSON, W. (1976). Selecting the gain of hearing aids for persons with sensorineural hearing impairments. *Scand. Audiol.* **5**, 51–59.

BYRNE, D. and WALKER, G. (1982). The effects of multichannel compression and expansion amplification on perceived quality of speech. *Aust. J. Audiol.* **4**, 1–8.

BZOCH, K.R. and LEAGUE, R. (1971). *Assessing Language Skills in Infancy: A Handbook for the Multidimensional Analysis of Emergent Language*. Baltimore, MD: University Park Press.

CACCAMISE, F., BREWER, L. and MEATH-LANG, B. (1983). Selection of signs and sign languages for use in clinical and academic settings. *Audiology* **8**, 31–44.

CACCAMISE, F., UPDEGRAFF, D. and NEWELL, W. (1990). Staff sign skills assessment – development at the Michigan School for the Deaf: achieving an important need. *J. Aud. Rehab. Assoc.* **23**, 27–41.

California Achievement Test (1977). Monterey, CA: CTB/McGraw-Hill.

CALVERT, D.R. (1986). Speech in perspective. In: Luterman (1986).

CALVERT, D.R. and SILVERMAN, S.R. (1975). Speech and Deafness. Washington, DC: Alexander Graham Bell Association.

CAMPBELL, R. and WRIGHT, H. (1989). Immediate memory in the orally trained deaf: effects of 'lipreadability' in the recall of written syllables. *Br. J. Psychol.* **80**, 299–312.

CAMPBELL, R. and WRIGHT, H. (1990). Deafness and immediate memory for pictures: dissociatons between 'inner speech' and the 'inner ear'. *J. Exp. Child Psychol.* **50**, 259–286.

CANTWELL, D.P., BARTAK, L. and RUTTER, M. (1978). A comparative study of infantile autism and specific developmental receptive language disorder IV: analysis of syntax and language function. *J. Child Psychol. Psychiat.* **19**, 351–362.

CARNEY, A.E. (1986). Understanding speech intelligibility in the hearing-impaired. *Topics Lang. Disord.* **6**, 47–59.

CARROW, E. (1974). *The Carrow Elicited Language Inventory*. Boston, MA: Teaching Resources Corporation.

CASELLI, M.C. (1983). Communication to language: deaf children's and hearing children's development compared. *Sign Lang. Stud.* **39**, 113–144.

CASTLE, D. (1984). *Telephone Training for Hearing Impaired Persons: Amplified Telephones, TTD, Codes*. Rochester, New York: NTID/RIT Press.

CATES, D.S. and SHONTZ, F.C. (1990). Role-taking ability and social behavior in deaf school children. *Am. Ann. Deaf* **135**, 217–221.

CATES, J.A. (1991). Comparison of human figure drawings by hearing and hearing-impaired children. *Volta Rev.* **93**, 31–39.

CAZALS, Y. and PALIS, L. (1991). Effect of silence duration in intervocalic velar plosive on voicing perception for normal and hearing-impaired subjects. *J. Acoust. Soc. Am.* **89**, 2916–2921.

CAZDEN, C. (1976). Play with language and metalinguistic awareness. In: Bruner et al. (1976).

CHALIFOUX, L.M. (1991). The implications of congenital deafness for working memory. *Am. Ann. Deaf* **136**, 292–299.

CHAMPIE, J. (1984). Is total communication enough? The hidden curriculum. *Am. Ann. Deaf* **129**, 317–318.

CHAPIN, P.G. (1988). American sign language and the liberal education. *Sign Lang. Stud.* **59**, 109–113.

CHARROW, V.R. (1975). A psycholinguistic analysis of 'deaf English'. *Sign Lang. Stud.* **7**, 139–150.

CHAZAN, D., MEDAN, Y. and SHAUDRON, U. (1987). Evaluation of adaptive multimicrophone algorithms for hearing aids. *J. Rehab. Res. Devel.* **24**, 111–118.

CHEN, K. (1976). Acoustic image in visual detection for deaf and hearing college students. *J. Gen. Psychol.* **94**, 243–246.

CHEROW, E. (Ed.) (1985). *Hearing-Impaired Children and Youth with Developmental Disabilities*. Washington DC: Gallaudet College Press.

CHI, M.T.H. and CECI, S.J. (1987). Content knowledge: its role, representation, and restructuring in memory development. *Adv. Child Dev. Behav.* **20**, 91–142.

CHILD, D. (1991). A survey of communication approaches used in schools for the deaf in the UK. *J. Br. Assn. Teachers of the Deaf* **15**, 20–24.

CHIPMAN, S.F, SEGAL, J.W., and GLASER, R. (Eds) (1985). *Thinking and Learning Skills: Current Research and Open Questions*. Hillsdale, NJ: Erlbaum.

CHOMSKY, C. (1986). Analytic study of the Tadoma Method: language abilities of three deaf–blind subjects. *J. Speech Hear. Res.*, **29**, 332–347.

CHOMSKY, N. (1957). *Syntactic Structures*. The Hague: Mouton.

CHOMSKY, N. (1965). *Aspects of the Theory of Syntax*. Cambridge, MA: MIT Press.

CHOMSKY, N. (1968). *Language and Mind*. New York: Harcourt, Brace and World.

CHOMSKY, N. (1971). Deep structure, surface structure and semantic interpretation. In: Steinberg and Jakobovits (1971).

CHOROST, S. (1988). The hearing-impaired child in the mainstream: a survey of the attitudes of regular classroom teachers. *Volta Rev.* **90**, 7–12.

CHOUARD, C.H., MEYER, B., JOSSET, P. and BUCHE, J.F. (1983). The effect of the acoustic nerve electrical stimulation upon the guinea pig cochlear nucleus development. *Acta Otolaryngol.* 95, 639–645.

CHRISTENSEN, K.M. (1988). I see what you mean: nonverbal communication strategies of young deaf children. *Am. Ann. Deaf* 133, 270–275.

CHRISTENSEN, K.M. (1990). Thinking about thinking: a discussion of the development of cognition and language in deaf children. *Am. Ann. Deaf*, 135, 222–226.

CLARK, G.M. and TONG, Y.C. (1982). A multiple-channel cochlear implant: a survey of results for two patients. *Arch. Otolaryngol.* 108, 214–217.

CLARK, T. (Ed.) (1975). *Programming for Hearing Impaired Infants through Amplification and Home Intervention.* Logan, UT: Utah State University.

CLARKE, A.D.B. (1958). The abilities and trainability of imbeciles. In: Clarke and Clarke (1958).

CLARKE, A.D.B. (1972). Commentary on Kulochova's 'Severe deprivation in twins: a case study'. *J. Child Psychol. Psychiat.* 13, 103–106.

CLARKE, A.M. and CLARKE, A.D.B. (Eds) (1958). *Mental Deficiency: The Changing Outlook.* London: Methuen.

CLARKE, A.M. and CLARKE, A.D.B. (1976). *Early Experience: Myth and Evidence.* London: Open Books.

CLARKE, B.R. and KENDALL, D.C. (1976). Communication for hearing-handicapped people in Canada. In: Oyer (1976).

CLARKE, B.R. and LING, D. (1976). The effects of using cued speech: a follow-up study. *Volta Rev.* 78, 23–34.

CLARKE, B.R., ROGERS, W.T. and BOOTH, J.A. (1982). How hearing-impaired children learn to read: theoretical and practical issues. *Volta Rev.* 84, 57–69.

CLAY, M.M. (1979). *Reading: The Patterning of Complex Behavior,* 2nd Edn. Exeter, NH: Heinemann educational Books.

COCHRANE, J. (1991). Some necessary skills for entering mainstream schooling. *Taralye Bull., Melbourne* 9, 22–23.

COHEN, E., NAMIR, L. and SCHLESINGER, I.M. (Eds) (1977). *A New Dictionary of Sign Language Employing the Eshkol-Wachmann Movement Notation System.* The Hague: Mouton.

COHEN, G. (1977). *Psychology of Cognition.* London: Academic Press.

COHEN, N.L., WALTZMAN, S.B. and SHAPIRO, W.H. (1989). Telephone speech comprehension with use of the Nucleus cochlear implant. *Ann. Otol. Rhinol. Laryngol. Suppl.* 142, 8–11.

COHEN, O.P., FISCHGRUND, J.E. and REDDING, R. (1990). Deaf children from ethnic, linguistic and racial minority backgrounds: an overview. *Am. Ann. Deaf* 135, 67–73.

COKELY, D. (1990). The effectiveness of three means of communication in the classroom. *Sign Lang. Stud.* 69, 415–422.

COLE, E.B. and MISCHOOK, M. (1985). Survey and annotated bibliography of curricula used by oral preschool programs. *Volta Rev.* 87, 139–154.

COLE, E.B. and ST CLAIR-STOKES, J. (1984). Caregiver–child interactive behaviors: a videotape analysis procedure. *Volta Rev.* 86, 200–216.

COLE, S.H. and EDELMANN, R.J. (1991). Self perception of deaf adolescents from three school settings. *J. Br. Assn. Teachers of the Deaf* 15, 86–89.

COLLINS, B.E. and RAVEN, B.H. (1969). Group structure: attraction, coalitions, communication and power. In: Lindzey and Aronson (1969).

COLLINS, M.J. and HURTIG, R.R. (1985). Categorical perception of speech sounds via the tactile mode. *J. Speech Hear. Res.* 28, 594–598.

COLLINS-AHLGREN, M. (1975). Language development of two deaf children. *Am. Ann. Deaf* 120, 524–539.

COMMISSION ON EDUCATION OF THE DEAF (1988). Commission on Education of the Deaf Recommendations. *Am. Ann. Deaf* 133, 79–84.

CONNARD, P. and KANTOR, R. (1988). A partnership perspective viewing normal-hearing parent/hearing-impaired child communication. *Volta Rev.* 90, 133–148.

CONNOR, L.E. (Ed.) (1971). *Speech for the Deaf Child: Knowledge and Use*. Washington, DC: Alexander Graham Bell Association.

CONRAD, R. (1970). Short term memory processes in the deaf. *Br. J. Psychol.* **61**, 179–195.

CONRAD, R. (1972a). Profound deafness as a psycholinguistic problem. In: Fant (1972).

CONRAD, R. (1972b). Speech and reading. In: Kavanagh and Mattingly (1972).

CONRAD, R. (1972c). Short-term memory in the deaf: a test for speech coding. *Br. J. Psychol.* **63**, 173–180.

CONRAD, R. (1976). Matters arising. In: Henderson (1976).

CONRAD, R. (1977a). The reading ability of deaf school leavers. *Br. J. Educ. Psychol.* **47**, 138–148.

CONRAD, R. (1977b). Lipreading by deaf and hearing children. *Br. J. Educ. Psychol.* **47**, 60–65.

CONRAD, R. (1979). *The Deaf School Child*. London: Harper and Row.

CONRAD, R. (1980). Let the children choose. *Internat. J. Pediat. Otorhinolaryngol.* **1**, 317–329.

CONRAD, R. (1981). Sign language in education: some consequent problems. In: Woll et al. (1981).

CONRAD, R. and RUSH, M.L. (1965). On the nature of short-term memory encoding by the deaf. *J. Speech Hear. Disord.* **30**, 336–343.

CONRAD, R. and WEISKRANTZ, B.C. (1981). On the cognitive ability of deaf children with deaf parents. *Am. Ann. Deaf* **126**, 995–1003.

CONWAY, D. (1985). Children (re)creating writing: a preliminary look at the functions of free-choice writing of hearing-impaired kindergarteners. *Volta Rev.* **87**, 91–107.

CONWAY, D.F. (1990). Semantic relationships in the word meanings of hearing-impaired children. *Volta Rev.* **92**, 339–349.

COOPER, A.F. (1976). Deafness and psychiatric illness. *Br. J. Psychiat.* **129**, 216–226.

COOPER, C. and ARNOLD, P. (1981). Hearing impairment and visual perceptual processes in reading. *Br. J. Disord. Commun.* **16**, 43–49.

CORINA, D.P. (1989). Recognition of affective and noncanonical linguistic facial expressions in hearing and deaf subjects. *Brain Cognit.* **9**, 227–237.

CORNELIUS, G. and HORNETT, D. (1990). The play behavior of hearing-impaired kindergarten children. *Am. Ann. Deaf* **135**, 316–321.

CORNETT, O. (1967). Cued speech. *Am. Ann. Deaf* **112**, 3–13.

CORNETT, O. (1972). Cued speech. In: Fant (1972).

CORNETT, R.O. (1985). Diagnostic factors bearing on the use of cued speech with hearing-impaired children. *Ear Hear.* **6**, 33–35.

CORRIGAN, R. (1978). Language development as related to stage 6 object permanence development. *J. Child Lang.* **5**, 173–189.

COSSU, G. and MARSHALL, J.C. (1990). Are cognitive skills a prerequisite for learning to read and write? *Cognit. Neuropsychol.* **7**, 21–40.

COSTELLO, M.R. (1957). *A Study of Speech-Reading as a Developing Language Process in Deaf and in Hard of Hearing Children*. Northwestern University: unpublished Doctoral Thesis.

COWAN, R.S.C., BLAMEY, P.J., ALCANTARA, J.I., CLARK, G.M. and WHITFORD, L.A. (1989). Speech feature recognition with an electrotactile speech processor. *Aust. J. Audiol.* **11**, 57–72.

CRAIG, W.N. (1964). Effects of pre-school training on the development of reading and lipreading skills of deaf children. *Am. Ann. Deaf* **109**, 280–296.

CRAIG, W.N. and COLLINS, J.L. (1969). *Communication Patterns in Classes for Deaf Students*. Research Report: US Office of Education, Project No. 70640.

CRAIG, W.N. and COLLINS, J.L. (1970). Analysis of communicative interaction in classes for deaf children. *Am. Ann. Deaf* **115**, 79–85.

CRAWFORD, J., DANCER, J. and PITTENGER, J. (1986). Initial performance level on a speechreading task as related to subsequent improvement after shortterm training. *Volta Rev.* **88**, 101–105.

CRICKMORE, B.L. (1988). Working with families of hearing impaired children as a cultural sub-group. *Proc. Nat. Conf. Aust. Early Childhood Assoc.* **88**, 1–6.

CRITCHLEY, E., DENMARK, J., WARREN, F. and WILSON, K. (1981). Hallucinatory experiences of prelingually profoundly deaf schizophrenics. *Br. J. Psychiat.* **138**, 30–32.

CRITTENDEN, J.B. (1974). Categorization of cheremic errors in sign language reception. *Sign Lang. Stud.* **5**, 64–71.

CRITTENDEN, J.B. (1986). Attitudes toward sign communication mode: a survey of hearing and hearing-impaired educators of the deaf. *Am. Ann. Deaf* **131**, 275–280.

CRITTENDEN, J.B., RITTERMAN, S.I. and WILCOX, E.W. (1986). Communication mode as a factor in the performance of hearing-impaired children on a standardized receptive vocabulary test. *Am. Ann. Deaf* **131**, 356–360.

CROSS, T.G. (1977). Mothers' speech adjustments: the contribution of selected child listener variables. In: Snow and Ferguson (1977).

CROSS, T.G. and MORRIS, J.E. (1980). Linguistic feedback and maternal speech: comparisons of mothers addressing infants, one-year-olds, and two-year-olds. *First Lang.* **1**, 98–121.

CRYSTAL, D. (Ed.) (1979). *Working with LARSP*. London: Edward Arnold.

CRYSTAL, D. and CRAIG, E. (1978). Contrived sign language. In: Schlesinger and Namir (1978).

CRYSTAL, D., FLETCHER, P. and GARMAN, M. (1976). *The Grammatical Analysis of Language Disability*. London: Edward Arnold.

CUNNINGHAM, J.K. (1990). Parents' evaluations of the effects of the 3M/House cochlear implant on children. *Ear Hear.* **11**, 375–381.

CURTISS, S. (1977). *Genie: A Psycholinguistic Study of a Modern-Day 'Wild Child'*. New York: Academic Press.

CURTISS, S., PRUTTING, C.A. and LOWELL, E.L. (1979). Pragmatic and semantic development in young children with impaired hearing. *J. Speech Hear. Res.* **22**, 534–552.

DALBY, J.T., GIBSON, D., GROSSI, V. and SCHNEIDER, R.D. (1980). Lateralized hand gesture during speech. *J. Mot. Behav.* **12**, 292–297.

DAMICO, J.S., OLLER, J.W. and STOREY, M.E. (1984). The diagnosis of language disorders in bilingual children: surface-oriented and pragmatic criteria. *J. Speech Hear. Disord.* **48**, 385–394.

DAMPER, R.I. (1982). Speech technology – implications for biomedical engineering. *J. Eng. Technol.* **6**, 135–149.

DANEMAN, M. (1988). Word knowledge and reading skill. In: Daneman et al. (1988).

DANEMAN, M., MACKINNON, G.E. and WALLER, T.G. (Eds) (1988). *Reading Research: Advances in Theory and Practice*. New York: Academic Press.

DARROW, A.A. (1984). A comparison of rhythmic responsiveness in normal and hearing-impaired children and an investigation of the relationship of rhythmic responsiveness to the suprasegmental aspects of speech perception. *J. Music Ther.* **21**, 48–66.

DATO, D.F. (Ed.) (1975). *Development Linguistics: Theory and Applications*. Washington DC: Georgetown University Press.

DAVEY, B. and KING, S. (1990). Acquisition of word meanings from context by deaf readers. *Am. Ann. Deaf* **135**, 227–234.

DAVEY, B., LASASSO, C. and MACREADY, G. (1983). A comparison of reading comprehension task performance for deaf and hearing subjects. *J. Speech Hear. Res.* **26**, 622–628.

DAVIES, D.G. (1984). Utilization of creative drama with hearing-impaired youth. *Volta Rev.* **86**, 106–113.

DAVIES, S.N. (1991). The transition toward bilingual education of deaf children in Sweden and Denmark: perspectives on language. *Sign Lang. Stud.* **71**, 169–195.

DAVIS, C. (1976) (Untitled). In: Henderson (1976).

DAVIS, C. and BULLIS, M. (1990). The school-to-community transition of hearing-impaired persons with developmental disabilities. *Am. Ann. Deaf* **135**, 352–363.

DAVIS, H. and SILVERMAN, S.R. (1964). *Hearing and Deafness*. New York: Holt, Rinehart and Winston.

DAVIS, H., STEVENS, S.S., NICHOLS, R.H., HUDGINS, C.V., MARQUIS, R.J., PETERSON, G.F. and ROSS, D.A. (1947). *Hearing Aids – An Experimental Study of Design Objectives*. Cambridge, MA: Harvard University Press.

DAVIS, J.M. (1977). Reliability of hearing impaired children's responses to oral and total presentations of the test of auditory comprehension of language. *J. Speech Hear. Disord.* **52**, 520–527.

DAVIS, J.M. and HARDICK, E.J. (1981). *Rehabilitative Audiology for Children and Adults.* New York: Wiley.

DAVIS, K. (1947). Final note on a case of extreme social isolation. *Am. J. Sociol.* **52**, 432–437.

DAVIS, S.M. and RAMPP, D.L. (1983). Normal and disordered auditory processing skills: a developmental approach. *Audiology* **8**, 45–58.

DAWSON, E. (1981). Psycholinguistic processes in prelingually deaf adolescents. In: Woll et al. (1981).

DAWSON, P. (1990). A music program to improve prosodic production and perception by profoundly deaf children. *Taralye Bull., Melbourne* **8**, 13–16.

DAWSON, P.W., BLAMEY, P.J., ROWLand, L.C., DETTMAN, S.J., ALTIDIS, P.M., CLARK, G.M., BUSBY, P.A., BROWN, A.M. and DOWELL, R.C. (1990). Speech perception results in children using the 22-electrode cochlear implant. *Aust. J. Audiol. Suppl.* **4**, 9.

DAY, P.S. (1986). Deaf children's expression of communicative intentions. *J. Commun. Disord.* **19**, 367–385.

DEAN, M. and NETTLES, J. (1987). Reverse mainstreaming: a successful model for interaction. *Volta Rev.* **89**, 27–34.

DE FILIPPO, C.L. (1982). Memory for articulated sequences and lipreading performance of hearing-impaired observers. *Volta Rev.* **31**, 134–146.

DE FILIPPO, C.L. (1984). Laboratory projects in tactile aids to lipreading. *Ear Hear.* **5**, 211–227.

DE FILIPPO, C.L. (1990). Speechreading training: believe it or not! *ASHA* April, 46–48.

DE FILIPPO, C.L. and SCOTT, B.L. (1978). A method for training and evaluating the reception of ongoing speech. *J. Acoust. Soc. Am.* **63**, 1186–1192.

DE FILIPPO, C.L. and SIMS, D.G. (Eds) (1988). New reflections on speechreading. *Volta Rev.* **90**, No. 5.

DE l'EPÉE, L'ABBÉ, C.M. (1784). *La Veritable Manière d'Instruire les Sourds et les Muets.* Paris: Nyon l'Aire.

DELGADO, G.L. (1982). Beyond the norm – social maturity and deafness. *Am. Ann. Deaf* **127**, 356–360.

DENCKLA, M.B. (1983). Learning for language and language for learning. In: Kirk (1983).

DENCKLA, M.B., RUDEL, R.G. and BROMAN, M. (1981). Tests that discriminate between dyslexic and other learning-disabled boys. *Brain Lang.* **13**, 118–129.

DENGERINK, J.E. and PORTER, J.B. (1984). Children's attitudes toward peers wearing hearing aids. *Lang. Speech Hear. Services in Schools* **15**, 205–209.

DENNIS, R., REICHLE, J., WILLIAMS, W. and VOGELSBERG, R.T. (1982). Motoric factors influencing the selection of vocabulary for sign production programs. *J. Assn. Severely Handicapped* **7**, 20–32.

DEPARTMENT OF EDUCATION AND SCIENCE (1964). *The Health of the School Child, 1962 and 1963.* London: HMSO.

DEPARTMENT OF EDUCATION AND SCIENCE (1972). *The Health of the School Child, 1969 and 1970.* London: HMSO.

DERMODY, P. and MACKIE, K. (1987). Speech tests in audiological assessment at the National Acoustics Laboratories. In: Martin (1987).

DEUCHAR, M. (1983). Is British sign language an SVO language? In: Kyle and Woll (1983).

DEVENS, J., HOYER, E. and MCGROSKEY, R. (1978). Dynamic auditory localization by normal and by learning disability children. *J. Am. Audiol. Soc.* **3**, 172–178.

DICKSON, W.P. (Ed.) (1981). *Children's Oral Communication Skills.* New York: Academic Press.

DICKSON, W.P. and MIOSKOFF, M.A. (1980). *A Computer Readable Literature Review of Studies of Referential Communication: A Meta-analysis.* Madison, WS: Research and Development Center for Individualized Schooling.

DIEFENDORF, A. and ARTHUR, D. (1987). Monitoring children's hearing aids: re-examining the problem. *Volta Rev.* **89**, 17–26.

DIEHL, R., WALSH, M. and KLUENDER, K. (1991). On the interpretability of speech/nonspeech comparisons. *J. Acoust. Soc. Am.* **89**, 2905–2909.

DI FRANCESCA, S. (1972). *Academic Achievement Test Results of a National Testing Program for Hearing Impaired Students, United States, Spring 1971.* Series D, No. 9, Washington, DC: Gallaudet College, Office of Demographic Studies.

DI PIETRO, L.J., KNIGHT, C.H. and SAMS, J.S. (1981). Health care delivery for deaf patients: the provider's role. *Am. Ann. Deaf* **126**, 106–112.

DITTMAN A.T. (1972). The body movement – speech rhythm relationship as a cue to speech encoding. In: Siegman and Pope (1972).

DI VESTA, F.J. (1966). A developmental study of the semantic structures of children. *J. Verb. Learn. Verb. Behav.* **5**, 249–259.

DIXON, R.F. and NEWBY, H.A. (1959). Children with non-organic problems. *Arch. Otolaryn.* **70**, 619–623.

DJOURNO, A. and EYRIES, C. (1957). Prothèse auditive par excitation électrique à distance du nerf sonoriel à l'aide d'un bobinage inclus à demeure. *Presse Med.* **35**, 14–17.

DODD, B. (1972). Effects of social and vocal stimulation on infant babbling. *Devel. Psychol.* **7**, 80–83.

DODD, B. (1976). The phonological systems of deaf children. *J. Speech Hear. Disord.* **41**, 185–198.

DODD, B. (1979). Lip-reading in infants: attention to speech presented in- and out-of synchrony. *Cognit. Psychol.* **11**, 478–484.

DODD, B. (1987). The acquisition of lip-reading skills by normally hearing children. In: Dodd and Campbell (1987).

DODD, B. and CAMPBELL, R. (1987). *Hearing by Eye: The Psychology of Lip-Reading.* Hillsdale, NJ: Erlbaum.

DODD, B. and HERMELIN, B. (1977). Phonological coding by the prelinguistically deaf. *Percept. Psychophys.* **21**, 413–417.

DODD, B., HOBSON, P., BRASHER, J. and CAMPBELL, R. (1983). Short-term memory in deaf children. *Br. J. Devel. Psychol.* **1**, 354–364.

DODD, B., PLANT, G. and GREGORY, M. (1989). Teaching lip-reading: the efficacy of lessons on video. *Br. J. Audiol.* **23**, 229–238.

DONALDSON, M. (1978). *Children's Minds.* London: Fontana.

DONOGHUE, R.J. (1968). The deaf personality – a study in contrasts. *J. Rehab. Deaf.* **2**, 37–51.

DORE, J. (1974). A pragmatic description of early language development. *J. Psycholing. Res.* **3**, 343–350.

DORMAN, M.F., DANKOWSKI, K., MCCANDLESS, G., PARKIN, J.L. and SMITH, L. (1991). Vowel and consonant recognition with the aid of a multichannel cochlear implant. *Q. J. Exp. Psychol.* **43A**, 585–601.

DORMAN, M.F., DANKOWSKI, K., MCCANDLESS, G. and SMITH, L. (1989). Identification of synthetic vowels by patients using the Symbion multichannel cochlear implant. *Ear Hear.* **10**, 40–43.

DORMAN, M.F., LINDHOLM, J.M. and HANNLEY, M.T. (1985). Influence of the first formant on the recognition of voiced stop consonants by hearing-impaired listeners. *J. Speech Hear. Res.* **28**, 377–380.

DOUGLAS, J.E. and SUTTON, A. (1978). The development of speech and mental processes in a pair of twins: a case study. *J. Child Psychol. Psychiat.* **19**, 49–56.

DOWELL, R.C., BROWN, A.M., SELIGMAN, P.M. and CLARK, G.M. (1985a). Patient results for a multiple-channel cochlear prosthesis. In: Schindler and Merzenich (1985).

DOWELL, R.C., SELIGMAN, P.M., BLAMEY, P.J. and CLARK, G.M. (1987). Speech perception using a two-formant 22-electrode cochlear prosthesis in quiet and in noise. *Acta Otolaryngol. (Stockh.)* **104**, 439–446.

DOWELL, R.C., TONG, Y.C., BLAMEY, P.J. and CLARK, G.M. (1985b). Psychophysics of multiple-channel stimulation. In: Schindler and Merzenich (1985).

DOWNS, M. (1966). *The Establishment of Hearing Aid Use: A Program for Parents*. Minneapolis, MN: MAICO Audiological Library Series 4.

DOWNS, M.P. (1967). Testing hearing in infancy and early childhood. In: Freeman and Ward (1967).

DOWNS, M.P. (1974). The Deafness Management Quotient. *Hear. Speech News* Jan–Feb.

DOWNS, M.P. (1976). Early identification of hearing loss: Where are we? where do we go from here? In: Mencher (1976).

DOYLE, J. (1987). Audiologists, the audiogram and the perception of hearing-impaired children's speech. *Aust. J. Audiol.* 9, 1–6.

DREVER, J. and COLLINS, M. (1944). *Performance Tests of Intelligence*, 3rd Edn. Edinburgh: Oliver and Boyd.

DUBNO, J.R. and DIRKS, D.D. (1983). Suggestions for optimizing reliability with the Synthetic Sentence Identification Test. *J. Speech Hear. Disord.* 48, 98–103.

DUBNO, J.R., DIRKS, D.D. and SCHAEFER, A.B. (1987). Effects of hearing loss on utilization of short-duration spectral cues in stop consonant recognition. *J. Acoust. Soc. Am.* 81, 1940–1947.

DUCKWORTH, E. (1979). Either we're too early and they can't learn it or we're too late and they know it already: the dilemma of applying Piaget. *Harvard Educ. Rev.* 49, 297–312.

DUFFY, A. (1984). Discourse in the classroom. *Aust. Teacher of the Deaf* 25, 4–10.

DUNLAP, W.R. and ICEMAN SANDS, D. (1990). Classification of the hearing impaired for independent living using the Vineland Adaptive Behavior Scale. *Am. Ann. Deaf* 135, 384–388.

DUNN, L.M. (1965). *Peabody Picture Vocabulary Test*. Circle Pines, MN: American Guidance Service.

DUNN, L. and DUNN, L. (1981). *Peabody Picture Vocabulary Test – Revised*. Circle Pines, MN: American Guidance Service.

DUNN, L.M. and MARKWARDT, F.C. (1970). *Peabody Individual Achievement Test Revised*. Circle Pines, MN: American Guidance Service.

EAGNEY, P. (1987). ASL? English? Which? Comparing comprehension. *Am. Ann. Deaf* 132, 272–275.

EDITORIAL (1981). Hearing loss and perceptual dysfunction in schizophrenia. *Lancet* ii, 848–849.

EFRON, R. (1990). *The Decline and Fall of Hemispheric Specialization*. Hillsdale, NJ: Erlbaum.

EHRI, L. (1975). Word consciousness in readers and prereaders. *J. Educ. Psychol.* 67, 204–212.

EILERS, R.E., OZDAMAR, O., OLLER, D.K., MISKIEL, E. and URBANO, R. (1988a). Similarities between tactual and auditory speech perception. *J. Speech Hear. Res.* 31, 124–131.

EILERS, R.E., WIDEN, J.E. and OLLER, D.K. (1988b). Assessment techniques to evaluate tactual aids for hearing-impaired subjects. *J. Rehab. Res. Devel.* 25, 33–46.

EIMAS, P.D., SIQUELAND, E.R., JUSCYK, P.W. and VIGORITO, J. (1971). Speech perception in infants. *Science* 171, 303–306.

EISENBERG, L.S. (1982). Use of the cochlear implant by the prelingually deaf. In: House and Berliner (1982).

EISENBERG, L.S. (1985). Training strategies for the post-implant patient. In: Schindler and Merzenich (1985).

EKMAN, P. and FRIESEN, W. (1978). *Facial Action Coding System*. Palo Alto, CA: Consulting Psychologists Press.

ELLENBERGER, R. and STEYAERT, M. (1978). A child's representation of action in American Sign Language. In: Siple (1978b).

ELLER, R.G., PAPPAS, C.C. and BROWN, E. (1988). The lexical development of kindergarteners: learning from written context. *J. Read. Behav.* 20, 5–23.

ELLIOTT, H., GLASS, L. and EVANS, J.W. (Eds) (1987). *Mental Health Assessment of Deaf Clients: A Practical Manual*. Boston, MA: Little, Brown and Co.

ELLIOTT, L.L. and HAMMER, M.A. (1988). Longitudinal changes in auditory discrimination in normal children and children with language-learning problems. *J. Speech Hear. Disord.* **53**, 467–474.

ELLIOTT, R. and POWERS, A. (1988). Preparing teachers to serve the learning disabled hearing impaired. *Volta Rev.* **90**, 13–18.

ELLIS, D. (Ed.) (1986). *Sensory Impairments in Mentally Handicapped People*. San Diego, CA: College Hill Press.

ELLIS, R.A.F. and WHITTINGTON, D. (1981). *A Guide to Social Skill Training*. London: Croom Helm.

EMMOREY, K. and CORINA, D. (1990). Lexical recognition in sign language: effects of phonetic structure and morphology. *Percept. Mot. Skills* **71**, 1227–1252.

ENGLISH, K. (1991). Best practice in educational audiology. *Lang. Speech Hear. Serv. Schools* **22**, 283–286.

EPSTEIN, J. (1980). *No Music by Request*. Sydney: Collins.

ERBER, N.P. (1972). Auditory, visual and auditory–visual recognition of consonants by children with normal and impaired hearing. *J. Speech Hear. Res.* **15**, 413–422.

ERBER, N.P. (1974). Pure-tone thresholds and word-recognition abilities of hearing-impaired children. *J. Speech Hear. Res.* **17**, 194–202.

ERBER, N.P. (1978). Vibratory perception by deaf children. *Internat. J. Rehab. Res.* **1**, 27–37.

ERBER, N.P. (1979). Auditory–visual perception of speech with reduced optical clarity. *J. Speech Hear. Res.* **22**, 212–223.

ERBER, N.P. (1980). Use of the Auditory Numbers Test to evaluate speech perception abilities of hearing-impaired children. *J. Speech Hear. Disord.* **45**, 527–532.

ERBER, N.P. (1983). Speech perception and speech development in hearing-impaired children. In: Hochberg et al. (1983).

ERBER, N.P. (1985). *Telephone Communication and Hearing Impairment*. London and Philadelphia: Taylor and Francis.

ERBER, N.P. (1988). *Communication Therapy for Hearing Impaired Adults*. Victoria, Australia: Clavis.

ERBER, N.P. and ALENCEWICZ, C.M. (1976). Audiological evaluation of deaf children. *J. Speech Hear. Disord.* **41**, 256–267.

ERICKSON, F. (1981). Timing and context in everyday discourse. In: Dickson (1981).

ERICKSON, F. and SCHULTZ, J. (1980). When is a context? In: Green and Wallat (1980).

ERLBAUM, S.J. (1990). A comprehensive PEL-IEP speech curriculum overview and related carryover and summary forms designed for speech therapy services for the hearing-impaired. *Lang. Speech Hear. Serv. Schools* **21**, 196–199.

ERTING, C. (1980). Sign language and communication between adults and children. In: Baker and Battison (1980).

EVANS, A.D. and FALK, W.W. (1986). *Learning to Be Deaf*. Berlin: Mouton de Gruyter.

EVANS, J. and ELLIOTT, H. (1987). The mental status examination. In: Elliot et al. (1987).

EVANS, J.W. (1989). Thoughts on the psychosocial implications of cochlear implantation in children. In: Owens and Kessler (1989).

EVANS, L. (1981). Psycholinguistic perspectives on visual communication. In: Woll et al. (1981).

EVANS, P.I.P. (1987). Speech audiometry for differential diagnosis. In: Martin (1987).

EVANS, T. (Ed.) (1977). *Psychophysics and Physiology of Hearing*. London: Academic Press.

EVERHART, V.S. and MARSCHARK, M. (1988). Linguistic flexibility in signed and written language productions of deaf children. *J. Exp. Child Psychol.* **46**, 174–193.

EWING, A.W.G. (Ed.) (1957). *Educational Guidance and the Deaf Child*. Manchester: Manchester University Press.

EWOLDT, C. (1985). A descriptive study of the developing literacy of young hearing-impaired children. *Volta Rev.* **87**, 109–126.

EWOLDT, C. and HAMMERMEISTER, F. (1986). The language–experience approach to facilitating reading and writing for hearing-impaired students. *Am. Ann. Deaf* **131**, 271–274.

EXLEY, S. and ARNOLD, D.P. (1987). Partially hearing and hearing children's speaking, writing and comprehension of sentences. *J. Commun. Disord.* 20, 403–411.

FAIRBANK, D., POWERS, A. and MONAGHAN, C. (1986). Stimulus overselectivity in hearing-impaired children. *Volta Rev.* 88, 269–278.

FAIRBANKS, G. (1958). Test of phonemic differentiation: the rhyme test. *J. Acoust. Soc. Am.* 30, 596–600.

FANT, G. (1962). Descriptive analysis of the acoustics of speech. *Logos* 5, 3–17.

FANT, G. (Ed.) (1972). *Speech Communication Ability and Profound Deafness.* Washington, DC: Alexander Graham Bell Association.

FANT, G. (Ed.) (1974). *Speech Communication.* New York: Halstead Press.

FANT, G. and TATHAM, M.A.A. (Eds) (1975). *Auditory Analysis and Perception of Speech.* London: Academic Press.

FARB, P. (1973). *Word Play: What Happens when People Talk.* New York: Bantam.

FARWELL, R.M. (1976). Speechreading: a research review. *Am. Ann. Deaf* 121, 19–30.

FASOLD, R. (1984). *The Sociolinguistics of Society.* Oxford: Blackwell.

FAULKNER, A., BALL, V. and FOURCIN, A. (1990). Compound speech pattern information as an aid to lipreading. *Speech Hear. Lang. Work in Progress, No. 3.* London: University College.

FEINSTEIN, C.B. (1983). Early adolescent deaf boys: a biosocial approach. *Adolesc. Psychiat.* 11, 147–162.

FENN, G. and ROWE, J.A. (1975). An experiment in manual communication. *Br. J. Disord. Commun.* 10, 3–16.

FENN, G. and SMITH, B.Z. (1987). The assessment of lipreading ability: some practical considerations in the use of tracking procedures. *Br. J. Audiol.* 21, 253–258.

FERGUSON, J.B., BERNSTEIN, L.E. and GOLDSTEIN, M.H. (1988). Speech training aids for hearing-impaired individuals: II. Configuration of the Johns Hopkins aids. *J. Rehab. Res. Devel.* 25, 63–68.

FERGUSON, N. and WATT, J. (1980). Professionals and the parents of mentally handicapped children. *Bull. Br. Psychol. Soc.* 33, 59–60.

FESHBACH, S. (1970). Aggression. In: Mussen (1970).

FESTEN, J.M. and PLOMP, R. (1990). Effects of fluctuating noise and interfering speech on the speech reception threshold for impaired and normal hearing. *J. Acoust. Soc. Am.* 88, 1725–1736.

FEYEREISEN, P. (1983). Manual activity during speaking in aphasic subjects. *Internat. J. Psychol.* 18, 545–556.

FISCH, L. (1983). Integrated development and maturation of the hearing system. *Br. J. Audiol.* 17, 137–154.

FISCH, L. (1990). Letter to the editor: the significance of early auditory stimulation. *Br. J. Audiol.* 24, 141–142.

FISCHER, S.D. (1978). Sign language and Creoles. In: Siple (1978b).

FISHER, E. and SCHNEIDER, K. (1986). Integrating auditory learning at the preschool level. *Volta Rev.* 88, 83–91.

FLANDERS, N. (1965). *Analyzing Teacher Behaviour.* Reading, MA: Addison-Wesley.

FLAVELL, J.H. (1968). *The Development of Role-taking and Communication Skills in Children.* New York: Wiley.

FLAVELL, J.H. (1977). *Cognitive Development.* Englewood Cliffs, NJ: Prentice-Hall.

FLAVELL, J.H. (1985). *Cognitive Development,* 2nd Edn. Englewood Cliffs, NJ: Prentice-Hall.

FLAVELL, J.H. and WELLMAN, H.M. (1977). Metamemory. In: Kail and Hagen (1977).

FLETCHER, H. (1953). *Speech and Hearing in Communication.* New York: Kreiger Publishing Corp.

FLETCHER, P. and GARMAN, M. (Eds) (1979). *Language Acquisition.* Cambridge: Cambridge University Press.

FLETCHER, S.G. (1986). Visual feedback and lip-positioning skills of children with and without impaired hearing. *J. Speech Hear. Res.* 29, 231–239.

FLETCHER, S.G., SMITH, S.C. and HASEGAWA, A. (1985). Vocal/verbal response times of normal-hearing and hearing-impaired children. *J. Speech Hear. Res.* **28**, 548–555.

FLEXER, C. and WOOD, L.A. (1984). The hearing aid: facilitator or inhibitor of auditory interaction? *Volta Rev.* **86**, 354–361.

FLEXER, C., WRAY, D. and BLACK, T. (1986). Support group for moderately hearing-impaired college students: an expanding awareness. *Volta Rev.* **88**, 223–229.

FLORES d'ARCAIS, G.B. (Ed.) (1973). *Advances in Psycholinguistics*. Amsterdam: North Holland Press.

FONTANA, J.M. (1990). Is ASL like Digueno or Digueno like ASL? A study of internally headed relative clauses in ASL. In: Lucas (1990).

FORCHHAMMER, G. (1903). *Om Nodvendigheden af Sikre Meddelelsesmidler i Dovstume Under Evisningen*. Copenhagen: J. Frimodts, Fortag.

FORNER, L.L. and HIXON, T.J. (1977). Respiratory kinematics in profoundly hearing-impaired speakers. *J. Speech. Hear. Res.* **20**, 373–408.

FOSTER, J.R. and HAGGARD, M.P. (1979). (FAAF) An efficient analytical test of speech perception. *Proc. Inst. Acoust.*, IA 3, 9–12.

FOSTER, J.R. and HAGGARD, M.P. (1984). *Introduction and Test Manual for FAAF II*. Nottingham: MRC Institute of Hearing Research.

FOSTER, S., BAREFOOT, S.M. and DECARO, P.M. (1989). The meaning of communication to a group of deaf college students: a multidimensional perspective. *J. Speech Hear. Disord.* **54**, 558–569.

FOSTER, S. and BROWN, P. (1989). Factors influencing the academic and social integration of hearing-impaired college students. *J. Postsec. Educ. Disabil.* **7**, 78–96.

FOURCIN, A.J. (1976). Speech pattern tests for deaf children. In: Stephens (1976).

FOURCIN, A.J. and ABBERTON, E. (1975). First applications of a new laryngograph. *Med. Biol.* **21**, No. 3.

FOURCIN, A.J., ROSEN, S.M., MOORE, B.C., DOUEK, E.E., CLARKE, G.P., DODSON, H. and BANNISTER, L.H. (1979). External electrical stimulation of the cochlea: clinical, psychophysical, speech-perceptual and histological findings. *Br. J. Audiol.* **13**, 85–107.

FOWLER, C.A. (1991). Auditory perception is not special: we see the world, we feel the world, we hear the world. *J. Acoust. Soc. Am.* **89**, 2910–2915.

FRAISSE, P. (1964). *The Psychology of Time*. London: Eyre and Spottiswoode.

FRANKS, J.R. (1979). The influence of exaggerated mouth movement on lipreading. *Audiol. Hear. Educn.* **5**, 12–16.

FREEDMAN, D.A. (1981). Speech, language, and the vocal–auditory connection. *Psychoanalyt. Study of the Child.* **36**, 105–127.

FREEMAN, M. and WARD, P.H. (Eds) (1967). *Deafness in Childhood*. Nashville, TN: Vanderbilt University Press.

FREEMAN, R., CARBIN, C. and BOESA, R. (1981). *Can't Your Child Hear? A Guide for Those Who Care about Deaf Children*. Baltimore, MD: University Park Press.

FREEMAN, S.T. (1989). Cultural and linguistic bias in mental health evaluations of deaf people. *Rehab. Psychol.* **34**, 51–63.

FREUD, S. (1915). Instincts and their vicissitudes. In: Institute of Psychoanalysis (1957).

FRIEDMAN, L. A. (1976). The manifestation of subject, object and topic in American Sign Language. In: Li (1976).

FRISHBERG, N. (1975). Arbitrariness and iconicity: historical change in American Sign Language. *Language* **51**, 696–719.

FRISHBERG, N. (1988). Signers of tales: the case for literary status of an unwritten language. *Sign Lang. Stud.* **59**, 149–170.

FROMKIN, V. A. (1988). Sign languages: evidence for language universals and the linguistic capacity of the human brain. *Sign Lang. Stud.* **59**, 115–127.

FROMKIN, V., KRASHEN, S., CURTISS, S., RIGLER, D. and RIGLER, M. (1974). The development of language in Genie: a case of language acquisition beyond the critical period. *Brain Lang* **1**, 81–107.

FROST, B. and BROOKS, P. (1983). Identification of novel words and sentences using a tactile vocoder. *J. Acoust. Soc. Am.* **74**, Suppl. 104(A).

FRUCHTER, A., WILBUR, R.B. and FRASER, J.B. (1984). Comprehension of idioms by hearing-impaired students. *Volta Rev.* **86**, 7–19.

FRY, D.B. (1961). Word and sentence tests for use in speech audiometry. *Lancet* **ii**, 197–199.

FRY, D.B. (1966). The development of the phonological system in the normal and the deaf child. In: Smith and Miller (1966).

FUCCI, D. (1972). Oral vibrotactile sensation: an evaluation of normal and defective speakers. *J. Speech Hear. Res.* **15**, 179–183.

FUCCI, D. and ROBERTSON, J.H. (1971). Functional defective articulation: an oral sensory disturbance. *Percept. Mot. Skills* **33**, 711–714.

FUGAIN, C., MEYER, B. and CHOUARD, C.H. (1985). Speech processing strategies and clinical results of the French multichannel cochlear implant. In: Schindler and Merzenich (1985).

FULLER, D.R. and WILBUR, R.B. (1987). The effect of visual metaphor cueing on recall of phonologically similar signs. *Sign Lang. Stud.* **54**, 59–80.

FURTH, H.G. (1961). Influence of language on the development of concept formation in deaf children. *J. Abnorm. Soc. Psychol.* **63**, 386–389.

FURTH, H.G. (1963). Conceptual discovery and control on a pictorial part–whole task as a function of age, intelligence, and language. *J. Educ. Psychol.* **54**, 191–196.

FURTH, H.G. (1964a). Research with the deaf: implications for language and cognition. *Psychol. Bull.* **62**, 145–164.

FURTH, H.G. (1964b). Conservation of weight in deaf and hearing children. *Child Devel.* **35**, 143–150.

FURTH, H.G. (1966a). *Thinking without Language: Psychological Implications of Deafness.* New York: Free Press.

FURTH, H.G. (1966b). A comparison of reading test norms of deaf and hearing children. *Am. Ann. Deaf* **111**, 461–462.

FURTH, H.G. (1970). A review and perspective on the thinking of deaf people. In: Helmuth (1970).

FURTH, H.G. (1971). Linguistic deficiency and thinking: research with deaf subjects 1964–1969. *Psychol. Bull.*, **74**, 58–72.

FURTH, H.G. (1973). *Deafness and Learning: A Psychosocial Approach.* Belmont, CA: Wadsworth.

FURTH, H.G. and YOUNISS, J. (1975). Congenital deafness and the development of thinking. In: Lenneberg and Lenneberg (1975).

FUSFELD, I.S. (1955). The academic programme of schools for the deaf. *Volta Rev.* **57**, 63–70.

GAINES, R., MANDLER, J. and BRYANT, P. (1981). Immediate and delayed story recall by hearing and deaf children. *J. Speech Hear. Res.* **24**, 463–469.

GALLAGHER, T.M. and MEADOR, H.E. (1989). Communication mode use of two hearing-impaired adolescents in conversation. *J. Speech Hear. Disord.* **54**, 570–575.

GALLAGHER, T.M. and PRUTTING, C.A. (Eds) (1983). *Pragmatic Assessment and Intervention Issues in Language.* San Diego, CA: College Hill Press.

GALLAWAY, C., APLIN, D.Y., NEWTON, V.W. and HOSTLER, M.E. (1990). The GMC project: some linguistic and cognitive characteristics of a population of hearing-impaired children. *Br. J. Audiol.* **24**, 17–27.

GANNON, J.R. (1981). *Deaf Heritage: A Narrative History of Deaf America.* Silver Spring. MD: National Association of the Deaf.

GANTZ, B.J., TYLER, R.S., KNUTSON, J.F., WOODWORTH, G., ABBAS, P., MCCABE, B.F., HINRICHS, J., TYE-MURRAY, N., LANSING, C., KUK, F. and BROWN, C. (1988). Evaluation of five different cochlear implant designs: audiologic assessment and predictors of performance. *Laryngoscope* **98**, 1100–1106.

GARDNER, E.F., RUDMAN, H.C., KARLSEN, G. and MERWIN, J.C. (1982). *Stanford Achievement Test*, 17th Edn. Cleveland, OH: Psychological Corporation.

GARMAN, M. (1990). *Psycholinguistics.* Cambridge: Cambridge University Press.

GARRETT, M.F. (1980). Levels of processing in sentence production. In: Butterworth (1980).

GARRISON, W.M. and TESCH, S. (1978). Self-concept and deafness: a review of research literature. *Volta Rev.* **80**, 457–466.

GATES, A.J. and MCGINITIE, W.H. (1965). *Gates–McGinitie Reading Test*. Chicago, IL: Riverside.

GATHERCOLE, S.E. (1990). Working memory and language development: how close is the link? *The Psychologist* **2**, 57–60.

GAULT, R.H. (1924). Progress in experiments on tactual interpretation of oral speech. *J. Abnorm. Soc. Psychol.* **14**, 155–159.

GAY, T. (1978). Effect of speaking rate on vowel formant movements. *J. Acoust. Soc. Am.* **63**, 223–230.

GAZZANIGA, M.S. (Ed.) (1979). *Handbook of Behavioral Neurobiology* Vol. 2, New York: Plenum.

GEERS, A. and MOOG, J. (1989). Factors predictive of the development of literacy in profoundly hearing-impaired adolescents. *Volta Rev.* **91**, 69–86.

GEERS, A., MOOG, J. and SCHICK, B. (1984). Acquisition of spoken and signed English by profoundly deaf children. *J. Speech Hear. Disord.* **49**, 378–388.

GEERS, A.E. and MOOG, J.S. (1987). Predicting spoken language acquisition of profoundly hearing-impaired children. *J. Speech Hear. Disord.* **52**, 84–94.

GEFFNER, D. and DONOVAN, N. (1974). Intelligibility functions of normal and sensorineural loss subjects on the W-22 lists. *J. Aud. Res.* **14**, 82–86.

GEFFNER, D.S. and FREEMAN, L.R. (1980). Speech assessment at the primary level: interpretation relative to speech training. In: Subtelny (1980).

GELDARD, F.A. (1972). *The Human Senses,* 2nd Edn. New York: Wiley.

GENTILE, A. and DI FRANCESCA, S. (1969). *Academic Achievement Test Performances of Hearing Impaired Students*. Washington, DC: Gallaudet College, Office of Demographic Studies.

GEOFFRION, L. (1982). An analysis of teletype conversations. *Am. Ann. Deaf* **127**, 747–752.

GEOFFRION, L.D. and GEOFFRION, O.P. (1983). *Computers and Reading Instruction*. Reading, MA: Addison-Wesley.

GEOFFRION, L.D. and GOLDENBERG, E.P. (1981). Computer–based exploratory learning systems for communication-handicapped children. *J. Spec. Educ.* **15**, 325–332.

GERBER, S.E. and MENCHER, G.T. (Eds) (1978). *Early Diagnosis of Hearing Loss*. New York: Grune and Stratton.

GETTY, D.J. and HOWARD, J.H. (Eds) (1981). *Auditory and Visual Pattern Recognition*. Hillsdale, NJ: Erlbaum.

GIBSON, E.J. (1972). Reading for some purpose. In: Kavanagh and Mattingly (1972).

GIORCELLI, L. (1985). Communication: the essential ingredient. *Aust. Teacher of the Deaf* **26**, 19–20.

GLASER, R. (Ed.) (1978). *Advances in Instructional Psychology*. Hillsdale, NJ: Erlbaum.

GLASER, R. and BASSOK, M. (1989). Learning theory and the study of instruction. *Ann. Rev. Psychol.* **40**, 631–666.

GLEASON, J.B. (1975). Fathers and other strangers: men's speech to young children. In: Dato (1975).

GODA, S. (1964). Spoken syntax of normal, deaf and retarded adolescents. *J. Verb. Learn. Verb. Behav.* **3**, 401–405.

GODFREY, J. and MILLAY, K. (1978). Perception of rapid spectral change in speech by listeners with mild and moderate sensorineural hearing loss. *J. Am. Audiol. Soc.* **3**, 200–208.

GOFFMAN, E. (1967). *Interaction Ritual: Essays on Face to Face Behavior*. Garden City, NY: Doubleday.

GOLD, T. (1980). Speech production in hearing-impaired children. *J. Commun. Disord.* **13**, 397–418.

GOLDBERG, D., NIEHL, P. and METROPOULOS, T. (1989). Parent checklist for placement of a hearing-impaired child in a mainstreamed classroom. *Volta Rev.* **91**, 327–332.

GOLDIN-MEADOW, S. and MYLANDER, C. (1984). Gestural communication in deaf children: the effects and noneffects of parental input on early language development. *Monogr. Soc. Res. Child Devel.* **49**, 1–151.

GOLDMAN, R., FRISTOE, M. and WOODCOCK, R.W. (1970). *Test of Auditory Discrimination*. Circle Pines, MN: American Guidance Service.

GOLINKOFF, R.M. and AMES, G.J. (1979). A comparison of fathers' and mothers' speech with their young children. *Child Devel.* 50, 28–32.

GONZALEZ, K.A. (1984). The content of practicum observation and supervized interaction. In: Northcott (1984).

GOODMAN, Y. and BURKE, C. (1980). *Reading Strategies: Focus on Comprehension*. New York: Holt, Rinehart and Winston.

GOODY, E.N. (1978). *Questions and Politeness: Strategies in Social Interaction*. Cambridge: Cambridge University Press.

GORELICK, P.B. and ROSS, E.D. (1987). The aprosodias: further functional–anatomical evidence for the organization of affective language in the right hemisphere. *J. Neurol. Neurosurg. Psychiat.* 50, 553–560.

GORGA, M.P. and THORNTON, A.R. (1989). The choice of stimuli for ABR measurements. *Ear Hear.* 10, 217–230.

GORMLEY, K. and SARACHAN-DEILY, A.B. (1987). Evaluating hearing-impaired students' writing: a practical approach. *Volta Rev.* 89, 157–169.

GORMLEY, K.A. (1981). On the influence of familiarity on deaf students' text recall. *Am. Ann. Deaf* 126, 1024–1030.

GORMLEY, K.A. (1982). The importance of familiarity in hearing-impaired readers' comprehension of text. *Volta Rev.* 84, 71–80.

GORMLEY, K.A. and FRANZEN, A.M. (1978). Why can't the deaf read? Comments on asking the wrong question. *Am Ann. Deaf* 123, 542–547.

GOTTLIEB, D.D. and ALLEN, W. (1985). Visual disorders in a selected population of hearing-impaired students. *Volta Rev.* 87, 165–170.

GOTTMAN, J.M. (1981). *Time Series Analysis*. Cambridge: Cambridge University Press.

GRANT, K.W. (1987a). Encoding voice pitch for profoundly hearing-impaired listeners. *J. Acoust. Soc. Am.* 82, 423–432.

GRANT, K.W. (1987b). Identification of intonation contours by normally hearing and profoundly hearing-impaired listeners. *J. Acoust. Soc. Am.* 82, 1172–1178.

GRAVES, D. (1983). *Writing: Teachers and Children at Work*. Portsmouth, NH: Heinemann.

GRAY, C., FYFE, R. and BANKS, J. (1991). Some approaches to the study of story-schematic inference in deaf readers: a review of picture arrangement tests. *J. Br. Assn. Teachers of the Deaf* 15, 1–8.

GREEN, J. and WALLAT, C. (Eds) (1980). *Ethnographic Approaches to Face to Face Interaction in Educational Settings*. Norwood, NJ: Ablex.

GREEN, W.B. (1974). The development of semantic differential scales for deaf children. *Am. Ann. Deaf* 119, 361–364.

GREEN, W.B. and GREEN, K.W. (1984). The process of speechreading. In: Northcott (1984).

GREEN, W.B. and SHEPHERD, D.C. (1975). The semantic structure in deaf children. *J. Commun. Disord.* 8, 357–365.

GREENBERG, M.T. and CALDERON, R. (1984). Early intervention: outcomes and issues. *Topics Early Child. Spec. Educ.* 3, 1–9.

GREENBERG, M.T., CALDERON, R. and KUSCHÉ, C. (1984). Early intervention using Simultaneous Communication with deaf infants: the effect on communication development. *Child Devel.* 55, 607–616.

GREENFIELD, P.M. and SMITH, J. H. (1976). *The Structure of Communication in Early Language Development*. New York: Academic Press.

GREENO, J.G. and SIMON, H.A. (1988). Problem solving and reasoning. In: Atkinson et al. (1988).

GREENSTEIN, J.M., GREENSTEIN, B.B., MCCONVILLE, K. and STELLINI, L. (1975). *Mother–Infant Communication and Language Acquisition in Deaf Infants*. New York: Lexington School for the Deaf.

GREGG, N. (1991). Disorders of written expression. In: Bain et al. (1991).

GREGORY, J.F. (1987). An investigation of speechreading with and without child speech. *Am. Ann. Deaf* 132, 393–398.

GREGORY, R.L. (1974). Perceptions as hypotheses. In: Brown (1974).

GREGORY, S. and HARTLEY, G.M. (Eds) (1991). *Constructing Deafness*. London: Pinter.

GREGORY, S. and MOGFORD, K. (1981). Early language development in deaf children. In: Woll et al. (1981).

GREVILLE, K.A., KEITH, W.J. and LAVEN, J.W. (1985). Performance of children with previous OME on central auditory measures. *Aust. J. Audiol.* 7, 69–78.

GRIFFITHS, C. (1967). *Conquering Childhood Deafness*. New York: Exposition Press.

GRIFFITHS, C. (1988). The importance of the critical age of hearing and its implications. In: Taylor (1988).

GRIMWADE, J.C., WALKER, D.W., BARTLETT, M., GORDON, S. and WOOD, C. (1971). Human fetal heart rate change and movement in response to sound and vibration. *Am. J. Obstet. Gynec.* 109, 86–90.

GRONER, R. and FRAISSE, P. (Eds) (1982). *Cognition and Eye Movements*. Amsterdam: North-Holland Publishing Co.

GROSJEAN, F. and GEE, J.P. (1987). Prosodic structure and spoken word recognition. *Cognition* 25, 135–156.

GROVE, C., O'SULLIVAN, F.D. and RODDA, M. (1979). Communication and language in severely deaf adolescents. *Br. J. Psychol.* 70, 531–540.

GROVE, C. and RODDA, M. (1984). Receptive communication skills of hearing-impaired students: a comparison of four methods of communication. *Am. Ann. Deaf* 129, 378–385.

GRUNEBERG, M.M., MORRIS, P.E. and SYKES, R.N. (Eds) (1988). *Practical Aspects of Memory*, Vol. 2. Chichester: Wiley.

GUBERINA, P. and ASP, C.W. (1981). *The Verbo-Tonal Method for Rehabilitating People with Communication Problems*. New York: World Rehabilitation Fund.

GUELKE, R.W. (1985). The performance of hearing aids in relation to their frequency response. *Volta Rev.* 87, 171–176.

GULIAN, E., HINDS, P. and NIMMO-SMITH, I. (1986). Modifications in deaf children's vowel production: perceptual evidence. *Br. J. Audiol.* 20, 181–194.

GURALNICK, M.J. and BENNETT, F.C. (1987a). A framework for early intervention. In: Guralnick and Bennett (1987b).

GURALNICK, M.J. and BENNETT, F.C. (Eds) (1987b). *The Effectiveness of Early Intervention for At-Risk and Handicapped Children*. Orlando, FL: Academic Press.

GUSTASON, G. (1981). Does Signing Exact English work? *Teaching English To The Deaf* 7, 16–20.

GUSTASON, G. (1983). Where do we go from here? In: Kyle and Woll (1983).

GUSTASON, G., PFETZING, D. and ZAWOLKOW, E. (1972). *Signing Exact English*. Rossmoor, CA: Modern Signs Press.

HADADIAN, A. and ROSE, S. (1991). An investigation of parents' attitudes and the communication skills of their deaf children. *Am. Ann. Deaf* 136, 273–277.

HAGBORG, W. (1987). Hearing-impaired students and sociometric ratings: an exploratory study. *Volta Rev.* 89, 221–228.

HAKES, D. (1980). *The Development of Metalinguistic Abilities in Children*. New York: Springer-Verlag.

HALL, E.T. (1989). Deaf culture, tacit culture and ethnic relations. *Sign Lang. Stud.* 65, 291–304.

HAMILTON, H. (1985). Development of sign-based perception by deaf children. *Percept. Mot. Skills* 60, 699–704.

HAMILTON, H. and HOLZMAN, T.G. (1989). Linguistic encoding in short-term memory as a function of stimulus type. *Mem. Cognit.* 17, 541–550.

HAMILTON, H. and LILLO-MARTIN, D. (1986). Imitative production of ASL verbs of movement and location: a comparative study. *Sign Lang. Stud.* 50, 29–57.

HAMMERMEISTER, F.K. (1971). Reading achievements in deaf adults. *Am. Ann. Deaf* 116, 25–28.

HAMP, N.W. (1972). Reading attainment and some associated factors in deaf and partially hearing children. *Teacher of the Deaf* 70, 203–215.

HANEY, W.V. (1973). *Communication and Organizatioal Behavior*, 3rd Edn. Homewood, IL: Irwin.

HANNLEY, M. and JERGER, J. (1985). Patterns of phoneme identification error in cochlear and eighth nerve disorders. *Audiology* 24, 157–166.

HANSEN, B. (1975). Varieties in Danish sign language and grammatical features of the original sign language. *Sign Lang. Stud.* 8, 249–256.

HANSON, V.L. (1982). Short-term recall by deaf signers of American Sign Language: implications of encoding strategy for order recall. *J. Exp. Psychol.: Learn. Mem. Cognit.* 8, 572–583.

HANSON, V.L. (1986). Access to spoken language and the acquisition of orthographic structure: evidence from deaf readers. *Q. J. Exp. Psychol.* 38A, 193–212.

HANSON, V.L. and FELDMAN, L.B. (1989). Language specificity in lexical organization: evidence from deaf signers' lexical organisation of American Sign Language and English. *Mem. Cognit.* 17, 292–301.

HANSON, V.L., GOODELL, E.W. and PERFETTI, C.A. (1991). Tongue-twister effects in the silent reading of hearing and deaf college students. *J. Mem. Lang.* 30, 319–330.

HANSON, V.L., SHANKWEILER, D. and FISCHER, F.W. (1983). Determinants of spelling ability in deaf and hearing adults: access to linguistic structure. *Cognition* 14, 323–344.

HARGIE, O., SAUNDERS, C. and DICKSON, D. (1981). *Social Skills in Interpersonal Communication*. London: Croom Helm.

HARNAD, S. (Ed.) (1976). *The Origins and Evolution of Language and Speech*. New York: New York Academy of Sciences.

HARRIS, L.J. (1989). Hand preference and gestures and signs in the deaf and hearing: some notes on early evidence and theory. *Brain Cognit.* 10, 189–221.

HARRIS, P.L., KRUITHOF, A., TERGWOGT, M.M. and VISSER, T. (1981). Children's detection and awareness of textual anomaly. *J. Exp. Child Psychol.* 31, 212–231.

HARRIS, R.I. (1978). The relationship of impulse control to parent hearing status, manual communication, and academic achievement in deaf children. *Am. Ann. Deaf* 123, 52–67.

HARRIS, R.W., BREY, R.H., ROBINETTE, M.S., CHABRIES, D.M., CHRISTIANSEN, R.W. and COLLEY, R.G. (1988). Use of adaptive digital signal processing to improve speech communication for normally hearing and hearing-impaired subjects. *J. Speech Hear. Res.* 31, 265–271.

HARRISON, D.R., SIMPSON, P.A. and STUART, A. (1991). The development of written language in a population of hearing impaired children. *J. Br. Assn. Teachers of the Deaf* 15, 76–85.

HARRISON, M.F., LAYTON, T.L. and TAYLOR, T.D. (1987). Antecedent and consequent stimuli in teacher–child dyads. *Am. Ann. Deaf* 132, 227–231.

HARTUP, W.W. (1976). Peer relations and the behavioral development of the individual child. In: Schopler and Reichler (1976).

HARTVIG JENSEN, J., BORRE, S. and ANGAARD JOHANSEN, P. (1989). Unilateral sensorineural hearing loss in children and auditory performance with respect to right/left ear differences. *Br. J. Audiol.* 23, 207–213.

HARVEY, M.A. (1984a). Family therapy with deaf persons: the systemic utilization of an interpreter. *Family Process.* 23, 205–213.

HARVEY, M.A. (1984b). Rejoinder to Scott. *Family Process.* 23, 216–221.

HARVEY, M.A. (1989). *Psychotherapy with Deaf and Hard-of-hearing Persons: A Systematic Model*. Hillsdale, NJ: Erlbaum.

HARVEY, N. (1991). British research into skill: what is going on? *The Psychologist* 4, 443–448.

HASS, E.J. and SAMS, K.M. (1987). A method for examining gestural language structure. *Percept. Mot. Skills* 64, 391–397.

HAWKINS, J.E. and STEVENS, S.S. (1950). The masking of pure tones of speech by white noise. *J. Acoust. Soc. Am.* 22, 6–13.

HAY, J. (1978). Courtesy, humour and adjustment to a mad world. In: Montgomery (1978).

HAYCOCK, G.S. (1933). *The Teaching of Speech.* Washington, DC: Alexander Graham Bell Association.

HAYES, J.R. (Ed.) (1970). *Cognition and the Development of Language.* New York: Wiley.

HAZAN, V., FOURCIN, A. and ABBERTON, E. (1991). Development of phonetic labeling in hearing-impaired children. *Ear Hear.* **12**, 71–84.

HEFFERNAN, C. (1990). A Kodaly-based music programme for hearing-impaired children. *Tarolye Bull., Melbourne* **8**, 12–18.

HEIDER, F. and HEIDER, G.M. (1940). A comparison of sentence structure of deaf and hearing children. *Psychol. Monogr.* **52**, 42–103.

HEIDER, F. and HEIDER, G.M. (1941). Studies in the psychology of the deaf. *Psychol. Monogr.* **53**, 1–56.

HEIDINGER, V.A. (1972). *An Exploratory Study of Procedures for Improving Temporal Features in the Speech of Deaf Children.* Columbia University: unpublished Doctoral Thesis.

HELLIGE, J.B. (1980). Visual laterality and cerebral hemisphere specialization: methodological and theoretical considerations. In: Sidowski (1980).

HELLMAN, S.A., CHUTE, P.M., KRETSCHMER, R.E., NEVINS, M.E., PARISIER, S.C. and THURSTON, L.C. (1991). The development of a children's implant profile. *Am. Ann. Deaf* **136**, 77–81.

HELMUTH, J. (Ed.) (1970). *Cognitive Studies,* Vol 1. New York: Brunner.

HENDERSON, L. (1982). *Orthography and Word Recognition in Reading.* London: Academic Press.

HENDERSON, P. (Ed.) (1976). *Methods of Communication Currently Used in the Education of Deaf Children.* London: Royal National Institute for the Deaf.

HENSHALL, W.R. (1972). Intrauterine sound levels. *Am. J. Obstet. Gynec.* **112**, 576–578.

HERMELIN, B. and O'CONNOR, N. (1975). The recall of digits by normal, deaf and autistic children. *Br. J. Psychol.* **66**, 203–209.

HESS, D.W. (1969). Evaluation of the young deaf adult. *J. Rehab. Deaf* **3**, 6–21.

HIDI, A. and HILDYARD, A. (1983). The comparison of oral and written productions in two discourse types. *Discourse Processes* **6**, 91–105.

HIGGINS, E.T., FONDACARO, R. and MCCANN, C.D. (1981). Rules and Roles. In: Dickson (1981).

HIRSH, I.J. (1952). *The Measurement of Hearing.* New York: McGraw-Hill.

HIRSH, I.J., DAVIS, H., SILVERMAN, S.R., REYNOLDS, E.G., ELDERT, E. and BENSON, R.W. (1952). Development of materials for speech audiometry. *J. Speech Hear. Disord.* **17**, 321–337.

HIRSH-PASEK, K. (1987). The metalinguistics of fingerspelling: an alternate way to increase reading vocabulary in congenitally deaf readers. *Read. Res. Q.* **22**, 455–474.

HIRSH-PASEK, K. and TREIMAN, R. (1982). Recoding in silent reading: can the deaf child translate print into a more manageable form? *Volta Rev.* **84**, 71–82.

HOCHBERG, I., LEVITT, H. and OSBERGER, M.J. (1983). *Speech of the Hearing-Impaired: Research, Training, and Personnel Preparation,* Baltimore, MD: University Park Press.

HOEMANN, H.W. (1972). The development of communication skills in deaf and hearing children. *Child Devel.* **43**, 990–1003.

HOEMANN, H.W. (1975). The transparency of meaning of sign language gestures. *Sign. Lang. Stud.* **7**, 151–161.

HOEMANN, H.W. (1976). *The American Sign Language: Lexical and Grammatical Notes with Translation Exercises.* Silver Spring, MD: National Association of the Deaf.

HOEMANN, H.W. (1978a). *Communicating with Deaf People: A Resource Manual for Teachers and Students of American Sign Language.* Baltimore, MD: University Park Press.

HOEMANN, H.W. (1978b). Categorical coding of sign and English in short-term memory by deaf and hearing subjects. In: Siple (1978b).

HOEMANN, H.W. (1988). Communication skills in deaf and hearing children: a theoretical model. In: Taylor (1988).

HOEMANN, H.W. and KOENIG, T.J. (1990). Categorical coding of manual and English alphabet characters by beginning students of American Sign Language. *Sign Lang. Stud.* **67**, 175–181.

HOFFMEISTER, R. and MOORES, D.F. (1987). Code switching in deaf adults. *Am. Ann. Deaf* **132**, 31–34.

HOLLAND, J.H., HOLYOAK, K.J., NISBETT, R.E. and THAGARD, P.R. (1986). *Induction*. Cambridge, MA: MIT Press.

HOLLINGSHEAD, A. (1982). Issues raised by some recent research for the teaching of language to hearing-impaired pupils. In: Power and Hollingshead (1982).

HOLTON, S.A. (1978). Not so different: spatial and distancing behavior of deaf adults. *Am. Ann. Deaf* 123, 920–924.

HORII, Y. (1982). Some voice fundamental frequency characteristics of oral reading and spontaneous speech by hard of hearing young women. *J. Speech Hear. Res.* 25, 608–610.

HORTON, K.B. (1975). Early intervention through parent training. *Otolaryngol. Clin. North Am.* 8, 144–157.

HORTON, K.B. (1976). Early intervention for hearing-impaired infants and young children. In: Tjossem (1976).

HOUDE, R.A. (1980). Evaluation of independent drill with visual aids for speech training. In: Subtelny (1980).

HOUSE, W.F. (1976). Cochlear implants. *Ann. Otol. Rhinol. Laryngol.* (Suppl. 27) 85, 1–93.

HOUSE, W.F. and BERLINER, K.I. (1982). Cochlear implants: progress and perspectives. *Ann. Otol. Rhinol. Laryngol. (*Suppl.91), 91, 1–124.

HOUSE, W.F. and BERLINER, K.I. (1986). Safety and efficacy of the House/3T cochlear implant in profoundly deaf adults. *Otolaryngol. Clin. North Am* 19, 275–286.

HOUSTON, S. (1972). *A Survey of Psycholinguistics*. The Hague: Mouton.

HOWARTH, C. and WOOD, D. (1977). Research into the intellectual abilities of deaf children. *J. Br. Assoc. Teachers of the Deaf* 1, 5–12.

HOYT, M.F., SIEGELMAN, E.Y. and SCHLESINGER, H.S. (1981). Special issues regarding psychotherapy with the deaf. *Am. J. Psychiat.* 138, 807–811.

HUDGINS, C.V. and NUMBERS, F. (1942). An investigation of the intelligibility of the speech of the deaf. *Genet. Psychol. Monogr.* 25, 289–392.

HUGHES, M.C. and JAMES, S.L. (1985). Deaf children's revision behaviors in conversations. *J. Commun. Disord.* 18, 227–243.

HULL, R.H. (Ed.) (1982). *Rehabilitative Audiology*. New York: Grune and Stratton.

HULL, R.H. and ALPINER, J.G. (1976). The effect of syntactic word variations on the predictability of sentence content in speechreading. *J. Acad. Rehab. Audiol.* 9, 42–56.

HULL, R.H. and DILKA, K.L. (1984). *The Hearing-impaired Child in School*. Orlando, FL: Grune and Stratton.

HULME, C. (1988). Short-term memory development and learning to read. In: Gruneberg et al. (1988).

HUMMEL, J.W. (1982). Description of a successful inservice program. *Teacher Educ. Spec. Educ.* 5, 7–14.

HUMMEL, J.W. and SCHIRMER, B.E. (1984). Review of research and description of programs for the social development of hearing-impaired students. *Volta Rev.* 86, 259–266.

HUMPHRIES, T. (1991). An introduction to the culture of deaf people in the United States: content notes & reference material for teachers. *Sign Lang. Stud.* 72, 209–240.

HUMPHREY, G. (1948). *Directed Thinking*. New York: Dodd and Mead.

HUNG, D.L., TZENG, O.J.L. and WARREN, D.H. (1981). A chronometric study of sentence processing in deaf children. *Cognit. Psychol.* 113, 583–610.

HUNTINGTON, A. and WHATTON, F. (1981). Language and interaction in the classroom (Part 1): Teacher Talk. *J. Br. Assn. Teachers of the Deaf* 5, 162–173.

HUNTINGTON, A. and WHATTON, F. (1984). Language and interaction in the education of hearing-impaired children (Part 2). *J. Br. Assn. Teachers of the Deaf* 8, 137–144.

HUNTINGTON, A. and WHATTON, F. (1986). The spoken language of teachers and pupils in the education of hearing-impaired children. *Volta Rev.* 88, 5–19.

HURFORD, D.P. (1988). *Assessment and Remediation of a Phonemic Discrimination Deficit in Reading Disabled Second- and Fourth-Graders*. University of Akron: unpublished Doctoral Thesis.

HURST, J. (1988). Metaphors of communication in the dreams of deaf people. *Psychiat. J. Univ. Ottawa.* **13**, 75–78.

HUTCHINSON, J.M. and SMITH, L.L. (1976). Aerodynamic functioning in consonant production by hearing-impaired adults. *Audiol. Hear. Educ.* **2**, 16–25.

HUTCHINSON, K. (1990). An analytic distinctive feature approach to auditory training. *Volta Rev.* **92**, 5–12.

INSTITUTE OF PSYCHOANALYSIS (1957). *The Standard Edition of the Complete Psychological Works of Sigmund Freud* (1957). London: Hogarth Press and the Institute of Psychoanalysis.

IRAN-NEJAD, A., ORTONY, A. and RITTENHOUSE, R. (1981). The comprehension of metaphorical uses of English by deaf children. *J. Speech Hear. Res.* **24**, 551–556.

ISRAELITE, N., SCHLOSS, P. and SMITH, M. (1986). Teaching proverb use through a modified table game. *Volta Rev.* **88**, 195–207.

ISRAELITE, N.K. (1986). Hearing-impaired children and the psychological functioning of their normal-hearing siblings. *Volta Rev.* **88**, 47–54.

IVIMEY, G.P. (1976). The written syntax of an English deaf child: an exploration in method. *Br. J. Disord. Commun.* **11**, 103–120.

IVIMEY, G.P. (1977a). The perception of speech: an information-processing approach. Part 1 – The acoustic nature of spoken utterances. *J. Br. Assn. Teachers of the Deaf* **1**, 40–48.

IVIMEY, G.P. (1977b). The perception of speech: an information-processing approach. Part 2 – perceptual and cognitive processes. *J. Br. Assn. Teachers of the Deaf* **1**, 64–73.

IVIMEY, G.P. (1977c). The perception of speech: an information-processing approach. Part 3 – lipreading and the deaf. *J. Br. Assn. Teachers of the Deaf* **1**, 90–100.

IVIMEY, G.P. (1981). The production and perception by profoundly deaf children of syntactic time cues in English. *Br. J. Educ. Psychol.* **51**, 58–65.

JACKSON, C.A. (1989). Language acquistion in two modalities: the role of nonlinguistic cues in linguistic mastery. *Sign Lang. Stud.* **62**, 1–22.

JACKSON, P.L. and KELLY-BALLWEBER, D. (1979). Auditory stress pattern recognition in sentences. *Proc. ASHA Convention*, November.

JEFFERS, J. and BARLEY, M. (1971). *Speechreading (Lipreading)*. Springfield, IL: Charles C. Thomas.

JENSEMA, C.J., KARCHMER, M. and TRYBUS, R.J. (1978). *The Rated Speech Intelligibility of Hearing-Impaired Children*. Washington, DC: Gallaudet College, Office of Demographic Studies.

JENSEMA, C.J. and TRYBUS, R.J. (1978). *Communication Patterns and Educational Achievements*. Washington, DC: Gallaudet College.

JERGER, J., SPEAKS, C. and TRAMMELL, J.L. (1968). A new approach to speech audiometry. *J. Speech Hear. Disord.* **33**, 318–328.

JERGER, S. and JERGER, J. (1984). *Pediatric Speech Intelligibility Test*. St Louis, MS: Auditec.

JERGER, S., JERGER, J. and ABRAMS, S. (1983). Speech audiometry in the young child. *Ear Hear.* **4**, 56–66.

JERGER, S., JERGER, J. and LEWIS, S. (1981). Pediatric speech intelligibility test. II: Effect of receptive language age and chronological age. *Int. J. Pediat. Otorhinolaryngol.* **3**, 101–118.

JERGER, S., MARTIN, R.C. and JERGER, J. (1987). Specific auditory perceptual dysfunction in a learning disabled child. *Ear Hear.* **8**, 78–86.

JOHANSSON, B., WEDENBERG, E. and WESTIN, B. (1964). Measurement of tone response by the human foetus. *Acta Otolaryngol.* **57**, 188–192.

JOHN, J.E.J., GEMMILL, J., HOWARTH, J., KITZINGER, M. and SYKES, M. (1976). Some factors affecting the intelligibility of deaf children's speech. In: Stephens (1976).

JOHN, J.E.J. and HOWARTH, J.N. (1965). The effect of time distortions on the intelligibility of deaf children's speech. *Lang. Speech* **8**, 127–134.

JOHNSON, D., WHALEY, P. and DORMAN, M.F. (1984). Processing cues for stop consonant voicing by young hearing-impaired listeners. *J. Speech Hear. Res.* **27**, 112–118.

JOHNSON, D.D., CACCAMISE, F., ROTHBLUM, A.M., HAMILTON, L.F. and HOWARD, M. (1981). Identification and follow-up of visual impairments in hearing-impaired populations. *Am. Ann. Deaf.* **126**, 321–360.

JOHNSON, D.D., TOMS-BRONOWSKI, S. and PITTELMAN, S.D. (1982). Vocabulary development. *Volta Rev.* **84**, 11–24.

JOHNSON, F.L. (1977). Role-taking and referential communication abilities in first- and third-grade children. *Hum. Commun. Res.* **3**, 135–145.

JOHNSON, H. and GRIFFITH, P. (1985). The behavioral structure of an eighth-grade science class: a mainstreaming preparation strategy. *Volta Rev.* **87**, 291–303.

JOHNSON, H.A. (1988). A sociolinguistic aassessment scheme for the total communication student. *J. Acad. Rehab. Audiol. Monogr. Suppl.* **21**, 101–127.

JOHNSTON, T.A. (1987a). *A Preliminary Signing Dictionary of Australian Sign Language (Auslan)*. Payneham, South Australia: TAFE National Centre for Research and Development.

JOHNSTON, T.A. (1987b). *A General Introduction to Australian Sign Language (Auslan)*. Adelaide: TAFE National Centre for Research and Development.

JONES, E.E. (1985). Interpersonal distancing behavior of hearing-impaired vs. normal-hearing children. *Volta Rev.* **87**, 223–230.

JONES, T.W. (1984). A framework of identification, classification, and placement of multihandicapped hearing-impaired students. *Volta Rev.* **86**, 142–151.

JORDAN, I.K. (1983). Referential communication amongst Scottish deaf school pupils. In: Kyle and Woll (1983).

JOY, C.B. (1989). Features of discourse in an American Sign Language lecture. In: Lucas (1989).

KAGAN, J. and LEWIS, M. (1965). Studies in attention in the human infant. *Merrill–Palmer Q. Behav. Devel.* **11**, 101–119.

KAIL, R.V. and HAGEN, J.W. (Eds) (1977). *Perspectives on the Development of Memory and Cognition*. Hillsdale, NJ: Erlbaum.

KALIKOW, D.N., STEVENS, K.N. and ELIOTT, L.L. (1977). Development of a test of speech intelligibility in noise using sentence materials with controlled word predictability. *J. Acoust. Soc. Am.* **61**, 1337–1351.

KALLMAN, F. (1963). Main findings and some projections. In: Rainer et al. (1963).

KAMPFE, C.M. (1989). Reading comprehension of deaf adolescent residential school students and its relationship to hearing mothers' communication strategies and skills. *Am. Ann. Deaf* **134**, 317–322.

KAMPFE, C.M. and TURECHECK, A.G. (1987). Reading achievement of prelingually deaf students and its relationship to parental method of communication: a review of the literature. *Am. Ann. Deaf* **132**, 11–15.

KANGAS, K.A. and ALLEN, G.D. (1990). Intelligibility of synthetic speech for normal hearing and hearing-impaired listeners. *J. Speech Hear. Disord.* **55**, 751–755.

KANTOR, R. (1980). The acquisition of classifiers in ASL. *Sign Lang. Stud.* **8**, 193–208.

KAPLAN, H. and PICKETT, J.M. (1982). Differences in speech discrimination in the elderly as a function of type of competing noise: speech-babble or cafeteria. *Audiology* **21**, 325–333.

KATZ, J. (Ed.) (1985). *Handbook of Clinical Audiology*, 3rd Edn. Baltimore, MD: Williams and Wilkins.

KATZ, J. and HARMON, C.H. (1981). Phonemic synthesis: testing and training. In: Keith (1981b).

KAUTZKY-BOWDEN, S.M. and GONZALES, B.R. (1987). Attitudes of deaf adults regarding preferred sign language systems used in the classroom with deaf students. *Am. Ann. Deaf.* **132**, 251–255.

KAVANAGH, J.F. and CUTTING, J.E. (Eds) (1975). *The Role of Speech in Language*. Cambridge, MA: MIT Press.

KAVANAGH, J.F. and MATTINGLY, I.G. (Eds) (1972). *Language by Ear and by Eye: The Relationships between Speech and Reading*. Cambridge, MA: MIT Press.

KEENAN, P.A., WHITMAN, R.D. and PEPE, J. (1989). Hemispheric asymmetry in the processing of high and low spatial frequencies: a facial recognition task. *Brain Cognit.* **11**, 229–237.

KEITH, R.W. (1981a). Audiological and auditory language tests of central auditory function. In: Keith (1981b).

KEITH, R.W. (Ed.) (1981b). *Central Auditory and Language Disorders in Children*. Houston, TX: College Hill Press.

KEITH, R.W. (1984). The basic audiologic evaluation. In: Northern (1984).

KELLY, M.S., BEST, C.T. and KIRK, U. (1989). Cognitive processing deficits in reading disabilities: a prefrontal cortical hypothesis. *Brain Cognit.* **11**, 275–293.

KEMP, D.T., BRAY, P., ALEXANDER, L. and BROWN, A.M. (1986). Acoustic emission cochleography – practical aspects. *Scand. Audiol. Suppl.* **25**, 71–95.

KENDALL, M. and ORD, J.K. (1990). *Time series.* London: Edward Arnold.

KENDON, A. (1981a). Introduction: current issues in the study of 'nonverbal communication'. In: Kendon (1981b).

KENDON, A. (1981b). *Nonverbal Communication, Interaction, and Gesture: Selections from Semiotica.* The Hague: Mouton.

KENWORTHY, O.T. (1986). Caregiver–child interaction and language acquisition of hearing-impaired children. *Topics Lang. Disord.* **6**, 1–11.

KIERNAN, C., REID, B. and JONES, L. (1979). Signs and symbols: who uses what? *Spec. Educ. Forward Trends* **6**, 32–35.

KIERNAN, C., REID, B. and JONES, L. (1982). *Signs and Symbols: Use of Non-Vocal Communication Systems.* London: Heinemann.

KIMURA, D. (1973a). Manual activity during speaking. I. Right handers. *Neuropsychologia* **11**, 45–50.

KIMURA, D. (1973b). Manual activity during speaking. II. Left handers. *Neuropsychologia* **11**, 51–55.

KIMURA, D. (1983). Speech representation in an unbiased sample of left-handers. *Hum. Neurobiol.* **2**, 147–154.

KIMURA, D. (1990). How special is language? *Sign Lang. Stud.* **66**, 79–84.

KIMURA, D. and HUMPHRYS, C.A. (1981). A comparison of left- and right-arm movements during speaking. *Neuropsychologia* **19**, 807–812.

KING, A.B. (1987). Speech perception tests for the profoundly deaf. In: Martin (1987).

KING, C.M. and QUIGLEY, S.P. (1985). *Reading and Deafness.* Basingstoke: Taylor and Francis.

KING, F. (1989). Assessment of pragmatic skills. *Child Lang. Teaching Ther.* **5**, 191–201.

KINGSLEY, P.R. and HAGEN, J.W. (1969). Induced versus spontaneous rehearsal in short-term memory in nursery school children. *Devel. Psychol.* **1**, 40–46.

KIRK, S., MCCARTHY, J. and KIRK, W. (1968). *Illinois Test of Psycholinguistic Abilities.* Urbana, IL: University of Illinois Press.

KIRK, U. (1983). *Neuropsychology of Language, Reading, and Spelling.* New York: Academic Press.

KISILEVSKY, B.S. and MUIR, D.W. (1991). Human fetal and subsequent newborn responses to sound and vibration. *Infant Behav. Devel.* **14**, 1–26.

KITSON, H.D. (1915). Psychological tests for lip-reading ability. *Volta Rev.* **17**, 471–476.

KITSON, N. and FRY, R. (1990). Prelingual deafness and psychiatry. *Br. J. Hosp. Med.* **44**, 353–356.

KLAHR, D. and KOTOVSKY, K. (Eds) (1989). *Complex Information Processing: The Impact of Herbert A. Simon.* Hillsdale, NJ: Erlbaum.

KLECAN-AKER, J. and BLONDEAU, R. (1990). An examination of the written stories of hearing-impaired school-age children. *Volta Rev.* **92**, 275–282.

KLIMA, E.S. and BELLUGI, U. (1979). *The Signs of Language.* Cambridge, MA: Harvard University Press.

KLUWIN, T. (1981). The grammaticality of manual representations of English in classroom settings. *Am. Ann. Deaf* **126**, 417–421.

KLUWIN, T. (1983). Discourse in deaf classrooms: the structure of teaching episodes. *Discourse Processes* **6**, 275–293.

KLUWIN, T.N. and GAUSTAD, M.G. (1991). Predicting family communication choices. *Am. Ann Deaf* **136**, 28–34.

KLUWIN, T.N. and KELLY, A.B. (1991). The effectiveness of dialogue journal writing in improving the writing skills of young deaf writers. *Am. Ann. Deaf* **136**, 284–291.

KNELL, S.M. and KLONOFF, E.A. (1983). Language sampling in deaf children: a comparison of oral and signed communication modes. *J. Commun. Disord.* 16, 435–447.

KNIGHT, T.K. (1989). The use of cumulative cloze to investigate contextual build-up in deaf and hearing readers. *Am. Ann Deaf* 134, 268–272.

KNIGHTS, R.M. and BAKKER, K.K. (Eds) (1976). *Neuropsychology of Learning Disorders: Theoretical Approaches.* Baltimore, MD: University Park Press.

KNUDSEN, V.O. (1928). 'Hearing' with the sense of touch. *J. Gen. Psychol.* 1, 320–351.

KNUTSON, J.F. and LANSING, C.R., (1990). The relationship between communication problems and psychological difficulties in persons with profound acquired hearing loss. *J. Speech Hear. Disord.* 55, 656–664.

KOH, S.D., VERNON, M. and BAILEY, W. (1971). Free-recall learning of word lists by prelingually deaf subjects. *J. Verb. Learn. Verb. Behav.* 10, 542–547.

KOLERS, P.A., WROLSTAD, N.E. and BOUMA, H. (Eds) (1979). *The Processing of Visible Language I.* New York: Plenum.

KOLUCHOVA, J. (1972). Severe deprivation in twins: a case study. *J. Child Psychol. Psychiat.* 13, 107–114.

KOLUCHOVA, J. (1976). The further development of twins after severe and prolonged deprivation: a second report. *J. Child Psychol. Psychiat.* 17, 181–188.

KRAKOW, R.A. and HANSON, V.L. (1985). Deaf signers and serial recall in the visual modality: memory for signs, fingerspelling and print. *Mem. Cognit.* 13, 265–272.

KRASHEN, S.D. (1973). Lateralisation, language learning and the critical period: some new evidence. *Lang. Learning* 23, 63–74.

KRASHEN, S.D. (1982). *Principles and Practice in Second Language Acquisition.* Oxford: Pergamon Press.

KREIMEYER, K. and ANTIA, S. (1988). The development and generalization of social interaction skills in preschool hearing-impaired children. *Volta Rev.* 90, 219–231.

KRETSCHMER, R. (Ed.)(1985). *Writing to Learn and Learning to Write: Implications for the Hearing-Impaired* Washington, DC: Alexander Graham Bell Association.

KRETSCHMER, R.E. (1982). Reading and the hearing-impaired individual: summation and application. *Volta Rev.* 84, 107–122.

KRETSCHMER, R. and KRETSCHMER, L. (1980). Pragmatics: development in normal-hearing and hearing-impaired children. In: Subtelny (1980).

KRETSCHMER, R.R. and KRETSCHMER, L.W. (1978). *Language Development and Intervention with the Hearing Impaired.* Baltimore, MD: University Park Press.

KRETSCHMER, R.R. and KRETSCHMER, L.W. (1986). Language in perspective. In: Luterman (1986).

KRETSCHMER, R.R. and KRETSCHMER, L.W. (1990). Language. *Volta Rev.* 92, 56–71.

KRICOS, P.B. and LESNER, S.A. (1985). Effect of talker differences on the speechreading of hearing-impaired teenagers. *Volta Rev.* 87, 5–14.

KRICOS, P., LESNER, S. and LAZARUS, G. (1990). Influence of visual information on speech assessment with hearing-impaired children. *Volta Rev.* 92, 213–222.

KRINSKY, S. (1990). The feeling of knowing in deaf adolescents. *Am. Ann. Deaf* 135, 389–395.

KRYTER, K.D. (1970). *The Effects of Noise on Man.* New York: Academic Press.

KUHL, P.K. (1980). Perceptual constancy for speech sound categories in early infancy. In: Yeni-Komishian et al. (1980).

KUSCHÉ, C.A., GREENBERG, M.T., CALDERON, R. and GUSTAFSON, R.N. (1987). Generalization strategies from the PATHS project for the prevention of substance use disorders. In: Anderson and Watson (1987).

KUSCHÉ, C.A., GREENBERG, M.T. and GARFIELD, T.S. (1983). Nonverbal intelligence and verbal achievement in deaf adolescents: an examination of heredity and environment. *Am. Ann. Deaf* 128, 458–466.

KYLE, J. (Ed.) (1987). *Sign and School: Using Signs in Deaf Children's Development.* Clevedon, PA: Multilingual Matters Ltd.

KYLE, J.G. (1977). Audiometric analysis as a predictor of speech intelligibility. *Br. J. Audiol.* **11**, 51–58.

KYLE, J.G. (1978). The study of auditory deprivation from birth. *Br. J. Audiol.* **12**, 37–39.

KYLE, J.G. (1980a). Auditory deprivation from birth – clarification of some issues. *Br. J. Audiol.* **14**, 30–32.

KYLE, J.G. (1980b). Reading development of deaf children. *J. Res. Read.* **3**, 86–97.

KYLE, J.G. (1981). Signs of speech. *Spec. Educ. Forward Trends* **8**, 19–23.

KYLE, J.G. (1983a). Looking for meaning in sign language sentences. In: Kyle and Woll (1983).

KYLE, J.G. (1983b). Meaning in sign: reading events in BSL and English. In: Rogers and Sloboda (1983).

KYLE, J.G. and ALLSOP, L. (1982). Communicating with young deaf people: some issues. *J. Br. Assn. Teachers of the Deaf* **6**, 71–79.

KYLE, J.G. and WOLL, B. (Eds) (1983). *Language in Sign: An International Perspective on Sign Language.* London: Croom Helm.

KYLE, J.G. and WOLL, B. (1985). *Sign Language: The Study of Deaf People and Their Language.* Cambridge: Cambridge University Press.

LADD, G., MUNSON, H. and MILLER, J. (1984). Social integration of deaf adolescents in secondary-level mainstream programs. *Except. Child.* **50**, 420–428.

LADEFOGED, P. (1962). *Elements of Acoustic Phonetics.* Chicago, IL: University of Chicago Press.

LADEFOGED, P. (1967). *Three Areas of Experimental Phonetics.* London: Oxford University Press.

LA GRECA, A.M. and MESIBOV, G.B. (1979). Social skills intervention with learning disabled children: selecting skills and implementing training. *J. Clin. Child Psychol.* **8**, 234–241.

LAKOFF, G. (1987). *Women, Fire and Dangerous Things: What Categories Reveal About the Mind.* Chicago, IL: University of Chicago Press.

LAMBERT, N. and BOWER, E. (1979). *A Picture Game.* Monterey, CA: Publishers Test Service.

LANE, H. (1988). Educating the American Sign Language speaking minority of the United States: a paper prepared for the Commission on the Education of the Deaf. *Sign Lang. Stud.* **59**, 221–230.

LANE, H. (1990). Cultural and infirmity models of deaf Americans. *J. Aural Rehab. Assoc.* **23**, 11–26.

LANE, H. and BAKER, D. (1974). Reading achievement of the deaf: another look. *Volta Rev.* **76**, 489–499.

LANE, H., BOYES-BRAEM, P. and BELLUGI, U. (1976). Preliminaries to a distinctive feature analysis of American Sign Language. *Cognit. Psychol.* **8**, 263–289.

LANE, H.S. (1948). Some psychological problems involved in working with the deaf and the hard-of-hearing. *J. Rehabil.* **24–29** and 36.

LARSON, C.O., DANSEREAU, D.F., O'DONNELL, A., HYTHECKER, V., LAMBIOTTE, J.G. and ROCKLIN, T. (1984). Verbal ability and cooperative learning. *J. Read. Behav.* **16**, 289–295.

LARTZ, M.N. and MCCOLLUM, J. (1990). Maternal questions while reading to deaf and hearing twins: a case study. *Am. Ann. Deaf* **135**, 235–240.

LASASSO, C. (1980). The validity and reliability of the cloze procedure as a measure of readability for prelingually, profoundly deaf students. *Am. Ann. Deaf* **125**, 559–563.

LASASSO, C. (1985). Visual matching test-taking strategies used by deaf readers. *J. Speech Hear. Res.* **28**, 2–7.

LASASSO, C. (1986). A comparison of visual matching test-taking strategies of comparably-aged normal-hearing and hearing-impaired subjects with comparable reading levels. *Volta Rev.* **88**, 231–241.

LASASSO, C. (1987). Survey of reading instruction for hearing-impaired students in the United States. *Volta Rev.* **89**, 85–98.

LASASSO, C.J. (1990). Developing the ability of hearing impaired students to comprehend and generate question forms. *Am. Ann. Deaf* **135**, 409–412.

LASASSO, C. and DAVEY, B. (1987). The relationship between lexical knowledge and reading comprehension for prelingually, profoundly hearing-impaired students. *Volta Rev.* **89**, 211–220.

LASS, N.J. (Ed.) (1983). *Speech and Language: Advances in Basic Research and Practice*, Vol. 9. New York: Academic Press.

LAWSON, R. (1978). Patterns of communication in intermediate level classrooms of the deaf. *Audiol. Hear. Educ.* 4, 19–23.

LECOURS, A.R. (1975). Myelogenetic correlates of the development of speech and language. In: Lenneberg and Lenneberg (1975).

LEDER, S.B., SPITZER, J.B. and KIRCHNER, J.C. (1987). Speaking fundamental frequency of postlingually profoundly deaf adult men. *Ann. Otol. Rhinol. Laryngol.* 96, 322–324.

LEDERBERG, A.R. (1984). Interaction between deaf preschoolers and unfamiliar hearing adults. *Child Devel.* 55, 598–606.

LEDERBERG, A.R. (1991). Social interaction among deaf preschoolers. *Am. Ann. Deaf* 136, 53–59.

LEDERBERG, A.R. and MOBLEY, C.E. (1990). The effect of hearing impairment on the quality of attachment and mother–toddler interaction. *Child Devel.* 61, 1596–1604.

LEE, L.L. (1966). Developmental Sentence Types: a method for comparing normal and deviant syntactic development. *J. Speech Hear. Disord.* 31, 311–330.

LEE, L.L. (1969). *The Northwestern Syntax Screening Test*. Evanston, IL: Northwestern University Press.

LEE, L.L. and CANTER, S.M. (1971). Developmental Sentence Scoring: a clinical procedure for estimating syntax development in children's spontaneous speech. *J. Speech Hear. Disord.* 36, 315–340.

LEINHARDT, G. and GREENO, J.G. (1986). The cognitive skills of teaching. *J. Educ. Psychol.* 78, 75–95.

LEMANEK, K.L., WILLIAMSON, D.A., GRESHAM, F.M. and JENSEN, B.J. (1986). Social skills training with hearing-impaired children and adolescents. *Behav. Modif.* 10, 55–71.

LENNEBERG, E.H. (1967). *Biological Foundations of Language*. New York: Wiley.

LENNEBERG, E.H. and LENNEBERG, E. (Eds) (1975). *Foundations of Language Development: A Multidisciplinary Approach*. New York: Academic Press.

LEOTTA, D.F., RABINOWITZ, W.M., REED, C.M. and DURLACH, N.I. (1988). Preliminary results of speech-reception tests obtained with the synthetic Tadoma system. *J. Rehab. Res. Devel.* 25, 45–52.

LESLIE, P.T. and CLARKE, B.R. (1977). A study of selected syntactic structures in the language of young deaf children. *J. Br. Assn. Teachers of the Deaf* 1, 128–133.

LESNER, S.A. (1988). The talker. In: De Filippo and Sims (1988).

LESNER, S., SANDRIDGE, S. and KRICOS, P. (1987). Training influences on visual consonant and sentence recognition. *Ear Hear.* 8, 283–287.

LEVELT, W.J.M. (1989). *Speaking: From Intention to Articulation*. Cambridge, MA: MIT Press.

LEVINE, E.S. (1960). *The Psychology of Deafness: Techniques of Appraisal for Rehabilitation*. New York: Columbia University Press.

LEVINE, S. (1986). Hemispheric specialization and implications for the education of the hearing impaired. *Am. Ann. Deaf* 131, 238–242.

LEVINSON, P.J. and SLOAN, C. (Eds) (1980). *Auditory Processing and Language*. New York: Grune and Stratton.

LEVITT, H. (1971). Speech production for the deaf child. In: Connor (1971).

LEVITT, H., MCGARR, N.S. and GEFFNER, D. (Eds) (1987). *Development of Language and Communication Skills in Hearing-Impaired Children*. Washington, DC: ASHA.

LEVITT, H., SMITH, C. and STROMBERT, H. (1974). Acoustic, perceptual and articulatory characteristics of the speech of deaf children. In: Fant (1974).

LEVITT, H., STARK, R.E., MCGARR, N., CARP, J., STROMBERT, M., GAFFNEY, R.H., BARRY, C., VILEZ, A., OSBERGER, M.J., LEITER, E. and FREEMAN, L. (1976). Language communication skills of deaf children. 1973/1975. *Proc. Language Assessment for the Hearing Impaired – A Work Study Institute*. New York: New York State Education Department.

LEWIS, M.M. (1968). *Language and Personality in Deaf Children*. Slough, Buckinghamshire: National Foundation for Educational Research in England and Wales.

LEWIS, T.K. and WILCOX, J.C. (1978). The perceptual use of semantic rules by normal-hearing and hard-of-hearing children. *J. Commun. Disord.* **11**, 107–118.

LI, C.N. (Ed.) (1976). *Subject and Topic*. New York: Academic Press.

LIBEN, L.S. (Ed.) (1978). *Deaf Children: Developmental Perspectives*. New York: Academic Press.

LIBEN, L.S. (1979). Free recall by deaf and hearing children: semantic clustering and recall in trained and untrained groups. *J. Exp. Child Psychol.* **27**, 105–119.

LIBERMAN, A.M., COOPER, F.S., SHANKWEILER, D.P. and STUDDERT-KENNEDY, M. (1967). Perception of the speech code. *Psychol. Rev.* **74**, 431–461.

LIBERMAN, I.Y., MANN, V.A., SHANKWEILER, D. and WERFELMAN, M. (1982). Children's memory for recurring linguistic and non-linguistic material in relation to reading ability. *Cortex* **18**, 367–375.

LIBERMAN, I.Y., SHANKWEILER, D., LIBERMAN, A.M., FOWLER, C. and FISCHER, F.W. (1977). Phonetic segmentation and recoding in the beginning reader. In: Reber and Scarborough (1977).

LIDDELL, S. (1978a). Nonmanual signals and relative clauses in American Sign Language. In: Siple (1978b).

LIDDELL, S. (1978b). An introduction to relative clauses in ASL. In: Siple (1978b).

LIDDELL, S. (1980). *American Sign Langauge Syntax*. The Hague: Mouton.

LIDEN, G. and KANKKUNEN, A. (1973). Hearing aid procedures in young deaf and hard of hearing children. *Scand. Audiol. Suppl.* **3**, 47–54.

LIEBERTH, A.K. (1982). Functional speech therapy for the deaf child. In: Sims et al. (1982).

LIEBERTH, A.K. (1990). Rehabilitative issues in the bilingual education of deaf children. *J. Aural. Rehab. Assn.* **23**, 53–61.

LIEBERTH, A.K. and GAMBLE, M.E.B. (1991). The role of iconicity in sign language learning by hearing adults. *J. Commun. Disord.* **24**, 89–99.

LIEBERTH, A.K. and WHITEHEAD, R.L. (1987). Orosensory perception and articulatory proficiency in hearing-impaired adults. *Percept. Mot. Skills* **64**, 611–617.

LIEMOHN, W., HARGIS, C., WRISBERG, C. and WINTER, T. (1990). Rhythm production/perception by hearing-impaired students. *Volta Rev.* **92**, 13–24.

LILES, B., SCHULMAN, M. and BARTLETT, S. (1977). Judgments of grammar by normal and language-disordered children. *J. Speech Hear. Disord.* **42**, 199–209.

LILLO-MARTIN, D. (1990). Parameters for questions: evidence from wh-movement in ASL. In: Lucas (1990).

LINDZEY, G. and ARONSON, E. (Eds) (1969). *Handbook of Social Psychology*. Reading, MA: Addison-Wesley.

LING, D. (1976). *Speech and the Hearing-Impaired Child: Theory and Practice*. Washington DC: Alexander Graham Bell Association.

LING, D. (1979). Principles underlying the development of speech communication skills among hearing-impaired children. *Volta Rev.* **81**, 211–223.

LING, D. (Ed.) (1984a). *Early Intervention for Hearing-Impaired Children: Total Communication Options*. San Diego, CA: College Hill Press.

LING, D. (Ed.) (1984b). *Early Intervention for Hearing-Impaired Children: Oral Options*. San Diego, CA: College Hill Press.

LING, D. (1989). *The Foundations of Spoken Language for Hearing-impaired Children*. Washington DC: Alexander Graham Bell Association.

LING, D. (1991). *Phonetic–Phonologic Speech Evaluation Form: A Manual*. Washington DC: Alexander Graham Bell Association.

LING, D. and LING, A.H. (1978). *Aural Habilitation: The Foundations of Verbal Learning in Hearing-Impaired Children*. Washington DC: Alexander Graham Bell Association.

LING, D. and NIENHUYS, T.G. (1983). The deaf child: habilitation with and without a cochlear implant. *Ann. Otol. Rhinol. Laryngol.* **92**, 593–598.

LIVINGSTON, S. (1989). Revision strategies of deaf student writers. *Am. Ann. Deaf* **134**, 21–26.

LIVINGSTON, S. (1991). Comprehension strategies of two deaf readers. *Sign Lang. Stud.* **71**, 115–130.

LLOYD, L.L. and DOHERTY, J. (1983). The influence of production mode on the recall of signs in normal adult subjects. *J. Speech Hear. Res.* **26**, 595–600.

LOCKE, J.L. (1978). Phonemic effects in the silent reading of hearing and deaf children. *Cognition* **6**, 175–187.

LOCKE, J.L. and LOCKE, V.L. (1971). Deaf children's phonetic, visual, and dactylic coding in a grapheme recall task. *J. Exp. Psychol.* **89**, 142–146.

LOEB, R.C., HORST, L. and HORTON, P. (1980). Family interaction patterns associated with self-esteem in preadolescent girls and boys. *Merrill-Palmer Q. Behav. Devel.* **26**, 205–217.

LOEB, R. and SARIGIANI, P. (1986). The impact of hearing impairment on self-perceptions of children. *Volta Rev.* **88**, 89–100.

LOTT, B.E. and LEVY, J. (1960). The influence of certain communicator characteristics on lip reading efficiency. *J. Soc. Psychol.* **51**, 419–425.

LOU, M.W. (1988). The history of language use in the education of the deaf in the United States. In: Strong (1988).

LOU, M.W., FISCHER, S. and WOODWARD, J. (1987). A language-independent measure of communicative competence for deaf adolescents and adults. *Sign Lang. Stud.* **57**, 353–370.

LUCAS, C. (Ed.) (1989). *The Sociolinguistics of the Deaf Community*. San Diego, CA: Academic Press.

LUCAS, C. (Ed.) (1990). *Sign Language Research: Theoretical Issues*. Washington, DC: Gallaudet University Press.

LUCAS, C. and VALLI, C. (1989). Language contact in the American deaf community. In: Lucas (1989).

LUCKNER, J. (1991a). The competencies needed for teaching hearing-impaired students. *Am. Ann. Deaf* **136**, 17–20.

LUCKNER, J.L. (1991b). Mainstreaming hearing-impaired students: perceptions of regular educators. *Lang. Speech Hear. in Schools* **22**, 302–307.

LUDDERS, B.B. (1987). Communication between health care professionals and deaf patients. *Health Soc. Work.* **4**, 303–310.

LUETKE-STAHLMAN, B, (1984). Replicating single-subject assessment of language in deaf elementary-age children. *Am. Ann. Deaf* **129**, 40–44.

LUETKE-STAHLMAN, B. and MOELLER, M.P. (1990). Enhancing parents' use of SEE-2: progress and retention. *Am. Ann. Deaf* **135**, 371–378.

LUFTIG, R.L. and LLOYD, L.L. (1981). Manual sign translucency and referential concreteness in the learning of signs. *Sign Lang. Stud.* **30**, 49–60.

LUFTIG, R.L., PAGE, J.L. and LLOYD, L.L. (1983). Ratings of translucency in manual signs as a predictor of sign learnability. *J. Child. Commun. Disord.* **6**, 117–134.

LUPTON, L.K. and ZELAZNIK, H.N. (1990). Motor learning in sign language students. *Sign Lang. Stud.* **67**, 153–173.

LUTERMAN, D. (1979). *Counselling Parents of Hearing-Impaired Children*. Boston, MA: Little, Brown and Co.

LUTERMAN, D.M. (Ed.) (1986). *Deafness in Perspective*. San Diego, CA: College-Hill Press.

LYON, R. (1977). Auditory perceptual training: the state of the art. *J. Learn. Disabil.* **10**, 564–572.

LYREGAARD, P.E., ROBINSON, D.W. and HINCHCLIFFE, R. (1976). *A Feasibility Study of Speech Audiometry, N.P.L., Acoustics Report Ac73*. Teddington, Middlesex: National Physical Laboratory.

LYXELL, B. and RONNBERG, J. (1987). Guessing and speechreading. *Br. J. Audiol.* **21**, 13–20.

LYXELL, B. and RONNBERG, J. (1989). Information-processing skill and speech-reading. *Br. J. Audiol.* **23**, 339–347.

LYXELL, B. and RONNBERG, J. (1991). Word discrimination and chronological age related to sentence-based speech-reading skill. *Br. J. Audiol.* **25**, 3–10.

MAASSEN, B. (1986). Marking word boundaries to improve the intelligibility of the speech of the deaf. *J. Speech Hear. Res.* **29**, 227–230.

MAASSEN, B. and POVEL, D.J. (1984). The effect of segmental and suprasegmental corrections on the intelligibility of deaf speech. *J. Acoust. Soc. Am.* **78**, 877–886.

McAFEE, M.C., KELLY, J.F. and SAMAR, V.J. (1990). Spoken and written English errors of postsecondary students with severe hearing impairment. *J. Speech Hear. Disord.* **55**, 528–634.

McALISTER, P.V. (1990). The effects of hearing aids on speech discrimination in noise by normal-hearing listeners. *J. Rehab. Res. Devel.* **27**, 33–42.

McANNALLY, P.L., ROSE, S. and QUIGLEY, S.P. (1987). *Language Learning Practices with Deaf Children*. Boston, MA: College-Hill Press.

McCANE, N.P. (1980). Responding to classroom behavior problems among deaf children. *Am. Ann. Deaf* **125**, 902–905.

McCARTNEY, B. (1984). Education in the mainstream. *Volta Rev.* **86**, 41–52.

McCARTNEY, B.D. (1986). An investigation of the factors contributing to the ability of hearing-impaired children to communicate orally as perceived by oral deaf adults and teachers of the hearing-impaired. *Volta Rev.* **88**, 133–143.

McCAULEY, R.W., BRUININKS, R.H. and KENNEDY, P. (1976). Behavioral interactions of hearing-impaired children in regular classrooms. *J. Spec. Educ.* **10**, 277–284.

McCONKEY ROBBINS, M.S. (1986). Facilitating language comprehension in young hearing-impaired children. *Topics Lang. Disord.* **6**, 12–24.

McCORMICK, B., CURNOCK, D.A. and SPAVINS, F. (1984). Auditory screening of special care neonates using the auditory response cradle. *Arch. Dis. Childhood* **59**, 1168–1172.

McDEVITT, T.M., SPIVEY, N., SHEEHAN, E.P., LENNON, R. and STORY, R. (1990). Children's beliefs about listening: is it enough to be still and quiet? *Child Devel.* **61**, 713–721.

McDONALD, E.T. (1980). Disorders of articulation. In: Van Hattum (1980).

MacDONALD, J. and McGURK, H. (1978). Visual influences on speech perception processes. *Percept. Psychophys.* **24**, 253–257.

McDONALD, J.L. and MacWHINNEY, B. (1991). Levels of learning: a comparison of concept formation and language acquisition. *J. Mem. Lang.* **30**, 407–430.

McGARR, N.S. and HARRIS, K.S. (1983). Articulatory control in a deaf speaker. In: Hochberg et al. (1983).

McGINNIS, M.D., ORR, C.D. and FREUTEL, J.M. (1980). Becoming a social being. *Volta Rev.* **82**, 370–379.

MacGREGOR, S.K. and THOMAS, L.B. (1988). A computer-mediated text system to develop communication skills for hearing-impaired students. *Am. Ann. Deaf* **133**, 280–284.

McGROSKEY, R. and KIDDER, A. (1980). Auditory fusion among learning-disabled, reading-disabled and normal children. *J. Learn. Disabil.* **13**, 18–25.

McGUIGAN, F.J. (1970). Covert oral behavior during the silent performance of language tasks. *Psychol. Bull.* **74**, 309–326.

McGURK, H. and MacDONALD, J. (1976). Hearing lips and seeing voices. *Nature* **264**, 746–748.

McINTIRE, M.L. (1977). The acquisition of American Sign Language hand configurations. *Sign Lang. Stud.* **16**, 247–266.

MacKAY, D.G. (1981). The problem of rehearsal or mental practice. *J. Motor Behav.* **13**, 274–285.

MacKAY, D.G. (1987). *The Organization of Perception and Action: A Theory of Language and other Cognitive Skills*. New York: Springer-Verlag.

MacKAY-SOROTA, S., TREHUB, S.E. and THORPE, L.A. (1987). Deaf children's referential messages to mother. *Child Devel.* **58**, 385–394.

McKEE, B.G. and DOWALIBY, F.J. (1985). The relationship between student, course, and instructor characteristics and hearing-impaired students' ratings of instruction. *Volta Rev.* **87**, 77–86.

McKEEVER, W.F., HOEMANN, H.W., FLORIAN, V.A. and VAN DEVENTER, A.D. (1976). Evidence of minimal cerebral asymmetries for the processing of English words and American Sign Language in the congenitally deaf. *Neuropsychologia* **14**, 413–423.

McKEOWN, M. and CURTIS, M. (Eds) (1987). *The Nature of Vocabulary Acquisition*. Hillsdale, NJ: Erlbaum.

MacKINNON, G.E. and WALLER, T.G. (Eds) (1981). *Reading Research: Advances in Theory and Practice. Vol. 3.* New York: Academic Press.

McKIRDY, L.S. and BLANK, M. (1982). Dialogue in deaf and hearing pre-schoolers. *J. Speech Hear. Res.* **25**, 487–499.

MacLEOD, A. and SUMMERFIELD, Q. (1987). Quantifying the contribution of vision to speech perception in noise. *Br. J. Audiol.* **21**, 131–141.

MacLEOD, A. and SUMMERFIELD, Q. (1990). A procedure for measuring auditory and audio-visual speech-reception thresholds for sentences in noise: rationale, evaluation and recommendations for use. *Br. J. Audiol.* **24**, 29–43.

McPHERSON, D.L. and DAVIS, M.S. (Eds) (1978). *Advances in Prosthetic Devices for the Deaf: A Technical Workshop.* Rochester, NY: National Technical Institute for the Deaf.

MAGEN, Z. (1990). Positive experiences and life aspirations among adolescents with and without hearing impairments. *Int. J. Disabil. Devel. Educ.* **37**, 57–69.

MAKI, J. (1980). Visual feedback as an aid to speech therapy. In: Subtelny (1980).

MAKI, J.D. (1983). Application of the speech spectrographic display in developing articulatory skills in hearing-impaired adults. In: Hochberg et al. (1983).

MANDELBAUM, D. (Ed.) (1949). *Selected Writings of Edward Sapir in Language, Culture, and Personality.* Berkeley, CA: University of California Press.

MANION, I.G. and BUCHER, B. (1986). Generalization of a sign language rehearsal strategy in mentally retarded and hearing deficient children. *Appl. Res. Ment. Retard.* **7**, 133–148.

MANN, V.A., LIBERMAN, I.Y. and SHANKWEILER, D. (1980). Children's memory for sentences and work strings in relation to reading ability. *Mem. Cognit.* **8**, 329–335.

MANNING, A.A., GOBLE, W., MARKMAN, R. and LABRECHE, T. (1977). Lateral cerebral differences in the deaf response to linguistic and nonlinguistic stimuli. *Brain Lang.* **4**, 309–321.

MARCEL, A.J., KATZ, L. and SMITH, M. (1974). Laterality and reading proficiency. *Neuropsychologia* **12**, 131–139.

MARCOTTE, A.C. and LA BARBA, R.C. (1985). Cerebral lateralization for speech in deaf and normal children. *Brain Lang.* **26**, 244–258.

MARGOLIS, H. (1986). Patterns, thinking, and cognition. In: Mason and Au (1986).

MARKIDES, A. (1967). *The Speech of Deaf and Partially-Hearing Children with Special Reference to Factors Affecting Intelligibility.* University of Manchester: unpublished Doctoral Thesis.

MARKIDES, A. (1970). The speech of deaf and partially-hearing children with special reference to factors affecting intelligibility. *Br. J. Disord. Commun.* **5**, 126–140.

MARKIDES, A. (1983). *The Speech of Hearing-Impaired Children.* Manchester: Manchester University Press.

MARKIDES, A. (1987). Speech tests of hearing for children. In: Martin (1987).

MARKIDES, A. (1988). Speech intelligibility: auditory–oral approach versus total communication. *J. Br. Assn. Teachers of the Deaf* **12**, 136–141.

MARKIDES, A. (1989a). Background noise and lipreading ability. *Br. J. Audiol.* **23**, 251–253.

MARKIDES, A. (1989b). Lipreading: theory and practice. *J. Br. Assn. Teachers of the Deaf* **13**, 29–47.

MARMOR, G. and PETITTO, L. (1979). Simultaneous communication in the classroom: how well is English grammar represented? In: Stokoe (1979).

MARSCHARK, M. and WEST, S.A. (1985). Creative language abilities of deaf children. *J. Speech Hear. Res.* **28**, 73–78.

MARSCHARK, M., WEST, S.A., NALL, L. and EVERHART, V. (1986). Development of creative language devices in signed and oral production. *J. Exp. Child Psychol.* **41**, 534–550.

MARSHALL, W.A. (1970). Contextual constraints on deaf and hearing children. *Am. Ann. Deaf* **115**, 682–689.

MARTELLO, A. (1981). The Ling approach to teaching speech as adapted in a day program for the hearing impaired. *Volta Rev.* **83**, 458–465.

MARTIN, D.S. (Ed.) (1984). *International Symposium on Cognition, Education and Deafness.* Washington DC: Gallaudet College Press.

MARTIN, D.S. (Ed.) (1985). *Cognition, Education and Deafness: Directions for Research and Instruction*. Washington DC: Gallaudet University Press.

MARTIN, E.S., PICKETT, J.M. and COLTEN, S. (1972). Discrimination of vowel formant transitions by listeners with severe sensorineural hearing loss. In: Fant (1972).

MARTIN, F.N., ABADIE, K.T. and DESCOUZIS, D. (1989). Counseling families of hearing-impaired children: comparisons of the attitudes of Australian and US parents and audiologists. *Aust. J. Audiol.* **11**, 41–54.

MARTIN, F.N., BERNSTEIN, M.E., DALY, J.A. and CODY, J.P. (1988). Classroom teachers' knowledge of hearing disorders and attitudes about mainstreaming hard-of-hearing children. *Lang. Speech Hear. Services in Schools* **19**, 83–95.

MARTIN, F.N. and FORBIS, N.R. (1978). The present status of audiometric practice: a follow-up study. *ASHA* **20**, 531–541.

MARTIN, M. (Ed.) (1987). *Speech Audiometry*. London: Taylor and Francis.

MARTINEK, T.J. (1980). Students' expectations as related to a teacher's expectations and self-concepts of elementary age children. *Percept. Mot. Skills* **50**, 555–561.

MARTONY, J. (1968). On the correction of the voice pitch level for severely hard of hearing subjects. *Am. Ann. Deaf* **113**, 195–202.

MARTONY, J. (1972). Visual aids for speech correction: summary of three years' experiences. In: Fant (1972).

MASHIE, J.J., VARI-ALQUIST, D., WADDY-SMITH, B. and BERNSTEIN, L.F. (1988). Speech training aids for hearing-impaired individuals: III. Preliminary observations in the clinic and children's homes. *J. Rehab. Res. Devel.* **25**, 69–82.

MASON, J.M. (1980). When do children begin to read: an exploration of four-year-old children's letter and word reading competencies. *Read. Res. Q.* **2**, 203–227.

MASON, J.M. and AU, K.H. (1986). *Reading Instruction for Today*. Glenview, IL: Scott, Foresman and Co.

MASON, M.K. (1942). Learning to speak after six and one-half years of silence. *J. Speech Disord.* **7**, 295–304.

MATEY, C. and KRETSCHMER, R. (1985). A comparison of mother speech to Down's syndrome, hearing-impaired, and normal-hearing children. *Volta Rev.* **87**, 205–213.

MATHER, S.A. (1989). Visually oriented teaching strategies with deaf preschool children. In: Lucas (1989).

MATKIN, N.D. (1981). Amplification for children: current status and future priorities. In: Bess et al. (1981).

MATZKER, V.J. (1960). Schizophrenie und Taubheit. *Z. Laryngol. Rhinol. Otol.* **39**, 43–52.

MAXON, A.B., BRACKETT, D. and VAN DEN BERG, S.A. (1991). Self perception of socialization: the effects of hearing status, age and gender. *Volta Rev.* **93**, 7–18.

MAXWELL, M. (1980). Language acquisition in a deaf child of deaf parents: speech, sign variations, and print variations. In: Nelson (1980).

MAXWELL, M.M. (1986). Beginning reading and deaf children. *Am. Ann. Deaf* **131**, 14–20.

MAXWELL, M.M. (1988). The alphabetic principle and fingerspelling. *Sign Lang. Stud.* **61**, 377–404.

MAXWELL, M.M. (1989). A signing deaf child's use of speech. *Sign Lang. Stud.* **62**, 23–42.

MAXWELL, M.M. (1990). Simultaneous Communication: the state of the art and proposals for change. *Sign Lang. Stud.* **69**, 333–389.

MAXWELL, M. and BERNSTEIN, M. (1985). The synergy of sign and speech in Simultaneous Communication. *Appl. Psycholing.* **6**, 63–81.

MAYBERRY, R.I. and EICHEN, E.B. (1991). The long-lasting advantage of learning sign language in childhood: another look at the critical period for language acquisition. *J. Mem. Lang.* **30**, 486–512.

MAYBERRY, R.I. and FISCHER, S.D. (1989). Looking through phonological shape to lexical meaning: the bottleneck of non-native sign language processing. *Mem. Cognit.* **17**, 740–754.

MAYER, P. and LOWENBRAUN, S. (1990). Total communication use among elementary teachers of hearing-impaired children. *Am. Ann. Deaf* **135**, 257–263.

MEAD, R.A. and LAPIDUS, L.B. (1989). Psychological differential, arousal, and lipreading efficiency in hearing-impaired and normal children. *J. Clin. Psychol.* **45**, 851–859.

MEADOW, K.P. (1968). Early manual communication in relation to the deaf child's intellectual, social and communicative functioning. *Am. Ann. Deaf* **113**, 29–41.

MEADOW, K.P. (1980). *Deafness and Child Development*. London: Arnold.

MEADOW, K. (1981). Studies of behavior problems of deaf children. In: Stein et al. (1981).

MEADOW-ORLANS, K.P. (1987). An analysis of the effectiveness of early intervention programs for hearing-impaired children. In: Guralnick and Bennett (1987b).

MEDICAL RESEARCH COUNCIL (1947). *Committee on Electroacoustics, Hearing Aids and Audiometers, MRC Special Report Series No. 261.* London: HMSO.

MEISELS, S.J. and SHONKOFF, J.P. (Eds) (1990). *Handbook of Early Childhood Intervention.* Cambridge: Cambridge University Press.

MENCHER, G.T. (Ed.) (1976). *Early Identification of Hearing Loss.* Basel: S. Karger.

MENCKE, E.O., OCHSNER, G.J. and TESTUT, E.W. (1984). Speech intelligibility of deaf speakers and distinctive feature usage. *J. Aud. Res.* **24**, 63–68.

MENCKE, E.O., OCHSNER, G.J. and TESTUT, E.W. (1985). Distinctive-feature analyses of the speech of deaf children. *J. Aud. Res.* **25**, 191–200.

MENDELSON, J.H., SIGER, L. and SOLOMON, P. (1960). Psychiatric observations on congenital and acquired deafness: symbolic and perceptual processes in dreams. *Am. J. Psychiat.* **116**, 883–888.

MERKLEIN, R.A. (1981). A short speech perception test for severely and profoundly deaf children. *Volta Rev.* **83**, 36–45.

MERTENS, D.M. (1989). Social experiences of hearing-impaired high school youth. *Am. Ann. Deaf* **134**, 15–19.

MERTENS, D.M. (1991). Teachers working with interpreters: the deaf student's educational experience. *Am. Ann. Deaf* **136**, 48–52.

METZ, D.E., SAMAR, V.J., SCHIAVETTI, N., SITLER, R.W. and WHITEHEAD, R.L. (1985). Acoustic dimensions of hearing-impaired speakers' intelligibility. *J. Speech Hear. Res.* **28**, 345–355.

METZ, D.E., SCHIAVETTI, N., SAMAR, V.J. and SITLER, R.W. (1990a). Acoustic dimensions of hearing-impaired speakers' intelligibility: segmental and suprasegmental characteristics. *J. Speech Hear. Res.* **33**, 476–487.

METZ, D.E., SCHIAVETTI, N., SITLER, R.W. and SAMAR, V.J. (1990b). Speech production stability characteristics of hearing-impaired speakers. *Volta Rev.* **92**, 223–235.

MEYER, A.S. (1990). The time course of phonological encoding of successive syllables of a word. *J. Mem. Lang.* **29**, 524–545.

MICHELSON, R.P. (1971). Electrical stimulation of the human cochlea. *Arch. Otolaryngol.* **93**, 317–323.

MILLER, G.A. (1947). The masking of speech. *Psychol. Bull.* **44**, 105–129.

MILLER, G.A., HEISE, G.A. and LICHTEN, W. (1951). The intelligibility of speech as a function of the context of the test materials. *J. Exp. Psychol.* **41**, 329–335.

MILLER, G.A. and NICELY, P.E. (1955). An analysis of perceptual confusions among some English consonants. *J. Acoust. Soc. Am.* **27**, 338–352.

MILLER, G.A. and TAYLOR, W.G. (1948). Perception of repeated bursts of noise. *J. Acoust. Soc. Am.* **20**, 171–182.

MILLER, L. (1981). Remediation of auditory language learning disorders. In: Roeser and Downs (1981).

MILLER, M.S. (1987). Sign iconicity: single-sign receptive vocabulary skills of nonsigning hearing preschoolers. *J. Commun. Disord.* **20**, 359–365.

MILLS, C. and WELDON, L. (1983). Effects of semantic and cheremic context on acquisition of manual signs. *Mem. Cognit.* **11**, 93–100.

MILLS, J.H. (1975). Noise and children: a review of literature. *J. Acoust. Soc. Am.* **58**, 767–779.

MINDESS, A. (1990). What name signs can tell us about deaf culture. *Sign Lang. Stud.* **66**, 1–23.

MISCHOOK, M. and COLE, E. (1986). Auditory learning and teaching of hearing-impaired infants. *Volta Rev.* **88**, 67–81.

MISHKIN, M. and FORGAYS, D.G. (1952). Word recognition as a function of retinal locus. *J. Exp. Psychol.* **43**, 43–48.

MITCHELL, G. (1978). Stigma, stereotype and rehabilitation. In: Montgomery (1978).

MOELLER, M.P. (1985). Developmental approaches to communication assessment and enhancement. In: Cherow (1985).

MOELLER, M.P. and LUETKE-STAHLMAN, B. (1990). Parents' use of Signing Exact English: a descriptive analysis. *J. Speech Hear. Disord.* **55**, 327–338.

MOELLER, M.P., MCCONKEY, A.J. and OSBERGER, M.J. (1983). Evaluation of the communicative skills of hearing-impaired children. *Audiology* **8**, 113–127.

MOERK, E.L. (1977). *Pragmatic and Semantic Aspects of Early Language Development*. Baltimore, MD: University Park Press.

MOHAY, H. (1982). A preliminary description of the communication systems evolved by two deaf children in the absence of a sign language model. *Sign Lang. Stud.* **34**, 73–91.

MOHAY, H. (1983). The effects of cued speech on the language development of three deaf children. *Sign Lang. Stud.* **38**, 25–49.

MONSEN, R. (1981). A usable test for the speech intelligibility of deaf talkers. *Am. Ann. Deaf* **126**, 845–852.

MONSEN, R.B. (1976). Normal and reduced phonological space: the production of English vowels by deaf adolescents. *J. Phonet.* **4**, 189–198.

MONSEN, R.B. (1978). Toward measuring how well hearing-impaired children speak. *J. Speech Hear. Res.* **21**, 197–219.

MONSEN, R.B. (1979). Acoustic qualities of phonation in young hearing-impaired children. *J. Speech Hear. Res.* **22**, 270–288.

MONTGOMERY, A.A. and EDGE, R.A. (1988). Evaluation of two speech enhancement techniques to improve intelligibility for hearing-impaired adults. *J. Speech, Hear. Res.* **31**, 386–393.

MONTGOMERY, A.A., WALDEN, B.E. and PROSEK, R.A. (1987). Effects of consonantal context on vowel lipreading. *J. Speech Hear. Res.* **30**, 50–59.

MONTGOMERY, G. (1976). The integration of the oral–manual language ability of profoundly deaf children. In: Henderson (1976).

MONTGOMERY, G. (Ed.) (1978). *Of Sound and Mind: Deafness, Personality and Mental Health*. Edinburgh: Papers on Scottish Workshop Publications.

MONTGOMERY, G., MITCHELL, G., MILLER, J. and MONTGOMERY, J. (1983). Open communication or catastrophe? A model for educational communication. In: Kyle and Woll (1983).

MONTGOMERY, G.W.G. (1966). The relationship of oral skills to manual communication in profoundly deaf students. *Am. Ann. Deaf* **111**, 557–565.

MONTGOMERY, G.W.G. (1968). A factorial study of communication and ability in deaf school leavers. *Br. J. Educ. Psychol.* **38**, 27–37.

MOOG, J. and GEERS, A. (1985). EPIC: a program to accelerate academic progress in profoundly hearing-impaired children. *Volta Rev.* **87**, 259–277.

MOOG, J.S. and GEERS, A.E. (1991). Educational management of children with cochlear implants. *Am. Ann. Deaf* **136**, 69–76.

MOORE, D.T. (1983). Perspectives on learning in internships. *J. Experient. Educn.* **6**, 40–44.

MOORE, N. (1981). Is paranoid illness associated with sensory defects in the elderly? *J. Psychosom. Res.* **25**, 69–74.

MOORES, D. (1970). Psycholinguistics and deafness. *Am. Ann. Deaf* **115**, 37–48.

MOORES, D.F. (1987). *Educating the Deaf: Psychology, Principles and Practices*, 3rd Edn. Boston, MA: Houghton Mifflin.

MOORES, D.F. (1991). The great debates: where, how, and what to teach deaf children. *Am. Ann. Deaf* **136**, 35–37.

MOORES, D.F. and SWEET, C.A. (1990). Reading and writing skills in deaf adolescents. *Internat. J. Rehab. Res.* **13**, 178–179.

MORARIU, J.A. and BRUNING, R.H. (1984). Cognitive processing by prelingual deaf students as a function of language context. *J. Educ. Psychol.* 76, 844–856.

MORGAN-REDSHAW, M., WILGOSH, L. and BIBBY, M.A. (1990). The parental experiences of mothers of adolescents with hearing impairments. *Am. Ann. Deaf* 135, 293–298.

MORRIS, C. (1946). *Signs, Language and Behavior*. New York: Braziller.

MORRIS, T. (1978). Some observations on the part played by oral teaching methods in perpetuating low standards of language achievement in severely and profoundly deaf pupils. *J. Br. Assn. Teachers of the Deaf* 2, 130–135.

MORTON, J. (1970). A functional model for memory. In: Norman (1970).

MORTON, J. (Ed.) (1971). *Biological and Social Factors in Psycholinguistics*. London: Logos Press.

MOSCOVITCH, M. (1979). Information processing and the cerebral hemispheres. In: Gazzaniga (1979).

MOSENTHAL, P., TAMOR, L. and WALMSLEY, S.A. (Eds) (1983). *Research on Writing: Principles and Methods*. New York: Longman.

MOUNTY, J.L. (1989). Beyond grammar: developing stylistic variation when the input is diverse. *Sign Lang. Stud.* 62, 43–62.

MURPHY, J. and HILL, J. (1989). Training communication functions in hearing-impaired adolescents. *Aust. Teacher of the Deaf* 30, 26–32.

MURPHY, J.S. and NEWLON, B.J. (1987). Loneliness and the mainstreamed hearing impaired college student. *Am. Ann. Deaf* 132, 21–25.

MURPHY, K.P. (1957). Test of abilities and attainments. In: Ewing (1957).

MURPHY-BERMAN, V., STOEFEN-FISHER, J. and MATHIAS, K. (1987). Factors affecting teachers' evaluations of hearing-impaired students' behavior. *Volta Rev.* 89, 145–156.

MUSIEK, F.E., BARAN, J.A. and PINHEIRO, M.L. (1990). Duration pattern recognition in normal subjects and patients with cerebral and cochlear lesions. *Audiology.* 29, 304–313.

MUSIEK, F.E. and PINHEIRO, M.L. (1987). Frequency patterns in cochlear, brainstem, and cerebral lesions. *Audiology* 26, 79–80.

MUSSELMAN, C. and CHURCHILL, A. (1991). Conversational control in mother–child dyads: auditory–oral versus total communication. *Am. Ann. Deaf* 136, 5–16.

MUSSEN, P.H. (Ed.) (1970). *Carmichael's Manual of Child Psychology*, 3rd Edn. New York: Wiley.

MYERS, T., BROWN, K. and MCGONIGLE, B. (1986). *Reasoning and Discourse Processes*. London: Academic Press.

MYKLEBUST, H.R. (1960). The psychological effects of deafness. *Am. Ann. Deaf* 105, 372–385.

MYKLEBUST, H.R. (1964). *The Psychology of Deafness: Sensory Deprivation, Learning and Adjustment*, 2nd Edn. New York: Grune and Stratton.

MYKLEBUST, H.R. (1966). The effect of early life deafness. *Proc. XVIIIth Internat. Congress of Psychology*, Moscow.

NAGY, W.E., ANDERSON, R.C. and HERMAN, P.A. (1987). Learning word meanings from context during normal reading. *Am. Educn. Res. J.* 24, 237–270.

NASH, J.E. and NASH, A. (1981). *Deafness in Society*. Lexington, MA: Lexington Books.

NATIONAL INSTITUTES OF HEALTH (1988). *Consensus Conference Report*. Baltimore, MD: National Institutes of Health.

NATIONAL UNION OF THE DEAF STEERING COMMITTEE (1982). *Charter of Rights of the Deaf, Part One: The Rights of the Deaf Child*. Guildford, Surrey: National Union of the Deaf.

NEISSER, U. (1976). *Cognition and Reality: Principles and Implications of Cognitive Psychology*. San Francisco: Freeman.

NELSON, K.E. (Ed.) (1980). *Children's Language*. Hillsdale, NJ: Erlbaum.

NELSON, T.O., LEONESIO, J., SIMAMURA, A., LANDWEHR, R. and NARENS, L. (1982). Overlearning and the feeling of knowing. *J. Exp. Psychol.: Learn. Mem. Cognit.* 8, 279–288.

NEWELL, A. and SIMON, H.A. (1972). *Human Problem Solving*. Englewood Cliffs, NJ: Prentice-Hall.

NEWELL, W., STINSON, M., CASTLE, D., MALLERY-RUGANIS, D. and HOLCOMB, B. (1990). Simultaneous Communication: a description by deaf professionals working in an educational setting. *Sign Lang. Stud.* **69**, 391–414.

NEWPORT, E. and BELLUGI, U. (1979). Linguistic expression of category levels. In: Klima and Bellugi (1979).

NEWPORT, E.L. and SUPALLA, T. (1980). Clues from the acquisition of signed and spoken English. In: Bellugi and Studdert-Kennedy (1980).

NEWTON, L. (1985). Linguistic environment of the deaf child: a focus on teachers' use of non-literal language. *J. Speech Hear. Res.* **28**, 336–344.

NICHOLLS, G.H. and LING, D. (1982). Cued speech and the reception of spoken language. *J. Speech Hear. Res.* **25**, 262–269.

NIEMEYER, W. (1972). Studies on speech perception in dissociated hearing loss. In: Fant (1972).

NIENHUYS, T., CROSS, T. and HORSBOROUGH, K. (1984). Child variables influencing maternal speech style: deaf and hearing children. *J. Comm. Disord.* **17**, 189–207.

NIENHUYS, T.G., HOSBOROUGH, K.M. and CROSS, T.G. (1985). A dialogic analysis of interaction between mothers and their deaf or hearing preschoolers. *Appl. Psycholing.* **6**, 121–139.

NIENHUYS, T.G. and TIKOTIN, J.A. (1985). Mother–infant interaction: prespeech communication in hearing and deaf babies. *Aust. J. Teacher of the Deaf* **26**, 4–12.

NIX, G.W. (1983). How total is total communication? *J. Br. Assn. Teachers of the Deaf* **7**, 177–181.

NOBER, E.H. (1967). Articulation of the deaf. *Except. Child.* **33**, 611–621.

NOLEN, S.B. and WILBUR, R.B. (1984). Context and comprehension: another look. In: Martin (1984).

NOOTEBOOM, S.G. (1973). The perceptual reality of some prosodic durations. *J. Phonet.* **1**, 25–45.

NORLIN, P. (1981). The development of relational arcs in the lexical semantic memory structure of young children. *J. Child Lang.* **8**, 385–402.

NORMAN, D.A. (Ed.) (1970). *Models of Human Memory.* New York: Academic Press.

NORTHCOTT, W. (1975). Normalization of the pre-school child with hearing impairment. *Otolaryngol. Clin. North Am.* **8**, 159–186.

* NORTHCOTT, W.H. (Ed.) (1984). *Oral Interpreting: Principles and Practice.* Baltimore, MD: University Park Press.

NORTHERN, J.L. (Ed.) (1984). *Hearing Disorders,* 2nd Edn. Boston, MA: Little, Brown and Co.

NORTHERN, J.L. and DOWNS, M.P. (1984). *Hearing in Children,* 3rd Edn. Baltimore, MD: Williams and Wilkins.

NOVELLI-OLMSTEAD, T. and LING, D. (1984). Speech production and speech discrimination by hearing-impaired children. *Volta Rev.* **86**, 72–80.

NOWICKI, S. and STRICKLAND, B.R. (1973). A locus of control scale for children. *J. Consult. Clin. Psychol.* **40**, 148–155.

OBERKLAID, F., HARRIS, C. and KEIR, E. (1989). Auditory dysfunction in children with school problems. *Clin. Pediat.* **28**, 397–403.

OBLOWITZ, N., GREEN, L. and HEYNS, I. de V. (1991). A self-concept scale for the hearing-impaired. *Volta Rev.* **93**, 19–29.

O'BRIEN, D.H. (1987). Reflection–impulsivity in total communication and oral deaf and hearing children: a developmental study. *Am. Ann. Deaf* **132**, 213–217.

OCHS, M.T., HUMES, L.E., OHDE, R.N. and GRANTHAM, D.W. (1989). Frequency discrimination ability and stop-consonant identification in normally hearing and hearing-impaired subjects. *J. Speech Hear. Res.* **32**, 133–142.

O'CONNOR, N. and HERMELIN, B. (1973). Short term memory for the order of pictures and syllables by deaf and hearing children. *Neuropsychologia* **11**, 437–442.

O'CONNOR, N. and HERMELIN, B.M. (1976). Backward and forward recall by deaf and hearing children. *Q. J. Exp. Psychol.* **28**, 83–92.

O'CONNOR, N. and HERMELIN, B. (1986). Sensory handicap and cognitive deficits. In: Ellis (1986).

ODOM, P., BLANTON, R. and NUNNALLY, J. (1967). Cloze technique studies of language capability in the deaf. *J. Speech Hear. Res.* **10**, 816–827.

OGDEN, P. (1984). Parenting in the mainstream. *Volta Rev.* **86**, 29–39.

OGDEN, P.W. and LIPSETT, S. (1982). *The Silent Garden: Understanding the Hearing Impaired Child*. New York: St Martin's Press.

OLÉRON, P. (1978). *Le Langage Gestuel des Sourds: Syntaxe et Communication*. Paris: Éditions du Centre National de la Recherche Scientifique.

OLLER, D.K., EILERS, R.E., BULL, D.H. and CARNEY, A.E. (1985). Prespeech vocalizations of a deaf infant: a comparison with normal metaphonological development. *J. Speech Hear. Res.* **28**, 47–63.

OLLER, D.K., EILERS, R., VERGARA, K. and LA VOIE, E. (1986). Tactual vocoders in a multisensory program training speech production and reception. *Volta Rev.* **88**, 21–36.

OLSON, D. (1977). Oral and written language and the cognitive processes of children. *J. Commun.* **27**, 10–26.

OLSON, D. (Ed.) (1980). *Social Foundations of Language and Thought: Essays in Honor of J.S. Bruner*. New York: Norton.

O'NEILL, J.J. (1954). Contributions of the visual components of oral symbols to speech comprehension. *J. Speech Hear. Disord.* **19**, 429–439.

O'NEILL, J.J. and OYER, H.J. (1961). *Visual Communication for the Hard of Hearing*. Englewood Cliffs, NJ: Prentice-Hall.

ORLANSKY, M.D. and BONVILLIAN, J.D. (1984). The role of iconicity in early sign language acquisition. *J. Speech Hear. Disord.* **49**, 287–292.

OSBERGER, M.J. (1983). Development and evaluation of some speech training procedures for hearing-impaired children. In: Hochberg et al. (1983).

OSBERGER, M.J. (1987). Training effects on vowel production by two profoundly hearing-impaired speakers. *J. Speech Hear. Res.* **30**, 241–251.

OSBERGER, M.J. (1990). Audition. *Volta Rev.* **92**, 34–53.

OSBERGER, M.J. and LEVITT, H. (1979). The effect of time errors on the intelligibility of deaf children's speech. *J. Acoust. Soc. Am.* **66**, 1316–1324.

OSBERGER, M. and MCGARR, N. (1982). Speech production characteristics of the hearing-impaired. *Speech Lang.* **8**, 221–283.

OWENS, E., KESSLER, D., TELEEN, E. and SCHUBERT, E. (1985). *Minimal Auditory Capabilities Battery* (Rev. Edn). St Louis, MO: Auditec.

OWENS, E. and KESSLER, D. (Eds) (1989). *Cochlear Implants in Young Deaf Children*. Boston, MA: Little, Brown and Co.

OYER, H.J. (Ed.) (1976). *Communication for the Hearing Handicapped: An International Perspective*. Baltimore, MD: University Park Press.

PAGE, J.L. (1985a). Relative translucency of ASL signs representing three semantic classes. *J. Speech Hear. Disord.* **50**, 241–247.

PAGE, J.M. (1985b). Central auditory processing disorders in children. *Otolaryngol. Clin. North Am.* **18**, 323–335.

PAGET, G. and GORMAN, P. (1968). *A Systematic Sign Language*. London: Royal National Institute for the Deaf.

PAIVIO, A. (1971). *Imagery and Verbal Processes*. New York: Holt, Rinehart and Winston.

PAIVIO, A. and BEGG, I. (1981). *Psychology of Language*. Englewood Cliffs, NJ: Prentice-Hall.

PALMER, L., BEMENT, L. and KELLY, J. (1990). Implications of deafness and cultural diversity on communication instruction: strategies for intervention. *J. Aural Rehab. Assoc.* **23**, 43–52.

PANIAGUA, F.A. (1990). Skinner's senses of 'Guessing'. *New Ideas Psychol.* **8**, 73–79.

PANOU, L. and SEWELL, D.F. (1984). Cerebral asymmetry in congenitally deaf subjects. *Neuropsychologia* **22**, 381–383.

PARADY, S., DORMAN, M., WHALEY, P. and RAPHAEL, L. (1981). Identification and discrimination of a synthesized voicing contrast by normal and sensorineural hearing-impaired children. *J. Acoust. Soc. Am.* **69**, 783–790.

PARASNIS, I. (1983). Effects of parental deafness and early exposure to manual communication on the cognitive skills, English language skill and field independence of young deaf adults. *J. Speech Hear. Res.* **26**, 588–594.

PARKHURST, B.G. and LEVITT, H. (1978). The effect of selected prosodic errors on the intelligibility of deaf speech. *J. Commun. Disord.* **11**, 249–256.

PARKINS, C.W. and HOUDE, R.A. (1982). The cochlear (implant) prosthesis: theoretical and practical considerations. In: Sims et al. (1982).

PATERSON, M. (1986). Maximising the use of residual hearing with school-aged hearing-impaired students – a perspective. *Volta Rev.* **88**, 93–106.

PAYNE, J.A. and QUIGLEY, S. (1987). Hearing-impaired children's comprehension of verb–particle combinations. *Volta Rev.* **89**, 133–143.

PEARSON, H.R. (1984). Parenting a hearing-impaired child: a model program. *Volta Rev.* **86**, 239–243.

PEIRCE, C. (1932). *Collected Papers* (edited by C. Hartshorne and P. Weiss). Cambridge, MA: Harvard University Press.

PENDERGRASS, R.A. and HODGES, M. (1976). Deaf students in group problem solving situations: a study of the interactive process. *Am. Ann. Deaf* **121**, 327–330.

PERIGOE, C. and LING, D. (1986). Generalization of speech skills in hearing-impaired children. *Volta Rev.* **88**, 351–365.

PERKINS, W.H. (Ed.) (1984). *Hearing Disorders*. New York: Thième Stratton.

PETER, M. and BARNES, R. (Eds) (1982). *Signs, Symbols and Schools*. London: National Council for Special Education.

PETERSON, L.N. and FRENCH, L. (1988). Summarization strategies of hearing-impaired and normally hearing college students. *J. Speech Hear. Res.* **31**, 327–337.

PETERSON, C.C. and PETERSON, J.L. (1989). Positive justice reasoning in deaf and hearing children before and after exposure to cognitive conflict. *Am. Ann. Deaf* **134**, 277–282.

PETKOVSEK, M. (1961). The eyes have it. *Hearing News* **29**, 5–9.

PHIPPARD, D. (1977). Hemifield differences in visual perception in deaf and hearing subjects. *Neuropsychologia* **15**, 555–561.

PIAGET, J. (1926). *The Language and Thought of the Child*. New York: Harcourt and Brace.

PIAGET, J. (1929). *The Child's Conception of the World*. London: Routledge and Kegan Paul.

PICHENY, M.A., DURLACH, N.L. and BRAIDA, L.D. (1985). Speaking clearly for the hard of hearing I: Intelligibility differences between clear and conversational speech. *J. Speech Hear. Res.* **28**, 96–103.

PICHENY, M.A., DURLACH, N.I. and BRAIDA, L.D. (1986). Speaking clearly for the hard of hearing II: Acoustic characteristics of clear and conversational speech. *J. Speech Hear. Res.* **29**, 434–446.

PICKETT, J. and DANAHER, E. (1975). On discrimination of formant transitions by persons with severe sensorineural hearing loss. In: Fant and Tatham (1975).

PICKETT, J.M. (1980). *The Sounds of Speech Communication: A Primer of Acoustic Phonetics and Speech Perception*. Baltimore, MD: University Park Press.

PICKETT, J.M. and MCFARLAND, W. (1985). Auditory implants and tactile aids for the profoundly deaf. *J. Speech Hear. Res.* **28**, 134–150.

PICKETT, J.M., MARTIN, E., JOHNSON, D., SMITH, S., DANIEL, Z., WILLIS, D. and OTIS, W. (1972). On patterns of speech feature reception by deaf listeners. In: Fant (1972).

PICKETT, J.M., REVOILE, S.G. and DANAHER, E.M. (1983). Speech-cue measures of impaired hearing. In: Tobias and Schubert (1983).

PIEN, D. (1985). The development of communication functions in deaf infants of hearing parents. In: Martin (1985).

PIERS, E.V. and HARRIS, D.B. (1964). Age and other correlates of self-concept in children. *J. Educ. Psychol.* **55**, 91–95.

PINHEIRO, M.L. and MUSIEK, F.E. (1985a). Sequencing and temporal ordering in the auditory system. In: Pinheiro and Musiek (1985b).

PINHEIRO, M.L. and MUSIEK. F.E. (Eds) (1985b). *Assessment of Central Auditory Dysfunction*. Baltimore, MD: Williams and Wilkins.

PINTNER, R. (1941). The personality of the deaf. In: Pintner et al. (1941).

PINTNER, R., EISENSON, J. and STANTON, M. (1941). *The Psychology of the Physically Handicapped*. New York: F.S. Crofts.

PINTNER, R. and PATERSON, D.G. (1917). The ability of deaf and hearing children to follow printed directions. *Am. Ann. Deaf* 62, 448–472.

PINTNER, R. and PATERSON, D.G. (1923). *A Scale of Performance Tests*. New York: Appleton, Century, Crofts.

PINTNER, R. and REAMER, J.F. (1920). A mental and educational survey of schools for the deaf. *Am. Ann. Deaf* 65, 277–300.

PITT, M.A. and SAMUEL, A.G. (1990). Attentional allocation during speech perception: how fine is the focus? *J. Mem. Lang.* 29, 611–632.

PLANT, G. (1984). A diagnostic speech test for severely and profoundly hearing-impaired children. *Aust. J. Audiol.* 6, 1–9.

PLANT, G. (1988). A comparison of five commercially available tactile aids. *Aust. J. Audiol.* 11, 11–19.

PLANT, G. and HAMMARBERG, B. (1983). Acoustic and perceptual analysis of the speech of the deafened. *Stockholm: Speech Transmission Lab., Q. Progress and Status Report* 2–3, 85–107.

PLANT, G., MACRAE, J., DILLON, H. and PENTECOST, F. (1984a). A single-channel vibrotactile aid to lipreading: preliminary results with an experienced subject. *Aust. J. Audiol.* 6, 55–64.

PLANT, G., MACRAE, J., DILLON, H. and PENTECOST, F. (1984b). Lipreading with minimal auditory cues. *Aust. J. Audiol.* 6, 65–72.

PLAPINGER, D. and KRETSCHMER, R. (1991). The effect of context on the interaction between a normally-hearing mother and her hearing-impaired child. *Volta Rev.* 93, 75–87.

POIZNER, H., BATTISON, R. and LANE, H.H. (1979). Cerebral asymmetry for perception of American Sign Language: the effects of moving stimuli. *Brain Lang* 7, 351–362.

POIZNER, H., KAPLAN, E., BELLUGI, U. and PADDEN, C.A. (1984). Visual-spatial processing in deaf brain-damaged signers. *Brain Cognit.* 3, 281–306.

POIZNER, H., NEWKIRK, D., BELLUGI, U. and KLIMA, E.S. (1981). Representation of inflected signs from American Sign Language in short-term memory. *Mem. Cognit.* 9, 121–131.

POIZNER, H. and TALLAL, P. (1987). Temporal processing in deaf signers. *Brain Lang.* 30, 52–62.

POLLACK, D. (1967). The crucial year: a time to listen. *Internat. Audiol.* 6, 243–247.

POLLACK, M. (Ed.) (1975). *Amplification for the Hearing Impaired*. New York: Grune and Stratton.

PORTER, K.A. and DICKERSON, M.V. (1986). Syllabic complexity and its relation to speech intelligibility in a deaf population. *Am. Ann. Deaf* 131, 36–42.

POVEL, D-J., and WANSINK, M. (1986). A computer-controlled vowel corrector for the hearing impaired. *J. Speech Hear. Res.* 29, 99–105.

POWER, A. and WILGUS, S. (1983). Linguistic complexity in the written language of hearing-impaired children. *Volta Rev.* 85, 201–210.

POWER, D. and HOLLINGSHEAD, A. (Eds) (1982). *Occasional Paper No. 4*. Brisbane: Mt. Gravatt College, Centre for Human Development Studies.

POWER, D. and QUIGLEY, S.P. (1973). Deaf children's acquisition of the passive voice. *J. Speech Hear. Res.* 16, 5–11.

POWER, D.J., WOOD, D.J., WOOD, H.A. and MacDOUGALL, J. (1990). Maternal control over conversations with hearing and deaf infants. *First Lang.* 10, 19–35.

POWERS, S. (1990). A survey of secondary units for hearing-impaired children – Part 2. *J. Br. Assn. Teachers of the Deaf* 14, 114–125.

POYATOS, F. (1983). *New Perspectives in Nonverbal Communication*. Oxford: Pergamon.

PRATT, S.R. (1988). *Some Prosodic Characteristics of Maternal Speech Directed to Hearing Impaired Toddlers*. University of Iowa: unpublished Doctoral Thesis.

PREMINGER, J. and WILEY, T.L. (1985). Frequency selectivity and consonant intelligibility in sensorineural hearing loss. *J. Speech Hear. Res.* 28, 197–206.

PRESSNELL, L. MCK. (1973). Hearing-impaired children's comprehension and production of syntax in oral language. *J. Speech Hear. Res.* 16. 12–21.

PRINZ, P.M. (1985). Language and communication development, assessment and intervention in hearing-impaired individuals. In: Katz (1985).

PRINZ, P.M. and FERRIER, L.J. (1983). 'Can you give me that one?': The comprehension, production and judgment of directives in language-impaired children. *J. Speech Hear. Disord.* **48**, 44–54.

PRINZ, P.M., PEMBERTON, E. and NELSON, K.E. (1985). The ALPHA interactive microcomputer system for teaching reading, writing and communication skills to hearing-impaired children. *Am. Ann. Deaf* **130**, 444–461.

PRINZ, P.M. and PRINZ, E.A. (1985). If only you could hear what I see: discourse development in sign language. *Discourse Processes* **8**, 1–19.

PRIOR, M.R., GLAZNER, J., SANSON, A. and DEBELLE, G. (1988). Temperament and behavioural adjustment in hearing-impaired children. *J. Child Psychol. Psychiat.* **29**, 206–216.

PROCTOR, A. (1990). Oral language comprehension using hearing aids and tactile aids: three case studies. *Lang. Speech Hear.Services in Schools* **21**, 37–48.

PRUTTING, C.A. and KIRCHNER, D.M. (1983). Applied Pragmatics. In: Gallagher and Prutting (1983).

PUDLAS, K.A. (1987). Sentence reception abilities of hearing impaired students across five communication modes. *Am. Ann. Deaf* **132**, 232–236.

PUGH, G. (1946). Summaries from appraisal of the silent reading abilities of acoustically handicapped children. *Am. Ann. Deaf* **91**, 331–349.

PUMROY, D. (1966). Maryland parent attitude survey: a research instrument with social desirability controlled. *J. Psychol.* **64**, 73–78.

QUENIN, C.S. and BLOOD, I. (1989). A national survey of cued speech programs. *Volta Rev.* **91**, 283–289.

QUIGLEY, S. (1978). *Test of Syntactic Abilities.* Beaverton, OR: Dormac.

QUIGLEY, S. and KING, C. (Eds) (1984). *Reading Milestones.* Beaverton, OR: Dormac.

QUIGLEY, S.P. (1969). *The Influence of Fingerspelling on the Development of Language, Communication, and Educational Achievement in Deaf Children.* Urbana, IL: Institute for Research on Exceptional Children.

QUIGLEY, S.P. (1982). Reading achievement and special reading materials. *Volta Rev.* **84**, 95–105.

QUIGLEY, S.P. and KRETSCHMER, R.E. (1982). *The Education of Deaf Children: Issues, Theory and Practice.* London: Edward Arnold.

QUIGLEY, S.P., MONTANELLI, D.S. and WILBUR, R.B. (1976a). Some aspects of the verb system in the language of deaf students. *J. Speech Hear. Res.* **19**, 536–550.

QUIGLEY, S.P. and PAUL, P.V. (1984). *Language and Deafness.* London: Croom Helm.

QUIGLEY, S.P. and POWER, D.J. (1971). *Test of Syntactic Ability, Rationale, Test Logistics and Instructions.* Urbana, IL: Institute for Research on Exceptional Children.

QUIGLEY, S.P., STEINKAMP, M.W., POWER, D.J. and JONES, B.W. (1978). *Test of Syntactic Abilities.* Beaverton, OR: Dormac.

QUIGLEY, S.P., WILBUR, R., POWER, D., MONTANELLI, D. and STEINKAMP, M. (1976b). *Syntactic Structures in the Language of Deaf Children.* Urbana, IL: Institute for Child Behavior and Development.

QUINSLAND, L.K. and VAN GINKEL, A. (1990). Cognitive processing and the development of concepts by deaf students. *Am. Ann. Deaf* **135**, 280–284.

RAIMONDO, D. and MAXWELL, M. (1987). The modes of communication used in junior and senior high school classrooms by hearing-impaired students and their teachers and peers. *Volta Rev.* **89**, 263–275.

RAINER, J.D. (1976). Some observations on affect induction and ego development in the deaf. *Internat. Rev. Psycho-Anal.* **3**, 121–128.

RAINER, J.D. and ALTSCHULER, K.Z. (1971). A psychiatric program for the deaf: experiences and implications. *Am. J. Psychiat.* **127**, 1527–1532.

RAINER, J.D., ALTSCHULER, K.Z. and KALLMANN, F.J. (Eds) (1963). *Family and Mental Health Problems in a Deaf Population*, 2nd Edn. Springfield, IL: Charles C. Thomas.

RANEY, L., DANCER, J. and BRADLEY, R. (1984). Correlation between auditory and visual performance on two speech reception tasks. *Volta Rev.* **86**, 134–141.

REBER, A.S. and SCARBOROUGH, D. (Eds) (1977). *Toward a Psychology of Reading: The Proceedings of the CUNY Conference*. Hillsdale, NJ: Erlbaum.

REDGATE, G.W. (1972). *The Teaching of Reading to Deaf Children*. Manchester: University of Manchester Press.

REED, C. (1975). Identification and discrimination of vowel–consonant syllables in listeners with sensorineural hearing loss. *J. Speech Hear. Res.* **18**, 773–794.

REED, C.M., RABINOWITZ, W.M., DURLACH, N.I., BRAIDA, L.D., CONWAY-FITHIAN, S. and SCHULTZ, M.C. (1985). Research on the Tadoma Method of speech communication. *J. Acoust. Soc. Am.* **77**, 247–257.

REES, N.S. (1973). Auditory processing factors in language disorders: the view from Procrustes' bed. *J. Speech Hear. Disord.* **38**, 304–315.

REES, N.S. (1981). Saying more than we know: is auditory processing disorder a meaningful concept? In: Keith (1981b).

REICH, C., HAMBLETON, D. and HOULDIN, B.K. (1977). The integration of hearing-impaired children in regular classrooms. *Am. Ann. Deaf* **122**, 534–543.

REINKING, D. and SCHREINER, R. (1985). The effects of computer-mediated text on measures of reading comprehension and reading behavior. *Read. Res. Q.* **20**, 536–552.

REISBERG, D. (1978). Looking where you listen: visual cues and auditory attention. *Acta Psychol.* **42**, 331–341.

REISBERG, D., MCLEAN, J. and GOLDFIELD, A. (1987). Easy to hear but hard to understand: a lipreading advantage with intact auditory stimuli. In: Dodd and Campbell (1987).

REISBERG, D., SCHEIBER, R. and POTEMKEN, L. (1981). Eye-position and the control of auditory attention. *J. Exp. Psychol. Hum. Percept. Perform.* **7**, 318–323.

RESNICK, L.B. (Ed.) (1989). *Knowing, Learning and Instruction: Essays in Honor of Robert Glaser*. Hillsdale, NJ: Erlbaum.

REVOILE, S., PICKETT, J.M., HOLDEN-PITT, L.D., TALKIN, D. and BRANDT, F.D. (1987). Burst and transition cues to voicing perception for spoken initial stops by impaired- and normal-hearing listeners. *J. Speech Hear. Res.* **30**, 3–12.

REVOILE, S.G., KOZMA–SPYTEK, L., HOLDEN-PITT, L., PICKETT, J.M. and DROGE, J. (1991a). VCV's vs. CVC's for stop/fricative distinctions by hearing-impaired and normal-hearing listeners. *J. Acoust. Soc. Am.* **89**, 457–460.

REVOILE, S.G., PICKETT, J.M. and KOZMA-SPYTEK, L. (1991b). Spectral cues to perception of /d, n, l/ by normal- and impaired-hearing listeners. *J. Acoust. Soc. Am.* **90**, 787–798.

REYNOLDS, H.N. (1986). Performance of deaf college students on a criterion-referenced modified cloze test of reading comprehension. *Am. Ann. Deaf* **131**, 361–364.

RICHARDSON, J.E. (1981). Computer assessed instruction for the hearing impaired. *Volta Rev.* **83**, 328–335.

RIEBER, R.W. and VOYAT, G. (1983). *Dialogues on the Psychology of Language and Thought*. New York and London: Plenum.

RIESEN, A.H. (1961). Critical stimulation and optimal period. Paper presented to American Psychological Association, New York.

RIKO, K., HYDE, M.L. and ALBERT, P.W. (1985). Hearing loss in early infancy: incidence, detection and assessment. *Laryngoscope* **95**, 137–145.

RINGEL, R.L., BURK, K.W. and SCOTT, C.M. (1968). Tactile perception: form discrimination in the mouth. *Br. J. Disord. Commun.* **3**, 150–155.

RINGEL, R.L., HOUSE, A.S., BURK, K.W., DOLINSKY, J.P. and SCOTT, C.M. (1970). Some relations between orosensory discrimination and articulatory aspects of speech production. *J. Speech Hear. Disord.* **35**, 3–11.

RISBERG, A. (1976). Diagnostic rhyme test for speech audiometry with severely hard of hearing and profoundly deaf children. *Stockholm: Speech Transmission Lab., Q. Progress and Status Report* **2–3**, 40–58.

RISBERG, A. and SPENS, K.E. (1967). Teaching machine for training experiments in speech perception. *Stockholm: Speech Transmission Lab., Q. Progress and Status Report* **2–3**, 72–75.

RITTENHOUSE, R.K. and KENYON, P.L. (1987). Educational and social language in deaf adolescents: TDD and school-produced comparisons. *Am. Ann. Deaf* **132**, 210–212.

RITTENHOUSE, R., MORREAU, L. and IRAN-NEJAD, A. (1981). Metaphor and conservation in deaf and normal hearing children. *Am. Ann. Deaf* **126**, 450–453.

RITTENHOUSE, R.K. and STEARNS, K. (1990). Figurative language and reading comprehension in American deaf and hard-of-hearing children: textual interactions. *Br. J. Disord. Commun.* **25**, 369–374.

RITTENHOUSE, R.K., WHITE, K., LOWITZER, C. and SHISLER, L. (1990). The costs and benefits of providing early intervention to very young, severely hearing-impaired children in the United States: the conceptual outline of a longitudinal research study and some preliminary findings. *Br. J. Disord. Commun.* **25**, 195–208.

ROBB, M.P. and SAXMAN, J.H. (1985). Developmental trends in vocal fundamental frequency of young children. *J. Speech Hear. Res.* **28**, 421–427.

ROBBINS, A. MCC. (1990). Developing meaningful auditory integration in children with cochlear implants. *Volta Rev.* **92**, 361–370.

ROBBINS, A. MCC., OSBERGER, M.J., MIYAMOTO, R.T., KIENLE, M.L. and MYRES, W.A. (1985). Speech-tracking performance in single-channel cochlear implant subjects. *J. Speech Hear. Res.* **28**, 565–578.

ROBBINS, R.M. and GAUGER, J. (1982). Hearing aid evaluation and orientation for the severely hearing-impaired. In: Sims et al. (1982).

ROBINSON, E.J. (1981). The child's understanding of inadequate messages and communication failure: a problem of ignorance or egocentrism? In: Dickson (1981).

ROBINSON, E.J. and ROBINSON, W.P. (1983). Communication and metacommunication: quality of children's instructions in relation to judgement about the adequacy of instructions and the focus of responsibility for communication failure. *J. Exp. Child Psychol.* **36**, 305–320.

ROBINSON, J.H. and GRIFFITH, P.L. (1979). On the scientific status of iconicity. *Sign Lang. Stud.* **25**, 297–315.

RODDA, M. and GROVE, C. (1987). *Language, Cognition and Deafness.* Hillsdale, NJ: Erlbaum.

RODRIGUEZ, G.P., DiSARNO, N.J. and HARDIMAN, C.J. (1990). Central auditory processing in normal-hearing elderly adults. *Audiology* **29**, 85–92.

ROESER, R.J. and DOWNS, M.P. (Eds) (1981). *Auditory Disorders in School Children.* New York: Thieme-Stratton.

ROGERS, D. and SLOBODA, J. (Eds) (1983). *The Acquisition of Symbolic Skills.* New York: Plenum.

ROMAINE, S. (1984). *The Language of Children and Adolescents.* Oxford: Basil Blackwell.

ROMMETVEIT, R. (1974). *On Message Structure: A Framework for the Study of Language and Communication.* New York: Wiley.

RONNBERG, J., ARLINGER, S., LYXELL, B. and KINNEFORS, C. (1989). Visual evoked potentials: relation to adult speechreading and cognitive function. *J. Speech Hear. Res.* **32**, 725–735.

ROSEN, S.M., FOURCIN, A.J. and MOORE, B.C.J. (1981). Voice pitch as an aid to lipreading. *Nature* **291**, 150–152.

ROSEN, S., WALLIKER, J.R., FOURCIN, A. and BALL, V. (1987). A microprocessor-based acoustic hearing aid for the profoundly impaired listener. *J. Rehab. Res. Dev.* **24**, 239–260.

ROSS, M. (1975). Hearing aid selection for pre-verbal hearing-impaired children. In: Pollack (1975).

ROSS, M. (1990). Verbal communication: the state of the art. *Volta Rev.* **78**, 324–328.

ROSS, M., BRACKETT, D. and MAXON, A. (1982). *Hard of Hearing Children in Regular Schools.* Englewood Cliffs, NJ: Prentice Hall.

ROSS, M. and GIOLAS, T.G. (Eds) (1978). *Auditory Management of Hearing-Impaired Children.* Baltimore, MD: University Park Press.

ROSS, M. and LERMAN, J. (1970). A picture identification test for hearing-impaired children. *J. Speech Hear. Res.* **13**, 44–53.

ROSS, P., PERGAMENT, L. and ANISFELD, M. (1979). Cerebral lateralisation of deaf and hearing individuals for linguistic comparison judgements. *Brain Lang.* 8, 69–80.

ROWE, J. (1982). The Paget–Gorman Sign System. In: Peter and Barnes (1982).

RUBEN, R.J. (1986). Unsolved issues around critical periods with emphasis on clinical application. *Acta Otolaryngol. (Stockh) Suppl.* 429, 61–64.

RUBIN, K.H. (1973). Egocentrism in childhood: a unitary construct? *Child Devel.* 44, 102–110.

RUDEL, R.G. (1985). Hemispheric asymmetry and learning disabilities: left, right or in-between? In: Best (1985).

RUGGIERI, V., CELLI, C. and CRESCENZI, A. (1982). Gesturing and self-contact of right and left halves of the body: relationship with eye-contact. *Percept. Mot. Skills* 55, 695–698.

RUSHMER, N. and SCHUYLER, V. (1984). The IHR model of parent–infant habilitation. In: Ling (1984a).

RUSSELL, W.K., QUIGLEY, S.P. and POWER, D.J. (1976). *Linguistics and Deaf Children: Transformational Syntax and Its Applications*. Washington, DC: Alexander Graham Bell Association.

RUTHERFORD, S.D. (1988). The culture of American deaf people. *Sign Lang. Stud.* 59, 129–147.

RUTTER, M.L. (1981). *Maternal Deprivation Reassessed,* 2nd Edn. Harmondsworth: Penguin.

RYAN, K.M. and LEVINE, J.M. (1981). Impact of academic performance pattern on assigned grade and predicted performance. *J. Educ. Psychol.* 73, 386–392.

SACKS, O. (1986). Mysteries of the Deaf. *New York Rev. Books* 33, 23–33.

SACKS, O. (1989). *Seeing Voices: A Journey into the World of the Deaf.* Los Angeles, CA: University of California Press.

SAKATA, S. (1989). A study on the development of message production in referential communication. *Shinrigaku Kenkyu (Japan)* 59, 365–368.

SALASOO, A. and PISONI, D.B. (1985). Sources of knowledge in spoken word identification. *J. Mem. Lang.* 24, 210–231.

SALEND, S.J. and JOHNS, J. (1983). Changing teacher commitment to mainstreaming. *Teaching Except. Child.* 15, 82–85.

SAMAR, V.J. and SIMS, D.G. (1983). Visual evoked-response correlates of speechreading performance in normal-hearing adults: a replication and a factor analytic extension. *J. Speech Hear. Res.* 26, 2–9.

SAMAR, V.J. and SIMS, D.G. (1984). Visual evoked-response components related to speechreading and spatial skills in hearing and hearing-impaired adults. *J. Speech Hear. Res.* 27, 162–172.

SANDERS, D.A. (1977). *Auditory Perception of Speech: An Introduction to Principles and Problems.* Englewood Cliffs, NJ: Prentice Hall.

SANDERS, G., WRIGHT, H.V. and ELLIS, C. (1989). Cerebral lateralisation of language in deaf and hearing people. *Brain Lang.* 36, 555–579.

SANTROCK, J.W. (1986). *Life-Span Development,* 2nd Edn. Dubuque, IA: W.C. Brown.

SAPIR, E. (1949). Language and environment. In: Mandelbaum (1949).

SARACHAN-DEILY, A.B. (1982). Hearing-impaired and hearing readers' sentence processing errors. *Volta Rev.* 84, 81–95.

SARACHAN-DEILY, A.B. (1985). Written narratives of deaf and hearing students: story recall and inference. *J. Speech Hear. Res.* 28, 151–159.

SAUR, R., COGGIOLA, D., LONG, G.L. and SIMONSON, J. (1986). Educational mainstreaming and the career development of the hearing-impaired students: a longitudinal analysis. *Volta Rev.* 88, 79–88.

SAUR, R., POPP-STONE, M.J. and HURLEY-LAWRENCE, E. (1987). The classroom participation of mainstreamed hearing-impaired college students. *Volta Rev.* 89, 277–286.

SAUR, R.E. and STINSON, M.S. (1986). Characteristics of successful mainstreamed hearing-impaired students. *J. Rehab. Deaf* 20, 15–21.

SAVAGE, R.D., EVANS, L. and SAVAGE, J.F. (1981). *Psychology and Communication in Deaf Children.* Sydney: Grune and Stratton.

SAVIN, H.B. (1972). What the child knows about speech when he starts to learn to read. In: Kavanagh and Mattingly (1972).

SCHAEFER, E.S. (1976). Scope and focus of research relevant to intervention: a socioecological perspective. In: Tjossem (1976).

SCHAEFER, R.P. (1980). *An Experimental Assessment of the Boundaries Demarcating Three Basic Semantic Categories in the Domain of Separation*. University of Kansas: unpublished Doctoral Thesis.

SCHAFFER, H.R. (Ed.) (1977). *Studies in Mother–Infant Interaction*. New York: Academic Press.

SCHICK, B.S. (1990). The effects of morphological complexity on phonological simplification in ASL. *Sign Lang. Stud.* 66, 25–41.

SCHILDROTH, A. (1988). Recent changes in the educational placement of deaf students. *Am. Ann. Deaf* 133, 61–67.

SCHILDROTH, A.N. and KARCHMER, M.A. (Eds) (1986). *Deaf Children in America*. San Diego, CA: College-Hill Press.

SCHILP, C. (1989). Correcting grammatical errors with MacWrite. *Volta Rev.* 91, 151–155.

SCHINDLER, R.A. and MERZENICH, M.M. (Eds) (1985). *Cochlear Implants*. New York: Raven Press.

SCHLESINGER, H.S. (1972). A developmental model applied to problems of deafness. In: Schlesinger and Meadow (1972).

SCHLESINGER, H.S. (1978). The effects of deafness on childhood development: an Ericksonian perspective. In: Liben (1978).

SCHLESINGER, H. (1986). Total communication in perspective. In: Luterman (1986).

SCHLESINGER, H.S. and MEADOW, K.P. (1972). *Sound and Sign: Childhood Deafness and Mental Health*. Berkeley, CA: University of California Press.

SCHLESINGER, I. (1977a). The role of cognitive development and linguistic input in language acquisition. *J. Child Lang.* 4, 153–169.

SCHLESINGER I.M. (1971). The grammar of sign language and the problems of language universals. In: Morton (1971).

SCHLESINGER, I.M. (1977b). Some aspects of sign languages. In: Cohen et al. (1977).

SCHLESINGER, I.M. and NAMIR, L. (Eds) (1978). *Sign Language of the Deaf: Psychological, Linguistic and Sociological Perspectives*. New York: Academic Press.

SCHNEIDER, W. (1985). Training high performance skills: fallacies and guidelines. *Hum. Factors* 27, 285–300.

SCHNEIDMAN, E.S. (1948). Schizophrenia and the MAPS test: a study of certain formal aspects of fantasy production in schizophrenia as revealed by performance on the Make-A-Picture Story (MAPS) test. *Genet. Psychol. Monogr.* 38, 145–223.

SCHOLES, R.J. and FISCHLER, I. (1979). Hemispheric function and linguistic skill in the deaf. *Brain Lang.* 7, 336–350.

SCHOPLER, E. and REICHLER, R.J. (Eds) (1976). *Psychopathology and Child Development: Research and Treatments*. New York: Plenum.

SCHOWE, B.M. (1979). *Identity Crisis in Deafness: A Humanistic Perspective*. Tempe, AZ: Scholars Press.

SCHOW, R.L. and NERBONNE, M.A. (1980a). Overview of aural rehabilitation. In: Schow and Nerbonne (1980b).

SCHOW, R.L. and NERBONNE, M.A. (Eds) (1980b). *Introduction to Aural Rehabilitation*. Baltimore, MD: University Park Press.

SCHUCHMAN, J.S. (1988). *Hollywood Speaks: Deafness and the Film Industry*. Chicago, IL: University of Illinois Press.

SCHULZE, G. (1965). An evaluation of vocabulary development by 32 deaf children over a 3-year period. *Am. Ann. Deaf* 110, 424–435.

SCHWARTZ, J.L., ROSS, L.J. and HOUCHINS, R.R. (1975). An investigation of the self-concept of expressive language of thirty adolescent hearing-impaired students using the Q-sort technique. *Am. Ann. Deaf* 120, 572–577.

SCOTT, B.A. (1984). Deafness in the family: will the therapist listen? *Family Process* 23, 214–216.

SCOTT, D. (1978). Stigma in and about the deaf community. In: Montgomery (1978).

SCOUTEN, E.L. (1964). The place of the Rochester Method in American education of the deaf. *Proc. Internat. Congr. Educ. Deaf* 429–433.

SCOUTEN, E.L. (1980). An instructional strategy to combat the word-matching tendencies in prelingually deaf students. *Am. Ann. Deaf* 125, 1057–1059.

SCOVEL, T. (1981). The effects of neurological age on nonprimary language acquisition. In: Anderson (1981).

SCROGGS, C.L. (1983). An examination of the communication interactions between hearing impaired infants and their parents. In: Kyle and Woll (1983).

SEAL, B.C. (1987). Working parents' dream: instructional videotapes for their signing deaf child. *Am. Ann. Deaf* 132, 386–388.

SEASHORE, R.H. (1951). Work and Motor Performance. In: Stevens (1951).

SEEWALD, R.C. and BRACKETT, D. (1984). Spoken language modifications as a function of the age and hearing ability of the listener. *Volta Rev.* 86, 20–35.

SEEWALD, R.C., ROSS, M., GIOLAS, T.G. and YONOVITZ, A. (1985). Primary modality for speech perception in children with normal and impaired hearing. *J. Speech Hear. Res.* 28, 36–46.

SELOVER, P.J. (1988). American Sign Language in the high school system. *Sign Lang. Stud.* 59, 205–212.

SERWATKA, T.S., HESSON, D. and GRAHAM, M. (1984). The effect of indirect intervention on the improvement of hearing-impaired students' reading scores. *Volta Rev.* 86, 81–88.

SHAND, M.A. (1982). Sign-based short term coding of American Sign Language signs and printed English words by congenitally deaf signers. *Cognit. Psychol.* 14, 1–12.

SHANKWEILER, D. and LIBERMAN, I.Y. (1976). Exploring the relations between reading and speech. In: Knights and Bakker (1976).

SHARP, C. (1984). Sex and deafness stereotyping by hearing and deaf adolescents – a preliminary survey. *Aust. Teacher of the Deaf* 25, 39–45.

SHATZ, M. and GELMAN, R. (1973). The development of communication skills: modifications in the speech of young children as a function of listener. *Monogr. Soc. Res. Child Devel.* 38, (Serial No. 152).

SHAW, R. and BRANSFORD, J. (Eds) (1977). *Perceiving, Acting, and Knowing: Toward an Ecological Psychology*. Hillsdale, NJ: Erlbaum.

SHEPHERD, D.C., DELAVERGNE, R.W., FRUEH, F.X. and CLOBRIDGE, C. (1977). Visual–neural correlate of speechreading ability in normal-hearing adults. *J. Speech Hear. Res.* 20, 752–765.

SHER, A.E. and OWENS, E. (1974). Consonant confusions associated with hearing loss above 2000Hz. *J. Speech Hear. Res.* 17, 669–681.

SHERIF, M. and SHERIF, C. (1964). *Reference Groups: Exploration into Conformity and Deviance in Adolescence*. New York: Harper and Row.

SHIMIZU, H. and INOUE, T. (1988). The effect of rehearsal strategies on free recall in the deaf. *Psychologia*. 31, 226–232.

SHUKLA, R.S. (1989). Phonological space in the speech of the hearing impaired. *J. Commun. Disord.* 22, 317–325.

SHULMAN, B.B. (1985). *Test of Pragmatic Skills*. Tucson, AZ: Communication Skill Builders.

SIDOWSKI, J.B. (Ed.) (1980). *Conditioning, Cognition and Methodology: Contemporary Issues in Experimental Psychology*. Hillsdale, NJ: Erlbaum.

SIEBERT, R. (1980). Speech training for the hearing impaired: principles, objectives, and strategies for preschool and elementary levels. In: Subtelny (1980).

SIEGEL, L.S. and LINDER, B.A. (1984). Short-term memory processes in children with reading and arithmetic learning disabilities. *Devel. Psychol.* 20, 200–207.

SIEGMAN, A.W. and POPE, B. (Eds) (1972). *Studies in Dyadic Communication*. New York: Pergamon.

SILVERMAN, S.R. (1983). Speech training then and now. In: Hochberg et al. (1983).

SILVERMAN, S.R. and HIRSH, I. (1955). Problems related to the use of speech in clinical audiometry. *Ann. Otol. Rhinol. Laryngol.* 64, 1234–1244.

SILVERMAN, S.R. and KRICOS, P.B. (1990). Speechreading. *Volta Rev.* **92**, 22–32.

SIMEONSSON, R.J., COOPER, D.H. and SCHEINER, A.P. (1982). A review of the effectiveness of early intervention programs. *Pediatrics* **69**, 635–641.

SIMMONS, A. (1962). A comparison of the type-token ratio of spoken and written language of deaf and hearing children. *Volta Rev.* **64**, 117–121.

SIMMONS, F.B. (1966). Electrical stimulation of the auditory nerve in man. *Arch. Otolaryngol.* **84**, 24–76.

SIMS, D.G. (1982). Hearing and speechreading evaluation for the deaf adult. In: Sims et al. (1982).

SIMS, D.G., GOTTERMEIER, J. and WALTER, C.G. (1980). Factors contributing to the development of intelligible speech among prelingually deaf persons. *Am. Ann. Deaf* **125**, 374–381.

SIMS, D.G., WALTER, G.G. and WHITEHEAD, R.L. (1982). *Deafness and Communication: Assessment and Training.* Baltimore, MD: Williams and Wilkins.

SIPLE, P. (1978a). Linguistic and psychological properties of American Sign Language: an overview. In: Siple (1978b).

SIPLE, P. (Ed.) (1978b). *Understanding Language through Sign Language Research.* New York: Academic Press.

SIPLE, P., FISCHER, S.D. and BELLUGI, U. (1977). Memory for non-semantic attributes of American Sign Language signs and English words. *J. Verb. Learn. Verb. Behav.* **16**, 561–574.

SISCO, F.H. and ANDERSON, R.J. (1980). Deaf children's performance on the WISC-R relative to hearing status of parents and child-rearing experiences. *Am. Ann. Deaf* **125**, 923–930.

SKARAKIS, E.A. and PRUTTING, C.A. (1977). Early communication: semantic functions and communicative intentions in the communication of the preschool child with impaired hearing. *Am. Ann. Deaf* **122**, 382–391.

SKINNER, M.W., BINZER, S.M., SMITH, P.G., HOLDEN, L.K., FREDRICKSON, J.M., HOLDEN, T.A., JUELICH, M.F. and TURNER, B.A. (1988). Comparison of benefit from vibrotactile and cochlear implant for postlinguistically deaf adults. *Laryngoscope* **98**, 1092–1099.

SKINNER, M.W., HOLDEN, L.K., HOLDEN, T.A., DOWELL, R.C., SELIGMAN, P.M., BRIMACOMBE, J.A. and BEITER, A.L. (1991). Performance of postlingually deaf adults with the wearable speech processor (WSPII) and mini speech processor (MSP) of the Nucleus multi-electrode cochlear implant. *Ear Hear.* **12**, 3–22.

SKUSE, D.H. (1984a). Extreme deprivation in early childhood – I. Diverse outcomes for three siblings from an extraordinary family. *J. Child Psychol. Psychiat.* **25**, 523–541.

SKUSE, D.H. (1984b). Extreme deprivation in early childhood – II. Theoretical issues and a comparative review. *J. Child Psychol. Psychiat.* **25**, 543–572.

SLIKE, S.B., CHIAVACCI, J.P. and HOBBIS, D.H. (1989). The efficiency and effectiveness of an interactive video system to teach sign language vocabulary. *Am. Ann. Deaf* **134**, 288–290.

SLOAN, C. (1980). Auditory processing disorders and language development. In: Levinson and Sloan (1980).

SLOAN, C. (1986). *Treating Auditory Processing Difficulties in Children.* San Diego, CA: College-Hill Press.

SLOBIN, D. (1979). *Psycholinguistics,* 2nd Edn. Glenview, IL: Scott, Foresman and Co.

SLOBIN, D.I. (1980). The repeated path between transparency and opacity in language. In: Bellugi and Studdert-Kennedy (1980).

SLOWIACZEK, L.M. (1990). Effects of lexical stress in auditory word recognition. *Lang. Speech* **33**, 47–68.

SLOWIACZEK, L.M., NUSBAUM, H.C. and PISONI, D.B. (1987). Phonological priming in auditory word recognition. *J. Exp. Psychol.: Learn. Mem. Cognit.* **13**, 64–75.

SMALE, A.G. (1988). The intelligibility of the speech of orally educated, prelingually deaf adolescents. In: Taylor (1988).

SMALL, L.H. and INFANTE, A.A. (1988). Effects of training and visual distance on speechreading performance. *Percept. Mot. Skills* **66**, 415–418.

SMITH, C.R. (1975a). Residual hearing and speech production in deaf children. *J. Speech Hear. Res.* **18**, 795–811.

SMITH, C.R. (1975b). Interjected sounds in deaf children's speech. *J. Commun. Disord.* **8**, 123–128.

SMITH, F. (1973). *Psycholinguistics and Reading.* New York: Holt, Rinehart and Winston.

SMITH, F. and MILLER, G. (Eds) (1966). *The Genesis of Language: A Psycholinguistic Approach.* Cambridge, MA: MIT Press.

SMITH, M. and RICHARDS, S. (1990). Some essential aspects of an effective audiological management programme for school age hearing-impaired children. *J. Br. Assn. Teachers of the Deaf* **14**, 104–113.

SNIDECOR, J.C., MALBRY, L.A. and HEARSEY, E.L. (1944). *Methods of Training Talkers for Increasing Intelligibility in Noise (ORSD Report 3178).* New York: Psychological Corporation.

SNOW, C.E. (1972). Mothers' speech to children learning language. *Child Devel.* **43**, 549–565.

SNOW, C.E. and FERGUSON, C.A. (Eds) (1977). *Talking to Children: Language Input and Acquisition.* New York: Cambridge University Press.

SOKOLOV, A.N. (1972). *Inner Speech and Thought.* New York: Plenum Press.

SONNENSCHEIN, S. and WHITEHURST, G.W. (1984). Developing referential communication: a hierarchy of skills. *Child Devel.* **55**, 1936–1945.

SPARKS, D.W., ARDELL, L.A., BOURGEDIS, M., WEIDMER, B. and KIHL. P. (1979). Investigating the MESA (Multipoint Electrotactile Speech Aid): the transmission of connected discourse. *J. Acoust. Soc. Am.* **65**, 810–815.

SPEAKS, C. and JERGER, J. (1965). Method for measurement of speech identification. *J. Speech Hear. Res.* **8**, 185–194.

SPEAKS, C., NICCUM, N. and VAN TASELL, D. (1985). Effects of stimulus material on the dichotic listening performance of patients with sensorineural hearing loss. *J. Speech Hear. Res.* **28**, 16–25.

SPELKE, E. (1976). Infants' intermodal perception of events. *Cognit. Psychol.* **8**, 553–560.

SPENCER, P. and DELK, L. (1989). Hearing-impaired students' performance on tests of visual processing: relationships with reading performance. *Am. Ann. Deaf* **134**, 333–337.

SPENCER, P.E. and GUTFREUND, M. (1990). Characteristics of 'dialogues' between mothers and prelinguistic hearing-impaired and normally-hearing infants. *Volta Rev.* **92**, 351–360.

SPENCER, S.J., DALE, J. and KLIONS, H.L. (1989). Deaf versus hearing subjects' recall of words on a distraction task as a function of the signability of the words. *Percept. Mot. Skills* **69**, 1043–1047.

SPERLING, G. (1978). Future prospects in language and communication for the congenitally deaf. In: Liben (1978).

SPETNER, N.B. and OLSHO, L.W. (1990). Auditory frequency resolution in human infancy. *Child Devel.* **61**, 632–652.

SPILLMAN, T. and DILLIER, N. (1989). Comparison of single-channel extracochlear and multichannel intracochlear electrodes in the same patient. *Br. J. Audiol.* **23**, 25–31.

SQUIRES, S. and DANCER, J. (1986). Auditory versus visual practice effects in the intelligibility of words in everyday sentences. *J. Aud. Res.* **26**, 5–10.

STALLER, S.J., DOWELL, R.C., BEITER, A.L. and BRIMACOMBE, J.A. (1991). Perceptual abilities of children with the Nucleus 22-channel cochlear implant. *Ear Hear. Suppl.* **12**, 34–47.

STAMM, K.R. and PEARCE, W.B. (1971). Communicative Behavior and Co-Orientational States. *J. Commun.* **21**, 208–220.

STANDING, L. and CURTIS, L. (1989). Subvocalization rate versus other predictors of the memory span. *Psychol. Rep.* **65**, 487–495.

STANOVICH, K. (1986). Matthew effects in reading: some consequences of individual differences in the acquisition of literacy. *Read. Res. Q.* **21**, 360–407.

STANOVICH, K.E. (1980). Towards an interactive-compensatory model of individual differences in the development of reading fluency. *Read. Res. Q.* **16**, 32–71.

STANOVICH, K. and WEST, R. (1979). Mechanisms of sentence context effects in reading: automatic activation and conscious attention. *Mem. Cognit.* **7**, 77–85.

STATHOPOULOS, E.T., DUCHAN, J.F., SONNENMEIER, R.M. and BRUCE, N.V. (1986). Intonation and pausing in deaf speech. *Folia Phoniat.* **38**, 1–12.

STATON, J. (1985). Using dialogue journals for developing thinking, reading, and writing with hearing-impaired students. *Volta Rev.* 87, 127–154.

STEIN, L., MINDEL, E. and JABALEY, T. (Eds) (1981). *Deafness and Mental Health*. New York: Grune and Stratton.

STEINBERG, D.D. and JAKOBOVITS, L.A. (Eds) (1971). *Semantics: An Interdisciplinary Reader in Philosophy, Linguistics and Psychology*. Cambridge: Cambridge University Press.

STEPHENS, S.D.G. (Ed.) (1976). *Disorders of Auditory Function II*. London: Academic Press.

STERNBERG, M.L.A. (1981). *American Sign Language: A Comprehensive Dictionary*. New York: Harper and Rowe.

STERNBERG, R.J. (1983). Criteria for intellectual skills training. *Educ. Researcher* 12, 6–12, 26.

STERNBERG, R.J. (1987). Most vocabulary is learned from context. In: McKeown and Curtis (1987).

STEVENS, K.N., NICKERSON, R.S. and ROLLINS, A.M. (1978). On describing the suprasegmental properties of the speech of deaf children. In: McPherson and Davis (1978).

STEVENS, S.S. (Ed.) (1951). *Handbook of Experimental Psychology*. New York: Wiley. (See also Atkinson et al. (1988).)

STEWART, D.A. (1983). The use of sign by deaf children: the opinions of a deaf community. *Am. Ann. Deaf* 128, 878–883.

STOCKARD, J.E. and CURRAN, J.S. (1990). Transient elevation of threshold of the neonatal auditory brain stem response. *Ear Hear.* 11, 21–28.

STOEFEN-FISHER, J.M. (1990). Teacher judgments of student reading interests: how accurate are they? *Am. Ann. Deaf* 135, 252–256.

STOKOE, W. (Ed.) (1979). *Sign Language Studies*. Silver Spring, MD: Linstok Press.

STOKOE, W.C. (1960). *Sign Language Structure: An Outline of the Visual Communication System of the American Deaf*. Studies in Linguistics, Occasional Paper 8, Buffalo, NY: University of Buffalo.

STOKOE, W.C. (1978). *Sign Language Structure*. Silver Spring, MD: Linstok Press.

STOKOE, W.C. (Ed.) (1980). *Sign and Culture. A Reader for Students of American Sign Language*. Silver Spring, MD: Linstok Press.

STOKOE, W.C. (1983). Sign languages, linguistics and related arts. In: Kyle and Woll (1983).

STOKOE, W.C. (1987). Tell me where is grammar bred?: Critical evaluation or another chorus of 'Come Back To Milano?'. *Sign Lang. Stud.* 54, 31–58.

STOKOE, W.C. (1991). Semantic Phonology. *Sign Lang. Stud.* 71, 107–114.

STOKOE, W.C. and BATTISON, R.M. (1981). Sign language, mental health and satisfactory interaction. In: Stein et al. (1981).

STOKOE, W., CASTERLINE, D. and CRONEBERG, G. (1965). *A Dictionary of American Sign Language on Linguistic Principles*. Silver Spring, MD: Linstok Press.

STONE, P. and ADAM, A. (1986). Is your child wearing the right hearing aid? Principles for selecting and maintaining amplification. *Volta Rev.* 88, 45–54.

STRASSMAN, B.K., KRETSCHMER, R.E. and BILSKY, L.H. (1987). The instantiation of general terms by deaf adolescents/adults. *J. Commun. Disord.* 20, 1–13.

STRENG, A.H., KRETSCHMER, R.R. and KRETSCHMER, L.W. (1978). *Language, Learning, and Deafness: Theory, Application and Classroom Management*. New York: Grune and Stratton.

STROHNER, H. and NELSON, K.E. (1974). The young child's development of sentence comprehension: influence of event probability, nonverbal context, syntactic form, and their strategies. *Child Devel.* 45, 567–576.

STRONG, C.J. and SHAVER, J.P. (1991). Modifying attitudes towards persons with hearing impairments. *Am. Ann. Deaf* 136, 252–260.

STRONG, M. (Ed.) (1988). *Language Learning and Deafness*. Cambridge: Cambridge University Press.

STRONG, M. and CHARLSON, E.S. (1987). Simultaneous Communication: are teachers attempting an impossible task? *Am. Ann. Deaf* 132, 376–382.

STRONG, M., CHARLSON, E.S. and GOLD, R. (1987). Integration and segregation in mainstreaming programs for children and adolescents with hearing impairments. *Except. Child.* 34, 181–195.

STUCKLESS, E.R. (1965). *National Research Conference on Behavioral Aspects of Deafness.* Washington, DC: US Department of Health, Education and Welfare, Vocational Rehabilitation Administration.

STUCKLESS, E.R. (1991). Reflections on bilingual, bicultural education for deaf children. *Am. Ann. Deaf* **136**, 270–272.

STUDEBAKER, G.A. and SHERBECOE, R.L. (1991). Frequency-importance and transfer functions for recorded CID W-22 word lists. *J. Speech Hear. Res.* **34**, 427–438.

SUBTELNY, J.D. (Ed.) (1980). *Speech Assessment and Speech Improvement for the Hearing Impaired.* Washington, DC: Alexander Graham Bell Association.

SUBTELNY, J.D. (1982). Speech assessment of the adolescent with impaired hearing. In: Sims et al. (1982).

SUBTELNY, J.D. (1983). Integrated speech and language instruction for the hearing-impaired adolescent. In: Lass (1983).

SUBTELNY, J.D,. WHITEHEAD, R.L. and ORLANDO, N.A. (1980). Description and evaluation of an instructional program to improve speech and voice diagnosis of the hearing impaired. *Volta Rev.* **82**, 85–95.

SUMBY, W.H. and POLLACK, I. (1954). Visual contribution to speech intelligibility in noise. *J. Acoust. Soc. Am.* **26**, 212–215.

SUMMERFIELD, A.Q. (1979). Use of visual information for phonetic perception. *Phonetica* **36**, 314–331.

SUMMERFIELD, A.Q. and MCGRATH, M. (1984). Detection and resolution of audio-visual incompatibility in the perception of vowels. *Q. J. Exp. Psychol.* **36A**, 51–74.

SUTY, K. A. (1986). Individual differences in the signed communication of deaf children. *Am. Ann. Deaf* **131**, 298–304.

SVIRSKY, M.A. and TOBEY, E.A. (1991). Effect of different types of auditory stimulation on vowel formant frequencies in multichannel cochlear implant users. *J. Acoust. Soc. Am.* **89**, 2895–2904.

SWAIKO, N. (1974). The role and value of an eurhythmics program in a curriculum for deaf children. *Am. Ann. Deaf.* **119**, 321–324.

SWANSON, H.L. (1987). The effects of self-instruction training on a deaf child's semantic and pragmatic production. *J. Commun. Disord.* **20**, 425–436.

SWISHER, M.V. (1990). Developmental effects on the reception of signs in peripheral vision by deaf students. *Sign Lang. Stud.* **66**, 45–59.

SWISHER, M., CHRISTIE, K. and MILLER, S. (1989). The reception of signs in peripheral vision by deaf persons. *Sign Lang. Stud.* **63**, 99–123.

TAIT, D.M. and WOOD, D.J. (1987). From communication to speech in deaf children. *Child Lang. Teaching Ther.* **3**, 1–17.

TAIT, M. (1986). Using singing to facilitate linguistic development in hearing impaired pre-schoolers. *J. Br. Assn. Teachers of the Deaf* **10**, 103–108.

TALLAL, P. (1976). Rapid auditory processing in normal and disordered language development. *J. Speech Hear. Res.* **19**, 561–571.

TALLAL, P. (1980). Auditory processing disorders in children. In: Levinson and Sloan (1980).

TALLAL, P. (1990). Fine-grained discrimination deficits in language-learning impaired children are specific neither to the auditory modality nor to speech perception. *J. Speech Hear. Res.* **33**, 616–617.

TALLAL, P., STARK, R.E. and MELLITS, D. (1985). The relationship between auditory temporal analysis and receptive language development: evidence from studies of developmental language disorder. *Neuropsychologia.* **23**, 527–534.

TANNEN, D. (1980). Implications of the oral/literate continuum for cross-cultural communication. In: Alatis (1980).

TATE, M. (1980). A study of patterns of language development in a sample of hearing-impaired children. *J. Br. Assocn. Teachers of the Deaf* **4**, 198–204.

TAYLOR, G. and BISHOP, J. (Eds) (1991). *Being Deaf: The Experience of Deafness.* London: Pinter.

TAYLOR, I.G. (Ed.) (1988). *The Education of the Deaf: Current Perspectives*, Vol. IV. London: Croom Helm.

TELLER, H.E. and LINDSEY, J.D. (1987). Developing hearing-impaired students' writing skills: Martin Buber's mutuality in today's classroom. *Am. Ann. Deaf* 132, 383–385.

TERNSTROM, S., SUNDBERG, J. and COLLDEN, A. (1988). Articulatory F_0 perturbations and auditory feedback. *J. Speech Hear. Res.* 31, 187–192.

TERRIO, L. and HAAS, W. (1986). A model for evaluating tactually assistive devices. *Volta Rev.* 88, 209–214.

TERVOORT, B. (1965). Development of language and critical period. In: Davis (1965).

TERVOORT, B.T. (1961). Esoteric symbolism in the communication behavior of young deaf children. *Am. Ann. Deaf* 106, 436–438.

TERVOORT, B.T. (1979). What is the native language for deaf children? *Studies in Honour of Prof. B. Siertsima*. Amsterdam: Institute for General Linguistics.

THIBODEAU, L.M. (1990). Electroacoustic performance of direct-input hearing aids with FM amplification systems. *Lang. Speech Hear. Ser. in Schools* 21, 49–56.

THOMAS-KERSTING, C. and CASTEEL, R.L. (1989). Harsh voice: vocal effort perceptual ratings and spectral noise levels of hearing-impaired children. *J. Commun. Disord.* 22, 125–135.

THOMPSON, M.D. and SWISHER, M.V. (1985). Acquiring language through total communication. *Ear Hear.* 6, 29–32.

TJOSSEM, T.D. (Ed.) (1976). *Intervention Strategies for High Risk Infants and Young Children*. Baltimore, MD: University Park Press.

TOBEY, E.A. and HASENSTAB, S. (1991). Effects of a Nucleus multichannel cochlear implant upon speech production in children. *Ear Hear.* 12, 48–54.

TOBIAS, J.V. and SCHUBERT, E.D. (Eds) (1983). *Hearing Research and Theory*, Vol. 2. New York: Academic Press.

TOBIN, H. (1985). Binaural interaction tasks. In: Pinheiro and Musiek (1985b).

TOGONU-BICKERSTETH, F. (1988). Prospects and challenges of educating deaf pupils in Nigeria: teachers' perceptions. *Int. J. Rehab. Res.* 11, 225–233.

TOLHURST, G.C. (1957). Effects of duration and articulation changes on intelligibility, word reception, and listener preference. *J. Speech Hear. Disord.* 22, 328.

TREIMAN, R. and BARRON, J. (1981). Segmental analysis ability: development and relation to reading ability. In: MacKinnon and Waller (1981).

TREIMAN, R. and HIRSH-PASEK, K. (1983). Silent reading: insights from second generation deaf readers. *Cognit. Psychol.* 15, 39–65.

TRELOAR, C. (1985). A survey of attitudes to the role of Auslan in the education of the deaf. *Aust. Teacher of the Deaf* 26, 21–33.

TRINDER, J., FOSTER, J., GLYNN, C. and HAGGARD, M. (1980). Parameters of spectral shape in speech intelligibility enhancement. *J. Acoust. Soc. Am.* 68, Suppl. 101.

TRUAX, R. (1985). Linking research to facilitate reading–writing–communication connections. *Volta Rev.* 87, 155–169.

TRUNE, D.R. (1982). Influence of neonatal cochlear removal on the development of mouse cochlear nucleus: 1. Number, size and its neurons. *J. Comp. Neurol.* 209, 409–424.

TRYBUS, R.J. (1980). National data on rated speech intelligibility of hearing-impaired children. In: Subtelny (1980).

TRYBUS, R.J. (1987). Century 21: Social trends and deafness. *Am. Ann. Deaf* 132, 323–325.

TRYBUS, R.J. and KARCHMER, M.A. (1977). School achievement scores of hearing-impaired children: national data on achievement status and growth patterns. *Am. Ann. Deaf* 122, 62–69.

TUCKER, I., HUGHES, M. and GLOVER, M. (1983). Verbal interaction with pre-school hearing-impaired children: a comparison of maternal and parental language input. *J. Br. Assn. Teachers of the Deaf* 7, 90–98.

TUNMER, W.E. and BOWEY, J.A. (1984). Metalinguistic awareness and reading acquisition. In: Tunmer et al. (1984).

TUNMER, W.E., PRATT, C. and HERRIMAN, M.L. (Eds) (1984). *Metalinguistic Awareness in Children: Theory, Research and Implications*. New York: Springer-Verlag.

TUREK, S., DORMAN, M. FRANKS, J. and SUMMERFIELD, Q. (1980). Identification of synthetic /bdg/ by hearing-impaired listeners under monotic and dichotic formant presentation. *J. Acoust. Soc. Am.* 67, 1031–1040.

TURNER, C.W. and HENN, C.C. (1989). The relation between vowel recognition and measures of frequency resolution. *J. Speech Hear. Res.* 32, 49–58.

TURNER, C.W., HOLTE, L.A. and RELKIN, E. (1987). Auditory filtering and the discrimination of spectral shapes by normal and hearing-impaired subjects. *J. Rehab. Res. Dev.* 24, 229–238.

TURNER, C.W. and NELSON, D.A. (1982). Frequency discrimination in regions of normal and impaired sensitivity. *J. Speech Hear. Res.* 25, 34–41.

TWENEY, R.D., HOEMANN, H.W. and ANDREWS, C.E. (1975). Semantic organization in deaf and hearing subjects. *J. Psycholing. Res.* 4, 61–73.

TYE-MURRAY, N. (1987). Effects of vowel context on the articulatory closure postures of deaf speakers. *J. Speech Hear. Res.* 30, 99–104.

TYE-MURRAY, N. (1991). The establishment of open articulatory postures by deaf and hearing talkers. *J. Speech Hear. Res.* 34, 453–459.

TYE-MURRAY, N. and FOLKINS, J.W. (1990). Jaw and lip movements of deaf talkers producing utterances with known stress patterns. *J. Acoust. Soc. Am.* 87, 2675–2683.

TYE-MURRAY, N. and WOODWORTH, B. (1989). The influence of final-syllable position on the vowel and word duration of deaf talkers. *J. Acoust. Soc. Am.* 85, 313–321.

TYE-MURRAY, N., ZIMMERMAN, G.N. and FOLKINS, J.W. (1987). Movement timing in deaf and hearing speakers: comparisons of phonetically heterogeneous syllable strings. *J. Speech Hear. Res.* 30, 411–417.

TYLER, R.S., LOWDER, M.W., OTTO, S.R., PREECE, J.P., GANTZ, B.J. and MCCABE, B.F. (1984). Initial Iowa results with the multichannel implant from Melbourne. *J. Speech Hear. Res.* 27, 596–604.

TYLER, R.S., MOORE, B.C.J. and KUK, F.K. (1989). Performance of some of the better cochlear implant patients. *J. Speech Hear. Res.* 32, 887–911.

TYLER, R.S., PREECE, J.P., LANSING, C.R., OTTO, S.R. and GANTZ, B.J. (1986). Previous experience as a confounding factor in comparing cochlear-implant processing schemes. *J. Speech Hear. Res.* 29, 282–287.

UPFOLD, L.J. and ISEPY, J. (1982). Childhood deafness in Australia: incidence and maternal rubella, 1949–1980. *Med. J. Aust.* 2, 323–326.

UPFOLD, L.J. and SMITHER, M.F. (1981). Hearing-aid fitting protocol. *Br. J. Audiol.* 15, 181–188.

UTLEY, J. (1946). Factors involved in the teaching and testing of lipreading through the use of motion pictures. *Volta Rev.* 38, 657–659.

VANDELL, D.L. and GEORGE, L.B. (1981). Social interaction in hearing and deaf preschoolers: successes and failures in initiations. *Child Devel.* 52, 627–635.

VAN HATTUM, R.J. (Ed.) (1980). *Communication Disorders: An Introduction*. New York: MacMillan.

VAN KLEECK, A. (1984). Metalinguistic skills: cutting across spoken and written language and problem-solving abilities. In: Wallach and Butler (1984).

VAN RIPER, C. (1978). *Speech Correction: Principles and Methods*, 6th Edn. Englewood Cliffs, NJ: Prentice-Hall.

VAN UDEN, A. (1986). *Sign Languages Used by Deaf People, and Psycholinguistics: A Critical Evaluation*. Lisse: Swets and Zeitlinger, B.V.

VELLUMNO, F.R. (1979). *Dyslexia: Theory and Research*. Cambridge, MA: MIT Press.

VELLUTINO, F. (1983). Childhood dyslexia: a language disorder. *Prog. Learn. Disabil.* 5, 135–173.

VERBRUGGE, R.R. (1977). Resemblances in language and perception. In: Shaw and Bransford (1977).

VERNON, MCC. (1969). Sociological and psychological factors associated with hearing loss. *J. Speech Hear. Res.* 12, 541–563.

VERNON, MCC. and ANDREWS, J. (1990). *The Psychology of Deafness: Understanding Deaf and Hard-of-Hearing People*. New York: Longman.

VERNON, MCC. and OTTINGER, P.J. (1980). Psychosocial aspects of hearing impairment. In: Schow and Nerbonne (1980).

VOLTERRA, V. and CASELLI, M.C. (1986). First stage of language acquisition through two modalities in deaf and hearing children. *Ital. J. Neurol. Sci. Suppl.* **5**, 109–115.

VOLTERRA, V. and ERTING, C.J. (Eds) (1990). *From Gesture to Language in Hearing and Deaf Children*. Berlin: Springer-Verlag.

WALDEN, B., ERDMAN, S., MONTGOMERY, A., SCHWARTZ, D. and PROSEK, R. (1981). Some effects of training on speech recognition by hearing-impaired adults. *J. Speech Hear. Res.* **24**, 207–216.

WALDEN, B.W. and MONTGOMERY, A.A. (1975). Dimensions of consonant perception in normal and hearing impaired listeners. *J. Speech Hear. Res.* **18**, 444–455.

WALDRON, M.B., DIEBOLD, T.J. and ROSE, S. (1985). Hearing impaired students in regular classrooms: a cognitive model for educational services. *Except. Child.* **52**, 39–43.

WALDSTEIN, R.S. (1990). Effects of postlingual deafness on speech production: implications for the role of auditory feedback. *J. Acoust. Soc. Am.* **88**, 2099–2114.

WALKER, D.W., GRIMWADE, J.C. and WOOD, C. (1971). Intra-uterine noise: a component of the fetal environment. *Am. J. Obstet. Gynec.* **109**, 91–95.

WALKER, G., BYRNE, D. and DILLON, H. (1982). Learning effects with a closed response set nonsense syllable test. *Aust. J. Audiol.* **4**, 27–31.

WALKER, M. (1976). *The Makaton Vocabulary*. London: Royal Association for the Deaf and Dumb.

WALKER, M. and ARMFIELD, A. (1982). What is the Makaton vocabulary? In: Peter and Barnes (1982).

WALKER, M. and BUCKFIELD, P.M. (1983). The Makaton vocabulary. *New Zealand Speech Lang. Ther. J.* **38**, 26–36.

WALLACE, G. and CORBALLIS, M.C. (1973). Short-term memory and coding strategies in the deaf. *J. Exp. Psychol.* **99**, 334–348.

WALLACH, G.P. and BUTLER, K.G. (Eds.) (1984). *Language Learning Disabilities in School-Age Children*. Baltimore, MD: Williams and Wilkins.

WALMSLEY, S. (1983). Writing disability. In: Mosenthal et al. (1983).

WALTZMAN, S., COHEN, N.L., SPIVAK, L., YING, E., BRACKETT, D., SHAPIRO, W. and HOFFMAN, R. (1990). Improvement in speech perception and production abilities in children using a multichannel cochlear implant. *Laryngoscope* **100**, 240–243.

WAMPLER, D. (1971). *Linguistics of Visual English*. Santa Rosa, CA: Early Childhood Education Department, Santa Rosa Schools.

WARREN, C. and HASENSTAB., S. (1986). Self-concept of severely to profoundly hearing-impaired children. *Volta Rev.* **88**, 289–295.

WARREN, R.M. (1970). Perceptual restoration of missing speech sounds. *Science* **167**, 393–395.

WARREN, Y., DANCER, J., MONFILS, B. and PITTENGER, J. (1989). The practice effect in speechreading distributed over five days: same versus different CID sentence lists. *Volta Rev.* **91**, 321–325.

WATKINS, S. (1984). *Long-Term Effects of Home Intervention on Hearing Impaired Children*. Unpublished Doctoral Thesis, Utah State University.

WATSON, B., GOLDGAR, D., KROESE, J. and LOTZ, W. (1986). Nonverbal intelligence and academic achievement in the hearing impaired. *Volta Rev.* **88**, 151–158.

WATSON, B.U. (1991). Some relationships between intelligence and auditory discrimination. *J. Speech Hear. Res.* **34**, 621–627.

WATSON, P. (1979). The utilization of the computer with the hearing impaired and the handicapped. *Am. Ann. Deaf* **124**, 670–680.

WATSON, R. (1985). Towards a theory of definition. *J. Child Lang.* **12**, 181–197.

WATSON, T.J. (1967). *The Education of Hearing-Handicapped Children*. London: University of London Press.

WEBSTER, A. (1986). *Deafness, Development and Literacy*. London: Methuen.

WEBSTER, A. (1988). Deafness and learning to read: theoretical and research issues. *J. Br. Assn. Teachers of the Deaf* **12**, 77–83.

WEBSTER, A., BAMFORD, J.M., THYER, N.J. and AYLES, R. (1989). The psychological, educational and auditory sequelae of early, persistent secretory otitis media. *J. Child Psychol. Psychiat.* **30**, 529–546.

WEBSTER, A. and ELLWOOD, J. (1985). *The Hearing-Impaired Child in the Ordinary School.* London: Croom Helm.

WEBSTER, A., SAUNDERS, E. and BAMFORD, J.M. (1984). Fluctuating conductive hearing impairment. *J. Assn. Educ. Psychol.* **6**, 6–19.

WEBSTER, A., WOOD, D.J. and GRIFFITHS, A.J. (1981). Reading retardation or linguistic deficit? (I): Interpreting reading test performances of hearing-impaired adolescents. *J. Res. Read.* **4**, 136–147.

WEBSTER, D.B. and WEBSTER, M. (1979). Effects of neonatal conductive hearing loss on brainstem auditory nuclei. *Ann. Otol. Rhinol. Laryngol.* **88**, 684–688.

WEBSTER, J.C. (1984). Interlist equivalencies for a numeral and a vowel/consonant multiple-choice monosyllabic test for severely/profoundly deaf young adults. *J. Aud. Res.* **24**, 17–33.

WEDENBERG, E. (1954). Auditory training of severely hard of hearing preschool children. *Acta. Otolaryngol. Stockh. Suppl.* **94**, 1–129.

WEIR, R.H. (1966). Some questions on the child's learning of phonology. In: Smith and Miller (1966).

WEISEL, A. (1988). Parental hearing status, reading comprehension skills and social-emotional adjustment. *Am. Ann. Deaf.* **133**, 356–359.

WEISS, A.L. (1986). Classroom discourse and the hearing-impaired child. *Topics Lang. Disord.* **6**, 60–70.

WEISS, A.L., CARNEY, A.E. and LEONARD, L.B. (1985). Perceived contrastive stress production in hearing-impaired and normal-hearing children. *J. Speech Hear. Res.* **28**, 26–35.

WEISS, K., GOODWIN, M. and MOORES, D. (1975). *Evaluation of Programs for Hearing Impaired Children, University of Minnesota, MN: Research Report 91.* University of Minnesota, MN: Research, Development and Demonstration Center in Education of Handicapped Children.

WELLS, C.G. (1981). *Learning Through Interaction: The Study of Language Development.* Cambridge: Cambridge University Press.

WELLS, G. (1979). Variation in child language. In: Fletcher and Garman (1979).

WELSH, L.W., WELSH, J.J. and HEALY, M.P. (1983). Effect of sound deprivation on central hearing. *Laryngoscope* **93**, 1569–1575.

WELLS, G. (1984). *Language Development in the Pre-School Years.* Cambridge: Cambridge University Press.

WEPMAN, J. (1958). *Auditory Discrimination Test.* Los Angeles, CA: Western Psychological Services.

WEPMAN, J. (1960). Auditory discrimination, speech and reading. *Element. Sch. J.* **60**, 325–333.

WEPMAN, J. (1975). *Auditory Discrimination Test.* Palm Springs, FL: Language Research Associates.

WERKER, J.F. and TEES, R.C. (1984). Cross language perception: evidence for perceptual reorganisation during the first year of life. *Infant Behav. Devel.* **7**, 49–63.

WEST, J.J. and WEBER, J.L. (1973). A phonological analysis of the spontaneous language of a four-year-old hard-of-hearing child. *J. Speech Hear. Disord.* **38**, 25–35.

WEST, J.J. and WEBER, J.L. (1974). A linguistic analysis of the morphemic and syntactic structures of a hard-of-hearing child. *Lang. Speech* **17**, 68–79.

WESTBY, C.E. (1984). Development of narrative language abilities. In: Wallach and Butler (1984).

WHETNALL, E. and FRY, D.B. (1964). *The Deaf Child.* London: Heinemann.

WHITE, A. (1990). Differences in teacher expectations. *Volta Rev.* **92**, 131–144.

WHITE, A.H. and STEVENSON, V.M. (1975). The effects of total communication, manual communication, oral communication and reading on the learning of factual information in residential school deaf children. *Am. Ann. Deaf* **120**, 48–57.

WHITE, S. and WHITE, R. (1987). The effects of hearing status of the family and age of intervention on reception and expressive oral language skills in hearing-impaired infants. In: Levitt et al. (1987b).

WHITEHEAD, R. (1987). Fundamental vocal frequency characteristics of hearing-impaired young adults. *Volta Rev.* **89**, 7–15.

WHITEHEAD, R. and BAREFOOT, S. (1980). Some aerodynamic characteristics of plosive consonants produced by hearing-impaired speakers. *Am. Ann. Deaf* **125**, 366–373.

WHITEHEAD, R.L. (1991). Stop consonant closure durations for normal-hearing and hearing-impaired speakers. *Volta Rev.* **93**, 145–153.

WHORF, B.L. (1956). *Language, Thought and Reality: Selected Writings of Benjamin Lee Whorf* (edited by J.B. Carroll). Cambridge, MA: MIT Press.

WICKHAM, C. and KYLE, J. (1987). Teachers' beliefs about BSL and their perceptions of children's signing. In: Kyle (1987).

WIEGERSMA, P.H. and VAN DER VELDE, A. (1983). Motor development of deaf children. *J. Child Psychol. Psychiat.* **24**, 103–111.

WIGHTMAN, F.L. (1981). Pitch perception: an example of auditory pattern recognition. In: Getty and Howard (1981).

WIGHTMAN, F., MCGEE, T. and KRAMER, M. (1977). Factors influencing frequency selectivity in normal and hearing-impaired listeners. In: Evans (1977).

WIIG, E.H. and SEMEL, E. (1984). *Language Assessment and Intervention for the Learning Disabled*. Columbus, OH: Charles E. Merrill.

WILBERS, S. (1988). Why America needs deaf culture: cultural pluralism and the liberal arts tradition. *Sign Lang. Stud.* **59**, 195–204.

WILBUR, R. (1977). An explanation of deaf children's difficulty with certain syntactic structures in English. *Volta Rev.* **79**, 85–92.

WILBUR, R.B. (1979). *American Sign Language and Sign Systems*. Baltimore, MD: University Park Press.

WILBUR, R.B. (1987). *American Sign Language: Linguistics and Applied Dimensions*. Boston, MA: College Hill Press.

WILCOX, B. (1969). Visual preferences of human infants for representations of the human face. *J. Exp. Child Psychol.* **7**, 10–20.

WILCOX, J. and TOBIN, H. (1974). Linguistic performance of hard-of-hearing and normal-hearing children. *J. Speech Hear. Res.* **17**, 288–293.

WILCOX, S. (1988). Introduction: academic acceptance of American Sign Language. *Sign Lang. Stud.* **59**, 101–108.

WILCOX, S. (1990). The structure of signed and spoken languages. *Sign Lang. Stud.* **67**, 141–151.

WILLIAMS, A. (1982). The relationship between two visual communication systems: reading and lipreading. *J. Speech Hear. Res.* **25**, 500–503.

WILLIAMS, C.E. (1970). Some psychiatric observations on a group of maladjusted deaf children. *J. Child Psychol. Psychiat.* **11**, 1–18.

WILLIAMS, D.M.L. and DARBYSHIRE, J.O. (1982). Diagnosis of deafness: a study of family responses and needs. *Volta Rev.* **84**, 24–30.

WILLIAMS, E. (1986). A use of LARSP in secondary units of hearing-impaired pupils. *Child Lang. Teach. Ther.* **2**, 154–169.

WILLIAMS, J.E. and DENNIS, D. B. (1979). A partially hearing unit. In: Crystal (1979).

WILLIAMS, J.S. (1976). Bilingual experiences of a deaf child. *Sign Lang. Stud.* **15**, 37–41.

WILSON, B.A., BADDELEY, A.D. and COCKBURN, J.M. (1989). How do old dogs learn new tricks: teaching a technological skill to brain injured people. *Cortex* **25**, 115–119.

WILSON, B.S., FINLEY, C.C., FARMER, J.C., LAWSON, D.T., WEBER, B.A., WOLFORD, R.D., KENAN, P.D., WHITE, M.W., MERZENICH, M.M. and SCHINDLER, R.A. (1988). Comparative studies of speech processing strategies for cochlear implants. *Laryngoscope* **98**, 1069–1077.

WITELSON, S.F. (1982). Hemisphere specialization from birth. *Int. J. Neurosci.* **17**, 54–55.

WITELSON, S.F. (1985). On hemisphere specialization and cerebral plasticity from birth: Mark II. In: Best (1985).

WITELSON, S.F. (1987). Neurobiological aspects of language in children. *Child Devel.* **58**, 653–688.

WITELSON, S. and PAILLIE, W. (1973). Left hemisphere for specialisation in the newborn. *Brain* **96**, 641–646.

WOLF, M. (1984). Naming, reading and the dyslexias: a longitudinal overview. *Ann. Dyslexia* **34**, 87–115.

WOLFF, A.B. (1985). Analysis. In: Martin (1985).

WOLFF, J.G. (1973). *Language, Brain and Hearing: An Introduction to the Psychology of Language with a Section on Deaf Children's Learning of Language.* London: Methuen.

WOLFF, S. (1977). Cognitive and communication patterns in classrooms for deaf students. *Am. Ann. Deaf* **122**, 319–327.

WOLFLE, D. (1951). Training. In: Stevens (1951).

WOLK, S. and SCHILDROTH, A. (1984). Consistency of an associational strategy used on reading comprehension tests by hearing impaired students. *J. Res. Read.* **7**, 135–142.

WOLL, B., KYLE, J. and DEUCHAR, M. (Eds) (1981). *Perspectives on British Sign Language.* London: Croom Helm.

WOOD, D. (1991). Communication and cognition: how the communication styles of hearing adults may hinder – rather than help – deaf learners. *Am. Ann. Deaf* **136**, 247–251.

WOOD, D.J. (1980). Teaching the young child: some relationships between social interaction, language and thought. In: Olson (1980).

WOOD, D.J., GRIFFITHS, A.J. and WEBSTER, A. (1981). Reading retardation or linguistic deficit? (II): Test-answering strategies in hearing and hearing-impaired school children. *J. Res. Read.* **4**, 148–156.

WOOD, D.J., WOOD, H.A., GRIFFITHS, A.J., HOWARTH, S.P. and HOWARTH, C.I. (1982). The structure of conversations with 6-to-10-year old deaf children. *J. Child Psychol. Psychiat.* **23**, 295–308.

WOOD, D., WOOD, H., GRIFFITHS, A. and HOWARTH, I. (1986). *Teaching and Talking with Deaf Children.* Chichester, Sussex: Wiley.

WOODCOCK, R.W. (1973). *Woodcock Reading Mastery Tests.* Circle Pines, MN: American Guidance Service.

WOODS, B.T. and CAREY, S. (1979). Language deficits after apparent clinical recovery from childhood aphasia. *Ann. Neurol.* **6**, 405–409.

WOODWARD, J. and ALLEN, T. (1987). Classroom use of ASL by teachers. *Sign Lang. Stud.* **54**, 1–10.

WRIGHTSTONE, J.W., ARONOW, M.S. and MOSKOWITZ, S. (1963). Developing reading test norms for deaf children. *Am. Ann. Deaf* **108**, 311–316.

YENI-KOMISHIAN, G.H., KAVANAGH, J.F. and FERGUSON, C.A. (Eds) (1980). *Child Phonology*, Vol. 2., *Perception.* New York: Academic Press.

YOSHINAGA-ITANO, C. (1986). Beyond the sentence level: what's in a hearing-impaired child's story? *Topics Lang. Disord.* **6**, 71–83.

YOSHINAGA-ITANO, C. and SNYDER, L. (1985). Form and meaning in the written language of hearing-impaired children. *Volta Rev.* **87**, 75–90.

ZAIDEL, E. (1980). Clues from hemispheric specialization. In: Bellugi and Studdert-Kennedy (1980).

ZAJONC, R.B. (1960). The process of cognitive timing communication. *J. Abnorm. Soc. Psychol.* **61**, 159–167.

ZORFASS, J.M. (1981). Metalinguistic awareness in young deaf children: a preliminary study. *Appl. Psycholing.* **2**, 333–352.

ZWIEBEL, A. (1987). More on the effects of early manual communication on the cognitive development of deaf children. *Am. Ann. Deaf* **132**, 16–20.

Index

Date Due

23-236 PRINTED IN U.S.A.

Jessie White Mario

Jessie White Mario
RISORGIMENTO REVOLUTIONARY

By

Elizabeth Adams Daniels

Ohio
University
Press
ATHENS

To Helen Drusilla Lockwood 1891-1971

Contents

Preface

Whenever I have mentioned to anyone that I was writing a book about Jessie White Mario, the inevitable first question has been, "Who in the world is she?" I had never heard of her either until I discovered her while looking into the background of one of George Meredith's little-known novels, *Vittoria*. In this novel Meredith describes the trials and tribulations of an Englishwoman, turned Italian, who has committed herself to the "cause" of Mazzini, founder of the Young Italy movement. Not only does Meredith draw heavily on the actual events of the Five Days of Milan, one of the early insurrections of the Risorgimento, but he also works from living European and English models in his portraitures of the 110 or so characters in the book. The prototype of the heroine, I found, is partially traceable to the women of the Friends of Italy Society circle in England. Although Vittoria, Meredith's heroine, is modeled on no one woman in particular, her enthusiasms for the "Chief" and the dedication of her life to Italian freedom could be found in several English Italophiles of radical inclination during the Victorian period. Meredith wrote *Vittoria* in 1864-66 and discussed its details in 1864 with his English friend, Madame Emilia Ashurst Venturi, whom he knew as the translator of Mazzini's works into English. His book does not undertake to present the accurate biographical details of the lives of Emilia Venturi or of Caroline Stansfeld, her sister and the wife of a Liberal member of Parliament. Nor does it recount the life of Jessie White, their fellow enthusiast, who first became interested in the possibility of revolution in Italy when she was studying with an English clergyman in Birmingham. But Meredith observed that a great idea had captured the minds of the Englishwomen of this circle; and he was interested in exploring

1

the conduct of the new political woman in his historical romance. The novel is fourth-rate; but the lives of certain of the principals who were working for the Italian cause are extremely interesting, and they constitute my subject. No one had studied the activities of these Englishwomen as a group; I planned to do just that when I began my research, but I found that there was so much to be done on the most versatile of these feminists, Jessie White Mario, that the more general book is still to be written.

Luckily most of the papers of Jessie White Mario came into the possession of the Italian government after her death in 1906, for she was a relentless collector, saving everything she could acquire to preserve the record of the Risorgimento. In addition to the vast archival collection now stored at the Museo Centrale del Risorgimento in Rome, Jessie White Mario left fifteen or so books, many newspaper reports, and hundreds of magazine articles as her response to the Risorgimento. Mazzini's edited papers, running to more than ninety volumes, include a twenty-five year correspondence with her, and papers in the Public Records Office in London and the Cowen Collection in Newcastle-upon-Tyne yield the English and Italian governments' versions of her espionage and propagandistic activities.

Jessie White Mario was a woman of many parts. I have written a book about her because I found her irresistible. Encouraged to be herself by a dissenting businessman father, she broke out of the conventional middle-class behavior while still an adolescent and thereafter never ceased to find new and creative uses for her energy. From the age of twenty she wrote for a living. Her earliest stories and essays dealt with working people in England and France. But as she became more actively engaged in the unification of Italy, the drama of the Risorgimento became her dominant theme. First Mazzini's propagandist in a losing cause, then Garibaldi's field nurse during his four Italian campaigns, later a peripatetic observer of the new Italy, she still had her pen in her hand when she died in Florence at the age of seventy-four.

As a correspondent for the American periodical, the *Nation*, from 1866 to 1906, Jessie offered her readers a far-ranging description of developments in Italy. Benedetto Croce, in his *History of Italy, 1871-1915* (translated by Cecilia Ady [London: Oxford University Press, 1929], pp. 100-101, the translator of which assumed that J. White Mario, author of a book on Dr. Agostino Bertani, was a man) mentions her as trying to dispel offenses against truth about Italy by the light of her common sense and elementary justice. To Americans of our own time, Jessie's articles for the *Nation* are intriguing not only for what they say about Italy but for what they imply about the range of interest of nineteenth-century subscribers to that periodical. For forty years the readers of the *Nation* followed Jessie's accounts of political, social and cultural developments in this distant European country. (A chronological listing of Jessie's articles for the *Nation* and annotated abstracts of their contents will be found in Appendix 3.)

I take this opportunity to thank all of those people and institutions that have made it possible for me to complete this work. I am indebted to the trustees of Vassar College who awarded me three semesters of fellowships to pursue my research and writing. Twice I enjoyed for lengthy periods the courtesies extended by Professor Emilia Morelli and her staff at the Museo Centrale del Risorgimento, Rome, where I was given access to the Archivio Jessie White Mario, consisting of various *buste* of raw material. Professor Morelli herself was kind enough to encourage me to think that I was suited to write this book and has been a helpful critic of the manuscript in its later stages. She made several valuable suggestions that rescued me in matters pertaining to Risorgimento history. I owe special thanks also to Professor Salvatore Saladino of Queens College, New York, whose close reading of my text proved most helpful, and to Luigi Sera, Assistant Professor of Italian at Vassar College, who patiently worked with me over difficult translations.

The following libraries courteously extended to me the privilege of using their resources, including in several cases, unpublished materials: The Widener Library and the Houghton Library, Harvard University; the Colindale Branch of the British Museum, and the British Museum Reading Room; the Risorgimento Archives in Milan; the Yale University Library; the New York Public Library; the Central Library of Newcastle-upon-Tyne, England; the Birmingham Public Library, England; the Public Records Office at Salisbury, England; the Public Records Office at Somerset House, London; and the Vassar College Library. Special acknowledgment is made to Harvard College Library for permission to publish a letter from Jessie White Mario to James Russell Lowell, and John Murray Publishers, Ltd., for permission to quote from Elizabeth Barrett Browning's *Letters to her Sister, 1846-1859* and Jane Welsh Carlyle's *Letters to her Family, 1839-1863*.

At various stages this book was read by Vassar colleagues: the late Helen D. Lockwood, Josephine Gleason, Jeane H. Geehr, and I have profited from their suggestions. I received helpful advice also from Mr. Noel Blakiston, formerly director of the Public Records Office—himself a student of Jessie's espionage activities—and from Professor Harry Hearder of the University of South Wales. Two student assistants, Sarah Plotz and Deirdre Henderson, aided me in early phases of my research. Delma Vander Veer arranged the index, and Mario Lovergine designed the book and jacket. Throughout the several years that I have worked on the book I have enjoyed the encouragement of my husband John and of my children, as well as of my colleagues. Finally, I would especially like to thank Fannia Weingartner and Susan Schulman for their unfailing insight and editorial help.

Prelude:
A Visit to Garibaldi

In the autumn of 1854 a rich middle-aged English widow named Emma Roberts set out on a romantic quest to Avignon, Nice, and Sardinia. She had taken seriously a passing flirtation with the Italian revolutionary, Giuseppe Garibaldi, whom she had recently met at a reception in England as he was returning to Nice from a four-year exile spent in Staten Island, South America, and as a member of a ship's crew. Upon meeting Mrs. Roberts, Garibaldi quite characteristically had led her to believe that he was infatuated with her. Considering herself engaged, Mrs. Roberts had offered to visit him at his hunting lodge on the island of Sardinia, since he was forbidden to set foot on the mainland of Italy because of his participation in the establishment of the short-lived Roman Republic in 1849.

A young Englishwoman of twenty-two studying in France accepted Emma Roberts's invitation to join her as she passed through Paris on her way by land to the south. This young woman was Jessie White, who for the preceding year or so had been studying radical philosophy and attending lectures at the Sorbonne. She jumped at the chance to see Italy, which she had known only at second hand until now. The opportunity to meet Garibaldi and to explore for herself the country which had increasingly absorbed her thoughts was irresistible.

Jessie White had by then lived in Paris long enough to be well aware of the forces that were stirring all over the Continent in the aftermath of the revolutions of 1848. Under the aegis of Victor Cousin, the head of the Sorbonne, to whom she had been recommended as a student by her previous teachers in Birmingham and London, she had become friendly with some of the leading Parisian liberals. She had lived in a *pension* with her sister Lou, and supported herself by writing articles and stories with French contemporary backgrounds for English magazines, and by teaching.

As a student of the liberal philosophers, Jessie had been directly exposed to the mainstream of revolutionary thought current during the years of the Second French Republic (1848-52) and the first two years of the Second Empire (1852-54). After 1849, she had listened to speculations about the failure of the Roman Republic. She had noted the irony of the suppression of this Mazzinian enterprise by the republican French army under General Oudinot, acting on orders from Louis Napoleon, the President of France.* She had begun to understand the intricacies of practical politics as she observed Louis Napoleon's abandonment of his Carbonarist sympathies under pressure from the French Catholics.

Her participation in Parisian life was deepened by daily association with the people who had played a part in the development of radicalism in the years after the Napoleonic Wars. She had met the Abbé Felicité de Lammenais, then an old man, who was thoroughly disillusioned by Louis Napoleon's capitulation and who, in his disgust with politics, had turned to literary criticism. In these last years before his death (on February 27, 1854) he was occupied with the translation of Dante's works into French, but he had not shed the traces of his earlier involvement in democratic politics and the movement towards the Left. He had been much engaged by a desire to free the French church from the papacy and after a period as an initiate in the priesthood, he had severed his connections with organized religion. As Pope Gregory XVI noted in the encyclical letter excommunicating Lammenais, he had written "a book small in size, but immense in its perversity." While president of the *Societé de la Solidarité Republicaine* he had started two radical journals (*Peuple-Constituent* and *Revolution democratique et sociale*). Jessie wrote a long appreciation of his life as he had recounted it to her and as she had observed it. This she published in *Biographical Magazine*.[1] At this time Jessie also knew well the historian Henri Martin, later in 1856 the Academy prizewinner for his earlier distinguished *History of France*, and Pierre Jean de Béranger, the socialist, who wrote patriotic songs and had served as a member of the Constituent Assembly in 1848. Her study with Victor Cousin himself brought her into the presence of an important influence on French philosophy of the nineteenth century. Since his release from imprisonment as a Carbonarist in Dresden in

* Louis Napoleon, a nephew of Napoleon Bonaparte, had espoused Carbonarist principles in his youth but became increasingly conservative as he saw the possibility of achieving political power. Elected president of the Second Republic in 1848, he made himself emperor in 1852, taking the name of Napoleon III.

1824, he had promulgated his views as titular head of the Sorbonne where his lectures were annual drawing cards. In his so-called philosophy of eclecticism, he was attempting to give new impetus to the teaching of the history of philosophy.

The general bent of Jessie's thought, however, was already clearly established as practical rather than speculative. She recognized that she was no scholar. Although she had gone to Paris to study philosophy, she was convinced after two years that she did not have the mind for it. She knew that her own intellectual preoccupations were superficial, ranging and facile, rather than profound. Accordingly, she felt a strong desire to begin to do some good rather than just to think about it. She had been trained by teachers committed to the cause of social reform. For years she had been prodded and challenged to develop her own sense of social responsibility. Much like students in our own time, she felt restless and useless in the role of student and observer and recognized in herself a penchant for engaging in more meaningful activity.

It was natural that when the opportunity to go to Italy presented itself, she would seize it as a touchstone. On all sides and for several years she had heard of the growing crisis in Italy. Her father's business as a loading-dock builder in Portsmouth took him frequently to Italy and Spain, and although she did not go along with him, she found much to interest her in his observations. Her childhood teachers, George Dawson and John Daniel Morell and their friends, had exposed her to the writings and ideas of Giuseppe Mazzini, who had been in exile in England since 1832.[*] Dawson and his associates in Birmingham had not only followed the uprisings of 1848 closely, but had taken practical steps to interest the English in republican politics and the possibility that a people's revolution might yet succeed in western Europe. He had whetted Jessie White's curiosity about Italian affairs and under the influence of his views she was prepared to love republicans and to hate the pope. But so far her acquaintance both with Italy and revolution had all been through hearsay.

Garibaldi had lingered in England early in 1854 just long enough to make arrangements for his return to his estate in Sardinia.[2] After his visit, Jessie in some way heard of Mrs. Roberts's projected trip— perhaps she was or had been her daughter's governess—and was asked to join the expedition as the Roberts's party left Paris in the fall of 1854. The women traveled through Touraine to Avignon—where they looked for the tomb of Petrarch's Laura—and after a fortnight

[*] See chapter 2.

arrived at their first stop, the Maison Garibaldi in Nice* on October 17, 1854. Jessie wrote of this trip:†

In the autumn of 1854 I accepted an invitation from the lady who was betrothed to Garibaldi to accompany her and her daughter on an Italian tour. This was the realization of a life-dream, and I not only made the acquaintance of the great General, but saw face to face many of the noble patriots whose names, since 1848, had been household words to me. I had read most of Mazzini's works, and in Paris I had known many Liberals—especially Cousin, the devoted friend of Santorre Santarosa, the Italian hero of Greek independence—who had imbued me with their reverence for Mazzini and their sense of shame at the part played by France in the destruction of the Roman Republic. These men were Constitutionalists, and expected more from the plucky little kingdom of Piedmont than from any popular uprising having for aim the proclamation of an Italian republic. It is worthy of note that this view was rapidly becoming general, even Daniele Manin,‡ who lived in Paris in extreme, though honoured, poverty, subscribing to it. In Nice, also, we found that the refugees from Naples, Modena, and Sicily, with the sole exception of Dr. Paolo Fabrizi, brother of Niccola, declared that nothing could be attempted in the way of insurrection until the part that Austria intended playing in the Oriental§ drama should be known. But in Sardinia, where we went with Garibaldi for a month, the young men thronging 'round him did not seem to share his opinions about the advisability of abstaining from action till they should see which way the wind blew. These young men— almost all ex-officers who had served under him in Rome—were also worshippers of Mazzini, whom they considered their spiritual father, and, moreover, with few exceptions, they were all in banishment from the mainland States of Piedmont, sent to Sardinia by the inexorable Cavour [prime minister of Piedmont-Sardinia], who had taken no pains to ascertain whether they had, or had not, been accomplices of the Milanese revolutionists, but who had expelled them as Republicans, as writers in the *Italia del Popolo*, or as individuals who, not having demanded Piedmontese citizenship, possessed absolutely no rights.

Sardinia is a delightful resort for a month's shooting, especially when the grandees of the island organize boarhunts, as they did for Garibaldi, with their retainers all in native costume; but as an all-the-year-round residence, the prevalence of malarial fever gives it another character, and none but those utterly destitute or compelled by the pressure of insurmountable circumstances would think of remaining there.[3]

* At that time part of the kingdom of Piedmont-Sardinia.

† Amplification of many of Jessie's allusions to various personalities and events in this letter will be found in chapter 2.

‡ Daniele Manin (1804-1857) led the Venetian uprising of 1848, but later became a supporter of Cavour's policy of constitutionalism (see chapter 2).

§ An odd choice of adjective—she is referring to relations with Russia and Turkey.

A spontaneous exclamation penned in her notebook while she was in Nice, speaks for her state of mind at the time: "Hail rain thunder howling round our new abode yet strangely enough never place felt more like home to me. . . . Is it true that after the weary hopeless toil and dissatisfaction and lonliness* of the last months a time of rest and peace & intercourse with loved ones is setting in for me? My precious friend—ah thou who knowest the wild depths of love walking in my heart let some of it avail for her† in strength and health and a change of melancholy for cheerfulness."[4]

Once Jessie's initial delirium of excitement at being in Italy had subsided, she set out to become acquainted with the Italian people. After a six-week sojourn with Garibaldi, Jessie and Emma Roberts were given letters of introduction to some of his friends in other parts of Italy from which, of course, Garibaldi himself was barred. Jessie noted that on all sides the attitudes of the Italians were "sullen or, after they felt they could trust us, passionately hostile to Austria, the Pope, the Cardinals, France, and their Dukes." The travelers went first to Florence in Tuscany where they were cordially received by their hosts, the Brownings. "All the people we met—chiefly at their house—were admirers of Piedmont, believing that the young King‡ would wipe out the stain of Novara: they thought that, once the Austrians should be turned out of Lombardy, the Tuscans would easily 'settle things with their Grand Duke.'"[5] They heard tales of the exploits of Felice Orsini,§ who while the visitors were in Italy, attempted to cause an insurrection in the province of Venetia.

Mrs. Browning was an admirer of Cavour,‖ who had been invited to form a new cabinet in Piedmont in November, 1852, and whose administration would eventually effect change through constitutional means. Her husband Robert was "sceptical" of political movements; their young son was already a "fierce Republican, an Austrian-and-French-hater." The Englishwomen heard about the death by shipwreck near the American coast of Margaret Fuller Ossoli, the American journalist who, with her Italian husband, had been active in the Roman Republic of 1849. In Rome, which they reached by Eastertime 1855, they encountered some members of the "international" set. Jessie met Barbara Leigh Smith whom she liked, and subsequently was introduced to the artistic circle of Hatty Hosmer. The artists and aes-

---

* Throughout the book the quotes from Jessie's works are reproduced as in the original, spelling mistakes and all.
† The reference is to herself—she was apparently smitten with Garibaldi.
‡ Victor Emmanuel II (1849-1878) of Piedmont-Sardinia. His father Charles Albert had abdicated in his favor in 1849 after a whopping defeat by the Austrians at Novara.
§ Felice Orsini (1819-1858) was for most of his career one of Mazzini's active followers. In 1858 he made an attempt on the life of Napoleon III for which he was executed on March 13, 1858.
‖ See chapter 2.

thetes of this group irritated Jessie in their imperviousness to political questions. She felt that they looked at Rome as the "exclusive heritage of art and artists," and to her that attitude seemed utterly false, inexcusable, and narrow. Jessie and her companions were lucky enough to see at least "one true Roman" who took them around the theatre of the Roman siege of 1849 and told them of the details of the recent holocaust as Republicans battled French. "So we mentally reenacted the entire tragedy in reverence and awe for that heroic defence." In the nearby countryside they encountered an Italian peasant who, Jessie said, whispered to them a prediction and prayer for Garibaldi: "He will return . . . he must return to free us from the assassins. . . . Bid him come quickly! . . . we are weary . . . so weary!"[6]

In April the women returned to Nice, and then in May, to England. At the Maison Garibaldi Jessie breathed out a farewell to the beautiful country and its hero. Both were now hers: "Here me my love my half soul I love thee thy country—is mine. thy country's—my only—. I *will* return."[7] She promptly set about making her plans to do so.

PART ONE
POSSESSED BY THE ANGEL

1

Jessie Meriton White grew up in a house which faced the sea on the Forton Inlet near Portsmouth, England. The many White kinsfolk who, like the generations before them, had always supported themselves by the craft of naval architecture, lived close by in the sea-bordered hamlets contiguous to Portsmouth—Gosport, Forton, and Alverstoke. Since the 17th century these "simple folk" had handed down their art "without theory and probably with as little knowledge of the science of forces or the principles of construction as the rest of their carpenter contemporaries."[1] The firm of John White and Son, owned by Jessie's grandfather and inherited by his sons, was well known in the 1820s, having prospered except for a brief decline during the post-Napoleonic era. When Jessie's father, Thomas White, took over the firm, it was engaged in both domestic and overseas trade, having expanded its activities of custom designing and building racing boats as well as simpler ships, to include the design, construction, and installation of loading slips in continental ports, particularly in Italy and Portugal.

Thomas White's personality, influenced by the combination of a straitlaced upbringing and a broadening profession, was an interesting amalgam of urbanity and rigidity. As a boy, he had been sent by his parents to a grammar school in Northhampton, where it was supposed that he might prepare himself for higher education. He worked diligently and headed his class until the age of fourteen, when the hostility of his Latin master led to friction and eventual academic failure. His family, unwilling to give him a second chance—unreasonably, he thought—forced him to drop out of school and return home as a shipbuilder's apprentice. Tom never forgave his father for this

13

drastic interruption of his schooling, and vowed that his own children would fare better. Throughout his childhood, he had been persistently subjected to his family's narrow views on religion. His mother's father, Stephen Peake, had founded the settlement of the Dissenting Church located in Ramsgate, and his own father had given young Tom sixpence for every one of Watts's hymns that he could repeat verbatim on Sunday.[2] It is perhaps not surprising, therefore, that following his departure from school, Tom became a religious zealot.

After a few years Thomas White decided to become a businessman in his own right. He began his own branch of the ship building firm in Gosport, and shortly afterwards married a young woman whom he had met in the household of the proselytizing missionary preacher, a Doctor Bogue, whose church he had joined. By 1825 he and his wife Elizabeth had produced a family of three boys and a girl.[3] Elizabeth died in 1826, and Thomas was remarried in 1827 to Jane Teage Meriton,* a woman of American descent, but a resident, with her widowed mother and brother's children, of Botley, a little village near Gosport.[4] Thomas's second wife at first had seemed reluctant to take on the responsibilities of becoming a stepmother, but she was prevailed upon by the handsome and appealing young widower.[5] Unlike him, she was little interested either in ecclesiastical affairs or in theological refinements, but was a woman of practical vision, who had taken a lead in the development of the Sunday School movement as an effective form of public education. She undertook to mother Tom's family and for the six years that remained to her, during which she bore four children of her own—two of whom died—she worked very hard to fulfill her responsibilities to all the White children. Jessie was born on May 9, 1832, two years before her mother's death.†

Jane White's desire to obtain good schooling for the children in her community bore fruit. She attended an annual examination of schools at Portsea and determined to acquire the same kind of examination for Gosport so that students whose parents could afford it could participate.[6] When by chance she communicated her desire to the local surgeon, he told her that the woman who had conducted the very

---

* Jane Teage Meriton's family came from New Orleans where they had owned vast lands on which the city was founded. Her uncle, Thomas Leader Harmon, who had freed his slaves in the early twenties, had been a member of the legislative council for the Territory of New Orleans and was an influential citizen. We do not know by what sequence of events Jessie's mother happened to be in England, or why Thomas' daughter Charlotte should have been sent to be educated with her English relatives except that presumably her mother was dead. Charlotte later married William Eaton, Lord Cheylesmore, who was a silk merchant engaged in the China trade. Sir Joshua Reynolds painted Mrs. Meriton.

† Another daughter Jessie White, an earlier offspring of this union, died in infancy of croup, before Jessie Meriton White was born and given the same name.

school in which she had witnessed the examination was thinking of resigning. Mrs. White followed this up and "settled everything at once," employing Jane Gain—the schoolmistress in question—as director of a school at Gosport. The White children who were old enough to begin their formal studies were subsequently sent there and Mrs. White continued to take an interest in the school, visiting it daily and encouraging the schoolmistress, a supporter of the Pestalozzi method, to experiment in her handling of the children's needs. Jane Gain was the recipient of Mrs. White's confidences and anxieties about the education of the White children. This must have placed her in good stead when shortly after Mrs. White's death, she became Thomas White's third wife. Jessie was two at the time, so that it was Jane Gain who actually reared her.[7]

We may speculate about various aspects of Jessie's childhood from the rare but penetrating glimpses provided in her fragmentary unpublished memoirs.[8] The influence of the father was pervasive in the household. His narrow Puritanism dominated his family's domestic routines. There were daily prayers, both familial and personal, daily collective Bible readings, church services to be attended several times a week, and incessant interrogations by the father as to the state of preparation of the children's souls for the life hereafter. Even Jane Meriton had been uneasy under her husband's unbending scrutiny, professing that she could not possibly bring herself to worry about her soul. This careless attitude on a matter of such importance caused her husband some concern. Fred—Thomas White's son by his second wife, and thus Jessie's true brother—became something of a religious fanatic in his adolescence, a state of affairs which pleased his father; but Jessie, rebellious and agnostic even from childhood, considered herself "depraved" and knew that she had no desire to be saved. She argued almost every day of her childhood with her father and brother and wrote analyses of the inconsistencies in the Puritan dogma which plagued her. Her father dealt with her patiently and heard her out, but he puzzled increasingly over her agnosticism. She wrote in her scratch book:

> To my father I tried once or twice to get explanations in the early morning when he was always up with the dawn and pleased with me for being an early bird. Would let me light the fire laid overnight and make the tea but he only said that all God did must be right and as I grew older I should understand better the ways of Providence. Freddy with whom I wished to try and have it out couldn't help me much either but agreed that it was mean not to share and share alike with your mothers and sisters that it was wicked to lie and worse to deceive.[9]

Jessie increasingly detested this ascetic regime of the household. She frankly hated Sunday and all that went with it, and often expressed a wish to be like her friend Billy, the Catholic yardboy who did not seem to be plagued about the state of his soul at all.[10] She found the endless sermons and moralizing lessons tedious and almost daily freshly rejected her father's single-minded concentration on the goal of getting into heaven. "I realized" she wrote, "that the Sabbath there which ne'er shall end would be spent in singing hymns, in the company of the good children who had died early and left last death bed utterances for the conversion of survivors, and of winged angels gazing upon the face of God, but it did not increase my desire to go to Heaven."[11] Her substantial doses of Bible reading were relentlessly administered by her father as regularly as physic, and once she was "delivered," it was many years before she opened an English Bible save on compulsion. (In her later years, though, she added, "Now . . . with Shakespeare and Mazzini it is the book I read oftenest.")

She persistently questioned her father's pious ethics. At the age of twelve or so, musing on the story of Cain and Abel, she wrote:

> Abel was a keeper of sheep but Cain was a tiller of the ground. And in process of time it came to fall that Cain brought of the fruit of the ground an offering unto the Lord And Abel he also brought of the firstlings of the flock and of the fat thereof and the Lord had respect unto Abel and to his offering But unto Cain he had not respect And Cain was very wroth and his countenance fell Naturally enough— Why did the Lord not respect his offering—Because he preferred roast lamb to green vegetables was the only explanation I could find. Then I used to wonder what happened in that field when Cain talked with Abel—probably the later crowed over him until he got into a passion and hit out—the moral lesson lay there in not being able to keep your temper and the awful consequence? It might lead even to killing your own mother As for Jacob he was a mean lot altogether a most wicked woman see the story revolted me the lie when his father asked him how he had found the venison so quickly and he answered Because the Lord thy God brought it to me—The Esaus home coming and the exceeding bitter cry of his entreaty Bless me even also oh my father—why didn't Isaac revoke his blessing and punish Jacob for his deceit—Why say I have blessed Jacob yea and he shall be blessed why condemn Esau to serve his deceitful brother—only—but sword and tell him that when he should have the dominion he should break his yoke from his neck If he had killed Esau it would have been his father's fault—then even the Lord was not wroth with him but promised to be with Esau although that in his seed all the families of the earth should be blessed.[12]

In her childhood reading of "profane literature" Jessie indeed found ample confirmation of the same selfish ethic which she discovered in her interpretation of the stories of the Bible. Among the "fairy stories which dear little Miss Pearce" told her, "Jack in the beanstalk confirmed (in its highly immoral proceedings of killing giant and living on ill gotten gains with his mother) the biblical teachings that the bad ones got the best of it. What a hash the moderns have made of these delightful incongruities."[13]

In spite of the family's Puritan morality, Jessie nevertheless spoke of her childhood as "bright" and of herself as "free." She was a mischievous girl who constantly provoked the disapproval of adults, and had the reputation of not being sufficiently ladylike or obedient. With her brother Harry, the second son of her father's first marriage, she romped and tossed about in boys' games. "My delight was to be on the lake, where he would row me in a boat," she said. "Sunshine, salt water and the lake at high tide were pure joy, but the lake at low tide was to be avoided, being all mud and nastiness to eye and nose." Harry took her to the duckpond where she more than once fell in. He fed her candies, which she was expressly forbidden as she herself was thought to be delicate and "croupish." Her nurse Sarah taught her to read and study. The nurse was a "superior person" in Jessie's judgment, but she was sent away because she spoiled Jessie.

When the time came, Jessie went into a schoolroom presided over by a governess whom she detested. By then Harry had gone off to sea, her next brother was absent, and her older sister Eliza, who was "born good, always was good, and did good according to her lights all the days of her life" afforded a painful contrast in behavior to Jessie. Jessie wrote of the developing friction:

> The last violent scene that I remember was when Momma who for the time was tching me and owing to her numerous duties accumulated the lessons so that one day I had to repeat them all I did forget one and it was nasty LINDLEY MURRAY so that it was quite a justifiable suspicion that made her say YOU did not forget it you have left it out on purpose Bang down all the books. I'm not a liar why should I be do you suppose I am afraid of YOU? Informed of this awful crime My father condemned me to the back bedroom on bread and water until I begged pardon.
>
> The consternation in the house must have been geat for the bread came untouched and there was no Harra to swarm up with goodies nor a friend houseboy or cook to smuggle food in. The struggle came. My father came up and prayed not a bit of use—then I said I am not wrong I won't beg pardon. I suppose he saw that somebody must cave in though I really think that the saving of my soul was predominamy over what ust have been the suffering he went through for the starving of my body. Think it over he said you ought to be sorry because I am and I wrote—long did Fred keep that letter but it is lost

17

FOR WHAT I HAVE DONE WRONG THE LORD MAKE ME TRULY SORRY AMEN! This clearly a paraphrase of the grace before meet but which seems to me a most jesuitical proceeding was fully accepted and I think it must have been decided that home discipline was insufficient for me.[14]

In due course Jessie graduated from the home schoolroom to a school at Buckingham House, High Street, in Portsmouth where she began a deeper phase of her education. At about this time she met John Daniel Morell, who preached a new and fascinating brand of religion that opened her mind to fresh possibilities.

Morell came to occupy the pulpit of the Independent Chapel in Gosport in 1842. Naturally Jessie was introduced to him very soon after his arrival, as her father was one of the deacons of the church and was himself on the committee that chose Morell. Much to her surprise, throughout the next three years—at which point Morell was ousted by his dissatisfied and shocked parishioners—Jessie found herself increasingly drawn toward the church. The magnet was Morell's religious philosophy, and beyond that, the character of the man himself. His fresh, invigorating ideas about the need for ethical action came as a pleasant contrast to her father's ambiguous questions about dogma. Overnight, the loathed requirement of going to church so often became pleasurable; sermons churned her ideas provocatively instead of sending her into reverie. Now aged ten, Jessie was introduced to a world of ideas and hence launched on the progressively broadening educational experience which was to lead her at last to the center of the revolutionary movement in Italy.

Unlike most men of his profession, John Daniel Morell had been educated by philosophers rather than theologians; he developed his unconventional liberal views on the Continent. His father was a Congregationalist minister, and young Morell had planned to enter the same calling after a period as probationer under Dr. Pye Smith at Homerton College. There he had indeed read theology, as well as studying Greek, Latin, French, and German. But deterred by ill health, he decided to continue his studies rather than to preach the Gospel. He went to Glasgow where he met and developed a friendship with a congenial and similarly inclined student, George Dawson. Subsequently, Morell took a first prize in logic and moral philosophy at Glasgow, receiving a Bachelor of Arts degree in 1840 and a Master of Arts degree in 1841. After acquiring the second degree, he spent the summer in Bonn, where he continued his work in theology and philosophy under the tutelage of Fichte. Then, dissatisfied with German idealism, he went to France, and immersed himself in Cousin's philosophy of eclecticism at the Sorbonne. He arrived in conservative Gosport newly converted to French thought. Although still nominally a Congregationalist, his point of view was essentially that of a Unitarian.

Morell's religious position was an outgrowth of his philosophical probing, and it soon became apparent that he was too much of a latitudinarian in his standards of religious belief to suit his parish. Jessie afterwards could never quite understand why the parish board in search for a new minister had chosen him in the first place; his philosophical and religious liberalism were perfectly patent in his every attitude; he made no attempt to conceal his views. When he was forced to give up the Gosport pulpit in 1845, he sent out to be published the first of his many books which were to include studies of "mental philosophy," a history of philosophy, a work on phrenology, and a treatise on grammar. This first book, called *An Historical and Critical View of the Speculative Philosophy of Europe in the Nineteenth Century*,[15] is a systematic study of what Morell considered to be the distinct systems of philosophy. He finds that of all systems he prefers eclecticism; in the book's conclusion he sums up his views:

> Eclecticism, in the sense we employ it, may be described as the *philosophy of progress*. Take any fixed philosophical method, and if it be in itself *complete*, it ought to give a complete result. . . . If there be *progress* in the development of truth, then there must be some principle out of and beyond the individual, which exerts its influence upon the human mind at large; that is, there must be some element, out of and beyond the individual, on which philosophical truth is partly grounded. The case is the same with regard to the principle of tradition. Here we have a truth, fixed and abiding, in which there can be no question of progress whatever. What has come to us verbally and objectively from above, can neither be further developed nor put into new relations, without admitting another, and that a human principle, by means of which the development takes place. . . .
> Regarding philosophy, then, as progressive, what appeal can we have as final—what ground of certitude on which we can fully rely? We answer that the one final appeal, and the ultimate ground of certitude in philosophy, is HUMANITY. Positivism gives us truth and error; . . . but humanity sifts the results of individual thinking, and hands us down a stream of truth, ever widening as it flows onwards. . . .[16]

He asserted that it was the problem of the philosopher to develop a speculative method so that the "truth of the age" might be exposed to light. The development of Christianity, Morell thought, was but one phase of the development of this truth. He rejected the concept of revealed theology maintaining: ". . . we must establish the philosophic value of our primary theistic conceptions by the light of a searching *psychology*; and it is only when we have laid firm our basis in the inviolable depths of the human consciousness, that we can proceed to build up the noble superstructure of a *sound theology.*"[17]

Among his parishioners there were few who would support his kind of view. However, Jessie responded affirmatively to Morell's thinking, although many of his ideas were at the time over her head. He was her first hero and, like the several who came after him, he troubled her conscience with the awareness that the world had many unsolved problems. Shortly after their acquaintance had bloomed into friendship, Jessie took her initial step into the arena of public welfare. Her father was forever distributing tracts obtained from the Bible Society; and on one occasion he felt called upon to save the souls of the poorer inhabitants of Stoke and Brockhurst by subjecting them to spiritual examination. Jessie overheard one of these locals—a woman who had listened to a searching sermon along the lines of her father's beliefs—say that she couldn't fathom why anyone should worry about sin unless he simultaneously concerned himself about empty bellies. The child considered the merits of this statement and after turning it over in her mind, consulted with her brother Fred who agreed with her that it was imperative that the bellies be filled. They decided to make a series of raids on their plentiful family larder and to deliver the stolen goods to the poor. Mr. White, however, discovered their purpose and suggested that although he was not going to forbid them to feed the poor, they must bear their own financial burdens; he couldn't support them in their chosen private philanthropy. "Mamma and I do what we can and in our own way," he said, "we can't afford to do any more. Now we have calculated you cost us something like sixpence a week each for butter and about the same sum for sugar, now these are luxuries. You can't go without your bread, or meat, or pudding for long without injury to your health, but you may have butter and sugar money instead of butter and sugar if you like."[18]

When Jessie recalled Mr. Morell's influence on her she later wrote:

> I know that to read the books that he chose for me or perhaps told Fred who became his pupil I forewent Byron's Gulnares and Conrads*—Byron never by the way—and did my proper lessons and learned to write properly and to construe sentences. But the sermons were the delight for a time. One I remember from Hebrew 12th Wherefore laying aside every weight and the sins that do most easily beset us let us run with patience the race that is set before us looking unto Jesus the author and finisher of your faith. He told the story of the Grecian Games which all the people went to see every year in the

* Characters in "The Corsair," 1814.

Amphitheatre and where the favorite diversion was that of running for the prize divested of all encumbrances straining every nerve animated by the plaudits of the spectators. It is from these games that the peculiar phraseology was derived we cannot hope to obtain moral strength any more than we gain physical strength without severe exercise and toil. That was the moral or all that I remember of it. Nothing that was worth doing was done easily or without trouble a lesson learnt and found true every day of life from then till now.[19]

In 1845 when Mr. Morell left Gosport, Jessie's family moved to Portsmouth and she was sent to a school in Reading, where her older sister was already apprenticed as a teacher. The director of the school, Miss Laurie, was a cultured woman "and the ablest of teachers" and the transformed Jessie, now fully enjoying schoolwork, desired adult approval. The studies which pleased her most were the lectures on English poetry. Of the poets, Shelley and Byron were committed to memory and enjoyed. Throughout her life she was always able to pull from her memory an appropriate quotation from one or the other—especially Shelley—as embellishment for political essays. In her school years, however, Jessie's lack of discipline, personal disorderliness, and unruliness at once got her into trouble:

> If order is heaven's first law Miss Laurie would say it assuredly ought to be the same on earth where disorder produces so much inconvenience confusion and loss of time. And theoretically I acquiesced in the doctrine from bitter experience. A Noah's ark was kept for every article found out of place and on Sundays every article was held up to view its nature explained and its owner expected to claim it in person. Horrible to relate on the second Saturday after my arrival all the beasts birds and fishes in the ark had to be claimed by me books pencils pens thimbles even stockings undergoing repairs a pair of house shoes and a garden hat were held up one after the other to the public gaze. It was no use mumbling mine. Mine is a possessive pronoun but here the personal noun is required. So Jessie had to be repeated over and over again until I hated the very sound of it and so deaded a repetition of the scene that while really trying to be more orderly I struck a bargain to do all the exercises and sums of two rather stuped girls for the exchange of their care and supervision of my personal property.[20]

After she left Reading, Jessie went to London and when she was seventeen, to Birmingham, where she enrolled at a school run by "two ladies." Possibly this was the school organized by the sister-in-law and the wife of George Dawson (Morell's friend), the electrifying Birmingham reformer whose teachings were already stirring the whole north of England in the 1840s. In Birmingham, Jessie began to apprehend the transforming power of the ideas that she had first encountered through Morell.

Dawson's liberalism like Morell's, had proved too heady a dose for the general membership of the church that had called him to the pulpit, but a group of parishioners who dissented from the orthodox majority banded together to build him a new chapel in Birmingham which he headed after 1846. The Squire of Rickmansworth had complained after Dawson's preliminary audition in Mt. Zion Chapel pulpit on August 4, 1844 that the church had been invaded by an atheist;[21] and so it must have seemed to all the parishioners who held to the notion that a minister must confine himself to doctrinal matters. For like Morell, Dawson was in no sense a theologian. He was profoundly convinced that a man of God must help his congregation to translate the spirit of the Gospels into their community relationships by reforming their institutions and improving the quality of their daily lives. He himself was intensely involved in a spate of community activities: he instituted frequent town meetings and organized public debates; he pleaded for reforms in laws regulating public houses and affecting public sanitation and hygiene. He encouraged the townspeople to band together and to plan for new facilities—a public library (the first in England), a town hall, daily schools and Sunday schools. He spoke against the slavery existing in civilized countries on both sides of the ocean and in favor of fuller education of women. He promoted a society for the Reformation of Juvenile Offenders, a Free Trade Association, and a plan called the Nine Hours Movement for the shortening of working hours and profitable use of leisure time.[22]

In all these activities, Dawson saw himself as a popularizer of knowledge, for he believed with John Stuart Mill that only with the democratization of education and growth of universal literacy could the members of a community prosper. His ideas ran directly counter to the Victorian money ethic. He delivered his lectures on history, art, literature, and current affairs throughout the north of England and the Midlands. He spoke to women and workingmen, often in private houses where a group of neighbors would gather informally to hear him. George Eliot reported that he gave a series of lectures at Coventry in 1848 and stayed at Rosehill with her friends the Brays. During that series, entitled "Historical Characters Reconsidered," he lectured on Pythagoras, Michelangelo, and George Fox. His host, Charles Bray, observed to George Eliot that Dawson was one of his heroes and added that he had really very few.[23] Dawson's favorite contemporary was Thomas Carlyle, whose works he knew inside out —some said better than Carlyle himself did. He continuously ana-

lyzed and expounded the Scotsman's theories, acting as his popularizer.

Dawson's chief aim was to stimulate his fellow citizens to read,
think, and act. He insisted on the desirability of making institutions
the instruments of the people. The ideal community, he thought,
would be one in which each citizen, from whatever stratum of society,
experienced a sense of responsibility toward the others within the
same community. In such a case, he stated in his address at the inauguration of the Birmingham Central Library, a moral purpose would
emerge in the community. Each individual would feel a heightened
sense of identity in perceiving that the community was an organism
in which he necessarily played an integral role. As institutions improved, so would the quality of life.

Although he was centrally concerned with these early definitions
of the relationships of community organizations to the lives of individuals, Dawson's interests were in no sense narrowly parochial. He
was vitally concerned with the broader contemporary developments
in political and social affairs on the European continent and in America, and advocated movements to fight against oppression wherever
it existed. He took a group of his congregation and some friends—possibly even Thomas White, whom he had met through Morell—to Paris
to witness firsthand the activities of the 1848 revolutionaries. With
his circle of liberal acquaintances—the Reverend William Crosskey of
Glasgow; the Reverend James Martineau (brother of Harriet); Joseph
Cowen, Jr., a newspaper publisher of Newcastle-upon-Tyne; and
George Holyoake of Manchester—he joined in the support of political
refugees who had fled to England from Poland and Italy. Jessie later
realized that during this period she had been profoundly influenced
by the many talks she had with Dawson about the problems of Italy,
the evils of the papacy, and the Bourbon and Austrian suppression of
freedom in their Italian territories.*

What might be called the Birmingham School of Social Theory is
the subject of two anonymously published stories written by Jessie
White before she was twenty-one. Both were published during 1853
in a feminist magazine, *Eliza Cook's Journal*.[24] Together with some
anonymous and some identified stories by Elizabeth Meteyard, also
a Birmingham liberal, who went by the name Silverpen, they constitute an interesting commentary on the Dawson movement, and—most
important for us—they reveal Jessie's attitudes after her exposure to
this teacher. The stories are about workingmen heroes who feel a call
to supply the needs of their community. Each of Jessie's tales is extremely unsophisticated. Her inventiveness was certainly never more

* See chapter 2.

23

meagre and the slight narrative interest dwindles while the author heatedly belabors her views on social progress. Nevertheless the tales reveal the expanding scope of their author's concern with social problems and ways to solve them.

The childishly simple story called "Alice Lane" is without significant invention. It examines the love of a young man preparing to become a schoolteacher for a young girl who wishes to dedicate her life to her community. Its interest for us lies in the fact that it embodies Jessie's uncritical acceptance of Dawson's ethics. The narrative rehearses the growth of the young couple's determination to serve their community—in this case a typical Midlands village of the 1840s. The population consists of agricultural victims of industrial society, the laborers and the poor who have little incentive to improve themselves. They are illiterate and drawn towards drunkenness and vice to escape the sordidness of their surroundings. Before the "Birmingham theory" reaches them, there are few spurs to their improvement of their self-image. But Alice Lane, a pupil of William Barnard (surely George Dawson), herself learning to teach the people of the community, hopes to enhance the quality of their lives. Together with her young friend Frank, whom she subsequently marries, she moves from one enterprise to another, convinced by the validity of the given argument that

> Temperance societies are of no use, churches are of no use, unless there be within the workingman's heart a source of right motive and right action—a sense of the awfulness of duty and the beauty of the lowliest station, when the work of it is bravely and wisely done.

The only way to achieve this state is to understand what one is and what one can do. Seeking to bring about this understanding, Alice Lane begins a campaign for the emancipation of the workers by teaching them to read and giving them books: "This book club if it can be managed, will be one great help against the many temptations to vice and indolence in a village. . . ." When necessary funds have been raised to initiate the adult literacy movement, she and Frank inaugurate evening classes for children, to stem early juvenile delinquency: ". . . Not mere book-words and old repetitions are taught now these children, but broad high principles, making all duties alike of beauty if done in the true spirit of Christ. . . . Some of the children are learning to write, some to keep accounts, others, the first principles of mathematics or even astronomy. . . ." After some years a new village emerges, a model of environmental improvement:

> The aspect of the village is so changed; paved well-kept streets seem to hold no kinship with those of twenty years ago, when heaps of filth and rubbish obstructed the entrance to all the poorer dwell-

24

ings. Neat airy cottages have taken the place of the wretched hovels, where two, three, and sometimes four families herded together. Four of the alehouses are replaced by a draper's shop, a chemist's, a grocer's, and a bookseller's; and to judge by the brisk cheering bearing of the shopmen, business is flourishing in them all. Could we look into some of the interiors of the homes, a change more precious still would delight us. Poor, very poor, many families still are; but in most of the houses there is an air of comfort and happiness that money cannot give; and this change is not difficult to account for. We remember that the heads of these families were mostly children in Mrs. Barnard's time. So terrible was the memory of many of their childhoods, so fearful the warning, that hard indeed must have been the heart that would not turn from such a state of things to teaching such as hers. Emigration had done much towards this; it had drained an overpopulated neighborhood of many starving inhabitants, leaving more work and higher wages for those who remained behind. Many too, who by dint of great labour and economy, had saved a little money, had left their native village,—being "stalled of England"—knowing that it was impossible to make ever so small an inheritance for their children. No wonder that the labouring man looks with disgust on the enormous estates belonging to the rich, when the mere possessions gives them the right to every scrap of waste land that the labourer would gladly buy. No wonder that the gardener, the farmer, and all the agricultural poor, grow weary of England and their profitless toil therein, when the very land that their labour has rendered fertile benefits the rich owner at the poor worker's course. Why should they fertilize the land that their rent may be raised? Why toil endlessly with no hope of toiling less? The question is answered; they will no longer do it; and if colonization has done no other good, the lesson of dependence that the rich will certainly learn every day more, is in itself blessing enough.

By their own teachings, by the books that they placed within the reach of the young around them, they [Frank and Alice] had worked on the individual minds, on the youth; each boy and girl felt stirred to do his and her part to make their home neat and cheerful. For the same reason, each child would work diligently to obtain ever so little money, that they might read the books that they saw were prized by those whom they looked up to. And thus alone can the masses of mankind be influenced; not as masses by one spasmodic effort. Benevolent societies and institutions are useless, if they fail to inspire each member with a special resolve to help himself; and this Frank knew full well, and his efforts lay more among the few kindred souls that he could discern among the people, than on the whole body;—not that he neglected outward help, as the institutions and library which that village contains today prove well.

Finally the village hall, symbol of the new community spirit, is dedicated:

> A very sacred building will it be to us; and by our past struggles to-
> gether and apart, to live down prejudice, and gain for ourselves
> and our children what we deem essential to the welfare of every hu-
> man being, namely, a true, deep education of mind and heart; so
> will we strive earnestly to keep these walls pure from the stigma of
> frothy, empty babbling that attaches to too many of the like; so will
> we strive to keep it ever open to heaven's light, that knowledge
> divine and pure may be the portion of our children.

Years later Alice's son, Frank, leaves the village for the university
and the narrator observes:

> To raise that village from its degradation—to help and elevate the
> minds and souls of poor sunken human beings—to do it simply by a
> true, earnest life, without the aid of rank, or wealth, or station; such
> had been the painfully-wrought, nobly achieved "mission of the
> lowly,"—one more proof of Ruskin's glorious words, that "God ap-
> points to every one of His a separate mission"; and if they discharge it
> honorably, if they quit themselves like men, and faithfully follow that
> light which is in them, withdrawing from its all cold and quenching
> influence, there will assuredly come of it such harmony as, in its ap-
> pointed mode and measure, shall shine before men, and be of service
> constant and holy. Degrees infinite of lustre there must always be, but
> the weakest among us has a gift, however seemingly trivial, which is
> peculiar to him, and which, worthily used, will be a gift also to his
> race forever.

The poetry of the community was further developed in Jessie's next
story. In "Roger Dale" the hero is a youngster who works in the coal
mines but who finds that his good master and "the greatest organist
in Europe" (who comes to Birmingham to give a concert) both recognize his latent musical ability and cooperatively help him to become
a fine musician. As the story opens, Roger is standing in front of the
new Town Hall, a powerful "glorious" structure built with two hard
years' work of laborers using power equipment. The building is
modeled after the temple of Jupiter Ammon at Rome: "The external
height of the hall is a hundred and sixty feet, its width ninety. The
only ornaments of the exterior are the thirty-two fluted Corinthian
columns which support the entablature. The total height from the
basement to the acroterium is eighty-three feet. . . . Here town meetings will be held, when the eager, wan, tossed multitude whom no
threats or oppression can silence, shall listen to the words and feelings of men strong of purpose and wise of heart who have thought and
suffered and struggled for the truth as it is." Roger's master gives him
a week off to attend the maestro's concerts and on his way to one
"Roger pressed onward eagerly, as though he would have wrapped,
with his child arms, in one wild embrace, his mighty native town;

each tall, towering chimney, with its pillar-wreath of smoke, was full of poetry for him, the ringing clanging wheels were music for his heart. . . ."

Roger becomes an accomplished organist himself through the co-operation of the others. He works out a plan whereby the "work-stained, vice-degraded men" of the Birmingham factories and mines can attend concerts in the Town Hall and enjoy other cultural experiences. At last, his fellow townspeople salute him for what he has brought about and he responds by encouraging them to self-culture:

> These concerts that are to be held every week at a price that will meet the purse of the poorest labouring man, are but one among the many means that lie around you at this end. There are your lectures at the Institution, your evening classes, and debating clubs, all organized by yourselves, needing now but the strength of mind and will to gain time to avail yourselves of them.

The writer of these tales took both heroism and self-help very seriously. Her hero was the workingman's teacher—Dawson himself—leading his followers toward a more beautiful life by creating new institutions. Jessie's insatiable appetite for social reform and her confidence that all obstacles could be overcome permeate her juvenilia. Whatever her oversimplifications, the idea that with leadership desired changes could be planned for and accomplished was an exciting discovery.

2

At the time that Jessie accompanied Mrs. Roberts on her visit to Garibaldi, in 1854, a number of the Italian states which would later be unified into the modern nation of Italy had been in various stages of political ferment for several decades. Since the cause of Italian unification—the Risorgimento—was to absorb Jessie's attention and energy for the next sixteen years it might be well to survey the political map of Italy prior to Jessie's arrival on the scene. It was a complicated terrain, and Jessie herself approached it from a partisan position.

From 1796 to 1814, the larger part of Italy had been dominated by France, Napoleon having deposed the existing rulers and reorganized the occupied territories under the government of candidates of his own choice. The victorious powers who met at the Congress of Vienna in 1814-15 sought to root out French influence in Italy and, above all, to stifle the ideas of liberalism and nationalism which had been sown during the French occupation and which threatened to grow even after the defeat of the French.

In part to curb the threat of these dangerous ideologies, the Congress, and Prince Metternich of Austria in particular, moved to restore the former "legitimate" rulers in the reconstituted Italian states wherever possible. In the north, Victor Emmanuel I of the House of Savoy, returned to rule the Kingdom of Sardinia, which included Piedmont, Sardinia, and the newly annexed territory of the former Genoese Republic, as well as Monaco. In the south, the Bourbon ruler, Ferdinand IV was restored to the throne of the Kingdom of Naples and in 1816 assumed the title of Ferdinand I, King of the Two Sicilies (Naples and Sicily). Pope Pius VII returned from long exile to rule the Papal States, including the Romagna; Duke Francis IV was restored to rule in the Duchy of Modena; Grand Duke Ferdinand III returned to the Grand Duchy of Tuscany. An Austrian-sponsored candidate, Maria Louisa, daughter of Francis II of Austria (and also Napoleon's wife), was given the Duchy of Parma; and her namesake, the Infanta Maria Louisa of Bourbon-Parma, was given the Duchy of Lucca. Austria annexed Lombardy and Venetia (which had been the ancient Venetian Republic until Napoleon's conquest) and organized these two territories under separate Austrian administrations. The Republic of San Marino completed the roster of Italian states set up by the Congress of Vienna. Since the Bourbons had been restored to the Kingdom of Naples by the force of Austrian arms, and since the rulers of the various duchies owed either their restoration or the bestowal of their thrones to Austria, only the Kingdom of Piedmont-Sardinia remained relatively free of that power's domination.

The period of French occupation of Italy had fanned two sets of expectations, both of which were to be disappointed by the settlement imposed by the Congress of Vienna. On the one hand, the very fact of occupation by an outside power had aroused a feeling of nationalism and a strong desire to be rid of foreign domination. On the other hand, the introduction of enlightened laws and the pursuit of administrative reforms under the French aegis had awakened a taste for more liberal government and, among some, a hope for a movement toward popular sovereignty. The settlement of Vienna substituted Austrian domination for that of the French; and the restored rulers not only failed to institute liberal political reforms—not one of them operated under a constitution—but in their fear of the growth of liberalism imposed a political climate that was in some ways even more oppressive than that which had prevailed under the Napoleonic occupation. In the Papal States, Pius VII set out to restore the semifeudal ecclesiastical rule which had marked his administration prior to his deposition by the French, and the power of the papacy in the rest of Italy—curbed during the French era—was now strengthened by a series of new alliances with the newly reconstituted states.

The period between 1815 and 1831 had been characterized by a handful of episodic insurrections against the established regimes and power structures in various parts of Italy. In the south a group called the Carbonari, originally organized to combat the repressions of the French-imposed Murat government, became active once more and before long Carbonarism spread not only to other parts of Italy, but to France as well. The Carbonarists had no established program, but advocated larger freedoms both for individuals and for nations. They organized uprisings and issued manifestos urging popular action in the Papal States in 1817; in 1820 in Naples (where a constitution was briefly granted by Ferdinand I but later revoked); in 1821 under Santorre di Santarosa in Piedmont-Sardinia (where Charles Albert of another branch of the House of Savoy, the reigning monarchs, took over as regent following the abdication of Victor Emmanuel I and granted a constitution, which his uncle, the new king, Charles Felix, promptly thereafter rescinded; and in Modena and Bologna in February, 1831. Each of these uprisings failed because the masses of the Italian people were not really ready to respond, and because the agencies of repression moved in quickly.

Between 1831 and 1848 there were new beginnings and a consolidation of liberal activism in Italy. This period saw the rise of Mazzinism in the form of the movement known as Young Italy and thereafter Young Europe, which replaced the earlier Carbonarism. The movement was guided by Giuseppe Mazzini (1805-1872) who came from Genoa, now part of the Kingdom of Piedmont-Sardinia. Mazzini had joined the Carbonari in 1827. Three years later, in November, 1830, he was arrested for his subversive political activities. He awaited trial for three months, and then, given the choice between imprisonment and lifelong exile, he picked the latter. Between 1831—when his exile began—and 1837, Mazzini developed his views about Italian nationalism into a platform for what he called the Party of Action. His peripatetic headquarters moved from France to Switzerland and finally, after 1838, to Great Britain, although he continued to make many undercover forays into Italy. The views he developed can be briefly described as follows (they are to be found elaborated in the ninety-four and some odd volumes of Mazzini's *Scritti*): Mazzini was concerned with making Italy an organic whole. He believed that the people should rise up and take their destinies into their own hands. Each man must strive to do his individual duty and thus the national mission would gradually be identified and accomplished as the work of the people, not of monarchs and dynasties. Just as Italy had had two republican periods in its early history, so would it have a Third Rome, a republic, in the future. The people must and would—with spontaneous leadership—work toward the ideal republic. Mazzini's notion was a moral one, for he saw government as an expression of conscience. Beyond Italy, there were repressed peoples everywhere hungering for the opportunity to belong to a better world. Italy would become the initiator, then, of a movement of people that would build a world of nations. Mazzini's concept was not political, or geographical, but spiritual. As such, however, it bore no relation to ideas prevalent in organized religions; for although he thought of his world as a kind of new Jerusalem, he had no use for the outworn forms and promises of Christianity.

During its active phase Mazzinism was responsible for several uprisings which its leader conducted largely from abroad. An insurrection was planned but aborted in Piedmont-Sardinia in 1833, during which Mazzini's close friend Jacopo Ruffini committed suicide. Giuseppe Garibaldi was involved in another failure in 1834, after which he accompanied other Italian exiles to South America where he placed his popular guerrilla tactics at the service of republican movements. In the course of the long struggle for Italian unification, Garibaldi frequently returned to Italy to participate in various campaigns, but Mazzini retained the role of master planner of the movement. While Mazzini never deviated from his original aims for unification, Garibaldi came to accept gradualism and compromise as the years went by.

Other radical-liberal views on the desirable conditions for Italian unification also came to the fore between 1830 and 1848. Carlo Cattaneo (1801-1869), a Milanese economist, espoused a gradualist position. He believed that governments should provide the rational means by which men could direct their own affairs through use of their intelligence. He envisaged a form of republican federalism in which the several states would develop reform programs based on sound economic, technical, and industrial planning. He was, indeed, opposed to the idea of a unitarian Italian state. Cattaneo was not so much an activist as a theorist, but his positivistic studies and empirical guidelines introduced an element of planning and foresight into Italian liberal ideology.

Still another path to unification was suggested by Vincenzo Gioberti (1801-1851), a cleric, who saw a revitalized Catholicism under the presidency of the pope as the most effective means of achieving this end. Those who supported his view—a group that called itself the neo-Guelphs*—were encouraged by the election of Giovanni Mastai Ferretti to the papacy on June 17, 1846, especially since the new pope —Pius IX—began his pontificate with a liberal gesture by declaring an amnesty for political prisoners.

Charles Albert, King of Piedmont-Sardinia (1831-1849), granted some administrative reforms in 1847-1848. On the heels of the action of the pope, Ferdinand II of the Kingdom of the Two Sicilies (1830-1859) was forced to grant a constitution to his subjects in 1848. Other constitutions followed in Piedmont-Sardinia, the Papal States, and Tuscany. Finally, the Milanese in Lombardy rose against the Aus-

---

* After the original Guelphs, the party which during the Middle Ages championed the cause of the Church against the Ghibellines, supporters of the German emperors.

trians (an event which took place in March, 1848, and became known as the Five Days of Milan) and expelled them from the city. Simultaneously the Venetians declared their independence from Austria and established a Venetian Republic. At these signals, Charles Albert attempted to aid the Milanese. He received no help from other quarters (the pope, for example) and meanwhile the king of the Two Sicilies retrenched his position. After a series of engagements in July 1848, Charles Albert was defeated by the Austrian forces under the leadership of General Radetzky and driven out of Lombardy back into his own territory. With no help in sight he was forced to ask for an armistice.

When the papal prime minister, Pellegrino Rossi, was murdered on November 15, 1848, the pope fled to Gaeta. Thereupon the Mazzinians enjoyed a brief triumph by seizing power in Rome and setting up a republic under the triumvirate of Mazzini, Carlo Armellini, and Aurelio Saffi. Meanwhile, Charles Albert broke his armistice with Austria and experienced a second defeat, this time at Novara, after which he abdicated in favor of his son, Victor Emmanuel II.

The Roman Republic was short-lived. French troops commanded by General Oudinot came to the aid of the pope, supported by reinforcements dispatched by the Kingdom of the Two Sicilies, as well as by Spain and Austria. Garibaldi led the volunteers of the Roman Republic against the foreigners, but on July 3, 1849 the French troops occupied Rome, and Mazzini once again returned to exile in England. Garibaldi marched north to Venice* with nearly 3,000 men to join the Venetian forces battling anew against Austria, but the Venetian Republic fell in August. Garibaldi made his way out of the country and eventually arrived in New York. It was on his way back from this exile that he visited England and met Mrs. Roberts before proceeding to Nice (then in Piedmont-Sardinian territory).

In spite of the defeat of so many liberal causes in 1848, the unification of Italy was now irrevocably under way. Between 1850 and 1859 Piedmont-Sardinia forged ahead under the guidance of the statesman Camillo di Cavour,† who was to dominate the Italian scene until his death in June, 1861. Cavour was an advocate of constitutional reform and the parliamentary process, and under Victor Emmanuel II, he achieved the evolutionary transformation of Piedmont-Sardinia's government. Cavour, unlike Mazzini, believed that Italy could not be independent of regimes and policies in Europe. He also believed, as did many others in Italy by then, including the newly formed National Society, that Piedmont-Sardinia, as the most enlightened state

---

* Garibaldi's South American wife, Anita, died on this march.
† Cavour was elected to the Piedmontese parliament in 1848 and by October 1850 he was minister for agriculture. He became prime minister in November, 1852.

in Italy, would have to take the lead in bringing about the unification of Italy.

Piedmont participated in the Crimean War in 1855 when England sought help. One of the considerations that prompted Piedmont to participate was Cavour's hope that this would provide the opportunity to bring the case of Italy to the attention of the continental powers. In the course of the Crimean War Austria adopted an ambiguous position that eventually alienated it from both sides in the conflict. After the war Cavour went to the peace table at Paris and during subsequent discussions raised the Italian Question with the purpose of further isolating Austria from the major European powers.

But while Cavour devoted himself to bringing about unification by diplomatic and constitutional means, the radical Mazzinians continued to believe that conspiracies, force, and revolution were necessary to achieve the desired end. It was to Mazzini's party, still capable of seriously interfering with Cavour's plans, that Jessie White's initial sympathies were attracted once she was drawn into the circle of Risorgimento sympathizers and activists.

In the spring of 1855, Jessie returned to her own country, bringing with her from Italy one of Garibaldi's children, Ricciotti, who needed treatment for an orthopedic problem. She had already decided to devote herself to the cause of Italian liberation, and it was inevitable that she would therefore soon encounter the members of the Ashurst circle and others engaged in the work of the Friends of Italy Society.[1] This group unofficially channeled volunteer aid for Mazzini, and some of its members became actively involved in his various plots to touch off a revolution in Italy. As a result, some very respectable Friends of Italy found themselves violating British laws as they pursued their undercover activities for Mazzini's cause. By 1856, the Society, which had flourished for five years, was beginning to lose some of its initial impetus but a core of influential and dedicated adherents remained active. Most of the ardent Italophiles in England —both in London and the provinces—were at one time or another members of this group.

The Ashurst family, who in a sense had founded the Friends of Italy Society, lived on Muswell Hill, northeast of London proper on the Hornsey side. Mr. William Ashurst was a barrister of liberal convictions and had been outraged when in 1844 it became known that Mazzini's mail had been tampered with by the British government. Mr. and Mrs. Ashurst had heard many interesting things about Mazzini and very much wished to convey to him their displeasure at the action of the British government and their personal sympathy for him. Since they knew no Italian, they decided to send their son and daughter, William and Eliza, as envoys to Mazzini's residence in Copley Street. The young Ashursts carried with them a warm invitation to dine at Muswell Hill. Mr. Duncombe, their friend and member of Parliament, who had risen in the House of Commons to criticize the government for its role in the mail case, had told them that Mazzini, extremely preoccupied with Italian affairs, was unwilling to go out much in English society. But in spite of their parents' hesitancy in proffering the invitation and Mazzini's general reluctance, Mazzini welcomed the younger Ashursts and agreed to come to Muswell Hill for Sunday dinner. He spoke to his callers in French and said that he would do his best to converse with Mr. and Mrs. Ashurst in English. Following this meeting, Mazzini had frequently visited Muswell Hill to be with those whom he came to call his "clan."*

Mr. Ashurst was a quiet but persevering promoter of refugee causes. Indeed his dedication to the cause of civil liberties and to the protection of minority groups was such that a story was told that once a persecuted Russian Jew addressed him not at the Old Jewry, where his office was, but simply as "Old Jew's Advocate, London." From their first meeting with Mazzini, the Ashursts were drawn to him and their esteem for him rose as they came to know him better. They entertained him often, trying to divert him and bring some gaiety into his life. Above all, they paved his way with the English—in spite of his barbed manners—and increased the circle of his supporters. The various members of the clan—including some in-laws—contributed significantly to the Mazzinian cause. Taken separately, their activities were extremely versatile; considered as a whole they provided Mazzini with a forceful pressure group in England.

Eliza Ashurst, the oldest daughter, engaged in Mazzini's cause fullheartedly until her early death. Soon after she had acted as spokesman in her family's first overture to him in July, 1844, Mazzini wrote a letter to her. (He had a habit of dropping notes to his friends, sometimes several times a day.) Eliza had already translated George Sand's *Spiriton* into English and in his letter Mazzini urged her to make a translation of Sand's *Letters of a Traveller*. Apparently the degree of intimacy between Mazzini and Eliza began to raise a "happy dream" in the minds of Eliza's parents. The letters reveal glimpses of an Eliza on the brink of infatuation and Mazzini attentive but cool. Meanwhile, some of the Italians in exile started a rumor that the relationship between Eliza and Mazzini was "shocking." Mr. and Mrs. Ashurst attacked this rumor, denying any liaison. Mrs. Carlyle, too, gossiped maliciously about the eccentric conduct of all the Ashursts, especially of Eliza, towards Mazzini. The Ashursts, she said, are a *"good* twadly

* Their nickname for him was "the Angel," a name given him by Mrs. Milner-Gibson, who was frequently present at the Muswell Hill gatherings.

family . . . who have plenty of money and help 'his things' and *toady* him until I think it has rather gone to his head. A Miss Eliza Ashurst —who does strange things—made his acquaintance first—by going to his house to drink tea with him alone, &, &!! and when she had got him to *her* house she introduced him into innumerable other houses of her kindred—and the women of them paint his picture—and send him flowers, and *work* for his bazaar, and make verses about him, and Heaven knows what all—while the men give him *capital* towards his *Institutions* and adopt 'the new ideas' at his bidding."[2] In the summer of 1846, having given Eliza some pointers about her reading, Mazzini added in a letter to her that she should not make plans about their future: "Be good and kind and friendly and sisterly, if you can and if I deserve it, with me from day to day, from week to week; you will have done a real good to me, but leave future in the dark and never attempt to lift its veil, or conquer it."[3]

That November Eliza and Mazzini corresponded to arrange a Sunday night lecture that he was to give at which Margaret Fuller would be present (she was on her way to Italy from America).[4] In 1847 Eliza went to Paris to be nearer George Sand and there, at the age of thirty-three, fell in love with a French artisan whom she married against the wishes both of her family and of Mazzini. The latter stopped to see her on his way to Geneva and reported to Mrs. Ashurst on October 2, 1848 that she was well and hoped to have somebody near her for the "crisis".[5] Unfortunately, the crisis came early—for Eliza's pregnancy terminated in a miscarriage and two years later, in November, 1850 she died during a subsequent confinement. "It was an unlucky marriage and we [meaning he and Emilie] were right, through presentiment, in seeing it with repugnance," said Mazzini.[6]

There were three other Ashurst sisters and of these, it was Caroline who enjoyed the most mature relationship with Mazzini. She was apparently very intelligent and warm hearted, less intense than Eliza and Emilie, less sceptical than Matilda. Always tagging his English and Italian friends with epithets and metaphors, Mazzini referred to her and her son as the "rose and her bud." She was a "ministering angel;"[7] endowed not only with intelligence and the capacity for empathy, she possessed a great deal of common sense. She was the "summary of the past and the initiator of the future."[8] Of all the Ashurst women, Caroline was the one who most nearly lived up to Mazzini's Italianate ideal of womanhood, and he displayed a particular kind of patient tenderness in his relationship with her.

Caroline had married James Stansfeld, on July 27, 1844. She had met him through William Shaen, his good friend at University College, London and future fellow officer of the Friends of Italy Society.

Stansfeld, who was introduced to Mazzini in 1847, was the best-connected and most influential member of the circle. This circumstance undoubtedly did not escape the notice of Mazzini, who managed to get Stansfeld into trouble when the latter held a government position later on.* Caroline and James had one child, a boy named after Mazzini, born in April, 1852. It was through James that Jessie White was introduced into the Ashurst circle, and of all its members, James was the one that she liked best.[9]

From Matilda Biggs, the third Ashurst daughter, Mazzini counted on publicity for the cause in the country districts of the north. Matilda's husband was a businessman in Manchester, known for his enlightened policies toward his laborers and his philanthropic works. Mazzini rather resented Matilda's physical remoteness and thought that she would be more helpful to him in London. He finally found a use for her by asking her to collect money for him through a shilling campaign in Leicestershire. He asked her also to circulate propaganda in various nearby newspapers: "If we are to plunge into the struggle, the want of organizing a public opinion is more and more pressing, and a correspondence—a *coup d'oeil* on the condition of Italy every ten days or every fortnight in one of your County papers would be valuable. It is done elsewhere."[10] Mazzini's demands on Matilda were never subtle, and at moments when he felt the special need for money, they were downright blunt. "It is the first time that I speak so openly," he said after asking her and Mr. Biggs to pay for the reproduction of Italian propaganda in the *Daily News*.[11] In 1854 Mazzini, indicating that he did not quite trust her, asked her if she would

---

* During the 1850s Stansfeld delivered many public addresses in the north of England in support of various liberal causes. He spoke at meetings of the Northern Reform Union, and was one of the promoters of the Association for the Repeal of Taxes on Knowledge. On April 29, 1859 he was elected to Parliament as a member from Halifax. As a member of the House of Commons, he did everything he could to promote Italian unity. In April, 1863 he was appointed Junior Lord of the Admiralty. Unfortunately soon afterwards his collaboration with Mazzini came home to roost. During the 1864 trial in France of one Greco, accused of conspiring to assassinate Napoleon III, the Procureur-Imperial of France declared that in 1855 Stansfeld had been appointed banker to Tibaldi and other conspirators who sought Napoleon's life. It was stated that a Mr. Flowers (It. *fiore*, i.e., Mazzini) had corresponded with the would-be assassins from Stanfeld's address at 35 Thurlow Square, London. On March 17, 1864 Disraeli referred to this matter in the House of Commons, charging Stansfeld with holding correspondence with assassins in Europe. Stansfeld denied complicity with Mazzini and was defended in Parliament by John Bright and Lord Palmerston. But the vote of censure lost by only ten votes, and Stansfeld resigned. His resignation was accepted by Prime Minister Palmerston, but he was reelected without opposition on July 11, 1865. In February, 1866, with Lord Russell as prime minister, Stansfeld became under-secretary of state for India. Subsequently, he held the posts of Third Lord of the Treasury under Gladstone, Privy Councillor, and President of the Poor Law Board. He sacrificed his career on the issue of the Contageous Diseases Law, working for its repeal, and joined as an ardent advocate the crusade for women's suffrage, to which the repeal of that law was related. He refused a peerage in 1888.

send him copies of the propaganda that she was writing prior to publication so that he could double-check its content.[12]

Of the four sisters, the most interesting—and the one who was to have the most intimate connection with Jessie White as their work and their associations drew them together—was Emilia Ashurst Hawkes (later Madame Carlo Venturi). Emilie, as she was called, dedicated her life to Mazzini. Her first marriage withered under the dazzlement of her new interest, and in spite of the very romantic nature of her later second marriage Emilie was to remain single-mindedly infatuated with Mazzini.[13] No wonder then, that when she met Jessie White in 1856, Emilie was quick to express her jealousy of Jessie behind the scenes. In the future she was to be highly critical of Mazzini's attentions to Jessie, though in fact, these were never any more intimate than need be, since Mazzini really never understood, nor liked Jessie.

The rich and complex portraiture of Emilie in the *Scritti* reveals the ripening relationship between her and Mazzini. Emilie had a polished writing style; she rightly considered that she had a gift for translation; and she spent untold hours correcting and reworking Mazzini's often laborious prose essays. She also acted as an undercover agent for him, often traveling alone under trying conditions even though her chronic respiratory trouble always kept her in delicate health. Her education had been emancipated and sophisticated. She subscribed to new ideas, among them utilitarianism, of which Mazzini strongly disapproved.

In 1846 Emilie, whose talent as a painter was well recognized in her circle and beyond, painted a portrait of Mazzini* for his mother in Genoa, for whom from time to time she also tried to supply information about his activities and his whereabouts. By the end of 1847 Emilie had begun to receive mail as a blind for Mazzini and was acting as his amanuensis and financial secretary. She and the other Ashursts were always embroiled in some sort of pecuniary transaction with him, of which the following letter of December 27, 1847 offers an example:

> Sydney [her husband] ought to have received a note from P. Taylor, protesting against the penny Subscription in favour of the International League; I suppose on grounds of dignity. I do not agree with him; but I now think that we have been rather rash in starting, and beginning to execute the scheme without asking the opinion of the other Members of the Council; moreover I *know* that, once the objection started, we shall be obliged to give it up. I do therefore propose, that,—unless Sydney and the others feel so convinced and hopeful

* Now in the Casa Mazzini in Genoa.

as to believe that they will persuade Taylor and Co.—the plan be followed but for the Italian National Fund, about which no body will have a right to start objections. The plausibility of the scheme is daily increasing from the visible interfering intentions of Austria. Should we succeed in collecting the £ 1000, we shall give as an offering from the Italian Association to the Leag[u]e £ 500: if less shall be collected, less, the half of the amount.

Be so kind as to tell this to Sydney: the scheme is our own; and we can change its features in a moment, if we choose. My own *centres* I will take care of. With *your* own and Caroline's, I anticipate no great difficulties. The dignity of the League will thus be saved. William has been written to in the same style, and perhaps you will take the trouble of communicating to him 'the change come o'er the spirit of my dream.'

I have fulfilled your commission with Eliza; I will see you, for a few minutes, to-morrow, give a full account, and hear about the Subscription.[14]

Emilie more than the others frequently helped Mazzini cope with his problems of contacting agents and making plans on the Continent. In 1847 she and Sydney made a trip to Paris on his behalf, and in February, 1848 she provided him with a falsely endorsed passport. Knowing that Emilie was acquainted with Frank Dillon, an artist just back from a year in Italy, Mazzini asked her to borrow Dillon's passport and have it signed for Paris by the French embassy. He promised to return it to her in one week.[15] Soon thereafter he wrote Emilie from Paris that he was staying at her hotel and asked a couple of favors of her.[16] Among other things, would she please arrange for him to have access to English papers when he arrived in Milan?[17]

In September, 1848 she set out alone for Italy, with the assigned task of giving some money to Mazzini's agent. En route, she received word from Mazzini that she must avoid the shores of Lake Como and Lake Maggiore at all costs since insurgents were about to take possession of the steamers on these lakes.[18] Proceeding from Bellinzona to Airolo, she found the route closed owing to an avalanche, and the suggestion was made to her by a fellow traveler that she retrace her steps and take a steamer on Lake Maggiore to Domo d'Ossola, thereafter attempting the pass at Simplon. She felt, as she later revealed to Mazzini, that to refuse this suggestion would mean premature revelation of Mazzini's plans and so she followed it. The steamer was seized at Lake Maggiore by Daverio* and his men. The passengers underwent physical hardship, including in Emilie's case, setting out over the mountains by herself after being rowed in a boat for nine hours. Nevertheless, she accomplished her mission.[19]

* Francesco Daverio was Garibaldi's chief of staff during the siege of Rome in 1849.

In 1850 Emilie was in England while Mazzini made clandestine trips back and forth to the Continent. She undertook miscellaneous tasks, including introducing the exiled Carlo Pisacane* to designated people, inserting false notices in the *Times* and *Chronicle* to the effect that Mazzini had arrived in England so that spies would be thrown off his trail,[20] and agreeing to nurse an Italian general sick with brainfever.[21] Later on in the year, Emilie—further estranged from Sydney—went back to the Continent to be near Mazzini. During that winter she visited signora Mazzini, who finally enjoined Emilie to write a biography of her son.[22] Emilie hesitated at first, but finally began to lay the plans which not only eventually resulted in the biography, but in the publication of many of Mazzini's works translated into English.† At the end of November 1853, Sydney and Emilie made a final break. Thus, as Mrs. E. F. Richards observed in one of her volumes of Ashurst-Mazzini correspondence, "Emilie alone, of all the Ashurst family, came finally to enter Mazzini's religion and therefore to comprehend the very groundwork of his politics and life."[24] With this development of her affairs, Mazzini spoke to Emilie a little more openly:

> Your letter to them [her family] is just what I would have guessed you would write. . . . Dear, my notes have been perhaps a little constrained; and you now know under what feeling I was labouring all the while; but never did I write reluctantly: never and less than ever, will I feel so, if you grant me to write. My feelings, for not being exactly what you would wish them to be, are not the less intense, the less fond: sadness and joy, if I had any, I would always feel inclined to express to you, to call forth your own feeling and to listen devoutly and with advantage to their expression.[25]

Still Emilie's state of mind took on a fairly desperate cast; she complained to Mazzini about her loneliness and her worries. Her mother's death in October, 1854 increased her sense of guilt and dispossession. When her father's mind began to fail shortly thereafter, she was almost beside herself. In 1855 Mr. Ashurst died; the Ashurst establishment at Muswell Hill broke up, and with it the Friends of Italy Society as well, unofficially if not officially.

Thus in the early months of 1856, when Jessie White was preparing to begin her activities for the Italian movement, Emilie was living at 22 Sloane Street, London, trying hard to work. Mazzini, meanwhile,

---

* Carlo Pisacane (1818-1857) a Neapolitan, was to play a role in the Genoese uprising of which we shall hear later.
† Emilie's work provided English scholars with many of the basic materials on Mazzini, especially before the Italian government made available the augmented materials of Mazzini's writings and letters. It was in part due to Emilie's work on Mazzini that George Meredith became interested in writing a book about Italy and Mazzini in the 1860s.[23]

distracted Emilie with writing assignments. A translation of Dante's *La vita nuova*[26] would be useful, he thought; and furthermore there was much to be done on the biography[27] although he felt that she would have her problems with that because the issues of his life were unresolved. He gave her directions about shortening articles: "Do not tell me silly things about your not knowing what to cut; do the thing, as I tell you, for my sake; do it as you would after a conversation in which the particulars have been told."[28] Many of Mazzini's communications to her were in code: "The Government being already on the alert, I must really be cautious. . . . V.6.III.3.12.7.5.I.10.V.6.IV.3.7.4.2-VII.12.2. . . ."[29]

In December, 1855 Mazzini prophetically wrote to Matilda Biggs: "Yes, Matilda, I am as convinced as you are that the Christian myth of the woman crushing the head of the snake is concealing a great truth: and an association of women for all our purposes has long been my dream. But it would require a little nucleus of four or five women free and daring to stand before the public with circulars, appeals, etc. Where are they to be found? Could they be summoned forth, I would gladly suggest the bases of the thing and sketch the grounds of the Appeal. *They* ought to write and publish."[30]

It was about this time that Jessie made her debut into the affairs of the English Italophile circle. The eager new proselyte, as Mazzini would soon discover, was scouting for a challenge of the type that he had just issued. During the next two years as popular sympathy for Mazzini in England waned while Cavour's sun rose, Jessie assumed the role of spokesman for republicanism and tried to revive the dying propaganda campaign.

3

Immediately following her return from Italy in 1855, Jessie took her first step—a very practical one—to equip herself to serve the Italian cause: early in 1856 she applied for admission to medical school. In her notes for the *Birth of Modern Italy*, she recalled:

> Certain of being summoned to fight against the Austrians or lead the Italians in revolution, Garibaldi had obtained my promise to be the nurse of his wounded, so, to fit myself for the task, I now resolved to secure the best medical education possible, Dr. Little and other eminent surgeons warmly encouraging me to carry out my plan.[1]

But the encouragement of the eminent surgeons notwithstanding, Jessie found herself unable to carry out her resolve. She recounted the sorry tale one year later in a letter dated March 3, 1857 to an ardent battler for women's rights, Barbara Leigh Smith,* who had asked for an account of her efforts.[2]

> Your letter requesting an account of the attempt made by M—— and myself to obtain a thorough medical education in England reaches me on my lecturing tour; I cannot, therefore, send you all the letters and documents, but I think the enclosed will answer your purpose.
>
> My desire to study medicine originated in the constant care required of me by my little brother, who, owing to some deficiency in the system, has broken his legs sixteen times, and by Ricciotti, Garibaldi's boy, both lame. On one occasion, when the former broke his leg early one Sunday morning, his own doctor being out of town, the child objected to a stranger being called in, and I had to set the broken bone myself. On Monday evening, the surgeon sent by Dr. Little commended the operation, and laughingly offered me a certificate for the

* Later Barbara Leigh Smith Bodichon.

Crimea. I asked him, instead, to assist me in obtaining an entrance to one of the hospitals—for study—but this he declined, and I continued the process of splint-making and bandaging for both boys as usual.

When, however, I consulted Dr. Little, he entered warmly into my project, gave me several introductions, and exerted his influence with his own medical friends. By his advice I made a formal application for admission to all the London Hospitals—fourteen in number.

The following are fair specimens of the questions sent to, and the answers received from, each. (See Appendix No. 1.)*

The request for private anatomical instruction was made at the suggestion of Dr. Bence Jones, who foresaw that in this department practical difficulties might arise. I owe him cordial thanks for the energy and generosity with which he advocated my cause throughout the discussions. On the day following the receipt of my letter, I received a long visit from Dr. ——, the head doctor of St. George's. From his conversation I augured favourably of the result, and was disappointed to receive the following. (See No. II.) Of course, the Weekly Board of Governors acted according to the advice of the Committee. Meanwhile, I called upon several influential doctors and surgeons connected with the different hospitals. Some received me kindly, and a few promised their vote. One individual informed me, that even if the Committee should consent to admit me to the hospital, the door of his ward should be for ever closed to me. Another reproached me with the indecency of my demand: in no single case did I receive either a sensible or logical reply to my question, "Why may not a woman study medicine?"

You will see by Mr. Balfour's letter, that even had I succeeded in entering the hospitals and in obtaining certificates, the Diploma necessary for commencing practice would have been denied. (See No. III.)

One more letter from St. Bartholomew's, and I think you will be convinced, that a little alteration in Dr. Johnson's lines gives the only reason why I was denied admission:—

> "We shan't admit you, Mistress Fell—
> The reason why we cannot tell;
> But this we all know very well,
> We shan't admit you, Mistress Fell!" (IV.)

Throughout May, June, and July, when I was receiving refusals from all the hospitals, one hope cheered me, namely, that the University of London, quite the most liberal community of modern times, would admit me as a candidate to the Matriculation Examination. Until such an examination has been passed, of course no degree can be taken. Moreover, I hoped that a promise of examination from the Senate would influence the decision of some of the Hospital Committees, or at least, should I present myself again, after having passed such an examination, they might choose to reconsider such a decision.

* See pp. 136-37 for the letters referred to by Jessie.

To my formal application I received the following letter (V.), and a few days after, Dr. Carpenter's (VI.), to which I replied (VII.) A long silence followed. I knew that I had one very influential friend in the Senate, and that several others were disposed to accede to my request. I received, too, private information, that the pervading feeling was, that a woman *would* be admitted as a candidate for examination if she presented herself prepared to pass, but that the authorities did not choose to commit themselves to a promise. Now, though quite disposed to matriculate on the chance of being *then* admitted to study in the hospitals, I could not afford to pass at least a year in the society of Xenophon and Livy, &c. on the chance of being allowed to matriculate. I still pressed for an official answer, and received the following. (See No. VIII.)

The receipt of this letter then dashed all my hopes of obtaining a thorough medical education in England. As I wished you know for a profession, as a means to an end, rather than as an end in itself, as I am preparing myself for future work in Italy, conceiving that the way to make other women work is for us each to achieve some practical work ourselves. I shall not therefore go to America for that education which England denies me. But for many reasons I am glad to have made the experiment. Several medical men have assured me, that if a band of women were now to apply for admission at one or more of the hospitals, such has been the feeling excited among some of the most liberal-minded in the profession by the discussions following on my request, that it is improbable they would be refused . . .[3]

Deflected from her original intention, Jessie now decided to find other ways to assist the cause. Commenting on the refusal of the University of London to consider her as a candidate for the degree she explained that this and other circumstances, "the decision that Ricciotti Garibaldi should go to school in Liverpool, the marriage of one sister, and the engagement of another—set me at liberty, with my father's hearty consent and blessing, to dedicate myself fully to the cause of Italy, fully conscious that it was a question of 'all in all or not at all.' "[4]

In July of 1855, Jessie had been introduced to James Stansfeld in the course of her attempt to establish whether an Italian patriot—Calvi by name—whom she had met in Sardinia, was the Pier Fortunato Calvi whom the Austrians had recently hanged in Mantua. He was not. But Jessie's meeting with Stansfeld led to her introduction to other members of the Ashurst circle. The news must have traveled quickly, because soon thereafter Mazzini wrote Emilie to ask how she liked Miss White. It seems that for a while Jessie lived with Emilie, but did not meet Mazzini for some time. Nevertheless, Mazzini had become aware of Jessie's interest in Italian affairs and she was becoming familiar with his views through his newspaper articles, as we shall see.

Jessie and Garibaldi were reunited in the spring of 1856, when the latter paid another visit to England. Since the ostensible purpose of his mission was to purchase a cutter to transport rock from Genoa to Caprera, where he intended to build a house, he visited Thomas White at Portsmouth to look over the shipbuilder's wares. But any step taken by Garibaldi could be expected to be semipublic in its political implications, and this one was no exception. He sounded out friends, including Jessie, in London and talked about English-Italian political alignments.

Jessie wrote about this visit:

> We had many long and earnest talks about Italian affairs. I asked him whether, now that the Crimean struggle* was over, without bringing any benefit to Italy, he still believed in the King of Sardinia's intention and capacity to wage war against Austria, and whether he did not think that a general rising in the subject provinces would put him [the king of Sardinia] on his mettle. I had, throughout 1855 and the commencement of 1856, received cuttings from newspapers with articles by Mazzini and speeches by friends of Italy, and daily and hourly the longing grew in me to be up and doing for them. Garibaldi answered me thus: "If a general rising of the people of Italy could be ensured, there would be no necessity to wait for kings or diplomacy, but, at this moment especially, no one will stir hand or foot: the bravery and patience under hardships of the Sardinian contingent in the Crimea has awakened the pride of our people. You know how unpopular the war was, how only the King and Cavour carried the day in the teeth of the opposition and the resignation of the Minister of War, Dabormida. . . . Well, they are all expecting great things from the Conference. (Peace Congress in Paris) Believe me, there could be no greater mistake than to choose this moment for a rising. We must wait. If nothing comes of the Conference, and I, personally, expect but very little, then, bad as things are in Lombardy and Venice, they are worse, as far as actual suffering and oppression go, in Sicily and Naples, and there some conflagration is bound to burst out soon. We shall see if we can succeed this time in liberating the Neapolitan prisoners, as you know I tried to do with Ripari, last year."[5]

Although he said that he did not believe that the time was ripe for an uprising against Austria, Garibaldi, while still in England, joined a scheme involving Sir William Temple (British ambassador at Naples), Sir James Hudson (British minister at Turin), and Anthony Panizzi (exiled Italian liberal and curator of the British Museum), designed to bring about the escape of the political galleyslaves of

* See p. 33.

King "Bomba" (Ferdinand II) ruler of the Kingdom of Two Sicilies. "For this purpose, Sir James Hudson had consulted his friend, Dr. Agostino Bertani,* well knowing that for such a risky affair he must apply to the 'Party of Action,' and Bertani lost no time in securing Garibaldi's consent."[6] Accordingly, some time later a republican named Medici came to England and purchased a ship called the *Isle of Thanet* for purposes of the rescue, but the ship was wrecked off Yarmouth and the mission consequently delayed. The upshot was that an English subscription was collected from several donors who wished a second rescue attempt to be made. It was rumored that Lord and Lady Palmerston subscribed anonymously. After some delay, Panizzi telegraphed to Bertani: "Our commercial speculations must be suspended," which meant, according to Jessie, that Sir William Temple had sent instructions from Naples countermanding the attempt at rescue, as he thought himself able to secure an amnesty on the condition that the released prisoners should be deported to the United States.[7] Although Sir William Temple died soon afterwards, the prisoners were finally released.

The long and friendly talks that Jessie and Garibaldi had during this visit—free from the encumbrance of Emma Roberts and the pretense of the engagement—turned around Italy. What was the best way for Italy to be freed from the Austrians? From the Bourbons? From the pope? Garibaldi's views were somewhat tempered by expediency bred of impatience and by a growing conviction that Mazzini's uncompromising attitudes were doomed to failure. Mazzini had long since decided that all monarchies were by definition oppressive, Piedmont-Sardinia included, and more than that, he loathed Victor Emmanuel. But Garibaldi now felt that perhaps salutary changes could be brought about under Victor Emmanuel. Not that he favored particular policies pursued by Cavour or by Victor Emmanuel—far from it. But he was a man of action, and he was impatient to have the issues resolved.

Although she was a student of Mazzini's political theories, Jessie had not yet perceived all the implications of his position and was thus inclined to support Garibaldi's changing attitude. It is quite probable that she did not even realize the extent to which these two men differed in their views. True, she had become interested in Italy through the ideas of Mazzini, but what she knew was what she had read and what people had said. Now she was already infected with a very intense admiration verging on hero worship for Garibaldi, whose charisma had touched her. In the future, as her political thought matured, she would free herself from Mazzini's doctrinaire republi-

* Agostino Bertani (1812-1886) later organized the expedition of the 1,000 to Sicily and was chief surgeon to the Garibaldians in 1859. Jessie wrote his biography.

45

canism as she saw the successive failures of his conspiratorial schemes. But not yet.

Ironically, it was Garibaldi who now brought Jessie one step closer to Mazzini's affairs. Upon his return to Italy, Garibaldi recommended to Dr. Paolo Fabrizi, a young Italian who had been expatriated for his revolutionary activity in 1831, that he arrange for a letter to introduce another expatriate, Felice Orsini, to Jessie White. Orsini had been involved in the revolutions in the Romagna and Bologna in 1843 and 1844. He was allied with Mazzini by 1845, and in 1849 had served as a deputy in the short-lived Roman Republic. He participated as a lieutenant and subplanner in several of Mazzini's aborted plots, including the Milanese failure in February, 1853, and a subsequent failure in the Gulf of Spezia a few months later. Even in an age of conspiracies, his adventures unfolded like the scenario of a soap opera. Ten years of working with Mazzini had exposed him to more personal danger than most of his insurrectionary compatriots ever faced. He reflected his anxieties in the fragility of his emotions, however, and by the time Jessie met him, he was very unstable. Furthermore, he lacked the messianic sense that made Mazzini regard his political philosophy as a religion. In 1856 he probably was philosophically and practically at odds with Mazzini, and tried to dissociate himself from his former leader.

Orsini, in his life of daring, had escaped from prison many times. In his most recent escape from the dungeons of Mantua, he had encountered some of the severest dangers of his career; and in the prison itself he had seen such bestial treatment of human beings by the Austrians that he felt impelled to make these atrocities public. After escaping to England in 1856, he wrote an account of his experiences, and it was suggested to him that it would be useful propaganda for the Italian cause in England if he were to have the book translated into English and published for British consumption. Furthermore, it would earn him some much needed money. Orsini's one concern was that the book be in no way connected with Mazzinian sponsorship. Since Jessie, as a friend of Garibaldi, appeared to be in the desired pristine condition, she was invited to do the translation.*

Jessie completed this task and added her own translator's preface to the book. After publication, Orsini was very distressed at some of the modifications he discovered in the work. When he had first been introduced to Jessie, he had thought she was a remarkable young woman, one whom he would like to know better. He wrote to his married German friend Emma Herwegh: "She does not seem English. . . . she is not beautiful, but worthy to be loved by an Italian with all

---

* Apparently Jessie knew enough Italian to make the translation even though her husband in the first few months of their marriage found her Italian imperfect.

his heart. I can say nothing: I feel much sympathy—perhaps she is the one who would live with me."[8] By the time he had completed his literary transaction with Jessie, he had not only changed his mind about her personal charms but also thought her very presumptuous and wanted nothing more to do with her. The book, however, was a best seller on the English market. It appeared on August 2, 1856 under the title *The Austrian Dungeons in Italy* and sold 35,000 copies that year. A second edition was published in 1859.

Jessie's passionate devotion to the cause of Italian freedom shines through the preface she wrote to Orsini's book, as the following excerpts clearly show:

> The English champions of the cause of Italian liberty, [Jessie concluded] losing sight altogether of Orsini as an individual, a hero of romance, well knowing that millions of his countrymen have done and suffered, and are doing and suffering, at least as much as he, will use his narrative as a telescope, and turning it towards those provinces, where whole populations are groaning beneath the yoke of the oppressor from whom he has escaped, will employ the revelations as fresh incentives to their own energies and as inducements to new volunteers to enlist in the holy cause. [There followed a summary of the state of affairs between the time of the Congress of Vienna and the current moment, with Cavour's statement that Italy was thoroughly under the Austrian yoke.]
>
> These statements appear very disheartening, but the fact that they are made by the Piedmontese minister is fraught with an importance that far outweighs the statements themselves. If the total separation of Sardinia from Austrian domination on one hand, and the Pope's temporal rule on the other, had been the only good resulting from the revolution of 1848, that war had not been declared in vain. But there are other results at least as important of which it would be impossible to convince the uninitiated reader in the short space allotted to me.
>
> If I have said sufficient to induce him to read the detailed accounts of Austria's usurpation in Italy, of which he will find plenty in his own language,—if I have inspired him with a wish to judge for himself whether the cause in which Italian martyrs suffer exile, imprisonment, and death, is a just cause, I have attained my object. And while every reform in a nation, as in an individual, must come from within; while the Italians themselves must set Italy free, neither leaning on the implied promise of aid from one foreign government, nor deterred by the fear of intervention from another; while it is certain that in the day when the twenty-two millions of Italians who inhabit, or are exiled from, the Peninsula, shall *unite* against their tyrants, they must succeed in driving them from the soil; there is yet work enough left for each Englishman and Englishwoman who desires to strengthen and to forward the cause of Italian liberty. It may be that an Italian

crisis is at hand; that an Italian prince may yet unfurl the nation's banner, and summon volunteers and exiles to his camp. It is in sending these exiles back to their land, fitly supplied and fitly armed for the journey and the battle-field, that the English people must set their seal on the sympathy manifested to them during their residence amongst us.

I do not pretend to discuss the merits and demerits of the different parties enlisted in this same cause, whose alleged *disunion* those who are indifferent and hostile to freedom and independence take as a pretext for asserting that the Italians have no right to liberty, and that they could not govern themselves if they were free. I simply assert, that as long as the Piedmontese government maintains its ground against Austria and the Pope; as long as the Italians in their own land and in exile, wage war against these declared enemies of their country, they are entitled to be respected and sustained by the free-born and free-governed, of every nation under heaven.

It may be that the day of Italy's redemption is at hand. If so, deeds, not words, must prove who are willing to purchase the redemption with their blood and with their lives.

Or if the prisoners still languishing in Austria's dungeons must die in their fetters before their country's chains are wrenched asunder; —if the exiles, grown old and haggard before their time, worn out by their giant struggles with injustice, bowed down by the still more painful desertion of friends turned traitors, of fellow workers who, unsustained by "their inward feeling of the glorious end," now scoff at and thwart their work;—if these, each and all, must die, without even a Pisgah view of the Promised Land, their children shall yet possess that land, redeemed and regenerated by their lives and by their deaths.[9]

Jessie apparently did not realize how deeply her interpolations[*] offended Orsini, but given his reaction we must assume that she felt free to correct what she considered mistakes in fact on Orsini's part without consulting him. At the same time, she believed—in her ignorance of Orsini's defection from the "leader"—that Orsini was devoted to Mazzini and so would not mind the occasional insertion of hyperbolic statements on behalf of Mazzini's cause. Orsini reported to his friend Carlo Arrivabene soon after the book came out that he was very disturbed about her distortions of his text, and that he felt she had added a Mazzinian bias where there was none.[10]

In spite of Orsini's assumption that Jessie was already very much under Mazzini's personal influence, the most that could have been true was that by the time the book was published on August 2 Jessie might have met Mazzini once. In the *Birth of Modern Italy* Jessie places

[*] Since the Italian original of Orsini's text is unavailable we have no way of checking Jessie's translation against it.

the meeting after she had done Orsini's translation, but Packe, Orsini's biographer, notes that the latter claimed that by then Mazzini was already calling Jessie his "Bianca" and passing along cigars of his own choosing to her.[11] However, in his correspondence with Emilie Ashurst, Mazzini was still referring to Jessie as "Miss White" on August 19, 1856 and from this first reference in the letters, it appears that he had not yet met her by that time but had merely heard about her interest in the Friends of Italy and in him personally. On that date, he sent along to Emilie a "few words" for Miss White, and the words might very well have been to the effect that he was willing to meet her or to have her call.[12]

According to her practice, Jessie made notes for herself a few minutes after her departure from his Cedar Road room where she saw him for what seems to have been the first time:

> My first visit to his tiny room in Cedar Road remains ever present to my heart and vision. Birds were flying about the apartment, a few lilies of the valley stood in a vase on the mantlepiece, books and papers were scattered everywhere, and there, writing on his knee on the smallest fragment of the thinnest imaginable paper, sat Mazzini. He rose at once: his hand-grasp and luminous eyes fascinated and encouraged you, yet filled you with momentary awe. But the simple greeting, the gladness shown in welcoming "one more volunteer to the noble band of English workers and lovers of Italy," put all fears to flight, and soon he was talking, and I was listening as a student to a master anxious to convince, but not in the least desirous of *imposing* his convictions.[13]

Jessie's notes about their conversation further reveal that during this first visit they discussed whether or not Piedmont-Sardinia should be the vehicle of Italy's liberation. Mazzini felt that Piedmont's assistance was necessary, but that it "could not initiate." Jessie then asked Mazzini whether he would accept the leadership of Piedmont-Sardinia and Italian unification under the Sardinian crown if that state were victorious in a confrontation with Austria. Mazzini responded that of course he was prepared to accept the will of the people, whatever form it took, be it the choice of republic or monarchy. He added, however, "if the latter, we Republicans shall carry on our republican propaganda, but without attempting to overthrow the government of the people's choice." Jessie then questioned him about how revolution could take place when Cavour seemed determined to keep revolutions down. Mazzini seemed to think that it could: "Lombardy will go on attempting; you see, she gives no quarter even to Maximilian,*

* At the age of twenty-five Maximilian (1832-1867), the younger brother of Francis Joseph I of Austria, was appointed governor general of Lombardy-Venetia. He was known for his liberalism both there and in Mexico, of which he was subsequently persuaded to accept the crown. In 1867, he was overthrown and executed by the Mexicans.

though he is doing all he can to win the Lombards over: the restoration of the sequestered property, the amnesty granted, have no effect. Sooner or later the revolution will be successful in Milan, then Piedmont will step in and annex Lombardy and Venice. But the rest of Italy will not remain quiescent." He pointed out that the English government, while it would not take an active step, was very sympathetic with the victims of the oppressions of the king of Naples and was in addition disgusted with the way the Crimean War had turned out. The English saw now "that if they had helped the Poles, Hungarians, and other oppressed nationalities to rise against Austria and Russia, they would have formed the best barrier against the Turks."[14] Mazzini added at the end of the interview that he was sorry that he had not seen Garibaldi when the latter was in England, and that he felt sure that when Garibaldi saw that nothing would come of Cavour's intervention at the Congress of Paris,* he would return to his senses and again take up a more active role as revolutionary leader.

Mazzini officially summoned Jessie to the Italian cause on September 12, 1856 when he wrote her as follows:

> Dear Friend,
>   You told me when I last saw you that you were ready at any time to work for the Italian Cause. The time *has* come. Never has help, material help, money, been more called for than at this moment.
>   Will you endeavour to collect from the English People such sums as they are willing to give to our National Fund? Some are, I know, collecting subscriptions for the 10,000 muskets, or for the cannons, which is good. We need, however, other materials quite as much, and there are many who would prefer aiding Italy in other ways than by sending arms.
>   If you take in your hands the list of the "Friends of Italy" there are some to whom I cannot now write, who would, I know, give to me for my Country what they can. Will you go or write to them for me, and show them, if you like, this hurried letter?
>   Any subscription, if paid to Adamo Doria, 24, Old Broad Street, will reach me safely, and I shall acknowledge it immediately.
>
> Ever faithfully yours,
> Joseph Mazzini[15]

This first written appeal to Jessie was supplemented by a longer letter in which Mazzini went into greater detail. He had felt rather discouraged, he admitted, that his previous attempts at interesting the English people in giving money to his cause had met with failure: "A few chosen individuals have, at all times, liberally helped our National Italian Cause; but never did we succeed in eliciting one of those

* See page 33.

outbursts of popular sympathy which make the helping Nation holy, and the helped one strong and brave. If you believe that the time has come, set at work and be blessed for it. Never before has the help, whatever it may be, been more called for." Mazzini maintained that the first period of Italian agitation in England was exhausted. The English now understood that the Italians were an oppressed people. What had to be done next was that they must be convinced that Italy must undergo revolution and that nothing short of that would solve her problems: "Neither Pope, nor King, nor Emperor can grant anything without their turning suicides. . . . The gulf is too wide between us; no bridge can be thrown across it." The Piedmontese government —whatever its intentions—was without power: "Leaving entirely aside every question of principle, how can a Monarchy bound in compact with all existing Governments, existing herself in virtue of certain public Treaties and a party to the actual territorial arrangements, break on a sudden every compact, violate all Treaties, and tear up, in the name of a revolutionary principle the actual map of Europe? *We must rise*, the Nation must openly manifest her own will and assert herself. Monarchy may *follow*, but in no case *begin*." After this statement of principle came the specific instruction to Jessie: "From these grounds you must start in your agitation. About the sort of compromise we have come to between the different sections of the Party, '*that we, leaving aside for the present all political discussion about forms of Governments, should endeavour to rise* WITH THE NATION FOR THE NATION, *and leave the Nation to settle about her own Fates, once emancipated*,' my own writing in the *Italia e*[*del*] *Popolo* will supply you with plenty of proofs if wished for."[16]

In the fall of 1856 Mazzini went surreptitiously to Genoa to lay plans for an insurrection. Having arrived there, however, he decided to postpone action for the time being. In the meantime Jessie had followed him and met many of his loyal partisans there. She had promised Mazzini, in response to his previous letter, that she would give a propaganda lecture tour around the provinces in England and Scotland, and she felt the need of further instruction from Mazzini himself before she started on this tour. Mazzini was rather annoyed at her having followed him, especially because he feared that this would give her time to see and be further distracted by Garibaldi; but actually Garibaldi was not free to come to Genoa, although Jessie met almost daily with Medici, his lieutenant. As Mazzini got to know Jessie a shade better, he began to appreciate her initiative and he wrote Emilie: "she means good, is earnest, and energetic . . . I dare say she will succeed more than 20 men who would put their strength together." Later in the same letter he said: "I like her more and more; on leaving me she was moved; and so was I. Everything for the scheme has been settled." He continued his evaluation of Jessie: "She is very absolute in her opinions; so you are: I mean about individuals. . . . Will you be so good as to repeat both to yourselves this little maxim morning and night: 'That there are, in the actual world, neither angels nor devils; that our task here down is not that of the Last Christian Judgment; but that of *saving*, if possible, from the devil those who have a leaning to him, and of helping up more and more those who aspire towards the angel'; . . . she called me *jesuitical*; if there is within me a real merit towards God and men, it is that I have scarcely ever played the part of the 'individual'. . . ."[17]

Jessie's life now became much more closely linked with that of the Italian circle in England and with Mazzini himself. With Mazzini's blessings, Jessie organized her campaign in England. She first interviewed Walter Savage Landor* and Louis Kossuth,† to ask the one for monetary support, the other for verbal endorsement. Joseph Cowen, who was a newspaper publisher in Newcastle-upon-Tyne and an interested Mazzinian, cooperated in setting up a series of lectures, to be given jointly by Jessie and Aurelio Saffi, one of Mazzini's cotriumvirs during the period of the Roman Republic, and now an exile in England. Before she actually launched her lecture tour, however, Jessie wrote a series of articles entitled "Italy for the Italians" for the *Daily News* which went over the same materials she intended to cover in her lectures. Her first article for the paper was published November 7, 1856, and its highly bombastic, rhetorical, and ornate style gave proof that she was not yet a skillful propagandist. The central subject of the article was the atomization of Italy at the Congress of Vienna. Jessie criticized England for her attitude towards Italy. If England could "feel assured that Poland, Hungary, and Italy will again become nations, will be restored to their own self-respect through their own exertions, when the despots of France, Austria, Russia, and their subordinates are buried dust to dust in the dead old past, she would not, in accordance with her own policy, subject herself to the ignominy of being found chained to a corpse, when the dawn of a new epoch shall reveal the actual state of European nationalities." Jessie announced that in her coming series she intended to examine the question of whether England was short-sightedly "swimming with the tide." She included a general survey of the recent history of Italy in this article and promised to give an accurate analysis of the developments in Italy between 1815 and

---

* The English poet, who was outspokenly sympathetic to the cause of republicanism.

† The Hungarian revolutionary leader exiled after the failure of the Hungarian revolt against Austria in 1848.

1856 in subsequent ones. This continuity of events she proceeded to relate during the next four articles. In the fifth she spoke of the formation of the Young Italy movement by Mazzini after his disillusionment with Carbonarism. The article turned into a eulogy of Mazzini, ending with a quotation from Carlyle: "When we remember that his doctrines, carried out, must end not only in Italian nationality, but in the triumph of European nationalities, from which must outbranch the freedom of the world, would it not be well to look closely before we take our stand with despotism against liberty, with falsehood and wrong against truth and justice?" By the seventh piece, Jessie had warmed up to her issue and she raked the English over the coals for their past foreign policy in respect to Italy.

Many of these articles and of Jessie's early speeches, like Emilie's articles for the *Westminister Review*,[18] were simply a pastiche of Mazzini's writings. But before long, as she began to get the feel of her propagandistic pen, she wrote more lucidly and independently. By the time she went on her lecture tour in December, 1856, when several of her articles had already been printed, she was ready to rebut the arguments of anyone in the audience. Each lecture included an appeal for funds. Often Jessie recommended that her listeners make an effort to inform themselves more adequately about current events by reading some liberal newspaper like the *Daily News* or *Morning Star*, rather than the unsympathetic *Times*.

Jessie spent several months in this mode disseminating Mazzini's propaganda. (Although their paths did not cross, Orsini was similarly employed in raising money for Italy under his own auspices.) She spoke—and her speeches were reported favorably in local provincial papers—in Manchester, Leeds, Newcastle, Edinburgh, Tyneside, Glasgow, Paisley, and others.* She rather consistently wrote to Mazzini for elucidation of certain points so that she could make her lectures more detailed and so that they would accurately reflect his opinions. She also forwarded him her own ideas about the way things might be done; these Mazzini was not so eager to receive, and finally he asked her to desist and to concentrate instead on her money-raising efforts.

For a lecture to a workingman's league, for example, Jessie wrote to ask Mazzini about duties and tariffs in Italy, and Mazzini responded:

> I cannot tell you about the amount of duties; they are heavy; and from one corner of the Peninsula to the other there are at least seven lines of customs to cross; the smallness of the market is the plague of

* As usual the Friends of Italy rallied to the occasion and drew attention to the cause by giving Jessie abundant publicity in the press.

Italy as far as the *material* improvement is concerned; there is, as you know, a great self-improving movement towards association in our working classes, at least in Piedmont and Liguria; but they will never be able to solve the economical problem of their emancipation before a great national market is opened to their activity; before 24 or 25 millions of consumers are ready for their products. Without any socialistic sectarian squabble, our National Insurrection would atchieve [*sic*] wonders for the "people," with only three measures; first: the reform of Taxation, starting from the principle, that Life cannot be taxed; that taxation must begin from the surplus, leaving the average of necessities for human life untouched; and the surplus being taxed in proportion of the amount:—secondly: the opening of works in all branches, roads, railways, arsenals, maritime establishments, docks, bridges, Pantheon, House of National Assembly, fortresses, drainage of the marshes, etc., which would afford employment to millions of men:—thirdly, the formation of a gigantic National Fund, the elements of which would be: the ecclesiastical property, amounting to something like two milliards of francs; only the Roman states yielding 400 milliards of Scudi!—the property (national) of the Kings, Princes, etc.—the Austrian property (they have vast lands, etc. which would partially compensate the immense sums of money they have been taking from us)—the property of the few high aristocratic families who would fight or plot against the nation in the ranks of the enemy—etc., etc. From this immense fund, once having deducted for justice's sake a pension to the really wanting priest, or pension to the children of the traitors, etc.—one part could be taken to form a "Fond de crédit" for all *voluntary* industrial and agricultural associations of working men having both capacity and morality, but no capital. The Government would advance, at the half-per-cent only, for the Office and management expenses; the advance to be given back in installments, on the profits of the "enterprises." I mention all this, because it would please your working hearers to know something about mine or our intentions.[19]

Some of the people Jessie met in the provinces may have been rather surprised at her deportment. "I am fond of the Revd. Crosskey," Mazzini wrote to her when she was in Scotland, "on account of his tract, which you did *not* send, but mostly on account of your smoking whilst he was composing."[20] But the chairman of one of her lectures commented that she had a voice "as musical as is Apollo's lute" and the reporter in the *Northern Daily Express* for April 25, 1857 remarked "that her quiet, graceful, and thoroughly feminine manners must have agreeably disappointed those who expected in a lady-lecturer something violent, out of keeping, and out of nature."

Meanwhile in Italy, the last months of 1856 and the beginning of 1857 were marked by uprisings in several regions. An attempted revolution in Sicily, organized by Rosalino Pilo and Nicola Fabrizi failed, but when the supply ship rushing to the aid of the Bourbon government exploded, the unrest flared up again. Mazzinians asked Garibaldi to undertake an expedition to Sicily, but he refused to take on this commission. Jessie, troubled by his attitude and wishing to persuade him to change his mind, wrote to him from England to ask why he had refused. Garibaldi replied in a letter (which Jessie cautioned the reader of her history not to think of as a love letter):

Sister beloved, whatever happens, I never meant to vex you and should be grieved at heart if I have done so. You certainly have no need of tenderness, and I am far from wasting it on you; but what you cannot hinder me from saying is the truth. Well, I love you, which matters very little to you; I love you for myself and for my boy, and for Italy, which I idolise and venerate above all earthly things. As to principles, Jessie, I know that your opinion of your brother is even too high. Well, I can assure you that if Garibaldi was sure to be followed by a goodly number on presenting himself, with a flag, on the field of action, to his country, with even a slight probability of success, Jessie mine, can you doubt that I should rush forward with feverish joy, to realise the ideal of my whole life, even knowing that the reward awaiting me should be the most atrocious martyrdom? If you doubt me, you must know me but ill, after all. Sister, I say with pride that I dare take rank with the most staunch of Italian patriots, and in writing this my conscience tells me that I am not making a vain boast. My life, all spent for Italy, is my witness; to unsheath a sword for her is the paradise of my belief: my wife, my children, the desire for rest, nothing has ever been able to restrain me from fighting for the holy cause. I will say one thing more, that all and any of the movements directed by your friend [Mazzini] although disapproved of by me, would have had one follower more if I had found myself on the spot. If I do not offer myself as chief of an attempt, it is because I see no probability of success; and you know enough of my past life to admit that I do understand something of daring enterprises. One word more about Piedmont. In Piedmont there is an army of 45,000 men and an ambitious king; these are elements for an initiative, and for success, in which the majority of the Italians believe today. Let your friend furnish similar elements, and show a little more practicability than he has done hitherto, and we will bless him also and follow him with fervour. On the other hand, if Piedmont hesitates and proves itself unequal to the mission which we believe it is called upon to fulfil, we shall repudiate it. Let any one, in short, commence the "Holy War" with temerity even, and you will see your brother first on the battlefield. Fight, I say, and I am with the fighter; but, sister mine, I will not say to the Italians: "Arise," just to give the curs . . . food for laughter. This is frank speaking, is it not? I shall remain at Genoa for a few

55

days, then I will return to Nice, and go to Sardinia towards the end of
the month. There and elsewhere, command your brother,

G. Garibaldi[21]

Garibaldi's reluctance to join them notwithstanding, Pilo and Pisacane undertook to execute a plot against the Bourbons in the spring
of 1857. The rather disappointingly limited funds that had been collected by Jessie in the north of England were used exclusively to fi-
nance their enterprise; and Mazzini decided that it would be convenient to have Jessie in Genoa to help with the plans. Garibaldi sent
messages to Jessie urging her not to have anything to do with this
foolish plot, which he guessed was bound to fail, but Jessie, as she
said, was convinced of the "righteousness" of the action. She felt that
many others approved even if Garibaldi did not.

Consequently, at Mazzini's suggestion, Jessie in May of 1857 applied to the editor of the *Daily News*, England's pro-Italian newspaper, asking that she be appointed its Italian correspondent. Mazzini thought it very desirable that the news reaching England from
Italy should go through the hands of a Mazzinian; but the editors
of the *Daily News* seem to have exercised due caution in not com-
mitting themselves definitely to Jessie although she set off for Italy
thinking that she was their representative. Beyond this, Mazzini intended to capitalize on her presence for favorable publicity, and he
saw to it that her arrival was greeted with enthusiasm in the republican newspaper *Italia del Popolo* and by workingmen's groups. The
Italia del Popolo noted her arrival in Genoa as follows:

> Yesterday evening the group of the Association of Workers at Al-
> bergo d'Italia, celebrated joyfully the arrival of the noted Miss Jessie
> Meriton White, who has propagandized in England and Scotland
> with great energy for the cause of the Italian people. The *Marseil-
> laise* was sung many times, salutes were given to the gentle traveler,
> who from the balcony of the inn, waved her handkerchief in thanks.
> A deputation of workers of Genoa and of Sampierdarena gave the
> following speech. 'Signora, we welcome you, noble daughter of Eng-
> land; we welcome you as one whom we have come to love as a sister
> and for whom we feel admiration and gratitude. For a long time our
> thoughts have accompanied you in your trip, holy pilgrim, that you
> undertook in covering England and Scotland to preach the truth and
> the justice of the Italian cause and we have committed to memory
> and repeated to our fellow-citizens the dear words that have come
> from your generous heart. Without knowing you, our imagination
> clothed your virtuous soul in a beautiful body—a harmonious nature
> —and now that we have the pleasure of meeting you in person, we
> feel that we already know you. You are to be congratulated because
> you have awakened in your people sympathy and justice, which have

previously been denied our cause. Be praised for having dissipated prejudice and error about our country, for having dared to say that Italy is unjustly oppressed, and for having the purpose and will to help free it. Be praised for having worked towards an alliance between your country and ours, which one day will be realized. Be praised, above all, for saying so emphatically that Italy must be for the Italians—and having seen that the Italian question is not a question of Venice, nor Genoa, nor Turin, nor Naples locally—nor a question of dynasties nor of partial amelioration, nor of material interests, but it is a question of a National Union, of a Fatherland united and free from the Alps to the sea, of an Italian people, keeper of its own destiny. Be blessed for all this, both you and your fellow Englishmen. You have come, fellow working pilgrim, to see whether we—the first Italians to greet you—justify the cementing of relationships between your country and ours. . . . One thing we can assure you . . . that we will not rest until Italy has been united—in all its provinces and cities there will be no rest until this has taken place. . . . The day of battle will come, and we promise that you will be able to say to your compatriots: The Italians love their country and are worthy of your alliance.' At midnight the gathering broke up and all carried away with them the most pleasing impression of this woman of saintly purpose towards our beautiful and dear country.[22]

Her sudden beatification must have surprised Jessie as much as anyone. Mazzini, who had undoubtedly prepared rough notes for the dedication himself, wrote Emilie asking her to see to it that the *Italia del Popolo* article about Jessie was translated so that it could be used for publicity purposes in England. As an afterthought which seemed understated even coming from Mazzini, he observed to Emilie that he must be very careful about his relationship with Jessie from that point on because she would be watched.

There was a similar reception for Jessie in Turin on May 23; in this case the crowd was noisier, the personal testimonials more effusive, and Giuseppe La Masa read a sonnet in her honor.[23] During the weeks that followed, Jessie was further feted in Montebruno's Villa, La Spezia, Allesandria, Savona, and Oneglia.

While Jessie traveled about, Mazzini hid out in Genoa in the rooms of Alberto Mario. Originally from Venetia, Alberto had been actively interested in the republican cause for some time. He had recently become sympathetic to the federalist position* but was still sufficiently loyal to Mazzini to help him with his plans for the now imminent insurrection. At some point during these weeks Alberto was introduced to Jessie by Mazzini and offered to guide her around in her peregrinations. Mazzini encouraged her to continue participating in various ceremonies undoubtedly hoping that this peripheral activity

* See chapter 2, p. 31.

would distract the authorities from what was really afoot. The ceremonies continued until June 22; by the end of that month Jessie discovered that her assumption that she would be working for the *Daily News* was incorrect, the paper having dispatched Luigi Mariotti from England to act as its official correspondent. Mariotti was not a Mazzinian, while Jessie's activities since she had set foot in Italy had made it perfectly clear that she was far from impartial.

On the eve of the attempted execution of the plot, Mazzini sent Jessie the following message:

> I write these words now, because I shall have scarcely time tomorrow. I have no exact information as yet. But all the probabilities are that, how is a mystery, the boats and the steamer have not yet met. If the Steamer is ours P [isacane] is deprived of 19 men, 100 muskets, etc. It is however one of those steps which one cannot retrace; and if they have acted, they *must* attempt something; it is a crime of *piraterie*. We had, of course, prearranged something for all cases; but it is a sad affair and may prove worse than sad. If the boats had met the small ones would have come back by day; their not having come, shows that, loaded as they are with men and muskets, they cannot come except by night. However, I shall know within a few hours, and I shall add one word.[24]

The course of the ill-fated Pisacane expedition followed an increasingly familiar pattern. On paper, as worked out in Mazzini's blueprint, the plan made sense, although it involved many risks. It was to consist of two phases. During the first, Carlo Pisacane was to seize a Piedmontese ship plying the waters between Genoa, Sardinia, and Tunis and force the crew of the ship to make landings at Ponza and Sapri in the south. Here political prisoners would be liberated, and the populace, recognizing their liberators, would immediately join with them and march against Naples to overthrow the government, thus lighting the fire of revolution that would sweep over the whole peninsula. The second part of the plan was that simultaneously a group of conspirators were to seize strategic points in the city of Genoa and there establish a supply base for the Neapolitan liberators.

Neither phase of this plan worked. Pisacane was able to seize the *Cagliari*, but when he landed with his handful of fellow conspirators expecting to be met by earnest supporters who would follow him on to victory, he encountered instead forces of the Neapolitan army and was killed. The Genoese phase of the plot proved equally unsuccessful.[25] The conspirators were not able to seize their objectives and were soon dispersed. Though Mazzini managed to escape and make his way to England, many of his co-conspirators were less fortunate and were apprehended by the police. Among those arrested and confined in Sant'Andrea prison in Genoa were Jessie White and Alberto Mario.

4

Jessie's engagement to Alberto Mario began under stress on the evening of June 28, 1857 while the outcome of Pisacane's mission was still undecided. The couple's entire courtship was thereafter conducted by correspondence while they were both prisoners at Sant' Andrea. They could not have known each other for more than two weeks before they were engaged. Jessie was twenty-five and Alberto thirty-two and he was, in her words, "blond, elegant."

Alberto had been in residence in Genoa for some time. Indeed he had been moving around the north of Italy since 1848, a self-exiled radical who could not endure the Austrian oppression of his native province of Venetia. He was born in Lendinara near Venice on June 4, 1825, the son of Francesco and Angela Baccelli Mario. At the age of nineteen, he went to Padua to study mathematics and afterwards law, but became involved in anti-Austrian plots at the university and was subsequently under almost continuous surveillance by the Austrian police. In February, 1848 he fled to Bologna, where he tried to continue his studies. This was the spring of revolutions* when Milan had enjoyed a brief period of independence from Austrian rule. Alberto had gone to Milan after Cattaneo had set up a provisional government in that city in March and had offered himself as an aide to Mazzini who had also made his way to Milan. Mazzini was hopeful that with Milan free the triumph of republicanism was now close at hand. These hopes were soon extinguished when General Radetzky reasserted Austrian control and regained Milan.† At this point Alberto

* See chapter 2, p. 30.
† See chapter 2, p. 32.

Mario fled to Genoa, then Florence, Bologna, and back again to Genoa where he was living at the time of the Pisacane plot.

In June, 1857, when Mazzini was using Alberto's apartment as his secret quarters, Alberto was deeply committed to the cause of Italian unification, though his politics lay neither with those of Mazzini nor of Garibaldi. He was, to be sure, one of the contributors to the underground newspaper sponsored by Mazzini, *Italia del Popolo*. (Perhaps it was he who wrote the notices about Jessie's arrival in Genoa.) But initially a Giobertist and neo-Guelphist* he had come to support the federalist position of Carlo Cattaneo,† believing that the unification of Italy could best be gained through the voluntary federation of autonomous states. Thus neither Cattaneo nor Alberto shared Mazzini's conviction that a unitarian state was essential. But Alberto, like many other liberals, realized that while his views differed from Mazzini's in several important respects, he could not afford to neglect any opportunity to work toward the ultimate goal of unification. Whenever there was a chance to throw off the restrictions imposed by the papacy, by Austria, or by the Bourbons the initiative had to be seized and Mazzini remained the chief plotter of such initiatives. Out of necessity then, many liberals joined in Mazzini's schemes even though they had reservations about them. Alberto, for example, later told Jessie that he had participated in the Pisacane conspiracy not because he fully supported Mazzini's tactics but because he felt it would have been treacherous to default.‡

Jessie was arrested on July 4, the same day as Alberto, and was subsequently held in prison for four months (two months longer than Alberto) because she would not promise to return immediately to England if released. During her imprisonment, she did everything she could to regain her freedom. The British ambassador in Turin at this time was Sir James Hudson. Since Hudson quite rightly considered Jessie guilty of collaborating in Mazzini's Genoese enterprise—although she vigorously denied that this was the case—he would do nothing to assist her in her bid for freedom. Her attempt to gain release from jail was handled by two Mazzinian lawyers—Carcassi and Brofferio§—who offered to defend her against the accusations‖ of the state tribunal.[1] Jessie claimed that she had been illegally detained;

---

* See chapter 2, p. 31.   †See same page.

‡ According to some sources, Pisacane himself had serious doubts about the whole proceeding; see Alberto Mario, *Scritti letterari e artistici di Alberto Mario* (Bologna: N. Zanichelli, 1901), 1:1. See also chapter 3, note 25.

§ Angelo Brofferio, republican deputy of the Piedmontese Chamber.

‖ Jessie claimed that Cavour wanted her proven insane "in which case no trial would be needed" since insanity would argue "irresponsible guilt" (*BMI*, p. 272). Presumably Cavour hoped to avoid friction with the English authorities by such a move. Jessie always held him accountable for her detention believing that he was furious that the Mazzinians had escaped his spy network (see Cavour's letter, pp. 64-65).

she indicated that she was an English newspaperwoman who had gone peacefully and lawfully about her business when, without provocation, she was seized and illegally imprisoned. She maintained that her passport was in order and that she had not conspired against the king of Sardinia. Throughout her imprisonment she insisted that she was not Mazzini's agent. In the account she later offered her interrogators concerning her activities prior to her arrest, she gave her reasons for coming to Italy, explained why she had picked Genoa, with whom she had stayed, and added other details.* Some of her testimony is in direct conflict with other available evidence, and it seems quite clear that Jessie edged more than a little embroidery on the truth. She may not have been essential to the execution of the Pisacane plot, but she was certainly a party to it. In the *Birth of Modern Italy*, for example, Jessie freely reveals her complicity in the insurrection:

> On June 26th we saw Pisacane for the last time, *and I wrote under his dictation a note for the two engineers of the steamer*—discovered at the last moment to be English—*in explanation of what was going to happen*. [translator's italics throughout] The two men, Walt and Park by name, were afterwards imprisoned for seven months in the Neapolitan dungeons, in consequence of which one lost his mind and the other became permanently afflicted with epileptic convulsions.
> . . .
> Pisacane gave me his political testament and other papers to be published in England, together with a magnificent letter of Cattaneo, which appeared, translated, in the *Daily News*, but the originals in my possession were sequestrated by the Piedmontese police.
> At 7 p.m. of the 26th, from the heights of Carignano, Alberto Mario and I watched the vessel steam out of harbour. . . . (Mazzini) slept in Alberto Mario's apartment (for the next three nights) and, from hour to hour, sent us little notes.[2]

The *Italia del Popolo* gave this substantial account of Jessie's arrest:

> On the evening of July 3rd, towards 11:30, the officer Ansaldo, accompanied by about twenty carabinieri and guards, entered Mr. Roggero's apartment, calling him to account. Miss Jessie Meriton White, who was living at Mr. Roggero's house, having by chance found herself in the entrance hall when the troops arrived, answered that Roggero, she believed, would return in a short time as usual. As soon as the officer entered the rooms of the young Englishwoman with part of his company, he started to read letters and other papers and to search the wardrobes and every corner of the rooms. Miss White asked him by what right he proceeded to search and asked him to show her the

* See Appendix 1.

written order. The officer pulled a tricolored scarf from his pocket, but no card of authorization. Meanwhile, the search continued and it became necessary to submit to this abuse. For that reason Miss White prepared to help Ansaldo and his followers who in their job were certainly not very brilliant. Nothing was found which could interest the meticulous officer; and in the meanwhile a polite conversation took place between the illustrious English speaker and the above-mentioned officer. And she concluded: *My dear Sir, if you and your men were one day to visit free England I assure you that you would not be greeted by a visitation like the one with which the liberal Sardinian government has honored me.* In the end, Ansaldo, by chance rather embarrassed because of this uneasy conversation, ordered her on the part of the Minister [of the Interior, Rattazzi] to leave the Kingdom of Sardinia. *And the reason?* she asked. *I don't know it,* replied Ansaldo. *Sir,* Miss White said then, *I will not go without a reasonable* explanation unless you use force. For this purpose I ask to meet the Minister and I give my word of honor not to leave *Genoa.* The officer accepted her word placing the distinguished Englishwoman under arrest in her house, guarded by several carabinieri and security guards. The next day Ansaldo returned, saying that the Minister ordered her to leave the realm because the mothers and the sisters and the wives of the prisoners of the recent political commotions were imprecating against her, saying she had incited them. And Miss White said to him: *I absolutely do not understand the meaning of your words: I came to Italy for literary work and for correspondence with several English papers, therefore your words are a mystery to me. I demand therefore to be submitted to legal process so that the truth of my affirmations can be demonstrated. I will submit myself with pleasure—if it is required—to preventative detention. And if it is true, as you maintain, that we are in a free state, I am certain that my request cannot and must not be refused. Otherwise, I repeat, you will be forced to use your carabinieri in order to transport me to the frontier. I am perfectly within the law; my passport has been signed by Clarendon. My conduct is above reproach; therefore I have nothing to fear.* Later the several-times mentioned officer Ansaldo came again, this time without his previously belabored courtesy; he brusquely ordered her to leave; she calmly replied—*I will not leave*—Madame, you will leave this evening—Sir, *I will not leave*—She was denied recourse to her own consul, to whom she turned with a letter: she sent an electrical dispatch to the ambassador residing in Turin asking to be legally arrested.* But, in view of the fact that the English government usually only protects its citizens' pocket-books, the consul and the ambassador answered her like Pilate. Asking him to represent her cause in the tribunals, she sent the following dispatch to Brofferio: "I am arrested in my house, I don't know why. My passport issued by Clarendon is in order. I am required to leave.

---

* See note 5, p. 138.

I will not leave unless they use physical force. I want a regular trial. Do you wish to defend me?" And here are the words with which Brofferio accepted the task: "I will be honored to defend you. This evening I will talk to the Minister. I am on your side now and always."—electrical dispatch.

On the 5th [of July] in the afternoon the public prosecutor and the judge went to the home of the illustrious prisoner and proceeded with the first interrogation.* It seems that a regular trial properly evoked by her will take place and since we trust in the integrity of our magistrates, we don't doubt at all that the blind and senseless arbitrariness of the government will clearly be revealed.

That day at 11 she was handed over to the prison of Sant' Andrea. Miss White throughout this distasteful incident continued to praise the respectful bearing and the courtesy of the guards, and in particular, of the carabinieri.—We, ashamed of the inhospitable conduct of the government towards a young foreigner who had consecrated herself with so much devotion to the Italian cause, conquering with the force of an innocent conscience all the obstacles—the prejudice of vulgar aristocrats and hypocrisy—we beg you to distinguish the lying and illiberal action of those who command us from the sentiments and inspiration of the *liguranian-subalpine* people who had given her frequent and sure signs of their gratitude and homage for the constant and intelligent work of creating favorable opinion for Italy, for her lively sympathy, sincere admiration, and the more and more efficacious aid of the English people. Don't forget, Madam, that the flag which has green, white, and red on it and which flies from our towers is not the true Italian flag.[3]

In the meantime, Camillo Cavour, prime minister of Piedmont-Sardinia, hastened to recount his version of the arrest to Emmanuel d'Azeglio, the ambassador from Piedmont-Sardinia to Great Britain. On July 6, 1857 he wrote

I regret that among the most compromised people is a young Englishwoman, Miss White. It appears certain that she has played an important role and that she devoted all her efforts to push for the struggle. The magistrates charged with execution of the law issued an arrest warrant against her yesterday morning. She was found hidden in the house of one of the most ardent of Mazzinians and they seized a correspondence which left no doubt of her participation in the most violent acts of the conspiracy. She tried to seduce the carabinieri who were guarding her by using feminine coquetry. But our fine soldiers are Josephs whom the wives of Potiphar do not disturb. We are not brutal, but we believe that under the actual circumstances we must be very severe since this is not simply a matter of political conspirators but rather madmen who want to reach their goal by murder, assassination and pillage. Hudson, to whom Miss White ap-

* See Appendix 1.

pealed, refused to become involved with her. Please inform Lord Clarendon [British secretary of state for foreign affairs] of this fact lest he receive a false impression about an act which is imposed on us by the sacred duty to reprove this most odious of attempts, the most blameworthy that has taken place since '48.[4]

Undoubtedly Cavour's prompt report to d'Azeglio was intended to stave off a protest from the British government about the arrest of Her Majesty's subject, Jessie White. But Cavour's fear of unpleasant diplomatic repercussions proved groundless, for Jessie's attempts to secure the intervention of Her Majesty's Ambassador to Piedmont-Sardinia, Sir James Hudson, turned out to be singularly unsuccessful. Immediately following her arrest, Jessie had sent off a telegram July 4, 1857 to Hudson in Turin:

> I am arrested. I do not know why. I am not allowed to see the British Consul. I am ordered to leave Genoa. I will not go unless compelled by brute force. I demand a trial. I have a passport from Lord Clarendon in order.[5]

Hudson's response, dated July 4, sent to Yeats Brown, the British consul at Genoa, was scarcely encouraging:

> Acquaint Miss White that her proceedings in this Country have had for their object the setting the King's authority at defiance & the subversion of the Law & Public Peace & therefore I decline to take any steps in her behalf.

In replying to Hudson's communiqué, Brown enclosed a letter (also dated July 4) he had received from Jessie. Brown was clearly no more sympathetic to Jessie than his superior:

> I have the honor to enclose to you the copy of a letter wh. I received at midday from Miss Jessie Meriton White. Immediately upon its being in my hands I hastened to the Intendente Generale, who showed me letters addressed to her & induced me to believe that she was compromised in the late attempt at rebellion here & he informed me that she had declared herself to be the wife of Mazzini. Of this I verbally informed her by her messenger, who appeared to be a French lady—Upon this she has sent me a note, saying that "if I refuse to give her reasons for her arrest" she will telegraph to you.
> Under the circumstances I do not hold that she is entitled to any protection, and believe that she will be forwarded to the frontier wh. I shall not oppose.

The tone of Jessie's letter to Yeats Brown combined injured innocence with brave defiance, but the evidence shown Brown by the authorities had naturally enough negated its effect on him:

> I have been residing a month in Genoa corresponding for English papers. Last night 21 gens d'armes visited me, searched my papers,

and requested me to leave Genoa. No motive is assigned for the request beyond vague hints whose meaning I am at a loss to discover. My passport from Ld. Clarendon is in order. I refuse to go. Will you have the kindness to enquire the meaning of this insult offered to a British subject. If I am accused of any crime against this free & constitutional gov. let me be arrested & tried. If found guilty I am willing to suffer the penalty. Until such proof be found, I shall remain in Genoa or be led thence by brute force. My passport is in the hands of Avo.Fis.*Ansaldo.

I am, &
Jessie Meriton White
Saturday, July 5/57

P.S. I should come to you instead of writing, but am guarded by four gens d'armes.

In a dispatch (July 10) to Lord Clarendon, a week after Jessie's arrest, Hudson made no bones about his view of Jessie's actions:

> With reference to my despatch marked no. 79 of the 5th instant upon the recent proceedings of Miss White I have the honor to inform your Lordship that this Government took into consideration the sex of that person and her exaggerated political opinions, and, having no wish to deal severely by her, hoped that the lesson she had received at Genoa would tend to moderate her opinions and her practice, and therefore, while they had the power they gave her the option of quitting this country before including her in a Process of Law.
>
> These humane and gallant intentions of the Minister of the Interior have been frustrated by the lady herself, who denounced the King and his Government as tyrants and declared her intention of sharing the fate of her associates.
>
> The Minister of the Interior told me that he regretted this conduct of Miss White and added that, as the Public Prosecutor has now commenced an action against those Persons who recently attempted to disturb the peace of Genoa, Miss White's name is included amongst them and she must, through her perverse and obstinate spirit, undergo whatever sentence the law may pass upon her.

This was followed by yet another dispatch from Hudson three days later which included material calculated to discourage any intervention by Clarendon on Jessie's behalf.

> With reference to my despatch marked No 80 of the 10th inst. upon the subject of the arrest of a British Subject, Miss White, for participation in the recent attempt of Mr. Mazzini to create disturbance at Genoa I have the honour to enclose herewith the Copy and Translation of a memo which has been addressed to me upon that matter by the Sardinian Minister of the Interior....

---

* Title designating Ansaldo as prosecuting lawyer.

[*Memo from Rattazzi*, Turin, July 12, 1857] In conformity with the understanding come to the undersigned Minister [he] hastens to communicate to H.E. the Min. of HBM. the reasons which have caused on the part of the judicial authority at Genoa the arrest of Miss White a Brit. subject. The English woman Miss White came to Genoa some months ago with the reputation of being a warm emissary of Giu. Mazzini and one who in England and especially Scotland had supported for several years at various meetings the cause of that party.

She was visited immediately on her arrival at Genoa by the Director of the Journal "Italia del Popolo," the organ of the party and by the Chiefs of the Workmen's Association, who gave her an ovation with a serenade & *evvivas*.

She afterwards was present at festivals and meetings of workmen, where she spoke frequently & placed herself in relation with Carlo Pisacane who commanded the expedition to Sapri; Luigi Stallo, Michele Tassara, the Hatter Luigi Roggero and Angelo Manzini, known as the warmest promoters of the late conspiracy. It is too now known that she was engaged in exciting [*sic*] to insurrection influential emigrants & on the very night of the movement Miss White went & took up her abode in the house of Roggero in whose shop there had been a distribution of bread wine and daggers to some of the conspirators.

This conduct left no doubt as to her complicity in the deplorable events wh. disturbed the city of Genoa, and consequently the Office of the Intendant General did not hesitate to order a perquisition in the house of Roggero against the said Miss White, and to warn her to leave Genoa. But as she refused to comply with this intimation, & as at the same time by a letter found directed to Miss White in the possession of a certain Enrichetta Lazzari, Pisacane's mistress, there was ample proof of her complicity in the movement that had been organized (wh letter of July 3rd is to be found joined to the judical proofs), she was arrested by a formal order of the judicial authority, to whom this letter had then been communicated, and a prosecution commenced against her.

Another proof of the complicity of Miss White in these deplorable conspiracies is furnished by a receipt given by her to the compromised Stallo of a thousand lire for the sum for which he had rendered himself responsible to the National Subscription.

That the Sardinian authorities were perfectly correct in attributing participation in the plot to Jessie we know from her own writing. But as her father could have told them from his own experience, Jessie was not one to give in easily once she had assumed a definite stance. Given her passionate adherence to the cause the matter of departing from the truth presented no problem to Jessie. The extent to which she was party to what was going on is further revealed in her introduction to Alberto Mario's literary works.[6]

I was then living with Elena Casati at the house of Roggero, one of the conspirators; there we were awaiting a signal to fulfill the parts assigned us. At first, the quiet of the city was reassuring, then oppressive: finally, after midnight, Alberto returned.—An hour earlier the government was warned, that is General Durando heard it from one of his friends, a leader among the conspirators who at the same time told Mazzini that the government was on the alert, and that surprise would be impossible. Mazzini instantly gave the counterorder, not wishing conflict between civilians and soldiers, and if Pisacane had succeeded, everything would have been postponed for a better time or, in the contrary case, things would remain as if nothing had happened.

But unfortunately, the counterorder did not reach the men in the far distant fort of Diamente in time; they, having made friends with the guard by playing ball and playing music with them for several weeks, had entered the fort that night, invited to a prearranged party, and they suddenly took possession of the fort and of the artillery. Seargent Pastrone fell, killed by a youth, one of the conspirators, who shot him in fear and quite unnecessarily.

If the surprise moves had succeeded, all the positions could have been taken without bloodshed. Alberto, having left his papers at my house, suddenly wished to reassure himself that Mazzini was not in danger and he descended the hill of Santa Brigida. Dressed to the hilt, with pearl gray gloves and a top hat, [and] despite the fact that he encountered many carabinieri and soldiers and that the garrison was alerted, no one suspected that the elegant young man who was walking slowly along, smoking, had several minutes before found himself on the point of assailing Saint Spiritus,* armed with a revolver and having in his pocket letters which proved his participation in the crime of rebellion, a crime which the code punished with death. During the night, the house, not suspect until then, filled with people who thought they were already denounced. Elena Casati, with her accustomed munificence, would have been most generous in helping send them all to safety if I had not been opposed until the time when we heard the fate of Pisacane and nothing else could then be done.

Mazzini answered my request for instructions immediately. "What did you think when the city remained silent at one o'clock? . . . If there are any poor threatened exiles there, make them leave. But don't give in to any extremists' fears, like those of R[oggero]. . . . If you have any certain and important news, send it to me. . . . Save the proclamation and everything but well hidden. . . . Almost every contact is interrupted here. Tomorrow I will perhaps be able to see further, clearness among the clouds."

The next day the news reached me in code from the Neapolitan region, that Pisacane had disembarked successfully at Ponza: ". . . It is enough that I could exit from Sardinian waters and that I was not

* The locale of an artillery position.

taken by Neapolitan ships, I'll take care of the rest." Nothing seemed lost then. The government had not discovered anything of importance in its search: none of the leaders was arrested. As usual, outsiders had to pay for the mistakes of all, but Mario's house was not suspected.

On July 3rd my apartment was searched with great show of force: the officer, a certain Ansaldo, was angry but not clever. He found none of the papers given to me: they contented themselves with threatening me with expulsion: I answered that that was an illegal order for an English citizen with her passport in order from the Foreign Office. After setting up a code with Elena and Mario, and just at the moment in which the guards were leading me to the prison of Sant' Andrea, news dispatches arrived. Pisacane had succeeded in freeing the prisoners on the isle of Ponza, all embarking at Cagliari and getting off at Sapri. Thus, the first night of prison, I was allowed a golden sleep which the anxiety and emotion of many days had not permitted me.

Although her Britannic Majesty's representatives proved cold and unfriendly, Jessie was not without other sources of comfort during her ordeal. Her engagement to Alberto blossomed into full romance during their imprisonment. Alberto and Jessie were both practical souls and they were already well versed in the art of subterfuge. They thriftily nourished their acquaintance into a much deeper relationship and they corresponded frequently by means of the prison grapevine. Jessie saved some of the letters at least long enough to copy them into the introduction to her two-volume edition of her husband's works, published after his death.

Alberto had recognized Jessie's quick wit and her readiness to learn. He decided at once that he would begin systematically to teach her Italian history and to introduce her to Italian literature, of which he found her abysmally ignorant. Italian grammar, in which she needed intensive instruction, he would save until they were released from prison. His letters to her over the course of the summer drew from his mental storehouse. He had no books with him—and he acknowledged that it was difficult to teach either history or literature without books—but he reproduced with ease examples from the great Italian scientists, philosophers, and poets of the past, among them Galileo, Vico, and Dante, who was his favorite poet. Each day—or each letter, for sometimes several were sent in the course of one day—he set before her his ordered thinking about some aspect of the course he was giving her in the culture of her adopted land. Often a letter that commenced as a serious treatise on a particular author or period of literature would end in a declaration of love: "My Bianca [a bird he had captured and named for Jessie] is the dearest, sweetest, most modest little sparrow that you can imagine. She cheerfully answers my every call. . . . I caress her and she answers my caresses almost I would say with a sense of gratitude and tenderness. . . . I only fear that one fine day she will go in search of a better companion than I."[7] His effusions of love were not lengthy, but they were frequent; and as the friendship ripened through the correspondence, the allusions became less and less veiled.

The problem that perplexed both Jessie and Alberto was the important and troublesome decision they must make about the future. If they were to marry, where would it be and when? Where would they live? Alberto had a warm and close relationship with his family, in spite of his prolonged wanderings, but he could not return to his native province, having been outlawed by the Austrians for his political activities; neither did he wish to remain in Genoa under the existing Sardinian government. On the other hand, he did not wish to leave Italy, even for a while. The thought of moving to England, although it was Jessie's home, did not appeal to him either, for he could not foresee a meaningful future in a country where he was isolated from everything he had worked for and known. Meanwhile Jessie's father implored her to return to England once she was released from prison. She had already given a formal promise to Mazzini and other English friends that she would undertake a new series of lectures there. Furthermore she was toying with the idea of taking a trip to America to acquaint the "slave haters" of the new world with the Italian movement against Austrian slavery, a movement she thought would certainly appeal to Americans.

As the year drew to an end, the Sardinian authorities finally moved to release Jessie. On November 14, Sir James Hudson reported to Clarendon:

> I have the honour to report to your Lordship that Miss White, who, as your Lordship will recollect was one of Mazzini's assistants in his attempt to disturb the peace of Genoa in June last,—has been set at liberty, and that she has been allowed five days to make her preparations for leaving this Country.

In a further dispatch, dated December 12, 1857, Hudson forwarded to Clarendon a final report on the case from the authorities in Genoa,[8] but by this time Jessie was already back in England.

Alberto, who had been released two months earlier, had come to realize that he could not provide a home for Jessie in Italy, and by the time of her release they had resolved their dilemma and decided to go to England together. They left Italy on December 1, 1857. Recalling this event years later, Jessie wrote with deep feeling of their leave-taking from Italy. "I feared for Alberto this real exile from his country," she observed, and then went on to describe their actual departure. "Saying a sad farewell to friends and to Italy, we passed the Alps covered with snow and Alberto was drawn to the spectacle of the new country. He observed the most minute things. In Geneva, he wanted to visit the places connected with Rousseau. When he went to present a letter of reference to General Klapka,* I suggested that he put on a black suit. Characteristically, he responded that he couldn't because there was a poor devil in prison without enough to eat and he had given him his suit."[9]

Although he could speak almost no English and was a complete stranger—a foreign revolutionary at that—Alberto was readily accepted by the White family, or at least so Jessie thought. He himself was very relieved to be so quickly placed at ease. He was pleased with his new friends and curious about their lives. He went around the dockyards and pried into the minute details of the family business. He was interested in everything he saw and "always asked, 'But how is it run? Where are the employees? The soldiers? The troops?' He felt liberty in the air and in the joyfulness."[10]

Jessie White and Alberto Mario were married on December 19, 1857. The civil ceremony, the first ever in the White family, was performed by a judge who carefully examined all of Alberto's documents. "It might be," the magistrate said to her father, "that he left other wives in Italy."[11] He insisted that Alberto repeat the solemn words in French because he didn't know Italian and Alberto didn't know English. "Alberto smilingly said to Jessie—'I am beginning to realize that your family feels relieved that I am not a Calabrian brigand.'" They received a letter from Mazzini, telling them that he was happy about their plans and giving them his blessing. (He could not resist the temptation to combine business with pleasure, however, and cautioned Jessie not to waste too much time in dawdling, for there were lectures to be given and money was needed.) Actually, Mazzini was aware that Mario was not as convinced as Jessie that his theories were workable. He must privately have taken a colder view of the implications of this marriage than he admitted.

The newlyweds spent a month on the Isle of Wight among the four generations of White relatives living there. Alberto was treated with constant affection by his new kinsmen, and he ended up as affectionate toward them as if they had been his own relatives. They had a family Christmas celebration. Alberto's toast "Beef, beer, and liberty!" brought the response "My new son Bertie" from Jessie's father. On the last day of the year they went up to London and spent New Year's Eve with Mazzini. Subsequently, they found a place to live near him.

* Exiled hero of the Hungarian rebellion.

The couple worked together by day on their writing and in gathering materials for Jessie's forthcoming lectures. They spent many evenings in the Stansfeld house where Mazzini and Saffi often gathered with various members of the clan for informal discussion. Mazzini would hold forth and Bertie—as he was now called by everybody—would not argue with him although by now he had discovered that they were poles apart in their opinions on almost everything except their basic faith in a united Italy.

London naturally offered Bertie many opportunities to become acquainted with English culture. He rode around the city on the top of omnibuses, talking with conductors and looking at monuments. He asked many questions of fellow travelers. When an Englishman expressed surprise at the amount of time Alberto spent on top of the bus, he answered with a customary joke, "Sir, it is the only way of seeing your sunlight." Not to have the beautiful Italian sun, his wife observed, was his one disappointment.

Alberto decided that he could profitably write articles about Italy for magazine publication in England. These were not propagandistic pieces but were concerned with Italian literary history. He wrote one such article for the *National Review* entitled "The Direction of Italian Thought in the Last Three Centuries" and another called "The Mind of Ugo Foscolo." Jessie, of course, rendered his articles into English.

Soon Jessie decided that she must go through with her promise to Mazzini to make a trip to Scotland. Although Alberto did not oppose this trip, Jessie felt his distaste for it, and entreated him to stay with her brother at Aylesbury, believing that he would mind the separation less if he were there. Each day, however, a disconsolate letter from Alberto reached Jessie on her tour, and at the end of the first week he decided to join her, undertaking his first venture alone on the English railway system.

Later Alberto wrote his father a letter in which he described the difficulties of English train travel from the point of view of a foreigner. He went from Aylesbury to Newcastle-upon-Tyne, an arduous trip. Since he did not speak English, he did not realize that there were not one but three Newcastles in England. Thus he addressed his suitcase through to "Mario, Newcastle." The station masters in the two wrong stations were sent telegrams, and eventually Alberto and his suitcase were reunited. In Newcastle-upon-Tyne, he stayed with Joseph Cowen, a newspaper editor and sponsor of Jessie's trip. Like Jessie, Alberto was moved by the genuine affection that her audiences in the north of England showed for Italy.

Jessie and Alberto had met and married under romantic and unusual circumstances, and given their personalities and commitments it was hardly to be expected that their life together would follow the pattern of a conventional Victorian marriage. But it appears to have been a very happy one. Jessie's writings give no more than glimpses of her innermost feelings for Alberto, but these—especially in her introduction to his first volume of posthumously published *Scritti*—suggest a very deep and congenial attachment between two very unlike people.

George Eliot had heard in Florence that Alberto was a great egoist and wondered whether Jessie had a difficult time of it;* but if she did, it was never revealed in anything she said in print. In one of the letters Alberto wrote Jessie while they were in prison he quite openly confessed that one of the qualities he most admired about her was her ability to stand alone and follow her own ideas. Explaining why he could not share her unreserved admiration for Mazzini he went on to say that he thought it quite proper for them to maintain their independent political positions unless the one could persuade the other of an error of judgment. Alberto could understand why Jessie with her passionate and impulsive nature was more drawn to Mazzini than he was. Indeed he found her absolute devotion to Mazzini in these first months of their acquaintance a sign of her "nobility of spirit accompanied by superior intelligence."[12] Life without the kind of enthusiasm she possessed, he said, would be of a flat quality—a flower without its fragrance. The formulation of independent judgments and the courage to live according to principle—these he considered the backbone of individuality, and he looked for this ideal in women as well as men.

However romantic the trappings, this was a marriage between equals. It was a marriage in the modern sense long before Ibsen's Nora had slammed the door of passage to the outside world. It would continue to be a peripatetic, unconventional, and very interesting marriage for more than a quarter of a century, until Alberto's death.

* See p. 141.

5

Jessie and Mazzini had for some time thought that it might be possible to collect money for the Italian cause in America. They knew that Garibaldi had been well received by the Italian colony in New York and they hoped that American public opinion could be mobilized toward more outspoken support for Italian revolution. Margaret Fuller's* adventures in Italy and the Anglo-American connections of such figures as Ralph Waldo Emerson had already created a strong nucleus of Yankee interest in Italian affairs†.

Nevertheless, Alberto approached this trip to America with reservations and caution. Though he agreed to go, he insisted that he and Jessie pay their own expenses and not be indebted to Mazzinian funds in case there were developments not to Mazzini's taste. Since the voyage was expensive and Alberto poor, one can only conclude that the White family contributed to the voyage of the Marios. (Jessie possibly helped her father with Italian in business matters, since she was fairly fluent in the language and had Alberto's aid, and it may be that she was reimbursed for her services.) Whatever the source, the Marios had money to travel—if not in style, at least comfortably.

They had arrived in New York City by November 25, 1858; the New York *Journal of Commerce* for that day, announcing their arrival, noted that in Great Britain Jessie was celebrated for her eloquent lectures on liberal causes. The voyage had been uneventful, except

*See p. 9.

† A perusal of the New York City daily newspapers of the 1840 and '50's, especially the *New York Tribune* and the *New York Herald*, yields many articles concerning the role of the French, the Austrians, and the English in Italian affairs. There was scornful criticism of the pope and general sympathy for the Kingdom of Piedmont-Sardinia and its policies.

that Alberto was seasick and Jessie paced the deck with "a third class Neapolitan." Like many European travelers to the new world, they were astonished and appalled by America's rapid tempo. They marveled at the diversity of population in New York, especially at the number of Irishmen. When they got to know some of the citizens, "they had nothing but respect for them." They began at once to confer with New York's Italians, offering to give lectures. Taking up their pens as well, they commenced an extensive propaganda campaign through letters to the editorial columns of the *New York Post*, the *Herald*, and the *Times*.

Jessie's first lecture was given on December 1, 1858 in Clinton Hall in the Bowery. The *New York Daily Tribune* for that day promised that she would speak with "entire freedom, ample knowledge, and signal power." "Few women," it went on to say, "have come to us from Europe more strongly indorsed as able, eloquent, and in every way worthy." Horace Greeley introduced her, pointing out that she had not come on a personal errand but to enlist American sympathy for the "cause of the downtrodden children of Europe." The title of this lecture was "Italy and the Papacy," and its purpose was to introduce to the audience the notion that the papacy was at the root of all the evils and miseries that plagued Italy. Signora Mario was described by the *New York Herald* for December 2, 1858 as:

> a rather delicately molded lady, of a fine intellectual cast of features, and gifted with great volubility of speech and persuasive earnestness of expression which fixes the attention of her hearers. She occasionally ascends to very chaste and poetical language, rolling out in an impassioned strain great volumes of eloquence, and throughout the whole of her learned and beautiful lecture her language was choice and refined and enunciation clear and distinct. When she spoke of the wrongs of Italy and of the efforts of the martyrs who sacrificed their life for liberty, her brilliant eyes flashed like fire, and the glow of sympathy mounted to her cheek. Her light brown hair [*sic!*—not red] was dressed according to the prevailing fashion, and she wore a silk dress, with a gauze tippet about the neck. Her appearance was very fine.

Jessie's second lecture, given at Clinton Hall on December 8, and reported by the *Times* of December 9, took up the theme of the martyrdom for Italian independence. The *Tribune* of December 7, 1858 had printed a letter from her sponsors about the forthcoming lecture saying "Dear Madam: We have heard of your perils and sacrifices in behalf of liberty—of your imprisonment in Genoa—of your labors in the Italian cause in England—of the eloquence, the instructiveness and the solidity of your lectures in the principal cities of

Great Britain. . . ." The letter went on to say that although Italian liberty was not yet America's special cause, instruction from Jessie was awaited. Jessie responded in the same issue that she was encouraged by the sympathy of her audiences and the friendly spirit of the press, and that she looked forward to increasing sympathy and strengthening good will for Italy. During this lecture she drew a sharp contrast between Mazzini and Louis Napoleon. Unfortunately, she said, the touchstone for fame in the Victorian period was success. Louis Napoleon had successfully waded through blood to the French throne, trampling the liberties of millions. On the other hand, Mazzini, who fought against Louis Napoleon's objectives, was not a practical man. The fact was, Mazzini was not successful by standard terms. The English government, Jessie insisted, was making a mistake in not helping Mazzini when it had helped Louis Napoleon to his throne. But, Jessie noted, despite people like Louis Napoleon, and despite the erroneous policy of the English government, "Italy would yet be free."

On December 13, the *Times* commented on Jessie Mario's position in an editorial. In general, the editors said, they sympathized with the woman who had:

> done much and suffered much in the cause of Italian freedom, and [who] has been one of the most active and ablest agents Mazzini has ever had. . . . There is nobody who has a particle of sympathy with human sufferings, or a particle of detestation for tyranny and wrong, who will not feel an interest in the lady's subject, and nobody who admires devotion in a good cause can avoid wishing her all possible success in her labours.
>
> But in spite of all our sympathy with her and her theme, we cannot help saying that the questions— What do the Italian patriots propose to do? What are their aims and how do they mean to achieve them? are continually forming themselves in our minds. We desire as much as anybody to see Italy free and happy, but so far as our knowledge goes, nothing is *doing* to make her either one or the other. As year after year of this agitation passes by, as lecture follows lecture, and speech speech, and dinner dinner, we look for some tangible proposition, or plan of campaign. A good speech is a fine thing; an able manifesto is a fine thing; and a noble thought is finer than either; and they all three have their place and do their work in the world; but these are not all that are needed to shake off the yoke of a foreign conqueror.

The *Times* expressed the conviction that Sardinia should be the nucleus of emancipation in Italy because its patriots fought well in open fields, it maintained a good army, a government, a treasury, and most of all, it had a *locus standi* in European courts, a voice that was respected in international councils. Therefore it was to be hoped that in the next "battle" Venice and Lombardy would unite under Piedmont, "taught by bitter experience the difference between the enthusiasm which wins a battle and the trained courage which wins lasting gains." The editorial ended by agreeing that although Louis Napoleon was clever, Mazzini was honest and conscientious.

Two days later, Jessie responded to the *Times* editorial, maintaining that her position had been misstated. Mazzini, the *Times* failed to see, had taught Italy for twenty-seven years that she had a duty to fulfill to herself and towards humanity. In order to fulfill this duty, Italy must first achieve her own liberty, independence, and national unity. Savoy* and Sardinia are only interested in expediency, whereas Mazzini is interested in an idea, his republican cause. Sardinia has "selfish aims." Jessie elaborated further: "Every inch of ground won by Italians for Italy in '48 and '49 was won by Republicans and at the close of that year Italy would have been free from foreigners, would have been free, independent, and united, had not monarchy stepped in and substituted the petty longings of dynastic ambition to the great national aim. . . . In 1849, 80,000 Piedmontese, with the exception of a few regiments, fled ignominiously before 60,000 Austrians and the farce of Novara sealed the fate of Italy. It was left for Republican Venice and Republican Rome to wipe off the stain of cowardice from the Italian name—left there by royal treachery and royal flight—and they fulfilled this task."

The *Times* did not like Madame Mario's answer. The next day (December 16) it spoke out more strongly: "We are sick of the groans of downtrodden peoples, they have been groaning for a century, and it has never done them any good, that we have ever heard of." It is so useless, the *Times* pointed out, to know and hear over and over again about suppression and domination: "Who is the better for our information? Suppose the whole United States were to join tomorrow in an unanimous declaration that the Italians were an oppressed people, and the Austrians remorseless tyrants. Would that effect any change in the condition of the Peninsula? Would the martyrs sleep more soundly in their dungeons or the Imperial troops parade less steadily at Milan?" The article went on to say that Italy must 'get Italy' before making itself into a republic. According to the cookery book recipe, 'a hare must be caught before it can be cooked.' Furthermore, Madame Mario's charge that the Piedmontese were cowards in 1848 is a strange one; they are after all Italians and are fighting for their country. It is, the *Times* suggests, as if Benjamin Franklin were to have debased Virginia and Boston in France. Bunker Hill was de-

---

* The king of Piedmont-Sardinia was of the House of Savoy.

fended, after all, and Washington was chief executive before the colonies settled their terms.

On December 17th, "an Italian" chimed into the debate. He thought Jessie had done an injustice to the Piedmontese army and said she was doing a great wrong to the country in which she professed so much interest by playing down everybody but Mazzini. "For those who do not think Mazzini is right—that on the contrary, believe that Mazzini is doing a great deal of harm to the Italian cause—are in a very great majority in Italy."

On Saturday, December 18th, Jessie published an extremely long letter in the *Times*, in which she took that paper to task for refuting statements she had never made. She wanted only to acquaint Americans with the facts about Italy; she was trying to denigrate no one. Her real hope was not to get active help for Italy here, but to sway public opinion so that despots all over Europe would yield to the force of pressure from America: "Since you believe it to be peculiarly the province of the American people to assist and defend the principles of individual liberty, you cannot, I think, with justice, complain of me for appealing to that same people in behalf of national liberty and the principles involved therein." The rest of her long letter was devoted to an analysis of the recent history of Sardinia, in which she showed that her point was not that the Sardinian people were against progress; they most certainly were not. There were among them brave patriots, but they were being curbed and misdirected by the kings, their rulers. In Sardinia there had been a regression: its history from 1849 to 1858 suggested the movement of a crab—backwards instead of forwards. Political and civil liberties and the freedom of the press had steadily diminished. Jessie's letter was forceful and clear, but somewhat tedious and long-winded. The *Times* (December 20) had the last word—for a few days—and the argument dwindled.

In January certain letters in various journals again expressed sentiments for and against Jessie's position. The leading editorial of the *New York Post* for January 5, suggested that Mazzini's stand was far too strong and that it would be much better for Italians to compromise with the political facts of life and really get somewhere. In one issue—January 10, 1859—Jessie was accused of hypocrisy; in another, three days later, the charge was refuted. The lecture schedule continued in the Metropolitan Room on January 14, when between one thousand and twelve hundred people each paid twelve cents for admission to hear her and other patriots speak at a mass meeting. The *New York Herald* reporter did not find this lecture to his taste.

> Her delivery was plain and clear but it wanted that fire which was necessary to make her audience feel that they had got to work, and

work eternally to gain the freedom that they had dreamed about, and of which they were ever speaking. The address was very lengthy and considering that nine persons out of ten present knew the language in which she spoke only very imperfectly [according to the reporter there were many refugees present], it is not surprising that the address was anything but enthusiastically received. Several of the gentlemen on the platform and others in the body of the hall, when a good point was obtained, would lead off the applause, which the mass took up, and now and again relieved the general dulness.

Jessie was followed by a signor Corradi, then Dr. Spetlech, a Pole, and Gustave von Strav and Herr Kapp, two Germans. At the conclusion there were three cheers for Orsini, and his attempt on the life of Louis Napoleon.

There was one additional contribution to the *Times* controversy, on January 27, written by Count Louis Kazinski, who was not at all sympathetic with the Marios (for by now Alberto had gallantly entered the controversy with a statement to the press that he would back his wife's position, with which he was in complete agreement, against anyone who took issue with her but did not wish to offend a lady). At the conclusion of this letter, the *Times* announced that it had given an airing to both sides and there it would let the matter drop.

During the month of January, the Brownings who were in Rome heard that Jessie Mario was using their names as an entrée to important circles in America. Although they had unquestionably been amicable in their earlier acquaintance, when Jessie was touring Italy with Emma Roberts, relations between the Brownings and Jessie were now no longer cordial. Elizabeth Barrett Browning idolized Louis Napoleon, and thought that Cavour and the king of Piedmont-Sardinia should be encouraged as the true leaders in Italy, believing that Mazzini and the republicans went too far in their revolutionary tactics. She had reacted passionately against Orsini's attempt to assassinate Napoleon III and had spoken out strongly against regicide. She was convinced that help from the French emperor was essential to bring about Italian unification. The letter, signed by both Elizabeth and Robert and printed in the *Post*, read as follows:

Rome, January 5, 1859

Having seen a statement in American newspapers that Madame Mario, late Miss Jessie Meriton White, has arrived in the United States—recommended by the Brownings, etc. etc., to lecture on "Orsini" and "Italian Politics" we feel ourselves forced to explain distinctly that, with a strong personal affection and esteem for Madame Mario, and a love for liberty and the democracy still better known to all who know us, we yet entirely dissent both from her views of Orsini and her opinions upon Piedmont, considering that every attack upon the Piedmontese government is levelled also against the general Italian cause. This is the first time we have noticed a printed observation on ourselves, and only a painful sense of duty constrains us to do so now.

Jessie responded in kind in a letter to the editors of the *Post* written from Washington on February 4 and published in the *Post* on Monday, February 7:

I have seen the letter from Mr. and Mrs. Browning published in your paper. I am not aware that any American paper has ever stated that I was "recommended by them to lecture on Orsini and Italian politics." My letters of recommendation to America were from Professor and Mrs. Nichol, Mrs. Mary Howitt, J. D. Morell, M.A., Kossuth, Mazzini, etc. etc. Mr. and Mrs. Browning have long been (and judging from their last letters to me still are) my intimate personal friends, but Mrs. Browning's opinions on Louis Napoleon, whom she calls in *Aurora Leigh* "no despot, though thrice absolute," suffice to prove that we differ entirely in our political views.

At the time of Orsini's execution, Mrs. Browning pleaded earnestly with me to make a public declaration of my hatred of political assassination. I replied by asking her whether she thought the murderer of Rome, the author of the 2,652 murders on the Boulevards of Paris, on the second of December, 1851; or the man who, having spent his life in telling and fighting for his country, risked that life, and lost it in his attempt to lay Rome's assassin low, the greater murderer of the two? And here the matter ended.

I have never lectured on Orsini in America, though in my lecture [in Clinton Hall] I expressed my surprise that those who blame him applaud the perjured tyrant who has waded through the blood of two nations to a throne. I have also affirmed that any attempt made by Piedmont, or any other power, at the instigation of Louis Napoleon, to change the condition of Italy will result, perhaps, in a change of tyrants; will, perhaps, lessen Austria's power to increase French sway in the Peninsula, but will never lessen Italian suffering nor advance Italian independence. Many of my best friends hold a contrary opinion; I respect theirs, but I retain my own, founded as it is on the experience of the past. Time will prove which is right.

I have never spoken on Mr. or Mrs. Browning in connection with politics. In my lecture on "Illustrious Italian Women," I referred to the latter as the "greatest poetess that has yet arisen in the world; one of the noblest women; one of the most devoted wives and mothers that any age has seen." If any American papers have spoken in any other sense, they have done so on their own responsibility.

Mrs. Browning wrote to her sister Henrietta in May of that year commenting on this conflict:

My poor headstrong friend Madame Mario is not to be quoted on any subject—not even against me to whom she has behaved ill. She wrote me quite an insulting letter intimating that Robert's and my printed statement (which she gave the whole credit of to me) was written as a care of our personal safety solely at Rome. So like me that was! And so likely too, to effect such an object!!! She is about as right in her estimate of Louis Napoleon—being governed absolutely in her soul by that man of a narrow head and unscrupulous conscience Mazzini. The whole party has perished out of Italy. We have been forced to make a final statement in print which you will all see in the Athenaeum.[1]

On this emphatic note, relations between the Brownings and Jessie ended.

Jessie spoke in Washington under the auspices of the American anti-slavery activists dominated at this time by the uncompromising personality of William Lloyd Garrison. It was owing to this introduction to Garrison, who had known the Ashursts in England, that Jessie was eventually to become a lifelong analyst for the *Nation* (which did not begin publication until 1865) on the development of the emerging Italian nation. Jessie described her experience in Washington in her biography of Alberto:

I agreed to give a lecture in Washington, where there was a tremendous burning question between the pro- and anti-slavery parties, I was asked to behave like Kossuth and not mention this subject at all. That was impossible both on principle and because Lloyd Garrison and Lucretia Mott were among the most devoted friends of the Italian cause. Alberto agreed with me about this, but was very distressed about it. The evening came, and I found in the first row a dozen of the most rabid pro-slavery senators, but they had invited me to propagandize in their state. That was enough, because I had undertaken the obligation; and I began—"I would not dare speak in this great country on behalf of the oppressed Italians without the strong belief in the right of every nation, every race, every man to his liberty." Senator Brown interrupted: "Liberty for niggers too?" "For White and Black, for all together." Noisy and prolonged applause. The lecture went on without any other interruption: the slave senators contributed generously for the oppressed Italians but Mr. Brown said— "you are wrong. Niggers don't want liberty. They wouldn't know what to do with it; but for you, silence would be cowardice." Alberto, who had listened to the lecture contrary to my wishes although I did not know it, said to me—"What a foul quarter of an hour I passed! I was prepared to defend you with my fists if you were offended."[2]

On March 4, Mazzini addressed a letter to Jessie in New York, telling her that he was forwarding her £ 100:

If more are wanted, we shall manage. At the same time, supposing you should collect beyond what you want, send them back when you can, even before the end of your tour: this merely, on account of the position of things; war or insurrection may break out unexpectedly, and I would immediately leave. But do not do it for this consideration, before you are sure of having all you want. Act with me as a dear and loving sister, bless you. I hope you are going on. I am overwhelmed by work, and this is the only excuse for my not writing often. The war will take place: The time is uncertain but it might be *very* near. Tell Mario that I have ventured to put his name in a collective Declaration of ours, because I know he would have signed it, if here. He will see it in the Paper which comes out tomorrow. Thank him for his unremitting activity.[3]

On the same day Stansfeld wrote Jessie in care of General Avezzana, New York, to the following effect: "I don't believe in Jessie failing, who knows but all this work and bother at New York may have after all laid the foundation for the start and that from the day she leaves it to try elsewhere it may be plain sailing." At the end of the letter he indicated that more money was available if the Marios needed it.[4] In a subsequent letter of March 26, Mazzini wrote:

I cannot, with all possible wishes to please you, write the few words to the People of New England. It looks too dictatorial, and bombastic. Feel my motives and forgive. I write *to you* some lines which might be useful and if so, you can do anything you like with them. As for the signatures, dear, how can I, by return of Post, have the signatures of Saffi who is in Oxford, of Quadrio who is abroad, etc.?

I *shall* write, as you like, within two days, to the Italians. To *them* I feel I have a right to speak.[5]

As this letter indicates, the Marios had intended to swing around a New England lecture circuit before returning to Italy. But an unpublished letter from Jessie Mario to James Russell Lowell in the spring of 1859 indicates that the outbreak of hostilities in Italy summoned them back sooner than they had expected:

Summoned suddenly to Europe we are prevented from visiting Boston and so from the pleasure of seeing you and several other Bostonians whom we desire much to know.

May I ask you to look through the accompanying article in case it should suit the *Atlantic Monthly*? My husband has written three articles which can be published separately, or in a series—the one I send —a second on Ugo Foscolo and a third on Italian literature from Foscolo's time to the present day. In the first please omit reading *Fra Paolo Sarpi*. I will send the missing pages from England.

I am writing an article on "Mazzini the Man of Letters," which I hoped to have completed for your inspection but alas we sail this morning!

My address in England will be care of

James Stansfeld Esq. M.P.

Walham Green

Fulham

London

May I hope to receive an answer from you? Trusting to have the pleasure of seeing you in the fall. I am my dear sir

Most respectfully yours,
Jessie White Mario[6]

Their last evening in America the Marios attended a spiritualist séance.[7] Alberto, with great gravity, made believe to be converted and before the end of the meeting, a "signor Mann" had been directed by the spirits to make a contribution of five hundred dollars to Mazzini. This was perhaps the most profitable financial reward of the whole trip for the cause. For herself, Jessie obtained assignments to write articles for certain newspapers, and in years to come, especially in the 1860s and '70s, she would have several pieces published in the American press. But above all, the trip was to result in Jessie's major employment as a journalist in the future—the commission to write on Italy for E. L. Godkin, founder of the *Nation*. As far as the cause of Mazzinian republicanism was concerned, it is unlikely that the Marios' trip to America had a significant effect in enlarging Mazzini's following there. It is very obvious that both in England and America, public opinion found Mazzini's role to be overplayed and passé, and one must assume that Jessie had been swept along by her own enthusiasms in continuing this fruitless pursuit. Yet, Jessie in many ways profited from her quasi-liberation from Mazzini on this trip. She could not depend on Mazzini for materials or quick answers as extensively as she had in the past, due to their geographical separation, and as a result her ability to fall back on her own resources and thinking was sharpened. She showed herself ready to rise to controversy; yet she was still without much insight into the narrowness of her position. But it became increasingly clear that Alberto Mario's views, much more bound to federalism than Mazzinism, were weaning her towards a more independent position.

PART TWO
GARIBALDI'S ENGLISHWOMAN

6

The Marios had been away from Italy since the early winter of 1857, and during the eighteen months that intervened before their return, Italy's internal and external political structure altered radically. The chief architects of this change were Cavour and Napoleon III, who had met secretly at Plombières in July, 1858 and agreed upon joint action to provoke a war with Austria and expel that power and its influence from Italy. If they were successful, Italy would be reorganized into a federation of four states under the presidency of the pope, including the Kingdom of Piedmont, a Kingdom of Central Italy, a Papal State consisting of Rome and the surrounding territory, and the Kingdom of Naples. Napoleon's condition was that the war should be provoked in such a way as to justify French intervention to the French populace and the major foreign powers, and that Piedmont-Sardinia cede the provinces of Nice and Savoy to France as its reward.

By December, 1858 this agreement had been formalized into a treaty and by March, 1859 the Piedmontese reserves were called up. Austria responded by mobilizing on April 7 and issuing an ultimatum to Piedmont-Sardinia to demobilize within three days. Cavour was delighted at having succeeded in goading the Austrians into taking this step and made no move to comply with the ultimatum. On April 29, the Austrians invaded Piedmont, and the war was on.

Active on the side of Piedmont was the special army of about 3,000 volunteers know as the *cacciatori delle Alpi*, led by Garibaldi. Many of the volunteers were veterans of the 1849 uprisings and had started to Piedmont from all over Italy when they heard that Cavour had summoned Garibaldi from retirement in Caprera to lead the *cacciatori delle Alpi.* When the war with Austria broke out, Garibaldi and his three regiments crossed the Ticino at Sesto Calende and advanced into enemy territory. They defeated the Austrians at Varese and continued on to Como. The major engagements between the Piedmontese-French forces and the Austrians were fought at Magenta on June 4, and Solferino on June 24, and proved costly to both sides. In the meantime, taking advantage of the situation, revolutionaries in Tuscany, Modena, and Parma had dislodged their rulers in May, and by mid-June insurrections erupted in Ravenna, Ferrara, and Bologna, which were under papal control.

By the end of June the Austrians began to withdraw and success seemed near. But Napoleon III had become alarmed at the spread of revolutionary activity as well as by the bloody losses at Magenta and Solferino and without consulting his ally Victor Emmanuel, he proposed an armistice to Austria on July 8, 1859. A few days later he met Emperor Franz Josef of Austria at Villafranca and arranged the terms of the settlement finally confirmed by the Treaty of Zurich on November 20.

Piedmont-Sardinia had no choice but to comply, but whatever their allegiance, all Italians were outraged at this betrayal by the French emperor. Under the terms of the settlement at Villafranca, Austria ceded Lombardy to France which might then cede it to Piedmont-Sardinia; Venetia was to remain Austrian; and the Italian princes of the revolting states were to be restored. Though Victor Emmanuel of Piedmont-Sardinia had no choice but to agree, Cavour resigned in protest and was succeeded by Rattazzi. Garibaldi spent the next few months in and near Bologna contemplating what his next move should be.

This was the troubled state of affairs when the Marios reached Milan on July 25, roughly a fortnight after the signing of the armistice with Austria. Undoubtedly they had given up their trip to Boston in the hope of joining Garibaldi for the final victory. How disappointed they must have been to find instead that all their hopes had been betrayed at Villafranca. Moreover, their own position proved highly precarious. Arriving at Pontelagoscuro on August 22 en route to Lendinara (where Alberto's father lay gravely ill) they were arrested on the suspicion of being Austrian spies. Released, they made their way to Ferrara only to be imprisoned again until they promised to leave that city. Their involvement in the Pisacane plot and their close association with Mazzini apparently marked them as suspicious. This became quite obvious when after leaving Ferrara, they were imprisoned in Bologna. Here one of Garibaldi's aides-de-camp tried to interview them, but was turned back by the prison guards. In September they were granted their freedom by the local governor, Leonetto Cipriani, on condition that they leave the Romagna for good. They went to Lodi and then Lugano, Switzerland, where they remained from September, 1859 to May, 1860 in an apartment above the post office. There was apparently no place for them in Italy.

Although they did not see either Mazzini or Garibaldi during these months, they kept in touch with both. Mazzini was able to trace them through his vast correspondence and spy network. There is no telling what Alberto's personal opinion of Mazzini was at this point nor Mazzini's of him. Mazzini's letters to Emilie Ashurst during this period imply that he felt that Jessie was no longer putting her full heart and soul into his cause and that she was being misled by her husband. In view of this growing coolness between Mazzini and the Marios it seems puzzling that Mazzini should have asked Alberto to take over the editorship of his new underground paper, *Pensiero e Azione*, which was to replace the old *Italia del Popolo*. Perhaps the obvious motive is the correct one—that Mazzini had very little choice; he needed whatever help he could find. At any rate he must have trusted that Jessie's attachment to him would be strong enough to maintain the arrangement. Besides, there was no question that since Alberto too sought liberation for Italy, he was basically on Mazzini's side. Alberto published several issues of this paper at irregular intervals. During September he wrote four articles that suggested that Italians should rally behind the Piedmontese government and strike a blow for unification, and Mazzini registered disgust at the evidence of opportunism. Increasingly Alberto spoke with an independent voice, and Mazzini was provoked because the views expressed in the paper were in some fundamental way at variance with his own ideas on the correct tactics for achieving unification. Alberto was strong willed, and now that he was closer to his native soil he regained the confidence of his own federalist convictions. (Jessie, who would soon be passing bodily between Scylla and Charybdis with Garibaldi, began to feel the force of the metaphorical pull while still in Switzerland.)

Circumstances placed Carlo Cattaneo in the Marios' close company in Lugano during this interim period. They took evening walks together, and Jessie found him a veritable encyclopedia. Like the Marios, Cattaneo, who was to remain the leading theoretical exponent of Italian federalism, had sought asylum in Switzerland with his frail English wife. Alberto was already predisposed to take his lead from Cattaneo. Now, associating with him constantly and exposed to his strong but rational views, both Marios found a new kinship. After

Cattaneo's death, when Jessie edited his works and finished the biography that she and Alberto had begun jointly, she spoke of his influence on her thought and perspective, as well as on her husband's.

Cattaneo's brand of federalism differed from Mazzini's republicanism in important aspects. The consistent failure of the various revolutionist plots had left Cattaneo with a profound distrust of such conspiracies. He continued to believe in an independent Italy consisting of a federation of communes. True unification, he thought, would only come about with time, through popular education and a gradual reevaluation by its leaders of Italy's role in the political life of Europe. His efforts were bent toward educating "a generation [of Italians] in all the arts, sciences, and modes of life that [had] made other nations free," Jessie wrote. He was a positivist, and his voluminous writings on economics, history, and geography investigated cultural forces and the laws of human development. While Mazzini urged Italians to think only of Italy and revolution, as Jessie put it, "Cattaneo, in the pages of the *Annali di statistica,* in the *Annali di giurisprudenza pratica,* in the *Politecnico,* in the *Memorie di economia publica*—periodicals which he edited personally—familiarized his countrymen with the progress of other nations."[1] Yet for the time being he was forced to support the movement for unification under Piedmont-Sardinia in the absence of what he considered a viable political alternative.

Meanwhile, in the fall of 1859, the assemblies of Tuscany, Parma, Modena, and the Romagna voted to be annexed to the constitutional monarchy of Piedmont-Sardinia. Fearful of incurring Napoleon's anger, Piedmont hesitated to act on this vote. In January 1860, Cavour returned to power and negotiated the annexations with Napoleon III, who agreed in return for the cession of Nice and Savoy to France. In mid-March, 1860, plebiscites in Tuscany, Modena, Parma, and the Romagna resulted in a second affirmative vote for annexation, and now the plebiscites were followed by the signing of the Treaty of Turin on March 24, 1860, according to the terms of which Piedmont-Sardinia ceded Nice and Savoy to Napoleon III. Garibaldi had begun to gather arms and men for an invasion of Sicily. Cavour, who knew of this plan, did not try to stop it, his own position being precarious because of his cession of Savoy and Nice to France. Garibaldi, for his part, was willing to undertake the venture only if he could do so under the aegis of Piedmont-Sardinia.

Mazzini had urged Garibaldi to invade the south, but doubtful that he would do so, conceived of yet another plot—it was to be his last. He selected Rosolino Pilo to lead an attempt to stir up an insurrection in Sicily. But this plot proved no more successful than earlier ones.

Pilo, who landed near Messina, was captured and killed sometime in May, 1860. But by now Garibaldi was finally ready to act. With the tacit approval of Victor Emmanuel and Cavour he sailed from Genoa with his army of a thousand Redshirts and landed in Sicily on May 11. Within a few weeks he had driven northeastward from Marsala to Palermo where he set up a provisional government at the end of May.

Meanwhile the Marios left Lugano, found their way to Genoa, and shipped on the *Washington* when it sailed for Sicily on June 10, along with the *Oregon* and the *Franklin*. A French volunteer—one of the many survivors of the campaign to write his version of the activities of the Redshirts—had this to say about a more frivolous side of Jessie's activities on ship:

> There was on board another woman who was less young and, if I may say so without overstepping the laws of gallantry, less attractive. . . . It was an English woman with long golden-colored hair, Miss W. . . . This woman came along with us with the generous intention of devoting herself to Italian independence by organizing an ambulance corps for the national army. To that end, she was to ally herself with an elderly physician of Turin, Doctor Ripari, whom she would meet in Palermo and who was named head of the medical corps for the expedition.
>
> Miss W, . . . with all her virtues, had two irresistible passions— one for Italian independence and the other for the game of checkers . . . and much as one would praise the one, one would regret the other. A few hours after our departure, an officer of the ship thought it his duty to ask her if the motion of the ship made her ill.
>
> —"Oh, no, sir," she said; "Quite the contrary, I am so little indisposed that I would like to play a game of checkers with you."
>
> —A single hope still remained to the officer. That was, that there wasn't any checker board on the ship! It wasn't likely that anyone would have thought to bring checkers—anymore than cards or dominoes since the *Washington* had a more meaningful cargo. But Miss W . . . was a woman of forethought. In the midst of her equipment, her trusses, and the unguents of all sorts which she had in her luggage, she had not forgotten to slip in a checkerboard.[2]

No doubt even as she was finishing a game, six days later, the ships stopped at Cagliari to take on additional arms and men. They left the port on the afternoon of June 16 with twenty-five hundred men, and between six thousand and eight thousand rifles and muskets. Shortly before nightfall when the boats were nearing the Sicilian coast and entering the zone of greatest danger from Neapolitan cruisers, the people on the *Washington* saw a Piedmontese war ship bearing down on them. When she came abreast, she turned out to be the ship *Gulnara*.

The commander came aboard the *Washington* to speak with Giacomo Medici, the veteran revolutionary and leader of the Garibaldian forces. He said that he had orders from Admiral Persano —who in turn had them straight from Cavour—to conduct the expedition safely to Castellamare, twenty-five miles west of Palermo, and in the meantime to effect the immediate arrest of Mazzini, who was thought by the Italian government to be on board, and the Marios. Mazzini was not there, of course, and Medici refused to give up the Marios. Alberto later described this incident in a magazine article:

> In 1860 we landed with Medici at Castellamare, and arrived at Alcamo. Garibaldi came to meet us on horseback . . . I had never yet been personally presented to him, but he at once held out his hand, saying, "You are Alberto Mario; I am glad to have you here, you did well to come." He had guessed who I was, because I was accompanied by my wife. . . . He placed a carriage at our service, and we returned with him to Palermo; where, on the morrow, he received me in his little bed-room at the splendid palace of the Normans, and attached me to his staff. . . . Offering me a cigar, he said,
> "Do you know this morning I had a visit from Admiral Persano, who is here in the bay with two frigates. Guess why he came? He was sent by Cavour to beg me to arrest you and your wife—to consign you to him on board the *Maria Adelaide*, to be sent back to Genoa. I looked at him with astonishment, and answered, indignantly, "Signor Ammiraglio, reply to Count Cavour that I am not his police agent, like his lieutenants—Ricasoli, Farini, Lionetto, or Cipriani—in Central Italy; that I do not arrest tried and honoured patriots who have come to our assistance, and that I feel much offended by the demand."[3]

Alberto thanked him and told him Cavour had sent the same orders to Colonel Medici, detaining the expedition at Cagliari on that account.

During the month they spent in Sicily, the Marios made frequent excursions on horseback with Garibaldi to the outskirts of Palermo to take notes about the abuses in the penitentiaries and foundling hospitals. The general at once ordered rigid inquiries into the administration of these institutions. He had the food tested and took steps to improve the inmates' health. One day they rode to the fort of Castellamare, formerly used as a prison, which the patriots were in the process of demolishing. From there they went to Monte Pellegrino, where from three to four thousand children belonging to the very poorest classes in Palermo were undergoing military drill, partly to keep them out of mischief, partly to help in further emergencies. Garibaldi asked Alberto to organize a regular military school for these children. So eager was Alberto to be of use, that he drew up the plans on the same day and presented them to the general. Garibaldi went forward with this school, which Alberto agreed to run if he could be relieved at the right moment in case of war.

While Alberto was thus occupied, Garibaldi asked Jessie to nurse those who had been wounded during the battles which had carried the Redshirts from Marsala to Palermo. The local conditions were extremely unhygienic and there was little to be gained in trying to get help from the Sicilian doctors. Several medical aides had arrived from abroad, both with the Marios on the *Washington* and earlier. Doctor Ripari improvised a makeshift hospital by ousting the monks from a monastery on the hill at Monte Pellegrino. It was up to the medical unit to discover ways to survive under very difficult conditions. The Sicilian summer was very hot and fostered the spread of hospital gangrene and typhus. The necessary opium, quinine, and chloride of lime, as well as charcoal, strapping, old linen for bandages and rollers were all in short supply. The hospital corps could not obtain sufficient ticking for the beds nor straw to put in the ticking.

Even so, the doctors, with Jessie assisting, did much to alleviate the suffering of the wounded. Jessie constantly aided the doctors at surgical operations. For most of the time she was the only woman attached to Garibaldi's hospital unit, though occasionally local women, especially nuns, would also help. Dr. Ripari gave Jessie the full responsibility for managing the patients. In this situation her maternal instincts were called into full play. Once, when her husband was visiting her in the hospital set up at Milazzo, he observed:

> As I passed down the left corridor, I heard a young voice crying, "Signor Comandante," and saw three lads lying on the straw, their once white uniforms stained with blood and mire.
>
> "They are your boys; they deserted to D—— [Dunne]," said my wife. "Come and see another," and she led me into a room opening out of the corridor, where, on one of the beds abandoned by the monks, lay a little fellow asleep, an ice-bladder on the stump of his lost left arm.
>
> "He was amputated this afternoon," said my wife. "Poor little mite, he is only twelve. He said . . . , 'I'll only cry a little.' I held him on my lap; he kept his word, and told me afterwards that I cried more than he did, which was quite true. Then he went fast asleep, as they nearly all do after an operation."[4]

By the end of July, the Neapolitans had been driven out of Sicily and in August, Alberto and a regiment of two hundred or so specially picked men crossed the straits of Messina to the mainland. Jessie and the ambulance corps were not far behind. Garibaldi gained control of a triangle of land to enable the transit of ships from the batteries of Faro (in Sicily) to the mainland. As they landed, Jessie asked the head

officer, Sirtori, for orders for the ambulance, and Garibaldi, who overheard, said, "What do we want with ambulances? See how politely
they are moving on. We shall reach Naples, Signora, without the aid
of your rags and plasters."[5]

The troops marched from San Giovanni to Naples. On their entry
into Palmi, as Alberto Mario was riding with Jessie in a "very humble
fourwheel," the crowd mistook them for Garibaldi and his daughter.
(Alberto commented that this happened to him quite often: the same
thing occurred the day after their entry into Naples at the feast of the
Piedigrotta when a half-mad friar made the same mistake and started
a riot.)[6] During the march on Monteleone, the Marios found themselves ahead of Garibaldi. Alberto wrote:

> Finding that my wife had secured for the ambulance a carriage
> drawn by four powerful horses, I seated myself therein, and taking a
> different road, we found ourselves in advance of the General, and as
> the inhabitants of the district told us that we were within a mile or so
> of the enemy, we halted at a road-side inn, and my wife proposed to
> the head chemist of the ambulance to go off on one of their foraging
> expeditions; they returned with a hundred eggs, a kid, and some very
> consumptive looking fowls. . . . Then, they went into the innkeeper's
> kitchen and discovered that he had all sorts of things hidden away
> from the soldiers of "Bombino." They were given delicious foods—
> sausage, bread, wine. Garibaldi arrived and said to Jessie, "So, you
> here! You have inverted the order of things—the ambulance at the van
> instead of the rear?"
>
> "Since you despised our rags and plasters we have changed our
> trade and set up as quartermasters," so saying she led him by an ex-
> ternal staircase to the dining hall, and a cry of joy rose from the suite
> as they beheld a smoking omelette in the centre, and plates of fresh
> figs and sausage and sundry carafes of wine. Yolks of eggs, beaten
> up with wine and sugar, completed the repast.[7]

On September 4, 1860, Garibaldi made a triumphal entry into
Naples and set up an interim dictatorship. Alberto and Jessie were in-
stalled in a "snug apartment overlooking the Largo delle Pigne." They
had just arrived, so Alberto later recounted, when Jessie observed:

> "Can it really be true, that, only fourteen in number, we entered
> Naples? That Garibaldi is Dictator? They say that the cannons of all
> the fortresses are pointed at the city; that 14,000 Bourbon soldiers
> are under arms. Did you notice how the General's eyes dilated, the
> solemn radiance that encircled his brow, as we neared the royal pal-
> ace, and the spell-bound soldiers presented arms? Did—"
>
> "Oh yes, of course I saw it all; don't rhapsodize," I answered, sur-
> veying with sleepy satisfaction the spring mattresses, the snowy
> sheets, the soft pillows inviting me from the alcove to their arms.

> After twenty five days from Aspromonte to Castrovillari passed on horseback, and four from Castrovillari to Naples, with the sky for canopy and the earth for couch, the prospect of a good bed and a long tranquil night seemed the acme of human bliss.

At that point a waiter came in and announced a gentleman. Alberto, alarmed, imagined that Garibaldi was taken. The waiter very kindly told them how to escape by a back passageway, but Alberto insisted that his wife detain the visitor in conversation while he made his way to warn Garibaldi. Jessie said: "Let me come too, else we shall again be separated in prison. . . ." Alberto responded, "No! You must receive them, else there'll be a search. Don't look so scared; you've been through worse than this, and I told you what to expect when you insisted on coming." Then Jessie regained her courage and told her husband to go. But as they were parting, a Redshirt friend revealed that this was a hoax, and then rewarded them by taking them off to much better quarters.[8]

Shortly thereafter, Alberto received instructions to undertake a special mission for Garibaldi at Ischia.[*] The purpose of the mission seems to have been to arouse the interest and goodwill of the islanders towards Garibaldi's campaign. Jessie was engaged in "assisting in the transformation" of the Jesuits' College in Naples into a hospital. But she pleaded with Alberto to let her accompany him. "Let me come, too," she begged; "there are no wounded in Naples, and we can't proceed with our preparations here until the ambulance arrives." "Jump in then," replied Alberto, just as if they were setting off on a pleasure jaunt.

They went to Santa Lucia and then on to Pozzuoli. There they alerted the National Guard to come to the aid of Garibaldi and then set sail for Cape Misen on the Gulf of Baja in the Governor of Pozzuoli's boat. They landed at Procida on the shore of San Cattolico, then went across the island on foot and came to the beach at Cornicella. From there they were transported to the Ischian shore. They were shown to a bedroom in a house opposite the landing place. At dawn they set out for Forio, riding around the northern base of Mount Epomeo on their beasts. There they were greeted as Garibaldians by the residents who enthusiastically surrounded Jessie and Alberto. ". . . one . . . held over her head a gold and damask umbrella, precisely similar to those used by priests when transporting the holy wafer." The Marios were treated like conquerors, provoking Jessie—never quite

---

[*] Mack Smith believes that Garibaldi was at this point intent on currying favor with Victor Emmanuel in the hope that he would be allowed to go on to conquer Rome. Cavour, however, was determined to prevent just that. See Denis Mack Smith, *Cavour and Garibaldi 1860: A Study in Political Conflict* (Cambridge: Cambridge University Press, 1954).

able to take ceremony very seriously, especially when she was at the receiving end—to whisper "viciously" in her husband's ear, "All hail! Roi d'Yvetot." Alberto said that the resemblance to the model king who

> Sur un âne pas apas
> Parcourit son royaume

struck him as so ludicrous that his lips bled from his effort to restrain his laughter. Afterwards, Alberto was forced to settle a local feud between two governing members of the island's aristocracy whose constant quarreling kept the island as a whole from cooperating with Garibaldi. A dinner party was planned by Alberto and Jessie as a banquet of reconciliation. It took place, and the two diplomats returned to Naples in time for the real campaign.[9]

Before Naples was finally assured to Piedmont-Sardinia, a month later, there were to be bloody battles between the Bourbon forces and the Piedmontese troops who had arrived from the north.* During this time Jessie resumed her role as director of hospital operations. The *Daily News* followed the campaign closely, and with it her whereabouts, apparently making use of her loose connection with the newspaper and her semiofficial status as a reporter.[10] Both the Neapolitan correspondent and the war correspondent (Arrivabene) paid special attention in their columns to signora Mario, and her nursing. During the Neapolitan campaign Jessie was in charge of the field hospitals at Caserta and Santa Maria. Conditions there were even more deplorable than those during the Sicilian campaign; only the most rudimentary attention could be given to less than half the sick and wounded; doctors and staff were overworked and underequipped.[11] Jessie had dragged ticking from Sicily, but had no stuffing for it. The Neapolitans seemed indifferent to the suffering of the troops and to their sick.

The *Daily News* of Tuesday, September 25, reported that Jessie was doing as good a job as she could under the circumstances. "Amongst our visitors who are well known to fame," it said, are

> Madame Mario and Alexander Dumas. Dumas has been chosen to head the archeological works. Madame Mario, whose husband is attached to the staff, and herself to the hospitals of Garibaldi, is also here. I utterly reject her principles, as fraught with danger to the peace and liberties of Italy† but I admire her merits in the management of hospitals, and in the sacrifice of time and repose which she made for a great benevolent object. At Palermo, where Miss Middle-

---

* Apparently there was little coordination between the forces of Garibaldi and of Piedmont.

† The Neapolitan correspondent of the *Daily News* was somewhat more conservative politically than the paper itself.

ton also gave her valuable services, the wounded presented Madame Mario with a small gold medal, bearing on one side the inscription 'Alla Signora Mario, dai feriti di Garibaldi, luglio 1, 1860,' on the other side the emblem of Trinacria.

Near Naples Jessie worked with an Englishman—Dr. Franklin—and also several Italian doctors—Ripari, Boldrini, and Stradivar. Commander Charles Forbes, who observed the conditions under which the group worked, scornfully stated that the Neapolitans

> did not fight and they did not open their doors to a single wounded officer or private. A few of the doctors gave their assistance to the overworked army surgeons. . . . With that exception, the grateful inhabitants of this government do not care whether the sufferers rot or where they are. . . . The very nurses (except for Jessie) plunder the dying and helpless, and embezzle their scarce food for their own use.[12]

In the *Daily News* for Friday, October 12, it was reported that during the battle of Santa Maria "Miss White, in a fantastic dress, devoted herself entirely to this mission . . . [of collecting the wounded and dressing their wounds]. The hospital of Santa Maria was full, and train after train brought wounded men into Caserta. There were 480 in the hospital of Santa Maria on the 2nd, and as many more in that of Caserta, without speaking of those who were carried into Naples."

The same correspondent in his column of Thursday, October 18, gave a description of the conditions in the hospitals, which were much more wretched than they need have been:

> There is noise, profession, and talk enough, but very little of practical ability, and I have heard of five patients lying neglected for a whole night. As to supplies, which are in great abundance, "they are stolen right and left," said a person to me, "and I am thoroughly disgusted. There is enough of everything if it were utilized, but it is made away with in some way or another, and what becomes of it Heaven only knows." In fact everything is external here—noise and spectacle—heart there is little. Some ladies have started a snug little hospital in the College of the Jesuits—a kind of genteel praesepe affair, where they seek nice and interesting patients. Twenty-five vacant beds wait for the patients . . . and amateur sisters of charity at tables arranged here and there with a certain amount of taste, waiting for the heroes who do not come. I expect there is a want of real feeling here, still more of the practical active talent, determined to do and to suffer. Madame Mario does well, spite her politics, and a few more like her would be invaluable.

In the same issue, another report, written on a different day, reiterates the theme of the degradation of the hospitals—singling out the work of Madame Mario as the exception. The hospital at Naples, the reporter says, is as bad as it can be. "At Santa Maria and Caserta, where they are more under the control of Madame Mario, it is better. But in Naples—They are all thieves."

> . . . "From the regular attendants down to the crowds of visitors who come under the affection of sympathy, it was the same; every one seeks some profit for himself, and things are stolen right and left. I never saw such confusion in my life;" said the correspondent's friend, "so numerous are the lazy curious who come in and out that it is impossible to do anything for those who suffer."

We know from other accounts that Jessie herself often went onto the field of battle as the war became more intensive. During the battle of Santa Maria Jessie, in the heat of the day, looked for Garibaldi on the field and fed him figs and a glass of water, which constituted his refreshment for the day. During the battle of the Volturno she made fourteen sorties under fire, it was reported, to bring back the wounded, and put in thirty-six consecutive hours working in the field hospital.[13]

Looking back on the experience of this campaign, Jessie saw it as typifying the demoralization of the Italian people of the south:

> As ill luck would have it, our hospital director, a Tuscan, engaged a gang of nurses and cooks after the battle of Volturno. The bill of fare was by Garibaldi's order to be *ad libitum*, to be regulated by the doctor's daily orders. Fish and fowl were in great demand, and to see the bills paid we ought to have had the freshest and the finest. But the food as a whole was uneatable; the fish stank, the *pasta* was mouldy, and, strangest phenomenon of all, the fowls were all *drumsticks* and necks—whereas all the patients demanded *petti di pollo*. One evening, exasperated beyond endurance, we made a descent into the kitchen. All the cooks and *infermieri* were feasting on the fat of the land; every fish of the sea and fowl of the air was on their board, and lo and behold on a tray, delicately egged and breadcrumbed, some forty or fifty of the missing *fowls' breasts*. These were set aside for the chiefs.* Every one of the delinquents was paid and turned out "neck and crop." There were plenty of volunteers glad to come and nurse their sick comrades. . . . Finally we had some "sisters of charity," and despite the curses and threats of the miscreants expelled, who vowed vengeance on us and our wounded, we did not take one of them back or treat with any of their emissaries.[14]

At the end of the campaign, after Garibaldi and Victor Emmanuel had entered freed Naples together, Garibaldi was once again forced into retirement at Caprera. Though his desire to extend his conquest to Rome had not abated, it was not shared by the king and his prime

* [Chefs?]

minister.* The hardest part of his labor was over, however, and Italy was finally almost united. For the time being there was to be a lull in the tactics of war.

On March 17, 1861, the Kingdom of Italy was proclaimed with Victor Emmanuel as king and a government based on the Piedmontese constitution of 1848 established. Less than three months later, Cavour, one of the chief architects of this achievement, died at the age of fifty-two.

* On October 21, 1860, a plebiscite was held in Sicily and Naples, in which the voters approved the merger of the south into the Kingdom of Italy governed by Piedmont. Garibaldi acceded to Cavour's plan for the plebiscite. One must not lose sight of the fact that during the summer months of 1860 a great battle of diplomacy was taking place behind the scenes, namely, as Denis Mack Smith puts it in *Cavour and Garibaldi* (pp. 47-56), a battle for and against the annexation of Naples to Piedmont—and Cavour was working for annexation through his various emissaries.

7

Jessie was now, in 1861, twenty-nine years old. She had already gained a reputation as an outspoken advocate of republicanism and unification. She was known on both sides of the Atlantic as a newspaper woman. She had had experience in using what would in the present century be described as the techniques of propaganda. She had many warm friends among the Italians, and some enemies. Accounts of her bravery in the face of battle during the Neapolitan campaign had reached the English public through the reporting of Henry Wreford, the London *Times* reporter on the scene. Even so, the future did not seem especially bright for Jessie and Alberto. They were no longer needed by Garibaldi since he had returned to Caprera after the Southern campaign. Like many of their fellow revolutionists and exiles, the couple had no place to go and nothing to do. Alberto tried once or twice to return to his native region of Venetia, but in vain, since Venetia still belonged to Austria and the problems of the exiles from that part of Italy had not been solved by the annexation of the south to the Kingdom of Sardinia. There had been no general amnesty for political refugees.

Consequently during the next few months the couple wandered rather aimlessly, trying to get their bearings. In January they went to Ferrara to meet and visit Alberto's relatives. In May they went to Lugano. On June 7, Alberto engaged in a duel with a man named Francesco Bisi, who had accused him of breaking up the *Veneti da Ferrara* (a society controlling emigration affairs) and had caused his arrest. Nothing came of it as both men gave up after a few minutes and shook hands. In September, Jessie heard that Garibaldi was in Milan and that he had received an offer from Abraham Lincoln to go to America and lead the Union troops. She urged him not to accept the offer.

After brief sojourns in Naples and Genoa, Jessie accepted a commission to write articles three times a week for the English *Morning Star*. She traveled between those two key cities several times during the fall. Earlier in the spring she wrote an article on the American slavery question which was published in *Nuova Antologia* in July, 1861.[1]

In December 1861 the Marios went to London. Alberto stayed with Mazzini in an apartment in the city, and Jessie spent the months from January through April, 1862, lecturing in England and Scotland. Some weeks she gave as many as six lectures, her energy apparently never failing. Mazzini was reassured by what he heard about these lectures;* Jessie was still talking without compromise about the ultimate unification of Italy. She asserted that even though Sicily and Naples had been wrested from Bourbon control, the pope was still in possession of his states and Austria had not been forced to give up Venice or the border territory; so long as these conditions prevailed, Italy was not free.

The couple's arrangements in England turned out to be profoundly disappointing. Alberto found that he could not make an accommodation with Mazzini; indeed, it was difficult to work with him at all since their ideas were so dissimilar and their temperaments clashed. Furthermore he was used to being with Jessie and regretted her continued absence. They went back to Italy, arriving by the middle of April, 1862, when Jessie resumed her correspondence for the *Star*.

In the summer of 1862, Garibaldi, still restive at the unsuccessful attempts to challenge the pope's power in central Italy, decided to take matters into his own hands. Once again he gathered a group of volunteers, this time in Palermo. The government issued orders for his arrest, and the island was placed under martial law when Giorgio Pallavicino, the prefect, resigned rather than have to arrest his old ally. Garibaldi escaped capture and marched to Catania where he embarked for the Calabrian coast. There Cialdini, the governor, ordered a column sent against Garibaldi and, near Aspromonte, Garibaldi was wounded in the ankle by a sharpshooter's bullet. The government insisted on Garibaldi's arrest and he was removed to the fortress of Varignano near La Spezia. This seemed the crowning insult from an ungrateful and heartless government which had been only too ready to use Garibaldi's services in the southern campaign two years earlier. Jessie was in Milan when these events took place,

---

* There can be little doubt, however, that Mazzini realized that by now the cause was no longer in the hands of the Party of Action.

collecting money and gifts for the cause. Mayor Beretta of Milan gave her the news and urged her departure from the area for he knew that the prefect had given orders for her arrest. She proceeded to Lake Como, where Lorenzo Valerio gave her a passport for the frontier. Arrived in Lugano, she found Mazzini and Cattaneo together, reviewing recent events and making plans. When she gave them the latest news, they were stunned. Mazzini wept. He had known of Garibaldi's proposed expedition and had disapproved of it, but had nevertheless urged his workers to help as best they could. Mazzini wanted to start for Milan immediately, but Jessie persuaded him that he would certainly be arrested if he did so. They were joined by Alberto, who was thoroughly disgusted with the ubiquitous apathy of the Italian people, and by their failure to capitalize on Garibaldi's initial success. During the gloomy days that followed, Mazzini kept reiterating: "Christ! . . . spare him to Italy! Take me instead!" He could not eat or sleep. His room was next to the Marios' and one night he called Alberto to him and said: "Bear witness that this blood of Garibaldi is not on my head."[2]

Very shortly thereafter the Ashursts visited Lugano on their way to Turin. James Stansfeld was with them and was determined to see Garibaldi in his prison at Varignano at all costs. He reported to the Marios that the English had raised £ 1,000 to send out a surgeon to take care of Garibaldi, and that a committee had already been formed to supervise the General's care. They wanted Jessie to be his nurse. Jessie reacted by commenting that to send a surgeon from England to Italy was like carrying coals to Newcastle: they already had the best in the world in Bertani (who had been the head of Garibaldi's surgical staff during part of the campaigns) and as for a nurse, Garibaldi had his own daughter Teresa and his sons. The money, she felt, could be better spent on the many others wounded at Aspromonte. Nevertheless the idea of an English doctor carried the day.

William Ashurst optimistically assured Mazzini that English hatred of Napoleon III would increase tenfold over this incident, since it was clearly the French ruler who had put Garibaldi in jeopardy.* "Decamp he must," he said of the Frenchman, and his mimicry of the monarch's departure from Rome made Mazzini laugh for the first time in days. Stansfeld was delighted to make the acquaintance of Carlo Cattaneo and had some chance to talk with him while the group was still together. Soon, however, William Ashurst continued on to Varignano and saw Garibaldi. While he was there the English surgeon, a Doctor Parkins, arrived. But his diagnosis and treatment did Garibaldi no good, since he failed to see that the bullet was still embedded

---

* The French maintained troops in Rome for the protection of the papacy.

in the flesh. Jessie commented that he departed as he came, leaving no trace of his presence save the receipt for £ 1,000 sterling.[3]

Stansfeld went to visit the leader several days later and found his health better than he had expected. He then returned to Lugano and took Mazzini with him to England. Garibaldi was released on October 5, 1862. The Marios and Dr. Bertani traveled to La Spezia to see him as soon as he was free. Bertani then discovered that the bullet was still in the wound. Teresa, Garibaldi's daughter, was obliged to return to Genoa to await her third child's birth and so Jessie, with Alberto's approval, volunteered to remain to nurse Garibaldi. One day Garibaldi said to Jessie: "I have decided to tell the whole story of the last three months. Can you find me an English publisher who will take it?" Through Stansfeld, Jessie opened negotiations with Mr. George Smith. Stansfeld was most eager to have the book published, but, as Jessie had suspected from the beginning, upon reflection (to put it in one of her clichés) Garibaldi decided that "though speech might be silver, silence was golden."[4] The memoirs remained unwritten for the time being.

At last Professor Zanetti, a medical man from Tuscany, operated on the wound, with Jessie holding chloroform to Garibaldi's nose. As soon as the forceps entered, Garibaldi cried, "Per Dio, c'é" [By God, it's there]. Zanetti's probing removed the bullet and Jessie "penned a joyful telegram" to the friends in England announcing that the bullet had been extracted and that the General was doing well. Soon afterwards sheets and bandages stained with the blood of the hero of Aspromonte were in great demand as souvenirs. Lady Palmerston, according to Jessie, sent Garibaldi an invalid bed which proved excellent in easing the pain he suffered from arthritis. Stansfeld now wrote to Jessie suggesting that Garibaldi visit England and receive the hero's welcome that awaited him. But this visit did not take place until April, 1864.

Meanwhile Mazzini asked Jessie to translate some of his Italian essays into English. Unfortunately, he forgetfully asked Emilie Ashurst (now Madame Carlo Venturi) to perform the same service, and thus stirred up the old trouble between the two. As the dispute continued Emilie and Jessie each proved inflexible, and Mazzini tried to solve his problem by suggesting that Jessie work on his political writings and Emilie on his letters. Emilie refused the proposed collaboration, while Jessie said she would consider it provided she remained free to make her own arrangements with a publisher. Mazzini finally threw up his hands in despair and decided not to be translated at all just then. But Emilie, who had already gone too far in what she was doing, persisted. Her works were subsequently published in England in 1864-1870, by Smith Elder and Company. (They were read before publication by George Meredith, who not only recommended them for publication, but also made use of them and of Emilie's knowledge for the potboiler *Vittoria* that he wrote during the next two years.[5] The incidents of the "Five Days of Milan," a laudatory portrait of Mazzini, and a knowledgeable description of the tactics of the conspirators provided raw materials for the novel.)

Jessie showed her displeasure over the translation fiasco by maintaining an adamant silence, refusing to have anything to do with Mazzini for several months. Although they were eventually reconciled, their relationship was never the same after this episode. That Alberto attacked Mazzini in an article in the weekly republican paper, *Dovere*, published in Genoa in May 1863, did not help the relationship. In the article, Alberto accuses Mazzini of resorting to "mysticism," saying that his doctrine of duty as developed was a doctrine of bondage. Mazzini wrote Jessie on July 10, that he still thought of her fondly and appreciated all she had done for him even though Alberto's behavior was inexplicable.

Several months earlier, on May 28, 1863, Jessie's father, Thomas White, had died of a fall on a loading dock in Lisbon, where he had gone on business. He had appointed Alberto his executor, and there was an unpleasant exchange of correspondence between Jessie and her brother Thomas White, Jr., on this subject. The latter was mystified by his father's choice of his Italian son-in-law as agent. On July 28, Jessie's stepmother, who had traveled to Portugal with Mr. White, wrote Jessie that she had sold her husband's business interest in Lisbon for £ 900 and that she was waiting for a boat to take her back to England. Once she was back, she settled at Southsea and said she never wanted to leave England again. Alberto's mother wrote Jane White in October inviting her for a visit to Italy, but she did not accept.

The Marios settled during the early winter of 1864 at Bellosguardo, near Florence, which was to be the new capital of Italy. There they made the acquaintance of a new circle of friends. They discovered that Thomas Adolphus Trollope (Anthony's brother) who was also an author lived there with his wife, herself a writer. Trollope had composed and published a life of Pius IX as well as several romantic novels about Florence and was an authority on Florentine history. The Trollopes had lived in Florence for a long time and knew many people there. They were very cordial to the Marios although they thought Alberto's ideas extreme.[6]

In April, 1864, Garibaldi made his long-delayed trip to England. He landed at the Isle of Wight where he stayed for ten days, and later visited Jane White at Southsea. Tennyson went to see him and listened to him recite Foscolo's *I Sepolcri*. The Duke of Somerset placed a steam yacht at his disposal. On April 11, he made a solemn entry into London. The crowds came out to see him in the equivalent of a Victorian ticker tape parade. He attended a banquet given in his honor by Alexander Herzen, the Russian revolutionary leader, at which Stansfeld and Mazzini were also present.* The English conservatives, however, were worried about what Napoleon III would think of this reception. Emmanuel d'Azeglio, the Italian ambassador to England, pointed out that it was strange that one who had rebelled against the king of Italy should be so cordially treated by important people in England. Consequently, the Duke of Sutherland summoned a surgeon named Ferguson who "gravely opined that the fatigue and excitement of the proposed tour would be fraught with danger"[7] to the general, and Gladstone told Garibaldi that this celebration was an embarrassment to the government. Garibaldi was smuggled out of England and back to Italy on the Duke's ship. The people of England were understandably confused by the whole procedure. Jane White wrote to Jessie on April 21: "All have seemed disappointed at the General's sudden departure. I do not fancy his health would permit the whole Tour that was proposed but I am grieved that he cannot go to Newcastle and Glasgow."[8]

In 1866, Jessie's stepmother died, terminating the Marios' immediate ties with England. Jessie was now completely free to think of Italy as her home. During this year she began her career as correspondent for the American periodical, the *Nation*, which had commenced publication under E. L. Godkin in New York six months earlier.[9] Her connection with Godkin was perhaps first established during her visit to America, when he was traveling through the South as representative of the *Daily News* (which had taken a pro-Northern position).

Meanwhile the political situation in Italy took a new turn when, encouraged by Napoleon III, the Kingdom of Italy entered into an alliance with Prussia which committed Italy to join Prussia within three months should war break out between that state and Austria. Italy's reward would be Venetia. Bismarck had embarked on his long-range plan to unify Germany, and Austria at this stage loomed as one of his chief obstacles. The Seven Weeks War against Austria broke out in June, 1866, but while Prussia proved victorious in her battles, the Italians were defeated at Custozza and in a battle at sea near Lissa. Nevertheless, when peace was concluded, with Napoleon acting as broker, Venetia was ceded to France which in turn ceded it to Italy, while Austria retained the Trentino.

* Actually the purpose of the banquet was to effect a reconciliation between Mazzini and Garibaldi since Mazzini had refused to see Garibaldi.

During the Seven Weeks War Jessie followed Garibaldi on his campaign in the Tyrol. Just before the commencement of hostilities, Austria had offered to give up the sought prize, Venetia, to Italy. But by that time, the Italian ministry was so entangled in negotiations with Prussia that it found itself unable to terminate them. Garibaldi was furious with the organizational chaos and the inept management of this whole affair. Although he did his best during the campaign, he always thought that he was betrayed by those above him. La Marmora, who was the commanding general, did not see to it that Garibaldi was provided with the equipment or support that he needed; and consequently Garibaldi's operation, including the conquest of the Lake of Garda and the fight at Bezzacca on July 21, 1866, were unsuccessful. Garibaldi regretted that he had ever been induced to participate. In his autobiography he said, nevertheless, that as in the previous campaign, he enjoyed the loyal support and devoted services of Jessie White Mario, who was again at hand to treat the wounded.

At the end of the war, Jessie and Alberto accompanied Garibaldi to the League of Peace meetings at Geneva (where they met Bakunin). Garibaldi had continued to fret ever since Aspromonte because the Italian government seemed to be moving in only the most cautious fashion to free Rome from the pope. Late in 1864 Napoleon had agreed to withdraw French troops from Rome gradually over the next two years if Piedmont would move the capital of Italy to Florence from Turin. In December, 1866 the last French troops were withdrawn, but Pope Pius IX retained a private army, consisting of volunteers drawn from all over the world. With the disappearance of the last French troops, Garibaldi again decided to place himself at the head of volunteers with the purpose of invading the papal territory. Quickly captured after an insurrectionary attempt in September, he escaped to Caprera, leaving his son Menotti in charge. The Rattazzi government was forced to resign on October 19, 1867, and Garibaldi took heart, again appeared in Florence, and boarded a train for Rome, soon afterwards crossing the frontier with seven thousand men. At the end of October French troops returned to Rome and on November 3, Garibaldi was defeated by the papal forces, reinforced by the French. He was arrested and returned to Caprera.

Three years were to pass before Rome was finally secured for the Italian nation. The French were forced to withdraw their troops in August, 1870, since they needed them in the Franco-Prussian war which had begun in July. France, in the hope of gaining Italy's support, offered Italy a free hand in Rome if she would aid her militarily.

King Victor Emmanuel was forced to refuse this offer for economic reasons and the Italian government accordingly chose to remain neutral. Thereupon Victor Emmanuel made a final appeal to Pius IX, in which he asked him to relinquish Rome, but Pius refused. Consequently, on September 12, General Raffaele Cadorna moved into the Papal State of the city of Rome and on September 20 the city surrendered to his army. In the plebiscite held on October 2, in the Roman provinces, a heavy majority voted in favor of annexation. Cavour's dreams of complete unification were at last realized nine years after his death.

But what of the remaining architects of Italian unification? Ironically, at the very time that Cadorna was breaking down the gates of Rome, Garibaldi was offering his services to the French Third Republic. On September 4, Napoleon III had abdicated and fled to England after being defeated at Sedan by the Prussians. The fall of the Second French Empire was immediately followed by the establishment of the Third Republic on September 4, with General Louis Jules Trochu as president. With the Prussians besieging Paris, Trochu found himself unable to cope with the critical situation that faced the new regime. Another member of the new government, Léon Gambetta, minister for interior, escaped to Tours, crossing the Prussian lines by balloon, and for the next five months directed the continuation of the war with Prussia as virtual dictator of France.

As soon as he heard of the establishment of the French Republic, Garibaldi offered to form a volunteer corps to aid it against the Prussians—a move which surprised many of his former supporters, who were incredulous that the general could find himself on the side of a country whose leaders and causes he had opposed for so long. The French hesitated to accept his offer, but after a month's delay, finally did so. Garibaldi then proceeded from Caprera through Marseilles to Dijon, where he was joined by some of his Redshirts.

Jessie decided to follow him once more, this time without her husband, who refused to have anything to do with the expedition. She attached herself to Garibaldi's forces as before, but now as a military correspondent, although in this campaign she also resumed her task as nurse to the wounded when the occasion arose. She reported on October 29, 1870, in an article in the *Scotsman*, that she had paused to see Mazzini on her way to France and that he had told her he was glad that the Italians were offering their services to republican France although he wished they had had as much enthusiasm about republicanism in their own country. Traveling by train to France through the snowcovered Mont Cenis pass, she arrived at Dijon after a confusing series of shuttles, then took a military train to Bardone and finally a dog cart through the rain to Amanges. Arrived, at last, at Garibaldi's headquarters, she joyously greeted her old friends.

Jessie recounted her experiences during this phase of the war in her book, published the next year, entitled *I Garibaldini in francia.*[10] Before she brought the work out as a single volume, however, she sent intermittent dispatches from the scene of Garibaldi's marches from September 8 through November 27, 1870, and again later to the *Scotsman* in Edinburgh, and the *Tribune* in New York. Her accounts were those of an eyewitness, and since she was privy to the secret gatherings of Garibaldi and his staff, her work provided the most detailed record of his participation in the Franco-Prussian war.

In her supplement to the *Autobiography of Garibaldi*, Jessie described her reunion with her old comrades:

> The Garibaldian Chiefs were beside themselves with vexation. To go and fight under De Failly, perhaps side by side with the Zouaves of Charette, seemed an impossibility; to leave Garibaldi alone in a foreign land was equally distasteful. On the other hand, there were the Ruth-like followers who each answered Garibaldi's appeal unhesitatingly. "Wither thou goest I will go; where thou diest I will die, and there I will be buried."
>
> "Arrivederci," said Castellazzi, one of my wounded of 1860, just liberated from the Papal dungeons of San Michele, with Petroni, who had been immured there eighteen years. "I wonder where *we* shall come up with Garibaldi?" "Speak for yourself, and take plenty of rags and plaster," I made answer, "for never a surgeon-soldier or Garibaldian nurse will you see unless you fall a prisoner into the hands of the Prussians." Then, "Chi lo sa?"
>
> Truly, if Garibaldi had summoned the rank and file to fight for Prussia against France, very few would have failed to answer, "Present." Still, "Arrivederci" was Castellazzi's only farewell; and, indeed, within a fortnight we did "meet again," at Dole, the beautiful capital of the Jura, whose heights command the country from Saone to the Doubs, where the Garibaldians were concentrated.
>
> I was told that it would be very difficult to see Garibaldi that night, as he had just returned to his head-quarters at Amanges; but at that moment an officer of Menotti's staff offered me a seat in an open vehicle, and, despite pouring rain and the coldest of north winds, I accepted it and arrived frozen at a little hut, dignified with the title of headquarters. Entering the kitchen, I was welcomed with that glad greeting only given by old comrades meeting in a foreign land. There was Canzio, who had left Italy without waiting for the arrival of his ninth child, whose birth Teresita announced by telegraph twelve days after his departure; and there was Castellazzi, gleefully triumphant. The Genoese dialect predominated, and the host was requested to

continue Béranger's "Song of The Conscript," which my entrance had interrupted. I listened politely, my eye fixed on the door opposite, where, as I expected, Basso appeared, followed by Garibaldi, who had recognized my voice. His face lit up with the radiant smile so exclusively his own, as he said, "This time I scarcely expected you."[11]

She recounted that Garibaldi at once asked after each of his followers, insisting that he had not wanted to force them to come, but that he was glad to hear that some had chosen to do so. Jessie commented on the peculiar position of the correspondents in this war, whereupon Garibaldi summoned his orderly and instructed him to make her out a laissez-passer as correspondent for English and American newspapers.

She commented later:

> As I looked at that man, at whose feet I had seen the populations he had liberated prostrate themselves—before whom the proudest heads in my own proud England uncovered in reverent admiration —there in that wretched room, regardless of the ambiguous post assigned to him, of the no sort of account in which he was held, intent only on discovering and seizing the moment in which he could avail for a people suffering and struggling for liberty, Béranger's lines came to my mind:
>
> "Je connais le secret de ses modestes vertues,
>   Bras, tête et coeur, tout était peuple en lui."
>
> And as I went to sleep in the house of the curate, where my friends had secured a lodging for me, I was more thoroughly penetrated with the true greatness of Garibaldi than I had ever been on the victorious banks of the Volturno, or on the triumphant heights of Monterotondo. And he *was* greater, greater than his greatest self, the greatest man in Italy at that hour (figuratively if not literally) right to the core when all his countrymen were wrong. After Sedan, the king, the court, and the moderate party cared not what became of republican France;* even the vengeance of the Italian republicans was far from being satiated; but he, the inborn liberator—Shelley transformed into a warrior—only felt that the French people were suffering, only saw the goal that must be attained through seas of blood, through years of expiating sacrifice.[12]

Garibaldi commanded his motley volunteer troops with moderate successes and many failures. According to the official historian of the Franco-Prussian war, the Garibaldians successfully restricted Prussian movements in the south.[13] After his part in this campaign—which was to be his last—Garibaldi returned to Caprera in 1871. There he worked on his memoirs and interested himself in a variety of subjects, including the Socialist International. He was elected, as he had been several

---

* Something of an exaggeration, as the diplomatic history of the period shows.

times since 1862, to Parliament. Voted a pension and a sum of money against impoverishment, he refused it once, only yielding at last to an offer from the leftist government. He died on June 2, 1882, at the age of seventy-four.

Mazzini's last few years were sadder. Even after the completion of Italian unification, he continued to feel that "the great soul of Italy still lay prostrate in the tomb dug for her three centuries ago by the papacy and the empire," Emilie tells us in her biography of him.[14] The unification of Italy under a monarchy had left his dream of the rebirth of the Roman Republic unrealized. A final humiliation awaited him. In 1870, having decided to stir up opposition to the regime in Sicily, he found himself under arrest on the orders of his former lieutenant in conspiracy, Medici, who had by now joined the establishment and had become governor of Palermo. Held at Gaeta, Mazzini was released two months later and returned to England.

In 1871 Mazzini settled in Lugano and founded *La Roma del popolo,* his last underground newspaper. During his last years he did ideological battle against the various socialist doctrines then becoming current. His opposition to socialism sprang from his disdain for the Benthamite view which he saw as basic to socialist doctrine, namely, the conviction that happiness was life's most important measure. While Garibaldi showed considerable sympathy for leftist movements at this time, Mazzini remained adamant in his disapproval.

Despite the failure of his many plots and the eclipse of his political influence during the later years of the unification struggle, the importance of his contribution to that struggle and its ultimate success cannot be overestimated. Gaetano Salvemini, one of the foremost Italian historians, maintains that it was Mazzini alone who imposed the dominating psychological pressures for unification on the Italian people.[15]

En route from Lugano to England, Mazzini was stricken with pleurisy and died in Pisa on March 10, 1872. His disciple, Emilie Ashurst Venturi, remained loyal until the end and her memoir reflects the sadness of his last years.

8

"Every tub has to stand upon its own bottom, and in the year of grace 1910 when we shall be eaten up by the worms, Italy will probably be in quite other hands than now."

—Busta 420, AJWM

Jessie's days on the battlefield were now over. At the end of Garibaldi's last campaign she rejoined Alberto, who had remained in Rome as a correspondent for various journals. For the remainder of their lives together they divided their time between Rome and Florence and after 1871, Lendinara, where they had inherited a small house and garden from an uncle of Alberto's. They were very hard pressed financially and payment for their numerous contributions to Italian and foreign periodicals, as well as for separate volumes of history and biography, provided their only income. Though Jessie became adept at driving sharp bargains with editors and publishers, there was very little money coming in even so. Nevertheless the Marios seemed to take pleasure in the simple joys of gardening, growing their own food for the table, and canning. They settled down for a few years into what must have seemed a comparatively unexciting daily life, but continued to work steadily at their writing wherever they were.

The very comprehensive private library that the Marios had amassed at their house in Lendinara[1] provided them with an invaluable resource for their research into recent history, political developments, and literature. But rather than rely entirely on library materials for their research, they traveled ubiquitously, especially Jessie, who enjoyed the stimulus and excitement of fresh experiences and was much more inclined to keep on the move than her more scholarly

111

husband. On her trips through Italy she often stopped to visit various workingmen's groups and friends whom she had known during the campaigns. She intensified her research on Naples and Sicily, begun during the Southern campaign, and wrote several articles on conditions there. In 1877, she published *La miseria di Napoli*, an account of the living conditions of the poor in Naples.[2] In the same year, George Henry Lewes (friend, and later husband of George Eliot) consulted a well-known London physician, Dr. Hughlings Jackson, on the subject of Madame Mario's health. It was decided that she needed absolute rest for what appeared to be a nervous ailment. George Eliot's friend, Barbara Bodichon,* who shared many of Jessie's intellectual commitments and had kept up with her ever since 1855, invited her for a visit to St. Ives in Cornwall. During this sojourn at the Bodichon house Jessie met George Eliot once or twice. But the chief purpose of the visit, to rest, was not fulfilled. Barbara Bodichon was herself taken ill and Jessie immediately undertook to nurse her, thus complicating her own convalescence.[3]

With the exception of this visit and a subsequent one in the 1890s, Jessie henceforth spent her time in Italy. In 1881, at the age of forty-nine, Jessie suffered a minor stroke, as a result of which three fingers of her right hand were paralyzed. Fortunately she was already a confirmed user of the typewriter, having acquired one early in the 1860s. Unreliable and unskilled as her typing was, it nevertheless produced readable copy. To aid her in gathering and editing materials during the next years, she employed an amanuensis, who remained with her until her death. Happily the stroke did not seem to have impaired her mental powers.

In spite of her ailment and physical handicap, Jessie continued to work steadily on a life of Garibaldi during 1881. It was published in Milan, in April 1882, under the title *Vita di G. Garibaldi*, two months before his death. Meanwhile Jessie discovered that a biography of Garibaldi in English had been published in October 1881 by James Theodore Bent, one of Longman's popular writers on Italian subjects. She felt that Bent had included materials injurious to the Garibaldi family's reputation and sought to have Longman's remove the work from circulation, a pursuit in which she apparently succeeded in April.[4] Without doubt, her action was not solely altruistic as she too had her eye on the English market. In July she corresponded with T. Fisher Unwin about the possibility of bringing out a popular book in their Log Cabin series. The following, dated July 26, 1882, is the personal letter she received from the publisher:

*See pages 141-142.

Your favour of the 20th to hand. From it, I gather that you are in treaty with an English firm. Of course, I do not desire to obtrude myself in the matter, but if you can submit your MS to me and thus give me an opportunity to make a proposal, I should be happy to do so. As requested, I send "Log Cabin." Personally, I should prefer a book of that character and size, believing that a popular life would sell best. A large and expensive work would be to a great extent sold through the Libraries and by the time a cheap edition of it could be published, I fear the interest in Garibaldi would have dropped, or rather, have been provided for by other and cheaper books.

The book "Log Cabin" was a success here with both old and young, because it was cheap, lively, and not too big. The Public bought it instead of borrowing it from Mudies.

On the question of terms, I would do my best to meet your views on the matter. Perhaps the most equitable and satisfactory would be to publish on the basis of a Royalty to the Author. *For instance*, if you provided a volume similar in size and contents to "Log Cabin," it could be arranged that I, as publisher, pay you a royalty of say 6 per copy sold. I should thus have to take all the risks and expenses. Such terms might be arranged for a first edition, say of 2,000, and re-arranged for future editions.

Publishers call the winter months the "Season": 'tis the time when most books are published, bought, and read, and to be successful your book, I consider, should be out of the Printer's hands by Oct. 1.

You will see by this how necessary it is to settle the question quickly, and I would ask that, if you are inclined to treat with me, to place in my hands all details and any proposition you may have to make, at once. I should also be glad if you can send me copies of Maps, Plates, & Portraits required. I do not think an English edition would need so many as the Italians, still if I had them before me I could the better judge what to use.

I am, Dear Madam,
Faithfully Yours,
T. Fisher Unwin[5]

On the back of this letter Jessie wrote, "I decline royalty leave terms to you can do the popular book size Log cabin but will not bind myself not to publish my other work illustrated will send portrait and maps as they come out guarantee the book in time for publication Nov." (Presumably this was the response which Jessie then copied onto another piece of paper and sent off to T. Fisher Unwin). There was often a rather unobliging dictatorial streak in Jessie's dealings with her publishers, of which the terms contained in her reply here are a sample. Since the publisher could not secure her book on his terms, he seems not to have proceeded in this matter further, for the book did not come out in England after all.

After 1868 Alberto Mario became increasingly unwell and eventually underwent twelve operations for cancer of the pharynx. Jessie nursed him throughout his long and agonizing illness. He died on June 2, 1883, and was buried in Lendinara. Alberto had left a number of uncompleted projects, and Jessie promised to carry these forward. Within the decade before he died, even though ill and frail, he had taken on editorial work for several reviews: *La Provincia* (in Mantua); *La rivista repubblicana*, and later, *La lega della democrazia*. During the same decade he had written four studies: *La mente di Carlo Cattaneo*, published in 1870; *Camicia Rossa*, 1875; *Teste e figure*, 1877; *Garibaldi*, 1879.

With Giosuè Carducci* Jessie collected and supplemented some of Alberto's works, and brought them out in Bologna in 1884 in a volume called *Scritti letterari e artistici*. This book contains an introduction of over a hundred pages in which Jessie describes the warmth of their relationship and the ties which had bound the Marios to each other. In 1901 Carducci brought out Alberto's *Scritti politici*.

Jessie seems to have had very little money at her disposal after Alberto's death. She was now totally dependent on the output of her own pen; the days of her political activism were over and she began to look with a critical eye at the young kingdom. She had begun writing for the *Nation* in 1866 and in the last decades of the century she sought to branch out into subjects that would take her to various parts of Italy for study and observation. Possibly under the influence of Stansfeld, who had written much about birth control, Jessie became interested in introducing this idea to Italy, as a means of solving overpopulation and poverty. She gave increasing thought and study to ways in which knowledge of birth control might be disseminated.

In 1886 Jessie had published *Della vita di G. Mazzini*, a compendious work that brought together many previously uncollected documents concerning the Risorgimento. For this work she relied very heavily on the letters exchanged by Mazzini and other Risorgimento figures. This biography was followed in 1887 by a two-volume life of Bertani, *Agostino Bertani e i suoi tempi* (Garibaldi's physician and one of his influential advisers). In 1889 she wrote a lengthy one-volume supplement to an English version of Garibaldi's life translated by A. Werner. In 1894 she published a biography based on memories and letters, *In memoria di G. Nicotera.*† In 1900 she brought out a volume of selected writings of Mazzini, *Scritti scelti di Giuseppe Mazzini*. When she died in 1906, she was in the midst of composing

---

* Poet and man of letters (1836-1907).

† Nicotera was one of the members of the Pisacane expedition who survived the event but was imprisoned by the Bourbons.

several studies; a life of Stansfeld, a history of her own family, a novel, and her own popular history of the unification of Italy posthumously edited by Count Arese and published in 1909 as *The Birth of Modern Italy*.

We know very little of the chronology of her last years except that she traveled inexhaustibly looking for material for her articles and making arrangements for her books. She worked hard, but for all that she was almost indigent. From 1896 to the year she died she was a teacher of English literature at the Normal School in Florence. No record remains of what in particular she taught or how she liked this final new profession, undertaken at the age of sixty-four.

Jessie died on March 5, 1906, just before her seventy-fifth birthday. Following her cremation at a civil ceremony, her ashes were buried next to those of her husband at Lendinara. But before that her funeral cortege traversed the city of Florence in solemn procession. A handful of surviving Garibaldians, one hundred schoolgirls carrying roses, and a group of university professors followed her casket, pausing now and then to praise her in spontaneous encomia.

W. P. Garrison, editor of the *Nation*, published the following eulogy of Jessie in the March 15, 1906 issue:

Jessie White Mario

For forty years this name has been familiar by its initials to readers of the *Nation*, as that of this journal's Italian correspondent by way of eminency. Last week we published her animated account of the new Italian ministry.

"The enclosed pages," ran her private note of February 15, "are the first that I have been able to write since I last sent a letter to the *Nation* (that is since September, 1905). I have been very ill, but the new hopes for Italy have wakened me a little. . . . Of course, my book on Stansfeld (the English Mazzinian Liberal) lies three-fourth finished on the shelf. This is to me a dire grief, as it tells of the pioneers who rendered possible the Liberal triumph of today. John Burns in the English, and Pantano in the Italian, Ministry—really, I have a Pisgah view, at the age of seventy-five, of the Promised Land."

Two days before her letter appeared in the *Nation*, her funeral procession, as the *Evening Post's* London correspondent telegraphs, "passed the Casa Guidi in Florence, which was decorated in honor of the centenary of Elizabeth Barrett Browning. The association was just, as well as striking." . . . In her *Nation* letters, as our files will show, she followed closely the political development of the peninsula, interspersing these comments with accounts of Florentine Mosaics, or Venetian Glass, or the Italian Industrial Exposition, or the opening of the St. Gothard Tunnel. Ever her thoughts were with the great idealist leaders of the Italian new birth, and she played the part of Old Mortality in editing their writings or memoirs. . . . On July 12 (in 1905) she wrote "I am better, but not well; have got through the heavy exams (at the Woman's College in Florence) at last, and am now ordered off to the seaside at Via Reggio, where I go on the 16th. If I could hope to get my Stansfeld-Mazzini book ready by the time the Liberals 'come back again', I would ask no more of fate. Surely, surely, we shall not return to 'protection' in old England??? If we do, then 'manhood suffrage' has proved a delusion and a snare."

To our deep regret we never met this admirable woman, an honor to her sex and to Britain's great name for ardent, worldwide philanthropy. She had a soul sensitive to all misery: our readers will recall her exposition of the horrors of the subterranean life of Naples, of the sulphur mines of Sicily. She was responsive to every proletary movement for the relief from oppression or distress, though opposed to violence in the justest cause. She was ever giving of her scanty income to the poor. Her mode of living was almost ascetic. A young American couple [Garrison's relatives] who brought her a letter of introduction from us, were so impressed at once by her nobility and by the bareness of her surroundings that they said to each other, at the foot of the stairs on leaving, Shall we not sell our letter of credit, give her the proceeds, and return by the next steamer? On this being reported to generous hearts on this side of the water, and a sum being forwarded to her on a pretext of previous acquaintance, she accepted it —for the orphans of the Garibaldian connection.

I always wanted to know about people who had done things— where they were born who taught them how they began doing—how often they failed—how they came to succeed.

Busta 419, *AJWM*

It is tempting to speculate that as a child Jessie sat by her father as he read and commented on the newspaper accounts of the activities of the Italian exiles in England and expressed the hope that his children would live to see the day when Italy was free. Or that Jessie joined her parents during the long winter evenings of the 1840s while they read aloud passages from Thomas Carlyle's *On Heroes and Hero-Worship*. Whatever Jessie's early experiences may have been, there are some peculiar inducements to find a line of internal consistency in her actions and attitudes from childhood on.

Looking back at the earnest characters of "Alice Lane" who believed in seeking their duty close at hand and in fulfilling it in their community, we can quickly identify the woman in her sixties who has just taken a trip down into a sulphur mine in the interior of Sicily in order to inform her *Nation* readers of a primary social evil in southern Italy. And we can pick up the echoes of the youthful voice of scepticism raised against the Protestant ethic of the story of Cain and Abel, in the insistent self-assurance of her argument with the editors of the *Nation* over Garibaldi's march on Aspromonte. Jessie believed that the salvation of people in a nation with problems was much more important than the salvation of man; and she spent much of her life speaking out to the Italians themselves about the nature of their needs and the deficiencies of their culture, and to the rest of the world about Italian affairs as she saw them. When she died she was still searching for the embodiment of her self-styled Pisgah View. She never relinquished her positive conviction that with information and courage members of society might reform themselves and their institutions. For years after political unification had been achieved in Italy, Jessie continued to press for the kinds of social reforms—especially a higher degree of literacy, and the freedom of enlightenment —that she saw as essential to the development of a strong and healthy society. Unlike many of her colleagues who took part in various phases of the Risorgimento, she resisted the stultification of her political thought and social action and remained free to deal with the realities of Italy's changing conditions.

Indeed what seems most interesting about Jessie Mario as a person is the unified vision with which she moved through life, dedicated to a single ideal and purpose, but varying her means of serving this according to the demands of the situation. She gave the streaming energy of her life to the Italian cause but she modified her course with versatility. Thus while other republicans—like Mazzini and Emilie Ashurst—assumed uncompromising attitudes, Jessie always found it possible to adapt herself to political developments. She was, in that sense, a realist and a pragmatist. Like a plant with a metabolic compulsion to flourish when the sunshine has been cut off on one side, she hungrily readjusted.

While she was an active member of the Friends of Italy Society— during her early years of propagandistic writing and lecturing—she believed whole-heartedly that Mazzinism and unadulterated republicanism were the sole means to achieve and maintain a unified Italy. But though she subscribed to the ideas of Mazzini, she felt personally attracted to the figure of Garibaldi. She thought at first that their causes were one and the same. Enthralled by the very idea of insurrections, she accepted uncritically and without reservation Mazzini's notion that all of Italy was ready to rise up against the Austrians, the pope and the Bourbons at the touch of the match to the tinderbox. She shared his belief that his message was inspired by some quasi-divine power, and in the posture of a convert, she looked to him for instruction and kept to his terms. At this point Mazzini's detestations were hers: all monarchs were anathema and any compromise with monarchy or the papacy was immoral. Neither Victor Emmanuel II, nor Cavour could be trusted since they were representatives of the old order, and any suggestion that Piedmont-Sardinia under Cavour's guidance might accomplish an effective revolution was automatically ruled out. Mazzini was convinced that the force of the revolution had to come from the people and that they were indeed ready to act if only the impetus of popular leadership could be provided. The persecution and exiling of political liberals from Italy following the restoration of the old order by the Congress of Vienna in 1815 had deprived the people of their leaders. It was now the task of the exiles to gather money, arms, and political support from abroad and to bring these back to the people. Once provided with the means to effect their liberation, the people would rise spontaneously and set up the new republic.

Lacking political sophistication but desperately anxious to serve the cause, Jessie passionately embraced the Mazzinian view. But as time went on and the complexity of the Italian situation became clearer to her, Jessie gradually tempered her commitment to Mazzinian strategy. She came to see that Mazzini's plans for insurrection would not precipitate the desired revolts because the Italian people were too apathetic. By contrast, Garibaldi seemed more realistic, and she came to regard the compromises that he often struck with the Italian governors as inevitable stages in the development of Italian unification. The slowness of the pace was frustrating, and like Garibaldi, Jessie thought that Victor Emmanuel was far too conciliatory to the French and the pope. But she accepted compromises where Mazzini rigidly refused them and was drawn away from Mazzinism by Garibaldism. The intensity of her first discipleship waned as that of the second waxed.

For a period Garibaldi's adventuresome spirit dominated Jessie's life and thought even though she perceived his weaknesses. She knew that he was no political idealist and that he was incapable of Mazzini's noble vision. What mattered to Jessie—herself a doer rather than a profound thinker—was that under Garibaldi's leadership things got accomplished. Garibaldi set out with a handful of men across the straits of Messina, and took the capital city from the Bourbons. During the period when he was unifying the south, he put heavy demands on his anointed followers and inspired by the intensity of his enthusiasm and will to succeed, they taxed themselves to the utmost. One need only recall Alberto's accomplishment in organizing, practically overnight, a military college to train the ragamuffins of Palermo, or Jessie's almost miraculous achievements in providing medical facilities and nursing care for the wounded, to get a sense of the energy and effort that Garibaldi's vigorous leadership evoked from his followers. The Southern campaign revealed Garibaldi at his best, and when in subsequent years his sense of timing and tactics began to falter—as at Aspromonte and after—Jessie once again had to struggle with the recognition that the man whose leadership she had chosen to follow could no longer be followed blindly. Moved by her devotion to him, she tried to cling to a sentimental hope that the old gifts would be restored, but she actually knew better. Her comments in *I Garibaldini* show that as soon as she joined Garibaldi in France she saw that some of his chiefs had become reluctant to follow him in what seemed to them a pointless enterprise, especially given the past French influence on Italian affairs.

Between the figures of Mazzini and Garibaldi, and consistently a temperate influence on his wife, stood Alberto Mario. Mazzini had treated Jessie to rather acid praise and exchanged flowers and letters with her, but he probably never really understood her ambitions. Garibaldi constantly whipped up her volatile emotions, her hopes and expectations by his ready references to her high position in his sisterhood. There was always conflict between Garibaldi and Mazzini, and Jessie unwittingly found herself caught in the undertow. But she was relieved from lasting dependence on either of these powerful personalities by the dimension of her relationship with Alberto Mario. It was in response to his influence that she developed her sense of herself and achieved genuine independence and maturity.

Alberto was a very complex man. Like his Milanese friend, Cattaneo, he was a gradualist, a positivist, and a federalist, as well as a republican. Supporting both Mazzini and Garibaldi insofar as they shared the common aspiration of a unified Italy, he resented Mazzini's arrogance in trying to impose his mystical notions of duty on the Italian people on the one hand, but was too committed to republicanism to join Garibaldi's acceptance of Victor Emmanuel's monarchy on the other hand. Unlike either of these, or Jessie herself, the scholarly and reflective Alberto tended to act rationally, and consequently much of what happened in both Mazzinian and Garibaldian circles must have distressed him. He had a sense of history and of reality that were often at variance with Mazzini's idealism and Garibaldi's impetuosity. Courageous and adventurous, he had a zest for personal participation in life as well as a sense of humor that saved him from losing his sense of proportion. This served him well in his relationship with Jessie, who had a tendency to take herself too seriously. Over the years Alberto and Jessie shared a close and affectionate relationship which was bracing to Jessie's intellectual as well as her emotional development. Under Alberto's influence, Jessie gradually assumed the more critical attitude towards Italian affairs which was to form her mature viewpoint.

Jessie's contribution as a writer on the affairs of the Risorgimento must of necessity be judged both by its quality and by its volume. It may seem strange to judge a writer's worth by the number of words written, but in Jessie's case it was the large number of publications that she saw to the press—whether she wrote them, edited them, urged others to edit them, or simply copied them from the original documents—that have provided present-day scholars of Italian history with a rich store of source materials.

As a reporter-critic Jessie spoke with a unique voice. She profited from her intimate association with Garibaldi, Mazzini, and others who were the propelling forces behind the struggle for liberty in the nineteenth century. Her personal commitment to the cause gave her a feeling for what was taking place that an uninvolved reporter would not have had. On the other hand, this intimacy with the chief figures of the movement might very well have violated the objectivity of her reporting. It is no easier for a reporter to pretend he is not affected by the outcome of personal issues than for a doctor to pretend that the patient under his scalpel is not his child. But if Jessie's early lectures and writing efforts for the Mazzinian cause were predominantly propagandistic in style and content, her reporting of the Garibaldian campaigns was much sounder and more objective.

Her closeness to Garibaldi gave her access to news that was not available to other reporters, but Jessie appears to have been generous in sharing this information with other reporters when she was too busy nursing to use the material herself. In the anniversary issue of the *Daily News* collection, for instance, Jessie observed that she forwarded materials to the paper during the Sicilian and Neapolitan campaigns. Yet a careful reading of the *Daily News* for this period (June through October 1860) yields very few articles that could have been written by Jessie herself, the majority clearly being identified as having been submitted by the paper's Neapolitan correspondent Carlo Arrivabene. What Jessie must have meant by her observation is that she shared her information with Arrivabene, who was her friend and with whom she was often together during the campaign.

During the French campaign Jessie was able to devote the major portion of her time to reporting and rewarded her employers with unique coverage of Garibaldi's part in this conflict. Her reports were detailed, including statistics on the numbers of dead and injured, descriptions of the battlefields, analyses of the tactics, and accounts of actual skirmishes. But beyond these concrete details they conveyed the nuances of the situation: for example, the strained relationship between the Garibaldians and their traditional enemies—now their allies—the French. They depicted Garibaldi's fading skill as a leader.

Jessie White Mari

Museo Centrale del Risorgimento, Ron

Jessie White Mario

Museo Centrale del Risorgimento, Rome

Alberto Mario

Museo Centrale del Risorgimento, Rome

Mazzini (*left*) and Garibaldi

Museo Centrale del Risorgimento, Rome

Garibaldi Visiting the Wounded

Museo Centrale del Risorgimento, Rome

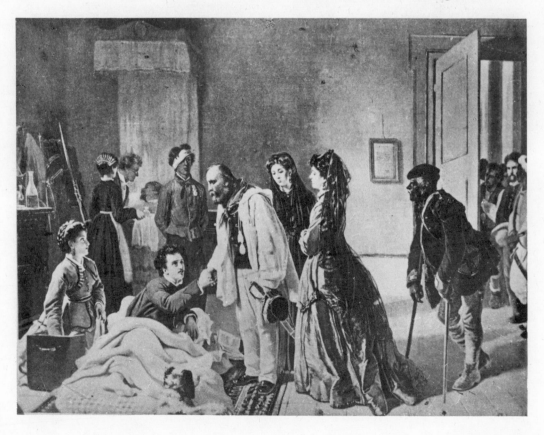

Alberto Mario in later years

Museo Centrale del Risorgimento, Rome

Jessie White Mario during her last years

Museo Centrale del Risorgimento, Rome

Edwin Lawrence Godkin

New York Public Library Photographic Collection

When an outsider looked at Garibaldi's last campaign it seemed a dismal failure from beginning to end. But why? Since much of Jessie's writing was explanatory as well as factual, a careful reading of her full narrative of this campaign provides the answer. Devoted as she was to him, she saw that Garibaldi was tired, debilitated by his arthritic condition, and in many ways living on his past reputation. He had lost his knack, his sense of timing. The popular stereotype of Garibaldi the infallible warrior is negated by Jessie's portrayal of a great leader confronted with a decline of those powers which have earned him renown and acclaim throughout the world. But her acknowledgement of the reality does not diminish her sympathy for him: she sees the sadness of the compromised situation in which he found himself, the poignancy of his refusal to recognize that he was finished.

In one of her communications to the English newspapers from France Jessie sent in to the editors an apology which showed that she was completely aware of her bias in favor of Garibaldi:

> Decidedly it is a bad lookout for a newspaper when its correspondents take a special interest in the events they simply ought to watch and narrate. I must plead guilty to caring more for the events themselves than for seeing the narrative in type. So, if you think fit to disown me, I can but pronounce the sentence just. I believe that I posted my last from this same place on the 18th November.
>
> How many things have passed since then
> How many changes have we seen.
>
> . . . . In fifteen days I have had but two nights' sleep, and have lost twice over my few personal belongings—That is my private history. And now for my diary.[6]

Jessie was up night and day during the French campaign—and undoubtedly during the Sicilian campaign too. She underwent the rigors of the soldiers' experiences and shared their deprivations with them.

> Never, never have I suffered so from the cold, and I thought that the Christmas of '58 spent in New York was the worst one could suffer. . . . Alack-a-day! instead of paying for our rooms, we must needs pass through the ordeal of going to the Mairie for a requisition. . . . But that my bones were aching with rheumatism and my vital energies frozen, I should have amused myself with compelling the Prussian-hearted Napoleonite to lodge me in his choicest apartment. . . . Early in the morning I saw the "proper authorities", learned from the prefect that the Prussians were not so far off as might be wished, and started for Daix, Durois, and Prenois. This journey had a double object. First, I wished to retrace the road of our day of victory and defeat, to ascertain for myself whether we did ill or well to retreat. Second, to see our wounded left along the road. The prefect, willingly I would fain believe, or compelled by the orders that I have, found

me horse and carriage—scarce articles in these days—and we made
our exit from Dijon. . . . Turning up the well-remembered avenue I
re-entered the chateau of the Mayor; found him and his wife still
terrified. Nor was my first abrupt question, "What have you done with
my wounded?" calculated to abate their fears.[7]

The nature of Jessie's reporting is best illustrated, finally, by the
following passages, which contain many of the attributes already discussed:

> The Prussians are concentrating in large numbers at Vesoul. They
> hold Dijon with 8000, Genlis with 15000, and stretch along the rail-
> road towards Lyons as far as Beaure. Between Genlis and Dôle is the
> fortress of Auxonne, garrisoned by 3000 regulars, if so one can style
> the raw young conscripts who now alone form the armies of France.
> This fortress, before the new mode of warfare rendered all much of a
> muchness, was considered a very important *place de guerre*. It was
> united to France after the death of Charles the Bold. Vauban con-
> structed its present works. Napoleon was there in garrison in 1788
> and 1789. In 1815 it was the centre of the movements of the Imperial
> Army and was besieged by the Austrians, who only entered after a
> long siege. But for the state of the Saone, swollen by the rains, the
> Prussians could turn this fortress, and come down to us across coun-
> try.[8]
>
> When I joined him [Garibaldi] again it was only in time to accom-
> pany him to Bordeaux, where he was reelected representative for
> four different departments. . . . [Of Garibaldi's new novel] he said,
> as at parting, he gave me a splendid bouquet of violets presented to
> him by the Marseillaise ladies—"and as you have done so much for me
> and mine, I shall strike out some passages which I know would vex
> you."
>
> "Thanks, General—" I answered; "that is a boon which I appreciate."
> "You would prefer my not publishing the book at all."[9]

Jessie's most valuable contributions to journalism were the 143 articles she wrote for the *Nation* between 1866 and 1906. A precis of their
contents reveals an energetic and far-reaching mind at work.* Taken
together these articles describe many aspects of life in post-unification
Italy. Writing about the economic development of both the north and
the south, describing and analyzing social changes and governmen-
tal reorganization, Jessie helped her American readers to understand
the nature and complexity of the problems which impeded successful
reconstruction. High among these problems, in Jessie's eyes, was a
conspicuous lack of both public and private leadership. Equally significant was the general apathy towards public affairs, which Jessie
attributed to two causes. First she stressed the lack of popular com-

* See Appendix 3, pp. 160-183.

prehension of the real meaning of unification; but above all she blamed the involvement of the papacy in temporal as well as spiritual affairs for the slow development and progress of effective civil government.

Jessie foresaw that the kingdom of Italy would be unified in name only until such time as the very deep chasm which separated the north from the south could be bridged—and prophetically, she was not sure that this would ever happen. The north was fairly prosperous; its entrepreneurs were open to new ideas and willing to seek the means to achieve good relations with their workers. They were making strides toward reforms in taxes and in voting laws. Many of the northerners were enlightened citizens, although the humanizing influence of the universities and of other institutions which promoted enlightenment had been dissipated or held in check during the Risorgimento. The south, on the other hand, was backward, impoverished, illiterate; its culture was more primitive. Many of its citizens, especially those in power, neither knew nor cared about the means of achieving social and economic progress. During the years of the wars no new leaders had been trained to assume parliamentary and legislative roles in the structure of the new state, and the Risorgimento heroes who moved in to fill the void were frequently less competent in the conduct of public affairs than they had been in the practice of warfare. Moreover, even after the pope had lost his stranglehold on temporal affairs and moved out of the Quirinal Palace in Rome, in 1877, the apathetic political climate that papal repression had created continued. For too many years, Jessie pointed out, there had been severe restrictions on suffrage, free speech, development of public facilities and education. It would take time to eradicate the depressing effects of such a heritage.

Jessie felt especially pessimistic about the south, and the analysis of its difficulties became her special concern and the dominant theme of her writing. She spent many hours walking over the miserable gutters of city slums and descending into mines and caves in which demoralized human beings worked and lived. She talked to the people in the country—the *analfabeti* who made their sparse livings from the soil and who paid their profits to the Mafia and the Camorra. When Jessie had been with Garibaldi in Sicily, she had seen countless examples of the unfortunate consequences of Bourbon rule. The economy was unhealthy; living conditions in the country hills were bestial, and in the city almost indescribable. The horror of her visit to the slum grottoes lived on in Jessie's mind long after. Here human beings copulated like pigs, sanitary measures were nonexistent, and disease was rampant. The ignorance and degradation of this part of

Italy haunted her, and publicizing the truth about it became a compulsion. She collected evidence in which no other writer was yet professionally interested; statistics on the birthrate; on the rate of infant mortality, and on the incidence of disease. She pleaded for the provision of elementary public hygiene. The sense of urgency and immediacy that sharpened her detailed reports on conditions in southern Italy makes these articles stand out as some of her most successful work.

Here, for example, is a passage from her article of December 12, 1891, which appeared in the January 14, 1892, issue of the *Nation*:

> All the descriptions penned by philanthropists, sensationalists, and Socialists of the sulphur mines of Sicily, and the work of children therein, which seemed sheer exaggeration when read in northern Italy or abroad, fall far short of the reality, which the pen of Dante could not portray. Not the slavery of the negroes in its worst aspect, nor the sweating of the whites as we know it in London and in all great cities, can compare in any least degree with the inhuman system of child torture openly and consistently practised in all the sulphur mines of the island, and especially in the central Province of Caltanisetta and the adjoining Province of Girgenti, bordering on the sea. This last week I have spent chiefly in and around the mines and in the mining district, as a penance for the pleasant tour through the Provinces of Trapani and Palermo, where the progress everywhere manifest, the healthy aspect of the country population, fill one with exultation, and dissipate the gloomy doubts which often assail one as to the benefits of liberty and civilization.
>
> Nor does your first arrival at Caltanisetta dispel these illusions. The town is built up the hilly slope, has some fine buildings old and new; the population, as you see it in the daytime, looks sturdy and healthy. Butchers' shops are plentiful, the fish market may vie with Palermo for the fine soles and enormous red mullet that comes from Terra Nuova direct by rail; the fruit and vegetables, artichokes and *finocchi*, the oranges, lemons, and mandarins, the figs and almonds and big loaves of wheaten bread exposed for sale, seem to promise that here is "bread and work for all." But wait until eventime; go up to the top of the city, and while chatting with the women who are preparing the evening meal of lentils or dried horse beans in dirty, airless, stinking hovels, watch for the first arrival of the *carusi*. Note the first batch of children, varying in age from six to ten, who work on the top of and about the mines, and who, if too young to be put to work at all, bear as yet no traces of it on their bright, impish, dirty faces, or thin, half-naked bodies; wait for the next batch of lads, varying from twelve to fifteen or seventeen years of age. The smaller and younger still retain the form and feature of human beings, though their eyes are red and bleared and their skin sallow and thick; but the older they

are, the more marked the result of hours and days and months and years of toil in the subterraneous caverns and galleries of the sulphur mines. All, or nearly all, have a bump on the left shoulder-blade; many a hacking cough; all are listless. . . .

When the price of sulphur is high, as at present, from fifty to sixty thousand men and children are employed in extracting and bringing to the surface the sulphur in its natural state, i.e., mixed with calcareous, clayey, or chalky soil; so it may be calculated that four times the number exist on the product of their toil. The proportion of the mineral to the soil varies from 8 to 40 per cent, the medium being 34 per cent, as the poorest mines are worked only at intervals and abandoned when prices fall. But the natural wealth of the mines adds nothing to the earnings of the *caruso* (literally a "boy" but now a term applied to all the toilers who bring the raw material to the surface of the pit). The mines all or nearly all belong to wealthy proprietors of the soil, of the old feudal estates; and though now the *feudi* are abolished, the *ex-feudi* as they are called, still remain in the same families. When a proprietor of the soil possesses, or believes that he possesses, a sulphur mine (the indications are various and of interest only to experts and owners) he is bound to inform the authorities and pay a small sum (about $25) for the right of working the mine. Here his duties end and his rights begin. Few proprietors work their own mines. They seek or are sought by a *gabellotto*, who hires the mine for four, nine, or even eighteen years. All the expenses of exploration, sinking pits, constructing galleries, etc., are assumed by the *gabellotto*. . . . [There follows a complete analysis of the function of the *gabellotto*.] Each miner or *picconiere* has so many *carusi*—boys of twelve, men up to sixty—who transport the material either to the cars or to boxes on wheels, or to the mouth of the pit. These cars run on inclined planes, but "lifts" are now introduced in some of the largest mines, and only where there are such contrivances can a stranger descend.

We have visited two mines during the past week, each time arriving at the surface with fervent resolve never again to seek such sickening sights. It is not the physical inconvenience which hurts, but the horror of the spectacle. . . . The boxes go down only about a third or half the depth of the mine; and from the bottom up to the level where the cars land, the children or men bring up the material in sacks, baskets, or even the huge blocks on their backs, in loads of 10, 20, 50, even 80 and 100 kilos per journey. Up the steep, slimy, slippery steps or paths they go, scarcely daring to rest a second, every one in three carrying a stinking oil-lamp stuck on his head, sweating, panting, moaning with a peculiar and specially heart-rending groan till he reaches the "magazine" or depot, flings down his load, then turns, and with lightning speed dashes down again—some of the little ones out of whose bodies life has not yet been crushed actually singing, capering with the sheer joy of the momentary relief from pain. Ten, eleven journeys these "bearers" make per day, and if the distances are short, twenty, and even thirty....

As yet we have spoken only of the mines where the material is brought up at least half way on trucks; but if the visitor who has come to the surface of one of these insists on the fact that in near spots the *carusi* do all the business, he will succeed in being taken there, and on a rough waste at the pit's mouth will see one after another the naked, sweating toilers reach the surface, bending under their load—the groaning, not dissimilar to the death-rattle, audible and continuous long before you *see* the scarcely human creatures who issue from the mouth of hell. It is said that the children are used gently and by degrees to the toil and danger . . . [and she proceeds to show that this is not so; they are ruthlessly exploited].

In a mining district some two miles from Caltanisetta, where there are seven important mines, in each of which the workers vary from 100 to 1,000 there is not a single doctor or surgeon on the spot. Sufferers (and they are numerous) taken ill or injured in the mines, and brought to the surface by their comrades, have to be taken into the town *on foot*, to be cared for or to die. As a rule, catastrophes are rare, yet they do happen when the mines are not properly ventilated or the airshaft is obstructed. One happened some years ago in the very mine we descended yesterday. [She then reviews the delinquency caused by the demoralization of these miners, and ends her article with a plea for sanity in the righting of this problem.]

It is safe to say that the passion for observation and discovery that gave vitality to her articles for the *Nation* also proved their greatest drawback. Jessie was so absorbed in the acquisition and presentation of detail that she often did not place it in perspective. Her vast collection of Risorgimento materials—diaries, journals, clippings, mementos, and notes—were drawn upon freely as was the unusually eclectic collection of books in the Marios' private library. Her archival collection was systematized after her fashion, and its resources were available whenever she needed statistics, reports of conversations, and minutiae of all sorts. She had an inexhaustible but careless memory about the events and figures of the Risorgimento at first remove, and she drew on this fund as well, as the occasion demanded. These materials, added to her personal observations in her travels about Italy and her conversations with the populace, were used voluminously in her monthly and weekly essays. They often ran away with her. An article that started out on one subject turned out to be about something quite different. She had very little discriminatory sense when it came to sacrificing detail, and consequently her prose style suffered. Her afterthoughts, analogies, and colloquialisms, rendered her syntax loose and rambling. Jessie's writing was in this respect like her mind—literal and unsubtle, but forceful in detail, vivid, and vigorous.

There are many aspects of these *Nation* articles, though, that even now seem amazingly modern. Jessie's desire to offer her American readers a full picture of Italy gave her writing a panoramic range. Her article on sulphur mining in Sicily is a fine example of the mode and depth of her reporting. She made a field trip to ferret out information; she used the words and phrases of her subjects and conveyed their sense of the realities of their lives. She placed the immediate scene against a carefully researched background which opened up the history of the Sicilian mining industry. She conveyed the nature of the social problem caused by the economic exploitation. And all of her findings were liberally seasoned with her own recognition that there were no easy solutions to the problems that had been described. Her writing was provocative, serious, and responsible. It was that of a lay social scientist who understood that where there were effects there were causes. She tried to depict the effects and discover their causes.

The view of Italy that Jessie gave in her *Nation* articles as a whole was remarkably more mature than the one she had given in 1856 in her preface to Orsini's *Austrian Dungeons*. Now her view reflected the awareness of complexity, the uncertainty of someone who spoke from the center of personal experience. As a consequence, the voice was much less self-assured than earlier. It raised many more questions than it offered solutions. Many conditional reservations tempered the assertions. But although the problems now seemed to loom larger than the vision, the remarkable integrity of Jessie Mario's belief in the perfectability of the social organism remained intact. The study of man's communal life was the continuum of her thought.

Yet it is not as a writer of newspaper and magazine articles alone that Jessie must be remembered. It is impossible to assess the importance of Jessie's contribution to Risorgimento history without remembering her role as collector and interpreter. Thanks to her assiduous preservation of the personal papers and documents of many of the Risorgimento figures, invaluable materials are available to our generation. An article describing the holdings of the Jessie White Mario collection indicates in brief its significant features.[10] The materials, which were placed in the Museo Centrale del Risorgimento in Rome after Jessie's demise, include such correspondence as: thirty-one letters from Agostino Bertani to Alberto Mario and one hundred nineteen to Jessie written during the period between 1857 and 1886; letters of Aurelio and Giorgina Saffi; and letters of the Nathan family, Pietro Ripari, Gabriele Rosa, Carlo Cattaneo, Francesco Crispi, Giuseppe Silingardi, the Cairoli family, and of Garibaldi. There were letters written by Mazzini which have since been used in the national edition of his writings. The correspondence that Jessie Mario carried on during the last years of the century with officials of flourishing political societies and of other organizations are included as well. In addition to the letters to and from these more significant figures and organizations, there is an interesting correspondence between Jessie and members of her family in England—with especially revealing letters "crosshatched"* in the Victorian manner—between Jessie and her father. These letters are illuminating in that they give the more personal details of her life and tell us a great deal about both correspondents.[11]

The collection contains many papers concerning the activities of numerous of the pivotal figures of the Risorgimento. It also includes many miscellaneous items which the more sentimental side of Jessie's nature prompted her to keep—a hardened drop of Garibaldi's blood, a poem in honor of Anita Garibaldi. Lastly, the collection contains Jessie's assorted personal papers—some of them never completed and some very carefully copied twice over—including fragments of her youthful compositions in which she revealed her passion for Garibaldi, the personification of the hero of her reveries.[12]

From these materials Jessie reconstituted the chronicle of the Risorgimento for public consumption. As we have indicated, she used her full resources for her newspaper and *Nation* articles. In addition she wrote many other works, which are listed in a full bibliography to be found at the end of this book.† She developed her materials in Italian, English, and French. Thus she published articles in *Nuova Antologia, Nineteenth Century, Scribner's,* and other magazines, and produced books for T. Fisher Unwin, Le Monnier, Scribner's, and Barbera, to name but a few.[13] She adapted her communications to prospective readers, knowingly taking stock of the particular interests of reading audiences. For her American audience she consistently drew connections between developments concerned with the slavery issue and American politics and developments in Italy. For English readers she remembered the figures of English liberalism and drew examples from Mill, Ruskin, Gladstone, and others. All told, she constantly readapted her thoroughly researched material and kept adding to it. The result was an encyclopedic supply.

Had the same audiences been reading everything she wrote, they would indeed have wearied of her repetition. But this cunning in

---

* Crosshatching was used to economize on paper. Longhand parallel lines were bisected in overwriting by another set of parallel lines. The effect produced makes the letters hard to read a hundred or so years later.

† See Appendix 2, p. 153-158.

adaptation enabled Jessie to supplement her income—in her later years always a major consideration. The ease with which Jessie practiced her profession on two continents and in several languages makes her accomplishment none the less noteworthy. Whenever she borrowed ideas in the interest of a publication, it was only from herself.

The legends surrounding Mazzini and Garibaldi sprang up even before their deaths, and Jessie contributed to the increasing sentimentality that was attached to both figures as the century moved to a close. She wrote several lives of Garibaldi, and a life of Mazzini as well as prefatory materials for a volume of his writings. Her method in drawing together these books is demonstrable. They began with a chronicle of the subject's life, in which Jessie documented her narrative with lengthy quotations and anecdotal illustrations from her many sources. She paused in every chapter and on every page to give the flavor of her subject's personality through direct quotation from his conversations or his writings. Wherever possible, she drew enthusiastically upon her own witness. Thus her biographies tended to be personalized, long, copiously documented, and without emphasis due to her inability to sort out the trivial from the significant. Yet withal they were often completely fresh in their particular perspective of the subject.

In all of the works the subjects are sympathetically drawn. But although these biographies abound in lavish tokens of Jessie's admiration for their subjects, they are also replete with frank revelations of their subjects' inconsistencies, motivations, and quirks of character and behavior. Jessie's reportorial training sent her in pursuit of whatever background material could be found, and in the process she was able to ferret out a great deal that was interesting and provocative. The result was a complex and colorful treatment of her subject.

The following passage, a translation from her French biography, *Garibaldi et son temps*, conveys the characteristic flavor of her biographical style. The time was June, 1860, immediately after Garibaldi had taken over Palermo. Jessie and Alberto had just arrived in Sicily from exile in Switzerland.

> The enthusiasm that followed this news [Garibaldi's coup] in all of Italy was indescribable: young men and even adolescent boys from all over tried to rush to Sicily. Bertani with great energy and speed, instituted supervisory committees in the villages, and put them in direct contact with the headquarters and the central committee at Genoa, and the volunteers flocked there to embark. Here is a letter from Garibaldi to Bertani on this subject: [In the book, the letter is reproduced in the original handwriting and then Jessie translates it from Italian into French in a footnote.] "Palermo, June 3rd, 1860— Office of the Dictator—Dear Bertani, I authorize you not only to un-

dertake all arrangements in connection with Sicily, but also to see that we have such an undertaking that everybody will be satisfied. See to it that we get as many arms, munitions, and soldiers as you can manage. Yours, G. Garibaldi."

Medici, who had been alienated from Cavour, realizing that the minister would oppose an expedition in central Italy,* took over the command of the second expedition of 4,000 men.

Garibaldi met with Medici at Alcamo and I will never forget the cordiality of his welcome to my husband and me.

Cavour, distrusting Garibaldi with the greatest injustice, had a network of agents acting for him in Palermo; La Farina† was trying to arrange it so that Garibaldi would have to allow the cession of the island to the kingdom of Sardinia immediately. But Garibaldi opposed this cession vigorously and with good sense. He knew very well that if such an act took place, the cause of liberty on the island, and certainly on the continent, would be lost.

One day, in his hall at the royal palace, Garibaldi laughingly said to us: "Count Cavour did you the honor of asking me to turn you over to Admiral Persano, to be extradited to Genoa. But, I don't want to insult him, so I will send him back his friend La Farina." And in fact he did expel La Farina, for he was tired of his machinations to obtain annexation.

Those who did not have the opportunity of seeing Garibaldi at Palermo lost the chance to see him in one of the happiest moments of his life. Everything was smiling on him: victory, the sun and the beautiful Palermians. He was radiant and exceedingly affable. When he revealed his ideas on the manner in which the people should be governed, it was obvious that the people in his hands would prosper and fare below no other people in intelligence and patriotism.[14]

What can be seen in her work on Mazzini or Garibaldi is duplicated in her other biographies—those on Nicotera, Cattaneo, Bertani, Dolfi, and Mario. For several of these figures, Jessie's edition of the biographical materials or writings or both constituted the basic publication until well into the twentieth century.[15]

In considering Jessie's career as a serious-minded journalist and biographer dedicated to the pursuit of political and social reform, one might be tempted to forget the Jessie of earlier days—the conspirator who lived through the tumultuous days of the Pisacane insurrection and defied the Sardinian authorities from her cell in Sant' Andrea prison. But the miscellaneous notes in her *buste* remind us that the early Jessie lived on behind the facade of the respectable correspondent and author of later days.

* Cavour's fear of international repercussions had led him to oppose the expedition.
† Giuseppe La Farina, a Sicilian, originally a republican but later a supporter of Cavour.

In 1877, two decades after the Pisacane conspiracy, Jessie made a deal with the *New York Herald* that she would provide them with a scoop in the event of the aging Pope Pius IX's death.* She and an unnamed "spy" in the Vatican then devised a code by means of which he would be able to smuggle out to Jessie veiled reports on the pope's state of health. Among the thirty-four possibilities provided for in the code are the following:

Please write	The Pope has fallen seriously sick
Come directly Gagliari	The Pope rallied slightly today, and engaged in conversation
When come Cremona	His Holiness had an attack of apoplexy at—— o'clock yesterday
Safely delivered Foggia	The physicians held a consultation today[16]

The code also made provision for the naming of the pope's successor:

Dishonor Draft Spezzia Cardinal Antonelli

Whether or not Jessie was able to keep her bargain with the *New York Herald* we do not know. But clearly she had not lost her taste for conspiratorial arrangements altogether.

"Miss Uragano"—"Miss Hurricane"—the Italians affectionately called her when she herself had become legendary. Their epithet cannot be improved on, for it strikes the heart of the figure. Unlike many dreamers with visions, this one attacked the central problems of her century. She was not only one of the most interesting participants in the Risorgimento but also one of that remarkable species, a "new woman" of the Victorian era.

* He died in 1878.

Notes

NOTES TO PRELUDE

1. Jessie said that she wrote an article on Lammenais "published somewhere." Since she wrote for *The Biographical Magazine,* one must assume that the article signed "G de F" ("Lammenais," *Lives of the Illustrious. The Biographical Magazine* 7(1855): 109-26) was hers. She never used this signature on any other occasion.

2. See Giacomo Emilio Curàtolo, *Garibaldi e le donne, con documenti inediti* (Rome: Imprimerie Polyglotte, 1913).

3. Jessie White Mario, *The Birth of Modern Italy* (posthumous), ed. Duke Litta-Visconti Arese (London: T. Fisher Unwin, 1909), pp. 249-50 (hereafter referred to as *BMI*).

4. Busta 417, Archivio Jessie White Mario in collection of Museo Centrale del Risorgimento, Rome (hereafter referred to as *AJWM*).

5. *BMI*, p. 250.

6. Ibid., pp. 251-52.

7. Busta 417, *AJWM*.

NOTES TO CHAPTER 1

1. Busta 419, *AJWM*.

2. Ibid.

3. Ibid.

4. *Hampshire Allegations for Marriage Licenses* (Harleian Society Publications, 1893), 2:342.

5. Busta 419, *AJWM*. Jessie records that neither regretted this decision.

6. Ibid.

7. Jane Teage Meriton, according to the rolls of the Church of Holy Trinity of Gosport, died May 21, 1834. The marriage of Thomas White and Jane Gain (*Hampshire Allegations*, 2: 343) was solemnized May 25, 1834.

8. See especially Busta 416, 419, *AJWM*.

9. Busta 416, *AJWM*.

10. Busta 419, *AJWM*.

11. Busta 417, *AJWM*.

12. Busta 419, *AJWM*.

13. Ibid.

14. Ibid.

15. 2d ed. (New York: Robert Carter & Bros., 1847). This book was first published in London in 1846.

16. Ibid., pp. 733-34.

17. Ibid., p. 741.
18. Busta 419, *AJWM*.
19. Ibid.
20. Ibid.
21. William Wright Wilson, *The Life of George Dawson, M. A.,* 2d. ed. (Birmingham: Percival Jones, 1905), p. 16.
22. Ibid. See also Elizabeth Meteyard, Introduction, *The Nine Hours Movement: Industrial and Household Tales* (London: Longmans, Green & Co., 1872).
23. Gordon S. Haight, ed., *The George Eliot Letters,* 7 vols. (New Haven: Yale University Press, 1954-1955), 1:243.
24. Jessie's Birmingham writings are so similar to those of Elizabeth Meteyard (Silverpen) as to be almost indistinguishable. Elizabeth Meteyard and Jessie both wrote stories that glorified the development of community life and the working-class hero. Two of Jessie's stories published in *Eliza Cook's Journal* can be positively identified since her authorship is mentioned in the Cowen Collection (A698, "Rome and Venice," pp. 8-15): "Jessie wrote 'Alice Lane, a tale of Yorkshire Humble Life' and "Roger Dale, a story of Birmingham.'" "Alice Lane," *Eliza Cook's Journal,* Aug. 27, 1853, pp. 276-83; "Roger Dale: A Story of Birmingham," *Eliza Cook's Journal,* Nov. 19, 1853, pp. 55-61, and Nov. 26, 1853, pp. 69-76. She also published a poem "The Home of Taste" in *Eliza Cook's Journal,* Sept. 11, 1852, p. 320. She may also have written "Jessie's Wisdom," (April 2, 1853, pp. 361-64), "Lilly Crossland" (May 31, 1851, pp. 73-75, June 7, 1851, pp. 93-95, June 14, 1851, pp. 106-9, June 21, 1851, pp. 116-18, and June 28, 1851, pp. 141-43), all published in *Eliza Cook's Journal.*

NOTES TO CHAPTER 2

1. About the Ashurst circle, just as about Jessie herself, there is an abundance of largely unexamined material in the ninety-four volumes of Mazzini's writings, including his letters (Giuseppe Mazzini, *Scritti editi ed inediti,* 94 vols. and 6 supplements [Imola, 1906-1948] hereafter referred to as Mazzini, *SEI*). Mrs. E. F. Richards brought some of these letters together (translating where necessary) in a three-volume series, *Mazzini's Letters to an English Family* (London: John Lane, 1920). Both works have been used extensively in this chapter for background. The papers relating to the movement in the Cowen Collection of the Central Reference Library at Newcastle-upon-Tyne, and the various materials cited about George Dawson were useful also. Similarly much can be learned from the newspaper columns of the time. Mazzini himself had seen to the founding of the Friends of Italy Society. In June, 1851 a manifesto announcing its inauguration was published in *Italia del Popolo* (Mazzini, Introduction, *SEI,* 46: xxvi) outlining the objectives of the society—to propagandize the Italian cause in the press, in lectures, and through meetings; to adopt all legal measures possible to increase English support of Italian republicanism. Seven people were charged with regularizing the organization: George Dawson, H. J. Slack, W. Shaen, W. H. Ashurst, S. Hawkes, J. Collett, and J. Stansfeld. To these names the membership of the society added, among others: Peter Taylor, W. MacCready, T. Duncombe, Thornton Hunt, and S. Courtauld. Although the public meeting place of the group was announced as 10 Southampton Street, many Sunday-night sessions at Muswell Hill, as well as others elsewhere, got the work of the organization done, and there was constant communication between London and the provincial units.
2. Jane Welsh Carlyle, *Letters to Her Family, 1839-1863,* ed. Leonard Huxley (London: J. Murray, 1924), p. 300. Despite this initial antipathy the Carlyles and Emilie Ashurst continued their friendship. In 1867 Emilie (Ashurst Venturi), writing to Joseph Cowen, described her weekly tea-taking with Carlyle after Mrs. Carlyle was dead: "Since his wife's death I had acquired a habit of taking tea with him once a week, and I had become much attached to him. It seemed very sad to see him—very grave and much bent, pouring out the tea himself, with a certain large, gentle awkwardness quite his own; asking one with serious intent brow, and suspended hand, how much sugar and milk one required, as if the matter were of stern import, and then holding each piece of sugar with a serious earnest face to the light, as if to judge of its capability of performing its mission before putting it into the cup."
3. *Mazzini's Letters,* 1:36.
4. Ibid., 1:42.
5. Ibid., 1:159.

6. Ibid., 1:169.
7. Ibid., 1:25.
8. Ibid.
9. In her later years Jessie was working on a biography of Stansfeld which was never published. See Busta 416, *AJWM*.
10. Mazzini, *SEI*, 47:309-10. It was indeed "done elsewhere." In Newcastle-upon-Tyne Joseph Cowen saw to publicity; in Birmingham, George Dawson; in Edinburgh and Glasgow, the Rev. Crosskey and others.
11. Ibid., 48:22.
12. Ibid., 50:335-38.
13. Mrs. Richards (*Mazzini's Letters*, 3:10-11) relates the first meeting between Emilie and Carlo Venturi:

> In the autumn of 1859 she had gone to Italy with her brother, William Ashurst, and his wife Bessie, travelling in less comfort than usual on account of the recent war. After a tedious night journey their train reached a station where it halted long enough for the passengers to breakfast. Emilie and the Ashursts, having obtained some refreshment, returned to their compartment prepared for several more wearisome hours, and William, to prevent any one else entering, leaned across his sister to close the door.
>
> "Don't shut it—he's coming!" Emilie exclaimed, with no consciousness at all of what she was saying. William looked at her in a surprise that scarcely surpassed her own, but he made no attempt to move the hand with which she had suddenly stopped his intention. The guard began shouting and doors were banging, when, just as the train started, a young man rushed along the platform, leapt into the Ashursts' compartment and almost collapsed upon the seat opposite to Emilie. She told the writer that the glance which passed between them at that moment seemed one of recognition, though she had not the remotest idea that any one was likely to appear when she spoke those unconscious words to her brother.
>
> Carlo Venturi [the visitor] journeyed in danger, for the Austrian military authorities had power to seize and shoot him, and at that moment a large Austrian force lay behind the Mincio. . . . The remarkable premonition that had forced an utterance through Emilie seemed to find its echo in the mind of the young Venetian. . . .

14. Mazzini, *SEI*, 33:178-80.
15. *Mazzini's Letters*, 1:73.
16. Ibid., pp. 75-76.
17. Ibid., p. 82.
18. Ibid., p. 98.
19. Ibid., pp. 98-99.
20. Ibid., p. 148.
21. Ibid., p. 151.
22. Ibid., p. 185 n.
23. Meredith read Emilie's tome on Mazzini for the publisher Smith, Elder & Co. In 1864 when he needed advice about *Vittoria*, Meredith sought out Emilie (by now remarried to Carlo Venturi) and asked for her judgment of his book [see *Letters of George Meredith*, ed. C. L. Cline (Oxford: The Clarendon Press, 1970), 1:152; 152 n; 244; 244 n; 252 n; 321; 331].
24. *Mazzini's Letters*, 1:317.
25. Mazzini, *SEI*, 52:310-11.
26. Ibid., pp. 127-28.
27. Ibid., p. 133.
28. *Mazzini's Letters*, 2:38.
29. Mazzini, *SEI*, 56:284-88.
30. Ibid., p. 35.

NOTES TO CHAPTER 3

1. *BMI*, p. 253.
2. Barbara Leigh Smith Bodichon, *Women and Work* (London: Bosworth & Harrison, 1857), pp. 40-42.
3. Ibid., pp. 53-56.

I.

To the Secretary of St. George's Hospital
From Jessie Meriton White
May 9, 1856

I wish, with another lady, to attend a three-years' course of lectures, and surgical and medical practice, commencing the October Term, in St. George's Hospital.

I presume my being a woman will prove no obstacle, as I can furnish you with certificates as to character and capacity from known London physicians.

Will you inform me whether I can have private anatomical instruction, and on what terms? An answer will oblige.

II.

To Jessie White
From Henry Wm. Fuller, M.D.
May 17, 1856

Your letter of the 9th instant, containing an application for permission "to attend with another lady a three-years' course of lectures, and surgical and medical practice, commencing the October Term, in St. George's Hospital," has been submitted to the Medical School Committee; and I am requested to inform you, that the Committee, not having the power to grant that permission, have referred your letter to the Weekly Board of Governors. At the same time, the Committee wish me to add that, having carefully and maturely considered the subject of your application in all its relations, they are of opinion that so many practical inconveniences would result from the admission of women as pupils of the Hospital and School that they do not intend to advise the Weekly Board of Governors to accede to your application.

III.

To Jessie White
From Edm. Balfour, Sec., Royal College of Surgeons
May 17, 1856

In reply to your letter of the 10th inst. inquiring, "Can a woman on producing certificates of having attended during three years the lectures and the medical and surgical practice in one of the London Hospitals, be admitted to examination for a diploma in surgery and midwifery?" I am desired by the Court of Examiners to acquaint you, that there is no instance of this College ever having admitted a female to examination for either of the said diplomas, and that the Court considers it would not be justified in adopting such a course.

IV.

To Jessie White
From James Paget, St. Bartholomew's Hospital
May 30, 1856

I have the honour to inform you that, this afternoon, at a meeting of the Medical Officers and Lecturers of this Hospital, your letter of the 19th inst. was read and considered; and, in reply to it, I am requested to state, that, in the opinion of the meeting, it is not expedient to admit ladies as students of the hospital.

V.

To Jessie White
From H. Moore, University of London
May 12, 1856

I have the honour to acknowledge the receipt of your letter of the 10th inst. The inquiry contained in it, however, being a novel one, I should wish to consult the Senate on the subject of it, which I will endeavour to do at their next meeting, and will communicate the result to you without delay.

VI.

To Jessie White
From William B. Carpenter, University of London
May 22, 1856

I am directed by the Senate to forward you a copy of the minutes of its proceedings on the 14th inst., by which you will perceive that your letter has been brought under its consideration with a view to a decision upon the question proposed in it, at an early meeting.

In the meantime, I beg to direct your attention to the regulations to which candidates for degrees in medicine are required to conform; and especially to those relating to the Matriculation Examination. These you will find in the Calendar herewith sent, pp. 35-41 and 58-60.

Should increased knowledge of the requirements of the University make any alteration in your views, I shall be obliged by an intimation to that effect.

VII.
To William B. Carpenter
From Jessie White
May 23, 1856

I thank you for your letter just received, and for the Calendar.

Before addressing you, on the 10th inst., I was aware of the regulations to which candidates for degrees in Medicine are required to conform, and shall be prepared to comply with all the requirements of the University should the Senate decide to admit me for examination.

VIII.
To Jessie White
From William B. Carpenter
July 10, 1856

I am directed by the Senate to inform you, that, acting upon the opinion of its legal advisers, it does not consider itself as empowered, under the Charter of the University, to admit females as candidates for degrees.

4. *BMI*, p. 260.
5. Ibid., pp. 254-55.
6. Ibid., p. 255.
7. Ibid., p. 256.
8. Michael St. John Packe, *Orsini: The Story of a Conspirator* (Boston: Little, Brown & Co., 1957), p. 220 n, quoting from Allessandro Luzio, ed., *Felice Orsini e Emma Herwegh, Nuovi Documenti* (Florence: Le Monnier, 1937), p. 69.
9. Felice Orsini, *The Austrian Dungeons in Italy*, trans. Jessie White (London: Routledge, Warnes, & Routledge, 1859), pp. vi-xvi.
10. Packe, *Orsini*, p. 220.
11. Ibid., p. 221.
12. Mazzini, *SEI*, 57:23.
13. *BMI*, p. 260.
14. Ibid., pp. 261-62.
15. Mazzini, *SEI*, 57:90-92.
16. Ibid., pp. 92-97.
17. Ibid., pp. 98-103.
18. See my article, "Collaboration of Mazzini on an article in the *Westminster Review*," *Bulletin of the New York Public Library*, 65(1961):577-82.
19. Mazzini, *SEI*, 58:30-33.
20. Ibid., p. 17.
21. *BMI*, p. 265.
22. Mazzini, *SEI*, 58: 132-33 n.
23. Ibid., p. 158, 158 n.
24. Ibid., pp. 228-29.
25. This incident has now been the subject of considerable scholarship, including the studies of Giuseppe Berti, *I democratici e l'iniziativa meridionale nel Risorgimento* (Milan: Feltrinelli, 1962); Noel Blakiston, "Sulla scia di Pisacane: un grattacapo per Hudson," (Estratti del volume *Atti del XXXVI congresso di Storia del Risorgimento Italiano*, n. d.; and Harry Hearder, "La cattura del Cagliari, una disputa tripartita fra Napoli, Piemonte e Inghilterra (1857-1858)," *Rassegna storica del Risorgimento* (April-June, 1960): 226-35.

NOTES TO CHAPTER 4

1. The text copied by Jessie from the state tribunal hearings (and saved in Busta 407, *AJWM*), is translated in full in Appendix 1.
2. *BMI*, pp. 268-69.
3. Mazzini, *SEI*, 58:244-46.

4. Camillo di Cavour, *Nuove Lettere Inediti* (Turin, 1895), pp. 534-35.

5. Miscellaneous papers relating to Jessie's involvement in the Pisacane incident, and subsequent imprisonment, Genoa, July-December, 1857, quoted from the collection in the Public Records Office, Somerset House, London, FO 67/227, 77-146, Sardinia-Hudson: JWM to Hudson, telegram, Genoa, July 4, 1857, p. 51; Hudson to Yeats Brown, telegram, Genoa, July 4, 1857, p. 53; Brown to Hudson, July 4, 1857, p. 55; JWM to Brown, July 5, 1857, p. 59; Hudson to Clarendon, dispatch, Turin, July 10, 1857, p. 61; Hudson to Clarendon, dispatch, Turin, July 13, 1857, p. 71; Rattizzi memorandum, Turin, July 1857, p. 73 [English translation, p. 75]; Hudson to Clarendon, Turin, Nov. 14, 1857, p. 251; Hudson to Clarendon, Turin, Dec. 12, 1857, p. 314; Viglioni memorandum, Genoa, Dec. 9, 1857, pp. 316-18, [trans.].

6. Alberto Mario, *Scritti*, ed. Giosuè Carducci (Bologna: N. Zanichelli, 1884), 1: lvi-lviii.

7. Ibid., p. lxvii.

8. FO 67/227:

Turin, Dec. 12, 1857
My Lord [Clarendon],
With reference to my despatch marked No. 123 of the 14th Ultimo reporting to Your Lordship that Miss White had been ordered by this government to leave this country in consequence of her guilty knowledge of the Plot by which Mazzini attempted to create a Revolutionary movement in Genoa in the month of last June —I have the honour to inclose herewith a report addressed by the Fiscal Advocate General of Genoa to the Minister of Grace and Justice which contains the grounds upon which that Law Officer caused Miss White to be arrested examined and subsequently discharged from custody.

[Hudson]

Genoa, 9 December 1857
The Advocate General of Genoa, being directed to report upon the trial of the English person Miss J. M. White concerned in the revolutionary attempt of 29th last June, thinks it right first to explain the motives for Miss White's arrest & secondly the motives for setting her at liberty. As soon as the authorities got wind of the revolutionary attempt of the Mazzini party, they took all steps to discover, arrest, & bring to justice the author. The night in question & the following days several persons with arms and cartouches were arrested, & domiciliary searches were made in the houses of those indicated by public voice [sic], by the revelation of those arrested, or by flight as having had a share in the attempt. One Luigi Roggero was generally suspected, & early took to flight—he was a hatter & warm supporter of Mazzini known as being one of the prime movers, & as having assembled in his shop the band which marched on the Citadel, & melted away on the alarm of "police coming" being raised. After a vast search for him, it was discovered that Miss White had lodged in his house for some days past, & she displayed much indignation at the search of his house. It was then thought prudent to have her watched by 2 Gendarmes, to whom she addressed questions about news from Naples, if the outbreak to take place there was known, & then referring to their function she said they did not do themselves credit, & could be more useful to Italy—To this behaviour, to these speeches which excited no slight suspicion were subsequently added still further proofs of complicity—It was proved that since her arrival at Genoa she had frequent relations with known Mazzinists. [sic] & especially with the lower classes now known most to admire Mazzini —that on the days preceding the 29 June the heads of the Workmen's Society were presented to her at Roggero's house in return for an address of thanks for her part for the part they took in liberating Italy—that the opinions she expressed were most exaggerated, & that twice at workmen's meetings she had talked of a Republic —On 4th July while Pisacane's house was being searched 2 letters were found & sequestrated, one from London to Henrietta Lazzari, Pisacane's mistress, contained a strong praise of Miss White [grounded] on the part she took on Italy's behalf. The other letter had been sent to di Lazzari shortly before for speedy delivery to Miss White, & was written by one Angelo Mangini, pastry Cook [sic] Genoa, & a Mazzinist who had hired two places at S. Andrea which could be placed in communication with the prison; there were found arms & munition. Mangini fled on discovery—this letter showed that Miss White was in close communication with the conspirators & Mangini told her they did not yet despair, but

still hoped to attain their end. These—words were in the letter *"I am with our Stallo" all is not lost*—"Stallo" is a Genoese merchant of woven goods & suspected, as others of the chiefs, he had arms and munitions in his house—He also early escaped. All this, together with the —— of Miss White who was much praised in the *Italia del Popolo* organ of Mazzini from whom it receives instruction, were sufficient to move the authorities to arrest Miss White on 5 July after the visit to Pisacane's house. From further particulars, while she was detained, & especially from her answers during examination it appeared that she denied having participated in the conspiracy, she had a devout admiration for Mazzini whom she considered the "Christ of the period," & she worshiped [*sic*] his portrait which she had in prison. In a further search at Stallo's house, a receipt from Miss White was seized, for 1000 lire paid to her, in payment of M's National Subscription—i.e. the subscription set on foot by Mazzini for the insurrection of the Italian Provinces. Miss White admitted the receipt & having received the money, but refusing to give an account of it to other than the London Committee, & declining further explanations. Talking of her arrest, in prison, she declared she would rather remain there, & be brought to trial, rather than abandon Italy by a decision which would prevent her being tried like the others. This was the state of Miss White's case, when the report was made as prescribed by law to the Court of Accusation, which altho not concealing from itself the gravity of the charges, still as the accused was a young stranger, evidently labouring under strong mental excitement, towards the Italian cause, & as her conduct was more imprudent & rash than criminal in intention— besides there being no proof of direct participation in the attempt—that Court indulgently decided not to bring her to trial, but simply to set her at liberty— What also contributed to induce this lenient decision was the reflexion that being a Stranger she might be expelled from these States and thus her misplaced excitement & zeal be rendered innocuous.

Vigliani AFG [Advocate Fiscal General in Genoa]

9. Mario, *Scritti*, p. lxxxii.
10. Ibid.
11. Ibid.
12. Ibid., lxxv-lxxvi.

NOTES TO CHAPTER 5

1. Elizabeth Barrett Browning. *Letters to Her Sister, 1846-1859* (London: John Murray, 1929), p. 316.
2. Mario, *Scritti*, 1:lxxxix.
3. Alberto Mario, *Scritti letterari e artistici*, 2 vols. (Bologna: N. Zanichelli, 1901), 1: Appendix 6, pp. 18-19.
4. Busta 912, *AJWM*.
5. Mario, *Scritti letterari e artistici*, 1:19-20.
6. Jessie White Mario to Lowell, May 21, 1859, #527, bMS Am 765, Houghton Library, Harvard University, Cambridge, Mass.
7. Mario, *Scritti*, 1: Preface, p. xc.

NOTES TO CHAPTER 6

1. Jessie White Mario, "Cattaneo," *Contemporary Review*, 26(August, 1875): 465-86. Cattaneo's influence on Jessie began to be reflected in her comprehensive analysis and criticism of the problems of the Italian economy. So different was this criticism from her earlier propaganda that one might wonder when it matured. The answer might well lie in Jessie's exposure to Cattaneo's thought during the nine-month interlude before the Southern campaign.
2. Clement Caraguel, ed., *Souvénirs et aventures d'un volontaire garibaldien* (Paris: A. Bourdilliait et cie, 1861), pp. 23-25.
3. Alberto Mario, "Personal Reminiscences of General Garibaldi," *Macmillan's Magazine*, 46(July, 1882):245-56.
4. Alberto Mario, "Garibaldi's Invisible Bridge," *Cornhill Magazine*, 9(May, 1864): 549.
5. Alberto Mario, *The Red Shirt. Episodes*, (London: Smith, Elder & Co. (1865), p. 143.

6. Ibid., p. 147.
7. Ibid., pp. 155-56.
8. Ibid., pp. 170-73.
9. Ibid.
10. John Hohenberg in his book *Foreign Correspondence, The Great Reporters and Their Times* (New York: Columbia University Press, 1964) says "Jessie covered Garibaldi in Sicily and during the march to Naples in 1860. On October 1 that year, at the Volturno battle, she was more nurse than correspondent . . ." (p. 102). [I tried to find evidence for Mr. Hohenberg's comment, but a careful reading of the *Daily News* between June 1 and November 1 of that year convinces me that the use of the word "covered" must be stretched to make his conclusion fit the events. In 1859, upon their return from America, the Marios were indeed accredited as special correspondents to the *Daily News*, with the caution that Jessie should not again get herself into prison. However, both Marios were imprisoned several times between their arrival in northern Italy and their retreat to Lugano. Meanwhile Carlo Arrivabene, a Neapolitan who spoke and wrote English perfectly, was appointed as the new Italian correspondent for the *Daily News*. During the 1860 Sicilian and Neapolitan campaigns the *Daily News* ran a great deal of Italian news, and it stemmed from three sources: 1) the reporter in Turin who gave news of the official government of Victor Emmanuel; 2) the reporter in Naples; and 3) Carlo Arrivabene, who wrote from general headquarters or the scene of battle. Only during the brief period of a few days when Arrivabene—because he was captured by the troops of the King of Naples—was prevented from composing his articles, did he fail to cover the campaign. At that time, the Neapolitan correspondent covered for him as best he could. At any rate, if Jessie wrote for the *Daily News* during those weeks, her correspondence was not published. It is most likely, though, that her proximity to Garibaldi and her association with the chief actors in the march on Naples enabled her to inform the *Daily News* writers of plans and occurrences at Garibaldi's headquarters. A reading of the *Daily News* from June 1 through October provides a fascinating day-by-day account of the campaign. The news lagged anywhere from a day or so (by telegraphic communication) to several days (by post or special messenger) behind the events, and the narrative was enlivened by many personal anecdotes and observations of the correspondents. The details, especially those about the hospitals, were probably often buttressed by Jessie's comments. But it is stretching a point to say that she "covered" the campaign for the *News*.]
11. Miriam B. Urban, *British Opinion and Policy on the Unification of Italy* (Scottsdale, Pa.: The Mennonite Press, 1938), p. 555.
12. Charles Stuart Forbes, *The Campaign of Garibaldi in the Two Sicilies: A Personal Narrative* (London: W. Blackwood & Sons, 1861).
13. Urban, *British Opinion*, pp. 554-58.
14. Jessie White Mario, "Italy and the United States," *Nineteenth Century*, 29 (Jan., 1891):707.

NOTES TO CHAPTER 7

1. Jessie White Mario, "La schiavitù e la guerra civile negli Stati Uniti d'America," *Nuova Antologia* (July 26, 1861):264-310.
2. *BMI*, p. 326.
3. Ibid., p. 327.
4. Ibid., p. 329.
5. See my article "Mazzini e la Vittoria di Meredith," *Rassengna storica del Risorgimento* 49 (1962): 1-22.
6. T. A. Trollope, *What I Remember* (New York: Harper & Bros., 1888), pp. 428-30. Trollope speaks of knowing the Marios well in Florence and through them being introduced to Garibaldi:

> My first acquaintance with him was through my very old and very highly valued, loved, and esteemed friend, Jessie White Mario. The Garibaldi *culte* had been with her truly and literally the object (apart from her devoted love for her husband, an equally ardent worshipper at the same shrine) for which she has lived, and for which she has again and again affronted death. For she accompanied him in all his Italian campaigns as a hospital nurse, and on many occasions rendered her inestimable services in that capacity under fire. If Peard has been called "Garibaldi's Englishman," truly Jessie White Mario deserves yet more emphati-

cally the title of "Garibaldi's Englishwoman." She has published a large life of Garibaldi, which is far and away the best and most trustworthy account of the man and his wonderful works. She is not blind to the spots on the sun of her adoration, nor does she seek to conceal the fact that there were such spots, but she is a true and loyal worshipper all the same.

Her husband, Alberto Mario, was—alas! that I should write so; for no Indian wife's life was ever more ended by her suttee than Jessie Mario's life has practically been ended by her husband's untimely death!—among the, I fear, few exceptions to Peard's remark on the men who were around Garibaldi. He was not only a man of large literary culture, a brave soldier, an acute politician, a formidable political adversary, and a man of perfect and incorruptible integrity, but he would have been considered in any country and in any society in Europe a very perfect gentleman. He was in political opinion a consistent and fearlessly outspoken Republican. He and I therefore differed *toto coelo*. But our differences never diminished our, I trust, mutual esteem, nor our friendly intercourse. But he was a born *frondeur*. He edited during his latter years a newspaper at Rome, which was a thorn in the side of the authorities. I remember his being prosecuted and condemned for persistently speaking of the pope in his paper as "Signor Pecci." He was sentenced to imprisonment. But all the government wanted was his condemnation; and he was never incarcerated. But he used to go daily to the prison and demand the execution of his sentence. The jailer used to shut the door in his face, and he narrated the result of his visit in the next day's paper.

It was as Jessie Mario's friend, then, that I first knew Garibaldi. ". . . Jessie (pronounced Jessee) told me I should find you up; but you are not so early as I am!" was his [Garibaldi's] salutation. . . . Then we talked about the Marios, of both of whom he spoke with the greatest affection; and of the prospects of "going to Rome," which, of course, he considered "the simplest and easiest thing possible."

7. *BMI*, p. 338.
8. Busta 437, *AJWM*.
9. Her articles on Italy in the *Nation* are annotated in Appendix 3.
10. (Rome: Giovanni Polizzi, 1871).
11. Giuseppe Garibaldi, *Autobiography of Giuseppe Garibaldi: Authorized Translation by A. Werner. With a Supplement by Jessie White Mario*, 3 vols. (London: Smith and Innes, 1889), 3:400-401.
12. Ibid., pp. 401-3.
13. General Carl Wilhelm von Werder quoted in Christopher Hibbert, *Garibaldi and His Enemies* (London: Longmans, Green & Co., 1965), p. 362.
14. Emilia Ashurst Venturi, *Joseph Mazzini, A Memoir* (London: Henry S. King & Co., 1875), p. 158.
15. Gaetano Salvemini, *Mazzini*, trans. I. M. Rawson (London: Jonathan Cape, 1956), p. 159.

NOTES TO CHAPTER 8

1. This library was catalogued by Jessie and the list of books can be consulted in Busta 415, *AJWM*.
2. (Florence: Le Monnier, 1877).
3. The interesting connections between Jessie Mario and the friends Marion Lewes (George Eliot) and Barbara Leigh Smith Bodichon are substantiated by the following references in Eliot, *Letters*:

My heart was warmed by that letter of Barbara's about Miss J. M. White, and I wished it had been in large print [a letter referring to activities in behalf of Mazzini]. (G. Eliot to Bessie Rayner Parkes, Richmond, 1 Sept. 1857 [2:379]).

Nannie's account of Madame Mario is delightful. What she says of the happiness between the husband and wife pleases me especially because I had heard at Florence that he was égoiste and allowed her to adore him. (G. Eliot to Mme. E. Bodichon, Redhill, July 1872 [5:289]).

Dear Barbara,
Fearing that in my medical ignorance I might have spoken too absolutely about Mad. Mario I yesterday went to consult Hughlings Jackson who has made the subject [central nervous diseases] his specialty, and he confirms everything I said

and more, for he insists that galvanism or any other local application is quite useless: "There is but one prescription—absolute rest."

In case Mad. Mario MUST write and can't dictate, let her by all means use
the left and not the right hand; but rest for the brain is the main point. Urge upon
her the fact that a short interval of rest now may save her from a very long forced
rest in a little while. (G. Eliot to Mme. E. Bodichon, London, 4 May 1877 [6:
367]).

Pray bring Madame Mario to see us again. . . . Please tell Madame Mario that
I have received an interesting parcel of books from Italy, with pretty words of her
husband's on his card. I am much pleased to have such a present from her and him.
(G. Eliot to Mme. Bodichon, London, 15 May 1877 [6:370]).

Will you oblige me by sending a copy of "Middlemarch," with a copy of
Smith and Elder's "Romola" to
Madame Mario/Poor House/ Zennor/ St Ives/ Cornwall? (G. Eliot to Joseph
M. Langford, Witley, 29 June 1877 [6:391]).

Mrs. Harrison asked with much interest about you, and was glad to hear of
Madame Mario, also, of whom Dr. Bridges had spoken very prettily to her. . . .
. . . I am wondering how long Madame Mario will be able to remain with you.
Please ask her to send me a line in case of her leaving you. But August is an in-
auspicious month for returning to Italy. (G. Eliot to Mme. E. Bodichon, Witley, 2
August 1877 [6:398]).

Do you know that our dear Madame Bodichon, whose life was so full of active
benevolence, was some months ago stricken with an attack of aphasia and other
symptoms of nervous weakness? She had gone to a cottage she has in Cornwall for
the sake of taking there Madam Mario, whose overtasked frame was much in need
of rest and change, and lo Barbara herself was stricken and Madame Mario became her energetic nurse. The attack has long passed its worst, and she is completely like herself in everything except strength. (G. Eliot to Sara Hennell, London, 16 Nov. 1877 [6:419-420]).

4. See Busta 438, AJWM, Ricciotti Garibaldi to Jessie Mario, letter dated Rome,
December 11, 1881. Apparently Jessie wrote offering to defend R. Garibaldi against the
slander in Bent's book if he would reply. He wrote her concerning the following:

1) His mother was not in a position to make the offer stated—"There are my
brother tells me letters existing in which she asks for financial help from my father
—as she was in great difficulties—and this is all I know about her"; 2) "The 'Osprey'
or 'Princess Olga' which was the yacht's name—was sold by my father during my
absence to the Italian government—nominally but was paid out of the king's civil
list and was used I believe by Prince Amadeus as a pleasure boat"; 3) A statement
that he had nothing to do with the schools at Caprera; 4) The Garibaldi boys had
an older sister who died from injuries caused by falling into a pan of lighted charcoal at Nice; 5) "The greater portion of Caprera was bought by the General himself—a piece equal to about a third or fourth of the whole—belonging to a Mrs.
Collins—was purchased by English subscribers and presented to my father"; 6) "A
contract was entered into between myself as representative of a Mr. Nicholson—(an English contractor) and the Roman Municipance for laying down a few
yards of Caprera granite for a trial—but Mr. Nicholson's death and there being no
capital to carry out the contract with—brought it to an untimely end—before a
single yard of stone was even cut"; 7) ". . . I have here a document executed by my
father—with the consent of my brother about that time—authorizing me to borrow
£ 20,000 upon Caprera—this does not look as if my father feared to entrust financial operations to me. I am afraid that most of the bitter pangs I may have caused
my father have mostly been caused by the officious kindness of friends—who have
not failed always to make the most of any youthful peccadiloe for what purpose
can be pretty well guessed—

My father has not only not objected to my presence in Caprera but it was his
always earnest wish that I should take it in hand and live there—and he was opposed to my departure for Australia from the first and even now speaks of it as a
mistake on my part"; 8) "I need not tell you that I am very much obliged for your

proposed defence of us. I have ordered the book and shall esteem it a great favour if you will let me know what you have done about it."

Two other letters in Busta 438, continue the episode. These letters were written to F. M. White, Jessie's brother, who was an editor of the *Fortnightly*, and who was acting in her behalf:

We have gone very fully into the subject of your letter and have been in communication with Mr Wm Bent. We are authorized to say on Mr. Bent's behalf that his only wish has been to give an unbiased view of Garibaldi's life: that if he has been led by false information into making any statements that are not true he much regrets it: and further that he will be happy to receive any information you may be inclined to give him on the part of Garibaldi's family with a view to correcting the book when it is reissued. We shall be happy to forward any communication to Mr. Bent. We may add that we shall be glad to get the matter settled with as little delay as possible, as the suspension of the sale of the book so soon after publication involves us in inconvenience and pecuniary loss.

We are, yours faithfully,
Longman's & Co.
Jan. 31, 1882

In answer to your letter of April 12th we beg to inform you that we have withdrawn Mr. Bent's Life of Garibaldi from sale in accordance with our undertaking to that effect. We did not consider it necessary to destroy all copies of our catalogue in which that book might be included.

We are, yours faithfully,
Longman's & Co.
April 12, 1882

There was a second edition of Bent's book in 1882. The records of Longman's Green indicate that the second edition contained errata sheets apparently to correct the misinformation. The publishers consulted a lawyer on this matter in June, 1882 and must have been advised at length to go ahead with their second edition.

5. Busta 437, *AJWM*.
6. Busta 425, *AJWM*.
7. Ibid.
8. Ibid.
9. Busta 417, *AJWM*. The book was a standing joke between them.
10. Emilia Morelli, *"L'Archivio di Jessie White Mario,"* published separately by Libreria della stato, Rome, 1938; extracted from *Rassegna storica del Risorgimento* 3 (March 1938): 3-4.
11. *AJWM* contains correspondence between Jessie White and various members of her immediate family. The correspondence, as well as the personal papers, have yielded the material upon which the events of Jessie's life have been reconstructed. Busta 419 and 437 especially contain many letters between Jessie and the following members of her family: Thomas White, her father; Thomas White, Jr., her brother; Jane White, her stepmother; Jessie Harvey, her aunt; M. Crisp, her aunt; Jennie Ridley, her cousin; Samuel White and George White, her brothers.
12. In particular the following papers:
Busta 417: "In my father's house." Busta 418: "Student's room overlooking town of Genoa, spirit of Dante enters"; Unfinished novel in English, untitled. Busta 419: Part of a biographical history: "In 1845 Mr. Morell left Gosport"; part of same biographical history, fragment beginning p. 68, "and made no end of resolutions"; "Venice in Winter," a descriptive passage; manuscript beginning "used to come sometimes to tea with nurse," an autobiographical passage; a novel, different copy untitled; "his constitution for life," part of an autobiographical statement; fifty sheets beginning with "He was one of the first advocates for popular education," a history of Dawson; "Ugo e Linda," a short story; parts of a story, marked 901978, purple typed sheets, beginning "When the old nurse came in"; parts of a story, purple typed sheets, beginning, "Of our dearest drenching the ground. . ."; large folio sheet, "perhaps if husband and son," part of a story.
13. See for example "Le miniere di zolfo in Sicilia," *Nuova Antologia*, 49(Jan. 15, 1894): 441-66; Ibid., (Feb. 15, 1894: 719-43. "In Sicilian Sulphur Mines," *Nation*, Jan. 14, 1892, pp. 29-31; "Italy and the United States," *Nineteenth Century*, 29(Jan., 1891): 701-18. "The Poor in Naples," in "The Poor in Great Cities," *Scribner's Magazine*, 13(Jan., 1893); *La Miseria di Napoli* (Florence: Le Monnier, 1877).

14. (Paris: Denoc, 1884). pp. 567-68.
15. Especially Cattaneo and Bertani. The Bertani has not yet been replaced; the Cattaneo only recently by the Yale University Press edition.
16. Busta 416, *AJWM*.

Appendix 1

Interrogation of Jessie Mario

These records were endorsed "Interrogatorio di Jessie Mario nel processo 29 vi, 1857 copiata dalla *Gazzetta dei Tribunali* [record of law court proceedings], 25 Febr, 1858" (Busta 407, AJWM).

Questioned on generalities. Answer: My name is Miss Jessie Meriton White, my father is Thomas. I am twenty-five years old, was born in Forton in England, county of Hampshire, traveler in this city, woman of letters.

Questioned for what reason she was in Genoa and for how long she had been there. Answer: I came to Genoa on March 15 in order to write for several English papers and to collect material for a history of Italy in accordance with a contract I have with Mr. Routledge, an English editor.

Questioned whether she stayed in Genoa for the whole time. Answer: After several days I went to Turin and stayed at the *Albergo della Gran-Bretagna* for three or four or perhaps a few more days. I went there out of mere curiosity.

Questioned on what day she came to live in this house. Answer: I came on Thursday June 25 because I was discontented with my lodging on via Assarotti. I asked my friend, Mrs. Isabella Roggero, to put me up for several days until I could find some place to live.

Questioned whether she knew Angelo Manzini, and in such case, what relations did she have with him. Answer: I believe that I know the said Manzini and I have no relations with him except that he visited me when I came to Genoa, as did many others.

Questioned if the said Manzini, when he came to see her, had spoken to her of some projected attempt in favor of Italy. Answer: I can say that Mr. Manzini, like others, spoke to me about the hope of Italy, but he spoke of no concerted project and no nearing attempt to bring it about.

145

Questioned if she knew a certain Mr. Checco, who is he, and what relations did she have with him. Answer: I don't think I know anyone named Checco or Francesco; I do know a certain Guecco, a middle-aged man of slight stature and dark hair, who came to see me with the others. I remember him especially because I saw him in the theater of San Carlo when I was with Mr. Ugo in his box. I remember thus that Mr. Guecco came into the box.

Questioned if she knew Luigi Stallo, how she knew him, and what relations she had with him. Answer: I know the said Stallo as I know the others, because he came to me while I lived on via Assarotti; and I have no particular relation with him.

Invited to indicate precisely the relations she had with the said Manzini and Luigi Stallo, since she really had a most intimate acquaintance with them. Answer: I can only reaffirm the answer I have already given and can only add that they seemed to me to be good Italians.

Questioned if when she came to Genoa she was equipped with letters of introduction, given by whom and addressed to whom. Answer: I came to Genoa with several letters of introduction from my friend Emilia Ashurst Hawkes. One was to signora Celisia whom I have not met because she hasn't been in Genoa. Another was to signora Enrichetta di-Lorenzo, and another to Albini Belcredi, whom I saw only once at my house and at other times in a shop.

They showed her a letter from London, dated May 13. Questioned if this was another of those given her by her aforesaid friend Emilia. Answer: It is one of my friend's letters, addressed to signora di-Lorenzo; one which she did not entrust to me but sent by post.

Questioned whether signora Enrichetta had not let her know that through Angelo Manzini the state had recovered a letter consigned to the correspondent. Answer: Signora Enrichetta gave me no plan; on the other hand, I haven't seen her since the second of this month.

Questioned how, when she came to Genoa, she established relations with so many people and why she was treated with so much confidence. Answer: I don't know what to say. As soon as I came to Genoa, as in Turin, I was the object of several demonstrations, and many people came to see me without my really knowing the reason except that I knew that my arrival had been announced in the newspaper *Italia del Popolo.*

Asked if she had closer rapport with Mr. Ugo with whom she said she went to the theater. Answer: I had no closer rapport with him than with the others, and as for the box—having encountered me one day, he asked me if I wanted to hear the *Prophet*, and upon the affirmative answer, got me a ticket and it was box twenty-one or twenty-two in the first row.

Asked why so many people came to visit her as soon as she reached Genoa. Answer: Probably because they knew my opinions on Italy, since some of my writings were printed in English papers and reproduced in *Italia del Popolo* and other papers.

Asked if she knew the reason for her detention. Answer: I know as much of the reason for my detention as there was in the warrant of arrest which reached me at the moment of my arrest which took place towards eleven o'clock in the evening in which I was conducted to the place of detention.

Asked if she had no foreknowledge of what happened in Genoa and if she had a plan of action for the days preceding June 30. Answer: I had absolutely no knowledge of how I came to be questioned, I refer myself on this question to the answers I gave the other day when examined by this illustrious sir.

A reading was given her of her examination of the day before and she was asked if she recognized and confirmed it and wanted to add anything to it or to change anything. Answer: I clearly recognize it and I confirm the answers I gave and I would repeat them in being examined.

Asked to kindly give some explanation of the signature on the letter of Angelo Manzini dated July 3. Answer: I don't know what explanation to give. The address is not really mine while the last name written above is mine. I don't know why Mr. Manzini has called me "my dearest Sister" if indeed it is true that he wrote this to me and greeted me using these words of confidence. I am certain that I, as an Englishwoman, have not used them on his behalf. I do not understand why Miss Enrichetta, if the letter was for me, did not send it to me since the letter is dated the third, and for the rest I can say no more than that which I said yesterday in my trial.

They showed her the aforesaid letter sent to signora Enrichetta di-Lorenzo on the evening of the third of the month. It could not be answered because the said lady was object of a search on the following day when this letter and the letter of introduction were intercepted: and again they asked her to kindly give a better explanation. Answer: I repeat that the letter was not addressed to me; that signora Enrichetta had all the means to send it on if it had been addressed to me, wherefore I believe it to have been otherwise directed. . . . On the other hand, perhaps you can question signor Manzini regarding this letter which is completely strange to me.

They then show her extracts from telegraphic dispatches pertaining to various acts, and ask her if she has any knowledge of them. Answer: I read the content of most of these dispatches in the second supplement of *Italia del Popolo*, which supplement, as I have said, gave the reason for the arrest of signor Savi, director of the above mentioned journal.

Questioned why she was not contented with the lodging she had in via Assarotti. Answer: I was content with the service and with the lodging; only the two rooms which I occupied became scorchingly hot because they were exposed to the sun all morning. I left the lodging to escape from that excessive heat.

Questioned if she had a close relation with Carlo Pisacane. Answer: I certainly was closer to him than to the others, the more I suppose because he is a friend of signora Emilia who recommended me to signora Enrichetta. However, this relationship consisted in walking with him several times and visiting him with signora Enrichetta, and being visited by them.

Questioned if Pisacane was signora Enrichetta's husband. Answer: I think so, but that's none of my business.

Questioned whether he had told her of certain deserving projects. Answer: He said nothing to me. On the other hand, men aren't accustomed to entrust confidences to mere women.

Questioned whether she came from London to Italy alone or in company of some Genoese. Answer: I came here alone.

Questioned if she knew Giuseppe Mazzini. Answer: I know him because he lived near me in London, and I hold him to be the Christ of the century.

Asked if she had constant business with the said Mazzini and if she saw him daily. Answer: No sir, I see him only too seldom, unfortunately.

Asked if she had seen him before leaving. Answer: I saw him several days before.

Asked if Giuseppe Mazzini had not informed her about the events which were to come next in Italy. Answer: He said nothing to me.

Reading given her of her interrogation on July 5 and 6. Asked if she recognized and confirmed it. Answer: I know and confirm it in its every word.

Asked for what reason she had qualified Giuseppe Mazzini the Christ of the century in her previous examinations and what that could mean. Answer: First, I don't hold Christ as divine and therefore I don't think that Mazzini is divine, and in qualifying him as the Christ of the century I wanted to say that he is the man chosen by God to give the new word of the age which is God and the People.

Asked what she meant by the new word of the age. Answer: I believe that the age of the tyrants is finished and the age of the People is about to begin.

Asked if during her stay in Genoa or in Turin she had occasion to see Mazzini and to speak with him. Answer: I have to tell the truth about what regards my person but in as far as others are concerned, I don't believe that I have to answer.

Asked if she had ever seen letters from Giuseppe Mazzini and if she knew his writing. Answer: I have seen his writing many times and can recognize it.

Afterwards they showed her a certain letter . . . dated 17 July, 1857 from the hand of Antonio Mosto. Asked to tell if she recognized the handwriting of Giuseppe Mazzini. Answer: The letter dated September '56, which you showed me, I recognize plainly as being by Mazzini.

Asked if she recognized as her own the signature placed on the receipt of June 9, 1857 reading as follows: I received from Luigi Stallo in Piedmont L 1,000 in receipt of his obligation to the National Subscription. Answer: I see the signature on the slip and I recognize it as being made by me; it is made by me.

Asked why she took that sum from Luigi Stallo and what she was to do with it. Answer: There were many subscriptions in England for Italian independence. Stallo gave me the sum for this reason.

Questioned as to what was the scope of this Italian independence. Answer: The general scope was that the state rid itself of tyrants.

Asked what she did with the said L 1,000. Answer: I hold myself responsible even now towards the person who paid it to me.

Observed that having received that sum from Luigi Stallo in payment of a promised gift to the National Subscription, why had she not categorically answered that she was not in fact responsible to Stallo. Answer: The Committee for the National Subscription is in London, and I didn't say whether I had paid them or not.

Questioned if she knew Alberto Mario and what relations she had with him. Answer: I know him and he is engaged to me.

Questioned if she knew him before she came to Italy. Answer: I have known him only since I came to Italy.

Questioned why they got along so easily and were now engaged. Answer: These aren't questions which concern the law. They are personal questions.

Questioned if she knew Francesco Savi. Answer: I know Francesco Savi only slightly since I've seen him three or four times in his office; he has never visited me at home.

Questioned if she knew a Michele Tassara, a saddler, who had a shop near Santa Caserina. Answer: I believe that a Michele Tassara came to visit me but I didn't know that he was a saddler and I don't remember his face.

Questioned if she had ever been in the location of the Workman's Society in Genoa, along the Strada della Maddalena, and in such a case what conversations did she hold there. Answer: I went to the living room of the Workman's Society once because I was curious to see the school. I was surprised that there were many workmen there and that they greeted me. I don't remember who they were but I thanked them in a few words for everything they said on my behalf but said that perhaps it would be better to think of our slave brothers for whom we were working in England.

Questioned if when she went to the said Workman's Society she had been accompanied by the said Michele Tassara among others. Answer: When I returned to my house from the Workman's Society, I was accompanied by seven or eight of the people who had been in the hall; it is probable that Tassara was among them but I cannot say for certain—now that I think about it I remember that he was a bearded man, pitted with smallpox; he was among the first deputation that came to visit me.

Questioned why she was living in Roggero's house after she left her lodging in via Assarotti. Answer: I met signora Isabella, whom I afterwards found to be the wife of Roggero, at the country feast of the Marassi ball. When she heard that I was not content with my lodging in via Assarotti, she offered to lend me her lodging for several days until I could find another place. I was living in that house near Castelletto when Roggero came there and I met him.

Questioned if she had met a certain Primo in Genoa. Answer: I remember that I saw Primo once or twice since he was a member of a deputation, but I do not think I have ever talked with him. After I was imprisoned he made haste to send me flowers.

Questioned if she had ever had the chance to meet Francesco Daneri in

Genoa. Answer: The name doesn't sound new to me but I am not absolutely sure that I know him.

Questioned if she knew a certain Cavalieri, a doctor in Sestri. Answer: I have never met him or even heard his name.

Questioned if she had received a certain delegation of the Society of Workers from Sestri toward the end of last June. Answer: I do not remember receiving such a delegation; on the other hand, those received are named in the *Italia del Popolo*.

Questioned if she knew a certain Pittalunga who was a brassworker at the strada Maddelena, the one called "il Rosso." Answer: I don't know his name or his person.

Questioned if she had met a Venetian ex-official after she had come to Italy, and in that case if she had ever planned anything with him. Answer: It seems to me that the only Venetian I know is Mario and I don't know who this ex-official is of whom you speak.

Questioned if, on the contrary she had not offered, at the beginning of last June to a Venetian ex-officer, the command of five hundred troops prepared to revolt in Genoa and if the officer had not agreed to assume command, provided that he could lead them in Lombardy, Venetia, and the Duchies, but having been informed that it was to consist only of operations in Genoa, negotiations were not concluded. Answer: Absolutely false.

Questioned if when she had been conducted to the prison she had not asked the royal carabinieri who were her guards of the news of the king of Naples' death—and of the destruction of the Swiss regiment. Answer: I don't precisely remember all the talks that I had with the carabinieri who led me to prison but it seems to me that I only asked them if the news of the death of the king of Naples which I had read about in the papers had been confirmed. I don't remember having talked to them about the Swiss regiments or that there were barracks threatened.

Questioned which people she had met in the few days that she was in Turin during the last few months. Answer: Many people came to visit me in Turin too but I am not willing to list their names.—Mostly I saw the deputation to Parliament.

Questioned if she had made the acquaintance of the lawyer Gianbattista, native of Venice. Answer: I did not meet the famed lawyer in Turin.

Asked if she had never written letters to the leaders of Italian emigration in Genoa, inviting them to take part in the conspiracy. Answer: No.

Questioned if she knew General Garibaldi and whether she had repeatedly contacted him for the purpose of having him accept the leadership of the forces ready to revolt. Answer: I know General Garibaldi very well. He spent several days in my home in London, inasmuch as he had a son by the name of Ricciotti who had been entrusted to my care as his tutor. But I never wrote letters of the kind that you talk about; I have written him only once since I have been in Italy and I directed the letter to Caprera (Sardinia) principally in order to ask him news of his son, but I did not discuss political matters, and he replied in a few lines, giving me news of himself and his family.

President: It appears that the Savio of whom Miss White talks is the lawyer Francesco Savio, not the imputed Francesco Bartolommeo Savi.

The Lawyer Cafano: I find Savi in the copy of the proceedings. On the other hand, there is talk of his office; the lawyer, Francesco Savio, I believe, does not have an office open in Genoa.

The president verified that Savi, not Savio, was written in the original proceedings.

Then followed a reading of the interrogation undergone by Giovanni Cavaliere, doctor in medicine, before the investigating judge on July 24.

Questioned if she knew Bartolommeo Francesco Savi. Answer: I know that I have seen Savi without ever having any business with him and I recognized him on the 28th of last June when he came to the inauguration of our Workingmen's Society in Sestri.

Questioned if Savi came there because he was invited or if he came spontaneously. Answer: Savi was invited there but I cannot say whether it was by written or by oral invitation as a member of the mutual aid society of Genoa. As a result of this invitation, various individuals came from Genoa whom I do not even know. . . .

Questioned if in this audience there was talk against the government and prediction of insurrection. Answer: No word was spoken in this regard. I heard someone say that ignorance gave evidence of the confessional, and other similar expressions.

Questioned if after the speeches at that gathering on the 28th she had spoken to Savi. Answer: I took him outside, persuading him to go since getting all heated up with wine and drinking does not please me. I was with him until the end of the meeting.

Questioned if she heard any cheers in such circumstances. Answer: I heard some cheers in the hall but they were without political significance—for example they said, viva our flag, viva associates of Genoa and similar cheers could be heard but they were without political coloring.

Questioned if they had not shouted instead viva Mazzini, viva Young Italy. Answer: I assure you that I heard no such cheers in the hall. I cannot say if there were any afterwards. If they had set about to do so in that hall I would politely have opposed it. . . .

Questioned if among those who spoke there was a certain Giovanni Prana. Answer: Perhaps, but I don't know him; but I can observe that I paid little attention to those discussions.

Asked if she was at that time told that on June 29 and on several days before that a flag flew in Sestri with "Dio e Popolo" written on a red field. Answer: I saw that flag long before it was flown in Sestri. I saw it flying on a building where a certain Pier, who was constructing it, had placed it. This flag did not have an entire red field with the inscription "Dio e Popolo," but was composed of four parts which joined in the middle as four points. Two of them were red and the other two white or yellow, which I believe might have been a signal flag, and upon which had been written that inscription for, who knows what purpose. I state absolutely that I am not involved in the matter of this flag.

Appendix 2

Jessie White Mario, Complete Bibliography

Many of the articles and books cited in this bibliography appear in varying stages of manuscript preparation in the Archivio Jessie White Mario (*AJWM*), Museo Centrale del Risorgimento, Rome. The published material is here listed in chronological order. Articles published in the *Nation* are numbered to key in with Appendix 3, "Abstracts of Jessie White Mario's Articles for the *Nation*."

"Augustin Thierry." *Eliza Cook's Journal*, Feb. 8, 1851, pp. 229-31.

"Association of French Workmen." *Eliza Cook's Journal*, Feb. 15, 1851, pp. 245-48.

"Lilly Crossland." *Eliza Cook's Journal*, May 31, 1851, pp. 73-75; June 7, 1851, pp. 93-95; June 14, 1851, pp. 106-9; June 21, 1851, pp. 116-18; June 28, 1851, pp. 141-43. [Unsigned, authorship likely.]

"The Old Man's Mystery." *Eliza Cook's Journal*, July 17, 1852, pp. 186-89 [Background identical to "People's Artist."]

"The Home of Taste." (poem) *Eliza Cook's Journal*, Sept. 11, 1852, p. 320. [Initialed "J. W."]

"Jessie's Wisdom." *Eliza Cook's Journal*, April 2, 1853, pp. 361-64.

"Alice Lane." *Eliza Cook's Journal*, August 27, 1853, pp. 276-83.

"The People's Artist." *Eliza Cook's Journal*, October 1, 1853, pp. 354-59; Oct. 8, 1853, pp. 372-76. [Identified as hers in the Cowen collection, but unsigned.]

"Roger Dale: A Story of Birmingham." *Eliza Cook's Journal*, November 19, 1853, pp. 55-61; Nov. 26, 1853, pp. 69-76.

"Lamennais." "Lives of the Illustrious." *Biographical Magazine* 7 (1855): 109-26. [Article signed "G de F," attributed to her in *AJWM* (Busta 419) where she says "published somewhere."]

"Beranger." In "Lives of the Illustrious." *Biographical Magazine* 6 (June-Dec. 1854): 241-47.

"Alphonse de Lamartine." In "Lives of the Illustrious." *Biographical Magazine* 6:177-92.

"Italy for the Italians." *Daily News* (London), series of 9 articles: Nov. 7, 1856; Nov. 13, 1856; Nov. 27, 1856; Dec. 11, 1856; Dec. 26, 1856; Dec. 29, 1856; Jan. 2, 1857; Jan. 8, 1857; Jan. 15, 1857.

Orsini, Felice. *Austrian Dungeons in Italy.* Translated with preface by Jessie White Mario. London: Routledge, Warnes, and Routledge, 1856.

"A Plan for Preventing Italian attempts on the Life of the French Emperor." Letter to the editor. *Morning Star and Dial*, Feb. 17, 1858.

Releases covering Sicily and the Southern campaign for the *Daily News*, 1859.

Correspondence, including bulletins, three times a week to the *Morning Star and Dial*, 1859.

"La schiavitù e la guerra civile negli Stati Uniti d'America." *Nuova Antologia* (July 26, 1861): 264-310.

"March on Rome." (Pamphlet) [Accepted for publication, November 28, 1862, by Smith, Elder & Co., London, but perhaps not printed.]

"Recent Italian Comedy." *North American Review* 99 (1864): 364-401. [Houghton Library, Norton papers April 15, 1864, F. Boot to Charles Eliot Norton, attributes it to her but most likely a rewriting of Alberto's work.]

1. "Parties in Italy." *Nation* 2(Feb. 22, 1866): 241-42.
2. "Italian Finances," *Nation* 2(Mar. 22, 1866): 369-70.
3. "Religious Intolerance in Italy." *Nation* 2(Apr. 26, 1866): 527-28.
4. "The Military Strength of Italy." *Nation* 2 (May 4, 1866): 567.
5. "The Warlike Preparations in Italy." *Nation* 2 (June 8, 1866): 727.
6. "Florentine Mosiacs." *Nation* 3 (Dec. 13, 1866): 476.

"Italy." *New York Tribune*, Sept. 16, 1867, unsigned.

7. "Garibaldi's Position." *Nation* 5 (Nov. 7, 1867): 378-79.
8. "The Daily Press in Italy." *Nation* 6 (Feb. 13, 1868): 129-30.
9. "Public Instruction in Italy." *Nation* 6 (Feb. 27, 1868): 167-68.
10. "The Volunteers of 1867." *Nation* 6(Mar. 12, 1868): 208-9.
11. "Italian Libraries." *Nation* 6 (Apr. 9, 1868): 287-88.
12. "What One Noble Family Has Done For Italy." *Nation* 6 (May 7, 1868): 369-70.
13. "The New Process of Mummification." *Nation* 7 (July 9, 1868): 29-30.
14. "The Abolition of Feudal Tenure in Venetia." *Nation* 7 (Sept. 17, 1868): 227-29.
15. "Venetian Glass." *Nation* 7 (Nov. 19, 1868): 413-14.
16. "Right and Wrong in Italy." *Nation* 9 (July 15, 1869): 48-49.
17. "Social Equality in Italy." *Nation* 9 (Sept. 30, 1869): 267-69.
18. "On The Position of Women in Italy." *Nation* 9 (Nov. 25, 1869): 456-57; (Dec. 2, 1869): 480-82.

Articles about French Republican war for Scotsman (Edinburgh), Sept. 8, 26; Oct. 6, 10, 16, 27; Nov. 6, 7, 10, 14, 15, 20, 21, 23, 27; Dec. 13, 23, 1870. [Some also published in the *Daily News* and *New York Tribune*. Duplicates in *AJWM*.]

I Garibaldini in Francia. Rome: Giovanni Polizzi, 1871. [Compilation of newspaper articles on Franco-Prussian war.]

"Cattaneo." *Contemporary Review* 26 (1875): 465-86.

La miseria di Napoli. Florence: Le Monnier, 1877. [Printed only after

Pasquale Villari assured her that London slums were better than those of Naples.]

[With Alberto Mario, posthumously.] *Carlo Cattaneo.* Cremona: Ronzi and Signori, 1877.

"Sepolcri Inglese in Roma." *Nuova Antologia* (May 14, 1879): 265-83.

"Sicily and Ireland." *Newcastle Chronicle,* Jan. 25, 1881, unsigned.

"A Mazzinian View of Mr. Gladstone." *Newcastle Chronicle,* Feb. 16, 1881.

Releases to the *Pall Mall Gazette* [no articles identifiable], 1881.

19. "Specie Payments in Italy." *Nation* 31 (Dec. 23, 1880): 440.
20. "Italian Industrial Exposition." *Nation* 32 (May 26, 1881): 369-70.
21. "The Vatican and the Extension of the Suffrage in Italy." *Nation* 33 (Aug. 11, 1881): 111-12.
22. "A Press Trial in Rome." *Nation* 33 (Dec. 29, 1881): 509-510.
23. "The *Scrutin de liste in Italy." Nation* 34 (Mar. 2, 1882): 181-82.
24. "The Opening of the St. Gothard Tunnel." *Nation* 34 (June 15, 1882): 498-99.
25. "The Last Days of the Italian Liberator." *Nation* 34 (June 29, 1882): 539-40.
26. "Garibaldi and Mazzini." *Nation* 35 (July 27, 1882): 71-72.
27. "Elements of Discord in Italy." *Nation* 36 (Feb. 1, 1883): 101-2.
28. "The Crown Prince in Rome. The Italian (Republican) View." *Nation* 38 (Jan. 10, 1884): 31-32.
29. "Carlo Cattaneo and the Five Days of Milan." *Nation* 38 (Apr. 17, 1884): 338-39.
30. "Cholera, Misery, and Superstition." *Nation* 39 (Oct. 9, 1884): 306-7.
    [Again uses *La Miseria di Napoli.*]

Life of Garibaldi. Milan: Treves, 1884.

[Carducci.] *Scritti di Alberto Mario.* Edited by G. C. and J. W. Mario. Bologna: N. Zanichelli, 1884.

[and Alberto Mario.] *Carlo Cattaneo, Cenni Reminiscenze.* Rome: Sommarnga, 1884.

Garibaldi et son Temps. Paris: Denoc, 1884.

31. "Italian Politics." *Nation* 41(Oct. 1, 1885): 274.
32. "Misery, Discontent, and Agitation in Italy." *Nation* 42 (Feb. 25, 1886): 165-67.
33. "The Trial of the Peasant Rebels." *Nation* 42 (Apr. 15, 1886): 316-17.
34. "Italy.—The General Elections." *Nation* 42 (May 13, 1886): 400-401.
35. "A Radical View of the Italian Elections." *Nation* 42 (June 24, 1886): 526-27.
36. "Among the Tuscan Hills." *Nation* 43 (Sept. 2, 1886): 193-94.
37. "Anti-Clerical Agitation in Italy." *Nation* 43 (Oct. 7, 1886): 288-89.
38. "The Cooperative Congress in Milan." *Nation* 43 (Nov. 11, 1886): 390-91.

Agostino Bertani e i suoi tempi. 2 vols. Florence: Barbera, 1886.

Della Vita di G. Mazzini, Milan: Sonzogno, 1886.

39. "The Daily and Periodical Press in Italy." *Nation* 44 (Jan. 6, 1887): 8-9.
40. "Carducci." *Nation* 44 (Feb. 3, 1887): 95-96.
41. "The Italian Army—1887." *Nation* 44 (Apr. 28, 1887): 360-61.

42. "The First Pilgrimage to Caprera." *Nation* 44 (June 30, 1887): 548-50.
43. "The New Italian Premier." *Nation* 45 (Aug. 4, 1887): 90-91.
44. "Agostino Depretis." *Nation* 45(Aug. 18, 1887): 130-31.
45. "The Last of the Gozzadini." *Nation* 45 (Sept. 29, 1887): 250-51.
46. "Italy and the Vatican." *Nation* 45 (Nov. 17, 1887): 390-91.
47. "Garibaldi's Memoirs." *Nation* 46 (Feb. 2, 1888): 97-98.
48. "Aurelio Saffi." *Nation* 46 (Apr. 19, 1888): 319-20.
49. "Poets and Cooperatives." *Nation* 47 (Sept. 13, 1888): 207-9.
Della Vita di Giuseppe Mazzini. Milan: Sonzogno, 1888.
50. "The Italian Fleet." *Nation* 48 (May 2, 1889): 362-64.
51. "Italy's Allies and War Scares." *Nation* 49 (Aug. 22, 1889): 146-47.
52. "Michele Amari." *Nation* 49(Aug. 29, 1889): 164-65.
Autobiography of Giuseppe Garibaldi. With a supplement by Jessie White Mario. Authorized translation by A. Werner. 3 vols. London: Walter Smith, 1889. Vol. 3 by Jessie White Mario.
53. "The Patrimony of the Poor in Italy." *Nation* 50 (Feb. 20, 1890): 149-51.
54. "Italy's Burdens under the Triple Alliance." *Nation* 50 (Apr. 17, 1890): 312-13.
55. "The Triumph of an Idea." *Nation* 50(May 8, 1890): 371-72.
56. "Public Instruction and Starvation in Italy." *Nation* 50 (June 26, 1890): 504-6.
57. "Venice and Liberty," *Nation* 51 (Sept. 11, 1890): 208-9.
58. "The Italian Elections." *Nation* 51 (Dec. 11, 1890): 459-60.
Scritti e discorsi di Agostino Bertani. Scelti e curati da Jessie White Mario. Florence: G. Barbera, 1890.
"Italy and the United States." *Nineteenth Century* 29 (Jan., 1891) 701-18.
59. "The Housing of the Poor in Naples." *Nation* 52 (Feb. 12, 1891): 134-36. [*Scribner's Magazine* article in process uses same material.]
60. "Mafia, Camorra, Brigandage—Alias Crime." *Nation* 52 (Apr. 16, 1891): 314-15.
61. "Peace or Death." *Nation* 53 (July 9, 1891): 25-26.
62. "The Jews and Italy." *Nation* 53 (July 30, 1891): 82-83.
63. "Italy on the Sea." *Nation* 53 (Sept. 3, 1891): 177-78.
64. "The Financial Condition of Italy." *Nation* 53 (Oct. 1, 1891): 255-56.
65. "The City of Initiatives." *Nation* 53 (Dec. 3, 1891): 422-24.
66. "Italian Wine-Making." *Nation* 53 (Dec. 31, 1891): 505-6.
67. "In Sicilian Sulphur Mines." *Nation* 54 (Jan. 14, 1892): 29-31.
68. "The Exhibition of Palermo." *Nation* 54 (March 17, 1892): 208-10.
69. "St. Joseph's Day in Naples." *Nation* 54(Apr. 14, 1892): 281-82.
70. "A Treasure Trove." *Nation* 54 (June 9, 1892): 426-28.
71. "Letters of Ippolito Pindemonte." *Nation* 55 (Aug. 11, 1892): 103-5.
72. "An Extra-Territorial Italian City." *Nation* 55 (Sept. 1, 1892): 162-63.
73. "Crime and Politics in Italy." *Nation* 55 (Nov. 10, 1892): 350-52.
74. "The Italian Elections." *Nation* 55 (Dec. 8, 1892): 427-28.
Cattaneo, Carlo, *Scritti, Politici ed epistolario.* 3 Vols. Florence: Barbera, 1892, 1901.
"The Poor in Naples." In "The Poor in Great Cities." *Scribner's Magazine* 13 (Jan. 1893); see 59 above.
75. "Bank Troubles in Italy." *Nation* 56 (Feb. 9, 1893): 98-100.
76. "The Italian Bank Scandal." *Nation* 56 (Mar. 9, 1893): 175-76.

77. "Carducci and His Critics." *Nation* 57 (July 6, 1893): 7-8.
78. "A True Realist." *Nation* 57 (Oct. 7, 1893): 305-7.
79. "The Social Unrest in Sicily." *Nation* 57 (Nov. 9, 1893): 344-46.
80. "The Dry Rot in Italy." *Nation* 57 (Dec. 21, 1893): 462-63.
Vita di Giuseppe Garibaldi. Milan: Fratelli Treves, 1893.
81. "Habemus Pontificem." *Nation* 58 (Jan. 4, 1894): 9-10.
82. "Martial Law in Sicily." *Nation* 58 (Jan. 25, 1894): 63-64.
"Le miniere di zolfo in Sicilia." *Nouva Antologia* 49 (Jan. 15, 1894): 441-66; (Feb. 15, 1894): 719-43.
83. "The Trade Between Sicily and the United States." *Nation* 58 (Mar. 22, 1894): 209-11. [Previous two articles use same materials.]
84. "Italy at the Cross-Roads." *Nation* 58 (Apr. 19, 1894): 287-88.
85. "Protectionism and Socialism in Italy." *Nation* 58 (May 24, 1894): 384-85.
"Prodotti del Suolo e Viticoltura in Sicilia." *Nuova Antologia* 136 (Aug. 15, 1894): 708-41.
86. "Lake Garda and Lake Iseo." *Nation* 59(Oct. 11, 1894): 267-68.
87. "Carducci at San Marino." *Nation* 59 (Oct. 25, 1894): 303-5.
88. "The Last Letters of Baron Ricasoli." *Nation* 59 (Dec. 20, 1894): 459-60.
[With Gabriele Rosa]. *In Memoria di G. Nicotera.* Florence: Barbera, 1894.
Scritti di Alberto Mario scelti e curati da Giosuè Carducci, con le memorie di lui scritte da Jessie vedova Mario. 2 vols. Bologna: Zanichelli, 1894.
"The Poor in Naples." In *The Poor in Great Cities.* New York: Charles Scribner's Sons, 1895.
89. "Italy in Africa." *Nation* 60 (Mar. 7, 1895): 178-80.
90. "A Grand Old Man." *Nation* 60 (Apr. 4, 1895): 254-55.
91. "On the Eve of the Italian Elections." *Nation* 60 (June 6, 1895): 441-42.
92. "Carducci—Tasso—Ferrara." *Nation* 60 (June 27, 1895): 497-98.
93. "Mazzini's Love Story." *Nation* 61(Aug. 1, 1895): 77-78.
94. "Carducci's Readings from the Italian Renaissance." *Nation* 61(Nov. 21, 1895): 361-62.
95. "A Doomsday Book Doomed." *Nation* 62(Jan. 2, 1896): 8-9.
96. "The Thirty-Fifth Anniversary of Carducci's Professorship." *Nation* 62(Feb. 27, 1896): 175-76.
97. "Italy's Humiliation and Prowess in Africa." *Nation* 62 (Apr. 9, 1896): 284-85.
98. "Social Regeneration in Italy." *Nation* 62 (May 7, 1896): 358-59.
99. "An Impenitent Republican." *Nation* 62(June 4, 1896): 431-32.
100. "The Triumphs of Leo XIII." *Nation* 63(July 2, 1896): 7-9.
101. "Italy and France in 1870." *Nation* 63(July 9, 1896): 33-35.
102. "The First Act of Social Justice to Sicily." *Nation* 63 (Aug. 6, 1896): 102-3.
103. "The Marriage of the Crown Prince of Italy." *Nation* 63 (October 29, 1896): 324-25.
"L'Italia, Roma, e la Guerra Franco-Prussania." Estratto dalla *Rivista storica del Risorgimento Italiano.* vol. 1. Turin, 1896.
"Italy, Rome and the War." *Cosmopolis.* London: T. Fisher Unwin, n.d.

104. "Italy and Crete." *Nation* 64(Mar. 11, 1897): 178-79.
105. "More Readings from the Italian Renaissance." *Nation* 64 (April 22, 1897): 300-301.
106. "Crime and Misery." *Nation* 64(June 24, 1897): 470-71.
"Le opere pie e l'infanticidio legale." Rovigo: A. Minelli, 1897.
"Il sistema penitenziario e il domicilio coatto in Italia." Dalla *Nuova Antologia*. Rome, 1897.
107. "Mazzini's Early Letters, 1834-1840." *Nation* 66 (Feb. 24, 1898): 146-47.
108. "Felice Cavallotti." *Nation* 66 (Mar. 31, 1898): 240-42.
109. "The Riots in Italy." *Nation* 66(May 26, 1898): 402-3.
110. "Carducci's Leopardi." *Nation* 67(Sept. 15, 1898): 201-2.
111. "One More Letter from Robert." *Nation* 68(Mar. 23, 1899): 220-21.
112. "Carducci's Petrarch." *Nation* 68(April 6, 1899): 254-56.
113. "Micromaniacs and Megalomaniacs." *Nation* 68(May 11, 1899): 350-51.
114. "The Villari Testimonial." *Nation* 69 (Dec. 7, 1899): 423-25.
Cenni biografici sulla vita di G. Dolfo. Florence: Elziviriana, 1899.
115. "Charles Albert—Legend and History." *Nation* 70 (April 5, 1900): 257-59.
116. "Carducci's Muratori." *Nation* 70(May 31, 1900): 414-15.
117. "Sunset or Dawn." *Nation* 71(Oct. 18, 1900): 305-6.
118. "Malta and the Question of Language." *Nation* 71(Dec. 20, 1900): 484-86.
Scritti scelti di Giuseppe Mazzini. Edited by Giosuè Carducci. Introduction by Jessie White Mario.
119. "Verdi, the Patriot." Nation 72(Mar. 31, 1901): 231.
120. "Unpublished Letters of Mazzini and Kossuth." *Nation* 72 (Apr. 11, 1901): 291-93.
121. "Giosuè Carducci." *Nation* 72(May 16, 1901): 392-94.
"Carlo Cattaneo." *Nuova Antologia* 177(June 16, 1901): 683-705.
122. "Carlo Cattaneo." *Nation* 73(July 18, 1901): 48-49.
123. "Cesare Abba's Von Quarto zum Volturno." *Nation* 73(July 25, 1901): 72-73.
"Cattaneo," *New York Evening Post*, August 17, 1901.
124. "Crispi." *Nation* 73(Aug. 29, 1901): 165-67.
125. "Tuscan Town and Country." *Nation* 73 (Nov. 14, 1901): 375-76.
Mario, Alberto. *Scritti letterari e artistici*. Edited by Giosuè Carducci. Bologna: N. Zanichelli, 1901. With a biography by Jessie White Mario.
126. "The Naples Tammany Overthrow." *Nation* 74(Jan. 23, 1902) :65-66.
127. "The Railway Strike in Italy." *Nation* 74 (Mar. 27, 1902) :245-47.
128. "Giosuè Carducci." *Nation* 74(May 15, 1902): 383-84.
129. "The General Strike in Florence." *Nation* 75 (Sept. 25, 1902): 241-43.
130. "The Rebuilding of the Campanile." *Nation* 75 (Oct. 16, 1902): 302-4.
131. "The Roman Strike." *Nation* 76(May 14, 1903): 391-92.
132. "Mazzini Redivivus." *Nation* 77(July 2, 1903): 7-9.
133. "The Italian Socialists." *Nation* 78(May 12, 1904): 367-68.
134. "Italy, France, and the Vatican." *Nation* 78(June 16, 1904) :467-68.
135. "Popular Education in Italy." *Nation* 79 (August 4, 1904): 97-98.

136. "The Great Political Strike in Italy. *Nation* 79 (Oct. 20, 1904): 312-14.
137. "The General Elections in Italy." *Nation* 79 (Nov. 10, 1904): 370-72; (Dec. 8, 1904): 456-58.
138. "Italy's Tribute to Carducci." *Nation* 80 (Feb. 2, 1905): 88-90.
139. "Monuments to Crispi." *Nation* 80 (Feb. 16, 1905): 130-31.
140. "Parliamentary Decadence in Italy." *Nation* 80 (Apr. 13, 1905): 285-87.
141. "The Sixteenth Volume of Carducci's Works." *Nation* 81 (Oct. 12, 1905): 297.
Garibaldi e i suoi tempi: Milan. n.p., 1905.
142. "The New Italian Ministry." (posthumous) *Nation* 82 (Mar. 8, 1906): 195-97.
The Birth of Modern Italy. (posthumous) Edited by Duke Litta-Visconti Arese. London: T. Fisher Unwin, 1909.

Appendix 3

Abstracts of Jessie White Mario's Articles for the *Nation*

The *Nation* was founded in the summer following the end of the Civil War, by Charles Eliot Norton, James Miller McKim, and E. L. Godkin, as a "newspaper" which would consider itself a friend of the freedmen. Godkin had come to America as a reporter for the *London Daily News*, James Miller McKim of Philadelphia and C. E. Norton undertook to float the stock for the publication. The magazine went through a rocky first year, with one financial crisis following another. [The Correspondence, E. L. Godkin to Charles E. Norton, Cambridge, Mass., Harvard University, Houghton Library, Norton papers, 30 letters, b Ms Am 1088, 2714-43, discusses the relationship between the two men in these and other matters, the editing of articles for the *North American Review*, the formation of the *Nation*, and Godkin's growing dissatisfaction with democracy.] After this first year, Godkin took over the magazine himself, forming the Nation Association, under the title of E. L. Godkin and Company.

Godkin's early life had been spent as a law scholar and newspaperman. He was in Hungary in 1854 and had been warmly welcomed by the revolutionists there; in 1854-1855 he served as correspondent for the *London Daily News* in the Crimea, and won himself recognition for letters from the front. In 1855 he delivered lectures in Belfast on the war and did editorial work on the *Northern Whig*. In 1856 he traveled to America where he reported on conditions in the South, then studied law in the office of David Dudley Field, and on February 6, 1858 was admitted to the bar. In 1881 Henry Villard bought the *New York Post*, a daily newspaper. Godkin became his assistant with Carl Schurz and Horace White, editors. Godkin soon linked the *Nation* with the *Post*, and thereafter the *Nation* became the weekly edition of the *Post*. In 1883 Godkin was appointed editor-in-chief of the whole enterprise; he held this position until January, 1900.

The first issue of the *Nation* was printed July 6, 1865. For the remainder of that year the editors devoted the political commentary largely to Reconstruction in the South. Early in 1866, however, they began to take note of political issues in Europe. With Godkin's early bias toward republicanism and revolution, it is not surprising that he should employ Jessie White Mario, his colleague on the *Daily News*, as a correspondent for his new weekly. During the span of years between 1866 and 1870 and again between 1880 and 1906 Jessie Mario wrote one hundred forty-three articles for the *Nation*.

The *Nation's* editors complemented Jessie Mario's view of Italy with articles by William J. Stillman and his wife, Marie Spartalli, William Roscoe Thayer, and Luigi Villari. Stillman and his wife wrote primarily about the antiquities of Italy—except for two or three occasions when Stillman's views were used to balance Jessie's assessment of various controversial issues. Villari wrote about art and literature, and Thayer's writings ranged over many subjects. For the steady, thorough coverage of current events and national developments, the magazine relied on Jessie, whose work it published anonymously or over the initials J. W. M. or W. M.

[The headnote gives the title of the article, the date of publication in the *Nation*, and Jessie White Mario's by-line, in brackets.]

1. "Parties in Italy." Feb. 22, 1866 [Florence, Jan. 22]

An analysis of the makeup of the new Parliament which first met on November 19, 1865. The present ministry, under Lamarmora, does not possess elements of success, "and if the proposed coalition of left and left centre is carried into effect, we shall have a radical ministry before the end of the session. I, for one, shall deeply regret such a premature event; the members of the left are chiefly new to parliamentary life; and of administrative routine they are totally ignorant . . . the radicals are in too great a hurry; they have no decisive financial programme; no war programme; no well organized system of internal reform, so necessary in this transition state, where administrative and legislative unification demands that the best laws of each state shall be extended to the whole." She raises questions about the financial structure of the new kingdom saying the greatest present enemy of Italy is the deficit. [In 1866 Italy was on the verge of bankruptcy.]

2. "Italian Finances." Mar. 22, 1866 [Florence, Feb. 19]

A discussion of a legislative proposal to dislodge funds from the clergy. Jessie describes how a bill is put through Parliament and how long it takes to be enacted. She contends that Italy has a choice between war or financial disaster. Public and newspapers alike cry for a solution to the problem; how not to solve it seems to be the motto of the cabinet and of the chambers. She includes a description of Florence at the time, and comments on the disappearance of the "good old days." Ambassadors, senators, deputies, fortune seekers, palace hunters, and pickpockets are changing the face of Florence, and workmen are destroying its time-honored stones to make new office buildings for government.

3. "Religious Intolerance in Italy." Apr. 26, 1866 [Florence, Mar. 29]

Analysis of disputes between Catholic and Protestant churches. How far, she asks, can the state go in separating itself from the Catholic church? She discusses examples of both the loosening of the grip of the church, and the strong fight by the prelates to strengthen theirs. The church clutches the "analfabeti." The church checks up on people who go to Easter services, trying to keep a tight hold. Breakdown of tie between the sacristy and the police bureau.

4. "The Military Strength of Italy." May 4, 1866 [Italy, Apr. 13]

"The sole topics of conversation and speculation are 'War or no war' and the fall of Italian funds." Article analyzes the conflicting statements by *Diritto* (the leading Parliamentary opposition newspaper) saying Italy could only bring 197,448 men to war with Prussia, and General De Pettinengo, saying Italy could bring 354,743 men to war (Cavour's half-million). She quotes from a report to the Chamber of Deputies giving statistics on state of Italian navy.

5. "The Warlike Preparations in Italy." June 8, 1866 [Florence, May 19]

An analysis of troop movements and army strength although war has not yet been declared. A discussion of the declaration by Mazzini called "The War": "The war for the emancipation of Venice was, up to the present moment a duty; now it is a necessity. Today all Italy is Venice; the life, the future, the honor of the nation await their ransom between the Alps and the lagunas. The war ought to be exclusively Italian." Quoting a statement from the *Nazione* of Florence on what American women did for their wounded in the Civil War, Jessie tells American readers that Soldiers' Aid Societies are being formed: "When I remember the careless way in which our wounded were thrown across mules or jolted in springless carriages in 1860, and read the accounts of your hospital cars and slung elastic beds, I feel that I would do a great deal to get one or even an exact model of one over here."

6. "Florentine Mosaics." Dec. 13, 1866 [Florence, Oct. 28]

She tells of visiting Dr. Salviati, who repairs old pictures and has a glassblowing works at Murano, and hopes that Italians will invest in the glass company, which could become a source of national pride.

7. "Garibaldi's Position." Nov. 7, 1867 [Florence, Oct. 9]

[Editors of the *Nation* in November '67 expressed confusion over cable reports from Rome, not knowing that the French are in Rome: "What curious notions of government his [Garibaldi's] followers have got into their head may be inferred from the letter of our correspondent at Florence, who is a warm friend and supporter of his. It appears, according to their theory, that whenever an established government does not make war at what appears to outsiders the proper time, anybody who conceives himself to be a 'good representative' of the 'popular idea' and can get a few thousand men to follow him, has a right to rise up and make war on his own account. After this, we may fairly expect to see the right of private war asserted before long."]

Article 7 invites the criticism offered against it by the *Nation's* editors. Jessie states that "individual initiative" reverted to its possessors after 1864 since the government did nothing to incorporate Rome into Italy. She chronicles Garibaldi's recent movements: he left Caprera to go to Florence and began his crusade against the papists and priests in the midst of frenzied crowds. Ricasoli, in the meantime, having dissolved the Chamber of Deputies, courted the Left asking them to persuade Garibaldi to return to Caprera, but Garibaldi refused to listen. Garibaldi went from city to city spreading his word. Garibaldi's old friends in the Left did everything they could to persuade Garibaldi to desist, but he could not be persuaded. "Whether he felt he could do without them or thought 'Let 'em alone, and they'll come home,' he alone knows. The Left believed that syrup rather than blood circulated in Roman veins and so, when Garibaldi suggested letting the Roman insurrection take place before free state intervention, the Left turned to him. "However, Garibaldi injected Marsala blood to create a chemical transformation of 'syrup' to 'blood.'" Garibaldi was made a government prisoner and conveyed back to Caprera, where he is now a continually guarded prisoner. Jessie surmises that if the troops and populace had been allowed to combine—which there was every evidence they were ready to do—the Pitti Palace cabinet would now be dissolved.

[The next issue of the *Nation* carries the cabled news, not from JWM, that the Garibaldians were defeated at Monte Rotondo owing to the assistance of the French;

Garibaldi is a prisoner and his son has escaped. There is little question, the news item says, that had Rattazzi boldly seized Civitavecchia before the arrival of the French, the latter would never have landed and the Roman problem would be solved. It was because of the king's anxiety about his "soul" that present relations with the pope were not severed. "The spectacle of a Christian bishop having people slain by the hundred on their own soil by foreign hirelings to enable him to retain possession of a city, is too revolting for this age." The November 21, 1867 *Nation* bears the editorial opinion that the Garibaldian expedition was a failure and that Garibaldi has lost his military prestige. The Italian government was not ready for the Roman affair. Cavour, who could have pulled it off, is dead, and Rattazzi is not up to it. For the next month and a half the *Nation* reports the chaos of disorganization and indecision on Rattazzi's part.]

8. *"The Daily Press in Italy."* Feb. 13, 1868 *[no by-line]*

Many Italian papers are one-sided and monotonous, have few readers, and consequently serve little purpose. Analysis of the *Unità Cattolica*, perhaps the best paper in Italy.

9. *"Public Instruction in Italy."* Feb. 27, 1868 *[no by-line]*

Jessie compares the state of public education in Italy with that in America, finding the Italian wanting in content.

10. *"The Volunteers of 1867."* Mar. 12, 1868 *[Florence, Feb. 20]*

The Garibaldian volunteers are destitute after the recent campaign. Mrs. G. P. Marsh and others have organized a Committee on the Wounded to alleviate the sufferings of the destitute volunteers, and no one in America can ever guess how much good they have done, but it is not enough. The government is doing nothing to take heed of the plight of these people. [Includes much firsthand information.]

11. *"Italian Libraries."* Apr. 9, 1868 *[Florence, Mar. 20]*

The Italian libraries have always been the best in the world, but now there is a shocking decline in the money being spent on these libraries. Only the equivalent of two hundred dollars a year currently is spent on books in the library in Florence; much more was spent under the grand dukes.

12. *"What One Noble Family Has Done for Italy."* May 7, 1868 *[Florence, Apr. 15]*

A discussion of the modern business techniques of the Ginori china manufacturing company at Doccia. It has weathered the storm and is improving. The relations between employers and employed are good: there has been no strike in 132 years. The Company has its own elementary schools, schools of design, land, cottages, and community improvements, yet there seems to be neither patronage nor servility: "And although Italy's real prosperity must lie chiefly in her fertile soil and tideless sea, there are signs which give fair hope that she may recover something of her old renown as a manufacturing country." [About one third of Italy's soil was arable. Was she ignorant or carried away?]

13. *"The New Process of Mummification."* July 9, 1868 *[Florence, June 20]*

Jessie investigates Professor Marini's discoveries about mummification, since the French and Italian papers were talking about them although the English were "pooh-poohing" them. Perhaps his process, which he is guarding as a jealous secret, can be used for the cure of cancer and of hospital gangrene: "He showed us petrified livers ... a petrified medal of Garibaldi's blood."

14. *"The Abolition of Feudal Tenure in Venetia."* Sept. 17, 1868 *[Venice, Aug. 26]*

Feudal tenure law may seem unimportant in Italy in such a place as Tuscany where tenure has never been a problem (certainly it would seem a pointless law in the U.S.), but in the Venetian territory it involves everyone. Jessie speculates on what the abolition of the inheritance law may mean in Venetia.

15. "Venetian Glass." Nov. 19, 1868 [Venice, Oct. 29]

Jessie had feared that British practicality would subordinate beauty to utility when the Anglo-Italian Company took over the Salviati business at Murano. This has not been the case; the British wisely separated administration from art.

16. "Right and Wrong in Italy." July 15, 1869 [Leghorn, June 10]

Jessie examines the relationship between the murder of Austrian general Crenneville, who was visiting the scenes of his earlier administration, and crime in Italy in general. The Italian hatred of flogging and love of immediate vengeance in a duel cited. The Italian hatred of law analyzed.

17. "Social Equality in Italy." Sept. 30, 1869 [Leghorn, Sept. 1]

Analysis of the relationships among serving classes. Relationships are free in Italy; one class does not kowtow to another even though no one refrains from cheating. The age is a fast age. She quotes "Redeunt Saturnia regna"; "veniet cordatior aetas." [Refers to herself as "sir" in this article.]

18. "On the Position of Women in Italy." Nov. 25, 1869 [Leghorn, Nov. 1]

An analysis of the differences between the Protestant and the Catholic attitude towards women.

18. Continued. Dec. 2, 1869 [Leghorn, Nov. 1]

Jessie continues the explorations of the previous article, asserting the equality of the sexes in Italy and discussing the lack of concern about the battle of the sexes. [During the years that Jessie was not writing, the Nation had three or four articles dealing with the removal of the seat of government to Rome; the loss of the pope's temporal power; the pope's 'excommunicatio major,' forbidding Catholics to take part in elections or government on threat of excommunication. "This is the most comprehensive of modern curses and leaves its victims in a very bad way."]

19. "Specie Payments in Italy." Dec. 23, 1880 [Rome, Nov. 24]

An examination of the bill which would resume specie payments and stop the banking confederation from issuing notes. The prosperity of Italy has not been increasing rapidly enough to cover the flow of gold from the country during the last fifteen years.

20. "Italian Industrial Exposition." May 26, 1881 [Milan, May 6]

The Milanese exposition for art and industry gives Jessie the first hope for the future since the proclamation of "one Italy with Rome for the capital." At the exposition she saw many gutta-percha articles which are used mostly in hospitals, and new railroad cars—in particular a car that could be used as a hospital. She discusses the battle to save the silkworm industry which has been devastated by disease. A description of a woolen factory that she has visited at Serio, which is a "model colony" with a nursery for children whose mothers work, a school, large and airy houses, and "a fair day's wages for a fair day's work." Here the workers feel they are human beings. The Italians are really talking about the silkworm industry and bills to abolish the export and salt taxes, not about Tunis, as the foreign press would have us believe.

21. "The Vatican and the Extension of the Suffrage in Italy." Aug. 11, 1881 [Rome, July 25]

A new law will extend suffrage to any male over twenty-one who can sign his name. Three million more people will now be eligible to vote. One-half million have previously been eligible. [Jessie was in error in her description of the franchise laws. Not until 1912 under Giolotti was universal manhood suffrage achieved. In the elections of 1882, barely two million males were eligible to vote.] Many don't vote because there seems to be little to choose from between the Left and the Right. The gradual loss of power of Pius IX and Leo XIII has left the voter rather puzzled. "Leo XIII shut himself up in the Vatican, and is now, like all prisoners and exiles, an irritable, suspicious man, beset with sick fancies and distrustful of all; leaning now to this, now to that counsellor; never able to see things and judge events and circumstances in their true light and comparative proportions." Jessie wonders if the extension of suffrage will bring about a reconciliation between the church and the state. If the church were to revoke its policy of *ne életti, ne élettori* ["Neither elected, nor electors," signifying the practice of many Catholics who stayed away from the polls since to vote would acknowledge the existence of the Italian state], it would possibly regain some of its power.

22. "A Press Trial in Rome." Dec. 29, 1881 [Rome, Dec. 1]

Alberto Mario has been placed on trial for things he said about Leo XIII in an article in *Lega della Democrazia*. In that article, Mario offered a resolution that "The Government should take possession of the apostolic palaces." (Prior to this, the Mazzinian radicals and the federalists had held meetings to bring about the abolition of the Law of Guarantees: it is "indecorous for an Italian Liberal government to continue these laws.") The pope has refused to avail himself of these laws, he has spoken against the new kingdom; he has appealed to foreign governments for aid: "His existence as a recognized and inviolable sovereign is a constant menace to Italy." (In his self-defense Alberto said "though a republican, he respected popular sovereignty too thoroughly to dispute the legitimate authority of the king chosen by plebiscite, but that his was the only legal authority in the realm, as the constitution ought to have been voted by a constituent assembly. The law of guarantees was a categoric negation of the national will.") [Trollope remarked that Alberto, though sentenced to imprisonment, was never incarcerated and would go to the prison daily to ask for the execution of his sentence. "The gaoler used to shut the door in his face, and he narrated the result of his visit in the next day's paper!"] Jessie commented that Mario's articles would have had far less publicity and a smaller audience if there had been no trial.

23. "The Scrutin de liste in Italy." Mar. 2, 1882 [no by-line]

A discussion of the reform bill to bring almost universal suffrage to Italy despite the conservatives' fear of the "inroads" of republicanism and the liberals' fear that Catholics, the most disciplined of the Italians, would predominate. The advantage of the *scrutin de liste* will be the end of the purchase of votes by promises and pledges and the end to undue government favoritism. Jessie recalls Cavour's previous objections to the *scrutin de liste*, thus lending body to her argument. She comments that after his supplication by the parishioners, the pope has decided to let the names of Catholics be entered on the electoral roles: "The first costly step taken, the rest will naturally follow."

24. "The Opening of the St. Gothard Tunnel." June 15, 1882 [Milan, May 22]

Jessie, an eyewitness, reports on the opening of the tunnel and gives a short history of its building. She praises Carlo Cattaneo who first promoted the tunnel, as the "greatest philosopher and political economist of modern Italy, the guide and inspirer of the five days of Milan in 1848, where the unarmed citizens defeated and drove out the entire Austrian army under Radetzky." The inaugurating train was warmly welcomed on its Swiss stops, but the Italians, doubtless because it was the silkworm season, seemed indifferent to the proceedings.

25. "The Last Days of the Italian Liberator." June 29, 1882 [Milan, June 7]

Jessie speaks from personal experience of Garibaldi's last days and of his wish to be cremated—counter to the nation's wish to embalm him. The grief of the nation is such, she says, that "it seems as if the pulse of the nation had ceased to beat." She quotes the king's letter praising Garibaldi. On a local note [she is in Milan], she speaks of the fact that the French consul at Milan has refused to fly a veiled tricolor and it is with difficulty that the workmen have been stopped from attacking the consul's office. She quotes a letter from Garibaldi to her written during the *Alabama* incident between the U.S. and England, expressing grief that England was opposed to the reestablishment of the Union and noting his hope for the future agreement of the two noble nations. [Jessie's article was supplemented by an article by A. V. Dicey suggesting that Garibaldi's death was the close of an era, noting that already men important in 1848 seem to belong to a past age. In fact, Victor Emmanuel II and Pope Pius IX had both died in 1878.]

26. *"Garibaldi and Mazzini." July 27, 1882 [Genoa, June 29]*

Reporting of controversy over whether Garibaldi was to be cremated or embalmed. There is a description of a ceremony at the monument to Mazzini.

27. *"Elements of Discord in Italy." Feb. 1, 1883 [Venetia, Jan. 9]*

Jessie suggests several elements of discord in this critical article: Only 49% of the electors have voted in this present (October-November 1882) election; the situation in the Chambers is unchanged. [In fact 60.7% had voted.] Depretis is trying to unite the progressives and conservatives so that the radicals have no influence, but he is using reactionary measures to do so, illustrated by the unseating of Deputy Fallaroni. The democratic party is reviving; it is not revolutionary but advocates respect for the will of the nation. It is against the centralization of Italy, which is divided into seven provinces, but Rome persists in trying to regulate every movement. This kind of coordination does not work, Jessie points out, at times of national disaster such as the inundations of the Po and Adige. Constant unalleviated hatred of Austria makes for hard feeling. Such hatred has been fanned recently by the Oberdank agitation. Leaders tried to quell demonstrations because Italy is not ready for a war with Austria. [The word is "Oberdan." The Oberdan incident involved a Triestean student Guglielmo Oberdan, who was found to have bombs with which he planned to assassinate Francis Joseph of Austria during a visit to Trieste. He was hanged on December 20, 1882, shouting as he died: "Long live Italy! Long live free Trieste."]

28. *"The Crown Prince in Rome, the Italian (Republican) View." Jan. 10, 1884 [Rome, Dec. 19, 1883]*

This article speculates on the meaning of the visit of the German crown prince to Rome. The Italians feel hostile toward the Italo-Austro-Hungarian-Germanic alliance. Italians are speculating on the meaning of the prince's visit to the Vatican. Such a visit is ominous because the Catholics are plotting to regain power, especially in their dealings with the king. They have already regained considerable power since the death of Pius IX.

29. *"Carlo Cattaneo and the Five Days of Milan." Apr. 17, 1884 [Milan, Mar. 23]*

Jessie praises Cattaneo as the leader of the Five Days, tells of the solace he offered to the Marios during their seclusion in Switzerland and points to the fact that her husband Alberto came to be considered as Cattaneo's chief exponent and disciple.

30. *"Cholera, Misery, and Superstition." Oct. 9, 1884 [Bologna, Sept. 20]*

Jessie takes up the theme which she plays on often of poverty in Naples. She describes a recent visit to Naples in the company of two ladies and a gentleman journalist. There she saw such sights as "could not be recounted to the ears of newspaper readers." Now a cholera epidemic has swept through the *bassi fondi* and grottoes of Naples where thousands of wretched people live in squalor and abject poverty. Prior to this time (even though she has cited it in her writing) people have failed to believe that such misery could exist in Italy. Now the epidemic has brought this matter out into the open. Jessie makes a few suggestions for helping the poor: "But alas! I have but the very faintest hope of this, and fear nothing will be done to better the condition of the poor classes of Naples, as of Italy, until when patient suffering has exceeded its utmost limit the people rise up in their own defence and take their rights into their own hands." She speaks of the most hideous aspect of Naples—legalized prostitution.

31. *"Italian Politics." Oct. 1, 1885 [Italy, Sept. 9]*

In this article, after a lapse of almost a year, Jessie writes of several specific matters which seriously affect the Italian economy. The first, the fight in Parliament over whether the state-owned railroads should be sold to private individuals; the second, that taxes fall too heavily on the land. There is a need for heavy taxation, in view of the necessary expenditures for the army, the navy, and education; but the agricultural depression, the failure of the silkworm crop and the recurrence of vine disease, and above all American competition in cereals, have depressed the economy. She cautions against colonization and alliances which will draw Italy's attention away from its problems.

32. "Misery, Discontent, and Agitation in Italy." Feb. 25, 1886 [Lendinara, Jan. 4]

The growing labor agitation in Italy and its connection with the workingman's vote, and the ineffectual charity organizations, and the increase in crime are discussed. Englishmen ask, she says, why the Italian people don't agitate for the vote. They don't understand why fifty percent of those who have the vote don't use it. The reason is simple. Leo XIII says, "Vote where you please as long as you vote for the right persons: only don't ask me to sanction your so doing." It is the working class and the peasants who don't vote because it makes no difference who is in power—they have the same taxes, the same ineffectual police protection, the same administration of justice "if ever they have the ill luck to need it." Voting only makes enemies, since it is not really secret. Only when the population are especially angry do they vote. Furthermore, Parliament passes no laws which affect people's daily lives. Charity institutions are not reformed. One can be put in jail without knowing of what one is accused. [She then cites two such trials.] Finally, it is a crime in Italy to organize to raise wages unless such a raise is proved necessary, and the working people are afraid to speak.

33. "The Trial of the Peasant Rebels." Apr. 15, 1886 [Venice, Mar. 27]

Jessie details the proceeding against some peasant rebels from Mantua and their imprisonment in Venice, using their trial as an opportunity to criticize administration of justice. She speaks of the growing discontent and the threat of a general conflagration if misery in Mantua continues to be suppressed and not dealt with.

34. "Italy—The General Elections." May 13, 1886 [Bologna, Apr. 28]

Depretis has been compelled to dissolve the Chambers. Social reform is badly needed. Depretis personally offended everybody by his arrogance and by his insistent following of his motto, *Piace a me e basta*. The ministry allowed African scientific expeditions to be sacrificed to political interests. The Italian government, in fact, has committed several imprudences in Africa.

35. "A Radical View of the Italian Elections." June 24, 1886 [Rovigo, May 29]

This article analyzes the history of the Radical party in Rovigo and dissects some of the surprising results of the recent election, including the loss by both parties of good men and the double election of Amilcare Cipriani.

36. "Among the Tuscan Hills." Sept. 2, 1886 [Capraia, Aug. 12]

As Jessie revisits Capraia she recalls a visit twenty years ago with Giuseppe Mazzoni, conspirator and liberal leader who stood for Prato, at the extreme Left. In Tuscany she finds a working demonstration of the *metayer* system advocated by John Stuart Mill. The Tuscan farmers and proprietors are prosperous, and their prosperty stems from the successful operation of the system, including a division of expenses and profits. In this system proprietors provide peasants with land and equipment in exchange for a large part of the profits.

37. "Anti-Clerical Agitation in Italy." Oct. 7, 1886 [Italy, Sept. 23]

For a long time there was hope in Italy that a "free church in a free state," Cavour's motto, could exist. This is seen to be impossible and there are fears that the Jesuits may one again take possession of the nation, especially by influencing youth.

38. "The Cooperative Congress in Milan." Nov. 11, 1886 [Italy, Oct. 16]

Jessie reports on the Cooperative Congress in Milan. The purpose of the Congress is to form a federation of Italian cooperatives. Delegates from France (M. Fougerousse), Italy (Vigano), England (Holyoake) have convened to discuss mutual problems. Cooperatives had been advocated by Mazzini, Garibaldi, Saffi, and Cavour, have not taken root in Italy because of "inherent defects in the Italian character"; there is no mutual trust, a man is guilty until found innocent. Italian co-ops started on a grand scale with fancy dinners and buildings, but they didn't keep to the first rule of co-ops—no credit.

39. "The Daily and Periodical Press in Italy." Jan. 6, 1887 [Lendinara, Dec. 4]

Jessie here comments on the diminishing press in Italy. With the deaths of their leaders, the radical newspapers died. The influence of the press has gradually declined since there are not enough readers and, with the exception of Vieusseux's Florentine library, no public reading rooms in Italy. She catalogues the former papers: *Roma del Popolo*, a weekly that died with Mazzini; *Emancipatore* and *Dovere*, Mazzinian papers that died with Maurizo Quadrio in 1876; *Lega della Democrazia*, that died with her husband. Surviving papers like *Diritto, Pungalo, Perseveranza, Opinione, Tempo, Nazione, Caffaro, Gazzetta di Torino* are scarcely read or heard of now. Depretis owns *Popolo Romano*; Crispi maintains *Riforma*. The only good paper of today is *Unità Cattolica*, edited by Don Margotto. The periodical *Nuova Antologia* is only a shadow of its former self "despite poems of Carducci, articles of Bonghi, Villari." In the face of this poverty, she personally reads American and English papers with delight.

40. "Carducci." Feb. 3, 1887 [Bologna, Jan. 10]

A tribute to Carducci, calling him the greatest living poet, one who loves Italy more than fame.

41. "The Italian Army—1887." Apr. 28, 1887 [Florence, Mar. 27]

Jessie describes the Italian standing army and its provisions for the draft; the army is organized according to three categories: permanent army; mobile militia; territorial militia. "Grievous is it to think that so large a portion of the population should spend their youth and strength in learning the art of killing; but, all things considered, the methods employed for the formation of the army and keeping it up to the regulation standard are as fair and equal as can be. A standing army is, alas, a costly affair."

42. "The First Pilgrimage to Caprera." June 30, 1887 [Genoa, June 7]

Jessie, traveling with a group of fellow pilgrims on a visit to Caprera, reports that the gardens at Caprera are being despoiled by souvenir hunters in "vandal English fashion." On the steamer to the island, the first- and second-class passengers voted to have a common table with the third class: "That trait of Garibaldian equality was a real bit out of the past." She quotes a sonnet of Carducci translated by an American lady which praises Garibaldi's nature. She recalls the flight of Garibaldi in October, 1867.

43. "The New Italian Premier." Aug. 4, 1887 [Italy, July 13]

An assessment of the career of Crispi, a survivor of the Mazzinian school, who has been constantly devoted to the idea that Italy must be united, and who finally gave his allegiance to monarchy. In 1864 Crispi broke with Mazzini; in 1870, Crispi, Bertani, Cairoli, and the entire Left saved Italy from a pro-French, anti-Prussian alliance and compelled monarchy to enter Rome. [Jessie erred here; this should have been credited to the Right, not the Left. Influential members of the government like Quintino Sella also opposed participation in the war.] Jessie assesses the accomplishments since the Left came into power in 1876: enlarged manhood suffrage; no more forced paper currency; no more grist tax; a decreased salt tax; an army drafted from the citizens, priesthood not excluded. She describes Crispi's program for the future— the projected reform of the Senate, the reform of prefectures or provincial governors, the employment of no civil servants in Parliament. She thinks that it will be a difficult task to effect these reforms and warns that there is many a slip "twixt the cup and the lip." [Jessie did not anticipate Crispi's policy of colonial expansion into Ethiopia.]

44. "Agostino Depretis." Aug. 18, 1887 [Italy, July 30]

Depretis is dead, and Jessie reviews his accomplishments. Cavour had said that Depretis would be a poor leader of men; his judgment proved correct. She writes of the good and bad acts of Depretis while he was in power and adds, "but these evils [demoralized police force, corruption of the moral sense by pressure on prefects, syndics and civil servants] can be remedied by his successors, and the good he did will not be interred with his bones—the reforms he effected will be associated with his name." Actually Jessie underestimated his accomplishment in being able to obtain a stable majority. Though he was not a charismatic leader, his policy of *trasformismo* was successful when measured by facts.

45. *"The Last of the Gozzadini." Sept. 29, 1887 [Italy, Aug. 28]*

Jessie traces the history of the Gozzadini family from 1256 on as a way of paying tribute to Count Gozzadini who had died and his wife, La Nina. Their villa was the resort of young Italian leaders and among their protégés had been the poet Aleardi, and Alberto Mario.

46. *"Italy and the Vatican." Nov. 17, 1887 [Italy, Oct. 25]*

Jessie uses the occasion of the Papal Jubilee to point out that there is no special question about the Vatican to be settled at the present. Instead of paying any attention to the pope, Crispi is meeting with Bismarck and trying to settle some matters related to the German-French question.

47. *"Garibaldi's Memoirs." Feb. 2, 1888 [no by-line]*

Jessie here reviews Garibaldi's just published memoirs, unedited and with only Garibaldi's preface. She suggests that this work ought to be translated and that a factual appendix and some letters should be added. She points out that Garibaldi has made a number of errors concerning Mazzini's career. "As in life so in his records, he never understands or appreciates Mazzini, and, with the fullest intention of being just and generous, falls into numerous errors of fact." Garibaldi, she says, is impartial in his military criticism and his simple narrative of the events of his years of service. She quotes at length from the book to give her readers a flavor of the work. [It is interesting that Jessie immediately set out to secure the editorial privileges of the "authorized translation" of this work that was translated by A. Werner and brought out by Walter Smith and Innes in London in 1889. She wrote a supplement in one volume to this three-volume work. In her preface to the work she commented:

"The biography of Garibaldi has yet to be written in English. There are excellent partial narratives, such as 'Garibaldi and Italian Unity,' by Colonel Chambers; 'The Life and Campaign of Garibaldi in the Two Sicilies,' by Charles Stuart Forbes, Commander, R. N.; 'H. M. S. *Hannibal* at Palermo and Naples,' by Admiral Mundy; 'Personal Recollections about Garibaldi,' by Karl Blind; 'The Red Shirt,' by Alberto Mario; but no complete history. 'The Life of G. Garibaldi,' 'Garibaldi: Recollections of His Public and Private Life,' containing more errors than facts, have been published, but they give no idea of the patriot, or the man Garibaldi, and are untrustworthy in the details of events in which he was one of the chief actors. The time may be at hand when . . . an alliance [between England and Italy] shall become an accomplished fact; then the great English people, whom Garibaldi loved next only to his own, will care to know the truth about him and his legion of heroes. I have not drawn largely on published books, with the exception of Guerzoni's 'Life of G. Garibaldi,' for some manuscripts of the General's to which he had access, and of Chiala's six volumes of Cavour's letters, which have rectified many errors and destroyed many fond beliefs of his friends and foes alike. I have used many unpublished documents, chiefly the 'Bertani Archives,' as they are called in the text. Some thirty years ago, I received from Dr. Bertani a collection of papers, letters, and documents, with a request that I should coordinate them. And throughout the following years, until his death in 1886, fresh contributions arrived, among them all the documents of 1860. When Dr. Bertani died in absolute poverty, he requested me to help two of his friends to sell this collection for the benefit of his widowed sister. This I was enabled to do by making a fourfold catalogue of over 17,000 letters, papers, and documents. These, examined by experienced directors of Archives in Milan, were purchased by the unanimous vote of the Municipal Council for the 'Tempio del Risorgimento' in that city, and 30,000 francs were paid to Bertani's widowed sister. The 'Bertani Archives' will be accessible to the public as soon as the authorities have organized their 'Temple.'" Jessie published her book on Bertani at this time. Her preface to that book had the materials which she had collected close at hand since she was deep in the reconstruction of the history. "Though," she says, "enjoying the high privilege of the friendship of Mazzini, Garibaldi, and the other leaders of the party of action, of which my husband was an active member from his boyhood to his death, I have, as well in my Italian works, 'The Life of Garibaldi,' 'Garibaldi and His Times,' 'The Life of Joseph Mazzini,' 'Agostino Bertani and His Times,' etc., as in the present sketch, relied as little as possible on memory, which is more tenacious of impressions than of facts, and in each successive work have corrected, by the light of new documents, the involuntary errors made in the former. All the letters of Garibaldi (saving those in the 'Bertani Archives') and of Mazzini, which I quote, in the hands of Aurelio Saffi, of the editors of Mazzini's works, of Adriano Lemmi, of other friends, or in my own, and can be shown in the original or photographed when required."]

48. *"Aurelio Saffi."* Apr. 19, 1888 [Bologna, Mar.]

This faithful disciple of Mazzini has spent fifteen years editing the works of his master. The sixteenth volume, just out, deals with Mazzini's last three years. Saffi is the highest example of Italian scholar, booklover, and thinker by nature, revolutionist by force of circumstances, conspirator through necessity. "It is a labor of love and patience, and will, when terminated, stand forth a noble monument to the noblest man that Italy has ever given birth to—as noble a one as any nation on earth can claim for her own." To write this piece, Jessie has recently interviewed Saffi, and she includes some of his current thoughts on the state of affairs, including his distrust of alliances.

49. *"Poets and Cooperatives."* Sept. 13, 1888 [Bay of Spezia, Aug.]

This strange marriage of topics in one article comes about because Jessie has been invited to La Spezia to launch a ship for the workingmen of that port. She has just visited Shelley's Casa Magni and is "writing in the shadow of the ilex and walnut trees under whose dark, massive, intermingled foliage Shelley wrote most of his poems after he left Pisa in 1822 till he suffered the sea change." "It would be difficult to imagine a more perfect poet's home, with the sea which (though tideless), owing to an almost constant ground swell, dashes and foams against its walls—a sea now gray and hoary, now violet or green or blue, oftenest golden, as the sturdy rowers cleave the waves with their oars, and the sun shines down into the clefts." Later on, in a few days, she visits the cooperative societies of Voltri. Her examination of their organization gives her the opportunity to comment on the condition of the workingmen's homes in Italy which are "unfit for human habitation—piggeries, dog-kennels, fowl-houses, not to speak of stables" are often cleaner and less populated. "How, we ask, is cleanliness or morality to be taught or learned? How can a tired workingman be expected to exchange the delights of a pot-house for the din, filth, and confusion of his so-called home?"

50. *"The Italian Fleet."* May 2, 1889 [Leghorn, Apr. 6]

Jessie employs some of her knowledge of the family business as she recounts the history of the Italian fleet and the history of iron shipbuilding in Italy.

51. *"Italy's Allies and the War Scares."* Aug. 22, 1889 [Lendinara, July 27]

There have been many war scares since 1870. The latest follows a season in which crops were devastated by rain, prices rose, able-bodied young men were drafted from farms—even the physically unfit were not safe from being called up. Italy drifted into the Triple Alliance which held false hopes of peace. [Italy joined the Alliance with Austria and Germany on May 20, 1882, to protect herself from France, which had occupied Tunis.] Because she is a member, Italy must maintain a large army which she finances by imposing crippling taxes. Jessie uses extensive evidence from Gladstone's writings about the Italian national debt.

52. *"Michele Amari."* Aug. 29, 1889 [no by-line]

This article is a tribute to Michele Amari, who died the month before. His most famous book, *The Sicilian Vespers*, originally called *A Period of Sicilian History in the XIII Century*, was a "tale of bygone days . . . addressed to the Italian slaves of the Bourbons in 1842. . . . Who can say how many hearts the author of the 'Vespers' had inspired, what swords he had sharpened?"

53. *"The Patrimony of the Poor in Italy."* Feb. 20, 1890 [Mantua, Jan. 26]

Jessie analyzes the pros and cons of a proposed law dealing with the administration of money for the poor left by "pious or remorseful men and women of olden time." She gives a history of poor law reforms and points to the need for further reform. The proposed law stipulates that the state shall have the right to redirect such money according to the changing situation in the recipient's needs, or social changes. The bill has been opposed by the Catholics and the moderate press.

54. "Italy's Burdens Under the Triple Alliance." Apr. 17, 1890 [Mantua, Mar. 28]

[In this article there is a recurrence of a theme that Jessie has long been concerned with.] The economy of Italy is suffering under the burden of its alliance with foreign powers in the Triple Alliance. At a recent labor conference in Berlin, Italy made a plea for a reduction of the burden on labor by a reduction of the standing armies. Because of the demands of the military budget, laws restricting child labor are evaded by deft manufacturers, who are aided by parents who need the money. The *metayer* system is declining; the government is undertaking public works, but this is not bringing prosperity because of the methods of contractors. The country, in short, is in a dismal financial plight.

55. "The Triumph of an Idea." May 8, 1890 [Forlì, Apr. 12, 1890 and Bologna, Apr. 14]

This article sums up the events of Saffi's career, and describes a Workingman's Society memorial ceremony in his honor which she attended in Bologna.

56. "Public Instruction and Starvation in Italy." June 26, 1890 [Italy, June]

This article brings together several thoughts about the times: the Italian population is increasing due to a decline in infant mortality, better care for the young and for unwed mothers, better sanitation and less disease. There is progress in education, especially in the infant schools for children from three to six. There is the possibility of free technical schooling but the children of the poor must leave school to work, or else they will starve. Jessie quotes from Professor Villari who points out that educating the masses without improving their cultural opportunities leads to social revolution. The prisons are filled with the unemployed. Italy is too much engaged in expenditures for foreign conquest in Africa and armed peace. Strikes are being fostered by professional agitators. Finally, Jessie ends the article with a quotation by Carlyle asking for work for men.

57. "Venice and Liberty." Sept. 11, 1890 [Lendinara, Aug.]

This article canvasses the progress in public and private works in Venice and gives an interesting on-the-spot commentary of life in this city. As a port, Venice is in the first category for military defence. Industry is increasing; a cotton factory is manufacturing goods on the *banchina* of Santa Maria, the glass factory at Murano is thriving. The repairs of San Donato cathedral are finished as are the restoration of St. Mark's and the Ducal Palace. In spite of Ruskin's disapproval of the steamers and water omnibuses and trams, Jessie thinks that they "increase" the traffic of the city and "add health and strength to the people." Steamers go to the Lido and special omnibuses carry sick children to the baths. New public health laws have been put into effect; the death rate is diminishing, cholera and smallpox have been "sturdily grappled with," the sources of pellagra are being questioned. Charitable institutions are being reformed.

58. "The Italian Elections." Dec. 11, 1890 [London, Nov. 25]

Jessie analyzes the previous general elections four years ago and compares them with the present one. [During the writing of this article, Jessie is staying in London, where she is surprised at the public excitement over the Gladstone-Parnell leadership. The excitement is "incomprehensible" to one who has been absent from England for thirty years.]

59. "The Housing of the Poor in Naples." Feb. 12, 1891 [London, Jan.]

Jessie [still writing from London] compares the condition of the poor in Naples —which has deteriorated—with the improvements in housing for the poor in London.

60. "Mafia, Camorra, Brigandage—Alias Crime." Apr. 16, 1891 [London, Mar. 28]

Jessie writes about organized crime and secret societies in Italy—the Camorra in

Naples and the Mafia in Sicily. [She had already used this material in an article published in the January issue of the English magazine, *Nineteenth Century*.] In Naples the honest police force instituted by signor Mele was "alas, like many things Garibaldian . . . dispersed and destroyed after the inauguration of the moderate governors and rulers in Naples." After speaking of conditions in Italy, Jessie recounts the narrative of the Italian immigrants in the United States, who although for the most part sober, hard-working people, are plagued by the Mafian crimes of a few objectionable immigrants. She recommends that the New Orleans community, which is having trouble with crime, establish a list of the Italians in the area.

61. "Peace or Death." July 9, 1891 [Italy, June 21]

A general assessment of Italy's position as a nation, and an analysis of the obstacles to progress. Jessie also gives an analysis of the mind of the middle class in Italy—its concern with education and the public budget. She speaks of the popularity of Villari.

62. "The Jews and Italy." July 30, 1891 [Italy, July 15]

Cattaneo was the exponent of the Jewish cause in Europe. In Italy today no distinction is made between Jews and Catholics: the Jews may hold office and marry Catholics in the civil ceremonies that are obligatory in Italy. Jews fought for Garibaldi and they were pioneers for Young Italy. At this time, Russian Jews are being persecuted and Jessie suggests that Russian immigrants in Italy colonize "the fertile, uncultivated territories of the peninsula and the islands." [Once again, she speaks of Italy's fertility!]

63. "Italy on the Sea." Sept. 3, 1891 [Italy, Aug. 15]

A description of the Italian navy.

64. "The Financial Condition of Italy." Oct. 1, 1891 [Sept. 9]

Italy's financial problems can be traced to centralization. Twenty years or more ago the country was in a state similar to England's several centuries ago. Cavour's policy was to borrow and to spend; he passed a mounting debt on to his successors. "In short, Italy in thirty years has done as much for the order, comfort, and decorum of her citizens, and for visitors, as other European nations have done in a hundred. Her poorer classes are miserable enough, but they are better paid, better clothed, and better fed than they were thirty years ago; and if they emigrate in ever-increasing numbers, it is because in the good old days, they were resigned to their misery, and now they are determined to better their own condition if they can, and at any rate to put their children in a condition to do so."

65. "The City of Initiatives." Dec. 3, 1891 [Palermo, Nov. 13]

Jessie describes contemporary Palermo. She finds that the dirt and poverty have been removed to a great extent since she was last there. She also visits Naples and compares it with Palermo.

66. "Italian Wine-Making." Dec. 31, 1891 [Marsala, Dec. 6]

Jessie visits Marsala to examine the wine-making industry. She finds that the three major firms have introduced modern employment practices, and that Marsala is a progressive society with much less drunkenness than in the north.

67. "In Sicilian Sulphur Mines." Jan. 14, 1892 [Caltanissetta, Dec. 12, 1891]

Jessie visits Caltanissetta, Sicily, and deplores the conditions in the Sicilian sulphur mines. Dante himself, she says, could not describe the suffering of the children who work in the mines. Here there is a high rate of delinquency, and strikers demanding better conditions are punished: "Here we want missionaries—a Mazzini, a Lloyd Garrison, Mrs. Fry, Lucretia Mott, the Rochdale pioneers." This could be an "ideal" for the young men who spout at clubs and twaddle in newspapers. . . . The time will come, but now one can only exclaim with wrung heart and harrowed soul, 'How long, oh Italy! how long!' "

68. "The Exhibition of Palermo." Mar. 17, 1892 [Palermo, Feb. 10]

While Jessie is viewing the fair at Palermo, on a return trip to that city, a workingman shows her the work done in the prisons: " 'See,' said a workingman who was taking me over some of the industrial sections, 'how the prison work undersells us. That bed in iron and gilt-bronze is sold at 150 lire; it can't be turned out by an honest craftsman for 250 lire, and so on to the end of the chapter. The prisoners are well housed, fairly fed and clothed; we starve in hovels, often don't get a decent meal a day, are at times a week or more without work, so that the temptation presents itself to commit some crime and to be taken in and cared for.' " Jessie also visits the gallery of Sala dei Ricordi Patria, and is especially interested in a curtain painted with a scene of Garibaldi's campaign.

69. "St. Joseph's Day in Naples." Apr. 14, 1892 [Naples, Mar. 19]

Jessie visits Naples on St. Joseph's Day, and makes the point that the two Josephs—Garibaldi and Mazzini—have worked so well in Naples. She visits an old folks' hospital run by the Sisters of the Poor, and a Froebelian Institute, school for infant strays and waifs. She discourses on the effects, which she has investigated, of the Royal Commissary on housing. "Some evicted poor have been moved to new houses with running water, light, air, and in less than two months had reduced the houses to a state of dirt and mess. The houses were for a better class of workmen and not at all adapted to this class of slummers, and their ironical allusions to the 'three and more charcoal stoves, with nothing to cook over them' are justifiable." Jessie reports a conversation with a "grave Piedmontese" who rebukes her for writing about the miserable conditions of the poor when the very poorest are, during the feast, eating macaroni and drinking wine.

70. "A Treasure Trove." June 9, 1892 [Venetia, May 20]

The letters of the Countess Isabella Albrizzi to Ugo Foscolo, and other letters of this fascinating woman who kept a salon in the early days of the fight for unification, have been published and are interesting to the student of history. Jessie quotes copiously from the contents of the letters.

71. "Letters of Ippolito Pindemonte." Aug. 11, 1892 [Italy, June 25]

This article discourses upon the letters of signor Pindemonte to the Countess Albrizzi, written as he traveled about Europe.

72. "An Extra-Territorial Italian City." Sept. 1, 1892 [Trieste, Aug. 1]

Trieste was granted an independent constitution in 1849 and permitted to become a free port by Austria. The Triestines look upon this as their "greatest treasure." In recent years there has been an increase in pro-Italian feeling in Trieste. Before the pope's temporal power was abolished in Italy, Triestines did not regard annexation to Italy as desirable, but since 1870 feelings have become more intense. Jessie, taking a trip from Venice to Trieste and remaining in Trieste a few days, surveys the institutions—especially the school system, the Poor Fund, and the reformatory for boys. Her article outlines the history of the country. [Trieste was divided between Yugoslavia and Italy on October 5, 1954.]

73. "Crime and Politics in Italy." Nov. 10, 1892 [Italy, Oct. 23]

Jessie analyzes the nature of the two most common crimes in Sicily, kidnapping and animal theft. The prisons are like the Black Hole of Calcutta, with two exceptions which she commends—the women's prison at Messina and the men's at Procida. [She uses the same materials in the Nuova Antologia articles on enforced domiciles on Mediterranean islands.] Men who have committed a series of misdemeanors are exiled up to five years, then returned to their homes subject to police surveillance. They are given one-half lira a day and required to return to their quarters at a certain time. They are not forced to work, and often commit new crimes. Social awakening has not yet come to Italy.

[In connection with this article, there is in the Risorgimento Museum in Milan, a letter on Nation stationery addressed to Madame Mario from W. P. Garrison, Godkin's successor:

I enclose a draft for your letter on Sicily in today's Nation.

We are rejoicing with all our might in the popular overthrow of our worse than Sicilian brigandage—the robbery of the masses by the baron industries of Protection. We have done the unprecedented thing of giving a second term to a President after an interval, and that, too, upon a defeat in the interval. The summits of our Presidential range are now Washington, Lincoln, and Cleveland—emancipation respectively from the yoke of England, of slavery, and of the tariff. It is not to be denied that our leader is much in advance of his party—strictly so-called—to which too often the lines of Petrarch, "Vinse Annibal, e non seppe usar poi/Ben la sua vittoriosa ventura," with its accompanying warning have been applicable.]

74. "The Italian Elections." Dec. 8, 1892 [Italy, Nov. 15]

Jessie reflects that Italy—like America and England—at the time of the elections has a government in which the champions of liberty, economical and political, have won the day. Giolitti's program will be a modification of Crispi's and will contain plans for reform which have been neglected or modified by Rudini. The program provides for the reform of charitable institutions, communal laws, old-age pensions, cooperative societies, and for internal colonization. It proposes no fresh taxation. It anticipates no change in the Triple Alliance; at the same time relations with France are much better under this new regime, than they were four years ago. [This refers to the conflict with France over her occupation of Tunis during Crispi's administration.]

75. "Bank Troubles in Italy." Feb. 9, 1893 [Italy, Jan. 22]

Jessie, referring her readers to her previous articles on Italian banking, explains the history of the nation's banking troubles. This background buttresses her discussion of the present bank scandal, in which a respected Neapolitan banker named Cuciniello decamped with two and one-half million lire. [The Bank Scandal was an important issue because it involved the government. A published report in January, 1893 revealed a deficit in cash, great numbers of bad debts, and many corruptions. Giolitti's Bank Act of August, 1893 introduced necessary reforms. Sonnino in 1894 and 1895 continued them.]

76. "The Italian Bank Scandal." Mar. 9, 1893 [Italy, Feb. 18]

This article suggests that the present time is the gloomiest period in Italian history since the "Borgian times" of the tobacco scandals. It is a "bitter winter" and the government, about which she was enthusiastic a few months ago, is losing its appeal.

77. "Carducci and His Critics." July 6, 1893 [Bologna, June 16]

Carducci has been called the poet laureate of Italy, but this is incorrect because his pen is not used to flatter.

78. "A True Realist." Oct. 7, 1893 [Italy, Sept.]

Verga's works on Sicily are true stories of Sicilian life. Jessie praises them for being absolutely faithful to reality: "All Verga's stories are sad, for life is so at this close of the nineteenth century. It is so especially in Italy, where the people are awakened to a sense of their suffering, of their misery, of the injustice that prevents them from bettering their condition." Verga takes no stand on the life he sees; he merely tries to represent the reality as it is.

79. "The Social Unrest In Sicily." Nov. 9, 1893 [Italy, Oct. 15]

Jessie suggests why the outlook for Sicily is becoming gloomier. Italy is severely in need of great statesmen. *Fascidei Lavori* have been formed and now have over 300,000 members. The leaders are collectivists or socialists who urge the peasants to vote, pressing on them the need for better wages, profit sharing cooperative societies, minimum wages, and revision of agricultural contracts. Female *fasci* have also been formed, Jessie adds that there is no truth to the rumor that Sicily is thinking of seceding from the Continent.

80. "The Dry Rot in Italy." Dec. 21, 1893 [Italy, Dec. 3]

Jessie agrees with an article by Professor Villari in *Nuova Antologia* which maintains that Italy is drifting. The moral excellence of the nation is at stake. The banking scandal has exposed the absence of statesmanship; the present government is corrupted.

81. "Habemus Pontificem." Jan. 4, 1894 [Italy, Dec. 16, 1893]

Crispi has been chosen by the king to become minister because Zanardelli could not form a ministry. The greatest difficulty for Crispi is to pacify Sicily, where there have been serious rebellions. Crispi must restore the people to the land and the land to the people; there must be an inspection of municipal administration. [The title refers to Crispi "at the helm."]

82. *"Martial Law in Sicily." Jan. 25, 1894 [Italy, Jan. 11]*

Sicily is in a state of siege and under martial law. Crispi must figure out how to alleviate the unbearable conditions in this area.

83. *"The Trade Between Sicily and the United States." Mar. 22, 1894 [Italy, Mar. 4]*

The amount of sulphur which the United States imports from Italy has declined owing to the increased cost of extracting sulphur. Furthermore, ten years ago, the price of green citrus fruits imported to the U.S. was high and it was a profitable business; today, although importation to America has not decreased, prices have fallen off because of the competition of Florida and California oranges, and the careless packing of fruit by middlemen which causes much of it to be spoiled.

84. *"Italy at the Cross-Roads." Apr. 19, 1894 [Italy, Mar.]*

Jessie confirms her earlier pessimistic reports about Sicily with the review of three books on the state of Italy.

85. *"Protectionism and Socialism in Italy." May 24, 1894 [Italy, May]*

Jessie speaks briefly of the new review *La Riforma Sociale*. It may be a good organ, but its theories are not new: Cavour, Mazzini, and Cattaneo had already laid the groundwork for the theories about the function of the state in social matters. Turning then to a discussion of protectionism, Jessie agrees with signor Nitti that protectionism is the result of class selfishness rather than a basic economic principle. Cavour was a free trader; Mazzini thought protection was absurd, unjust, and evil; Cattaneo also favored free trade. Mazzini did not want free trade carried to the limits, but rather wanted Italian workmen to become capitalists.

86. *"Lake Garda and Lake Iseo." Oct. 11, 1894 [Castiglione delle Stiviere, Sept. 15]*

This piece describes a sentimental journey to places Jessie had known several decades earlier. "Recalling those good old days, the three hours' drive passed all too quickly; and alighting at the Albergo d'Italia, where we used to halt with the wounded before taking them to the hospital, it seemed indeed impossible that thirty-five and twenty-four years had come and gone since the last battles to oust the foreigners were fought and won."

87. *"Carducci at San Marino." Oct. 25, 1894 [Mount Titan, Sept. 30]*

Carducci's speech at the inauguration of the town hall of San Marino indicates that, like Mazzini, he is "a believer, not a Christian." He believes in the divine idea, the unseen, the eternal.

88. *"The Last Letters of Baron Ricasoli." Dec. 20, 1894 [Italy, Nov.]*

Ricasoli's letters, which have now been edited, taken together with the six volumes of Cavour's letters, allow the history student to obtain insight into the men who set up a solid foundation for Italian unity.

89. *"Italy in Africa." Mar. 7, 1895 [Mantua, Feb. 11]*

Governor Baratieri at the moment is doing a good job in Africa. In 1890 there were military disorganization, a want of roads, wasteful expenditure. Since 1891, there has been a great change in Italy's "moral and material methods" because of this governor's policy. "How Italy drifted into Africa is now a matter of history; that she means to remain there . . . with or without the consent of the Abyssinians, is a stubborn fact."

90. *"A Grand Old Man." Apr. 4, 1895 [Mantua, Mar. 16]*

Cesare Cantù has died, and this is a great loss, for he contributed vastly to the intellectual progress of Italy. For as long as possible he advocated a federal republican movement with the pope as head of the government.

91. "On the Eve of the Italian Elections." June 6, 1894 [Italy, May 15]

This article is generally unfavorable to Crispi. It discusses the proposed trial of Giolitti precipitated by Crispi, and the inadequacies of Crispi's handling of voting procedures behind the scenes. [The *Nation* (11 July 1895) contained an angry response from a correspondent "W," with a rebuttal to Jessie's article. "Nothing could be more curiously indicative of the demoralization which political passion has produced in Italian affairs than the letter of 'J. W. M.' in the *Nation* of June 6, and the writer's evident blindness to the conclusion which must be drawn as to the hopeless degradation of Italian politics." Almost ungovernable license and the plotting of the social revolution, thinks W, make Crispi the only man who can restore order. W thinks Jessie has entirely misjudged Crispi. He is privy to information which voids her analysis, and so he gives a completely different insight into the man. "W" is W. J. Stillman, *London Times* Italian correspondent, and a very close friend of Crispi.]

92. "Carducci—Tasso—Ferrara." June 27, 1895 [Bologna, June]

Jessie reviews Carducci's *Ode to the City of Ferrara*, a history of that city. Tasso is represented as a man driven mad by the "moral and material terrors of the Vatican." Carducci writes from the conviction that "only to the greed and foulness of the Papacy, the constant summons of foreigners by the Popes, are due Italy's three hundred years of slavery and degradation."

93. "Mazzini's Love Story." Aug. 1, 1895 [Italy, July 14]

Jessie denies a claim in the *Nineteenth Century* (May) that Mazzini was in love with a seventeen-year-old Swiss, "Magdalen," but affirms his love for Giuditta Sidolo, an Italian patriot with children, with whom he lived in Turin for a while in 1857. Mazzini wrote her a letter just before her death in 1871 praising her saintly conduct.

94. "Carducci's Readings from the Italian Renaissance." Nov. 21, 1895 [Italy, Nov. 6]

A review of Carducci's three-volume writings, including a review of the contents of each volume.

95. "A Doomsday Book Doomed." Jan. 2, 1896 [Italy, Dec. 11, 1895]

Jessie here studies the history of the *catasto*, the land survey. Sonnino, minister of the treasury, has announced that the *catasto* must stop because it is too expensive. Jessie gives various suggestions as to how to tax land without this survey. Then she appraises the general state of affairs in Italy—it is "holding its own." She is disinclined to reexamine old grievances or decayed scandals, but she feels that there is only a languid interest in the social reforms proposed for Sicily. Italy is proceeding sensibly in Africa; and, she approves of the ecclesiastical policy of the government, which is keeping the pope from infringing on civil power.

96. "The Thirty-Fifth Anniversary of Carducci's Professorship." Feb. 27, 1896 [Bologna, Feb. 9]

Jessie calls for special notice of the services of Carducci, who is not merely a genius of a poet, but more especially a "professor who has educated several generations in the worship of intellectual greatness and civic virtue." The king and his former students have honored him.

97. "Italy's Humiliation and Prowess in Africa." Apr. 9, 1896 [Italy, Mar. 19]

This article assesses the complicated situation in Africa. [Lately the Jingoes have criticized Italy's foreign policy, saying that "every nation of Europe had obtained something and Italy nothing." These murmurings went against the spirit of the unification which had concentrated on peace within the country and not been concerned with expansion. Once France took Tunis, however, Italy could not help drifting into Africa. After the fall of Crispi's first ministry, the Rudinì-Nicotera ministry opposed the military occupation of Africa, but did not propose withdrawal from the Eritrean colony. They reduced the African budget. General Oreste Baratieri, the governor, obeyed the non-expansion instructions. Italy in 1895 had trouble with Tigré and Agame, immense provinces of Abyssinia belonging to Menelik, but armed by Italy. Should Italy give up these provinces or hold them was the question. "You must bear in mind the state of Italy during these months—the galleys, the prisons full of political offenders; every day fresh suspects sent by the exceptional tribunal to *domicilio coatto*, amid protests and menaces from their friends and champions, the banking scandals smothered, but resuscitating the most violent indignation and clamor throughout the country, and in the House a nominal majority for the Government of four-fifths of the Deputies. The financial difficulties, too, must not be forgotten, nor now nor hereafter would it be just to forget that, but for this African episode, Sonnino would have succeeded in laying the foundations for a budgetary equilibrium in a not far distant future. To have asked the House for supplies for expansion in Africa would have been suicide for the ministry when you consider the frightful state of taxation, the misery of the populations, the increasing emigration, the fact that there is a tax on wheat of 7 lire per quintal, that salt is 40 centiares per kilo, that commerce is stagnant and industry gagged at every point." The Rudinì-Nicotera government decided not to expand in Africa, but a kind of creeping expansion took place anyhow involving the country in protecting the old and new in Africa. Money had to be voted to relieve the war. A disaster followed and between seven thousand and ten thousand soldiers were lost. The news plunged Italy into a convulsion. Then the king accepted the resignation of the Crispi ministry and Rudinì was to succeed him. This produced comparative calm. "Now the new Ministry is composed of the staunchest opponents of African extension."

98. "Social Regeneration in Italy." May 7, 1896 [Italy, Apr. 16]

This article once more takes up the problems of Sicily, especially its economic distress and competition with other nations for exports. Jessie records that while some administrative changes are helping tax adjustment and are improving transportation, nothing has been done to reform the land laws. Jessie says that she writes about Sicily not because it is the most miserable part of Italy but rather because "those islanders do not choose to suffer in silence and therefore force their grievances and their demands for redress on the public."

99. "An Impenitent Republican." June 4, 1896 [Italy, May 16]

The grand old hero, Enrico Cernuschi, who was the arm as Cattaneo was the head, of that first great uprising of March 1848, is dead. He was made the object of vituperation by the supporters of the government during the elections of 1890 because he gave money to republican associations for their propaganda and candidates. He paid an editor to publish Cattaneo's writings.

100. "The Triumphs of Leo XIII." July 2, 1896 [Italy, June 10]

Leo has been pope for over eighteen years now (since 1878) and is the most talked of and most respected person in Europe, a fact which appeals to Italian national vanity. Jessie speaks of some of the matters that have come up for consideration and action in his time; the question of education by church or state, the revival of feasts and festivals, the war against the Freemasons, the negotiations to return the Anglican church to the Holy Mother church, the demands for the Africans to restore Italian prisoners. [The pope's encyclical *Rerum novarum* condemned socialism and liberalism and instead opposed the class conflict implicit in socialism and the competition implicit in liberalism. It proposed the collaboration of classes. This was a very important nucleus of the doctrine of the Catholic political movement after 1912.]

101. "Italy and France in 1870." July 9, 1896 [no by-line]

A review of a new book, *Souvenirs Militaires, 1866-70*, by General Lebrun in which he criticizes Italy for breaking a pledge to aid France in the war on Prussia. Lebrun says Victor Emmanuel had said he would encourage an alliance between France and Italy on the condition that French troops would leave papal territory, but pursued a foreign policy contrary to that of his ministry. Jessie assesses this theory in light of what actually happened.

102. "The First Act of Social Justice to Sicily." Aug. 6, 1896 [Italy, July 13]

Report of a debate in the House of Parliament on the bill appointing a civil commissioner in Sicily.

103. *"The Marriage of the Crown Prince of Italy."* Oct. 29, 1896 [Italy, Oct. 7]

A report on the projected marriage between the crown prince of Italy and the daughter of the prince of Montenegro.

104. *"Italy and Crete."* Mar. 11, 1897 [Italy, Feb. 20]

Italy must support the efforts of Crete to reject the Turks and rejoin Greece. The article summarizes history of the relations between Italy and Crete.

105. *"More Readings from the Italian Renaissance."* Apr. 22, 1897 [Italy, Mar. 31]

A review of the second volume of Carducci's readings in the history of the Italian Renaissance.

106. *"Crime and Misery."* June 24, 1897 [Italy, May 31]

"It is sad to realize that, after five and thirty years of national life, these two words crime, misery sum up the history of Italy." This article discusses the characteristics of crime and the handling of criminals. Crimes in Italy are committed by people who come from towns or families which have been criminal for generations. Pietro Acciarito, who tried to kill King Humbert, is from such a town. His father had warned the police that he was dangerous and they paid no heed. Now the public is censuring the police, so they are arresting scores of young men and accusing them without cause of being anarchists. They beat them ruthlessly. Some crimes are committed by public officials. Such crimes surpassed the "crimes committed by the populace against the security of the state" by thirteen to one during the years 1890-1894. The enforcement of sentences and trying of prisoners is very carelessly handled in Italy. Three-quarters of the condemned prisoners do not undergo sentencing in the way that is prescribed by the law. Jessie points out that police reforms must be accompanied by the end of hunger. She refers her readers to the discussion of the "Law for patrimony" reform that she has already written about in 1890.

[In the December 23, 1897 issue of the *Nation*, the editors record the receipt of two pamphlets from Jessie Mario which deserve the attention of students of social questions. One is *Il sistema penitenzario e il domicilio coatto in Italia*, which speaks of the inhumanity of prisons. In this pamphlet Jessie compares the penal systems in Italy, France, Belgium, England, and the United States. She suggests that criminals be sent out to reclaim the land. The second pamphlet is entitled *Le opere pie e l'infanticidio legale*. In it she suggests that the care of foundlings be taken away from the pious fraternities and given to disinterested philanthropists. She ends by saying that the women who, in the Red Cross societies, prepare to help the wounded in battles which may never be fought ought to make war on this slaughter of the innocents (in Italy, foundlings are called *innocenti*).]

107. *"Mazzini's Early Letters, 1834-1840."* Feb. 24, 1898 [Florence, Feb.]

Reviews of two new volumes of letters of the Ruffinis and Gaspare Rosales.

108. *"Felice Cavallotti."* Mar. 31, 1898 [Florence, Mar. 26]

Cavallotti [a leading figure in the Italian Radical party] was killed in a duel. Jessie hopes duels will be completely done away with. He was the last survivor of the Garibaldian legend.

109. *"The Riots in Italy."* May 26, 1898 [Florence, May 7]

Jessie describes the riots in heretofore peaceful Tuscany and attributes them to the rise in the price of bread. [In the May 19, 1898 *Nation*, E. L. Godkin wrote an unsigned article entitled "The Italian Trouble," in which he asserted that the "wheat" riots are really a long-planned insurrection. Class hatred is showing up in Italy for the first time. Thus, he seems not to accept Jessie's argument that the riots are a temporary phenomenon. At the same time W. J. Stillman, writing from Rome, says: "The present trouble in Italy should not be taken as an indication of the poverty of the country, or of a general distress due to class-poverty inducing real suffering more than that which is found at all times in any population where public resources are ill-administered." In other years, he says, when the price of grain was much higher there has been perfect quiet, and the proof that the present disturbances are not due either to the want of bread or want of work is that they are the most grave where there is the least want of either. [Thus Jessie presented a controversial opinion here. It is remarkable that JWM says nothing of the far more serious riots in Milan (*I fatti di maggio*, May 6-9, 1898). True, her article is dated Florence, May 7, but no reference is made in subsequent articles to the *fatti*.]

110. "Carducci's Leopardi." Sept. 15, 1898 [Pisa Marina, Aug.]

A review of Leopardi's *Literary and Philosophical Thoughts*, as edited by Carducci. Jessie states that Leopardi foresaw the necessity of moral, material, and intellectual as well as political regeneration for Italy.

111. "One Letter More From Robert." Mar. 23, 1899 [Florence, Mar. 2]

In reference to the publication of Browning's letters, Jessie quotes a letter from Robert to Mrs. Anna Jameson [a prolific writer on art history]. The main tenor of Jessie's discussion is that the Brownings, especially Robert, had a great antipathy to the publication of their letters and up until the present moment this has been largely respected. Now that a volume of letters has been published, she will reveal a heretofore unpublished letter which shows the wonderfully warm relationship between Robert and Elizabeth. But the Brownings are probably turning over in their graves. At the end of this article Jessie adds that Mrs. MacPherson, Mrs. Jameson's niece, spent the last year of her life in Rome with the Marios. Mrs. MacPherson was Jessie's secretary at this point and died in Jessie's arms on 24 June 1878. She had just completed a biography of her aunt, Mrs. Jameson, and was disappointed that Mr. Browning would not allow her to publish his wife's letters to Mrs. Jameson. "She gave them to me, with his, and this is the first one to come to light."

112. "Carducci's Petrarch." Apr. 6, 1899 [Florence, Mar. 16]

The history of the commentators of Petrarch is included in this edition of *Rime*, published by Carducci and his disciple, Severino Ferrari.

113. "Micromaniacs and Megalomaniacs." May 11, 1899 [Florence, Apr. 20]

Jessie takes her key from a recent speech on Sicily given by Crispi, the "last of the old guard who united Italy." Jessie felt that the audience had no sympathy for Crispi, as he insisted that micromaniacs were undermining Italy by not setting her on the path of greatness as he, who had often been accused of being a megalomaniac, had tried to do. Crispi was through: "That mirage faded at Abba Carima [in Africa]; since then the nation has sat down to count its dead, to bemoan the 400 millions squandered in Africa, which signify insupportable taxation, its next to impossible reduction, squalor, discontent, rebellion at home, the emigration of the sturdiest, ablest, and most needed citizens from a country which denied them work or bread." Jessie herself seems to have no sympathy for Crispi.

114. "The Villari Testimonial." Dec. 7, 1899 [Florence, Nov. 17]

Jessie covers a ceremony honoring Villari, a figure familiar to the *Nation* readers, for all his good works.

115. "Charles Albert—Legend and History." Apr. 5, 1900 [Florence, Mar. 14]

While reading documents which Cantù, custodian of Mazzini's archives, gave her to help her in her writing of the life of Mazzini, Jessie discovered documents to show that the legend of calling the tragic king Carlo Alberto a traitor was untrue. This legend originated in a *History of the Piedmontese Revolution* written by Carlo Alberto's war minister, Santarosa.

116. "Carducci's Muratori." May 31, 1900 [Florence, May 6]

A review of Carducci's new edition of the eighteenth-century scholar's *Rerum Italicarum*. She dwells at length on Muratori's original ideas in bringing together the medieval materials of humanism, rather than on the particular characteristics of Carducci's work. She quotes lavishly from Carducci's preface, on which she has leaned heavily in her assessment of the book.

117. "Sunset or Dawn." Oct. 18, 1900 [Florence, Sept. 24]

At the turn of the century, Jessie seems in a state of deep pessimism. She reports in this article about the congress of socialists and the congress of clerics in Rome. By their behavior at the death of King Humbert, she thinks, the clerics have done a great deal to revive old grievances and open new wounds. She proceeds to an analysis of the recent elections and the growth of the socialist party. "That which is called scientific socialism" spread in eight years but few believe, she says, in extreme socialism. She thinks socialism is merely a continuation and repetition of Mazzini's program. Her main objection to the socialists is that they have broken up the workingmen's societies and the class harmony preached by patriots. In addition to these two major sources of conflict and irritation at the present moment, the government for two years has been "illegal"—the voters have not been educated to the use of the vote; the government is rife with bribery and corruption. She hopes that "the darkest hour that precedes the dawn" has passed.

118. "Malta and the Question of Language." Dec. 20, 1900 [Florence, Nov. 25]

Jessie blames Mr. Chamberlain, the British colonial secretary in Malta, for making the language question the burning one in Malta. She discusses relations between England and Malta and the problems of making either English or Italian the official language.

119. "Verdi the Patriot." Mar. 31, 1901 [Florence, Feb. 28]

Verdi, the "last genius of [Italy's] renaissance" is dead. As much as Mazzini and Garibaldi he contributed to inspire the people with the will to be a nation, and the belief that their will would triumph.

120. "Unpublished Letters of Mazzini and Kossuth." Apr. 11, 1901 [Florence, Mar.]

Jessie comments that these newly issued letters of Mazzini and his fellow workers, despite their "monotonous reiteration of the duty of action, the necessity of a war fund, the formation of plans destined to certain success" are interesting; she quotes letters from Kossuth, the Hungarian revolutionary, to Mazzini, and Mazzini to Nicola Ferrai.

121. "Giosuè Carducci." May 16, 1901 [Florence, Apr. 21]

A review of the *Reminiscences and Critical Essays* by Giuseppe Chiarini, a friend of Carducci. [In the January 3, 1901 issue of the *Nation*, W. R. Thayer makes special mention of Jessie White Mario's splendid new volume of writings of Mazzini, *Scritti scelti di Giuseppe Mazzini*, which has been brought out for the series of Italian classics of which Professor Carducci is the general editor. Into these four-hundred pages Jessie has put the best of Mazzini. "No other living person is so well qualified as she to do this work; for she not only knew Mazzini intimately and plotted with him, in the days of conspiracy, but she also knew thoroughly the conditions amid which he lived in England, and the acquaintances and friends with whom he passed more than half his life there." Jessie has written for this book an introduction of more than sixty pages in which she surveys rapidly Mazzini's life down to 1847 and prints passages from letters and memoirs, some of which have not hitherto been made public. "The briefer notices with which she introduces the selections are also full of important information.]

122. "Carlo Cattaneo." July 18, 1901 [Florence, June 23]

A monument to Cattaneo has been dedicated in Milan on the centenary of his birth. She speaks of the difficulty she has had in finding publishers for Cattaneo's works. Professor Pulle vindicated Cattaneo's right to be considered the discoverer of certain truths in almost all branches of science. Cattaneo, indeed, laid the cornerstones for anthropological, geographical, and sociological geography. Jessie suspects that Cattaneo would not be satisfied with today's Italy.

123. "Cesare Abba's Von Quarto zum Volturno." July 25, 1901 [no by-line]

A book entitled *Von Quarto zum Volturno*, by Cesare Abba, has just been translated from Italian into German. It is the chronicle of the Garibaldian expedition.

124. "Crispi." Aug. 29, 1901 [Romola, Aug. 13]

"The last, not the least, of the makers of Italy has left us." We can't deny his faults now that he is dead "any more than we did when his staunch, enthusiastic, thoroughly honest champion, W. J. Stillman . . . challenged our right to judge this 'greatest of all Italians in modern times.'" If Crispi had died after the second ministry of August 1887-March 1889 he would have been in better repute. [Jessie's comment in this article that Italy, of late, seems a cemetery, is a reflection of her own age and the fact that she had outlived most of the figures of the Risorgimento.]

125. "Tuscan Town and Country." Nov. 14, 1901 [Florence, Oct. 15]

Commenting on a letter about socialism in a recent issue of the *Nation* Jessie writes "[I] was glad to see that the writer is not one of the timid crew who thinks that a country must be going to the dogs because of a few strikes, where the masters and workmen are allowed to settle things between themselves without any interference on the part of the government. Had this system been adopted in 1880, when strikes became fashionable in Italy, very possibly, in this new century, we should not have heard of any more." Jessie further describes the recent bakers' strike—agitation for the abolition of night work and changes in the method and time of pay—and describes how the strike was peacefully resolved without the police. She adds to this letter from Castello di Gabbiano on October 17, saying that the peasants in Tuscany are presently happy since there is an unparalleled wine crop and the *metayer* system is working well. She predicts, however, that socialism will come.

126. "The Naples Tammany Overthrow." Jan. 23, 1902 [Rome, Dec.]

[In many ways, this is one of Jessie's most solid and representative articles.] Here Jessie deals with the current conditions of the city of Naples in an historical context, attempting to make her American readers feel comfortable with the details by introducing the idea that the corruption in Naples has been like the corruption in Tammany Hall in New York. She begins with the Royal Decree of November 8, 1900 which set up a commission to investigate conditions in the city of Naples. She confesses to having felt somewhat incredulous about this decree, given the stultification and decline of effective government action in this city for forty years. Things had been going from bad to worse culminating in the rule of King Camorra [a secret society] which would be not unknown to those acquainted with Tammany Hall. Under Humbert, King Camorra was the "uncontested, uncontestable, inviolable monarch of Naples and the provinces." She comments that *Nation* readers should be familiar with the misery of Naples from Villari's letters from the southern provinces as well as from her own letters: "Nor has your present correspondent failed to expose the situation, which could not be exaggerated, either in itself or in its fatal consequences to the entire life of Italy, even as cancer taints the whole system, poisoning its very heart's blood." She then reviews the reign of terror in Naples from 1793 to 1860, giving detailed information about Naples under the Bourbons. Garibaldi and Bertani set to work to reorganize the police, abolish the secret service fund, establish twelve infant schools in the twelve quarters of the city, establish a military college for the sons of the poor, abolish the lotteries, introduce a system of savings banks, sequester ecclesiastical property, introduce sanitation—in fact, to implement all of those changes which a progressive government should entertain. Cavour was always occupied by the Neapolitan problem. "But June, 1861 deprived Italy of the great statesman, and his successors managed in a very short space of time to efface every trace of Garibaldi's efforts and of Cavour's good intentions."

She goes on to say that her readers' experience of Tammany Hall proceedings can give but a faint idea of the state of Naples at the death of King Humbert. Just before the Royal Commission was decreed, *La Propaganda*, a socialist newspaper in Naples, attacked on "the front, rear, and flank the communal administration personified in the Syndic Summonte." Deputy Casale, who was in the pay of this syndic, was attacked by the paper and he brought suit for libel. The public minister soon discovered, however, that Casale was completely corrupt. He was given a severe sentence and deprived of all his public responsibility. The commission report, eighteen hundred pages long, subsequently shows the growing corruption in Naples from 1876 to the present. "The details are all too nauseous to continue." A subsequent general election has proved that the hold of Camorra is loosened—the Camorra candidate has failed. Zanadarelli, the prime minister, on December 13 pledged the government and the nation to use every effort for the redemption of the southern provinces at any cost or sacrifice—not by "violent, spasmodic measures, but by a gradual system of necessary public works." Meanwhile, the investigation of charitable institutions and of provincial administration is to be carried out without delay: "Italy on the whole is looking up. Her finances have never been in such flourishing condition as at the present moment. . . . It was a fitting moment for this moral inquiry to be set on foot at the moment of her ascertainment to a certain amount of hopefulness, but, it is accompanied by a much larger portion of fear and trembling."

127. "The Railway Strike in Italy." Mar. 27, 1902 [Rome, Mar. 10]

In general, Jessie favors arbitration and peaceful settlement of strikes at the bargaining table. She is therefore unhappy about the plight of the railway men in Italy who do not have the opportunity to negotiate their differences with the railroad companies. She speaks about other strikes in Italy and gives evidence about their settlement.

128. "Giosuè Carducci." May 15, 1902 [Florence, Apr. 16]

Notice of the one-volume edition of Carducci's poems.

129. "The General Strike in Florence." Sept. 25, 1902 [Florence, Sept. 2]

A report on the recent strike threat at the iron and steel works of Pignone. She criticizes the Socialists for not providing funds to support the strike which failed for lack of financial resources.

130. "The Rebuilding of the Campanile," Oct. 16, 1902 [Venice, Sept. 20]

Specifically concerned with the collapse and rebuilding of the Venetian Campanile.

131. "The Roman Strike." May 14, 1903 [Florence, Apr. 24]

Describing the general strike in Rome, Jessie points out that this attempt at a general strike has split the Socialists into two camps. Revolutionists, led by Ferrari, think that there should be strikes in the separate trades. Reformists, led by Turati, think that a general strike is useful to protest political measures, but is inexpedient as an economic weapon. They are opposed to "unorganized, sudden, unjustified strikes in the several trades," the Socialist stand at the Congress of Imola. Italy has many strikes; England, practically none. Clearly every country and every class, says Jessie, must buy its own experience.

132. "Mazzini Redivivus." July 2, 1903 [Florence, May 26]

A controversy is now going in Italy about the use of Mazzini's *Duties of Man* in the public schools. The Republicans object to the use of this work because it is "too theological, too dogmatic, too mystical." The Catholics object on principle; the Socialists' venom and calumny exceed all. Jessie also points out that the second volume of Mazzini's correspondence is going to be published. She gives an account of the events that the correspondence chronicles.

133. "The Italian Socialists." May 12, 1904 [Florence, Apr. 24]

Jessie further analyzes the Italian socialist movement, continuing from her May 14 article. She shows that at the present moment the Reformists are ascendant.

134. "Italy, France, and the Vatican." June 16, 1904 [Florence, May 28]

On the occasion of the visit of French President Loubet to Italy, certain members of the Vatican hierarchy created a fuss about whether visitors should be received in the Quirinal, the pope's former residence. This matter has been settled amicably.

135. "Popular Education in Italy." Aug. 4, 1904 [Florence, July 12]

Jessie tells of the successes and failures of the public school system in Italy. There is still a shocking amount of illiteracy in Italy. The Socialists, Republicans, and Radicals think that the army's expenses should be reduced and that the money saved should be turned over to the schools. "Strange as it is, but Italy clings to the 'idea' of military greatness and glory as did old Rome herself, and until this dream shall vanish, it is useless to strive against it." There is a new meagre school bill up before the people.

136. *"The Great Political Strike in Italy."* Oct. 20, 1904 [Florence, Oct. 2]

Jessie tells of the strikes all over Italy and notes the failure of the strike to accomplish its aim, namely, to have the ministry dismissed, the chambers dissolved, the general election called.

137. *"The General Elections in Italy."* Nov. 10, 1904 [Florence, Oct. 19-22]

Discussion of new alignments in the general election which is taking place because Parliament has been dissolved by royal decree [see article 138].

137. *Continued* Dec. 8, 1904 [Florence, Nov. 14]

Jessie presents an analysis of the recent election. The Giolitti ministry won the most votes but some unusual elements entered into the struggle. There was "participation of the real proletary *in propria persona*, without recognized leaders, or in despite of their mandates; . . . the open, acknowledged, numerous affluence of clerical citizens and parties at the urns." She speaks about the divisions between the Conservatives and the Socialists. Then she traces the course of church-state relations during the last three pontificates: under Pius IX each was the other's arch enemy; under Leo XIII, the church tried hard to woo France to intervene in Italian affairs; under Pius X, the situation has changed again in that, although he has not officially abolished the ban against Catholics running for office and voting he has no real objection to such behavior. [Leo XIII had died August 30, 1903.]

138. *"Italy's Tribute to Carducci."* Feb. 2, 1905 [Florence, Jan. 13]

After describing Carducci's life in detail, Jessie observes that Italy could shower no higher honors on Carducci "had he already joined the mystic realms 'where the immortal are.' "

139. *"Monuments to Crispi."* Feb. 16, 1905 [Florence, Jan. 25]

Crispi was responsible for both good and bad developments in Italy. The good survives him; much of the bad was buried with him. "No present or future statesman will ever dare again to attempt to coerce a whole people, in Italy at least, while the mobocracy also is learning that neither shall they gain by violence." [Perhaps this should be described as Jessie's worst prediction!]

140. *"Parliamentary Decadence in Italy."* Apr. 13, 1905 [Florence, Mar. 22]

Jessie discusses Giolitti's resignation after the fiasco which followed the state's attempt to take over the railway. It was announced that Giolitti resigned because of bad health; but Jessie doubts this. "Italy offers a spectacle that grieves her friends and rejoices her enemies." [Actually Jessie's political judgment was not at its keenest here: Giolitti's resignation was neither wholly nor largely due to the railway fiasco.]

141. *"The Sixteenth Volume of Carducci's Works."* Oct. 12, 1905 [Florence, Sept. 14]

A comprehensive review of the volume.

142. *"The New Italian Ministry."* Mar. 8, 1906 [Florence, Feb. 15]

The last article and probably the last piece of formal writing by Jessie was published the week that she died. In many ways it was typical of her articles. It begins: "Uninteresting as are the details of ministerial changes in Italy, the late crisis has awakened such unusual excitement throughout the country, and is so seriously commented on by the Continental press, that a succinct account may be welcome to the readers of *The Nation*." She proceeds to give a synopsis of Prime Minister Sonnino's first speech to Parliament and comments on how astonishing it is that Sonnino has been made the head of the government in view of his checkered career, which she then describes in detail. With great skill Jessie conveys a sense of the variety of public opinion in Italy at that moment. After discussing the backgrounds of the members of the cabinet, she goes on to speculate as to what they may be expected to accomplish and work for separately and together. Her remarks about Edward Pantano are characteristic of her approach. She shows how he has moved from the position of a rigid Garibaldian to that of a forward-looking political liberal. The article throughout is a combination of fact and comment, well grounded in a knowledge of the political situation.

Anthony, Katharine Susan. *Margaret Fuller: A Psychological Biography*. New York: Harcourt, Brace & Howe, 1920.

Arnould, Arthur. *Béranger, ses amis, ses ennemies et ses critiques*. 2 vols. Paris: Joel Cherbuliez, 1864.

Auchmuty, James Johnston. *Sir Thomas Wyse, 1791-1862: The Life and Career of an Educator and Diplomat*. London: P. S. King & Son, Ltd., 1939.

Baldasseroni, F. *Pasquale Villari: Profilo biografico e bibliografia degli scritti*. Florence: A cura del comitato per le onoranze a P. Villari, 1907.

Barbiera, Raffaello. *La principessa belgiojoso, da memorie mondane inedite o rare e da archivi segriti di stato*. Milan: Fratelli Treves, 1930.

————. *Passioni del Risorgimento*. Milan: Fratelli Treves, 1903.

Barr, Stringfellow. *Mazzini: Portrait of an Exile*. New York: Henry Holt & Co., 1935.

Beales, Derek. *England and Italy, 1859-60*. London: Thomas Nelson & Sons, 1961.

Bell, Margaret. *Margaret Fuller, a Biography*. New York: Charles Boni, Inc., 1930.

Bent, James Theodore. *The Life of Giuseppe Garibaldi*. 2d ed. London: Longmans Green & Co., 1882.

Béranger, Pierre Jean de. *Oeuvres complètes de P.-J. Béranger*. Paris: Perrotin, 1834.

Berti, Giuseppe. *I democratici e l'iniziativa meridionale nel Risorgimento*. Milan: Feltrinelli, 1962.

Bevington, Merle M., ed. *Matthew Arnold's England and the Italian Question*. Durham, North Carolina: Duke University Press, 1953.

Blakiston, Noel. *Sulla scia di Pisacane: un grattacapo per Hudson*. Atti del XXXVI Congresso di Storia del Risorgimento Italiano, n.d.

Boris, Ivan. *Gli 'anni di Garibaldi in sud-america, 1836-1848*. Milan: Longanesi & Co., 1970.

Bourne, H. R. Fox. *English Newspapers: Chapters in the History of Journalism*. 2 vols. London: Chatto & Windus, 1887.

Brand, C. P. "A Bibliography of Travel-Books Describing Italy Published in England 1800-1850." *Italian Studies* 11 (1956): 108-117.

————. *Italy and the English Romantics: The Italianate Fashion in Early Nineteenth-Century England*. Cambridge: Cambridge University Press, 1957.

Bremner, Christina Sinclair. *Education of Girls and Women in Great Britain.* London: Swan Sonnenschein & Co., 1897.

Briguglio, Letterio. "Caratteri del movimento operaio a Venezia dopo l'unità." In vol. 3 *Miscellanea in onore di Roberto Cessi.* pp. 355-375. Rome: 1958.

Browning, Elizabeth Barrett. *Letters to Her Sister, 1846-1859.* London: John Murray, 1929.

Bryce, James Bryce. *Studies in Contemporary Biography.* New York: Macmillan Co., 1903.

Burton, Hester. *Barbara Bodichon, 1827-1891.* London: J. Murray, 1949.

Caraguel, Clement, ed. *Souvénirs et aventures d'un volontaire garibaldien.* Paris: A. Bourdilliat et cie, 1861.

Carducci, Giosuè. *Confessioni e battaglie di Giosuè Carducci.* Bologna: N. Zanichelli, 1902.

Carlyle, Jane Welsh. *Letters to Her Family, 1839-63.* Edited by Leonard Huxley. London: J. Murray, 1924.

Castelar, Emilio. "The Republican Movement in Europe." *Harper's New Monthly Magazine* 45 (1872): 47-60, 215-224, 372-385, 581-592, 722-732, 849-860.

Cattaneo, Carlo. *Dell'insurrezione di Milano nel 1848 e della successiva guerra.* Florence: F. Le Monnier, 1949.

———. *Notizie naturali e civili su la Lombardia.* Milan: G. Bernardoni di Giovanni, 1844.

———. *Opere edite e inedite di Carlo Cattaneo.* Edited by Agostino Bertani. 7 vols. Florence: Le Monnier, 1881-1892.

———. *Scritti economici.* Edited by Alberto Bertolino. Florence: F. Le Monnier, 1956.

———. *Scritti storici e geografici.* Edited by Gaetano Salvemini and Ernesto Sestan. 4 vols. Florence: Le Monnier, 1957.

Cavour, Camillo di, *Nuove lettere inedite.* Turin: n.p., 1895.

Chambers, O. W. S. *Garibaldi and Italian Unity.* London: Smith, Elder & Co., 1864.

Clark, William George. "Naples and Garibaldi." *Vacation Tourists and Notes of Travel in 1860.* Edited by Francis Galton. Cambridge: Macmillan & Co., 1864.

Clough, Arthur Hugh. *The Poems of Arthur Hugh Clough.* Edited by H. F. Lowry, A. L. P. Norrington, and F. L. Mulhauser. Oxford: Clarendon Press, 1951.

———. *Prose Remains: With a Selection from his Letters and a Memoir.* Edited by his wife. London: Macmillan & Co., 1888.

Clough, Shephard B. and Saladino, Salvatore. *A History of Modern Italy; Documents, Readings, & Commentary.* New York: Columbia University Press, 1968.

Cobbe, Frances Power. *Italics: Brief Notes on Politics, People, and Places in Italy, in 1864.* London: Tübner and Co., 1864.

———. *Life of Frances Power Cobbe, as Told by Herself.* London: Sonnenschein & Co., 1904.

Collins, Irene. *Liberalism in Nineteenth-Century Europe.* London: Published for the Historical Association by Routledge and K. Paul, 1957.

Comandini, Alfredo. *L'Italia nei cento anni del secolo XIX, 1801-1900.* Vol. 3 (1850-1860). Milan: Villardi, 1900-1917.

Corbellini, Piero. *Diario di un Garibaldino: della spedizione Medici in Sicilia, 1860.* Edited by Riccardo Gagliardi. Como: Libreria Anti-quaria, 1911.

Croce, Benedetto. *A History of Italy, 1871-1915.* Translated by Cecelia M. Ady. Oxford: The Clarendon Press, 1929.

Curàtulo, Giacomo Emilio. *Garibaldi e le donne, con documenti inediti.* Rome: Imprimerie Polyglotte, 1913.

Daily Chronicle (Newcastle), 1880-1881.

Daily News (London), 1856-1861.

Daily News, (London), *The War Correspondence of the Daily News, 1870.* 2 vols. London: Macmillan & Co., 1871.

Dale, Robert William. *History of English Congregationalism.* Completed and edited by A. W. W. Dale. London: Hodder & Stoughton, 1907.

Daniels, E. A. "Collaboration of Mazzini on an Article in the *Westminster Review.*" *Bulletin of the New York Public Library* 66 (1961): 577-583.

———. "Mazzini e la Vittoria di Meredith." *Rassegna storica del Risorgimento* 49 (1962): 1-22.

Dawson, George. *Biographical Lectures.* Edited by George St. Clair. London: K. Paul, Trench & Co., 1886.

———. Two Lectures on the "Papal Aggression" Controversy. Delivered in the Town Hall, Birmingham, 6, 12 February, 1851. Published in two pamphlets.

———. *Shakespeare and Other Lectures.* Edited by George St. Clair. London: K. Paul Trench & Co., 1888.

dePalnay, Peter. *Garibaldi: The Man and the Legend.* New York: Thomas Nelson & Son, 1961.

Derby and Chesterfield Reporter, Derby. 1856-1857.

Drummond, James. *The Life and Letters of James Martineau.* 2 vols. New York: Dodd, Mead & Co., 1902.

Duncan, William. *Life of Joseph Cowen.* London & Newcastle-upon-Tyne: Walter Scott Publishing Co., 1904.

Eliza Cook's Journal, London. 1849-1854. 12 vols.

Elliot, Frances. *Roman Gossip.* London: John Murray, 1894.

Eliot, George. *The George Eliot Letters.* Edited by Gordon S. Haight. 7 vols. New Haven: Yale University Press, 1954-1955.

Faedella, G. *I Fratelli Ruffini.* Turin: Roux-Frassati, 1895.

Fincham, John. *A History of Naval Architecture.* London: Whittaker & Co., 1851.

Forbes, Archibald. *My Experiences of the War between France and Germany.* 2 vols. London: Hurst and Blackett, 1871.

———. *Souvenirs of Some Continents.* New York: Harper & Bros., 1885.

Forbes, Charles Stuart. *The Campaign of Garibaldi in the Two Sicilies: A Personal Narrative.* London: W. Blackwood & Sons, 1861.

Forgues, P. E. D. "Le Roman Anglais Contemporain." *Revue des Deux Mondes* 64 (1867): 1007-1027.

Fortier, Alcée. *A History of Louisiana.* Vol. 3. *The American Domination.* New York: Goupil & Co. of Paris, 1904.

Foscolo, Ugo. *Poesie: con uno studio di Carlo Cattaneo.* Milan: Istituto editoriale italiano, n.d.

Fratta, Arturo. *Garibaldi, Passioni e battaglie. Collana di cultura Napoletana.* Naples: Fausto Fiorentino, 1960.

Fuller, Margaret [Ossoli]. *The Writings of Margaret Fuller.* Edited by Mason Wade. New York: The Viking Press, 1941.

Gallaupesi, Giuseppe. "British Friends of the Italian Risorgimento." *Contemporary Review* 136 (1929): 354-364.

Garibaldi, Giuseppe. *Cantoni il volontario romanzo storico.* Milan: 1873.

———. *Clelia. Il governo del monaco.* Milan: Fratelli Rechiedei, 1870.

———. *La domination du moine.* Paris: 1873.

———. *The Memoirs of Garibaldi.* Edited by Alexandre Dumas. Translated by R. S. Garnett. London: E. Benn, Ltd., 1931.

———. *The Rule of the Monk: or, Rome in the Nineteenth Century.* 2 vols. London: Cassell, Petter, & Galpin, 1870.

Garrison, Wendell Phillips. *Letters and Memorials of Wendell Phillips Garrison, Literary Editor of "The Nation" 1865-1906.* Cambridge, Mass.: The Riverside Press, 1908.

Gatti, Carlo. *Verdi: The man and his music.* Translated by Elizabeth Abbott. New York: G. P. Putnam's Sons, 1955.

Gay, Harry Nelson. *Scritti sul Risorgimento.* Edited by Tomaso Sillani. Rome: La Rassegna Italiana, 1937.

Gilfillan, George. *Sketches of Modern Literature and Eminent Literary Men.* New York: D. Appleton & Co., 1846.

Gladstone, William Ewart. *Two Letters to the Earl of Aberdeen on the State Prosecutions of the Neapolitan Government.* London: John Murray, 1851.

Gladstone, W. E.; St. Aubyn, G. R.; Rees, Brian. *The Unification of Italy.* Oxford: Basil Blackwell, 1955.

Glasgow Sentinel, 1856.

Gill, Conrad. *History of Birmingham.* 2 vols. London: Published for the Birmingham City Council by Oxford University Press, 1952.

Godkin, Edwin Lawrence. *Life and Letters of Edwin Lawrence Godkin.* Edited by Rollo Ogden. 2 vols. London: Macmillan & Co., Ltd., 1907.

———. *Reflections and Comments: 1865-1895.* New York: Charles Scribners' Sons, 1895.

"Godkin." Obituary *Evening Post* (New York), 21 May 1902.

"Godkin." Obituary *Nation,* 22 May 1902.

"Godkin." Obituary *New York Times,* 22 May 1902.

Great Britain, Foreign Office. *Correspondence Respecting the Affairs of Italy, 1846-1849.* 4 vols. London: Printed by Harrison and Son, [1849?]

Great Britain, *Parliamentary Papers,* Vol. 59 (*Accounts and Papers,* 1857).

Greenfield, Kent Roberts. *Economics and Liberalism in the Risorgimento: A Study of Nationalism in Lombardy, 1814-1848.* Baltimore: The Johns Hopkins Press, 1934.

Grew, Raymond. *A Sterner Plan for Italian Unity.* Princeton: Princeton University Press, 1963.

Griffith, Gwilym Oswald. *Mazzini: Prophet of Modern Europe.* London: Hodder & Stoughton, 1932.

Grimes, Alan Pendleton. *The Political Liberalism of the New York Nation, 1865-1932*. Chapel Hill: University of North Carolina Press, 1953.

Guérard, Albert Leon. *French Civilization in the Nineteenth Century; A Historical Introduction*. New York: Century Co., 1914.

Hales, Edward Elton Young. *Pio Nono, A Study in European Politics and Religion in the Nineteenth Century*. London: Eyre & Spottiswoode, 1954.

———. *James Stansfeld: A Victorian Champion of Sex Equality*. London: Longmans, Green & Co., 1932.

Hammond, John Lawrence. *The Bleak Age*. London: Longmans, Green & Co., 1934.

Hardman, Sir William. *The Hardman Papers: A Further Selection (1865-1868) from the Letters and Memoirs of Sir William Hardman*. Edited by S. M. Ellis. London: Constable & Co., Ltd., 1930.

———. *The Letters and Memoirs of Sir William Hardman*. Second Series, 1863-1865. Edited by S. M. Ellis. New York: H. Doran Co., 1925.

———. *A Mid-Victorian Pepys: The Letters and Memoirs of Sir William Hardman*. Edited by S. M. Ellis. London: Carl Palmer, 1923.

Hearder, Harry. "La cattura del Cagliari, Una Disputa Tripartita fra Napoli, Piemonte e Inghilterra (1857-1858)." Estratto dalla *Rassegna storica del Risorgimento* 48 (April-June, 1960).

———. "Napoleon III's threat to break off Diplomatic Relations with England during the Crisis over the Orsini Attempt in 1858." Reprinted from *EHR*, July 1857.

———. "La Politica di Lord Malmesbury verso L'Italia nella primavera del 1859." Estratto dalla *Rassegna storica del Risorgimento* 43 (Jan.-Mar., 1956).

Hibbert, Christopher. *Garibaldi and His Enemies*. London: Longmans, Green & Co., 1965.

Hinton, R. J. *English radical leaders*. New York: G. P. Putnam's Sons, 1875.

Hohenberg, John. *Foreign Correspondence, The Great Reporters and Their Times*. New York: Columbia University Press, 1964.

Holt, Edgar. *The Making of Italy, 1815-1870*. New York: Atheneum, 1971.

Holt, Raymond V. *The Unitarian Contribution to Social Progress in England*. London: Lindsey Press, 1952.

Holyoake, George Jacob. *Bygones Worth Remembering*. London: T. F. Unwin, 1905.

———. *Sixty Years of an Agitator's Life*. London: T. F. Unwin, 1893.

Hostetter, Richard. *The Italian Socialist Movement*. Princeton: Van Nostrand Co., 1958.

Hughes, Henry Stuart. *The United States and Italy*. Cambridge: Harvard University Press, 1953.

Hutton, R. H. *Essays in Literary Criticism*. Philadelphia: J. H. Coates & Co., 1876.

Istituto Italiano di Cultura di Londra. *Conferenze tenute all'istituto in occasione della mostra sui rapporti anglo-italianá dal 1815 al 1848*. London: Pubblicazione dell'Istituto Italiano di Cultura di Londra, 1954.

189

Jackson, Abraham Willard. *James Martineau: A Biography and Study*. Boston: Little, Brown & Co., 1900.

James, Henry. *William Wetmore Story and His Friends*. 2 vols. Boston: Houghton, Mifflin & Co., 1903.

Jameson, Anna. *Letters and Friendships*. Edited by Beatrice Erskine. New York: E. P. Dutton & Co., 1916.

Jarrin, Jules. *Béranger et son temps*. 2 vols. Paris: Rene Pincebourde, 1866.

Jewsbury, Geraldine. "Vittoria." *Athenaeum* 2052 (1867): 248-49.

"Jessie White Mario." *Nation* 82 (March 15, 1906): 218.

Klein, Viola. *The Feminine Character: History of an Ideology*. London: K. Paul, Trench, Trubner & Co., Ltd., 1946.

King, Bolton. *A History of Italian Unity, being a political history of Italy from 1814 to 1871*. 2 vols. London: J. Nisbet & Co., 1899.

————. *The Life of Mazzini*. New York: E. P. Dutton & Co., 1911.

King, Harriet E. B., *Letters and Recollections of Mazzini*. London: Longmans, Green & Co., 1912.

Lancet (London), July 7-Sept. 1, 1860.

Lang, Elsie M. *British Women in the Twentieth Century*. London: T. W. Laurie, Ltd., 1929.

Langford, John Alfred. "An Examination of the Rev. George Gilfillan's Notice of George Dawson, M. A." 2d ed. London: Simpkin, Marshall & Co., 1850.

————. "George Dawson." London: Simpkin, Marshall & Co. Reprint from *Truth Seeker*, March 1849.

The Leader (London), 1-11 (30 March 1850-30 June 1860).

Leigh Smith, Barbara. *Women and Work*. London: Basworth & Harrison, 1857.

Levi, Alessandro. *Il positivismo politico di Carlo Cattaneo*. Bari: Laterza, 1928.

Linton, William James, ed. *The English Republic*. 4 vols. London: J. Watson, 1851-1855.

————. *European Republicans: Recollections of Mazzini and his Friends*. London: Lawrence & Bullen, 1892.

————. *Memories*. London: Lawrence & Bullen, 1895.

"Lives of the Illustrious." *The Biographical Magazine*, 1852-1855.

Luzio, Alessandro. *Carlo Alberto e Giuseppe Mazzini: studi e ricerche di storia del risorgimento*. Turin: Fratelli Bocca, 1923.

————, ed. *Felice Orsini e Emma Herwegh, Nuovi Documenti*. Florence: Le Monnier, 1937.

McCarthy, Justin. *The "Daily News" Jubilee, A Political and Social Retrospect of Fifty Years of the Queen's Reign*. London: Sampson, Low, Marston & Co., 1896.

————. *Reminiscences*. 2 vols. New York: Harper & Bros., 1899.

Mack Smith, Denis. *Cavour and Garibaldi, 1860: A Study in Political Conflict*. Cambridge, England: Cambridge University Press, 1954.

————. *Garibaldi: Una grande vita in breve*. Milan: Lerici, 1959.

Maison, Émile. *Journal d'un volontaire de Garibaldi*. Paris: Lagnay, 1861.

Mario, Alberto. *Dante e i codici danteschi*. Mantua: V. Guastalla, 1869.

————. "Garibaldi's Invisible Bridge." *Cornhill Magazine* 9 (1864): 537-54.

————. *Il libro dei profeti dell'idea in Italia*. Milan: L. Bartistelli, 1898.

————. *I mille*. Genoa: Regio stabilmento L. Lavagnino, 1876.

———. "Personal Reminiscences of General Garibaldi." *Macmillan's Magazine* 46 (May-October, 1882): 245-56.

———. *The Red Shirt. Episodes.* London: Smith, Elder & Co., 1865.

———. *Scritti.* Edited by Giosuè Carducci. 2 vols. Bologna: N. Zanichelli, 1884.

———. *Scritti letterari i artistici di Alberto Mario.* Edited by Giosuè Carducci, con biografia di J. vedova Mario. 2 vols. Bologna: Nicolas Zanichelli, 1901.

———. *Scritti politici di Alberto Mario.* Edited by Giosuè Carducci. Bologna: N. Zanichelli, 1901.

Marriott, Sir J. A. R. *The Makers of Modern Italy: Napoleon-Mussolini.* Oxford: The Clarendon Press, 1931.

Martinengo-Cesaresco, Evelyn. *Italian Characters.* New York: Charles Scribner's Sons, 1901.

———. *The Liberation of Italy 1815-1870.* London: Seeley & Co., 1902.

Masi, Ernesto. *Il Risorgimento italiano.* Florence: G. C. Sansoni, 1937.

Marraro, Howard R. *American Opinion on the Unification of Italy, 1846-1861.* New York: Columbia University Press, 1932.

Mazzini, Giuseppe. *The Duties of Man.* Translated by Emilia Ashurst Venturi. London: Chapman & Hall, 1862.

———. *Edizione nazionale degli scritti editi ed inediti di Giuseppe Mazzini.* 94 vols. and 6 supp. Imola: Cooperativa P. Galeati, 1906-1948.

———. *Letters to an English Family.* Edited by Mrs. E. F. Richards. 3 vols. London: John Lane, 1920-1922.

———. *The Life and Writings of Joseph Mazzini.* 6 vols., rev. ed. London: Smith, Elder & Co., 1890-1898.

———. *Royalty and Republicanism in Italy: or Notes and Documents Relating to the Lombard Insurrection, and to the Royal War of 1848.* London: C. Gilpin, 1850.

Mead, William Edward. "Italy in English Poetry." *PMLA* 23 (1908): 421-70.

Meredith, George. *Letters.* Edited by C. L. Cline. 3 vols. Oxford: The Clarendon Press, 1970.

———. *Vittoria.* New York: Charles Scribner's Sons, 1910.

Merrill, Walter M. *Against Wind and Tide: A Biography of W. Lloyd Garrison.* Cambridge: Harvard University Press, 1963.

Meteyard, Elizabeth. *The Nine Hours Movement: Industrial and Household Tales.* London: Longmans, Green & Co., 1872.

Mill, John Stuart. *Letters of John Stuart Mill.* Edited by Hugh S. R. Elliott. 2 vols. London: Longmans, Green & Co., 1910.

Montini, Domenico. *Scene e figure del Risorgimento veneto, 1848-1862.* Lapi: Città di Castello, 1913.

Morelli, Emilia. "L'Archivio di Jessie White Mario." Rome: La Libreria della Stato, 1938.

———. *L'Inghilterra di Mazzini.* Rome: Istituto per la storia del Risorgimento Italiano, 1965.

———. *Mazzini in Inghilterra.* Florence: Le Monnier, 1938.

Morning Star and Dial (London), 1861-1869.

Morrell, John Daniel. "Atheism." *National Review* 3 (1856): 97-123.

———. *An Historical and Critical View of the Speculative Philosophy of*

Europe in the Nineteenth Century. New York: Robert Carter & Bros., 1847.

Muirhead, John Henry, ed. *Nine Famous Birmingham Men: Lectures Delivered in the University.* 2d ed. Birmingham: Cornish Bros., Ltd., 1909.

"Muswell Hill, Past and Present, Hornsey Public Libraries." (Pamphlet) 1936.

Nation papers. Cambridge, Mass. Houghton Library, Harvard University.

Newman, Francis William. *Essays, Tracts or Addresses Political and Social.* Vol. 3. *Miscellanies,* London: Kegan Paul, Trench & Co., 1889.

New York Times, 1858-1859.

New York Tribune, 1858-1870.

Nightingale, Florence. *Notes on Nursing: What It Is, and What It Is Not.* New York: D. Appleton & Co., 1860.

Northern Evening Express (Newcastle-upon-Tyne), August 1, 1866-October 16, 1886.

Orsini, Felice. *The Austrian Dungeons in Italy: A Narrative of Fifteen Months' Imprisonment and Final Escape from the Fortress of S. Giorgio.* Translated by J. Meriton White. London: Routledge, Warnes, & Routledge, 1859.

Osbourne, J. E. *Arthur Hugh Clough.* Boston: Houghton Mifflin Co., 1920.

Packe, Michael St. John. *Orsini: The Story of A Conspirator.* Boston: Little, Brown & Co., 1957.

Paisley Herald (Paisley, England), 1857.

Pall Mall Gazette (London), 1880, 1881.

Parkhurst, Richard K. "Saint Simonism in England." *Twentieth Century* 152 (1952): 449-513; 153 (1953): 47-58.

Parris, John. *The Lion of Caprera.* New York: David McKay Co., Inc., 1962.

Perkins, Alice J. G. *Frances Wright, Free Inquirer: The Study of a Temperament.* New York: Harper & Bros., 1939.

Pollak, Gustav, ed. *Fifty Years of American Idealism: The New York Nation, 1865-1915.* Boston: Houghton Mifflin Co., 1915.

Pollard, A. F. "James Stansfeld." *DNB* Supplement, 22. London: Oxford University Press, 1937-1938, pp. 1224-1226.

Pratt, Edwin A. *Pioneer Women in Victoria's Reign.* London: G. Newnes, Ltd., 1897.

Ramm, Agatha. "The Risorgimento." London: Published for the Historical Association by Routledge & Kegan Paul, 1962.

Rhodes, James Ford. "Edwin Lawrence Godkin." *Atlantic Monthly* 102 (1908): 320-334.

Robertson, Priscilla. *Revolutions of 1848, a Social History.* Princeton: Princeton University Press, 1952.

Robinson, Henry Crabb. *Diary, Reminiscences, and Correspondence.* Edited by Thomas Sadler. Boston: Fields, Osgood & Co., 1870.

Ross, Ishbel. *Ladies of the Press: The Story of Women in Journalism by an Insider.* New York: Harper & Bros., 1936.

Rosselli, Nello. *Mazzini e Bakounine: dodici anni di movimento operaio in Italia (1860-1872).* Turin: Fratelli Bocca, 1927.

——. *Saggi sul Risorgimento italiano.* Turin: Einaudi, 1946.

Rossetti, William M. *Some Reminiscences of William Michael Rossetti.* New York: Charles Scribner's Sons, 1906.

Royal British Commission, Chicago Exhibition, 1893. *Women's Mission: A Series of Papers on the Philanthropic Work of Women.* New York: Charles Scribner's Sons, 1893.

Rudman, Harry W. *Italian Nationalism and English Letters; Figures of the Risorgimento and Victorian Men of Letters.* Columbia University Studies in English and Comparative Literature, no. 146. New York: Columbia University Press, 1940.

Ruffini, Giovanni Domenico. *I fratelli Ruffini: Lettere di Giovanni e Agostino Ruffini alla madre, dall'esilio francese e svizzero.* Serie del Risorgimento, Vol. 2. Genoa: Atti della Societa Ligure di Storia Patria, 1925.

Saffi, Aurelio. *Ricordi e scritti.* 14 vols. Florence: pubblicati per cura del Municipio di Forlì, 1898.

Saint Clair, George. "Mr. Dawson's Teaching and Its Tendency." Two Discourses Delivered in the Church of the Saviour, Sunday, August 6, 1882. (Pamphlet) Birmingham, 1882.

———. "Our Lost Leader." A Discourse Preached in the Church of the Saviour, December 17, 1876 on the Occasion of the Death of George Dawson, M. A., Birmingham. (Pamphlet) Birmingham, 1877.

Salvadori, Massimo. *Cavour and the Unification of Italy.* New York: Van Nostrand, Inc., 1961.

Salvatorelli, Luigi. *The Risorgimento, Thought and Action.* Translated by Mario Domandi. New York: Harper & Row, 1970.

Salvemini, Gaetano. *Mazzini.* Translated by I. M. Rawson. London: Jonathan Cape, 1956.

Sand, George. *Correspondence 1812-1876.* 6 vols. Paris: Calmann Levy, 1883-1895.

———. *Letters of a Traveller.* Edited by Matilda M. Hays. Translated by Eliza Ashurst. London: E. Churton, 1847.

———. *The Mosaic Masters: and Fanchette.* Translated by Eliza Ashurst. London: E. Churton, 1847.

———. *The Mosaic Workers; A Tale. To Which is Added The Orco; A Tradition.* Translated by Eliza Ashurst. London, 1844.

Sarderi, G. *La Sicilia et gl'Inglesi.* Rome, 1943.

The Scotsman (Edinburgh), 1850-1860.

Seton-Watson, Christopher. *Italy from Liberalism to Fascism, 1870-1925.* London: Methuen & Co., 1967.

Seymer, Lucy Ridgely, ed. *Selected Writings of Florence Nightingale.* New York: Macmillan Co., 1954.

Sharp, Evelyn. *Hertha Ayrton, 1854-1923, A Memoir.* London: Edward Arnold & Co., 1926.

Shiavo, Giovanni. *The Italians in America Before the Civil War.* New York: Vigo Press, 1934.

Smalley, George W. *Anglo-American Memoirs.* London: Duckworth & Co., 1911.

Spallicci, Aldo. *Alberto Mario.* Milan: Gastaldi, 1957.

Stanton, Elizabeth (Cady); Anthony, Susan B.; Gage, Mathilda Joselyn. *History of Women Suffrage.* Vol. 1. New York: Fowler & Wells, 1881-1922.

Stephen, Barbara (Nightingale). *Emily Davies and Girton College.* London: Constable & Co., Ltd., 1927.

Stern, Madeline B. *The Life of Margaret Fuller.* New York: E. P. Dutton & Co., Inc., 1942.

Stillman, William James. *The Autobiography of a Journalist, William James Stillman.* 2 vols. Boston: Houghton Mifflin Co., 1901.

———. *Francesco Crispi, Insurgent, Exile, Revolutionist and Statesman.* London: Grant Richards, 1899.

———. *The Union of Italy, 1815-1895.* Cambridge: Cambridge University Press, 1898.

Taplin, James. "A Discourse Preached in the Baptist Chapel, King's Norton, On Sunday Evening, December 10th, 1876 on the Occasion of the Lamented Death of George Dawson, M. A., Birmingham, 1877." (Pamphlet).

Thayer, William Roscoe. *The Dawn of Italian Independence, Italy from the Congress of Vienna, 1814, to the Fall of Venice, 1849.* 2 vols. New York: Houghton Mifflin & Co., 1893.

———. *The Life and Times of Cavour.* 2 vols. Boston: Houghton Mifflin Co., 1911.

Times (London), 1850-1870.

Toye, Francis. *Rossini; A Study in Tragi-Comedy.* New York: A. A. Knopf, 1934.

Trevelyan, George Macaulay. *Englishmen and Italians: Some Aspects of Their Relations Past and Present.* Published for the British Academy. London: Oxford University Press, 1919.

———. *Garibaldi and the Making of Italy.* New York: Longmans, Green & Co., 1911.

———. *Garibaldi and the Thousand.* London: Longmans, Green & Co., 1909.

———. *Garibaldi's Defence of the Roman Republic.* New York: Longmans, Green & Co., 1907.

Treves, Guiliana Artom. *The Golden Ring: The Anglo-Florentines, 1847-1862.* Translated by Sylvia Sprigge. London: Longmans, Green & Co., 1956.

Trollope, Theodosio. *Social Aspects of the Italian Revolution.* Reprinted from the *Athenaeum.* London: Chapman & Hall, 1861.

Trollope, Thomas Adolphus. *Diamond cut Diamond, A Story of Tuscan Life.* New York: Harper & Bros., 1883.

———. *Filippo Strozzi: A History of the Last Days of the Old Italian Liberty.* London: Chapman & Hall, 1860.

———. *Gemma. A Novel.* Philadelphia: T. B. Peterson & Bros., 1868.

———. *A History of the Commonwealth of Florence, From the Earliest Independence of the Commune to the Fall of the Republic in 1531.* 4 vols. London: Chapman & Hall, 1865.

———. *A Lenten Journey in Umbria and the Marches.* London: Chapman & Hall, 1862.

———. *The Papal Conclaves, as They Were and as They Are.* London: Chapman & Hall, 1876.

———. *Tuscany in 1849 and in 1859.* London: Chapman & Hall, 1859.

———. *What I Remember.* New York: Harper & Bros., 1888.

Urban, Miriam B. *British Opinion and Policy on the Unification of Italy.* Scottsdale, Pa.: Mennonite Press, 1938.

Urquhart, D., ed. *The Portfolio.* 5 vols. n.s. London, 1843-1845.

[Venturi, Emilia Ashurst.] "Europe: Its Conditions and Prospects." *Westminster Review* 57-58 (1852): 237-50.

[———.] *Joseph Mazzini, A Memoir.* London: Henry S. King & Co., 1875.

[———.] "Joseph Mazzini: What Has He Done for Italy?" *Contemporary Review* 15 (1870): 383-407.

[———.] "State of Parties in Italy Since 1848." *Westminster Review* 67 (1857): 54-73.

Viglione, F. *L'Italia nel pensiero degli scrittori inglesi.* Milan: Bocca, 1946.

Villari, Luigi. *Italian Life in Town and Country.* New York: G. P. Putnam's Sons, 1902.

Villari, Pasquale. *The Barbarian Invasions of Italy.* Translated by Linda Villari. New York: Charles Scribner's Sons, 1902.

———. *Life and Times of Girolamo Savonarola.* Translated by Linda Villari. London: T. F. Unwin, 1888.

———. *Life and Times of Niccolò Machiavelli.* Translated by Linda Villari. London: T. F. Unwin, 1898.

———. *Studies, Historical and Critical.* Translated by Linda Villari. London: T. F. Unwin, 1907.

———. *The Two First Centuries of Florentine History: The Republic and Parties of the Time of Dante.* Translated by Linda Villari. London: T. F. Unwin, 1894.

Victoria, Queen of Great Britain. *Early Letters.* Edited by John Raymond. New York: Macmillan Co., 1963.

Whitehouse, Henry Remsen. *Une Princesse revolutionnaire.* Lausanne: n.p., 1907.

Whyte, Arthur James. *The Evolution of Modern Italy.* Oxford: Basil Blackwell, 1950.

Wicks, Margaret C. W. *The Italian Exiles in London, 1816-1848.* Manchester, England: Manchester University Press, 1937.

Wilson, William Wright. *The Life of George Dawson, M.A.* 2d ed. Birmingham: Percival Jones, 1905.

Williams, Roger L. *Modern Europe, 1660-1945.* New York: St. Martin's Press, 1964.

Woodham-Smith, Cecil. *Florence Nightingale.* New York: McGraw-Hill Book Co., Inc., 1951.

Index

197

Index